THE WRITERS' AND ARTISTS'
YEAR BOOK 1971

The Writers' and Artists' Year Book

SIXTY-FOURTH YEAR OF ISSUE **1971**

A Directory for writers, artists, playwrights,
writers for film, radio and television,
photographers and composers

ADAM & CHARLES BLACK · LONDON

PRINTED IN GREAT BRITAIN BY BILLING AND SONS LTD.

GUILDFORD AND LONDON

PREFACE

Every entry in the Year Book has been submitted to the appropriate editor, publisher or author since the publication of the previous edition, and innumerable changes have resulted. The information given in the Reference Section and elsewhere has also been brought up to date. Immediate notification of any changes in entries, at any time of the year, will be welcomed by the publishers so that enquiries by post or telephone may be answered as accurately as possible at all times.

The publishers have to emphasise that they cannot provide a gratuitous advisory service in connection with the Year Book, nor can they give legal advice. Reasonable complaints about entries in the Year Book, however, are always investigated.

There is continuing evidence that the advice we have given to authors in every edition for many years past is still necessary: **never pay for publication, whether of a book, an article, a piece of music or a lyric.** This advice is repeated at greater length later in this Preface under the heading *Warning to Authors*.

In the interests of the users of the Year Book, and indeed of those agents who have a long and well-deserved reputation for their integrity and honest dealing, only those agents are included who are prepared to state their terms of business and who do not charge a marketing or placing fee.

We strongly recommend all writers and would-be writers who are contemplating writing to an agent to note carefully the information given at the head of the agents' section on page 238. It should also be noted that short manuscripts, unless they are of an exceptional nature, are unlikely to be profitable or even to pay an agent for the work involved. Writers must not expect agents, publishers or editors to comment at length on unsuitable work submitted to them, although often they are asked to do so. Every writer must expect disappointments, especially at the outset of his career, but if he has something to say and knows how to say it, then eventually (if he is patient) he will learn how to satisfy an editor's requirements, or alternatively he will learn that he should give up attempting to write and turn to some other form of activity. He must not expect other people to tell him his mistakes, although not infrequently a new writer is helped in this way by an agent, editor or publisher who has detected a spark of promise in a manuscript submitted to him.

Writers and artists, and others, are advised not to accept from editors less than a fair price for their work and, moreover, to ascertain exactly what rights they are being asked to dispose of when an offer is made.

Magazine editors frequently complain to us about the unsuitability of many manuscripts submitted to them. Not only are the manuscripts unsuitable, but no postage is sent for their return. In their own interests, writers and others are advised to enclose postage for the return of unsuitable material. Equally important, before submitting manuscripts writers should study carefully the editorial requirements of a magazine; not only for the subjects dealt with, but for the approach, treatment, style and length. Obvious though these comments may be to the practised writer, the beginner would be spared much disappointment if he studied markets more carefully (though he must not expect editors to send him free specimen copies of their magazines).

Similar care should be taken when submitting manuscripts to book publishers. A suitable publisher should be chosen, by a study of his list of publications, or an examination in the bookshops of the type of books in which he specialises. It is a waste of time and money to send the typescript of a novel to a publisher who publishes no fiction, or poetry to one who publishes no verse, though all too often this is done. A preliminary letter is appreciated by most publishers, and this should outline the nature and extent of the typescript and enquire whether the publisher would be prepared to read it (writers have been known to send out such letters of enquiry in duplicated form, an approach not calculated to stimulate a publisher's interest). Finally, it is desirable to enclose the cost of return postage when submitting the typescript.

The risks of loss, or at best of delay, through using an out-of-date issue of the Year Book must be emphasised. For this, the sixty-fourth edition, many thousands of corrections, alterations and additions have been made, and every effort is made to keep the book up to date at the time of going to press.

The omission of a journal from the Year Book is not due to any editorial discrimination but solely because it offers little or no scope for the free-lance writer or artist. In addition, as is pointed out on page 1 and elsewhere, it is impossible to include most of the many technical and specialist journals, for the benefit of only a small proportion of the Year Book's purchasers, without substantially increasing its price.

It has always been our aim to obtain and publish the rates of payment offered for contributions by journals and magazines.   Certain journals of the highest standing and reputation are reluctant, for reasons that are understandable, to state a standard rate of payment, since the value of a contribution may be dependent not upon length but upon the standing of the writer or of the information he has to give.   Many journals when giving a rate of payment indicate that it is the "minimum rate"; others, in spite of efforts to extract information from them, prefer to state "usual terms" or "by arrangement".

WARNING TO AUTHORS AND OTHERS

No reputable publisher asks an author to pay for the production of his work, or to contribute to its cost, or to undertake to purchase copies.   The only exception is in the case of a book of an extremely specialised nature, with a very limited market; in such instances, especially if the book is a good one making a contribution to its subject, an established and reliable publisher will be prepared to accept a subvention from the author to make publication possible, and such financial grants often come from scientific or other academic foundations or funds. This is a very different procedure from that of the *vanity publisher* who claims to perform, for a fee to be paid by the author, all the many functions involved in publishing a book.

In his efforts to secure business the vanity publisher will usually give exaggerated praise to an author's work and arouse equally unrealistic hopes of its commercial success.   The distressing reports we have received from embittered victims of vanity publishers underline the importance of reading extremely carefully the contracts offered by such publishers. Often these will provide for the printing of, say, two thousand copies of the book, usually at a quite exorbitant cost to the author, but will leave the "publisher" under no obligation to bind more than a very limited number.   Frequently, too, the author will be expected to pay the cost of any effective advertising, while the "publisher" makes little or no effort to promote the distribution and sale of his book.   Again, the names and imprints of vanity publishers are well-known to literary editors, and their productions therefore are rarely, if ever, reviewed or even noticed in any important periodical. Similarly, such books are hardly ever stocked by the booksellers.

We repeat, therefore, except in rare instances never pay for publication, whether for a book, an article, a lyric or a piece of music.   If a work is worth publishing, sooner or later a publisher will be prepared to publish it at his own expense.   But if a writer cannot resist the temptation of seeing his work in print, in book form, or in an anthology, even though he has to pay a substantial sum, he should first discover just how much or how little the publisher will provide and will do in return for the payment he demands.

THE SOCIETY OF AUTHORS

History and Aims

The Society of Authors is a non-profit making organisation founded in 1884 by Sir Walter Besant, at a time when the law of copyright was cumbrous and confused and conditions in publishing far from favourable or even honest.   The original aim of the Society was to further the interests of authors and defend their rights whenever and wherever they were challenged.   This aim remains unchanged today.   Much time was spent in the early days in defining and protecting literary property and in working for the reform of the copyright law, national and international.   By the time Besant died in 1904 a sound start had been made.   George Meredith had followed Tennyson as President (to be succeeded by Hardy, Barrie and John Masefield, and Sir Alan Herbert who holds the office today).   Administration was in the hands of a small staff and a Council and Committee manned, then as now, by leading writers of the day.   Among the most active of these during the first half-century of the Society's life were Galsworthy, Rider Haggard, Ian Hay, Anthony Hope, W. B. Maxwell, Shaw, Walpole and Wells.

Between the wars the advent of new media—films, radio and television—with their attendant problems meant that extra staff had to be taken on and specialist sub-committees appointed.   The process of sub-division within the membership continued after the last war with the need again to increase staff.   Today the society is administered by a Secretariat, aided by senior personnel with many years' experience who are in charge of departments.

Services

The Society serves authors in the following ways:

Individually: It gives members legal and business advice in all matters affecting their rights as authors.   This constitutes the bulk of its routine work and includes clause-by-clause vetting of contracts and the provision of expert advice on every aspect of the marketing of literary work at home and abroad.   Every year, at a risk quite beyond the resources of most members, the Society takes up some 20 or 30 cases concerned with breach of contract, infringement of copyright, and claims in liquidation or bankruptcy in this country and overseas.

Specially: The present subsidiary organisations within the membership for those who write for particular *media* are The League of Dramatists, The Radiowriters Association and The Translators Association; and for particular markets The Childrens Writers Group and The Educational Writers Group. By identifying the problems of specialist writers the Society has been able both to press for improvement in their conditions and also to reveal the pattern of authorship now emerging. Few authors make a living from writing, least of all from book royalties, and this can have serious implications. For instance, a teacher writing an occasional schoolbook, on which he does not have to rely for income, tends to be careless about his publication contracts and accepts bad terms, damaging thereby not only himself but his fellow authors, by lowering professional standards.

Generally: It advances the cause of authorship by discussion with Government departments, Members of Parliament, the BBC, the Publishers Association, the Arts Council and other organisations. For example, it pressed for safeguards for authors in the 1954 Television Act and is playing a prominent part in the current crisis concerning the future of radio. It is active in promoting legislation benefiting the profession, e.g. the Copyright Acts of 1911 and 1956, the Defamation Act of 1952, the Obscene Publications Act of 1959, and Taxation concessions under the Finance Acts of 1944, 1953, 1956 and 1967. It pursues in and out of Parliament such projects as Public Lending Right, is represented on the British Copyright Council, and is deeply concerned with the protection of authors' rights abroad following the International Copyright Conference at Stockholm in 1967. All these and other questions affecting the business of writing are dealt with in *The Author*, the Society's quarterly journal; and in a series of booklets devoted to specialist subjects, list on application to 84 Drayton Gardens, S.W.10.

The Society is also responsible for a number of awards, grants and literary prizes, including two Travel Awards: The Somerset Maugham for authors under 35 and the Travelling Scholarship, which has no age restriction; the Tom-Gallon award for short story writers; the Crompton Bequest for aiding the publication of original work of high quality; the Eric Gregory Award for poets under 30; the Margaret Rhondda Award for women journalists; and two prizes for translations. From its Contingency Fund "first-aid" assistance is given and from its Pension Fund small life pensions (there are now twelve) are granted. It helped found and now administers the Phoenix Trust for the support of literary and artistic effort and research. It has established a Retirement Benefits Scheme into which members have paid more than £200,000, a B.U.P.A. group sickness benefit arrangement, and a shopping discount service.

Admission to membership is at the discretion of the Committee of Management, but normally an author will be made a full member if he has had a full-length work published by a member of the Publishers Association, or has an established reputation in another medium, e.g. stage or radio. Associate membership is open to those, for example, who have had radio scripts broadcast or articles published, but no full length work to their credit. The annual subscription is £10·50. There is no entrance fee.

CONTENTS

JOURNALS SECTION

PUBLISHERS' SECTION

GHANA	PAKISTAN
HONG KONG	RHODESIA
KENYA	TANZANIA
MALAWI	UGANDA
MALAYSIA	ZAMBIA
NIGERIA	

INDEXES, ETC.

BRITISH AND IRISH JOURNALS AND MAGAZINES

The days of the week given in brackets are the actual, not the advertised, date of publication.

Many journals do not appear in this list because the market they offer for the free-lance writer is either too small or too specialised, or both. It is impossible to include all such publications in the Year Book, for the benefit of only a small proportion of its purchasers, without substantially increasing its price. Those who wish to offer contributions to technical, specialist or local journals are likely to know their names and can ascertain their addresses; before submitting a manuscript to any such periodical they are advised to communicate with its editor.

ABERDEEN EVENING EXPRESS, R. SMITH, Lang Stracht, Aberdeen AB9 8AF T. 40222.

2½p. D.—Lively evening paper reading. *Payment:* by arrangement. *Illustrations:* mainly half-tone.

(ABERDEEN) THE PRESS AND JOURNAL (1748), J. C. GRANT, Lang Stracht, Aberdeen, AB9 8AF. *T.* 40222. London Office, Thomson House, W.C.1.

2½p. D.—Contributions of Scottish interest. *Payment:* by arrangement. *Illustrations:* half-tone.

ACCOUNTANCY (1889), WALTER TAPLIN, M.A., B.COM., The Journal of The Institute of Chartered Accountants in England and Wales, 56–66 Goswell Road, E.C.1. *T.* 01–253 1090.

20p. Ann. Sub. U.K. £2·40; abroad £3. M.—Articles (*length* 1000 to 5000 words, occasionally longer) and notes (*length* 100 to 1000 words) on accounting, financial, management, taxation, and economic subjects. *Payment:* £10 per 1000 words. *Illustrations*: photographs of accountants in the news, of accounting activities, machines, etc.; illustrative diagrams, graphs and charts.

ACCOUNTANT, THE (1874), ARTHUR E. WEBB, 151 Strand, London, WC2R 1JJ. *T.* 01–836 0832.

14p. W.—Authoritative articles on accountancy, taxation, costing, management accounting, electronic data processing, finance and economics. *Length:* up to 3500 words (four pages).

ACCOUNTANT'S MAGAZINE (1897) (Official Publication of The Institute of Chartered Accountants of Scotland), E. H. V. McDOUGALL, 27 Queen Street, Edinburgh EH2 1LA. *T.* 031–225 3687.

20p. M. £2·10 per annum post free.—Has articles on accounting in practice and theory, taxation, economics, and law, etc. *Length preferred:* 3000 to 6000 words. *Payment:* about £6 per 1000 words.

ACHIEVEMENT, 13 New Bridge Street, London, E.C.4. *T.* 01–353 1751.

17½p. M.—Lively articles relating to British business acheivements of direct interest to American company presidents. *Illustrations:* first-class photographs. *Payment:* by arrangement.

A

ADAM INTERNATIONAL REVIEW (1941), Miron Grindea, 28 Emperor's Gate, London, S.W.7. *T.* 01–373 7307. Publishers: University of Rochester, New York.

52½p., £2 p.a. Q.—Poetry, fiction, articles and essays on comparative literature in English and French, drama, art and music.

ADVERTISER'S WEEKLY: The Journal of Advertising and Marketing (1913), Derrick Jolley, 110 Fleet Street, London, E.C.4. *T.* 01–353 6961.

15p. W.—News of advertising and marketing. Technical articles on advertising subjects. *Length:* 750 to 1500 words. *Payment:* articles from £8·40 per 1000 words; news at generous rates. *Illustrations:* line and 100 screen half-tone.

AEROMODELLER (1935), R. G. Moulton, Model and Allied Publications Ltd., 13/35 Bridge Street, Hemel Hempstead, Hertfordshire. *T.* Hemel Hempstead 2501.

15p. M. (3rd Friday). (Annual subscription, £2·05.)—Articles and news concerning model aircraft and radio control of model aircraft. Suitable articles and first-class photographs by outside contributors are always considered. *Length:* 750–2000 words, or by arrangement. *Payment:* about £3·15 to £5·25 per page. *Illustrations:* photographs and line drawings to scale.

AGENDA, William Cookson, 5 Cranbourne Court, Albert Bridge Road, London, S.W.11. *T.* 01–228 0700.

£1·50 p.a. ($4.00 in USA). Q.—Poetry and criticism. *Payment:* £2·50 per poem or per page of poetry, occasionally higher. *Illustrations:* half-tone.

AGRICULTURAL MACHINERY JOURNAL, Agricultural Press Ltd., 161–166 Fleet Street, London E.C.4. *T.* 01–353 5011.

£2·30 p.a. M. (1st)—Articles on all significant developments within the agricultural engineering industry. *Payment:* by arrangement.

AIR-CUSHION VEHICLES (1962), J. B. Bentley, P.O. Box 39, Bagshot, Surrey. *T.* Bagshot 2707.

25p. M.—An international journal for news and technical features on the design, construction and operation of all classes of hovercraft and air-cushion systems. Articles general and technical, illustrated by photographs and engineering drawings, also news paragraphs, reports of lectures, etc. *Payment:* varies; cheques 20th of month following publication. *Illustrations:* half-tone and line.

AIR PICTORIAL, 142 Sloane Street, London, S.W.1.

15p. M.—Journal of the Air League a magazine of wide aviation coverage. Many articles commissioned, and the Editor is glad to consider competent articles exploring fresh ground or presenting an individual point of view on technical matters. *Payment:* up to £5·25 per 1000 words. *Illustrations:* half-tones and line drawings; new photographs of unusual or rare aircraft considered.

AIRCRAFT ENGINEERING, D. P. L. Scallon, 4 Ludgate Circus, E.C.4. *T.* 01–353 4353.

37½p. M.—Scientific and technical articles of interest to aeronautical engineers and research workers. Special importance is attached to international outlook. *Length:* preferred: 3000 to 5000 words. *Payment:* £3·15 to £5·25 per 1000 words. *Illustrations:* photographs, diagrams, and scale drawings.

A.M.A.; The Journal of the Incorporated Association of Assistant Masters in Secondary Schools (1896), M. C. CONSTABLE, Gordon House, 29 Gordon Square, W.C.1. *T.* 01–387 5238–9. *Editorial:* (all communications) 6 Grayland Close, Birmingham B27 7NE.

$7\frac{1}{2}$p. 8 times a year—Articles of educational interest, particularly to masters in secondary schools, of 1000 to 1500 words. *Payment:* minimum, $62\frac{1}{2}$p. to £1·05 per column. *No illustrations.*

AMATEUR GARDENING (1884), A. J. HUXLEY, 189 High Holborn, London WC1V 7BA *T.* 01–242 3344.

5p. W. (Thursday).—Articles up to 800 words about any aspect of gardening. *Payment:* £6·30 per 1000 words. *Illustrations:* line or half-tone.

AMATEUR PHOTOGRAPHER (1884), R. H. MASON, M.A., F.I.I.P., F.R.P.S., 161–166 Fleet Street, London, E.C.4. *T.* 01–353 5011.

10p. W. (Wednesday).—Original articles of pictorial or technical interest, preferably illustrated with either photographs or diagrams. *Length preferred:* (unillustrated) 400 to 800 words; cine articles up to 1500 words; (illustrated) 2 to 4 pages. *Payment:* from £5·25 per page, according to interest, illustrations counting as text. Illustrations unaccompanied by text are considered, especially for covers.

AMATEUR STAGE (1946), ROY STACEY, 1 Hawthorndene Road, Hayes, Bromley, BR2 7DZ. *T.* 01–462 6461.

15p. M.—Articles on all aspects of the amateur theatre, preferably practical and factual. *Length:* 600–2000 words. *Payment:* minimum of £2·10 per 1000 words. *Illustrations:* photographs and line drawings, *payment* for which varies.

AMBASSADOR, THE, BARRY TOLFREE, 49 Park Lane, W1Y 6BT. *T.* 01–499 4871. £4·87$\frac{1}{2}$ per annum. M.—Textile and fashion news. *Payment:* varies. *Illustrations:* half-tone and line, some full colour.

AMBIT (1959), Dr. MARTIN C. O. BAX, 17 Priory Gardens, London, N6 5QY. *T.* 01–340 3566.

20p. Q.—Poems, short stories (up to 5000 words), occasionally reviews and critical articles on the Arts, but a preliminary letter advisable for this type of material. *Payment:* by arrangement. *Illustrations:* line and half-tone.

ANGLER'S MAIL, JOHN INGHAM (IPC Magazines Ltd.) 69–76 Long Acre, London, WC2E 9QF. *T.* 01–836 2468.

5p. W.—Features, cartoons and news items about sea, coarse and game fishing. 850 to 1500 words. *Payment:* £6·30 per 750 words and pro-rata. *Illustrations:* Colour transparencies £7·35. Black and white £1·05 to £1·58. Half-tones, colour transparencies, line and wash drawing. (Offset litho printing.)

ANGLING (1959), (incorporating **CREEL**), BRIAN HARRIS, Aldwych House, 81 Aldwych, London, W.C.2. *T.* 01–242 8621.

17$\frac{1}{2}$p. M.—Angling articles and photographs. *Length:* 550; 1200 words. *Payment:* £5·25 per 1000 minimum. *Illustrations:* line and half-tone; colour transparencies.

ANGLING TIMES (1953), RUSSELL HOLE, EMAP, Oundle Road, Peterborough, PE2 9QR *T.* Peterborough 61471.

5p. W.—Articles, pictures, news stories, on all forms of angling. *Payment:* £5·25 per 800 words. *Illustrations:* half-tone, line.

ANGLO-WELSH REVIEW, THE (1949) (formerly **DOCK LEAVES**), WILLIAM SMITH (Dock Leaves), 2 Croft Terrace, Pembroke Dock, Wales. *Editorial:* ROLAND MATHIAS, Deffrobani, Maescelyn, Brecon. *T.* Brecon 3385.

38p. Twice yearly.—Short stories, plays, poetry, satire, and articles on literature, the arts, history, travel, education, having some relation to Wales. Reviews of books in English by Welsh authors, and with a Welsh setting. *Payment:* by arrangement. *Illustrations:* four pages of blocks or photographs.

ANIMAL WAYS (1935), 105 Jermyn Street, S.W.1. *T.* 01–930 0971.

1p. M. (1st)—Official Magazine of the Animal Defenders, R.S.P.C.A. Articles and notes about animals up to 300 words, and photographs are considered. Short verses are used. Puzzle drawings considered. Continuous stories and animal-adventure tales; cartoons (strip, showing kindness to animals). Readers are mainly children from 8 to 16 years old. *Payment:* according to value. *Illustrations:* line and half-tone.

ANIMALS (1963), NIGEL SITWELL, 21–22 Great Castle Street, London W1N 8LT *T.* 01–499 4383.

17½p. M.—Serious, scientifically-oriented articles about wild life. *Length:* 1000–3000 words. *Payment:* from £10·50 per 1000 words. *Illustrations:* top quality colour and black-and-white photographs used extensively; little art work.

ANIMALS' DEFENDER AND ANTI-VIVISECTION NEWS. Official Organ of the National Anti-Vivisection Society, J. EVANS, 51 Harley Street, W1N 1DD *T.* 01–580 4034. *T.A.* Zoophilist, London, W.1.

8p. 6 issues a year.—First rate articles dealing with the human treatment of animals in regard to necessary reform, legislative and otherwise, occasionally accepted. *Length:* 1000 to 1500 words. *Payment:* £3·15 per 1000 words. No verse.

ANIMALS MAGAZINE, M. I. M. GODDARD, P.D.S.A. House, South Street, Dorking, Surrey. *T.* Dorking 81691.

3p. M. (43p. a year).—Articles and short stories on non-controversial topics of interest to all animal lovers. *Maximum length:* 1000 words. *Payment:* by arrangement, on acceptance. *Illustrations:* line and half-tone, black-and-white.

ANNABEL (D. C. Thomson & Co. Ltd.), 80 Kingsway East, Dundee DD4 8SL, and Thomson House, 12 Fetter Lane, London, E.C.4.

10p. M.—Colour gravure monthly for the modern woman with wide interests. Personal experience stories, biographical stories of well-known personalities, controversial topics, fashion, cookery, knitting, fiction. Art *illustrations* and photographs in full colour and black and white. *Payment:* on acceptance.

ANTIQUE COLLECTOR (1930), G. W. WHITEMAN, M.A., 16 Strutton Ground, Victoria Street, S.W.1. *T.* 01–222 2150.

37½p. (Published every other month.)—Articles of 1500 to 2500 words on antiques and collecting. *Illustrations:* half-tone from finely produced photographs.

ANTIQUITY, GLYN DANIEL, St. John's College, Cambridge CB2 1TP. *T.* 61621. (Publisher: W. Heffer & Sons Ltd., 104 Hills Road, Cambridge CB2 1LW. *T.* Cambridge 51571.)

75p.; £2·50 p.a. Q. (March, June, Sept., Dec.)—General articles on archaeology of all parts of the world. *Length:* 2000 to 5000 words. *Payment:* free offprints supplied. *Illustrations:* half-tones and line blocks.

APOLLO (1925) (Apollo Magazine Ltd.). *Editorial:* DENYS SUTTON, 22 Davies Street, London, W1Y 1LH *T.* 01–629 3061.
75p. M.—Knowledgeable articles of about 2500 words on art, ceramics, furniture, armour, glass, sculpture, and any subject connected with art and collecting. *Payment:* by arrangement. *Illustrations:* colour and half-tone.

AQUARIST AND PONDKEEPER, THE (1924) (The Buckley Press, Ltd.), The Butts, Half Acre, Brentford, Middlesex. *T.* 01–568 8441. Editor: LAURENCE E. PERKINS.
15p. M.—Illustrated authoritative articles by professional and amateur biologists, naturalists and aquarium hobbyists on all matters concerning life in and near water. *Length:* about 1500 words. *Payment:* by arrangement. *Illustrations:* photographs and line.

ARCHITECT & BUILDING NEWS, THE, R. J. BARFOOT, 32 Southwark Bridge Road, London, S.E.1. *T.* 01–928 2060.
Controlled circulation. Fortnightly. Articles of interest to architects. *Length:* 1000 to 2000 words. *Payment* by arrangement.

ARCHITECT AND SURVEYOR, THE, RICHARD RAYNER, 29 Belgrave Square, London, S.W.1. *T.* 01–235 3755.
17½p. Bi-M. (20th February and alternate months).—The Journal of the Incorporated Association of Architects and Surveyors. Matter required: architectural, surveying, and allied matters. Preliminary letter desirable. *Payment:* by arrangement. All kinds of *illustrations* used.

ARCHITECTS' JOURNAL (1895), D. A. C. A. BOYNE, 9–13 Queen Anne's Gate, Westminster, S.W.1. *T.* 01–930 0611.
10p. W. (Wednesday).—Articles on architecture, town planning and associated arts. Authoritative articles, preferably illustrated, on technical subjects. *Payment:* by arrangement. *Illustrations:* high standard photographs of new buildings and architectural subjects of general and technical interest.

ARCHITECTURAL DESIGN (1930), M. PIDGEON, 26 Bloomsbury Way, London, WC1A 2SS *T.* 01–405 6325. *T.A.* Britstanex.
40p. M. (7th).—Fully illustrated articles by qualified writers on architectural and allied subjects. *Length:* up to 1500 words. *Payment:* by arrangement. *Illustrations:* line and half-tone; photographs or line drawings of current architectural work at home or abroad.

ARCHITECTURAL REVIEW (1896), 9–13 Queen Anne's Gate, Westminster, S.W.1. *T.* 01–930 0611.
37½p. M. (1st.)—Contains articles (up to 5000 words in length) on architecture and the allied arts. Must be by thoroughly qualified writers. *Payment:* by arrangement. *Illustrations:* photographs, drawings, etc.

ARGOSY (1926), Fleetway House, Farringdon Street, EC4A 4AD *T.* 01–634 4444.
20p. M.—Only the very highest standard of fiction is accepted. Present *length:* short stories of 1500 to 7000 words; or full length and short complete novels. The magazine consists of stories which are acknowledged to be the best, British or foreign, and mostly contemporary.

ARMY QUARTERLY AND DEFENCE JOURNAL, Major General R. F. K. GOLDSMITH. C.B., C.B.E., c/o Clowes and Sons Ltd., Dorland House, 14 and 16 Lower Regent Street, London, S.W.1. *T.* 01–839 3301.
88p., £3 p.a. Q.—Devoted to all matters connected with the Army and Imperial defence. Articles should deal with military topics of the day, personal experiences and lessons gained in war, military history, strategy, tactics, and administration; they should be from 2000 to 5000 words. Articles from the younger generation of officers are particularly welcome. *Payment:* £1 per 1000 words. *Illustrations:* maps if essential.

ART AND ARTISTS (1966), CHARLES SPENCER, Hansom Books, Artillery Mansions, 75 Victoria Street, London, S.W.1. *T.* 01–799 4452.

40p. M.—Articles on contemporary art, serious but readable. *Length:* from 1000 to 2000 words with photographs. *Payment:* by arrangement. *Illustrations:* line, half-tone and colour.

ART AND CRAFT IN EDUCATION (1946), HENRY PLUCKROSE (Evans Brothers Ltd.), Montague House, Russell Square, WC1B 5BX *T.* 01–636 8521.

17½p. M.—Articles must be of a practical nature and deal with the various phases of art and craft in Primary and Secondary Schools. *Payment:* by arrangement. *Illustrations:* line, half-tone.

ARTIST, THE (1931), Managing Editor: FREDERICK PARKINSON, 33 Warwick Square, S.W.1. *T.* 01–834 0272.

25p. M.—Instructional articles relating to every branch of fine and commercial art. Articles are mainly commissioned from artists of highest repute. *Length:* 1500 to 2000 words. *Payment:* by arrangement. *Illustrations:* must relate to articles. Line, half-tone, and colour.

ARTS REVIEW, (1949), Richard Gainsborough Periodicals Ltd., 8 Wyndham Place, London, W1H 2AY *T.* 01–262 7278.

20p. F.—Art criticism and reviews. Commissioned work only. *Illustrations:* half-tone and line.

ASHORE AND AFLOAT (1876), Rev. E. J. R. BENTLIFF, M.A., Agnes Weston House, 32 Western Parade, Southsea, Hants PO5 3JE. *T.* Portsmouth 23126.

5p. M.—Short stories and articles with a nautical flavour, and excluding reference to gambling, drinking and strong language. *Length:* 1000 to 1500 words. *Payment:* £1·25 per 1000 words. *Illustrations:* half-tone.

ASSEMBLY AND FASTENER ENGINEERING (1963), FRANKLIN KEELEY, Riverside House, Hough Street, Woolwich, London, S.E.18. *T.* 01–855 7001.

Controlled circulation. M.—Aimed at technical management executives responsible for product design and assembly production. *Length:* 500–2000 words. *Payment:* by arrangement. *Illustrations:* line and half-tone, photographs and diagrams.

AUTHOR, THE (1890), RICHARD FINDLATER, 84 Drayton Gardens, London, S.W.10. *T.* 01–373 6642. *T.A.* Auctoritas, London.

20p. Q.—Organ of The Society of Authors. Commissioned articles from 1000 to 2000 words on any subject connected with the legal, commercial, or technical side of authorship. *Payment:* by arrangement. (Little scope for the freelance writer: a preliminary letter is advisable.)

AUTOCAR (1895), PETER GARNIER, Dorset House, Stamford Street, S.E.1. *T.* 01–928 3333. *T.A.* Autocar, Iliffepres 25137, London, Telex.

12½p. W. (Thursday).—All aspects of cars, motoring and motor industries. Articles, general, practical, touring, competition and technical. *Payment:* varies; mid-month following publication. *Illustrations:* tone, line (litho) and colour. Press day news: Monday.

AUTOMOBILE ENGINEER (1910), T. K. GARRETT, Dorset House, Stamford Street, S.E.1. *T.* 01–928 3333. *T.A.* Engineer, Iliffepres 25137, London, Telex.

50p. M. (last Friday, previous month).—Technical articles, on design, production, research and materials, in relation to road vehicles. Press day, first Thursday each month. *Payment:* £6·30 minimum per 1000. *Illustrations:* line and half-tone.

AUTOMOTIVE DESIGN ENGINEERING, JOHN FENTON, Hermes House, 89 Blackfriars Road, London, S.E.1. *T.* 01–928 0181.
£7 p.a. M.—Specialist technical articles 1500 to 3000 words. *Illustrations:* half-tone and line. *Payment:* by arrangement.

AV TIMES, official organ of the British Union for the Abolition of Vivisection, 47 Whitehall, S.W.1. *T.* 01–930 7698. *T.A.* Abolition, London, S.W.1. Editor: JOHN PITT.
4p. M. (15th).—Intelligent articles on any aspect of the anti-vivisection standpoint may be accepted. *Length:* 500–1200 words. *Payment:* by arrangement but not less than £2.10 per 1000. No verse. *Illustrations:* half-tone, animal studies or features.

BALLET TODAY, ESTELLE HERF, 33 Shepherd Street, London, W1Y 7LH *T.* 01–499 2230.
15p. 6 issues a year.—Articles on ballet and dancing. *Length:* 400 to 1000 words. *Payment:* £1·05 and up per 1000 words. *Illustrations:* photographs, tone and line drawings.

BALLROOM DANCING TIMES (1956), ALEX MOORE, Editorial Adviser, MARY CLARKE, Executive Editor, 18 Hand Court, High Holborn, W.C.1. *T.* 01–405 1414.
13p. M.—Dealing with ballroom dancing from every aspect, but chiefly from the serious competitive, teaching and medal test angles. Well informed free-lance articles are occasionally used, but only after preliminary arrangements. *Payment:* from £2·10. *Illustrations:* half-tones preferably, occasional line.

BANER AC AMSERAU CYMRU (Banner and Times of Wales), (1843), GWILYM R. JONES, 11 Bryn Teg, Denbigh. *T.* 074–571 2819.
3½p. Weekly.—National weekly newspaper in Welsh; articles of economic literary and political interest. Non-party. *Length:* 800 words. *Payment:* Minimum £1·05 per article. *Illustrations:* line and photographs.

BANKER, THE (1926), WILLIAM M. CLARKE, Editorial Office: Bracken House, 10 Cannon Street, E.C.4. *T.* 01–248 8000.
35p. M.—Articles on economic policy, finance and banking, home and overseas, 1500 to 3000 words. Outside contributions are accepted on banking and general economic subjects. *Payment:* by arrangement. *Illustrations:* half-tones of people, buildings, office equipment.

BANKERS' MAGAZINE, THE (1844), DR. G. W. MAYNARD, 12 Vandy Street, London, E.C.2. *T.* 01–247 0151.
22½p. M.—Articles of from 200–3000 words. *Payment:* by arrangement.

BAPTIST TIMES (1855), Revd. W. W. BOTTOMS, 4 Southampton Row, WC1B 4AA *T.* 01–405 5516. *T.A.* Preacher, London, W.C.1.
4p. W. (Th.).—Religious or literary matter, 1000 words. Standard rate of *payment. Illustrations:* half-tone.

BATTLE PICTURE LIBRARY (1961), New Fleetway House, Farringdon Street, London, EC4A 4AD *T.* 01–634 4444.
5p. Four each month.—All picture war stories. Artists and authors invited to submit sample work to the Editor.

BEANO, THE (D. C. Thomson & Co., Ltd.), Courier Place, Dundee, DD1 9QJ, and Thomson House, 12 Fetter Lane, London, E.C.4.
2p. W. (Thursday).—Picture paper for young folk. Comic strips series, sets of 12–14 pictures. Also picture stories, 6–10 panels per page. *Payment:* on acceptance.

BEDFORDSHIRE MAGAZINE (1947), JAMES DYER, 6 Rogate Road, Luton, LU2 8HR   T. Luton 24808.
12½p. Q.—Articles of Bedfordshire interest. *Length:* up to 1500 words. *Payment:* £1·05 per 1000 words. *Illustrations:* line and half-tone, photographs, 52½p. per reproduction.

BEEZER, THE (D. C. Thomson & Co., Ltd.), Courier Place, Dundee, DD1 9QJ, and Thomson House, 12 Fetter Lane, London, E.C.4.
2½p. W. (Tuesday).—Picture paper for children. Stories told in pictures in 14–20 panels per instalment. Also comic strips in series, 6–15 pictures each number. Interest drawings—history, geography, general—suitable for full colour reproduction. *Payment:* on acceptance.

(BELFAST) NEWS-LETTER (1737), COWAN WATSON, Donegall Street, Belfast, BT1 2GB   T. 44441.
2½p. D.—Conservative.

BIMBO (D. C. Thomson & Co., Ltd.), Courier Place, Dundee, DD1 9QJ, and Thomson House, 12 Fetter Lane, London, E.C.4.
2½p. W. (Monday).—Picture stories and feature comics for younger children. Drawings in wash or line. Also full colour work for gravure on children's subjects. *Payment:* On acceptance. Special encouragement to promising artists.

BIO-MEDICAL ENGINEERING (1965), 9 Gough Square, Fleet Street, London, E.C.4.   T. 01–353 3172.   *T.A.* Markeba, London, E.C.4.
£5 p.a. M.—Original and review articles of such a scientific standard as to be understandable by both medically and technologically qualified specialists. *Length:* varies considerably, usually between 1000 and 3000 words. *Payment:* by arrangement. *Illustrations:* line and half-tone.

BIRDS AND COUNTRY MAGAZINE, HOCKLEY CLARKE, Managing Editor, 79 Surbiton Hill Park, Surbiton, Surrey.   T. 01–399 7809.
15p. Q.—Original observations on bird life and natural history subjects all over the world, articles up to 1000 words. *Payment:* by arrangement. *Illustrations:* half-tone and line.

BIRMINGHAM EVENING MAIL (1870), FRANK OWENS, Colmore Circus, Birmingham 4.   T. 021–236 3366 (30 lines).   *T.A.* Mail, Birmingham. London Office, 88 Fleet Street, E.C.4.   T. 01–353 0811.
2½p. D.—Ind. Crisp, topical articles considered, generally of 300–700 words, Midland interest preferred. *Payment:* on merit.

BIRMINGHAM POST, THE, DAVID HOPKINSON, Post & Mail House, Colmore Circus, Birmingham 4.   T. 021–236 3366.
2½p. D.—Original articles up to 1100 words for leader page; submissions (up to 600 words) considered for women's page. No stories or verse. *Payment:* by arrangement. Topical news photographs and occasional pictorial photographs of Midland interest used.

BLACKWOOD'S MAGAZINE (1817) (William Blackwood and Sons, Ltd.), 45 George Street, Edinburgh, EH2 2JA.   T. 031–225 5835; and 6 Buckingham Street, London, WC2N 6BU   T. 01–839 6191.
25p. M. (last Friday of each month).—*Original* work of all kinds: fiction, adventure, travel, history, and biography; as well as miscellaneous articles treating in a fresh manner any unhackneyed subject of general interest. Short stories should be strong in plot and characterisation. Not illustrated. *Length:* 3000–9000 words. *No preliminary letter* is required, but would-be contributors are advised to study the magazine before submitting material. *Payment* is good and is made on publication.

BOARD (1958), JACK R. D. HEMING, Pressmedia Ltd., Ivy Hatch, Sevenoaks, Kent. *T.* Plaxtol 316.

32½p., £3·65 per annum. M.—Well-informed articles of up to 1500 words of a technical or practical nature of interest to architects and builders, as well as manufacturers, importers, distributors, industrial and commercial users of fibreboard, plywood, chipboard and allied products; machinery, tools, accessories and services. *Illustrations:* photographs and line drawings. *Payment:* by arrangement.

BOLTON EVENING NEWS AND LANCASHIRE JOURNAL SERIES (1867), T. H. COOKE, Mealhouse, Lane Bolton, Lancashire, BL1 1DE *T.* Bolton 22345. *T.A.* Newspapers, Bolton.

2½p. D. and W.—Articles, particularly those with South Lancashire appeal. *Length:* up to 1000 words. *Illustrations:* photographs; considered at usual rates. *Payment:* from £3·15; on 15th of month following date of publication.

BOOK COLLECTING AND LIBRARY MONTHLY (1968), B. HUTCHISON, 42 Trafalgar Street, Brighton, Sussex. *T.* 66120.

£1·50 per annum. M.—Articles on book collecting and bibliography, not elementary. *Length:* up to 5000 words. *Payment:* £3·15 to £10·50 per 1000 words.

BOOK COLLECTOR, THE (1952) (incorporating **BIBLIOGRAPHICAL NOTES AND QUERIES**), Editorial Board: PERCY MUIR, JOHN CARTER, C.B.E., NICOLAS BARKER (Editor), ALASTAIR SHAND (Publisher), The Collector Ltd., 58 Frith Street, London, W1V 6BY. *T.* 01–734 2731.

75p. Q.—Articles, biographical and bibliographical, on the collection and study of printed books and MSS. *Payment:* by arrangement.

BOOK TRADE see **THE PUBLISHER**

BOOKS AND BOOKMEN (1955), JAMES GORDON, Hansom Books, Artillery Mansions, 75 Victoria Street, London, S.W.1. *T.* 01–799 4452.

25p. M.—Articles on authors and their books. *Payment:* by arrangement. *Illustrations:* half-tone.

BOOKSELLER, THE (1858), EDMOND SEGRAVE (J. Whitaker and Sons, Ltd.), 13 Bedford Square, London WC1B 3JE *T.* 01–636 4748 (2 lines).

7½p. W.—An organ of the publishing and bookselling trades. While outside contributions are always welcome (especially news paragraphs, payment from 50p. each), most of the journal's contents are commissioned. *Length:* about 1000 to 1500 words. *Payment:* from £4·50 per 1000 words and by arrangement.

BREWING TRADE REVIEW (incorporating **BOTTLING**) (1886), 42 Portman Square, London, W1H 0BB *T.* 01–486 4831.

17p. M.—Official organ of The Brewers' Society. *Payment:* by arrangement. *Illustrations:* line and half-tone; 120 screen.

BRISTOL EVENING POST (1932), G. B. FARNSWORTH, Broadmead, Bristol, BS99 7HD. *T.* Bristol 20080.

2½p. D. Articles up to 800 words with strong West-country interest. *Payment:* at recognised rates.

BRITANNIA (1950), M. BRIMICOMBE (Brimicombe Publications Ltd., 8 St. John's Park, Blackheath, London, S.E.3. *T.* 01–858 3581.

9p. M. (not published during the summer months, June–September). —A magazine for students of English all over the world. Very lively, well-informed articles dealing with the British and every aspect of life in Great Britain and the British Commonwealth. *Length:* 900 to 1000 words. *No preliminary letter necessary. Payment:* by arrangement on acceptance of article. *Illustrations:* photographs and line drawings (on request).

BRITANNICA (1953), M. BRIMICOMBE (Brimicombe Publications Ltd., 8 St. John's Park, Blackheath, London, S.E.3. *T.* 01–858 3581.

9p. M.—(not published June–September).—For junior students of English all over the world. Very lively, well-informed articles on the British and British customs, written in simple English. *Length:* 500 to 700 words. *Payment:* by arrangement on acceptance of article. *Illustrations:* photographs and line drawings (on request).

BRITISH CHEMICAL ENGINEERING, J. O. S. MACDONALD, B.SC., C.ENG. M.I.CHEM.E., ASSOC.I.MECH.E., (E. C. & M. Press Ltd.), 33–40 Bowling Green Lane, E.C.1. *T.* 01–837 1277.

30p. £3·60 p.a.   U.K., M.—High-level articles on process design, processing and handling methods and processing equipment. Apply to Editor for notes on preparation of articles.

BRITISH CHESS MAGAZINE (1881), B. P. REILLY, 9 Market Street, St. Leonards-on-sea, Sussex. *T.* Hastings 4009.

15p. Annual subscription £2·10 post free. M. (1st).—Photographs used.

BRITISH ENGINEER (1928), DOROTHY HENRY, Windsor House, 46 Victoria Street, London, S.W.1. *T.* 01–799 5585.

20p. Bi-M.—Technical articles on all engineering or allied subjects. *Payment:* £10·50 per 1000 words. *Illustrations:* line and half-tone.

BRITISH ESPERANTIST, THE (Journal of the British Esperanto Association) (1905), E. P. OCKEY, 140 Holland Park Avenue, London, W11 4UF   *T.* 01–727 7821.

10p.+postage. (£1·25 p.a. post free). M.—Articles in English or Esperanto, by arrangement, on the applications of the International Language, Esperanto, to education, commerce, travel, international affairs, scouting, radio, television, literature, linguistics, etc. *Illustrations:* photos by arrangement. *Payment:* by arrangement.

BRITISH FARMER (1948), BRIAN FREESTONE, Agriculture House, Knightsbridge, S.W.1. *T.* 01–235 5077. *T.A.* Farmesuni, London Telex.

M. to members.—Articles on all aspects of agriculture and horticulture. *Length:* 600–1000 words. *Payment:* £4·20 to £15·75 per article. *Illustrations:* line and half-tone.

BRITISH FOOD JOURNAL (1899), C. R. A. MARTIN, M.B., B.S., D.P.H., Peterson Publishing Co. Ltd., Peterson House, Livery Street, Birmingham 3. *T.* 021–236 2706–7–8–9.

£2·75 annual subscription. Alt. months (15th).—Articles of a serious and authentic kind dealing with the quality control of foods, food engineering, food technology, packaging, etc., length two or three columns, 1200 to 2000 words. Press day, 1st. *Payment:* varies.

BRITISH JOURNAL OF CHIROPODY, THE (1933), J. C. DAGNALL, M.CH.S., 300 Bramhall Lane South, Bramhall, Stockport, Cheshire, SK7 3DJ. *T.* 061–439 1138.

14p. (£1·30 per annum). M.—Authoritative articles on chiropody and foot problems, history of foot care and shoes, nothing humorous required. *Length:* 1000 to 1500 words. News items. *Payment:* by arrangement. *Illustrations:* line and half-tone.

BRITISH JOURNAL OF PHOTOGRAPHY, THE (1854), G. W. CRAWLEY, 24 Wellington Street, Strand, WC2E 7DG *T.* 01–836 0731–4.
   7½p. W. (Friday).—Articles on professional, commercial and press photography, and on the more advanced aspects of amateur, technical, industrial, medical, scientific and colour photography. *Payment:* by arrangement. *Illustrations:* in line and half-tone are used.

BRITISH LEGION JOURNAL (1921), R. L. PENNELLS, Pall Mall, S.W.1. *T.* 01–930 8131.
   5p. M.—Authoritative articles preferably with ex-Service interest (including Air or Naval), also vignettes, features concerning British Legion. *Length:* not more than 1000 words. *Payment:* £1·05 to £5·25. *Illustrations:* occasional cartoons.

BRITISH MEDICAL JOURNAL (1840), MARTIN WARE, M.B., F.R.C.P., British Medical Association House, Tavistock Square, W.C.1. *T.* 01–387 4499.
   35p. W. (Saturday).—Medical articles only.

BRITISH PLASTICS (1929), RICHARD ROWLAND, 33–40 Bowling Green Lane, London E.C.1. *T.* 01–837 1277. *T.A.* Pressimus, London, E.C.1.
   37½p. £5·50 per annum. M.—Technical articles dealing with plastics and allied subjects. *Length:* depending on subject. *Payment:* by arrangement. *Illustrations:* half-tone blocks 120 screen, line.

BRITISH PRINTER (1888), ROY BREWER, 30 Old Burlington Street, London, W1X 2AE *T.* 01–437 0644.
   25p. £3·50 p.a. M.—Articles on technical and aesthetic aspects of printing processes and graphic reproduction. *Payment:* by arrangement. *Illustrations:* letterpress from photographs, line drawings and diagrams, or wood engravings.

BRITISH RACEHORSE, THE (1949), JOHN HISLOP, 55 Curzon Street, London, W1Y 7PF *T.* 01–499 4391.
   90p. February, May, August, September, November.—Preliminary letter essential. Articles on breeding of racehorses and ancillary subjects by recognised experts.

BRITISH-SOVIET FRIENDSHIP (formerly **RUSSIA TO-DAY**) (1927), 36 St. John's Square, E.C.1. *T.* 01–253 4161.
   2p. M.—An illustrated magazine on British-Soviet relations. Good photographs and well-informed news items and articles up to 900 words (on Soviet Russia). *Payment:* for articles and photographs only by special arrangement.

BRITISH STEELMAKER, THE (1935), J. F. S. RUSSELL, M.A., B.LITT., 65–66 Turnmill Street, E.C.1. *T.* 01–253 8201.
   27p., £3·25 p.a. M. (23rd of month).—Technical, general, or historical articles, preferably illustrated on all aspects of steel production. *Payment:* by arrangement (average £6·30 per 1000 words). *Illustrations:* line and half-tone.

BRITISH VEGETARIAN, THE (1959), GEOFFREY L. RUDD, Parkdale, Dunham Road, Altrincham, Cheshire. *T.* 061–928 0793.
   10p. Bi-M.—Articles on nutrition and humanitarianism. *Payment:* by arrangement. *Illustrations:* photographs of foods growing, nature studies, etc.

BRITISH WEEKLY AND CHRISTIAN WORLD (1886), DENIS DUNCAN, 69 Fleet Street, London, E.C.4. *T.* 01–583 7915–6, and 38 Melville Street, Edinburgh, EH3 7HA *T.* Caledonian 7927.

4p. W. (Thursday).—A Christian inter-denominational journal of news and comment specialising in religious, social, political and economic questions in their relation to Christianity, written by authorities. No short stories or verse. Uses commissioned work mostly, but always welcomes articles of topical interest and importance, news items, etc. Study of paper desirable. *Payment:* £1·05 to £5·25 per 1000 words.

BROWNIE, THE, Official Organ of The Girl Guides Association, Mrs. J. V. RUSH, 17–19 Buckingham Palace Road, S.W.1. *T.* 01–834 6242.

2½p. W.—Short articles about training for Brownies (girls 7–10 years). Serials with Brownie background (500–700 words per instalment). Puzzles, Line Drawings, "Things to make," etc. *Payment:* by arrangement. *Illustrations:* line and half-tone.

BRUSHES (1915), ARTHUR DOWSETT, 157 Hagden Lane, Watford, WD1 8LW. *T.* Watford 32308.

£3 per annum, including Directory of the Brush and Allied Trades. M.—Technically accurate articles on brush-making or brush-selling. *Payment:* £4·20 and upwards per 1000 words. Submit synopsis. *Illustrations:* half-tone and line.

BUCKS LIFE AND CHILTERN LIFE AND COUNTRYSIDE (1966), JOHN ROTHEROE, 12b Temple Square, Aylesbury, Bucks. *T.* Aylesbury 83999.

15p. M.—Articles on Buckinghamshire and Chiltern history, scenery, sociology, economy, etc. *Length:* 500 to 1500 words. *Payment:* £2·10 to £3·15 per 1000 words. *Illustrations:* line, half-tone black and white.

BUILDING (formerly THE BUILDER) (1842), ANTHONY R. DAVIS, The Builder House, Catherine Street, W.C.2. *T.* 01–836 6251.

10p. W. (Friday).—A newspaper covering the entire professional side of the building industry with special emphasis on construction. Articles on architecture and techniques at home and abroad considered, also news and photographs. *Payment:* by arrangement.

BUILDING MATERIALS (incorporating FLOORS), (1939), CHRISTOPHER SYKES, A4 Publications Ltd., Press House, P.O. Box 7, Church Road, Woldingham, Surrey, CR3 7YE. *T.* Woldingham 205011.

£7·50 per annum. M.—Information on building materials, in particular on new materials and methods. components and equipment, and their application. *Length:* up to 1200 words. *Payment:* by arrangement. *Illustrations:* line and half-tone.

BUILDING SOCIETIES, GAZETTE, THE (1869), ERIC HOLMES, Franey & Co. Ltd., Burgon Street, EC4V 5DP *T.* 01–236 0855 (5 lines).

30p. (13 issues per year inc. 1 Special Number). Subscriptions £3·90 per annum pre-paid. M. (7th).—Articles on matters of interest to building societies, financial rather than on house construction. *Length:* up to 2000 words. *Average payment:* £10·50 per 1000 words. *Illustrations:* line and half-tone.

BULLETIN OF HISPANIC STUDIES (1923), GEOFFREY RIBBANS, School of Hispanic Studies, The University, P.O. Box 147, Liverpool, L69 3BX. *T.* 709 6022. Published by the Liverpool University Press, 123 Grove Street, Liverpool, L7 7AF.

52½p. £2 p.a. Q.—Specialist articles on the languages and literatures of Spain, Portugal and Latin America, written in English, Spanish, Portuguese or Catalan. *No payment* made.

BUNTY (D. C. Thomson & Co., Ltd.), Courier Place, Dundee, DD1 9QJ; and Thomson House, 12 Fetter Lane, London, E.C.4.

2½p. W. (Tuesday).—Picture-story paper for young girls of school age. Vividly told stories in picture-serial form, 16–18 panels in each 2-page instalment; 27–28 panels in each 3-page instalment. Comic strips and features. *Payment:* on acceptance. Special encouragement to promising script-writers and artists.

BUNTY LIBRARY (D. C. Thomson & Co., Ltd.), Courier Place, Dundee, DD1 9QJ, and Thomson House, 12 Fetter Lane, London, E.C.4.

5p. M. (2nd Tuesday each month).—Stories told in pictures, for schoolgirls; 64 pages, (about 140 line drawings). Ballet, school, adventure, theatre, sport. Scripts considered; promising artists and script-writers encouraged. *Payment:* on acceptance.

BURLINGTON MAGAZINE (1903), BENEDICT NICOLSON, 49 Park Lane, London, W.1. *T.* 01–493 2622. *T.A.* Rariora, London, W.1.

65p. M. (1st).—Deals with the history and criticism of art. Rate of *payment:* £3·15 per page. Average length of article, 500 to 3000 words. The Editor can use only articles written by those who have special knowledge of the subjects treated, and cannot accept MSS. compiled from works of reference. Reviews and a monthly chronicle. No verse. *Illustrations:* almost invariably made from photographs.

BUSES (1949), JOHN F. PARKE, ASSOC.INST.T., Terminal House, Shepperton, Middlesex. *T.* Walton-on-Thames 28484.

18p. M.—Articles of interest to both road passenger transport operators and bus enthusiasts. *Illustrations:* half-tone, line maps. *Payment:* on application.

BUSINESS CREDIT and HIRE PURCHASE JOURNAL, Quaintance & Co. (Publishers) Ltd., 24A Chertsey Street, Guildford, Surrey. *T.* Guildford 67965.

Subscriptions £2·25 M.—Articles on any aspect of Credit, preferably by contributors with practical or professional experience. *Length:* 1500 to 2500 words. *Payment:* from £8·40 per 1000 words. *Illustrations:* half-tone or line.

BUSINESS MANAGEMENT (1913), M. C. WADE, Mercury House, Waterloo Road, London, S.E.1; *City Office:* 180 Fleet Street, E.C.4. *T.* 01–928 3388. *T.A.* Sysmaga, London, S.E.1.

37½p., £4·50 p.a. M.—Feature articles, particularly case histories of improved management methods of real firms. *Length:* 1500–3000 words. *Payment:* £10·50 per 1000 words, sometimes higher. *Illustrations:* line, half-tone, two-colour.

BUSTER (1960), New Fleetway House, Farringdon Street, London, EC4A 4AD *T.* 01–634 4444.

3p. W. (Monday).—Juvenile comic. Comedy characters and adventure stories in picture strips. For boys and girls ages 8 to 14. Full colour, and black-and-white.

BUSY BEES' NEWS, M. I. M. GODDARD, P.D.S.A. House, South Street, Dorking, Surrey. *T.* Dorking 81691.

3p. M. (43p. a year).—Short stories (max. *length* 800 words) and articles (max. *length* 700) about animals suitable for children up to eleven; educational nature articles welcomed. *Payment:* by arrangement, on acceptance. *Illustrations:* Line and half-tone, black-and-white.

CABINET MAKER AND RETAIL FURNISHER (incorporating **FURNITURE RECORD**), PETER DARK, (Benn Brothers Ltd.), Bouverie House, 154–160 Fleet Street, EC4A 2DL *T.* 01–353 3212. *T.A.* Benbrolish, London, Telex. *Telex:* 887026.

15p., £6·50 p.a. W. (Wednesday press day).—Matter required: news of the furniture, furnishing fabric, bedding, and floor-covering trades and of all subsidiary trades, including machinery and supplies.

CAGE AND AVIARY BIRDS (1902), W. J. PAGE, 161–166 Fleet Street, London, E.C.4. *T.* 01–353 5011.

6p. W. (Thursday).—Practical articles on aviculture. First-hand knowledge only. *Payment:* by arrangement. *Illustrations:* line and photographic.

CAMPAIGN, PETER ELMAN, Gillow House, 5 Winsley Street, London, W1N 7AQ. *T.* 01–636 7766/3600.

15p. W. (Friday).—News and articles covering the whole of the mass communications field, including advertising in all its forms, marketing, newspapers and publishing, public relations, television and printing. News items and exclusive information particularly welcome. Articles should not exceed 2000 words. Press day, Wednesday. *Payment:* by arrangement.

CAMPING (1961), PETER JORDAN, Link House, Dingwall Avenue, Croydon, CR9 2TA *T.* 01–686 2599. *T.A.* Aviculture, Croydon.

15p. M.—Articles based on real camping experiences, all aspects, illustrated with photographs if possible. *Length:* 1000 to 2000 average. *Payment:* from £4·20 per 1000 words. *Illustrations:* line and half-tone.

CANDOUR (1953), A. K. CHESTERTON, M.C. 92 Fleet Street, London, E.C.4. *T.* 01–353 1723.

10p. M.—Politico-economic articles with a national and Commonwealth appeal. *Length:* 1200–1500 words. *Payment:* £5 per 1000 words.

CANVAS (formerly **AMATEUR ARTIST**) (1966), JOHN GAINSBOROUGH, 8 Wyndham Place, W1H 2AY *T.* 01–262 7278.

20p. F.—Articles on all aspects of art. *Length:* up to 1500 words. *Payment:* by arrangement. *Illustrations:* half-tone and line.

CAR (1962), DOUG BLAIN, The National Magazine Co. Ltd., 21 Ebury Street, London, S.W.1. *T.* 01–730 0344.

20p. M.—Top-grade journalistic features on car driving, car people and cars. *Length:* 1000–2500 words. *Payment:* £10·50 per 1000 words minimum. *Illustrations:* black-and-white and colour photographs to professional standard.

CAR MECHANICS, JOSS JOSELYN, Mercury House, Waterloo Road, London, S.E.1. *T.* 01–928 3388. *T.A.* Sysmaga, Souphone London.

15p. M.—Practical articles on car maintenance and repair for the non-technical motorist with limited facilities. *Length:* Average 1500 words of hard fact. *Payment:* £7·35 per 1000 words; pictures £1·05 each. *Illustrations:* line and half-tone. *Preliminary letter outlining the article is advisable.*

CARAVAN, THE (1933), A. W. BRADFORD, Link House, Dingwall Avenue, Croydon CR9 2TA *T.* 01–686 2599. *T.A.* Aviculture, Croydon.

15p. M.—Lively articles based on real experience of caravanning, any aspect, especially if well illustrated by photographs. Also single decorative pictures. General countryside or motoring material not wanted. *Payment:* usually £5·25 per 1000 words, and higher for commissioned technical work.

CARITAS (1934), Granada, Stillorgan, Co. Dublin. *T.* 880509, 880049.
5p. Q.—Matter on mental and physical health, family and community well being. Short stories with a moral. Articles of topical interest. *Length:* 700 to 1500 words. *Payment:* £1·05 to £6·30. *Illustrations:* photographs, and line; black and white only.

CARPETS & TEXTILES (1965), JEAN SHERIDAN, Textile Business Press Ltd., 30 Finsbury Square, London, E.C.2. *T.* 01–628 7901–11.
25p., £2·50 p.a. M.—News, features and articles of interest to carpet and domestic textile retailers. *Payment:* by arrangement. *Illustrations:* half-tone, colour.

CATERER AND HOTELKEEPER (1878), R. O. BAKER, 1 Dorset Buildings, Salisbury Square, E.C.4. *T.* 01–353 1555. *T.A.* Pracpress, London, E.C.4.
10p. W.—Mainly news, plus practical and technical articles. *Length:* up to 1500 words. *Payment:* 2½p. to 5p. line: articles £10·50 to £12·60 per 1000 words. *Illustrations:* photographs (mainly news) and special covers.

CATERERS' ASSOCIATION BULLETIN (Caterers' Association of Great Britain), G. C. HEDGES, Victoria House, Vernon Place, Southampton Row, London, WC1B 4DD *T.* 01–405 1795.
12½p. M.—Articles of about 800–1400 words, news items and paragraphs appertaining to the catering, hotel restaurant, and café trades. *Payment:* by arrangement. *Illustrations:* photographs of interest to above trades.

CATERING & HOTEL MANAGEMENT (1948), MICHAEL DUKE, 167 High Holborn, London, WC1V 6PH *T.* 01–836 9551.
10p. M.—Illustrated features of professional interest to all managers in large-scale catering establishments and welfare feeding. *Length:* 750-word illustrated articles preferably. *Payment:* by arrangement on publication.

CATERING TIMES (1963), MILES QUEST, Elm House, 10–16 Elm Street, London, W.C.1. *T.* 01–837 1234.
2½p. W.—News items and authoritative feature material on all aspects of the food service and hospitality industries, written in crisp concise style. *Payment:* by arrangement. *Illustrations:* photographs.

CATHOLIC EDUCATION TODAY (1967), JAMES McGIBBON and JOSEPH RHYMER, St. Mary's College, Strawberry Hill, Twickenham, Middlesex. *T.* 01–892 0051, ext. 85.
20p. Alt. months.—Articles on all aspects of educational theory and practice, particularly the teaching of religion. *Payment:* £5·25 per 1000 words *Illustrations:* half-tone and line.

CATHOLIC FIRESIDE (1879), P. CHARLES WALKER, 8B Spencer Hill, London, S.W.19. *T.* 01–947 2495.
3p. W.(Friday).—Combines instruction, information and amusement for home reading. Short stories, serials, brightly written articles on subjects of Catholic interest, travel, etc. Should be from 1500 to 3000 words. Illustrated articles always given preference. *Illustrations:* half-tone and line.

CATHOLIC GAZETTE, THE, The Mission House, 114 West Heath Road, N.W.3. *T.* 01–458 3316.
5p. M.—Articles on recent theology, current affairs concerning the Church and Church history are considered. *Length* of articles: 1000 to 2000 words. *Payment:* by arrangement at time of submitting MS.

CATHOLIC HERALD, DESMOND ALBROW, 67 Fleet Street, E.C.4. *T.* 01–353 6264–5.

4p. W.—An independent lay newspaper, topical news and articles of Catholic and Christian interest, but no "parish pump paragraphs." Articles (1100 to 1500 words) about *new* developments in this field and life of Church anywhere. *Payment:* £5 to £15. *Illustrations:* Topical photographs illustrating Catholic life, but not "The little Church in the Austrian Valley" type of thing.

CATHOLIC PICTORIAL (1961) NORMAN CRESSWELL, 12 Prescot Road, Liverpool L7 0LQ *T.* 051–263 9551–2–3.

4p. W.—News and photo features of Lancashire interest.

CATHOLIC STANDARD, THE (1938 Ltd.), DONAL MOONEY, 11 Talbot Street, Dublin 1. *T.* 49478.

4p. W.—Exclusive news stories and pictures of Catholic and general interest. Short contributions preferred. Articles mainly on social and family affairs with special reference to agricultural communities, must be of high literary standard. *Length:* 500 words average; 1000 words maximum. *Payment:* articles at Editor's rating.

CEMENT, LIME AND GRAVEL (1926), BRIAN G. FISH, 62–64 Baker Street, London, W1M 2BN. *T.* 01–486 2547. *T.A.* Ruspamac, London, W.1.

20p., £2·25 p.a., post free. M. (16th.).—Technical material directly relevant to the production of limestone, lime, cement, sand and gravel, ready-mixed concrete, and concrete products. *Payment:* £7·35 per 1000 words for good, original material. *Illustrations:* photographs and line drawings.

CEMENT TECHNOLOGY, 52 Grosvenor Gardens, London, S.W.1. *T.* 01–235 6661.

20p. Alternate months.—Articles on the manufacture, chemistry and marketing of cement; descriptions of modern cement factories in any part of the world. *Illustrations:* photographs and drawings.

CENTRE POINT (formerly **LONDON TEACHER**) (1883), Mrs CHRISTINE ZWART, 40 Belitha Villas, London, N.1. *T.* 01–607 5138.

30p. per annum. 3 issues per year. Organ of the Inner London Teachers' Association. Contributions of interest to teachers in London considered. *Illustrations:* Educational cartoons and photographs.

CERAMIC DIGEST, J. E. ROBERTS, F.R.S.A. (Ceramic Digest Ltd.), 34 Townsend Drive, St. Albans, Herts. *T.* St. Albans 57628 and Hyde Park 3379.

22½p. Q. (at present). £2·50 subscription for twelve copies; £3 overseas.—The Journal of the Ceramic Industry at Home and Overseas. *Payment:* by arrangement.

CERAMICS, Turret Press Ltd., Stamford House, 65–66 Turnmill Street, London, E.C.1. *T.* 01–253 8201–10.

£2·50 per annum. M. (18th.).—Articles on works processes and plant in clay, glass, pottery and porcelain industries. *Length:* 2000 to 3000 words. *Payment:* £4·20 per 1000 words. *Illustrations:* half-tone and line blocks.

CERTIFIED ACCOUNTANTS JOURNAL, ROBERT BELL, (Association of Certified and Corporate Accountants), 22 Bedford Square, W.C.1. *T.* 01–636 5163–4.

12p. M. (except August)—Articles of accounting and financial interest. *Preliminary letter* to Editor before submitting MSS.

CHARTERED SECRETARY, THE (founded as The Secretary, 1904), 16 Park Crescent, London, W1N 4AH   *T.* 01–580 4741.

12½p.   M. (excluding August).—Articles of business interest to members of the Institute: Law, economics, local government, etc.   *Length:* about 2500 words.   *Payment:* £6·30 per page (approx. 800 words).   *Illustrations:* half-tone.

CHEMICAL AGE (incorporating **CHEMICAL TRADE JOURNAL**) (1887), M. C. HYDE, Editor. (Benn Bros., Ltd.), Bouverie House, 154 Fleet Street, EC4A 2DL   *T.* 01–353 3212.   *T.A.* Benformula, London.

17½p., £8 p.a.   W. (Friday).—News relating to chemical industry and chemical engineering.   Articles on market trends, economics.   *Length:* 500 to 1200 words.   *Payment* by agreement.   *Illustrations:* diagrams, news and personal photographs.

CHEMICAL AND PROCESS ENGINEERING (1950), I. L. HEPNER, PH.D., M.I.CHEM.E., Morgan-Grampian (Publishers) Ltd., 28 Essex Street, Strand, London, W.C.2.   *T.* 01–353 6565.   *T.A.* Induspres, London, W.C.2.

£4 per annum.   M.—Articles on chemical engineering subjects such as evaporation, absorption, distillation, extraction, size reduction, filtration, plant design, materials of construction, process operation, etc.   Also articles relating to other process industries.   Most articles are commissioned.   *Length:* 1000–3000 words.   *Payment:* by arrangement.   *Illustrations:* line and half-tone, photographs and diagrams.

CHEMICAL PROCESSING, CLIVE HOPKINS, 33–40 Bowling Green Lane, London, E.C.1.   *T.* 01–837 1277.

Controlled Circulation.   M.—Technical and managerial articles on process operations, processing equipment and materials of construction.   *Length:* 2500 words.   *Payment:* by arrangement.   *Illustrations:* photographs and line drawings.

CHEMIST AND DRUGGIST (1859), A. WRIGHT, M.P.S., D.B.A., 12 Dyott Street, London, WC1A 1DA.   *T.* 01–240 0855.

25p. (£6 per annum, including Year Book).   W.—News of the trade, technical articles (up to 1500 words), and commercial information respecting the practice of pharmacy and the pharmaceutical, chemical, drug, cosmetic, and allied industries.   *Illustrations:* usually half-tone blocks.   *Payment:* by arrangement.

CHESHIRE LIFE (1934), LESLIE N. RADCLIFFE, The Whitethorn Press Ltd., Thomson House, Withy Grove, Manchester M6O 4BL.   *T.* 061–834 1234.

15p.   M.—Articles of country interest only.   No fiction.   *Length:* 800–1500 words.   *Payment:* £4·20 per 1000 words minimum.   *Illustrations:* line and half-tone, 4-colour block for cover.   Photographs of news value and definite Cheshire interest.   £1·05 minimum payment.

CHILD EDUCATION (1924), MISS MARY E. BINGLEY (Evans Brothers, Ltd.), Montague House, Russell Square, London, WC1B 5BX   *T.* 01–636 8521.   *T.A.* Byronitic, London, W.C.1.

20p.   M. (25th for following month).   Also 4 Quarterly Numbers, 15p. For teachers and adults practically interested in the education of young children. Articles by specialists on teaching methods, psychology, etc., also plays, music, and short stories for young children (*length:* 1000 to 2000 words).   *Payment:* by arrangement.   Profusely illustrated in line, and by photographs; also large pictures in full colour.

CHINA QUARTERLY, THE, DAVID C. WILSON, Contemporary China Institute, 24 Fitzroy Square, London, W.1.   *T.* 01–387 9044.
    75p., £3 p.a.   Q.—Articles on Contemporary China.   *Length:* 8000 words approx.   *Payment:* £50·40 per articles of 8000 words.   No *illustrations.*

CHRISTIAN ACTION (1957), MRS. DIANA COLLINS, 2 Amen Court, London, E.C.4.   *T.* 01–248 3747.
    23p.   Q.—Articles, 1500–2500 words.   Reviews, short stories, poems.   *Payment:* £7·35 per article.   *Illustrations:* occasional photographs.

CHRISTIAN HERALD (1866), 4 Western Esplanade, Portslade, Brighton, BN4 IWP   *T.* Brighton 47288.
    4p.   W. (Saturday).—Contributions, about 1500 words, should be bright, accompanied by photographs if possible.   Topical articles should be received at least a month in advance of date concerned.   Christian serial stories with plenty of movement, 20,000–40,000 words, will be considered, also short stories, 1600 words.   The paper is strictly evangelical and definitely upholds the Reformed Faith.   *Payment:* varies according to length and interest.

CHRISTIAN NOVELS (1905), L. PALK (Wm. Stevens Publications, Ltd.), 53 Fetter Lane, London E.C.4.   *T.* 583 9027.
    2½p.   W. (Monday).—Contains fiction with plenty of incident and action, of about 21,000 words in length.   No sex questions or controversial matter.   *Payment:* on acceptance.   *No illustrations.*

CHRISTIAN RECORD (Interdenominational Weekly) (1969), 69 Fleet Street, London, EC4Y 1NN.   *T.* 01–583 7915.
    4p.   W.—Articles of religious and social interest.   A *Preliminary* letter is advisable.   *Length:* 1500 word maximum.   *Payment:* £3·15 per 1000.   *Illustrations:* photographs and drawings.

CHURCH OF ENGLAND NEWSPAPER (1894), 182 Fleet Street, E.C.4.   *T.* 01–242 9694.
    4p.   W. (Friday).—The newspaper contains articles of religious and social interest.   A *preliminary letter* is advisable.   *Length:* normally 1500 words maximum.   *Payment:* £3·15 per 1000.   *Illustrations:* photographs or drawings.

CHURCH OF IRELAND GAZETTE (1885, New Series 1963), Canon F. A. G. WILLIS, 20 High Street, Belfast, 1.   *T.* Belfast 29321.
    2½p.   W. (Friday).—Church news, articles of religious and general interest.   *Length:* 600 to 1000 words.   *Payment:* according to length and interest.

CHURCH NEWS (1948), 11 Ludgate Square, London, E.C.4.   *T.* 01–248 2872.
    2p.   M. (25th).—An Illustrated Church magazine inset.   Articles of popular Church interest (500 to 1000 words); occasional short stories and verse.   *Illustrations:* photographs and line drawings of religious and ecclesiastical subjects.   *Payment:* by arrangement.

CHURCH QUARTERLY, THE (1968) (incorporating **LONDON QUARTERLY AND HOLBORN REVIEW** and **CHURCH QUARTERLY REVIEW**): Editors: The Rev. M. C. PERRY, M.A., SPCK, Holy Trinity Church, Marylebone Road, London, N.W.1.   *T.* 01–387 5282, The Rev. G. S. WAKEFIELD, M.A., B.LITT., Epworth Press, 27 Marylebone Road, London, N.W.1.   *T.* 01–935 2549.
    42½p.   Q.—Articles on Christian doctrine, sociology, ethics, church history, ecumenical thought, philosophy and comparative religion, literature and the arts.   *Length:* up to 4000 words maximum.   A small nominal *payment* is made for most articles.

CHURCH TEACHER (1956), Church Information Office, Church House, Dean's Yard, S.W.1. *T.* 01–222 9011. Editor: MRS. PAMELA EGAN, Children's Council, Church House, Dean's Yard, S.W.1.

5p. M.—Short, practical or topical articles dealing with all forms of voluntary religious education and concerned with the development and psychology of children. *Illustrations:* half-tone and line. *Length:* up to 1200 words. *Payment:* usually £2 per 1000 words.

CHURCH TIMES (1863), 7 Portugal Street, WC2A 2HP *T.* 01–405 0844.

3½p. W. (Friday).—Articles on ecclesiastical and social topics are considered. Usual *length:* 750 to 1500 words. No verse or fiction. *Payment:* £4·20 per 1000 words minimum. *Illustrations:* news photographs.

CHURCHMAN, THE (1879), G. E. DUFFIELD, Appleford House, Appleford, Abingdon, Berks. *T.* Sutton Courtenay 319.

20p. per copy, 75p. p.a. (post free). Q.—A quarterly journal of Anglican theology, evangelical in emphasis. Religious and literary articles on subjects of current interest and significance in theology and ecclesiastical life. *Length:* 2000 to 5000 words. *Payment:* honorarium. No illustrations.

CITY PRESS (1857), RICHARD LAMB, 4 Moorfields, London, E.C.2. *T.* 01–628 6331.

2½p. W. (Thursday).—Contributions invited of City of London interest, and on economic, financial and industrial subjects. *Payment:* £5·25 to £21 per 1000 words.

CIVIL ENGINEERING AND PUBLIC WORKS REVIEW (1906), DAVID LIGHT, 8 Buckingham Street, London, W.C.2. *T.* 01–839 6661.

25p. M.—Contains highly technical articles on subjects of current interest to Civil Engineers. From 1000 words upwards. *Payment:* by arrangement. *Illustrations:* line blocks of sectional drawings and photographs of engineering works, either recently completed or in various stages of progress. *A preliminary letter is essential.*

CIVIL SERVICE OPINION (founded as **THE QUILL**, 1923), TREVOR WOOLSTON, 19 Surrey Street, London, WC2R 2NR *T.* 01–836 5303.

5p. M.—Anything of interest to senior Civil Servants, articles on trade union problems and public administration, humorous articles on Service topics. *Length:* up to 2000 words. *Payment:* £5 per page (about 1000 words) but higher payment by arrangement. *Illustrations:* line and half-tone blocks. Cartoons on Civil Service themes.

CLAYCRAFT AND STRUCTURAL CERAMICS (1927), J. E. ROBERTS, F.R.S.A., Stamford House, 65–66 Turnmill Street, London, E.C.1. *T.* 01–253 8201.

37p. M. (£4 Ann. Sub., £4·50 overseas).—Welcomes reviews and notices of current literature, biographical notices, and technical articles, which must be authoritatively written, of interest to the clay industry. *Length:* approximately 1000 words. *Payment:* by arrangement.

CLEANING AND MAINTENANCE, Turret Press Ltd., Stamford House, 65–66 Turnmill Street, London, E.C.1. *T.* 01–253 8201–10.

£3 per annum, post free, including the Cleaning and Maintenance Year Book. M.—Articles on all aspects of industrial and commercial maintenance cleaning. Technical articles on plant, equipment and materials relating to cleaning, including flooring, seals, polishes, disinfectants, detergents, etc. *Length:* 1000 to 2500 words. *Payment* £4·20 per 1000 words. *Illustrations:* half-tone and line.

CLERGY REVIEW, The Rev. M. RICHARDS, S.T.L., B.LITT., M.A., St. Edmunds College, Ware, Herts. *T.* 0920–821 223.
    30p. M. (by subscription, £3·25 a year; U.S.A. $7.00).—A journal of information, dialogue and research for Catholics of the English-speaking countries. *Length* and *payment* by arrangement.

CLIMBER AND RAMBLER (1962), R. R. BUTCHART, 56–57 Fleet Street, London E.C.4. *T.* 01–583 5671.
    12½p. M.—Articles on all aspects of mountaineering and hill walking, in Great Britain and abroad, and on related subjects. *Length:* 500 to 3000 words, preferably illustrated. *Payment:* according to merit. *Illustrations:* photographs and line drawings.

CLUB SECRETARY (1953), DAVID FIELD, B.A., Legal Editor, 9 Gough Square, Fleet Street, London, E.C.4. *T.* 01–353 3172. *T.A.* Markeba, London, E.C.4.
    £3 p.a. M.—Feature articles and news items slanted to inform people concerned with the management of clubs of every type. *Payment:* by arrangement. *Illustrations:* line and half-tone.

COACHING JOURNAL & BUS REVIEW, J. F. SPEED, M.I.MECH.E., ASSOC.INST.T., 2 Mumford Court, E.C.2. *T.* 01–606 8465.
    17½p. M.—News and views of the road passenger transport industry. No stories. Articles of from 800 to 1000 words. *Payment:* from £4·20 per 1000. *Illustrations:* coaches, coach stations, etc.

COAL MERCHANT AND SHIPPER (1900), KEITH WHITWORTH, John Adam House, 17–19 John Adam Street, London, W.C.2. *T.* 01–839 6171. *T.A.* Zacatecas, London, WC2N 6JH.
    £2·40 per annum, single copies 10p. M. Wholesale and retail coal trade; coal export trade; commercial aspects of the coal industry. This is a specialised journal, and a prior letter is advisable. News items and features welcomed. *Payment:* by arrangement. *Illustrations:* special aspects of the interests covered; generally in connection with special articles. Line and half-tone.

COINS (1964), HEATHER SALTER, Link House, Dingwall Avenue, Croydon, CR9 2TA *T.* 01–686 2599. *T.A.* Aviculture, Croydon.
    15p. M.—Articles of high standard on coins and medals. *Length:* up to 1000 words. *Payment:* by arrangement. *Illustrations:* line and half-tone.

COLLECTORS WEEKLY, The Antiques and Art Newspaper (1970), WILLIAM F. SPICER, Aldwych House, 81 Aldwych, London, WC2B 4HL *T.* 01–242 8621.
    10p. W.—Features, personality profiles, specialist articles with pictures on furniture, silver, porcelain, glass, works of art etc. *Length:* 800–1500 words. Also news and diary items from world of art and antiques. *Payment:* £1·05 per 100 words. *Illustrations:* line, half-tone, colour.

COLLIERY GUARDIAN (1858) (incorporating the mining interests of **STEEL AND COAL,** formerly the **IRON AND COAL TRADES REVIEW**), KEITH WHITWORTH, John Adam House, 17–19 John Adam Street, Adelphi, London, WC2N 6JH *T.* 01–839 6171. *T.A.* Zacatecas, London, W.C.2.
    50p., £6·50 (inc. Annual Review Issue) p.a. M. (8th)—Coal industry and its ancillary trades and interests. Matter of interest to the coal industry from a trade and technical standpoint. News items and features welcomed. *Payment* by arrangement. *Illustrations:* line, half-tone.

COMING EVENTS IN BRITAIN (1930), D. A. YOUNG, The British Travel Association, 64 St. James's Street, London, S.W.1. *T.* 01-629 9191.

15p. M. (£1·95 annual subscription).—Articles 400-1200 words occasionally accepted on all aspects of life in Britain, written to attract the overseas visitor. *Payments:* £3·15 to £10·50. *Illustrations:* half-tone (photographs normally provided by staff.)

COMMANDO (D. C. Thomson & Co., Ltd.), Courier Place, Dundee, DD1 9QJ, and Thomson House, 12 Fetter Lane, London, E.C.4.

5p. Six each month.—War stories of World War II told in pictures. Line drawings. Scripts should be of about 140 pictures, 63 pages. New artists and writers encouraged. *Payment:* on acceptance.

COMMERCE INTERNATIONAL, K. GRUNDY, 69 Cannon Street, London, E.C.4. *T.* 01-236 2675.

30p. M.—Authoritative outside contributions are accepted on commercial and industrial subjects. *Payment:* by arrangement. *Illustrations:* half-tone. *Preliminary letter essential.*

COMMERCIAL GROWER (1895), H. G. WARR (Benn Brothers Ltd.), 154 Fleet Street, E.C.4. *T.* 01-353 3212.

7½p., £3·75 p.a. W. (Friday).—Trade and news pictures and practical and informative articles on production and distribution for those engaged in fruit, flower and vegetable growing on a commercial scale, both outdoors and under glass. *Length:* up to 1000 words. *Payment:* 2½p. a line for general news: exclusive news and technical articles by arrangement. *Illustrations:* half-tone or line.

COMMERCIAL MOTOR (1905), H. BRIAN COTTEE, IPC Transport Press Ltd., Dorset House, Stamford Street, London, S.E.1. *T.* 01-928 3333.

12½p. W. (Friday).—*Payment:* varies for articles (technical and road transport only), maximum length 2000 words, drawings, and photographs. Photos of commercial vehicles (including buses and coaches) in service, with life and incident, most likely to be accepted.

COMMERCIAL VEHICLES (1947), JOHN ALDRIDGE, Dorset House, Stamford Street, S.E.1. *T.* 01-928 3333. *T.A.* Commveh, Iliffepres 25137, London, Telex.

Controlled circulation. M.—Articles dealing with the professional operation of road transport vehicles. *Payment:* by arrangement. *Illustrations:* half-tone or line.

COMPASS NEWSPAPERS (formerly NATIONAL CHRISTIAN NEWS), Rev. GEOFFREY BROWN, 319 Gazette Buildings, Corporation Street, Birmingham 4. *T.* 021-236 2275.

M.—Tabloid newspaper for issuing in bulk to parishes and groups of churches. Illustrated articles and news stories. *Length:* 300-800 words. *Payment:* £1 per 100 words for first 300, 50p. per 100 words thereafter. *Illustrations:* half-tone.

COMPUTER SURVEY (1962), Miss MABOTH MOSELEY, 9 Gough Square, Fleet Street, London, E.C.4. *T.* 01-353 3172.

£1. Bi-M.—Devoted mainly to surveys of the digital computer industry in Britain and British-built computers overseas; but authoritative articles on the financial and economic aspects of the computer industry, world-wide, are considered. *Payment:* by arrangement. *Illustrations:* line and half-tone.

COMPUTER WEEKLY (1966), J. C. HIPWELL, M.A., IPC Electrical–Electronic Press Ltd., Dorset House, Stamford Street, S.E.1. *T.* 01–928 3333.
Controlled circulation. W.—Specialised news and features on computer subjects. *Payment:* £1 per 100 words published. *Illustrations:* line and half-tone.

CONCRETE (1967) 52 Grosvenor Gardens, London, S.W.1. *T.* 01–235 6661.
25p. M. Articles on the theory and practice of reinforced and prestressed concrete and descriptions of important concrete contracts. *Illustrations:* photographs and drawings.

CONFECTIONERY AND TOBACCO NEWS, (incorporating **BRITISH STATIONER**) LEN BRIGHT (NTD Business Journals Ltd.), 33–39 Bowling Green Lane, London, E.C.1. *T.* 01–837 1277.
4p. F. (alt. Thursdays).—£1·25 p.a. Trade news and brief articles illustrated when possible with photographs or line drawings. Must be of live interest to retail confectioner-tobacconists and newsagents. *Length:* Articles 600–800 words. *Payment:* news lineage rates £5·25 per 1000 words, articles at negotiated rates.

CONGREGATIONAL MONTHLY, THE (1924), F. W. BELL, 11 Carteret Street, Westminster S.W.1. *T.* 01–930 0061. *T.A.* Indpress, London.
2½p. M.—Articles religious or educational in character. *Length:* 750–1250 words. *Illustrations:* half-tone and line drawings. *Payment:* by arrangement.

CONNOISSEUR (1901), L. G. G. RAMSEY, Chestergate House, Vauxhall Bridge Road, London, S.W.1. *T.* 01–834 2331.
75p. 12 times a year.—Articles on all subjects interesting to art collectors are considered, but a *preliminary letter* should be sent. *Length:* Articles about 2000 words. Writers are held responsible for all dates and facts mentioned. *Payment:* according to arrangement. *Illustrations:* all kinds suitable to subjects dealt with; photographs preferred. Illustrations are essential.

CONTEMPORARY REVIEW (incorporating the **FORTNIGHTLY**) (1866), Editor: ROSALIND WADE. Literary Review: A. G. de MONTMORENCY, Editorial Advisers: SIR DENIS BROGAN, SIR HERBERT BUTTERFIELD. Fine Arts Correspondent: ERNLE MONEY. Manager: MARGARET FREAN, 38 Farringdon Street, London, E.C.4. *T.* 01–248 5824.
25p. M. (1st).—Independent, but slightly left of centre. A review dealing with all questions of the day, chiefly politics, theology, history, literature, travel, poetry, the arts. A great part of the matter is commissioned, but there is scope for free-lance specialists. Articles submitted should be typewritten and should be about 2000 to 3000 words. If refused, articles are returned, *if a stamped envelope is enclosed. Payment:* £2·50 per 1000 words, 2 complimentary copies. Potential contributors should study journal before submitting MSS.

CONTRACT JOURNAL (1879), BERNARD DONOVAN, 32 Southwark Bridge Road, London, S.E.1. *T.* 01–928 2060. *T.A.* Beandcejay, London, S.E.1.
17½p. W.—Technical articles on construction projects; news of forthcoming building work. *Length:* 1000 to 2000 words. *Payment:* by arrangement. *Illustrations:* line and half-tone.

CONTRACTOR, 151 Dulwich Road, London, S.E.24. *T.* 01–733 6201.
35p. M. 1–2000 word articles on practical construction methods, concerning the use, management and maintenance of contractors mechanical plant. *Payment:* £10·50 per 1000 words min. *Illustrations:* line and half-tone.

CONTRIBUTOR'S BULLETIN. See Freelance Press Services on p. 207.

CONTROL & INSTRUMENTATION (1958), D. SIMS, (Morgan-Grampian (Publishers) Ltd.), 28 Essex Street, Strand, London, W.C.2. *T.* 01–353 6565.
£5 p.a. M. (last Thursday of preceding month). Authoritative main feature articles on automation, control systems, instrumentation, and data processing. Also political, economic or engineering news connected in any way with control. *Payment:* according to value. *Length of articles:* 500 words for highly technical pieces. 2000 to 5000 words main features. Serial articles to greater length. *Illustrations:* half-tone and photographs and drawings of equipment using automatic techniques, control engineering personalities.

CONVERTING INDUSTRY, J. F. TOWNSEND (S. C. Phillips & Co. Ltd.), Alliance House, 50–51 Fetter Lane, E.C.4. *T.* 01–353 7076-7.
30p. M.—Practical articles on all forms of conversion of paper, paperboard, transparent films, laminates and aluminium foils. Features on all new developments, including machinery and equipment and materials used in the converting industries. About 2000 words unless otherwise agreed. *Payment:* by arrangement.

CO-PARTNERSHIP (1884), IAN GORDON BROWN, 60 Buckingham Gate, London, S.W.1. *T.* 01–828 8754.
Q. £1·50 per annum post free.—Journal of the Industrial Co-partnership Association. Articles on co-partnership and profit-sharing in industry, employee shareholding, joint consultation, the sharing of information, labour-management relations, workers participation, and kindred industrial subjects from the operational angle, with emphasis on the practice of particular enterprises, usually written by a member of the management team involved, and with a strong factual background. *Payment:* is seldom required.

CORDAGE, CANVAS AND JUTE WORLD, ARTHUR DOWSETT, 157 Hagden Lane, Watford, WD1 8LW. *T.* Watford 32308.
44p. M.—Technically accurate articles on hemp, jute, flax and sisal (the "long" fibres and manufactures therefrom). Articles with photos particularly welcome on the ropemakers, tent and canvas makers and hirers, and sack and bag makers in various towns. Submit synopsis. *Payment:* £4·20 and upwards per 1000. *Illustrations:* half-tone and line.

CORK WEEKLY EXAMINER AND WEEKLY HERALD, J. A. CULLEN, F.J.I., 95 Patrick Street, Cork. *T.* 26661 (10 lines).
2½p. W.—Short stories, 1500 words. Stories should preferably possess an *Irish* interest. *Illustrations:* photographs, line or wash drawings. *Payment:* short stories from £4·20; poems £2 to 25p.

CORNHILL MAGAZINE (1860), 50 Albemarle Street, W1X 4BD. *T.* 01–493 4361.
25p. Illustrated. Four issues a year with occasional Supplements containing work of up to 35,000 words in length. Fiction, verse, articles, belles-lettres, criticism of a high literary standard. No contribution previously published in this country is accepted. Contributions should be typewritten and accompanied by a stamped addressed envelope. *Payment:* by arrangement. *Illustrations:* line and half-tone.

CORSETRY AND UNDERWEAR (1935), N. ROGER PARKER, 47 Hertford Street, Mayfair, W1Y 8EH *T.* 01–493 7557.
Controlled circulation. M. (1st).—Trade articles, technical and trade news. *Length:* 1500 words maximum. *Payment:* 1½p. per line.

COUNTRY GENTLEMEN'S MAGAZINE, THE (1901), Country Gentlemen's Association, 54–62 Regent Street, London, W1R 6AQ *T.* 01–437 0244. £2·10 per annum. M.—Journal of the Country Gentlemen's Association. Practical and authoritative articles of general country interest. From 500 to 1500 words. *Payment:* varies: from £8·40 per 1000 words. *Illustrations:* line and black-and-white.

COUNTRY LIFE (1897), J. K. ADAMS, 2–10 Tavistock Street, Covent Garden. WC2E 9QX *T.* 01–836 4363.
20p. W. (Thursday).—An illustrated journal, chiefly concerned with English country life, natural history, agriculture, architecture and the fine arts. *Length of articles:* about 700, 1000, 1350 or 1800 words; short poems are also considered. *Payment:* according to merit. Press day, Thursday. *Illustrations:* mainly photographs.

COUNTRYMAN, THE (1927), JOHN CRIPPS, Editorial Office: Burford, Oxford OX8 4LH. *T.* Burford 2258. Advertising: 23–27 Tudor Street, E.C.4. Publishing: Watling Street, Bletchley, Bucks.
30p. Q.—Every department of rural life and progress except field sports. Party politics and townee sentimentalising about the country barred. Copy must be trustworthy, well written, brisk, cogent and light in hand. Articles up to 2500 words. Good paragraphs and notes, first-class poetry, and skilful sketches of life and character from personal knowledge and experience. Dependable natural history based on writer's own observation. Really good matter from old unpublished letters and MSS. *Payment:* £9·45 per 1000 words and upwards according to merit. *Illustrations:* photographs and drawings, but all must be exclusive and out of the ordinary, and bear close scrutiny. Humour welcomed if genuine.

COUNTRY QUEST, GLYN GRIFFITHS, Caxton Press, Oswestry, Salop. *T.* 4321.
15p. M.—*Illustrated* articles on matters relating to country-side of Wales and Border counties. *Length:* 1000 to 1500 words. Short poems. No fiction. *Payment:* by arrangement. *Illustrations:* half-tone and line.

COUNTRY-SIDE (1905), ANTHONY WOOTTON, 13 Bishopstone Road, Stone, Nr. Aylesbury, Bucks.
50p. per annum. Published every 4 months. Official organ of The British Naturalists' Association (B.E.N.A.). Original observations on wild life and its protection, and on natural history generally, but not on killing for sport. *Payment:* not usually made. *Illustrations:* photographs and drawings. *Preliminary letter* advisable.

COVENTRY EVENING TELEGRAPH, K. WHETSTONE, Corporation Street, Coventry, CV1 1FP *T.* Coventry 25588. London Office: 192 Fleet Street, E.C.4.
2p. D.—Illustrated articles of topical interest, those with a Warwickshire interest particularly acceptable. *Maximum length:* 800 words.

CRANES (1966), CHRIS WILSON, 28 Essex Street, Strand, London, W.C.2. *T.* 01–353 6565.
£3 p.a. Twelve issues a year.—Covers the design, manufacture, operation, hire and maintenance of cranes. *Length:* 1000 to 3000 words. *Payment:* by arrangement. *Illustrations:* line and half-tone, photographs and diagrams.

CREATIVE CAMERA (formerly **CAMERA OWNER**) (1964), COLIN OSMAN, Coo Press Ltd., 19 Doughty Street, London. WC1N 2PT *T.* 01–405 7562.
17½p. M.—Illustrated articles and single pictures, particularly modern creative photography. *Payment:* £5·25 per page. *Illustrations:* black and white half-tone.

CRIMINOLOGIST, THE, (1966), NIGEL MORLAND, Forensic Publishing Co., 9 Old Bailey, London, E.C.4.

55p. post free or £2 yearly. Q.—Specialised material designed for an expert and professional readership. Covers nationally and internationally criminology, the police, forensic science, the law, penology, sociology and law enforcement. Articles (2000 to 6000 words) by those familiar with the journal's style and requirements are welcomed. *A preliminary letter* with a brief résumé is preferable. *Payment:* is wholly governed by the nature and quality of manuscripts. *Illustrations:* line, and photographs.

CRITICAL QUARTERLY, THE (1959), C. B. COX and A. E. DYSON, The University, Manchester. *T.* 061–273 3333.

40p. Q.—Literary criticism, poems. *Length:* 2000–10,000 words. *Payment:* by arrangement. Interested contributors should study magazine before submitting MSS.

CROSS, THE (1910), Rev. BRIAN D'ARCY, C.P., Mount Argus, Dublin, 6. *T.* Dublin 971469 and 971165.

5p. M. (90p. yearly, post free).—Illustrated magazine of Catholic and general interest. Articles, 1200 to 1500 words on general topics of Catholic interest. Illustrated articles especially welcome. No Fiction. *Payment:* £2·50 to £5·50, on publication. *Illustrations:* half-tone from photos.

CRUSADE (1955), DAVID B. WINTER, 30 Bedford Place, London, WC1B 5JN *T.* 01–636 1132.

10p. M.—News and feature articles on evangelism, social and other issues from evangelical viewpoint; missionary and other Christian biography; small amount of fiction and poetry with Christian or moral emphasis. *Payment:* £3·15 per 1500 words.

CUMBRIA (1951), HARRY J. SCOTT, Dalesman Publishing Company, Ltd., Clapham, via Lancaster. *T.* Clapham (Lancaster) 225.

7½p. M.—Articles of genuine rural interest concerning Lakeland. Short *length* preferred. *Payment:* according to merit. *Illustrations:* line drawings and first-class photographs.

CUSTOM CAR (1970), MICHAEL HILL, Link House, Dingwall Avenue, Croydon, CR9 2TA *T.* 01–686 2599. *T.A.* Aviculture, Croydon.

15p. *Payment:* by arrangement. *Length:* 1000–2000 words.

CYCLETOURING (1878), H. JOHN WAY, Cotterell House, 69 Meadrow, Godalming, Surrey. *T.* Godalming 7217–8.

Alt. months from Dec. 1st. 15p. including postage. (free to members of the Cyclists' Touring Club). Articles, 500 to 2000 words—preferably well illustrated with photographs or sketches—relating to recreational cycling, travel, and countryside. *Payment:* by arrangement. Few outside contributors.

CYCLING (1891), KEN EVANS, IPC Specialist and Professional Press Ltd., 161 Fleet Street, London, E.C.4. *T.* 01–353 5011.

10p. W. (Thursdays)—Touring, technical, and short humorous articles not exceeding 1300 words are invited. Topical photographs and a limited amount of fiction with a pronounced cycling interest also considered. *Payment:* by arrangement.

DAILY EXPRESS, DEREK MARKS, Fleet Street, London, E.C.4. *T.* 01–383 8000; Great Ancoats Street, Manchester. *T.* Manchester Central 2112; Albion Street, Glasgow. *T.* Glasgow Bell 3550.

2½p. D.—Exclusive news; striking photographs. Leader page articles, 600 words; facts preferred to opinions. *Payment:* according to value.

DAILY MAIL (1896) (Now incorporating **NEWS CHRONICLE**), ARTHUR BRITTENDEN, Northcliffe House, E.C.4.   *T.* 01–353 6000.

2½p.   D.—Highest payments for good, exclusive news.   Leader Page articles 500–800 words average.   Ideas for these welcomed.   Exclusive news photographs always wanted.

DAILY MIRROR (1903), L. A. LEE HOWARD, Holborn Circus, London, E.C.1.   *T.* 01–353 0246.

2½p.   D.—Top payment for exclusive news and news pictures.   Few articles from free-lances used, but ideas bought.   Send only a synopsis.   "Unusual" pictures and those giving a new angle on the news are welcomed.

DAILY RECORD, 67 Hope Street, Glasgow.   *T.* Glasgow City 7000.   London: 33 Holborn, London, E.C.1.   *T.* 01–353 0246.

2½p.   D.—Topical articles of from 300 to 700 words.   Exclusive paragraphs of Scottish interest and exclusive photographs.

DAILY SKETCH (formerly **DAILY GRAPHIC**) (1890), DAVID ENGLISH, New Carmelite House, London, E.C.4.   *T.* 01–353 6000.

2½p.   D.—Exclusive news, pictures, cartoons and news-projection ideas welcomed.   *Payment:* very generous.

DAILY TELEGRAPH (1855) **AND MORNING POST** (1772), MAURICE GREEN, 135 Fleet Street, E.C.4.   *T.* 01–353 4242.

2½p.   D.—Independent.   Authoritative articles, 600 to 1400 words, arising out of current topics are welcome.   *Illustrations:* topical photographs.

DAIRY FARMER, D. A. GOMERY, Lloyds Chambers, Ipswich.   *T.* Ipswich 54081–3.

10p.   M.—Authoritative articles dealing in practical, lively style with dairy farming.   Topical controversial articles invited.   Well-written, illustrated accounts of new ideas being tried on dairy farms are especially wanted.   *Length:* up to 1500 words.   *Payment:* according to merit.   *Illustrations:* half-tone or line.

DAIRY INDUSTRIES (1936) (including **DAIRY AND ICE CREAM INDUSTRIES DIRECTORY**), Editor: Miss DALLAS FAWDRY, B.A. (United Trade Press Ltd.), 9 Gough Square, Fleet Street, London, E.C.4.   *T.* 01–353 3172.

50p.   M. (£5 post free; Canada and U.S.A. 15.00 dollars; other countries £6).—Covers the entire field of milk processing, the manufacture of products from liquid milk, and ice cream.   Articles relating to dairy plant, butter and cheese making, ice cream making, etc.   *Payment:* by arrangement; special lineage rates.   *Illustrations:* glossy prints and indian ink diagrams.

DALESMAN, THE (1939), HARRY J. SCOTT, Dalesman Publishing Company Ltd., Clapham, via Lancaster.   *T.* Clapham (Lancaster) 225.

10p.   M.—Articles and stories of genuine rural interest concerning Yorkshire and the North Country.   Short *length* preferred.   *Payment:* according to merit.   Colour reproductions, line drawings and first-class photographs.

DANCE AND DANCERS (1950), Editor/Art Director: PETER WILLIAMS, Hansom Books, Artillery Mansions, 75 Victoria Street, London, S.W.1.   *T.* 01–799 4452.

30p.   M.—Articles and photographs on classical ballet, modern dance and national dancing in theatre, films and television. (No ballroom dancing.)

DANCING TIMES (1910), Editor: MARY CLARKE, Editorial Adviser: IVOR GUEST, 18 Hand Court, Holborn, London, W.C.1.   *T.* 01–405 1414–5.

20p.   M.—Dealing with ballet and stage dancing, both from general, critical and technical angles.   Well informed free-lance articles are occasionally used, but only after preliminary arrangements.   *Payment:* from £2·10.   *Illustrations:* half-tone, occasional line, action photographs always preferred.

DANDY, THE (D. C. Thomson & Co., Ltd.), Courier Place, Dundee, DD1 9QJ, and Thomson House, 12 Fetter Lane, London, E.C.4.
2p. W. (Tuesday).—Comic Strips for boys and girls. Stories told in pictures (16–20 drawings). *Payment:* on acceptance.

DATA JOURNAL, K. GILL, Onslow Hall, Little Green, Richmond, Surrey. *T.* 01–940 3341–43.
M.—Technical, trade union and industrial matter. *Payment:* £5 per 1000 words. *Illustrations:* line and half-tone blocks.

DATA PROCESSING (1959), E. P. BAILEY, IPC Electrical–Electronic Press Ltd., Dorset House, Stamford Street, London, S.E.1. *T.* 01–928 3333. *T.A.* Data Iliffepres 25137, London, Telex.
£1·50 Bi-monthly.—Articles on data processing methods and machines including descriptions of new computers and peripheral equipment, the application of computers in business and industry, software developments, and computer-based management techniques. *Length:* 2000 to 5000 words. *Payment:* £12·60 per 1000 words published. *Illustrations:* Half-tone and line.

DATA SYSTEMS, GRAHAM WEINER, Mercury House, Waterloo Road, London, S.E.1. *T.* 01–928 3388.
60p., £6 p.a. M.—Authoritative, well-written articles, addressed to senior businessmen, company directors, managers, accountants, systems analysts, programmers, etc., on aspects of business information technology, e.g. cybernetics, operations research and data retrieval. A very high standard is required. *Length:* 1500 words and upward. *Payment:* by arrangement, normally £10·50 per 1000 words. *Illustrations:* Line and 120 screen half-tone.

DECORATING CONTRACTOR formerly **DECORATOR** (1902) (incorporating **PAINT AND WALLPAPER**), GODFREY STAINES (Trade Publications Ltd.). John Adam House, 17–19 John Adam Street, Adelphi, London, WC2N 6JH *T.* 01–839 6171.
£2·40 per annum, M. (mid-month).—Technical articles on decorating, including the use of cladding materials; articles on performance and handling of new materials, and on design. *Length:* 1500 to 2000 words. *Illustrations:* photographs, good line drawings and, when applicable, diagrams, welcome. *Payment:* by arrangement.

DERBYSHIRE LIFE AND COUNTRYSIDE (1931), Lodge Lane, Derby DE1 3HE *T.* Derby 47087–8–9.
15p. M.—Articles, preferably illustrated, about Derbyshire life, people, and history. *Length:* 1000–1500 words. Short stories and verse little used. *Payment:* according to nature and quality of contribution. *Illustrations:* photographs of Derbyshire subjects.

DESIGN (1949), CORIN HUGHES-STANTON, The Council of Industrial Design, The Design Centre, 28 Haymarket, S.W.1. *T.* 01–839 8000.
25p. M.—Articles on industrial design at home and abroad: case-histories of new products and company design policy (by arrangement with the editor). *Payment:* £12·60 per 1000 words. *Illustrations:* line, halftone and drawings.

DESIGN AND COMPONENTS IN ENGINEERING, C. ROBINSON, P.O. Box 42, 33–39 Bowling Green Lane, London. EC1P 1AH. *T.* 01–837 1277.
Controlled Circulation. Twice Monthly.—Articles on engineering design, new components, materials, and processes in engineering industry. *Length:* up to 2500 words. *Payment:* £10·50 per 1000 words. *Illustrations:* line and half-tone.

DESIGN ELECTRONICS, Editor: J. HILLARY; Editorial Director: G. H. MANSELL, IPC Electrical–Electronic Press Ltd., Dorset House, Stamford Street, London, S.E.1. *T.* 01–928 3333.

Controlled circulation journal within the U.K. only. Illustrated features up to 2500 words on design and production aspects of electronic equipment and systems, news relating to new materials, development, etc.

DIANA (D. C. Thomson & Co., Ltd.), Courier Place, Dundee, DD1 9QJ, and Thomson House, 12 Fetter Lane, London, E.C.4.

3p. W. (Monday).—Picture-story paper for schoolgirls. Stories, in serial or series form, told in pictures, in line, or line and wash, also in full colour, for gravure printing. Features, full page size, interest, informative; series or singly; in line or full colour. *Payment:* on acceptance. Special encouragement to promising artists and script-writers.

DICKENSIAN, THE, MICHAEL SLATER, M.A., D.PHIL, Birkbeck College, Malet Street, London, WC1E 7AT.

50p. 3 times a year.—Published by The Dickens Fellowship. Welcomes articles on all aspects of Dickens' life, works and character. *No payment.*

DIGESTS with one or two exceptions are not included since they seldom use original material, but reprint articles previously published elsewhere and extracts from books. But see **THE READERS' DIGEST.**

DISC & MUSIC ECHO (formerly **DISC WEEKLY**) (1958), Disc Echo Ltd., 161–166 Fleet Street, London, E.C.4. *T.* 01–353 5011.

5p. W.—Articles to appeal to the young record enthusiast.

DISPLAY (1919), ALLAN PLOWMAN, 167 High Holborn, W.C.1. *T.* 01–836 9551.

20p. M.—Articles, news, etc., appertaining to window display and exhibitions, point-of-sale, screen process printing. *Length:* 750–1250 words or short paragraphs. *Features:* by arrangement. *Payment:* by arrangement. *Illustrations:* photographs or line drawings of window displays, interior store displays, point-of-sale display units; colour transparencies.

DISPOSABLES INTERNATIONAL AND NON-WOVEN FABRICS REVIEW (1969) Joint Managing Editors: E. F. J. DEAN and E. HAYLOCK (Stonhill and Gillis Ltd.), Lincoln House, 296–302 High Holborn, London, WC1V 7JS *T.* 01–405 7055. *T.A.* Stongillis, London, W.C.1.

25p. Q. (December, March, June, September).—Coverage of all aspects of the manufacture, conversion and marketing of disposables, whether they are made of paper, plastics, or nonwovens; interests primarily aimed at those products manufactured and marketed in bulk to large volume consumers: hotels, hospitals, motels, catering establishments, and the large chains of department stores and supermarkets. Outside contributions. *Payment:* according to merit. *Illustrations:* half-tone.

DO IT YOURSELF (1957), DAVID G. JOHNSON, Link House, Dingwall Avenue, Croydon, CR9 2TA *T.* 01–686 2599. *T.A.* Aviculture, Croydon.

12½p. M.—Authoritative articles on every aspect of do-it-yourself in the house, garden, workshop and garage. Leaflet describing style, requirements, available on request. *Payment:* by arrangement. *Length:* up to 1000 words. Press 3 months ahead.

DOCK AND HARBOUR AUTHORITY, THE (1920), BILL REID, 19 Harcourt Street, London, W1H 2AX *T.* 01–723 0077.

30p. M.—Authoritative articles on port engineering subjects, and port operation and administration. Preliminary letter desirable. *Payment:* £5·25 per 1000 words, or more by special arrangement for articles. *Illustrations:* photographs and line diagrams.

DOMESTIC SCIENCE (1964), ARTHUR J. FEARON, 33 Wykeham Avenue, Hornchurch, Essex. Fearon Publications Ltd. *T.* Hornchurch 51698.
12½p. M.—Articles on food, nutrition, cooking, hygiene, textiles, grooming, home management, furnishing, domestic appliances, laundry. *Length:* 1000 words. *Payment:* by arrangement. *Illustrations:* line, half-tone, colour.

DOWNSIDE REVIEW, THE, DOM DANIEL REES, Downside Abbey, Stratton on the Fosse, nr. Bath, Somerset. *T.* Stratton-on-the-Fosse 295.
45p. post free; £1·80 per annum. Q.—Articles and book reviews on theology, metaphysics and monastic history. *Payment:* by arrangement.

DRAMA (1919), Executive Editor: WALTER LUCAS, 9 Fitzroy Square, W1P 6AE. *T.* 01-387 2666.
18p. Q.—A magazine of the theatre. Articles, 1000 to 3000 words. *Payment:* by arrangement. *Illustrations:* photographs.

DRAPERS' RECORD (1887), LESLIE BECKETT, 20 Knightway House, Soho Square, London, W1V 6DT *T.* 01-734 1255.
7½p. W. (Friday).—Matter should be of special interest to retail and wholesale drapers. *Length* of articles from 500 to 1000 words. *Payment:* by arrangement. *Illustrations:* drawings or photographs.

DRAPERY & FASHION WEEKLY, (1959), GEORGE WHITE, Textile Business Press (Ltd.), 30 Finsbury Square, London, E.C.2. *T.* 01-628 7901.
4p. W. (Friday, Press day Wednesday). (£2·75 a year post free).—News and features of interest to women's and children's wear retailers. *Payments* on publication. *Illustrations:* line and half-tone.

DUBLIN MAGAZINE, THE, JOHN RYAN and KEVIN O'BYRNE, 2-3 Duke Street, Dublin 2 *T.* 773055.
25p. Q.—Poetry, fiction, articles on literature and art. *Length:* up to 5000 words. *Payment:* by arrangement.

DUNDEE COURIER AND ADVERTISER (1816 and 1801) (D. C. Thomson & Co., Ltd.), 7 Bank Street, Dundee, DD1 9HU, and 186 Fleet Street, London, E.C.4. *T.* Dundee 23131 and 01-242 5086.
2p. D.—Independent.

DUNDEE EVENING TELEGRAPH AND POST (D. C. Thomson & Co. Ltd.), Courier Place, Dundee, DD1 9QJ, and Thomson House, 12 Fetter Lane, London, E.C.4. *T.* Dundee 23131 and 01-353 2586.
2p. D.—Topical articles up to 700 words.

DYER, TEXTILE PRINTER, BLEACHER AND FINISHER INTERNATIONAL, G. W. BEDNALL, Textile Business Press Ltd., 30 Finsbury Square, London, E.C.2. *T.* 01-628 7901.
15p. (£3 per annum). 1st and 3rd Fridays—Articles, photographs and news relating to the trades covered. *Payment:* by arrangement. *Illustrations:* line and half-tone.

EAST COAST YACHTSMAN (1968), MAURICE HEDGECOCK, Coastal Publications, Claire House, Burns Avenue, Lexden, Colchester, Essex. *T.* Colchester 79805.
12½p. Q.—Technical articles and cruising yarns, relevant to the East Coast. *Length:* 2000 to 3000 words. *Payment:* by arrangement. *Illustrations:* line and half-tone.

EAST WEST DIGEST, D. G. STEWART–SMITH, 139 Petersham Road, Richmond, Surrey. *T.* 01–940 2885.
12½p. M.—News stories and authoritative articles on the Communist world, international affairs, defence, political warfare, subversion and East-West relations. Articles and reviews are written on request. *Payment:* by arrangement.

EASTERN DAILY EXPRESS (1870), P. J. ROBERTS, Prospect House, Rouen Road, Norwich, NOR 87A *T.* Norwich 28311; London Office, Aldwych House, W.C.2.
2½p. D.—Independent. Limited market for articles of East Anglian interest not exceeding 850 words.

EASTERN EVENING NEWS (1882), M. BEALES, EEN, Prospect House, Rouen Road, Norwich, NOR 87A *T.* Norwich 28311; London Office, Aldwych House, Aldwych, W.C.2.
2½p.—Independent.

EASTERN WORLD (1946), H. C. TAUSSIG, 58 Paddington Street, W.1. *T.* 01–935 7439. *T.A.* Tadico, London, W.1.
12½p. M. (£1·50 per annum).—Authoritative, political, economic and cultural articles on S.E. Asia and the Far East. *Length:* 500 to 2000 words. *Payment:* by arrangement. *Illustrations:* photographs and maps.

ECONOMIC JOURNAL (1891), W. B. REDDAWAY, D. G. CHAMPERNOWNE, and P. M. DEANE, The Marshall Library, Sidgwick Avenue, Cambridge. *T.* Cambridge 57815.
Quarterly. Subscription, £5 per annum.—The organ of the Royal Economic Society. The kind of matter required is economic theory and the development of economic thinking in relation to current problems. *Payment:* varies with the nature of the contributions. Statistical and economic diagrams. Sundry publications.

ECONOMICA (1921: New Series, 1934), Professor B. S. YAMEY and others, London School of Economics and Political Science, Houghton Street, Aldwych, London, WC2A 2AE *T.* 01–405 7686.
Q. Subscription, £3 per annum.—A learned journal covering the fields of economics, economic history, and statistics.

ECONOMIST, THE (1843), ALASTAIR BURNET, 25 St. James's Street, London, S.W.1. *T.* 01–930 5155. 15p. W. Articles staff-written.

EDINBURGH EVENING NEWS, MAX MCAUSLANE, 20 North Bridge, Edinburgh, EH1 1YX. *T.* 031–225 2468. London Office, 200 Gray's Inn Road, W.C.1.
2½p. D.—Independent. Articles, preferably of Scottish slant, on social, industrial, sporting subjects, and women's interests may be submitted. *Length:* 700 to 1000 words. *Payment:* according to value.

EDUCATION (1903) (Official Journal Association of Education Committees), TUDOR DAVID, 10 Queen Anne Street, W1M 9LD. *T.* 01–580 8197.
7½p. W. (Friday).—Special articles on educational administration, all branches of education; technical education; universities; school building; playing fields; rural studies; physical education; school equipment; school meals and health; teaching aids. *Length:* 1000 to 1500 words. *Payment:* by arrangement. *Illustrations:* photographs and drawings.

EDUCATION AND TRAINING (1959), ROGER BEARD, Turnstile Press Ltd., Great Turnstile, London, WC1V 7HJ. *T.* 01 405 8471.
60p. M.—Authoritative articles of 1500–3000 words on all aspects of further education and industrial training. *Payment:* by arrangement. *Illustrations:* half-tone and line.

ELECTRICAL AGE, THE (1926), 25 Fouberts Place, W1V 2AL
5p. plus postage. Q. (28p. yearly, post free).—Articles dealing mainly with domestic electricity but also with all aspects of electricity of interest to women. *Length:* about 1000 words. *Payment:* £2·10 per 1000 words. *Illustrations:* photographs and line.

ELECTRICAL AND ELECTRONIC TRADER (formerly **Wireless and Electrical Trader**) (1929), Managing Director, K. TETT; Editor: E. ICKINGER, Dorset House, Stamford Street, S.E.1. *T.* 01–928 3333. *T.A.* and *Telex:* Electrader, Iliffepress 25137, London.
Annual subscription, £3·75 W. (Friday).—Items of radio, television, domestic electrical and gramophone record trade news; general trade articles invited of interest to retailers; articles on selling, service and maintenance of domestic radio, television and electrical equipment. Regular Audiotopics supplements concerned with the high quality audio and public address markets. *Length:* articles of 1000–2000 words. *Payment:* trade news, 1½p. per line; articles by arrangement. *Illustrations:* line and half-tone.

ELECTRICAL AND ELECTRONICS MANUFACTURER, A. J. POTTER, Trade News Ltd., Drummond House, 203–209 North Gower Street, London, N.W.1. *T.* 01–387 9611.
20p. (post free). Ann. sub. £2·50. Overseas £2·50. M.—Articles up to about 2000 words, with illustrations dealing with all phases of production or development work in the electrical and electronic industries and evaluation of materials used. *Payment:* by arrangement. *Illustrations:* line and half-tone.

ELECTRICAL & RADIO TRADING (1890 as **ELECTRICITY**), OWEN PAWSEY, IPC Electrical–Electronic Press Ltd., Dorset House, Stamford Street, London, S.E.1. *T.* 01–928 3333.
12½p. W. £3·50 post free for 12 months.—Covers trade in domestic electrical, appliances, radio and television. Articles 500 to 1000 words on product design, technical development, distribution, trade promotion, service, maintenance and repairs. Contributors are required to have experience in electrical and radio industry. *Payment:* by arrangement. Prior consultation with editor essential.

ELECTRICAL EQUIPMENT, REX NARRAWAY, C.ENG., Broadwall House, Broadwall, Stamford Street, London, S.E.1. *T.* 01–928 3388. *Telex:* 21977.
Controlled circulation.—Short technical features. *Length:* approx. 2500 words. *Payment:* approx. £10·50 per 1000 words. *Illustrations:* line and half-tone.

ELECTRICAL REVIEW (1872), R. F. MASTERS (Editor), T. C. J. COGLE, B.SC.(ENG.), A.M.I.C.E., F.I.E.E. (Technical Editor), IPC Electrical–Electronic Press Ltd., Dorset House, Stamford Street, S.E.1. *T.* 01–928 3333. *T.A.* Review, Iliffepres 25137, London, Telex.
12½p. W. (Friday).—Articles on electrical engineering and trade; outside contributions considered. Electrical news welcomed. *Illustrations:* photographs and drawings.

ELECTRICAL TIMES, THE (1891), K. C. POUNDS, 33–39 Bowling Green Lane, London, E.C.1. *T.* 01–837 1277. *T.A.* Organigram, London, E.C.1.
12½p. W.—Technical articles about 2000 to 2500 words, with illustrations as necessary. *Payment:* by arrangement. *Illustrations:* line and half-tone.

ELECTRONIC COMPONENTS (1959), R. G. ATTERBURY, 9 Gough Square, Fleet Street, London, E.C.4. *T.* 01–353 3172. *T.A.* Markeba, London, E.C.4. U.K. Registered Readers—free. All others—£3 p.a.; overseas £7 p.a. M.—Technical articles of approx. 3000 words concerned with the design, manufacture and testing of electronic components. Articles on associated materials and test equipment will also be considered. *Payment:* by arrangement. *Illustrations:* Line and half-tone.

ELECTRONIC EQUIPMENT NEWS, GEOFFREY DUBBINS, Broadwall House, Broadwall, Stamford Street, London, S.E.1. *T.* 01–928 3388. Controlled circulation. M.—Technical articles on electronics. *Payment:* £10·50. per 1000 words. *Illustrations:* line and half-tone. Some colour.

ELECTRONICS WEEKLY (1960), Editor: ROGER WOOLNOUGH. Editorial Director: G. H. MANSELL (IPC Electrical–Electronic Press Ltd.), Dorset House, Stamford Street, London, S.E.1. *T.* 01–928 3333. 4p., £2·25 p.a. W.—News and articles by arrangement with editor. *Payment:* by arrangement. *Illustrations:* line and half-tone.

ELECTROPLATING AND METAL FINISHING (1947), JOHN H. ATTWATER, 65/66 Turnmill Street, London, E.C.1. *T.* 01–253 8201. £3·25 per annum. M.—Technical articles and news of the industry. *Payment:* varies. *Illustrations:* line and half-tone.

ELIZABETHAN, LEWIS SHERINGHAM (Brontpress Ltd.), P.O. Box 7, Ashford Road, Staines, Middlesex. *T.* Ashford (Middx.) 52181. 15p., £2·05 p.a. post free. M.—Short stories up to 2000 words, articles up to 1000 words and short informative features; also cartoons and photographs. Suitable for boys and girls between ten and eighteen. *Payment:* by arrangement. *Illustrations:* line and half-tone.

EMBROIDERY (1932), Embroiderers' Guild, 73 Wimpole Street, London, W1M 8AX *T.* 01–935 3281. 29p. £1·15 p.a. including postage. Overseas: £1·15 p.a. and $4 including, postage. Q.—Articles dealing with embroidery; contemporary, historical, foreign. *Payment:* by arrangement. *Illustrations:* line and half-tone.

ENCOUNTER (1953), MELVIN J. LASKY and NIGEL DENNIS, Panton House, 25 Haymarket, London, S.W.1. *T.* 01–839 4561. 35p. M. (20th preceding).—Reportage, stories, poems. *Length:* 3000–5000 words. *Payment:* £9 per 1000. Interested contributors should study magazine before submitting MSS.

ENGINEER, THE (1856), JOHN MORTIMER, D.C.AE., C.ENG., M.I.MECH.E., A.F.R.AE.S., 28 Essex Street, London, W.C.2. *T.* 01–353 6565. £12 p.a. W. (Friday).—Outside contributions paid for if accepted.

ENGINEERING (1866), F. B. ROBERTS, M.B.E., C.ENG., 33–39 Bowling Green Lane London, E.C.1. *T.* 01–837 1277. 12½p. W. (Fridays).—Contributions considered on technology of public interest. *Payment:* by arrangement. Photographs and drawings used.

ENGINEERING MATERIALS AND DESIGN, D. H. FEARS, C.ENG., M.I.MECH.E., A.F.R.AE.S., Engineering, Chemical and Marine Press Ltd., 33–40 Bowling Green Lane, E.C.1. *T.* 01–837 1277. 25p. £3 p.a. M.—Technical articles on engineering design and on materials and components. *Payment:* by arrangement. *Length:* from 1000 words. *Illustrations:* line and half-tone.

ENGINEERING PRODUCTION, Roy D. Cullum, P.O. Box 42, 33–39 Bowling Green Lane, London, EC1P 1AH *T.* 01–837 1277.

Controlled circulation. F.—Technical articles on new machines, accessories, methods, materials used by planning and production personnel. *Length:* 1000–2000 words. *Payment:* by arrangement. *Illustrations:* half-tone and line.

ENGLAND, The Royal Society of St. George, 4 Upper Belgrave Street, London, S.W.1. *T.* 01–235 1714.

Q.—Circulation at present restricted to Members of the Society. Articles on all aspects of English life, history, travel, industry, entertainment, sport, arts and crafts. *Length:* up to 1200 words. *Payment:* by arrangement in exceptional circumstances only. (Contributions normally obtained from the Society's membership.) *Illustrations:* photographs.

ENGLISH, the Magazine of the English Association, Margaret Willy, f.r.s.l., 1 Brockmere, 43 Wray Park Road, Reigate, Surrey.

52½p. Three times a year.—Articles on literature and teaching of English, reviews of books, and poetry. *Length of articles:* from 2000 to 3000 words. *Payment:* by arrangement.

ENGLISH HISTORICAL REVIEW (1886), J. M. Wallace-Hadrill, m.a., d.litt., and J. M. Roberts, m.a., d.phil. (Longman Group Ltd.), Burnt Mill, Harlow, Essex,

£1·05, £4·20 p.a. Four times a year.—This journal contains high-class articles (such as are usually found in quarterlies), documents, and reviews. Contributions are not accepted unless they supply original information and should be sent direct to J. M. Wallace-Hadrill, Editor, E.H.R., Merton College, Oxford. *No payment.*

ENTOMOLOGIST'S MONTHLY MAGAZINE (1864), Dr. B. M. Hobby and others, 7 Thorncliffe Road, Oxford, OX2 7BA *T.* Oxford 58976.

75p. (triple issue) £2·25 p.a.; overseas £2·50 ($7) p.a. M.—Articles on all entomological subjects, foreign and British. *No payment.*

ENVOI (1957), John Scott, Seven Levels, Marle Hill Parade, Cheltenham, GL 50 4LJ.

£1 p.a. Three times a year.—Poetry. *Payment:* 40p. for a short poem, with two specimen copies.

ESPERANTO TEACHER, THE (Journal of the Esperanto Teachers Association), Audrey Childs, 19 Cranbury Road, Eastleigh, Hants. *T.* Eastleigh 3845.

10p. 3 times a year (25p. p.a.)—Articles and news items, in English or Esperanto, concerning the teaching of Esperanto in schools, training colleges and universities. *Illustrations:* photographs. *Payment:* by arrangement. Intending contributors should contact the editor in advance.

ESSEX COUNTRYSIDE (1952), Leslie Bichener, Letchworth Printers Ltd., Norton Way North, Letchworth, Hertfordshire. *T.* 2501–4.

15p. M.—Articles of county interest. *Length:* approximately 1000 words. *Illustrations:* half-tone and line. *Payment:* £3·50 per 1000 words.

EUROPEAN CHEMICAL NEWS (1962), Michael Buckingham (E. C. & M. Press Ltd.), 33–40 Bowling Green Lane, London, E.C.1. *T.* 01–837 1277. *T.A.* Pressimus London E.C.1. Telex: 23839.

22½p. W.—News and background to current events. *Length:* maximum 1000 words. *Payment:* by arrangement.

B

EVANGELICAL QUARTERLY (1929), F. F. BRUCE, D.D., The Crossways, Temple Road, Buxton, Derbyshire. *T.* 3250. Published from Paternoster House, 3 Mount Radford Crescent, Exeter, Devon. *T.* Exeter 58977.

22½p. Q.—A Theological review, international in scope and outlook in defence of the historic Christian faith. Articles on the defence or exposition of Biblical theology as exhibited in the great Reformed Confessions. *No payment.*

EVENING CHRONICLE (Newcastle), ERIC B. DOBSON, Newcastle Chronicle and Journal, Ltd., Thomson House, Groat Market, Newcastle upon Tyne. *T.* 27500. London: Thomson House, Gray's Inn Road, W.C.1. *T.* 01–837 1234.

2½p. D.—Topical news articles invited; 500 to 800 words. Exclusive news and photographs. *Payment:* according to value.

EVENING ECHO (Watford); Published by Echo and Post Ltd., Mark Road, Hemel Hempstead, Herts. *T.* Hemel Hempstead 2277. London: Thomson House, Gray's Inn Road, W.C.1. *T.* 01–837 1234. 2½p. D.

EVENING NEWS (1881) (now incorporating STAR), JOHN GOLD, Harmsworth House, E.C.4. *T.* 01–353 6000.

2½p. D.—Independent. Uses factual topical articles, 300 to 800 words; London, social, political, and home subjects. Short stories, 1200 to 1300 words. News photographs.

EVENING POST, 123 Week Street, Maidstone. *T.* Maidstone 58444.

2½p. Monday to Friday.—Personal and Local news covering the Medway towns. Pictorial paper with emphasis on news and sport. *Illustrations:* line and half-tone.

EVENING POST (Luton and North Herts.). Published by Echo and Post Ltd., Mark Road, Hemel Hempstead Herts. *T.* Hemel Hempstead 2211. London: Thompson House, Gray's Inn Road, W.C.1. *T.* 01–837 1234. 2½p. D.

EVENING POST (Reading) (1965), GEOFFREY RICH, 8 Tessa Road, Reading, RG1 8NS. *T.* Reading 55833.

2½p. D.—Topical articles based on current news. *Length:* 1000 to 1200 words. *Payment:* £4·20 to £8·40 per 1000 words. *Illustrations:* half-tone.

EVENING STANDARD (1827), Editor: CHARLES WINTOUR, Shoe Lane, E.C.4. *T.* 01–353 3000.

2½p. D.—Independent. Articles of general interest considered, 1000 words or shorter; also news, pictures and ideas.

EXCHANGE AND MART (1868), Pembroke House, Wellesley Road, Croydon, CR9 2BX. *T.* 01–686 7181. *T.A.* Aviculture, Croydon.

4p. W. (Thursday).—No editorial matter used.

EXPORT MANAGEMENT, S. SELF (Benn Brothers Marine Publications Ltd.) 7–17 Jewry Street, London, EC3N 2HJ *T.* 01–480 5322. *T.A.* Shipping World, London, E.C.3.

£3 p.a. M.—Contributions on export finance, marine insurance, international law, shipping and aviation specially arranged. *Payment:* by arrangement. *Illustrations:* half-tone.

FABRIC FORECAST (1962), NINA HIRST, 40 New Oxford Street, W.C.1. *T.* 01–637 2211 (ten lines).

(Circulates to manufacturers of women's ready-to-wear, fabric retailers, textile producers, converters and fibre producers only.) Articles on fabrics, fibres, export markets, technical information of interest to the textile trade. *Length:* 1000–1500 words. *Illustrations:* half-tone and line.

FABULOUS (1964), BETTY HALE, New Fleetway House, Farringdon Street, London, EC4A 4AD *T.* 01–236 8080.

6p. W. (Monday).—Pop articles of 500–1000 words. *Payment:* £10·50– £20 according to length and arrangement. *Illustrations:* black-and-white and colour photographs.

FAIRPLAY INTERNATIONAL SHIPPING JOURNAL (1883), W. D. EWART, M.I.MAR.E., A.M.R.I.N.A., Palmerston House, 51 Bishopsgate, E.C.2. *T.* 01–588 3844.

20p. W. (Thursdays).—Paragraphs or articles dealing with shipping, ship-building, marine insurance, etc., up to three columns. *Payment:* by arrangement. *Illustrated.*

FAITH AND FREEDOM: A Journal of Progressive Religion (1947), Manchester College, Oxford. Editor: E. SHIRVELL PRICE, M.A., Bank Street, Chapel Vestry, Crown Street, Bolton, Lancashire BL1 2RU *T.* 0204 28633.

50p. ann. sub., 3 issues (Oct. Feb., June).—Articles on philosophy and religion from free, non-dogmatic point of view, 3000 to 4000 words. *No payment.*

FAMILY CIRCLE, CHRISTINE BRADY, Elm House, Elm Street, London, WC1X 0BJ *T.* 01–837 1234.

7½p. M.—Service features of all kinds, homecraft ideas, occasional human interest, 500–1500 words. *Payment:* by arrangement. *Illustrations:* colour, black-and-white.

FAMILY STAR (D. C. Thomson and Co., Ltd.), Courier Place, Dundee, DD1 9QJ and Thomson House, 12 Fetter Lane, London, E.C.4.

2½p. W. (Tuesday).—Serials up to 40,000 words with strong emotional and dramatic interest. Opening instalments up to 5000 words. Shorts, 1000 to 3000 words with good romantic interest. *Payment:* on acceptance. *Illustrations:* straight dramatic pictures in half-tone; colour covers with dramatic incident.

FAR EAST TRADE & DEVELOPMENT (1946), 3 Belsize Crescent, London, N.W.3. *T.* 01–794 4481.

15p. M.—Economics, management, technology—of concern to developing countries. *Preliminary letter advisable. Length:* 800–1200 words, or longer by arrangement. Photographs and short news items of 200 words about contracts, projects, developments. *Payment:* £10·50 per 1000 words if suitable. *Illustrations:* line and half-tone.

FAR EAST WEEK BY WEEK, 3 Belsize Crescent, London, N.W.3. *T.* 01–794 4481.

Annual subscription (48 issues): U.K. £26, Europe £28, outside Europe £30— Reports from the ECAFE area, plus People's Republic of China. Designed for quick reading, contents range from Outlooks, Newsleads, Projects and Developments, Contracts and Orders, to Guidelines. *Payment:* for original material of high news value: £5·25 for up to 250 words, if suitable. No *illustrations.*

FARM AND COUNTRY, PHILIP HASSALL, Elm House, Elm Street, London, W.C.1. *T.* 01–837 1234.

25p. M.—Management and marketing aspects of agriculture; articles and photographs with authoritative and informative captions. *Payment:* by arrangement. *Length:* 1000–2000 words. *Illustrations:* line and half-tone.

FARMER AND STOCKBREEDER (1843), ROBERT TROW-SMITH, 161–166 Fleet Street, London, E.C.4. *T.* 01–353 5011. *T.A.* Agricultural Press London.
7½p. W. (Tuesday).—Photographs of farming interest and practical articles on agriculture and livestock are welcomed. 800 to 1200 words. Also articles (400–800 words) of interest to country people and photographs of country subjects for the Home Pages. *Payment:* £8·40 per 1000 words or more; illustrations, £1·50 to £2 for reproductions, more for special assignments and for exclusive pictures.

FARMERS WEEKLY (1934) (Agricultural Press Ltd.), TRAVERS LEGGE, 161–166 Fleet Street, E.C.4. *T.* 01–353 5011.
7½p. W. (Friday).—Articles on agriculture from freelance contributors will be accepted subject to negotiation.

FARMING NEWS AND NORTH BRITISH AGRICULTURALIST (1843), IAN MORRISON, 3 Clairmont Gardens, Glasgow, C.3. *T.* 041–332 3792–6.
2½p. W.—Agricultural features of interest to Scotland. *Payment:* £8·40 per 1000 words.

FASHION FORECAST (1945), ANN CHUBB, 33 Bedford Place, London WC1B 5JH *T.* 01–637 2211 (ten lines).
£5 in U.K., £8 overseas. M.—Factual articles on fashions and accessories with forecast trend. Articles on textiles, display, promotion, export markets, etc. *Length:* 800 to 1000 words. *Illustrations:* half-tone and line.

FEED & FARM SUPPLIES (formerly **FERTILISER AND FEEDING STUFFS JOURNAL**) (1919), Stamford House, 65–66 Turnmill Street, London, E.C.1. *T.* 01–253 8201.
30p. M.—Technical, general, and market news dealing with the Fertiliser, Feeding Stuffs, Farm Seeds, and Insecticides Industries, with suitable illustrations, 1000 to 2000 words. *Payment:* about £3·15 per 1000 words. *Illustrations:* photographs.

FIELD, THE (1853), (incorporating **LAND AND WATER** and the **COUNTY GENTLEMAN**), 8 Stratton Street, W1X 6AT *T.* 01–499 7881. *T.A.* Field Newspaper, London.
15p. W.—Specific and informed comment on the British countryside and country pursuits, including natural history, field sports, gardening and farming. Overseas subjects are considered but opportunities for such articles to appear in *The Field* are limited. No fiction or children's material. Articles, *length* 800–1200 words, by outside contributors are considered, and there are occasional openings for brief news items. *Payment:* on merit. *Illustrations:* photographs illustrating above subjects: some colour if sufficiently high standard.

FILM AND TELEVISION TECHNICIAN (1935), ROY C. LOCKETT, B.A., (The Association of Cinematograph, Television and Allied Technicians), 2 Soho Square, London, W1V 5DE *T.* 01–437 8506–7–8.
7½p. M.—Technical and general articles of interest to professional film and television technicians. *Length:* 1000 to 2000 words. *Payment:* no payment made to technicians and members of the Association of Cinematograph, Television and Allied Technicians; by arrangement for other articles accepted. *Illustrations:* film technique, technicians at work, cartoons dealing with film and television industry. Usual agency rates paid.

FILM MAKING (formerly **8 MM MAGAZINE**) (1962), Haymarket Press Ltd., Gillow House, 5 Winsley Street, London, W1N 7AQ. *T.* 01–636 3600.
17½p. M.—Exclusively for the cine enthusiast. *Length:* 1500–2000 words. *Payment:* by arrangement. *Illustrations:* line, half-tone.

FILM USER (incorporating **INDUSTRIAL SCREEN**), STANLEY W. BOWLER, P.O. Box 109, Croydon, CR9 1QH *T.* 01–688 7788.
15p. M.—Articles (1000 to 2500 words) and news items on applications of film and other audio-visual techniques in education, industry, public relations, etc. *Payment:* by arrangement. *Illustrations:* line and half-tone.

FILMS AND FILMING (1954), ROBIN BEAN, Hansom Books, Artillery Mansions, 75 Victoria Street, London, S.W.1. *T.* 01–799 4452.
30p. M.—Articles on serious cinema, preferably with illustrations. *Length:* 1500–2000 words. *Payment:* by arrangement. *Illustrations:* photographs.

FILTRATION & SEPARATION (1964), W. G. NORRIS, 1 Katharine Street, Croydon, CR9 1LB *T.* 01-686 6330.
60p. Bi-M.—Articles on the design, construction and applications of filtration and separation equipment and dust control and air cleaning equipment for all industrial purposes; articles on filtration and separation and dust control and air cleaning operations and techniques in all industries. *Payment:* by arrangement. *Illustrations:* line and half-tone.

FINANCIAL TIMES, THE (incorporating **THE FINANCIAL NEWS**) (1888), Sir GORDON NEWTON, Bracken House, 10 Cannon Street, E.C.4. *T.* 01–248 8000.
5p. D.—Articles of financial, commercial, industrial, and economic interest from 800 to 1400 words. *Payment:* by arrangement. *Illustrations:* industrial subjects.

FINANCIAL WORLD (1886), BRIAN NAYLOR, 74 Temple Chambers, London, E.C.4. *T.* 01–353 5681.
10p. F. (Saturday).—Review of fortnight's finance. Articles on general financial topics. *Length* preferred, about 1200 words. Average rate of *payment:* £4·20 per column.

FIRE (1908), HARRY KLOPPER, L.I.FIRE.E., A.I.L., Unisaf House, 32–36 Dudley Road, Tunbridge Wells, Kent. *T.* Tunbridge Wells 23184–6.
20p. M. (30th of preceding month).—Principal aim: Promotion and propagation of fire engineering, fire prevention, fire extinction, and fire salvage. Original technical articles, personal paragraphs and suitable photographs accepted. *Payment:* at editor's valuation. *Illustrations:* drawings or photographs.

FIRE INTERNATIONAL (1963), HARRY KLOPPER, L.I.FIRE.E., A.I.L., Unisaf House, 32–36 Dudley Road, Tunbridge Wells, Kent. *T.* Tunbridge Wells 23184–6.
50p. Q. (12th of month, July, October, January, April).—Promotion and propagation of international fire prevention, extinction and salvage. Printed in English, French and German. Original highly technical articles and suitable photographs accepted. *Payment:* at editor's valuation. *Illustrations:* drawings or photographs.

FIRE PROTECTION REVIEW (1938), J. L. EADES (Benn Brothers, Ltd.), Bouverie House, 154 Fleet Street, EC4A 2DL *T.* 01–353 3212.
20p., £2·50 p.a. M.—Fire prevention, protection and fighting on land, sea and in the air; industrial safety. News of public Fire Service and industrial brigades at home and abroad. *Length of technical articles:* 1000–2000 words. *Payment:* on merit. *Illustrations:* drawings and photographs.

FLAIR, BERYL DOWNING, Tower House, Southampton Street, London, WC2E 9QX *T.* 01-836 4363.
15p. M.—Fashion and beauty magazine, mainly relying on specialist staff. Buys some freelance features, 850–1000 words, on fashion and associated subjects, largely on humorous angle. *Payment:* by arrangement.

FLIGHT INTERNATIONAL (1909), J. M. RAMSDEN, Dorset House, Stamford Street, S.E.1. *T.* 01–928 3333. *T.A.* Flight, Iliffepres 25137, London, Telex. 15p. W. (Thursday).—Deals with aviation in all its branches. Articles general and technical, illustrated by photographs, engineering cutaway drawings, also news paragraphs, reports of lectures, etc. *Payment:* varies; cheques 20th of month following publication. *Illustrations:* tone, line, occasionally two- and four-colour. News press day: Monday.

FLUID POWER INTERNATIONAL (incorporating **COMPRESSED AIR AND HYDRAULICS**), RAYMOND D. HEY Morgan-Grampian (Publishers) Ltd., Riverside House, Hough Street, Woolwich, London, S.E.18. *T.* 01–855 7001. £6 p.a. post paid. M.—Technical articles of interest to users of pneumatic, hydraulic and related control equipment in all industries. Latest information about new equipment and details of increasingly diversified new applications. *Length:* 1000 to 3000 words. *Payment:* by arrangement. *Illustrations:* photographs, line diagrams and half-tone.

FOLKLORE (1878), MISS CHRISTINA HOLE, c/o University College, Gower Street, London, WC1E 6BT. *T.* 01–387 5894. Published by the Folk-Lore Society; Distributed by W. Glaisher Ltd., 294 Croxted Road, Herne Hill, S.E.24. 90p. Q.—*No payment* is offered for contributions which should be of a scientific and not of a popular character. *Length:* 1000 to 9000 words. Occasional photographs, maps, etc.

FOOD MANUFACTURE (1927), ANTHONY WOOLLEN, B.SC., A.R.C.S., F.R.I.C., Morgan-Grampian (Publishers) Ltd., 28 Essex Street, Strand, London W.C.2. *T.* 01–353 6565. £10 per annum. £20 per 3 years. M.—Technical articles 1000 to 5000 words on food manufacture and technology; packaging and preservation. *Payment:* by arrangement. *Illustrations:* line and half-tone, photographs and diagrams.

FOOD PROCESSING INDUSTRY, R. DE GIACOMI, IPC Consumer Industries Press Ltd., 33–39 Bowling Green Lane, London, E.C.1. *T.* 01–837 1277. M.—Technical articles devoted to food processing, packaging, and marketing, and new developments in technology. *Length:* from 1000 to 3000 words. A *preliminary letter* is desirable. *Payment:* by arrangement. *Illustrations:* photographs or line drawings.

FOOD TRADE REVIEW (1931) (incorporating **FOOD INDUSTRIES REVIEW**), Editor-in-chief RAYMOND BINSTED; Editor: HOWARD BINSTED, 7 Garrick Street, London, W.C.2. *T.* 01–836 4295 and 8232. £5 per annum. M. (1st).—Technical articles on the manufacture, processing and packing of all kind of foods and food products.

FOOTWEAR WEEKLY, M. PROUT, IPC Consumer Industries Press Ltd., 33–39 Bowling Green Lane, London, E.C.1. *T.* 01–837 1277. 4p., £2·50 p.a. W. (Wednesday; Press day, Monday).—News and feature articles on all matters relating to footwear fashion, production, retailing and repairing. *Length:* up to 800 words. Prior consultation essential. *Payment:* on publication. *Illustrations:* line and half-tone.

FORD TIMES, JOHN EBBLEWHITE (Ford Motor Company, Ltd.), Warley, Brentwood, Essex. *T.* 01–592 7300.

2½p. M. Annual Subscription 50p., post free.—Top-class articles of from 500 to 1000 words on subjects associated with motoring. *Payment:* negotiable. *Illustrations:* first-class photographs essential, black-and-white. Intending contributors are advised to study the newspaper.

FOUNDRY TRADE JOURNAL (1902), A. R. PARKES, John Adam House, Adelphi, WC2N 6JH *T.* 01–839 6171. *T.A.* Zacatecas, London, W.C.2.

10p. W. (Thursday).—Accurate, up-to-date articles relating to the industries represented, consisting of from 1000 to 5000 words, are accepted and paid for by arrangement; as are articles (illustrated or otherwise) describing new processes, new plant laid down, and new works erected, whether at home or abroad. Original news paragraphs, relating to the important personnel or events of the industry, are also acceptable. *Illustrations:* line, half-tone and colour.

FREELANCE REPORT see Writers' Publishing Association, p. 209.

FREE-LANCE WRITING (1965), ARTHUR WAITE, Freelance Press Services, Forestry Chambers, 67 Bridge Street, Manchester, M3 3BS. *T.* 061–832 5079.

15p. Q.—Articles on the writing and selling of short stories, articles, poems, etc. Biographical and interview articles relating to successful authors and freelances. Contributions of practical assistance to the writer with a camera and photographers wishing to sell their pictures. *Length:* 500–1200. *Payment:* from £2·50 per 1000 words. *Illustrations:* half-tone.

FREE TRADER, THE (1903–1914 and since 1921), S. W. ALEXANDER, Free Trade League and Cobden Club, 177 Vauxhall Bridge Road, London, S.W.1. *T.* 01–628–7594.

15p. Q.—Journal of the Free Trade movement. Articles on the fiscal question, and on trade policy generally, will be carefully considered. Some scope for the free-lance specialist who has studied the journal. *Length:* preferably 1200–1800 words. *Payment:* by arrangement in special cases.

FREIGHT MANAGEMENT (1966), NORMAN TILSLEY, IPC Transport Press Ltd., Dorset House, Stamford Street, London, E.C.1. *T.* 01–928 3333.

Controlled circulation. M. (First week in the month)—*Payment:* varies for articles (case studies in particular) dealing with total distribution economics involving all modes of transport.

FREIGHT NEWS WEEKLY (1954), H. PEARCE SALES, 167 High Holborn, London, W.C.1. *T.* 01–836 9551.

W.—Illustrated trade news, technical features. *Payment:* by arrangement.

FRIEND, THE (1843), CLIFFORD HAIGH, Drayton House, Gordon Street, WC1H 0BR *T.* 01–387 7549. Publishing: Headley Brothers Ltd., Ashford, Kent.

6½p. W. (Friday).—The Quaker weekly paper. Matter of interest to the Society of Friends, devotional or general, considered from outside contributors. No fiction. 1200 words maximum length. No payment.

FRONTIER, Sir JOHN LAWRENCE, BT., O.B.E., 157 Waterloo Road, London, S.E.1. *T.* 01–928 5858. Published by Pergamon Press on behalf of Frontier Publications Ltd.

£1·50 p.a. Q.—Articles on the Church and the World, on the growth and expansion of the Christian faith, and on the Ecumenical Movement. *Payment:* by arrangement. *Length:* up to 2000 words.

FRUIT, FLOWER, AND VEGETABLE TRADES' JOURNAL (1895), BILL SANDFORD, 6-7 Gough Square, Fleet Street, E.C.4. *T.* 01-583 1003-5.

7½p. W.—Articles dealing with above trades on the marketing aspects of production but particularly importing and distributing sides; articles should average 500-700 words, and are paid for at the rates of 17½p. to 27½p. a (2⅛ in.) column inch, or by arrangement. *Illustrations:* half-tone or line blocks.

FUNERAL SERVICE JOURNAL, W. K. HOENES, Messrs. King & Hutchings Ltd., Cricketfield Road, Uxbridge, Middlesex. *T.* Uxbridge 37161.

£1·25 p.a. M.—Articles of interest to funeral directors and the funeral trade in general. *Payment:* £2·10 per 1000 words. *Illustrations:* photographs.

FURNISHING WORLD (1931), B. ARNOLD, Ludgate House, 110 Fleet Street, London, E.C.4. *T.* 01-353 6961.

5p. Fortnightly.—News, stories and features dealing with the furnishing industry. *Payment:* on news value; features by agreement. *Illustrations:* half-tone or line.

FURNITURE AND BEDDING PRODUCTION (1935), D. G. WESTLAND, 33 Furnival Street, London, E.C.4. *T.* 01-405 9556.

Annual subscription only (£2), published monthly.—Any trade information regarding supplies for and manufacturing of bedding, mattresses, seatings, upholstery, cabinet furniture, etc. *Length:* governed by subject-matter. *Payment:* £5·25 per 1000 words or more according to interest.

GAMBIT (1963), Calder & Boyers Ltd., 18 Brewer Street, London, W1R 4AS *T.* 01-734 1985.

£1·87 p.a. (U.S.A. and Canada $6.25 p.a.). Q.—Plays by contemporary writers, neglected authors, translations of foreign works. Full length and short. Also articles of theatrical interest and reviews. *Payment:* by arrangement. *Illustrated.*

GAMEKEEPER AND COUNTRYSIDE (1897), edited for the Proprietors, Gilbertson & Page, Ltd., Hertford, Herts. *T.* Hertford 2268 (2 lines).

15p. £1·80 per annum. M.—Informative articles of from 100 to 800-900 words on game preservation, shooting, and natural history. *Payment:* according to merit.

GAMES AND TOYS (1914), H. RICHARD SIMMONS Ltd., 30-31 Knightrider Street, St. Paul's Churchyard, London, E.C.4. *T.* 01-236 0681. *T.A.* Appressolo, London, E.C.4.

20p. M. (1st).—A trade journal specialising, as its name implies, in everything to do with games and toys. *Length:* 800 words. *Payment:* £3·15 per 800 to 1000 words, or according to the value of articles accepted. *Illustrations:* photographs, accompanying articles.

GARAGE (1913), GRAHAM DYMOTT (Ridgway Publications Ltd.), 277-279 Grays Inn Road, London, WC1X 8QF *T.* 01-278 6328 *T.A.* Arator, London.

10p. W. (Saturday). (Annual sub. £4·50).—Articles and news items on every aspect of the motor trade and industry, particularly on garage management. *Length:* 1000 to 3000 words. Short news items. *Payment:* by arrangement. Illustrations according to importance. *Illustrations:* technical and other drawings or photographs of general trade interest.

GARDEN NEWS (1958), TONY IRESON, 117 Park Road, Peterborough. *T.* Peterborough 69201.

5p. W. (Friday).—Gardening news and human features on gardeners and their methods of success. *Payment:* £6·30 per 750-1000 words. Higher rate for good short pieces suited to our style. *Illustrations:* line, half-tone and colour.

GARDEN SUPPLIES RETAILER, 4 Ludgate Circus, London, E.C.4. *T.* 01–353 4353.

Controlled circulation. Eight issues a year. All articles commissioned, but short news items on premises and activities of retailers of garden suppliers welcomed.

GARDENERS CHRONICLE, the Horticultural Trade Journal, COLIN PARNELL, Gillow House, 5 Winsley Street, London, W1N 7AQ. *T.* 01–636 3600.

12½p., £5·20 p.a. W. (Friday).—A scientific and practical horticultural journal for professionals. Outside contributions considered and, if accepted, paid for; they should contain from 500 to 1000 words. No fiction. *Payment:* by arrangement. *Illustrations:* in half-tone and line.

GAS AND OIL POWER (1905), G. R. HUTCHINSON (Managing), G. G. MACLENNAN (Editorial Director), Wrotham Place, Wrotham, Sevenoaks, Kent. *T.* Borough Green 3232–5.

50p. Bi-monthly.—Technical articles on the design, construction and operation of all forms of internal and external combustion reciprocating engines, and gas turbines. *Length:* 1000 to 2500 words. *Payment:* by arrangement. *Illustrations:* tone or line.

GAS JOURNAL (1849), G. W. BATTISON, Holborn Hall, 100 Grays Inn Road, London, W.C.1. *T.* 01–242 9700.

15p. £5·75 p.a. W.

GAS SERVICE, G. W. BATTISON, Holborn Hall, 100 Grays Inn Road, London, W.C.1. *T.* 01–242 9700.

20p. £2 per annum. M.—Articles dealing with all aspects of gas marketing and service.

GAS SHOWROOM, P. J. HALLS (Benn Brothers Ltd.), 2nd Floor, Hanover House, 73–78 High Holborn, London WC1V 7JS

15p., £1·75 p.a. M. (1st Sat.)—Devoted entirely to selling methods of gas board showrooms, new domestic appliances, heating installations. *Length:* features from 1000 to 2000 words, plus pictures. *Payment:* by arrangement.

GAS WORLD (1884), P. J. HALLS (Benn Brothers Ltd.), 2nd Floor, Hanover House, 73–78 High Holborn, London, WC1V 7JS.

15p., £6 p.a. W. (Saturday).—Full news coverage and technical articles of all aspects of the gas and associated industries. *Length:* from 2500 to 4000 words. Pictures and news items of topical interest are paid for at standard rates. *Payment:* by arrangement.

GEMS (1969) R. LAMBERT, 29 Ludgate Hill, London, EC4M 7BQ *T.* 01–248 3430.

12½p. Bi-M.—Articles about minerals, semi-precious stones and lapidary work, especially as applied to Britain. *Length:* 800 to 1000 words. *Payment:* by arrangement. *Illustrations:* line and half-tone.

GEOGRAPHICAL JOURNAL (1893), Royal Geographical Society, Kensington Gore, S.W.7. *T.* 01–589 5466.

£1·40 (post free), £4·30 p.a. Q.—Papers read before or contributed to the Royal Geographical Society. Academic Geography; travel. *Length:* 5000 words. Edited by the Director and Secretary, R.G.S. *Payment:* for reviews. *Illustrations:* photographs, maps and diagrams.

GEOGRAPHICAL MAGAZINE, THE, DEREK WEBER, 128 Long Acre, London, WC2E 9QH *T.* 01–836 2468.

25p. M.—Informative, readable, well-illustrated, authentic articles, from 1500 to 2500 words in length, dealing with people and their environment in all parts of the world; modern geography in all its aspects; kindred subjects such as hydrology, meteorology, communications, civil engineering, space, etc.; man's control of the environment in which he lives, works and plays; travel, exploration, research; plant and animal life in their relationship with mankind. A *preliminary letter* is recommended. *Payment:* ranges from £8·40 per 1000 words. *Illustrations:* at least 6 photographs to each 1000 words submitted, of high technical and artistic quality and covering as many aspects of subject as possible. Groups of specially interesting photographs unaccompanied by articles are considered. *Payment:* colour, from £7·35 upwards, covers by negotiation; black and white, from £3·15 upwards, depending on size of reproduction.

GEOLOGICAL MAGAZINE (1864), Professor O. M. B. BULMAN, Dr. S. R. NOCKOLDS and Mr. W. B. HARLAND, Cambridge University Press, 200 Euston Road, London N.W.1. *T.* 01–387 5030.

£4 per annum, single numbers £1. Bi-M. (January etc.).—Original articles on general and stratigraphical geology, petrology, palaeontology, mineralogy, etc., containing the results of independent research by experts and amateurs. Also reviews and notices of current geological literature, correspondence on geological subjects—illustrated. *Length:* about 5000 words; maximum 10,000 words. *No payment* made.

GIFTS, ANGELA HARLING (Benn Bros., Ltd.), Bouverie House, 154 Fleet Street, EC4A 2DL. *T.* 01–353 3212. *T.A.* Benbrolish London. Official journal of the Giftware Association.

30p., £3·50 p.a. M.—News of gifts industry—products, trends, shops. *Articles:* retailing, exporting, importing, manufacturing, crafts (U.K. and abroad). *Payment:* by agreement. *Illustrations:* products, news, personal photographs.

GLASGOW EVENING CITIZEN, WILLIAM STEEN, Albion Street, Glasgow C.1. *T.* 041–552 3550. London Editorial Office: c/o *Evening Standard*, 47 Shoe Lane, London, E.C.4.

2½p. D.—Informative articles on topical subjects. Woman-appeal articles for housewives' page. *Length:* 500 to 1000 words. *Payment:* according to importance of the article.

GLASGOW EVENING TIMES (1876), S. L. MCKINLAY, 70 Mitchell Street, Glasgow. *T.* 041–221 9200. London Office, 56–57 Fleet Street, E.C.4. *T.* 01–583 5671.

1½p. D.—Welcomes well-written short topical articles. 500–700 words. *Payment:* £4·20 per column (600 words). *Illustrations:* half-tone and line.

GLASGOW HERALD (1783), ALASTAIR K. WARREN, 70 Mitchell Street, Glasgow, C.1. *T.* 041–221 9200; London Office, 56–57 Fleet Street, E.C.4. *T.* 01–583 5671.

4½p. D.—Independent. Articles up to 1200 words.

GLASS, DONALD GRIMMER, John Adam House, 17–19 John Adam Street, Adelphi, London, WC2N 6JH. *T.* 01–839 6171.

25p. M.—Technical articles. *Length:* Under 6,000 words. *Payment:* by arrangement. *Illustrations:* half-tone and line.

GLOUCESTERSHIRE LIFE AND COUNTRYSIDE, D. J. N. GREEN, 6 Lillington Avenue, Leamington Spa. *T.* Leamington Spa 22003 and 22372. *Publisher:* Whitethorn Press Group of Manchester.

10p. M. Articles of interest to the county concerned based on first-hand experience dealing with the life, work, customs and matters affecting welfare of town and country. *Length:* articles 500 to 1200 words. *Payment:* by arrangement. Photographs also by arrangement. *Illustrations:* preference given to articles accompanied by good photographs relating to subject.

GOAL (1968), ALAN HUGHES, IPC Specialist and Professional Press Ltd., 161 Fleet Street, London, E.C.4. *T.* 01–353 5011.

9p. W.—Articles on all football subjects. *Length:* 500–600 words. *Payment:* £1 per 100 words. *Illustrations:* half-tone and colour at usual agency rates.

GOLF ILLUSTRATED (1890), TOM SCOTT, 8 Stratton Street, W1X 5FD *T.* 01–499 7881. *T.A.* Golfirst, London, W.1.

6p. W.—Articles on golf and of interest to golfers. *Payment:* by arrangement. *Illustrations:* photographs of golfers and golf courses.

GOLF MONTHLY (1911), PERCY HUGGINS, 94 Hope Street, Glasgow. *T.* 041–248 4667.

15p. M. (24th).—Original articles on golf considered (not reports). *Payment:* by arrangement. *Photographs* of important current golf events at standard reproduction fees are used.

GOLF WEEKLY (1969), JOHN INGHAM, 1–3 Brixton Road, London, S.W.9.

9p. W.—Profiles of great players, hard news, feature articles of 1200 or 600 words. *Payment:* £20 per 1000 words. *Illustrations:* colour, black and white, cartoons.

GOLF WORLD (1962), KEITH MACKIE, Golf House, South Road, Brighton, BN1 6SY *T.* Brighton 553027.

17½p. M.—Expert golf instructional articles 500–3000 words; general interest articles, personality features 500–3000 words. Little fiction. *Payment:* by negotiation. *Illustrations:* line, half-tone.

GOOD HEALTH (1902), R. D. VINE, Alma Park, Grantham, Lincolnshire. *T.* Grantham 4284–6. *T.A.* Stampress, Grantham.

12½p. Bi-M.—Articles on health topics. *Length:* 750 to 1250 words. *Payment:* £2·10 (basic) per article. *Illustrations:* half-tone and line.

GOOD HOUSEKEEPING, LAURIE PURDEN; *editorial*, Chestergate House, Vauxhall Bridge Road, S.W.1. *T.* 01–834 2331.

20p. M. (15th).—Articles of 1000–3000 words from qualified writers are invited on topics of interest to intelligent women. Domestic subjects covered by staff writers. Short stories and humorous articles also used. *Payment:* good magazine standards. *Illustrations:* mainly commissioned.

GOOD MOTORING (1935), R. O. HOWELL, 2 Ellis Street, Sloane Street, London, S.W.1. *T.* 01–730 2229.

7½p. M.—Articles on all motoring subjects. *Length:* varies. *Payment:* by arrangement. *Illustrations:* half-tone and line.

GRAMOPHONE, THE, ANTHONY POLLARD, 177–179 Kenton Road, Harrow, Middx., HA3 0HA. *T.* 01–907 2010.

15p. M.—Outside contributions are occasionally used. Features on recording artists, technical articles, and articles about gramophone needs. 1600 or 2000 words preferred. *Payment:* by arrangement. *Illustrations:* line and half-tone.

GROCER, THE (1861), A. DE ANGELI, 19 Eastcheap, E.C.3.   *T.* 01–626 0493.
3½p.   W.(Saturday).—This journal is devoted entirely to the trade.   Contributions accepted are articles or news or illustrations of general interest to the grocery and provision trades.   *Payment:* by arrangement.

GROWER, THE (1923), JOHN BLOOM, 49 Doughty Street, London, WC1N 2LP   *T.* 01–405 0364.
10p.   W.—News and practical articles on commercial horticulture, preferably illustrated.   *Payment:* from £9·45 per 1000 words.   *Illustrations:* photographs, line drawings.

GUARDIAN, THE (1821), 192 Grays Inn Road, W.C.1.   *T.* 01–837 7011 and 164 Deansgate, Manchester, M60 2RR   *T.* 061–832 7200.
4p.   D.—Independent.   The parts of the paper for which outside contributions are chiefly desired are the feature pages and the Women's page.   Articles should not exceed 1200 words in length and sketches 900 words.   *Payment:* from £12·60 a column.   *Illustrations:* news photographs, landscapes, art; topical drawings (for line or half-tone).

GUIDEPOSTS (1966) (American edition: 1946), RAYMOND W. CRIPPS, The Witney Press Ltd., Marlborough Lane, Witney, Oxon OX8 7DZ.   *T.* Witney 3981–2.
7½p.   Every two months.   Articles and features written for and by people of all faiths, in simple, anecdotal style with emphasis on human interest.   Intending writers should study magazine.   *Payment:* from £2 to £10.   *Illustrations:* line and half-tone.

GUIDER, THE, Official Organ of the Girl Guides Association, Mrs. J. V. RUSH, 17–19 Buckingham Palace Road, S.W.1.   *T.* 01–834 6242.
5p.   M.—Short articles of interest to adult readers, 500–1500 words, mostly by experts in the wide range of training subjects.   Cartoons about Guide Movement.   *Payment:* £3·67½ per 1000 words.   *Illustrations:* line and half-tone.

GUILD GARDENER, THE (1926).   Official organ of the National Gardens Guild.   Editor, H. G. WITHAM FOGG, 33 Cambanks, Cambridge CB4 1PZ.
7½p.   Q.—Articles on organic or natural gardening, country topics, growing flowers, fruit, etc., without artificial fertilisers or poisonous insecticides. *Length:* not more than 1000 words.   *Payment:* by arrangement.   *Illustrations:* half-tone front cover only.

GUILD NEWS, M. I. M. GODDARD, P.D.S.A. House, South Street, Dorking, Surrey.   *T.* Dorking 81691.
Free.   Articles about animals for age group 12–18.   Maximum *length:* 1000 words.   *Payment:* by arrangement, on acceptance.   *Illustrations:* line, half-tone.

HAIRDRESSERS' JOURNAL, DON TILLEY, IPC Consumer Industries Press Ltd., 33–39 Bowling Green Lane, E.C.1.   *T.* 01–837 1277.
10p.   W. (Friday).—Trade news and complete technical articles connected with the Trade.   *Payment:* by arrangement.   *Illustrations:* trade functions, hair styles, technical, beauty and fasion.   Prior consultation with editor essential.

HAMPSHIRE—THE COUNTY MAGAZINE, DENNIS STEVENS, 39 Above Bar, Southampton, SO1 0DX   *T.* Southampton 23591.
15p.   M.—Factual articles concerning all aspects of Hampshire and Hampshire life, past and present.   *Length:* 500–1500 words.   *Payment:* £5·25 per 1000 words.   *Illustrations:* photographs and line drawings.

HARDWARE MERCHANDISER (1968), PETER HEAD, 28 Essex Street, Strand, London, W.C.2. *T.* 01–353 6565. *T.A.* Iron, Estrand, London.

37p., £2·50 p.a. M.—Merchandising in depth; legal; financial; premises—all relating to hardware promotion and business management. *Payment:* £9·45 per 1000 words. *Illustrations:* line, half-tone.

HARDWARE TRADE JOURNAL, ALBAN HILLS (Benn Brothers Ltd.), Bouverie House, 154 Fleet Street, EC4A 2DL *T.* 01–353 3212.

15p., £5·50 p.a. W. (Friday).—General news of ironmongery, hardware, tool, D.I.Y., and builders' merchant trade interest, shop improvements, personal chat, obituary, legal, etc. Also practical articles up to 1500 words on display, shop layout, retail law, and marketing. *Payment:* by arrangement. *Illustrations:* half-tone and line.

HARPER'S BAZAAR, JOAN HORNSEY, Chestergate House, Vauxhall Bridge Road, London, S.W.1. *T.* 01–834 2331.

30p. M. (last Thursday).—Fashion, beauty, art, theatre, films, travel, decoration, cookery, mainly commissioned features. *Illustrations:* line, wash, full colour and two- and three-colour, and photographs.

HEADLIGHT (1950), J. KELSON, 8 Bloomsbury Way, London, W.C.1. *T.* 01–242 6605-6.

7½p. M.—Any subject on Commercial Road Transport; especially short reports on court cases and news items affecting lorry drivers. *Payment:* according to its value. *Illustrations:* line and half-tone.

HEALTH (1962) J. H. HARLEY WILLIAMS, M.D., Tavistock House North, Tavistock Square, London, WC1H 9JE *T.* 01–387 3012.

25p. Q.—Medical articles in non-medical terms up to 2000 words. *Payment:* by arrangement.

HEALTH EDUCATION JOURNAL (1943), Dr. A. J. DALZELL-WARD, Health Education Council, Lynton House, 7–12 Tavistock Square, London, W.C.1. *T.* 01–387 0581.

17½p. Q.—Matter on mental and physical health, health education and social well-being; reports of surveys of people's knowledge of health; educational method and material; anthropology; nutrition; educational psychology and preventive psychiatry. Book reviews. *Length:* 1500 to 3000 words. *No payment. Illustrations:* half-tone and line blocks are used where required.

HEALTH FOR ALL, PETER LIEF, Gateway House, Bedford Park, Croydon, CR9 2AT *T.* 01–688 5528–9.

10p. M.—Popularly written, practical articles, 2200 words, on nature cure, diet reform, exercise, fasting, osteopathy, etc. *Payment:* £3·15 per 1000 words or by arrangement. Relevant *illustrations.* A *Preliminary letter* is desirable.

HEARING (official journal of the Royal National Institute for the Deaf), ROY COLE, 105 Gower Street, London, W.C.1. *T.* 01–387 8033.

5p. M.—Articles and stories dealing in a bright and intelligent way with deafness. Special consideration given to deaf or hard-of-hearing contributors. *Payment:* by arrangement. *Illustrations:* photographs and line.

HEATING AND VENTILATING ENGINEER, THE, H. SWINBURNE, B.SC.(ENG)., A.K.C., 11–13 Southampton Row, London, W.C.1. *T.* 01–242 7676 7688–9.

17½p. (postage 6p.).—M.—Technical articles, length according to subject-matter. *Payment:* £5·25 per 1000 words. *Illustrations:* line and half-tone.

HEREDITY: AN INTERNATIONAL JOURNAL OF GENETICS (1947), Professor J. L. JINKS (General Editor), Department of Genetics, University of Birmingham, P.O. Box 363, Edgbaston, Birmingham 15. *T.* Selly Oak 1301.

£6. Four times yearly.—Research and review articles in genetics of 1000 to 15,000 words with summary and bibliography. Book reviews and abstracts of conferences. Occasional supplements. *No payment. Illustrations:* line, half-tone and colour.

HERE'S HEALTH, Abbot Close, Byfleet, Weybridge, Surrey. *T.* Byfleet 44402.
7½p. M.—Articles on nutrition; dieting; slimming; health foods and diet reform; natural food cookery; natural health and healing therapies; pollution; organic husbandry. *Length:* 1200–1800 words. *Payment:* by arrangement. Preliminary letter advisable.

HERS (1966), Executive Editor: MARGARET PALFREY, Editor: KATHY WALKER, Fleetway House, Farringdon Street, London, E.C.4. *T.* 01–236 8080.
15p. M.—Stories in first-person fictionalised form reflecting human problems and situations. To have strong appeal to women readers. *Length:* 2000 words upwards. *Payment:* by arrangement.

HERTFORDSHIRE COUNTRYSIDE (1946), LESLIE BICHENER, Letchworth Printers Ltd., Norton Way North, Letchworth. *T.* 2501–4.
15p. M.—Articles of county interest, 800 to 1000 words. *Illustrations:* line and half-tone.

HEYTHROP JOURNAL, THE (1960), Rev. Dr. B. R. BRINKMAN, Heythrop College, University of London, 11 Cavendish Square, London, W1M 0AN *T.* 01–580 6941.
75p. post free or £2·75 yearly. Q.—Articles (3000–6000) in: philosophy, theology speculative and positive, scripture, canon law, church relations, moral and pastoral psychology of general interest but of technical merit. *Payment:* from £8·40 with 25 offprints.

HI-FI NEWS (1956), JOHN CRABBE, Link House, Dingwall Avenue, Croydon, CR9 2TA *T.* 01–686 2599. *T.A.* Aviculture, Croydon.
17½p. M.—Articles on all aspects of high quality sound recording and reproduction; also extensive record review section and supporting musical feature articles. Audio matter is essentially technical, but should be presented in a manner suitable for music lovers interested in the nature of sound. *Payment:* from £8 per 1000 words. *Length:* 2000 to 3000 words. *Illustrations:* line and/or half-tone; cartoons.

HI FI SOUND (1967), CLEMENT BROWN, Gillow House, 5 Winsley Street, London. W1N 7AQ *T.* 01–636 3600.
15p. M.—Semi-technical articles on aspects of high fidelity sound. *Length:* 400–1200 words. *Payment:* by arrangement. *Illustrations:* line and half-tone. Preliminary letter advisable.

HIBERNIA (1936), JOHN MULCAHY, 179 Pearse Street, Dublin 2. *T.* 776317–8.
12p. Fortnightly—Articles, features, comments on Irish politics, current affairs, and everything of interest to Irish people at home and abroad, including books, writers, theatre, the arts, etc. *Payment:* by arrangement. *Illustrations:* line and half-tone.

HISTORY (1916), R. H. C. DAVIS, M.A., Editorial: The Department of History, The University, Birmingham. Business: 59a Kennington Park Road, S.E.11.
75p. Three times yearly.—Published by the Historical Association. Historical articles and reviews by experts. *Length:* usually up to 6000 words. *No payment. No illustrations.*

HISTORY TODAY (1951), PETER QUENNELL and ALAN HODGE, Bracken House, 10 Cannon Street, E.C.4. *T.* 01–248 8000.

20p. M.—History in the widest sense—political, economic, social, biography, the social scene, relating past to present; World history as well as English. *Length:* about 3500 words. *Payment:* by agreement. *Illustrations:* prints and original photographs.

HOME AND COUNTRY (1919), PEGGY MITCHELL, 11A King's Road, Sloane Square, S.W.3. *T.* 01–730 0307.

5p. M.—A good deal of the material published relates to the activities of the National Federation of Women's Institutes, whose official journal it is, but articles of general interest to women, particularly country women, of 800 to 1000 words are considered. *Payment:* by arrangement. *Illustrations:* photographs and drawings.

HOME WORDS (1870) (incorporating **CHURCH STANDARD, CHURCH MONTHLY** and **THE SENTINEL**), 11 Ludgate Square, London, E.C.4. *T.* 01-248 2872.

2p. M. (25th).—An illustrated Church magazine inset. Articles of popular Church interest (500 to 1000 words); occasional short stories and verse. *Illustrations:* photographs of religious and ecclesiastical subjects. *Payment:* by arrangement.

HOMEMAKER (1959), ROBERT TATTERSALL, 189 High Holborn, London, WC1V 7BA *T.* 01–242 3344.

12½p. M.—Practical features on all aspects of homemaking and inspired do-it-yourself. *Illustrations:* colour, half-tone, line. *Payment:* by arrangement.

HOMES AND GARDENS (1919), MRS PSYCHE PIRIE, 2–10 Tavistock Street, Covent Garden, W.C.2. *T.* 01–836 4363.

20p. M.—Fiction of the highest quality and articles of general interest to every intelligent woman. *Length:* articles, 900–1750 words; stories, 2000–5000 words. *Payment:* generous, but exceptional work required. *Illustrations:* all types.

HONEY (1960), GILLIAN COOKE, Fleetway House, Farringdon Street, E.C.4. *T.* 01–236 8080.

15p. M.—The magazine for teens and twenties: young, gay, lively. The emphasis is on service to the reader. Fashion and beauty are handled by staff editors, but we welcome fresh, original ideas from free-lance writers for profiles, humour, travel, careers, hobbies, the art of living—and loving. If it's new, we are interested. Fiction: first-rate writing, well plotted, with situations and problems with which the reader can identify herself. Particularly the short short story. *Payment:* for topflight material, thoroughly researched: top rates. *Length:* depends on merit of ideas, which should be submitted in outline form in the first place. *Illustrations:* photographs and sketches.

HORNET, THE (D. C. Thomson & Co., Ltd.), Courier Place, Dundee, DD1 9QJ, and Thomson House, 12 Fetter Lane, London, E.C.4.

2½p. W. (Tuesday).—Picture-stories, in line, for boys. Subjects—adventure, sport, war, mystery, wild west. Instalments of 2 to 4 pages; 8 to 10 frames per page. *Payment:* on acceptance.

HORSE AND HOUND, W. O. CASE, 189 High Holborn, London, WC1V 7BA *T.* 01–242 3344.

12½p. W. (Friday).—Special articles, news items, photographs, on all matters appertaining to horses, hounds.

HOSPITAL, THE, N. W. CHAPLIN, M.A., 75 Portland Place, W1N 4AN *T.* 01–580 5041.
25p. M.—Technical articles on hospital management and administration, construction, equipment, maintenance, finance, etc. *Length:* 500 to 3000 words. Articles accepted from outside contributors. *Payment:* by arrangement. *Illustrations:* views of hospitals and hospital equipment.

HOSPITAL MANAGEMENT, Wrotham Place, Wrotham, Sevenoaks, Kent. *T.* Borough Green 3232–5.
50p. M.—Articles on all aspects of hospital management, hospital architecture, engineering, equipment and electrical services. *Illustrations:* half-tone and line.

HOTEL & CATERING INSTITUTE JOURNAL (1950), M. A. NIGHTINGALE, M.H.C.I., Hotel and Catering Institute, 191 Trinity Road, London, S.W.17. *T.* 01–672 4251.
37½p., £1·50 p.a. Q.—Articles on the hotel and catering industry. *Payment:* £1 per 100 words published.

HOTEL & RESTAURANT CATERING (1969), R. O. BAKER, 1 Dorset Buildings, Salisbury Square, London, EC4Y 8ER *T.* 01–353 1555.
M.—Articles dealing with new products and developments in hotels and restaurants, food service and management techniques. *Length:* up to 1500 words. *Payment:* by arrangement. *Illustrations:* line and tone.

HOTSPUR, THE (D. C. Thomson & Co., Ltd.), Courier Place, Dundee, DD1 9QJ, and Thomson House, 12 Fetter Lane, London, E.C.4.
2½p. W. (Thursday).—Picture-stories for boys—adventure, sport, war, school, air and sea. Line drawings only. Instalments 2 to 3 pages, 8 to 10 panels per page. Also stories (in type) suitable for boys. *Payment:* on acceptance.

HOUSE & GARDEN, ROBERT HARLING, Vogue House, Hanover Square, W1R 0AD *T.* 01–499 9080.
25p. M.—Articles, always, commissioned on subjects relating to domestic architecture, interior decorating, furnishing, gardening, household equipment.

HOUSE-BUILDER AND ESTATE DEVELOPER, THE, ANDREW DEG, 82 New Cavendish Street, W1M 8AD. *T.* 01–580 1415.
20p. M.—A technical journal for those engaged in house and flat construction and the development of housing estates. The Official Journal of the Federation of Registered House-Builders. Articles on design, construction, and equipment of dwellings, estate planning and development, and technical aspects of house-building. *Length:* articles 500 words and upwards, preferably with illustrations. *Preliminary letter* advisable. *Payment:* by arrangement. *Illustrations:* photographs, plans, constructional details.

HOUSECRAFT, Official journal of the Association of Teachers of Domestic Science, PATRICIA HEDLEY, 10 Queen Anne Street, London, W1M 9LD *T.* 01–580 8197.
12½p., £1·80 p.a. (including postage). M.—Articles on the teaching of domestic science and social and technical background information for teachers. *Length:* 1000 words. *Payment:* approx. £5·25 per 1000 words. *Illustrations:* line and half-tone. Most articles are commissioned from teachers.

HUMANIST (1885), HECTOR HAWTON, 88 Islington High Street, London, N.1. *T.* 01–226 7251–2.

10p. M.—Articles (850–2000 words) with a humanist/rationalist outlook on current problems of religion, philosophy, ethics, science and art. *Payment:* by arrangement. *Illustrations:* half-tone.

HYDRAULIC PNEUMATIC POWER, JOHN A. W. BURROWS, Trade and Technical Press Ltd., Crown House, Morden, Surrey. *T.* 01–540 3897. *T.A.* Tratec, Morden, Surrey. *Telex:* 27526.

£6 p.a. post free, UK and overseas. M.—Technical articles and commercial news. *Payment:* by arrangement. *Illustrations:* line and half-tone.

IDEAL HOME and Gardening (1939), MONICA TYSON, 189 High Holborn, London, W.C.1. *T.* 01–242 3344.

20p. M.—Articles dealing with all practical aspects of the house and garden: house planning, conversion, heating and lighting, decoration, furnishing and equipment, cookery, housekeeping, garden design and maintenance. Synopses only should be submitted. *Payment:* according to material. *Illustrations:* photographs, drawings in line, wash.

ILLUSTRATED CARPENTER AND BUILDER (1877), LESLIE BLACK, Elm House, 10–16 Elm Street, London, WC1X 0BP *T.* 01–837 1234.

4p. W.—Contains well-illustrated technical articles by experts, dealing with any of the building trades, aspects of site, project and business management. Architectural designs with brief explanatory notes. Photographs and line drawings used, all by arrangement. *Preliminary* or *covering letter* with MSS. desirable. *Payment:* generally £2 per column of 300 words. *Length:* 1500 to 2000 words, with about 2 *illustrations*, either photos or line drawings.

ILLUSTRATED LONDON NEWS (1842), Holborn Hall, 100 Grays Inn Road, London, W.C.1. *T.* 01–242 9700.

15p. W. (Thursday).—A news weekly dealing chiefly with current affairs of British and international interest. Stories for the Christmas number are usually accepted only from authors of established repute. Interesting articles dealing with politics, social issues, science, art, archaeology, ethnology, travel, exploration, are particularly acceptable. *Payment:* for illustrations at the usual rates, or by special arrangement; special prices for exclusive material. Photographs (especially exclusive).

IMPACT OF SCIENCE ON SOCIETY (1950), Unesco, Place de Fontenoy, Paris 7e. *T.* 566–5757. *T.A.* Unesco, Paris.

30p. (annual subscription £1·05). Q.—Articles and original studies on the social, political and economic aspects of science. A *preliminary letter* to the Editor is requested. *Length:* 4000–10,000 words. *Payment:* £50 to £100 on acceptance. *Illustrations:* graphs and drawings. Intending contributors are advised to study the magazine.

INCORPORATED LINGUIST, THE, The Institute of Linguists, 91 Newington Causeway, London, S.E.1. *T.* 01–407 4755/6.

60p., £2 p.a. Q.—Articles of interest to professional linguists in translating, interpreting and teaching fields. Articles usually contributed, but *payment* by arrangement. All contributors have special knowledge of the subjects with which they deal. *Length:* 2000–2500 words. *Illustrations:* line.

INDUSTRIA BRITANICA, VICENTE SOTO, Benn Brothers Ltd., Bouverie House, Fleet Street, EC4A 2DL *T.* 01–353 3212.

£1 p.a. (£2 for 3 years) or $3 p.a. Q.—Articles and information on British industrial, technical and scientific achievements of interest in the Spanish speaking countries in Spanish. 4 issues a year including the Special Annual Edition. *Payment:* by arrangement. *Illustrations:* photographs.

INDUSTRIAL AND SCIENTIFIC COMMUNICATION, A. C. CLEGG, Orchard House, Mutton Lane, Potters Bar, Herts. *T.* Potters Bar 50911.

Controlled circulation. M.—Articles, preferably technical, on the communication of technical information by the printed word, illustrations, or other means. Information on new techniques of communication, new reprographic etc. devices. *Length:* up to 2000 words unless otherwise arranged. *Payment:* £8·40 per 1000 words, or by arrangement. *Illustrations:* line or half-tone.

INDUSTRIAL & WELFARE CATERING (1969) R. O. BAKER, 1 Dorset Buildings, Salisbury Square, London, EC4Y 8ER *T.* 01–353 1555.

M.—Articles dealing with new products and developments, food service and management techniques in industrial and institutional catering. *Length:* up to 1500 words. *Payment:* by arrangement. *Illustrations:* line and tone.

INDUSTRIAL ARCHAEOLOGY, The Journal of the History of Industry and Technology (1964), Dr. JOHN BUTT, Department of Economic History, University of Strathclyde, McCance Building, Richmond Street, Glasgow, C.1. *T.* 041–552 4400. Published by David & Charles, Newton Abbot.

54p., £2·10 p.a. Q.—Articles on industrial archaeology of approx. 3000 to 5000 words. No *payment*, but 15 offprints. *Illustrations:* line and half-tone.

INDUSTRIAL DIAMOND REVIEW, PAUL DANIEL, 7 Rolls Buildings, Fetter Lane, London, E.C.4. *T.* 01–242 2800.

20p. M. (10th).—Original articles and translations of foreign-language articles dealing with industrial diamonds from all aspects: also reviews of new equipment, books and exhibitions. *Length:* 500–5000 words. *Payment:* £10·50 per 1000 words. *Illustrations:* photographs and line drawings; colour photographs for cover.

INDUSTRIAL EQUIPMENT NEWS (1952), R. A. HEBBERT, 22 Greville Street, London, E.C.1. *T.* 01–242 1655. *T.A.* Frazette, London, E.C.1.

Free. Controlled circulation. Twice monthly.—Reviews new products; also short, preferable illustrated, feature articles on engineering production and equipment matters. *Length:* up to 2000 words. *Payment:* by arrangement. *Illustrations:* line and half-tone.

INDUSTRIAL FINISHING, Wheatland Journals Ltd., 157 Hagden Lane, Watford, WD1 8LW *T.* 32308.

£5 per annum, including Industrial Finishing Year Book. M. (12th).— Articles describing works processes in paint, plating, vitreous enamelling and finishing generally. *Length:* 2000 to 3000 words. *Payment:* £4·20 to £5·25 per 1000 words. *Illustrations:* half-tone and line.

INDUSTRIAL GAS, C. F. DEWBURY (Benn Brothers Ltd.), 2nd Floor, Hanover House, 73–78 High Holborn, London WC1V 7JS

£1 p.a. M. (3rd Saturday).—Descriptive articles dealing with the uses of gas for industrial and large-scale commercial purposes. *Illustrations:* essential: half-tone and line. *Payment:* by arrangement.

INDUSTRIAL SAFETY (1955), E. W. HODGSON (United Trade Press Ltd.), 9 Gough Square, Fleet Street, London, E.C.4. *T.* 01–353 3172.

30p., (£3 per annum including Industrial Safety Equipment and Clothing Catalogue). M.—Devoted to the interests of industrial safety, health and welfare, including safety equipment and protective clothing. Technical and general articles on all aspects of industrial accident prevention, industrial fire prevention, factory safety organisation, etc. *Payment:* by arrangement. *Illustrations:* high-quality photographs and drawings illustrating the relevant subjects.

INDUSTRIAL SOCIETY (formerly INDUSTRIAL WELFARE) (1918), ELIZA-
BETH McLEOD (The Industrial Society), 48 Bryanston Square, London, W1H
8AH T. 01-262 2401.
  20p., to members of the Society, 30p. to non-members. M.—Technical articles,
news items and photographs concerning developments in business and industry
connected with people at work, working conditions, and human relationships.
Length: 800 to 2500 words. *Payment:* £7 for 1000 words, or by arrangement.
Illustrations: half-tones.

INDUSTRIALISED BUILDING, SYSTEMS AND COMPONENTS, A. T.
GODWIN, 32 Southwark Bridge Road, London, S.E.1. T. 01-928 2060.
T.A. Beandcejay, London, S.E.1.
  M.—Controlled circulation.—Technical articles describing prefabricated
methods of building construction. *Payment:* by arrangement. *Illustrations:*
line and half-tone.

INQUIRER, THE (1842), Rev. TONY CROSS, 1-6 Essex Street, London, W.C.2.
T. 01-240 2384.
  4p. W. (Thursday).—A journal of news and comment for Unitarians.
Articles 700 to 1100 words of general religious, social, cultural, and international
interest. Religious articles should be liberal and progressive in tone.

INSTRUMENT AND CONTROL ENGINEERING, R. S. SQUIRES, I.P.C. Electrical-
Electronic Press Ltd., Dorset House, Stamford Street, London, S.E.1. T.
01-928 3333.
  Controlled circulation.—M.—Articles describe mechanical, pneumatic,
hydraulic, electrical, electronic or hybrid control schemes with their attendant
instrumentation. Each subject angled for readers who are not specialists in
that subject. Also covers instrument and test equipment. *Preliminary letter*
recommended. *Payment:* by arrangement. *Illustrations* line and half-tone
essential.

INSTRUMENT PRACTICE, P. D. RUSH, United Trade Press Ltd., 9 Gough
Square, Fleet Street, London, E.C.4. T. 01-353 3172-3-4-5.
  35p. M. (£3·50 per annum).—Articles of a high technical standard in the
fields of measuring and control instrumentation, process control systems and
automation. *Length:* 1000 to 2000 words. *Payment:* by arrangement. *Illustrations:* line and half-tone.

INSULATION—THERMAL, ACOUSTIC, VIBRATION, 8 Buckingham Street,
London, WC2N 6DA T. 01-839 6661.
  £1 p.a. (post free); overseas £1·50 (post free). Bi-Monthly.—Technical
articles only on all aspects of thermal, acoustic and vibration insulation. *Payment:* by arrangement. *Illustrations:* line and half-tone. A preliminary letter
is essential.

INSURANCE BROKERS' MONTHLY (1950), J. C. N. SADLER, Lower High
Street, Stourbridge, Worcs. T. Stourbridge 3011.
  20p. M. (1st of month).—Articles of technical and non-technical interest to
insurance brokers and others engaged in the insurance industry. Occasional
articles of general interest to the City, on finance, etc., and short stories of about
2000 words are also considered, but limited scope for stories which *must* have
strong insurance flavour. Humorous material with stong insurance flavour
specially welcomed. *Length:* 1000 to 1500 words. *Average payment:* £3·15
per 1000 words on last day of month following publication. Authoritative
material written under true name and qualification receives highest payment.
Illustrations: line and half-tone, 100-120 screen.

INTERNATIONAL AFFAIRS (1922), N. P. MACDONALD, Royal Institute of International Affairs, Chatham House, St. James's Square, London, S.W.1. *T.* 01–930 2233.

65p. Annual subscription: £2·50 in this country; $7.00 in U.S.A., and Canda. Q.—Serious long-term articles on international affairs. *Length:* 5000 words. *Illustrations:* none. *Payment:* by arrangement. A *preliminary letter is necessary.*

INTERNATIONAL ASSOCIATIONS (1949), G. P. SPEECKAERT, The Conference Centre, 43 Charles Street, Mayfair, London, W.1. *T.* 01–499 1101.

£3·75 p.a. (including Congress Calendar). 12 times a year.—Articles up to 3000 words on international organisation. *Payment:* up to £5·25 per 1000 words. *Illustrations:* of international activities.

INTERNATIONAL BREWERS' JOURNAL (1865), V. S. JONES, 19 Eastcheap, E.C.3. *T.* 01–626 0493–4–5.

20p. M. (1st of month).—This journal is devoted to the interests of Brewers Maltsters, Hop Growers, Barley Growers, Distillers, Soft Drinks Manufacturers and Allied Trades, circulating in over 100 countries. Trilingual Summaries of articles are printed. Contributions (average 1500 words) accepted are technical and scientific articles written by authors with a special knowledge of the subjects dealt with. Such articles may be illustrated by line drawings and photographs. *Payment:* by arrangement.

INTERNATIONAL BROADCAST ENGINEER, F. R. SIMMINS (Publisher), 31 St. George Street, London, W1R 9FA *T.* 01–493 3931. *Cables:* Inteevee, London.

25p. M.—Articles of interest to television, radio and audio engineers on new techniques and developments. Circulates to over 190 countries and international aspect is stressed. Preliminary letter advisable. *Illustrations:* line and half-tone. *Payment:* by arrangement.

INTERNATIONAL BULLETIN FOR THE PRINTING AND ALLIED TRADES (1930), 9 Railway Street, London, N.1. *T.* 01–723 7530.

4 times a year. Annual subscription £1.—The official organ of the International Master Printers Association (IMPA). Reports about the services of IMPA. Reports about international conferences concerned with the printing, binding and allied trades. *Payment:* by arrangement. *Illustrations:* line and half-tone.

INTERNATIONAL CONSTRUCTION, A. J. K. MOSS, 32 Southwark Bridge Road, London, S.E.1. *T.* 01–928 2060. *T.A.* Construction, London, S.E.1.

M.—Articles dealing with new techniques of construction, applications of construction equipment and use of construction materials in any part of the world. *Length:* maximum 1500 words plus illustrations. *Payment:* from £7·35 per 1000 words. *Illustrations:* half-tone and line. Some two-colour line illustrations can be used.

INTERNATIONAL HERALD TRIBUNE, 21 Rue de Berri, Paris-8e. *T.* 225–28–90. London Office: 28 Great Queen Street, W.C.2.

7½p. appears Mon-Sat.

INTERNATIONAL RAILWAY PROGRESS (formerly **OVERSEAS RAILWAYS**), Dorset House, Stamford Street, London, S.W.1. *T.* 01–928 3333.

52½p. Annually (November).—Illustrated survey of world railways development; contributed by General Manager and Senior executives of railway administrations.

INVERNESS COURIER (1817), Miss EVELINE BARRON, M.A., P.O. Box 13, 9–11 Bank Lane, Inverness. *T.* Inverness 33059. *T.A.* Courier, Inverness.
2p. Bi-W. (Tuesday and Friday).—Short articles (no stories or verses) of Highland interest. *Payment:* by arrangement. No *illustrations.*

INVESTORS CHRONICLE AND STOCK EXCHANGE GAZETTE, A. W. SMITH, 30 Finsbury Square, London, E.C.2. *T.* 01–628 4050.
15p. W. (Friday).—The leading journal for investors covering the field from a world-wide standpoint. Only occasional outside contributions are accepted. *Payment:* £15 per 1000 words.

IRELAND OF THE WELCOMES, Baggot Street Bridge, Dublin, 2. *T.* Dublin 65871.
18p. Bi-M.—Irish items with cultural background designed to arouse interest in Irish holidays. No fiction. *Length:* 1200 to 1500 words. *Payment:* by arrangement. *Illustrations:* scenic and topical. Preliminary letter preferred. Mostly commissioned.

IRELAND'S OWN (1902), M. J. WALL, 39 Lower Ormond Quay, Dublin 1.
3p. W.—Short stories (1500 to 4000 words); articles of interest to Irish readers at home and abroad (1000 to 3000 words); general and literary articles (1000 to 2500 words). Special issues for Christmas and St. Patrick's Day. Cartoons, adventure strips for family reading. Suggestions for new features considered. *Payment:* varies according to quality, originality and length. Serials, of novel length, preliminary letter advisable, enclosing synopsis and S.A.E., payment by arrangement. *Illustrations:* half-tone and line.

IRISH BUILDER AND ENGINEER (1859), 11 Findlater Place, off Upper O'Connell Street, Dublin, 1. *T.* Dublin 44235.
5p. F.—Articles relating to building, architecture, and civil engineering are chiefly required. *Length:* up to 2000 words. *Payment:* 1½p. a line. *Illustrations:* photographs or sketches.

IRISH INDEPENDENT, AIDAN J. PENDER, Independent House, 90 Middle Abbey Street, Dublin 1. *T.* 46841.
2½p. D.—Special articles on topical or general subjects. *Length:* 1000 words maximum. *Payment:* Editor's estimate of value.

IRISH JOURNAL OF MEDICAL SCIENCE (1st series 1832, 6th series January 1926), CHARLES DICKSON, M.B., F.R.C.S. General Publications Ltd., 59 Merrion Square, South Dublin, 2. *T.* 63581.
17½p. Subscription Great Britain and Ireland £2·70 post free; overseas £3·50 post free. M. (1st).—Official organ of the Royal Academy of Medicine in Ireland. Original contributions in medicine, surgery, midwifery, public health, etc.; reviews of professional books, reports of medical societies, etc. Outside contributions not paid for. *Illustrations:* half-tone, line and colour.

IRISH PRESS, THE, T. P. COOGAN, Burgh Quay, Dublin. *T.* 757931.
2½p. D.—Topical articles, about 800 words. *Payment:* by arrangement. *Illustrations:* topical photographs.

IRISH TIMES, DOUGLAS GAGEBY, 31 Westmoreland Street, Dublin, 2. *T.* Dublin 775871.
3½p. (4p. in England.) D.—Articles of Irish and general interest. *Length:* 800 to 2000 words. *Payment:* at editor's valuation, on publication. *Illustrations:* photographs and line drawings.

JACK AND JILL (1954), New Fleetway House, Farringdon Street, EC4A 4AD *T.* 01–634 4444.
3½p. W. (Monday).—Age appeal 3 to 8. All pictures. Four-colour front back and centre. Artists invited to submit specimen drawings to the Editor.

JACKIE (D. C. Thomson & Co., Ltd.), Courier Place, Dundee, DD1 9QJ, and Thomson House, 12 Fetter Lane, London, E.C.4.
3p. W. (Thursday).—Colour gravure magazine for teen girls. Complete picture love stories. Type stories up to 2000 words dealing with young romance. Pop pin-ups and show biz features of folk of teen interest. Fashion and beauty advice. *Illustrations:* transparencies, picture story art work, colour illustrations for type stories. *Payment:* on acceptance.

JEWISH CHRONICLE, THE (1841), WILLIAM FRANKEL, C.B.E., 25 Furnival Street, E.C.4. *T.* 01–405 9252 (15 lines).
7½p. W. (Friday).—Authentic and exclusive news stories and articles of Jewish interest from 500 to 1200 words are considered. There is a weekly children's page. *Payment:* average rate £1·50 per 1000 words. *Illustrations:* of Jewish interest, either topical or of notable persons or historic events.

JEWISH TELEGRAPH (1950), FRANK HARRIS, Levi House, Bury Old Road, Manchester 8. *T.* 740 9321 (4 lines).
1½p. W. (Friday).—Articles of Jewish interest, especially humour. *Length:* 1500–2000 words. *Payment:* £3·15 or by arrangement. *Illustrations:* half-tone and line.

JOURNAL, THE, IAN FAWCETT, Thomson House, Groat Market, Newcastle upon Tyne. London Office, Thomson House, W.C.1. *T.* 01–837 1234.
2½p. D.—Independent. No fiction, but topical articles of north-country interest.

JOURNAL OF THE BRITISH INTERPLANETARY SOCIETY (1934), Dr. G. V. GROVES, 12 Bessborough Gardens, London, S.W.1. *T.* 01–828 9371. *T.A.* Britintsoc, London.
£1. M.—Technical articles on space research and technology. *Maximum length:* 10,000 words. *Payment:* none. *Illustrations:* line and half-tone.

JOURNAL OF FUEL AND HEAT TECHNOLOGY (Turret Press Ltd.), Stamford House, 65–66 Turnmill Street, London, E.C.1. *T.* 01–253 8201–10.
£6 p.a. Bi-M. (16th).—Technical articles on the efficient use of fuel, also on insulation, instrumentation and other fuel-saving equipment. *Length:* up to 5000 words. *Payment:* £4 to £6 per 1000 words. *Illustrations:* line.

JOURNAL OF PARK AND RECREATION ADMINISTRATION, L. E. MORGAN, Consultant Editor, Lower Basildon, Reading, RG8 9NE. *T.* Goring-on-Thames 2314.
15p. M.—Articles on park, recreation and horticultural subjects. *Payment:* £7 per 1000 words (according to type of material). *Illustrations:* line and half-tone.

JOURNAL OF REFRIGERATION, THE (1957), W. B. GOSNEY, 19 Harcourt Street, London, W1H 1DT *T.* 01–723 0077.

25p. M.—Articles dealing with all aspects of the Technology of refrigeration. *Payment:* £6·30 per 1000 words. *Illustrations:* photographs and line drawings. *Preliminary letter* advisable.

JOURNAL OF THE ROYAL UNITED SERVICE INSTITUTION, H. P. J. HANNING, Whitehall, S.W.1. *T.* 01–930 5854.

75p. Q. (March, June, September, December).—Articles, from 2000 to 4000 words, connected with the Fighting Services, or of professional value or interest to them. *Illustrations:* maps or diagrams in each issue. *Payment:* £4·20 per printed page.

JOURNALIST, G. A. HUTT, Acorn House, 314 Gray's Inn Road, London, W.C.1. *T.* 01–278 7916.

2½p. M.—Official organ of the National Union of Journalists. Relating to journalism, journalists, and general conditions in the newspaper industry. Mainly contributed by members, and outside work is not paid for.

JUDY (D. C. Thomson & Co. Ltd.), Courier Place, Dundee, DD1 9QJ, and Thomson House, 12 Fetter Lane, London, E.C.4.

2½p. W. (Thursday).—Picture-story paper for schoolgirls. Stories in pictures, line drawings, as serials or series, 16–20 panels in each instalment of 2 pages. Also stories (in type) written to appeal to girls of school age. *Payment:* on acceptance. Encouragement to young artists and writers of promise.

JUDY LIBRARY (D. C. Thomson & Co. Ltd.), Courier Place, Dundee, DD1 9QJ, and Thomson House, 12 Fetter Lane, London, E.C.4.

5p. M. (2nd Tuesday each month).—Stories told in pictures, for schoolgirls; 64 pages (about 140 line drawings). Ballet, school, adventure, theatre, sport. Scripts considered; promising artists and script-writers encouraged. *Payment:* on acceptance.

JUNE AND SCHOOL FRIEND (1961), New Fleetway House, Farringdon Street, EC4A 4AD *T.* 01–634 4444.

3p. W. (Tuesday).—A picture-story paper for schoolgirls. Most of contents commissioned, but the Editor is always interested to see ideas and picture scripts by authors who have made a close study of the paper.

JUNIOR AGE (1936), ALICE M. GUPPY, 167 High Holborn, W.C.1. *T.* 01–836 9551.

15p. M. £1·87 a year, post free—Articles, news, etc., appertaining to children's clothes and equipment. *Length:* 1000 words, or short paragraphs. *Payment:* by arrangement. *Illustrations:* photographs.

JUNIOR BOOKSHELF, Marsh Hall, Thurstonland, Huddersfield, HD4 6XB. *T.* Huddersfield 21467.

25p. Six issues p.a. (Annual subs, £1·25 inland; £1·40 ($4.25) overseas). Articles on children's books and authors. *Length:* about 2000 words.

JUNIOR CHURCH PAPER (1947), JOAN SELBY-LOWNDES, 60 Hatch Lane, Windsor, Berks. *T.* Windsor 64279.

2½p. M.—Stories averaging 1000 words. Prayers, puzzles, ideas for competitions; visual ideas for teaching aids. *Payment:* by arrangement. *Illustrations:* line, black-and-white or two colour. Strips, picture puzzles, models to colour and cut out, and line drawings for colouring competitions are especially welcome.

JUSTICE OF THE PEACE AND LOCAL GOVERNMENT REVIEW (1837), BARRY ROSE, Little London, Chichester, Sussex. London: 11–12 Bell Yard, W.C.2. *T.* Chichester 87841, Holborn 6900. *T.A.* Justlocgov, Chichester.

22p. W.—Articles on magisterial law and local government practice including Children and Young Persons, Criminology, Housing, Road Traffic, Police, Probation, Town and Country Planning, Rating and Valuation (length preferred, 1200 to 1400 words). Short reports of Conferences, Meetings, etc. Rates of *payment:* articles minimum £1·50 per column except when otherwise commissioned. *Preliminary letter welcomed although not essential.*

KARATE AND ORIENTAL ARTS MAGAZINE (1966), PAUL H. CROMPTON, 638 Fulham Road, London, S.W.6. *T.* 01–736 2551.

25p. Bi-M.—Short stories with oriental background. True adventures in the East. *Payment:* £3·15 per 1000 words. *Illustrations:* half-tones, line.

KENT (The Journal of the Men of Kent and Kentish Men), *Hon. Editor:* ALAN RYE, K.C.S.G., Cornwallis House, Pudding Lane, Maidstone. *T.* 58722.

5p. (free to members). Q.—Articles referring to County of Kent, 500 to 600 words. *Payment:* by arrangement. *Illustrations:* photographs.

KENT LIFE (1962), H. R. PRATT BOORMAN, C.B.E., M.A. (Editor in-Chief), 129 Week Street, Maidstone, Kent. *T.* Maidstone 52986. (News Editor) R. F. SONGHURST, 3 Yew Tree Cottages, Sandling, Maidstone, Kent. *T.* Maidstone 57635.

15p. M.—Occasional fiction with a Kent background accepted. All articles and pictures must have a Kent connection. *Length:* articles and fiction 300 to 1000 words, 1–2 sharp black-and-white pictures with articles. *Illustrations:* half-tone or line drawings. *Payment:* £2·10 to £5·25.

KENT MESSENGER, H. R. PRATT BOORMAN, C.B.E., M.A. Head Office: Maidstone. *T.* 58444. Branch Offices: Ashford, Chatham, Sittingbourne, Tenterden, and 80 Fleet Street, E.C.4.

4p. Friday and Saturday.—Articles of special interest to Kent and referring to Kent. *Length:* up to 1000 words. *Payment:* state price. Articles dealing with film, stage, radio, or T.V. stars who are in any way connected with Kent. *Illustrations:* all types, line and half-tone are used.

KEYBOARD, VIC HAMMETT, Tofts & Woolf (Publishers) Ltd., 64a Lansdowne Road, South Woodford, London, E18 2BD *T.* 01–989 1774 & 2297.

30p. (£2 per annum). Bi-monthly.—Articles on piano and organ playing and about people who play those instruments. Articles on historical keyboard instruments. All must be of general appeal to players of all styles of music although articles explaining specialist aspects are also sought. Also musical arrangements for keyboard instruments. *Payment:* £5 to £15 per page (more by arrangement). *Illustrations:* black-and-white photographs and line drawings, also colour pictures suitable for cover use.

KINE WEEKLY, W. G. ALTRIA, IPC Specialist and Professional Press Ltd., 161 Fleet Street, London, E.C.4. *T.* 01–353 5011.

15p. W. (Thurs.).—Trade articles dealing with the production, distribution, and presentation of films and film publicity. *Payment:* by arrangement. **The Ideal Kinema,** incorporated in Kine, appears monthly and contains technical articles on the building, equipment, and maintenance of picture theatres and the projection of films. Special articles by arrangement. *Illustrations:* line drawings, diagrams, plans, and photographs. **Kine Studio Review,** dealing with studio technique, is published six times a year. *Payment:* by arrangement. **Kine Sales and Catering Review,** incorporated in **Kine,** is published on alternate months.

KNITWEAR AND STOCKINGS (1947), N. ROGER PARKER, 47 Hertford Street, Mayfair, W1Y 8EH *T.* 01–493 7557–8.

Controlled circulation. M. (13th).—News of store and shop developments, executive appointments, and new garments. *Payments:* 1½p. per line and by arrangement. *Illustrations:* line, half-tone, and colour.

LABORATORY PRACTICE (1952), 9 Gough Square, Fleet Street, London, E.C.4. *T.* 01–353 3172.

50p., £4 p.a. (U.K.) £7 overseas. M.—Articles on original scientific work. *Payment:* by arrangement. *Illustrations:* line and half-tone.

LABOUR MONTHLY (1921), R. PALME DUTT, 134 Ballards Lane, N.3. *T.* 01-346 5135.

18p. M. (1st of month).—A Magazine of International Labour. Well-informed special articles, 1200 to 3000 words, or shorter news items. *Preliminary letter* desirable. No payment is made.

LADY, THE (1885), Miss MARGARET E. WHITFORD, 39 and 40 Bedford Street, Strand, WC2E 9ER *T.* 01–836 8705.

7½p. W. (Thursday).—A preliminary letter is essential, as suitable MSS submitted ('Sketches', Holiday Travel, Careers, Commemorative articles, Country, Animals, Cookery 700–1850 words) are always far in excess of space available. 'Occasional' verse considered, though same applies. *Payment:* by arrangement; about £6·30 per 1000 words plus payment for *illustrations* (line, line and wash, half-tone) according to size.

LANCASHIRE EVENING POST, B. ASKEW, 127 Fishergate, Preston. *T.* 54841.

2½p. D. (except Sunday).—Topical articles on all subjects. Area of interest: Wigan to Lake District and coast. 600 to 900 words. *Payment:* by arrangement. *Illustrations:* half-tones and line blocks.

LANCASHIRE EVENING TELEGRAPH (1886), IAN A. JACK, Telegraph House, Blackburn, Lancashire BB1 5BA *T.* Blackburn 55291. 2½p. D.

LANCASHIRE LIFE, WILLIAM AMOS (The Whitehorn Press, Ltd.), Thomson House, Withy Grove, Manchester, M60 4BL. *T.* 061–834 1234.

15p. M.—Articles of county interest; no fiction. *Length:* 1000 words. *Payment:* £4·20 per 1000 words minimum. *Illustrations:* line and half-tone; four-colour block on cover. Photographs of news value and definite Lancashire interest. £1·05 minimum payment.

LANCET (1823), I. DOUGLAS-WILSON, M.D., 7 Adam Street, Adelphi, W.C.2. *T.* 01–836 7228.

15p. W. (Saturday).—Mainly from medical profession.

LAUNDRY & CLEANING, J. A. D. KERR, IPC Consumer Industries Press Ltd., 33–39 Bowling Green Lane, London, E.C.1. *T.* 01–837 1277.

Applied-for circulation, distribution alternate Fridays.—Short technical articles, must be authoritative. *Length:* 1000 to 1200 words. *Illustrations:* half-tone and line.

LAUNDRY & CLEANING INTERNATIONAL, J. A. D. KERR, IPC Consumer Industries Press Ltd., 33–39 Bowling Green Lane, London, E.C.1. *T.* 01–837 1277.

Controlled circulation. 6 times a year.—In German, French and English. Short authoritative technical articles. *Length:* 1000 words maximum. *Illustrations:* half-tone and line.

LAWN TENNIS (1893 as **Lawn Tennis and Badminton**), C. M. JONES, Lowlands, Wenhanston, Halesworth, Suffolk, *T.* 0502–70 264.   (Blythburgh 264).
15p.   M.—Unusual features about tennis, not about current events.   *Payment:* N.U.J. Freelance rates.   *Illustrations:* half-tone.

LEATHER, EDWIN HAYDON (Benn Brothers Ltd.), Bouverie House, 154 Fleet Street, EC4A 2DL   *T.* 01–353 3212.
£3 p.a.   M.—Trade news: technical and commercial articles; ideas invited.   *Payment:* by arrangement.   *Illustrations:* photographs and diagrams.

LEATHERGOODS (incorporating **LEATHER GOODS MANUFACTURER** and **SADDLERY & HARNESS**) (1917), NEIL HIRD (Benn Bros., Ltd.), Bouverie House, 154 Fleet Street, EC4A 2DL   *T.* 01–353 3212.   *T.A.* Benbrolish, London, E.C.4.
30p., £3·50 p.a.   M. (First of the month).—News and articles relating to the handbag, luggage and small leather goods manufacturing and retailing trades, with special emphasis on market trends and fashion.   *Length:* 500 to 1200 words.   *Payment:* by agreement.   *Illustrations:* sketches, fashion and personal photographs.

LEISURE, M. L. WOOD, 22 Shaftesbury Avenue, Piccadilly, London, W1V 8AP.   *T.* 01–437 0356.
2½p.   W. (Friday).—News items concerning bingo and social recreation. Articles mainly commissioned.   *Payment:* by arrangement.   Action photographs.

LIBERAL NEWS, 7 Exchange Court, Strand, London, WC2R 0PR.
5p.   Fortnightly (Thursday).   The official newspaper of the Liberal Party. Political and social features.   *Payment:* nominal, unless specifically agreed otherwise.

LIBRARY (1889), R. A. SAYCE, Worcester College, Oxford.   For the Bibliographical Society.
£1·25 net.   Q.—Articles up to 15,000 words, as well as shorter Notes, embodying original research on subjects connected with bibliography.   *Illustrations:* half-tone and line.

LIBRARY REVIEW, W. R. AITKEN, M.A., PH.D., F.L.A., W. & R. Holmes (Books), 98–100 Holm Street, Glasgow, C.2.   *T.* 041–221 8184.
£1·80 per annum.   Q.—Articles, light or serious, on library subjects and literary and bibliographical topics.   From 2000 to 3000 words preferred.   *Payment:* from £4·50 per 1500 words.   *No illustrations.*

LIBRARY WORLD, THE, 10 New Fetter Lane, London, E.C.4.   *T.* 01–583 0951.
£3·50 per annum.   M. (20th).—Professional and bibliographical articles. *Illustrations: Payment:* £4·20 per 1000 words.

LIFE AND WORK: RECORD OF THE CHURCH OF SCOTLAND, L. J. A. BELL, 121 George Street, Edinburgh, EH2 4YN.   *T.* 031–225 5722.
3p.   M.—Articles and news not exceeding **1200** words.   *Illustrations:* photographs and line drawings.   Seldom uses poems or stories.   Study the magazine.   *Payment:* on publication; up to £12·60 per 1000 words, or by arrangement.

LIGHT AND LIGHTING (1908), G. F. COLE, York House, Westminster Bridge Road, S.E.1.   *T.* 01–928 7651.
35p.   M. (1st).—The only journal in this country devoted to all aspects of lighting.   Contains illustrated scientific and technical articles on natural and artificial illumination and their application.   Contributions considered.   Such articles should not exceed 2000 to 3000 words in *length.   Payment:* variable.

LIGHT HORSE, THE (incorporating **SHOW JUMPING**) (1950), Lt.-Col. C. E. G. HOPE, 19 Charing Cross Road, London, W.C.2. *T.* 01-930 3957.

15p. M.—Deals with show jumping, polo, hunting, breeding and activities connected with the light horse. Articles of technical, veterinary and personality interest are usually commissioned. *Length:* up to 1000 words. *Payment:* by arrangement. *Illustrations:* good action photographs.

LION AND EAGLE (1952), New Fleetway House, Farringdon Street, London, EC4A 4AD *T.* 01-634 4444.

3p. W. (Monday).—Scripts for picture stories and picture articles, suitable for boys 9 to 15 years.

LISTENER, THE, KARL MILLER, Broadcasting House, London, W1A 1AA *T.* 01-580 4468.

9p. W. (Thurs.).—Articles based on, or relating to BBC radio and television broadcasts. General articles on the media. Poems, book reviews and reviews of the arts. *Payment:* at market rates. *Illustrations:* fully illustrated in half-tone and line.

LITHOPRINTER, THE (1957), GERRY WITHERS, Gillow House, 5 Winsley Street, London, W1N 7AQ *T.* 01-636 3600.

25p. M.—Technical articles on reproduction and photo-litho, printing research. *Payment:* by arrangement. *Illustrations:* half-tone and line.

LIVERPOOL DAILY POST (1855), JOHN PUGH, P.O. Box 48, 48 Victoria Street, Liverpool, L69 1AR. *T.* 051-227 2000. London: 132-4 Fleet Street, E.C.4. *T.* 01-353 7656.

2½p. D.—Independent. Takes articles of general interest and topical features of special interest to North West England and North Wales. *Payment:* month following publication; according to value. News and feature photographs used. No verse or fiction.

LIVERPOOL ECHO, THE, KENNETH STAMP, Victoria Street, Liverpool, L69 1AR. *T.* 051-227 2000.

2½p. D.—Chiefly takes articles of up to 600-800 words of local or topical interest. *Payment:* according to merit; special rates for exceptional material. Independent. This newspaper is connected with, but independent of, **THE LIVERPOOL DAILY POST.** Articles not interchangeable.

LIVING (1967), VERA SEGAL, Elm House, Elm Street, London, W.C.1. *T.* 01-837 1234.

6½p. M.—General interest and human interest features. *Payment:* by arrangement.

LLOYD'S LIST, J. D. PRINCE, Lloyd's, P.O. Box No. 111, E.C.3. *T.* 01-623 7644.

4p. D.—Special articles dealing with Shipping, Shipbuilding, Marine Engineering and Insurance. Contributions, 800 to 1750 words in length, must be based on professional knowledge of these subjects, and lucidity of presentment is essential. *Payment:* by arrangement. *Illustrations:* half-tone and line blocks.

LOCAL GOVERNMENT CHRONICLE (1855), Miss M. E. FITZGERALD, 11-12 Bury Street, London, E.C.3. *T.* 01-626 5477. *T.A.* Together, London.

12½p. W.—Technical articles relating to financial, legal and administrative work of the local government officer and public service administrator. *Payment:* by arrangement. *Illustrations:* half-tone.

LOCAL HISTORIAN, THE (formerly **THE AMATEUR HISTORIAN**), (1952). LIONEL MUNBY, 16 Carisbrooke Road, Cambridge, CB4 3LR *T.* 0223 62909. Standing Conference for Local History, 26 Bedford Square, London, WC1B 3HU.

27½p., £1·05 annually, post free. Q.—Articles, popular in style but based on knowledge of research, covering methods of research, sources and background material helpful to local and family historians—histories of particular places, people or incidents *not* wanted. *Length:* maximum 3000 words. *Payment:* none. *Illustrations:* line and photographs.

LONDON MAGAZINE: A Monthly Review of the Arts (1954), ALAN ROSS 30 Thurloe Place, London, S.W.7. *T.* 01–589 0618.

35p. M.—Poems, stories, literary memoirs, critical articles, features on theatre, cinema, music, architecture, events. *Payment:* by arrangement.

LONDON MYSTERY MAGAZINE (1949), NORMAN KARK, Norman Kark Publications, 268–270 Vauxhall Bridge Road, London, S.W.1. *T.* 01–834 8851.

17½p. Q.—Macabre, ghosts and whodunits. Must be strong and novel in plot. *Length:* maximum 4000 words. *Payment:* by arrangement. *Illustrations:* line.

LONDON WELSHMAN, TUDOR DAVID, London Welsh Association, 157–163 Gray's Inn Road, London, W.C.1. *T.* 01–837 3722.

5p. M.—Articles concerning Wales & London, either with a London-Welsh angle or by London Welshmen. Verse (in English or Welsh) must be top class. *Length:* 400 to 1200 words. *Payment:* by arrangement; minimum rate £1·05 per 1000 words. No *illustrations.*

LOOK AND LEARN (1962), New Fleetway House, Farringdon Street, London, EC4A 4AD *T.* 01–634 4444.

7½p. W. (Monday).—Weekly educational magazine that informs as it entertains. Educational articles, particularly science, literature and history written in an exciting yet informative style and suitable for both girls and boys aged between 9 and 15.

LOOK AND LISTEN (1956), Hansom Books, Artillery Mansions, 75 Victoria Street, London, S.W.1. *T.* 01–799 4452.

25p. M.—Articles of interest to the television viewer and radio listener. *Payment:* by arrangement. *Illustrations:* line and half-tone.

LOVE STORY LIBRARY (1952), Fleetway House, Farringdon Street, London, E.C.4. *T.* 01–236 8080.

Four issues every month, 5p. each. Picture stories of 130–140 frames with minimum wordage. Bright, light, romantic themes presented from point of view of modern young heroine.

LUCIE ATTWELL'S ANNUAL (Dean & Son, Ltd.), 43 Ludgate Hill, London, E.C.4. *T.* 01–236 4674.

Short stories of from 500 to 700 words appealing to children from five to seven years of age. The annual is illustrated throughout by Mabel Lucie Attwell. *Payment:* by arrangement on acceptance.

MACHINE DESIGN AND CONTROL (1963), BOB HERSEE, Hermes House, 89 Blackfriars Road, London, S.E.1. 01–928 0181.

Controlled circulation—Free to senior designers. 75p. where available. Specialist technical articles 1500 to 3000 words. *Illustrations:* half-tone and line. *Payment:* by arrangement.

MACHINERY & PRODUCTION ENGINEERING (1912), C. H. BURDER, M.B.E., B.A., Head Office: New England House, New England Street, Brighton BN1 4HN *T.* Brighton 61334. Editorial Office: Clifton House, Euston Road, London, NW.1. *T.* 01–387 8441.

10p. W. (Wednesday).—Articles covering all phases of production engineering, particularly the design, development and use of machine tools and allied equipment. These may be of reasonable length. Short articles of a practical nature are particularly acceptable. *Illustrations:* photographs and line drawings.

MACHINERY LLOYD, G. KINGSLEY, 33–39 Bowling Green Lane, E.C.1. *T.* 01–837 1277.

Controlled circulation. World-wide distribution. M.—Technical articles on new engineering products and processes of interest to mechanical, electrical and civil engineers. *Length:* 250 words maximum. *Payment:* by arrangement. *Illustrations:* half-tone and line.

MACHINERY MARKET (1879), W. E. J. BEECHING, A.C.G.I., F.I.MECH.E., 146A Queen Victoria Street, London, E.C.4. *T.* 01–248 1642. *T.A.* Wadham, London, E.C.4.

6p. W. (Thursday).—Articles on the commercial and technical aspects of engineering, and also details of new machinery. Press day Monday. *Illustrations:* line and half-tone, 120 screen.

MAIDSTONE GAZETTE (South Eastern Newspapers, Ltd.), 123 Week Street, Maidstone. *T.* Maidstone 58444.

2½p. W. (Tuesday).—Personal and local news covering Maidstone, Medway Towns and mid-Kent. Pictorial paper with emphasis on news and sport. *Illustrations:* line and half-tone.

MAKER-UP (1939), MARIE SCOTT (United Trade Press, Ltd.), 42 Gerrard Street, London, W.1. *T.* 01–437 5353. *T.A.* Tailcutta.

25p. (£4 per annum). M.—Covers the whole field of light clothing manufacture at home and abroad. Technical articles dealing with mass production of outerwear, underwear, etc., for women and children. *Length:* 1000 and 3000 words and continued articles. *Payment:* from £4·20 to £10·50 per 1000 words. *Illustrations:* pattern lays accurately drawn to exact scale; drafts drawn to scale; photographs interiors of garment works at home and in the Commonwealth; fashion photographs, cloth samples.

MAKING MUSIC (1946), LIONEL NUTLEY, Little Benslow Hills, Hitchin, Herts. *T.* Hitchin 3446.

15p. plus postage; 50p. per annum, post free. Three times yearly (Spring, Summer, Autumn).—Articles up to 2000 words by authoritative writers on music and allied subjects. *Payment:* by arrangement. *Illustrations:* line and half-tone.

MANAGEMENT IN ACTION (1969), P.O. Box. 109, Davis House, 69–77 High Street, Croydon, CR9 1QH *T.* 01–688 7788.

35p. M.—Articles on modern management sciences, methods and techniques. *Length:* 1000–3000 words. *Payment:* by arrangement. *Illustrations:* line and half-tone.

MANCHESTER EVENING NEWS, BRIAN REDHEAD, 164 Deansgate, Manchester M60 2RD *T.* 061–832 7200.

2½p. D.—Feature articles of up to 1000 words, topical or general interest and illustrated where appropriate, should be addressed to the Features Editor. *Payment:* on acceptance.

MANDY (D. C. Thomson & Co. Ltd.), Courier Place, Dundee, DD1 9QJ, and Thomson House, 12 Fetter Lane, London, E.C.4.

2½p. W. (Thursday).—Picture-story paper for schoolgirls. Serials and series in line drawings. 2 and 3 page instalments, 9–10 panels per page. Editorial co-operation offered to promising scriptwriters. *Payment:* on acceptance.

MANKIND QUARTERLY, Dr. R. GAYRE of GAYRE, 1 Darnaway Street, Edinburgh EH3 6DW *T.* 031–225 1896.

37½p., £1·25 p.a. Q.—Articles on ethnology, human heredity, ethno-psychology, anthropo-geography. *Payment:* £1·05 per printed page. *Illustrations:* line and half-tone.

MANUFACTURING CHEMIST AND AEROSOL NEWS (1964), PATRICK MOXEY, Morgan-Grampian (Publishers) Ltd., 28 Essex Street, Strand, London W.C.2. *T.* 01–353 6565.

£6 per annum. M.—Technical articles on pharmaceuticals, cosmetics, perfumery, soap and detergents, pesticides, disinfectants, analytical chemistry and aerosols. *Length:* 500–5000 words. *Payment:* by arrangement. *Illustrations:* line and half-tone, photographs and diagrams.

MANUFACTURING CLOTHIER (1946), BASIL WARDMAN, Editor (United Trade Press Ltd.), Tailor and Cutter House, 42 Gerrard Street, London, W1V 8BB *T.* 01–437 4672. *T.A.* Tailcutta.

27½p. (£3 p.a.). M.—Devoted to the production of men's clothing, shirts and overalls. Technical articles on clothing production. *Payment:* £4·20 to £10·50 for 1000 words. *Illustrations:* of clothing factories; drafts and lays drawn to exact scale.

MARINE AND AIR CATERING (founded 1907 as **THE CHIEF STEWARD AND SHIP STORES GAZETTE**), S. SELF (Benn Brothers Marine Publications Ltd.), 7–17 Jewry Street, London, EC3N 2HJ *T.* 01–480 5322. *T.A.* Shipping World, London, E.C.3.

£2 p.a. (1st Friday). M.—Contributions considered on international transport catering. *Length:* 750–1500 words. *Payment:* by arrangement. *Illustrations:* line half-tone.

MARINE ENGINEER AND NAVAL ARCHITECT (1879), G. G. MACLENNAN, Wrotham Place, Wrotham, Sevenoaks, Kent. *T.* Borough Green 3232–5.

50p. M.—Technical and practical articles on marine engineering. Articles from 1000 to 2500 words. *Payment:* by arrangement. *Illustrations:* tone or line.

MARKETING, Haymarket Press, Gillow House, 5 Winsley Street, London, W1N 7AQ *T.* 01–636 7766/3600.

£5 p.a. (free to members of the Institute of Marketing). M.—Articles on all aspects of industrial and consumer marketing and sales management at home and abroad. *Length:* 2000–3000 words. *Payment:* according to value.

MATERIALS HANDLING NEWS (1955), J. I. HYAM, P.O. Box 42, 33–39 Bowling Green Lane, London, ECIP 1AH. *T.* 01–837 1277.

M. (15th).—Provides a wide survey of the latest developments in materials handling equipment used in production, transport, packaging, storage and distribution. *Length:* up to 2000 words. *Payment:* by arrangement. *Illustrations:* line and half-tone.

MEAT INDUSTRY (1930), MALCOLM CHAMBERLIN (Practical Press Ltd.), 1 Dorset Buildings, Salisbury Square, E.C.4. *T.* 01–353 1555. *T.A.* Pracpress.

10p. M.—Features and articles on meat retailing, wholesaling, importation and production. *Payment:* by arrangement. *Illustrations:* photographs, and line drawings.

MECCANO MAGAZINE (1916), DAVE ROTHWELL, 13–15 Bridge Street, Hemel Hempstead, Herts. *T.* 0442 2501.

15p. M.—Short stories, mechanical inventions written to suit 10–16 year olds. *Payment:* £3·15 to £5 per page; i.e. 800 words + 2 photographs. *Illustrations:* line and half-tone, colour on cover only.

MECHANICAL HANDLING (18191), J. I. HYAM, P.O. Box 42, 33–39, Bowling Green Lane, London, ECIP 1AH. *T.* 01–837 1277.

37½p. M.—A journal containing practical articles on mechanical handling of materials of all kinds. Special articles contributed by experts on modern methods of handling all descriptions of merchandise by mechanical equipment. Articles from 1500 to 3000 words. *Payment:* by special arrangement. *Illustrations:* line or half-tone.

MEDICAL NEWS, Dr. DAVID CARRICK, Bracken House, Cannon Street, London, E.C.4. *T.* 01–248 8000.

2½p. W. (Friday).—News items of medical interest which must be reliable and accurate. Articles generally by medical practitioners of note. *Payment:* by arrangement. *Illustrations:* line and half-tone.

MEDICAL NEWS-TRIBUNE, Dr. RAANAN GILLON, 87 New Bond Street, London, W.1. *T.* 01–629 9402.

6p. W. (Friday).—News items of medical interest which must be accurate and reliable. Features generally by medical practitioners. Photographs of medical interest always welcome. *Payment:* by arrangement.

MEDICAL OFFICER (1908), G. L. C. ELLISTON, M.A., F.R.S.H., Macmillan (Journals) Ltd., 4 Little Essex Street, London, W.C.2. *T.* 01–836 6633.

10p. W. (Friday).—A journal for medical men and women in the Community Health Services. Written by salaried staff and invited contributors.

MEDICAL WORLD (1913) (incorporating **NEWSLETTER**), Medical Editor, Dr. W. C. LETTINGTON, MPU Publications Ltd., 55–56 Russell Square, London, W.C.1. *T.* 01–580 6235.

20p. M.—A professional journal of clinical and medico-political interest. Articles on medical, scientific and socio-medical subjects of specific interest to the G.P. and the hospital doctor. *Length:* variable, but averaging 1500–2000 words. *Payment:* by arrangement.

MELODY MAKER, RAY COLEMAN, IPC Specialist and Professional Press Ltd., 161 Fleet Street, London, E.C.4. *T.* 01–353 5011.

5p. W. (Thursday).—Technical, instructional and informative articles on, jazz and pop music. *Length:* 250–750 words. *Payment:* by arrangement. *Illustrations:* half-tone and line.

MEN ONLY, VAL HOLDING, Mowbray House Publishing Co. Ltd., 14 Norfolk Street, London, W.C.2. *T.* 01–836 6921.

25p. Monthly.—Features up to 4000 words on controversial topics of interest to men. Cartoons, short stories of 3,500 words, short articles on unusual subjects. Picture features, colour and black and white. *Payment:* by arrangement, on publication.

MEN'S WEAR (1902), J. F. GOULD, Knightway House, 20 Soho Square, London, W1V 6DT *T.* 01–734 1255.

7½p. W. (Thursday).—Matters should be of special interest to all engaged in men's wear trade. Length of articles from 500 to 1000 words. The Editor is always glad to have suggestions for articles in the first place and to advise whether they would be suitable. *Payment:* by arrangement. *Illustrations:* drawings and photographs.

MENTAL HEALTH (1940), HUGH L. FREEMAN, M.A., B.M., D.P.M., National Association for Mental Health, 39 Queen Anne Street, London, W1M 0AJ   *T.* 01–935 1272.

10p. 50p. p.a. 4 times yearly.—Articles on various aspects of mental health. News of developments in mental health movement. Reviews, etc. *Length:* 1000–2000 words. *Payment:* by arrangement. *Illustrations:* photographs and drawings.

MERCANTILE GUARDIAN (1885), D. GOOZÉE, Bouverie House, 154 Fleet Street, London, E.C.4.   *T.* 01–353 3212.

£2 per annum. M.—Well-informed matter required of genuine interest to importers abroad and exporters in this country. Candour, special information, conciseness expected. *Length:* 500 to 1500 words. *Payment:* promptly on publication at fair rates. *Illustrations.*

METAL FORMING, DONALD GRIMMER, John Adam House, 17–19 John Adam Street, Adelphi, London, WC2N 6JH   *T.* 01–839 6171.

25p. M.—Technical articles only. *Length:* Under 10,000 words. *Payment:* by arrangement. *Illustrations:* half-tone and line.

METALWORKING PRODUCTION (incorporating **THE MACHINIST**) (1900) RONALD IREDALE, 28 Essex Street, London, W.C.2.   *T.* 01–353 6565.

£10 p.a.—Practical articles dealing with engineering production methods and factory management. Subjects include facilities planning, machining, heat treatment, presswork and tooling; also production control, quality control, training and method study. *Payment:* by arrangement. *Illustrations:* line and half-tone, colour and black and white.

METHODIST RECORDER (1861), W. E. PIGOTT, 176 Fleet Street, E.C.4.   *T.* 01–353 4748.

4p. W. (Thursday).—This journal is devoted to the interests of World Methodism. Articles which have some bearing on religion, particularly in the ecumenical field, up to 600 words. Paragraphs, notes on subjects of Methodist interest. A *preliminary letter* is not necessary. Ordinary *payment:* £1·52½ per column. Special terms by arrangement. Photographs used. Press day, Tuesday.

MICROSCOPE, THE, Microscope Publications Ltd., 2 McCrone Mews, Belsize Lane, London, N.W.3.   *T.* 01–435 0804 and 2282–3.

£5 p.a. Q.—Authoritative scientific articles and papers on any subject embraced by the journal. Papers should present the matter in as concise a manner as possible. *Payment:* none; authors receive 100 separates free if they pay page charges. *Illustrations:* line and half-tone.

MIDLAND HISTORY (formerly **UNIVERSITY OF BIRMINGHAM HISTORICAL JOURNAL**), RICHARD C. SIMMONS, University of Birmingham, Birmingham, B15 2TT.   *T.* 021–472–1301.

£2. Twice yearly.—Articles of historical research on Midland history. *Length:* up to 8000 words.

MIDLAND INDUSTRIALIST, THE (1965), Peterson Publishing Co. Ltd., Peterson House, Livery Street, Birmingham, B3 2PH   *T.* 021–236 2706.

18p. M.—Authoritative articles on subjects of interest to management. Must be specially written with definite Midland slant. *Payment:* by arrangement. *Illustrations:* line and half-tone.

MILK INDUSTRY, THE (1920), W. F. R. DUXBURY, 37 Queen's Gate, London, S.W.7. *T.* 01–584 8736–8.

15p. M. (8th).—Well-written and factual articles of interest to dairymen, covering whole field of milk handling and distribution, including information on research and technical developments. *Length:* up to 1800 words. *Payment:* according to merit, on publication. *Illustrations:* half-tone.

MILLINERY AND BOUTIQUE (1938), Fashion Editor: GRACE BRADNICK. Publisher: Herbert W. Bradnick, 22 Cross Street, Islington, London, N.1. *T.* 01–226 2312. Editorial: 01–866 9585.

£3·25 per annum. M.—Only trade journal devoted to millinery and ladies' hats for guidance of retail buyer. Complete fashion coverage; sales and display technique; co-ordination of dress, style and colour.

MIND (1876), Professor G. RYLE, Magdalen College, Oxford.

37½p. Q.—A quarterly review of psychology and philosophy intended for those who have studied and thought on these subjects. Articles from about 5000 words. No articles paid for. Critical notices and reviews, £1·50 a page.

MINING AND MINERALS ENGINEERING (incorporating **COLLIERY ENGINEERING**), DAVID BUNTAIN, 10 Laystall Street, London, E.C.1. *T.* 01–837 5541.

M.—Technical articles on economic geology, modern methods of prospecting, the mining and quarrying of ore, coal and other industrial minerals, and processing methods. *Length:* up to 3500 words. *Illustrated.*

MINING JOURNAL (1835), JOHN SPOONER, 15 Wilson Street, Moorgate, London, E.C.2. *T.* 01–606 2567.

7½p. W. (Friday).—Covers all branches of the mineral industry, including geology, mining, smelting, refining, together with the financial and metal markets. Outside contributions, with or without illustrations, are considered. *Payment:* average £10 per 1000 words.

MINING MAGAZINE (1909), BRIAN LORD, 15 Wilson Street, Moorgate, London, E.C.2. *T.* 01–606 2567.

£4·20 p.a., £8·25 p.a. (combined subscription with Weekly Mining Journal and Annual Review, overseas: £9·35) M.—International technical and politico-economic articles by mining engineers and mineral specialists. *Illustrations:* line and half-tone.

MINING WORLD (1871), D. J. KEMSLEY, Mining World Ltd., 13–14 Charterhouse Square, London E.C.1. *T.* 01–253 2922. *T.A.* Quinland, Cent, London.

15p. W.—Journal of mining, banking, assurance, and joint stock enterprise. Outside contributions occasionally accepted.

MIRABELLE, PAUL COHEN, Fleetway House, Farringdon Street, London, EC4A 4AD *T.* 01–236 8080.

3½p. W. (Monday).—Complete and serial first-person romantic picture stories with strong appeal to teenagers; simple, direct plots. Personality and text articles on popular stars. *Illustrations:* line drawings and photographs. *Payment:* by arrangement on acceptance.

MODEL ENGINEER (1898), MARTIN EVANS (Model & Allied Publications Limited), 13/35 Bridge Street, Hemel Hempstead, Herts. *T.* Hemel Hempstead 2501.

15p. (1st and 3rd Friday).—Detailed description of the construction of models, small workshop equipment, machine tools and small electrical and mechanical devices; articles on small power engineering, mechanics, electricity, radio control, workshop methods and experiments. *Payment:* by arrangement. *Illustrations:* half-tone and line drawings.

C

MODEL RAILWAY CONSTRUCTOR (1934), S. W. STEVENS-STRATTEN, F.R.S.A., Terminal House, Shepperton, Middlesex. *T.* Walton-on-Thames 28484.

15p. M.—Short or medium length feature articles on relevant subjects; photo features. *Payment:* £4 per 1000 words. *Illustrations:* line and half-tone.

MODEL RAILWAY NEWS (1925), J. B. BREWER (Model & Allied Publications Ltd.), 13/35 Bridge Street, Hemel Hempstead, Herts. *T.* Hemel Hempstead 2501–2–3.

15p. M. (preceding 2nd Friday).—Descriptive articles on model railways and prototype railways suitable for modelling. Articles covering all aspects of construction, planning, electrical wiring and operation of model layouts. *Length:* 1000–2000 words. *Payment:* by arrangement. *Illustrations:* photographs and line drawings.

MODERN CARAVAN (1950), DENIS ARGENT, Pembroke House, 44 Wellesley Road, Croydon, CR9 2DY *T.* 01–686 8551.

12½p. M.—Authoritative articles on any aspect of caravan living or caravanning. *Length:* 1500 words ideal, but no limit either way so long as well written and informative. *Payment:* £5 to £20. *Illustrations:* half-tone, two colour line, and line monotone.

MODERN CHURCHMAN (1911), The Modern Churchmen's Union, The Vicarage, Caynham, Ludlow, Shropshire.

37p. Q. (15th). £1·25 per annum.—To maintain the cause of truth, freedom, and comprehensiveness in the Church of England. 1500 to 3500 words. Most contributions voluntary.

MODERN LANGUAGE REVIEW (1905), Professor T. J. B. SPENCER, The Shakespeare Institute, The University of Birmingham, Birmingham, 15.

£1·75 Q. (£6 per annum).—Contains articles and reviews of a scholarly or specialist character, on English, Romance, Germanic, and Slavonic languages and literatures. No payment is made, but offprints are given.

MODERN LANGUAGES (Journal of the Modern Language Association) (1905) Dr. CONSTANCE E. HURREN, 2 Manchester Square, W1M 5RF *T.* 01–935 7097.

50p. net. Four times yearly. All aspects of modern language study, pedagogic, and literary. Articles by arrangement. *No payment.*

MODERN MOTHER, ROSEMARY GARLAND, 38 North Audley Street, London W1Y 2HH. *T.* 01–629 3168.

20p. M.—Authoritative articles on child care; interesting personal stories on parenthood, about 800 words. *Payment:* by arrangement. *Illustrations:* line and half-tone.

MODERN RAILWAYS (1944), G. FREEMAN ALLEN, Ian Allan Ltd., Terminal House, Shepperton, Middlesex. *T.* Walton-on-Thames 28484.

20p. M.—Technical articles of 1000 to 4000 words. *Payment:* by arrangement. *Illustrations:* line and half-tone.

MONOGRAPHS OF THE SOCIOLOGICAL REVIEW, Editor: PAUL HALMOS, University of Keele, Staffs., ST5 5BG. *T.* Keele Park 371.

At least once a year, prices variable.—Articles of up to 10,000 words treating social subjects in a scientific way. *No payment* is made.

MONTH, THE (1864), PETER HEBBLETHWAITE, S.J., 114 Mount Street, London, W1Y 6AH *T.* 01–493 7811.

20p. M.—A Catholic review of theology, literature and world affairs. *Length:* 2500–3000 words. *Payment:* by arrangement.

MORNING ADVERTISER (1794), LESLIE FORSE, 18–20 St. Andrew Street, E.C.4. *T.* 01–353 8651 (six lines).

3p. D.—Independent and Anti-prohibitionist. 150-word diary paragraphs about people in brewing industry, licensed and allied trades. Trade news stories.

MORNING STAR (formerly **DAILY WORKER**, 1930), GEORGE MATTHEWS (The Morning Star Co-operative Society Ltd.), 75 Farringdon Road, London, E.C.1. *T.A.* Workadai, Telex, London, *T.* 01–405 9242.

2½p. D.—Articles of general interest. *Length:* not more than 1000 words. *Payment:* £3·15. *Illustrations:* photos, cartoons and drawings.

MORNING TELEGRAPH, J. D. MICHAEL HIDES, York Street, Sheffield, S1 1PU *T.* 0742 78585. London Office: 23–27 Tudor Street, E.C.4. *T.* 01–583 9199.

3p. D.—Special factual articles, 700–1000 words, of topical interest are considered. No short stories. *Payment:* by arrangement. *Illustrations:* picture news features and topical news photographs.

MOTHER (1936), VERONICA SNOBEL, 189 High Holborn, London, WC1V 7BA *T.* 01–242 3344.

15p. M.—Articles on practical child subjects, medical, educational, etc. *Length:* 1000 words. Short stories of 3500 words. *Payment:* by arrangement. *Illustrations:* photographs and sketches.

MOTHER AND BABY (1956), SYLVIA HULL, Saracen's Head Buildings, West Smithfield, London, E.C.1. *T.* 01–236 0014–5–6.

12½p. M.—Articles on baby care and management, pregnancy problems, etc. *Length:* 600–2000 words. *Payment:* by arrangement. *Illustrations:* line and half-tone; colour for cover.

MOTOR (1902), CHARLES H. BULMER, B.SC., C.ENG., A.F.R.AE.S. (IPC Transport Press Ltd.), Dorset House, Stamford Street, London, S.E.1. *T.* 01–928 3333.

12½p. W. (Wednesday).—Offers scope for topical and technical motoring articles and photographs. Colour photographs considered. *Payment:* varies.

MOTOR BOAT AND YACHTING (1904), JOHN LILEY (IPC Transport Press Ltd.), Dorset House, Stamford Street, London, S.E.1. *T.* 01–928 3636.

17½p. (Alt. Fridays).—General interest as well as specialist yachting material welcomed. Features up to 2000 words considered on all aspects sea-going and inland waterways. *Payment:* varies. *Illustrations:* photographs and line. Colour photographs considered.

MOTOR CYCLE (1903), H. W. LOUIS (Editor-in-Chief); NORMAN SHARPE (Editor), 161–166 Fleet Street, London, E.C.4. *T.* 01–353 5011.

6p. W. (Wednesday).—Anything of general interest to motor cyclists. Articles up to 1200 words. *Payment:* minimum £5·25 per 1000 words. Press days, Friday and Monday. *Illustrations:* photographs, pen-and-ink and wash drawings.

MOTOR CYCLE & CYCLE TRADER (1895), Editor: H. BRIERCLIFFE, 161–166 Fleet Street, London, E.C.4. *T.* 01–353 5011.

Subscription £3·15 p.a. Alternate Tuesdays.—Articles on any aspect of trading particularly servicing, repairing and selling. They should be written from a strictly practical angle and preferably by contributors who have had practical experience. *Length:* 1000 to 1750 words. *Payment:* £5 per 1000 words. *Illustrations:* half-tone and line.

MOTOR CYCLE NEWS (1955), ROBIN MILLER, Drysland Street, Kettering. *T.* Kettering 81651–6. *T.A.* Emap 34557, Telex.

5p. W. (Wednesday). Features (up to 1000 words), photographs and news stories of interest to motor cyclists. *Payment:* minimum £5·25 per 1000 words.

MOTOR INDUSTRY, R. T. DELLOW, John Adam House, 17–19 John Adam Street, Adelphi, London, W.C.2. *T.* 01–839 6171.
  M. Subs. £3 per annum.—Articles on business organisation, sales methods, and service matters of interest to the motor industry. *Length:* 1000 to 2000 words. *Payment:* by arrangement. *Illustrations:* half-tone, 100 screen, line.

MOTOR SHIP, THE (1920), W. WILSON (Engineering, Chemical and Marine Press Ltd.), 33–39 Bowling Green Lane, E.C.1. *T.* 01–837 1277.
  40p. M. (1st Tuesday).—Articles up to 3000 words in length—especially when illustrated—on motor ships or oil engines and equipment or services including repair facilities for such vessels. Also articles on other allied subjects dealing with the equipment and operation of all classes of commercial ships from tugs up to large ocean-going motor-ships.

MOTOR TRADER (1905), B. C. CAMBRAY, A.M.I.M.I., Dorset House, Stamford Street, S.E.1. *T.* 01–928 3333. *T.A.* Motrader, Iliffepres 25137, London, Telex.
  Subscription (U.K.) £4·25 p.a. W. (Wednesday).—Articles on any aspect of motor trading—particularly servicing, repairing and selling, written from a strictly practical angle and preferably by contributors who have had practical experience. *Length:* 800 to 1200 words. *Payment:* varies according to merit. *Illustrations:* half-tone and line.

MOTOR TRANSPORT (1905), PHILIP EDWARDS, Dorset House, Stamford Street, S.E.1. *T.* 01–928 3333.
  7½p. W. (Friday).—Information or photographs relating to the use of commercial and public service motor vehicles. *Payment:* 1½p. a line news; £6·30 minimum per 1000 words for articles. Press day, Thursday.

MOTOR WORLD, THE (1899), ROSS FINLAY, 73 Dunlop Street, Glasgow, C.1. *T.* 041–221 9535.
  5p. F. (alternate Fridays).—Articles about motoring rather than about individual cars. *Length:* 800–1500 words. *Payment:* varies. *Illustrations:* half-tone and line.

MOTORING LIFE, AUSTEN D. CHANNING, 39 Lower Ormond Quay, Dublin. *T.* 40098 and 46556.
  10p. M.—Technical and semi-technical articles on motoring up to 3000 words. *Payment:* £6·30 and upwards. *Illustrations:* photographs or line, half-tone. £1·05 illustrations: 52½p. photographs.

MOVIE MAKER (1967), TONY ROSE, 46–47 Chancery Lane, London, W.C.2. *T.* (*Editorial*) 01–242 1411. *T.A.* Nufotog, Holb, London.
  17½p. M.—Articles on narrow-gauge cinematography (silent and sound)—technical, constructional, cultural and educational. *Length:* 1000–2000 words. *Illustrations:* half-tone and line. Articles should preferably be illustrated.

MUCK SHIFTER (1939), JOHN OSBORNE, Morgan-Grampian (Publishers) Ltd., 28 Essex Street, Strand, London, W.C.2. *T.* 01–353 6565.
  £5 p.a. M.—The only technical journal written for civil engineering contractors and plant users. Specialist articles on the application and performance of contractors equipment. *Length:* 1000 to 3000 words. *Payment:* by arrangement. *Illustrations:* line and half-tone, photographs and diagrams.

MUNICIPAL AND PUBLIC SERVICES JOURNAL (incorporating the **MJ Gazette** of official ciculars, published in collaboration with Government Departments.) Editor: C. J. COSSEY 3–4 Clement's Inn, London WC2A 2DB *T*. 01–242 1200. *Telex* 262568.

12½p. W. (Friday).—Independent journal for professional and technical staff in local government and other public services. Articles considered for publication, subject to preliminary discussion with the editor. *Payment:* £12 (standard) per 1000 words or by arrangement. *Illustrations:* line and half-tone.

MUNICIPAL ENGINEERING, CLEANSING AND PUBLIC HEALTH, Managing Director: M. RODENBURG; Editor: C. BIRCH, 4 Clement's Inn, Strand, WC2A 2DB *T*. 01–242 1200.

10p. W. (Friday).—Outside contributions dealing with municipal engineering, public cleansing or public health accepted. *Preliminary letter* preferred. *Payment:* by arrangement.

MUNICIPAL REVIEW (1930), The official publication of the Association of Municipal Corporations. Managing Editor: DAVID PESCHEK, 36 Old Queen Street, Westminster, S.W.1. *T*. 01–930 9861.

£1·20 per annum, including postage. M.—Articles on the current local government scene with particular reference to new developments and management reforms. *Length* and *payment* by arrangement with the editor who prefers to discuss topics with contributors before copy is submitted.

MUSEUM (1948), Miss RAYMONDE A. FRIN, Unesco House, 9 Place de Fontenoy, Paris 7e. *T*. 556–57. 57, and 705–97. 49. *T.A.* Unesco, Paris.

90p. (annual subscription £3) Q.—Articles on museum programmes in popular education for adults and children; on research achievements of museum laboratories; on planning, preparation and installation of exhibitions; on architectural designs and construction of museum buildings; on techniques of restoration, cleaning of paintings, etc. *Length:* 1500–2000 words. *Payment:* 4 cents per word. *Illustrations:* photographs, plans, diagrams.

MUSEUMS JOURNAL, THE (1901), Hon. Editor, FRANK GREENAWAY, M.A., M.SC., F.R.I.C., F.M.A., The Museums Association, 87 Charlotte Street, London, W1P 2BX *T*. 01–636 4600.

75p. Q. to non-members.—Articles on Museum and Art Gallery policy, administration, research, architecture and display, notes on technical developments, book reviews. *Length:* unlimited. *Payment:* none; contributions voluntary. *Illustrations:* half-tone, line blocks.

MUSIC (1966), RUDOLPH SABOR, 24 Langton Road, East Molesey, Surrey. *T*. 01–387 4455.

12½p. Bi-Monthly.—Authoritative articles on all aspects of music. *Length:* 750 to 1500 words. *Payment:* £3·15 per 1000 words. *Illustrations:* line and half-tone; also cartoons.

MUSIC AND LETTERS (1920), Editorial: J. A. WESTRUP, 32 Holywell, Oxford, OX1 3SL. For other matters: 44 Conduit Street, London, W1R 9FB

60p. Q.—Scholarly articles, 2000–5000 words, on musical subjects, neither merely topical nor purely descriptive. Technical, historical, and research matter preferred. *Payment:* £1. per page. *Illustrations:* music quotations and plates.

MUSIC AND MUSICIANS (1952), FRANK GRANVILLE BARKER, Hansom Books, Artillery Mansions, 75 Vcitoria Street, London, S.W.1. *T.* 01–799 4452 (7 lines).

25p. M.—Commissioned articles on composers, conductors, players and singers of serious music. *Length:* 1000 to 4000 words. *Payment:* by arrangement.

MUSIC BUSINESS WEEKLY (1969), RODNEY BURBECK, 161 Fleet Street, London, EC4P 4AA *T.* 01–353 5011.

12½p. W.—News and feature articles pertaining to the business of making, promoting and selling music in all its forms—gramophone records, instruments, tape, sheet music, etc. *Payment:* £1·05 per 100 words or by arrangement for special features. *Illustrations:* line and half-tone.

MUSIC IN EDUCATION, GORDON REYNOLDS (Novello & Co., Ltd.), 27–28 Soho Square, W1V 6BR *T.* 01–437 1222.

15p. Bi-M.—Articles and lesson-material. *Length:* about 1250 words. *Payment:* £3 per 1000 words.

MUSIC INDUSTRY (1964), GORDON WOOLF, Tofts & Woolf (Publishers) Ltd., 64a Lansdowne Road, South Woodford, London, E18 2BD *T.* 01–989 1774 and 2297.

£2 per annum (£6 airmail). M. (8th).—News and technical articles of home and international interest to dealers, wholesalers, manufacturers, importers and exporters of musical instruments, pianos, organs, accessories, and music publishers and sellers. Also articles on general retailing principles (such as management and stock control) angled at the music dealer. *Payment:* £5 to £15 per page (800 to 1000 words approx.); news items from 25p. per 50 words approx. *Illustrations:* black-and-white photographs and line drawings.

MUSIC REVIEW, THE (1940), Editorial: GEOFFREY SHARP, Herons, Barnston, Dunmow, Essex. *T.* Felsted 268. Other matters: W. Heffer & Sons Ltd., 104 Hills Road, Cambridge CB2 1LW.

£1·60, £5 per annum. Q. (Feb., May., Aug. and Nov.).—Articles from 1500 to 8000 words, of some literary merit, dealing authoritatively with any historical or topical aspect of standard or classical music (no jazz). Theses developed from the results of musicological research, and comprehensive bibliographical compilations are particularly welcome. Music, line and half-tone illustrations are employed as required. *Payment:* small, by arrangement.

MUSIC TEACHER (1908), Mrs. BARBARA REES-DAVIES (Evans Brothers, Ltd.) Montague House, Russell Square, WC1B 5BX *T.* 01–636 8521.

15p. M. (5th).—A magazine for the teacher and student of music. Deals fully with all examinations in music. Answers readers' technical questions. Page about 1000 words. Average rate of *payment:* by arrangement. Articles and illustrations must have a *teacher*, as well as a musical, interest.

MUSICAL OPINION (1877), LAURENCE SWINYARD, 87 Wellington Street, Luton, Beds. *T.* Luton 30963.

15p. M.—Musical articles, 500 to 2000 words of general musical interest, organ and church matters. *Payment:* (small) on publication. No verse. *Illustrations:* line and half-tone occasionally.

MUSICAL TIMES (1844), STANLEY SADIE, 27 Soho Square, W1V 6BR *T.* 01–437 1222.

20p. M. (1st).—Musical articles, reviews, etc., 150 to 3000 words. *Payment:* by arrangement. *Illustrations:* photographs and music. Intending contributors are advised to study recent numbers of the journal.

MY HOME AND FAMILY (1928), PAMELA WESTLAND, 189 High Holborn, London WC1V 7BA *T.* 01–242 3344.

12½p. M.—A magazine devoted to family interests—child welfare, education, home-making, cookery and furnishing, knitting, fashion, fiction and features. Complete stories 1500 to 5000 words; serials in three to six instalments of up to 10,000 words each. Fiction with strong romantic or period interest. Family and biographical features considered.

MY WEEKLY (1910) (D. C. Thomson & Co. Ltd.), 80 Kingsway East, Dundee, DD4 8SL, and 186 Fleet Street, London, E.C.4.

3p. W. (Monday).—Serials, from 30,000 to 80,000 words, suitable for family reading. Short complete stories of 1500 and 4000 words with strong emotional theme. Articles on prominent people and on all subjects of feminine interest. All contributions should make their appeal to the modern woman. *No preliminary letter* required. *Payment:* on acceptance. *Illustrations:* colour and black-and-white.

NATIONAL BUILDER, THE (1921), W. SEKULES, 82 New Cavendish Street, W1M 8AD *T.* 01–580 4041. *T.A.* Natbuild, Westcent, London.

25p. M.—The official journal of the National Federation of Building Trades Employers. Articles on building and constructional methods, management techniques, materials and machinery used in building. Articles, 1000–3000 words, preferably with illustrations. *Preliminary letter* advisable. *Payment:* by arrangement. *Illustrations:* on subjects mentioned above.

NATIONAL NEWSAGENT (Efficient Retailing) (1902), GEORGE A. ADAMSON, Lennox House, Norfolk Street, WC2R 2HJ *T.* 01–836 8111.

Short articles on general retailing subjects. Features with photographs (approx. 3 with each article) of modernised shops are especially welcomed. *Payment:* £4·20 for 750 words (longer articles pro rata), plus extra for photographs. *Illustrations:* line or half-tone.

NATURALIST (1875), W. A. SLEDGE, PH.D., B.SC., The University, Leeds, LS2 9JT. *T.* 31751; Courier Printers, Arches Street, Halifax.

50p., £2 per annum. Q.—Original papers on Natural History subjects of all kinds relating to this country; length immaterial. *No payment.* *Illustrations:* photographs and line drawings.

NATURE (1869), JOHN MADDOX (Macmillan (Journals) Ltd.), Little Essex Street, WC2R 3LF *T.* 01–836 6633. *T.A.* Phusis, London, W.C.2.

20p. W. (Saturday).—This journal is devoted to scientific matters and to their bearing upon public affairs. All contributors of articles have special knowledge of the subjects with which they deal. *Illustrations:* half-tone and line.

NAUTICAL MAGAZINE (1832), R. INGRAM-BROWN, F.R.A.S., M.I.N., 52 Darnley Street, Glasgow, S.1. *T.* 041–429 1234. *T.A.* Skipper.

11p. M. (1st). Per annum, including postage: £1·65; 3 years, £4·50.—Articles relating to nautical and shipping profession, from 1500 to 2000 words, also translations. *Payment:* average rate £1·50 per 500 words. *No illustrations.*

NAVY, G. WOOD, Broadway House, Broadway, Wimbledon, London, S.W.19. *T.* 01–540 8222.

12½p. M.—Articles on topical and technological matters of maritime interest—Royal Navy, Merchant Navy, Maritime Air, Shipping and Shipbuilding. Occasional historical articles and short stories with nautical flavour. *Length:* 1000 to 2000 words. *Payment:* by arrangement. *Illustrations* are used.

NEW BEACON (1930) (as BEACON 1917), DONALD BELL, R.N.I.B., 224–228 Great Portland Street, London, W1N 6AA   *T.* 01–387 5251.

    5p., 60p. p.a.   M.—Authoritative articles on all aspects of blind welfare. *Length:* from 800 words. Also original contributors in prose and verse by blind authors. *Payment:* £2·10 per 1000 words; verse by arrangement. *Illustrations:* half-tone. Also Braille edition.

NEW BLACKFRIARS (1920), THE ENGLISH DOMINICANS (Rev. HERBERT McCABE, O.P.), St. Dominic's Priory, Southampton Road, London, N.W.5.   *T.* 01–485 5491. Editorial: Blackfriars, Oxford.   *T.* Oxford 57607.

    20p. net.   M.—A critical review, surveying the field of theology, philosophy, sociology and the arts, from the standpoint of Christian principles and their application to the problems of the modern world. Incorporates *Life of the Spirit*. *Length:* 2000 to 3000 words. *Payment:* by arrangement.

NEW COMMONWEALTH (incorporating **THE CROWN COLONIST**, 1931), DON TAYLOR, 4/5 Fitzroy Square, London, W.1.   *T.* 01–387 4455.

    £3 p.a.   M.—Scope embraces all countries which are members of, or associated with, the British Commonwealth. Deals especially with trade, development, industrial progress. Articles up to 1800 words, with illustrations. *Payment:* by arrangement. A *preliminary letter* is essential. *Illustrations:* half-tone and line. Good photographs wanted.

NEW ERA (incorporating **WORLD STUDIES QUARTERLY BULLETIN**) (1920), ELSIE FISHER, Yew Tree Cottage, Roundabouts, Five Ashes, Mayfield, Sussex. *T.* Hadlow Down 389.

    15p. Subscription £1·50.   M. (10 issues a year).—This is a magazine devoted to experiments in education. Material is generally supplied by psychologists or educational specialists. The articles and reviews are often written on request. *Length:* 1600–3000 words.   *No payment.*

NEW LAW JOURNAL, THE (founded 1965 under that title on amalgamation of **Law Journal** and **Law Times**, both dating from early 19th century), THOMAS HARPER, 4 & 5 Bell Yard, Temple Bar, London, W.C.2.   *T.* 01–405 6900.

    12½p.   W.—Articles of interest to the legal profession. *Payment:* by arrangement. Not normally *illustrated.*

NEW MOON (1931) ANNE BRODIE, (Wm. Stevens Publications, Ltd.), 53 Fetter Lane, London, E.C.4.   *T.* 01–583 9027.

    4p. Two numbers monthly.—Contains one long story, 22,000–25,000 words. No illustrations required.

NEW MUSICAL EXPRESS, ANDREW GRAY, Fleetway House, Farringdon Street, London, E.C.4.   *T.* 01–634 4444. Editorial and Advertising: 112 Strand, London, W.C.2. *T.* 01–240 2266.

    4p.   W.—Authoritative articles and news stories on record stars. *Length:* 500–1000 words. *Payment:* by arrangement. *Illustrations:* action photos with strong news-angle of recording personalities. *Preliminary letter* desirable.

NEW OUTLOOK, RICHARD LAMB, 4 Moorfields, London, E.C.2.   *T.* National 6331.

    17½p.   Bi-M.—A Liberal Bi-monthly. Political and sociological articles of interest to liberals. A preliminary letter is advisable. *Payment:* by arrangement.

NEW SCIENTIST, BERNARD DIXON, 128 Long Acre, WC2E 9QH *T.* 01–836 2468. *T.A.* Newscient, London, W.C.2.

10p. W.—Authoritative articles of topical importance on all aspects of science and technology are considered. *Length:* 1000 to 3000 words. Preliminary letter or telephone call is desirable. Short items from specialists also considered for *Notes on the News, Trends and Discoveries* and *Science in Industry.* Intending contributors should study recent copies of the magazine. *Payment:* varies but average £1·05 per 100 words. *Illustrations:* line and halftone.

NEW SOCIETY, PAUL BARKER, 128 Long Acre, London, WC2E 9QH *T.* 01–836 2468.

10p. W.—Devoted to the social sciences and society.

NEW STATESMAN (1913), RICHARD CROSSMAN, 10 Great Turnstile, London, WC1V 7HJ *T.* 01–405 8471.

10p. W.—As the political and economic articles are mainly written by the staff, the most welcome outside contributions are "middles", social reporting and studies. This does not exclude expert contributions on scientific or other topics or articles from foreign correspondents. *Length:* 1000 to 1500 words. Usual *payment:* £15·75 to £25 per article.

NEW UNIVERSITY AND NEW EDUCATION (1969), TERRY PAGE, M.A., 22 Gray's Inn Road, London, W.C.1. *T.* 01–405 2580.

15p. M.—Articles dealing with new techniques in education. *Length:* 2000 words. *Payment:* by agreement. *Illustrations:* line and half-tone.

NEW WORLD, ROBIN GURNEY, United Nations Association, 93 Albert Embankment, London, S.E.1. *T.* 01–735 0181. 4p. M.

NEW WORLDS, MICHAEL MOORCOCK, 271 Portobello Road, London, W.11.

25p. M.—Experimental fiction of high quality, any *length,* poetry; speculative articles on "hard and soft" science or the arts. 1,000–3000 words approx. *Artwork:* highest quality, imaginative, not standard 'commercial'. Any monotone medium. *Payment:* by arrangement. Potential contributors should study journal before submitting MSS.

NEW ZEALAND NEWS (Est. London 1927), RAY LOUSICH, 97 Fleet Street, London, E.C.4. *T.* 01–583 4974.

2½p. W.—*Matter required:* of interest to New Zealanders in Europe and exporters/importers in both U.K. and N.Z. *Length:* 50 to 500 words. *Payment:* according to value.

NEWS EXTRA (1964), G. E. DUFFIELD, Marcham Manor Press, Appleford, Abingdon, Berkshire. *T.* Sutton Courtenay 319.

75p. per 100 (carriage extra). M.—Monthly church magazine inset, evangelical, mainly Anglican but also nonconformist, religious and cultural articles of current popular interest. Methodist edition. *Maximum length:* 925 words. *Payment:* honorarium. *Illustrations.*

NEWS OF THE WORLD (1843), C. J. LEAR, 30 Bouverie Street, E.C.4. *T.* 01–353 3030. 3½p. W.

19 (1968), MARGARET KOUMI, Fleetway House, Farringdon Street, London, E.C.4. *T.* 01–236 8080.

15p. M.—A glossy, sophisticated fashion magazine for young women, including general features of strong contemporary interest.

NOTTINGHAM EVENING POST AND NEWS (1878), Forman Street, Nottingham, NG1 4AB. London Office: 67 Fleet Street, E.C.4. *T.* 01–353 7252. London Editor: *T.* 01–353 0880.

2½p D.

(NOTTINGHAM) GUARDIAN JOURNAL (1861), Forman Street, Nottingham NG1 4AB   London Office: 67 Fleet Street, E.C.4.   *T.* 01–353 7252.   London Editor: *T.* 01–353 0880.
2½p.   D.—Topical articles of 700 words are considered.   *Illustrations:* line and half-tone.

NOVA (1965), PETER CROOKSTON, Tower House, Southampton Street, London, WC2E 9QX   *T.* 01–836 4363.
20p.   M.—Limited market for the freelance.   Careful study of magazine is advised.   Send *preliminary letter*.   *Payment:* by arrangement.

NUCLEAR ENGINEERING INTERNATIONAL (1956) (previously **Nuclear Engineering**), S. E. RIPPON, I.P.C. Electrical Electronic Press Ltd.), Dorset House, Stamford Street, London, S.1.   *T.* 01–928 3333.
£1·25   M. (last Tuesday previous month.)—Articles, preferably illustrated, about all aspects of the industrial applications of nuclear energy.   *Payment:* varies.   *Illustrations:* half-tone and line.

NUMISMATIC CHRONICLE (1839), R. A. G. CARSON, M.A., F.S.A., c/o The British Museum, WC1B 3DG.
£5 per annual volume.—The Journal of the Royal Numismatic Society. Articles on coins and medals.   Memoirs relating to coins and medals are unpaid, and contributions should reach a high standard of quality.

NURSERY WORLD, IVY GODFREY, 2 Salisbury Court, Fleet Street, London, E.C.4.   *T.* 01–353 9781.
7½p.   W.—For mothers, all grades of nursery and child care staff, nannies, foster mothers and all concerned with the care of expectant mothers, babies and young children.   Authoritative and informative articles, 750–1200 words, and photographs, on all aspects of child welfare, especially from 0–7 years, in the U.K. and abroad.   Also personal family stories, light humorous articles and practical ideas.   Short stories for young children approx. 500–750 words. *Payment:* by arrangement.   *Illustrations:* line and half-tone.

NURSING MIRROR AND MIDWIVES JOURNAL (1888), YVONNE CROSS, 161–166 Fleet Street, London, E.C.4.   *T.* 01–353 5011.
6p.   W. (Friday).—Contains news, educational, technical, and descriptive articles and pictures of interest to all nurses and midwives.   *Length:* 250 to 1800 words.   *Payment:* by arrangement.   *Illustrations:* line and half-tone.

NURSING TIMES (1905), PEGGY D. NUTTALL, S.R.N., M.C.S.P. (Teacher's Cert.), Macmillan (Journals) Ltd., 4 Little Essex Street, WC2R 3LF   *T.* 01–836 1776.
5p.   W.—Articles of clinical interest, nursing education and nursing policy. Illustrated articles not longer than 1500 words.   Contributions from other than nurses and doctors rarely accepted.   *Payment:* about £10·50 per 1200 words.   Press day, Monday.

NUTRITION, Newman Books Ltd., 68 Welbeck Street, London, W1M 8HD *T.* 01–935 3335.
50p.   Q.—Journal of Dietetics, Food, Catering and Child Nutrition, incorporating official news of the British Dietetic Association.   Technical, scientific and practical articles.   Material is highly specialised and intending contributors are advised to study the journal.   *Length:* up to 4000 words. *Payment:* by arrangement.

OBSERVER, THE (1791), The Hon. DAVID ASTOR, 160 Queen Victoria Street, E.C.4.   *T.* 01–236 0202.   *T.A.* Observer, Fleet, London.
6p.   W. (Sunday)—Independent.   Some articles and illustrations are commissioned.

OCCUPATIONAL HEALTH (formerly **JOURNAL FOR INDUSTRIAL NURSES**) (1949), M. MARGARET WILLIAMS, S.R.N., O.H.N.TUTOR CERT., F.R.S.H., c/o Macmillan (Journals) Ltd., Little Essex Street, W.C.2. *T.* 01–836 6633.

25p., £2·75 p.a. M.—Published by Macmillan publishers of *Nursing Times* associated with the Occupational Health Section, Royal College of Nursing and National Council of Nurses of the United Kingdom. Articles on occupational and environmental health, occupational diseases, safety, industrial injuries, conference reports, notations and reviews contributed from all parts of the World. Main article 1000–1200 words.

OCCUPATIONAL PSYCHOLOGY (National Institute of Industrial Psychology), 14 Welbeck Street, WIM 8DR *T.* 01–935 1144.

£6 per annum, overseas £7·50. Q.—Articles on industrial psychology, the human factor in occupational life, working conditions, vocational guidance, etc., from 1000 to 5000 words. *Illustrations:* occasional photographs. *No payment.*

OFF LICENCE NEWS AND WINE AND SPIRIT TRADE REVIEW (1863), J. R. THOMAS, Eastcheap Buildings, E.C.3. *T.* 01–626 0493–4–5.

5p. £2 p.a. W. (Friday).—This journal is entirely devoted to the wine, cyder, and spirit trades. Contributions and illustrations accepted and articles or news of general interest to the trades concerned. *Payment:* by arrangement.

OFFICIAL ARCHITECTURE AND PLANNING, CORNELIUS M. MURPHY, The Builder House, P.O. Box 135, 4 Catherine Street, London WC2B 5JN *T.* 01–836 9484.

17½p. (£1·50 annual subscription). M.—Articles about architecture, planning and the built environment, with particular reference to work carried out on behalf of Government Departments and Local Authorities. *Length:* 1000 to 3000 words. *Payment:* by arrangement. *Illustrations:* photographs and line drawings. A preliminary letter is advisable.

OPERA, HAROLD ROSENTHAL, 6 Woodland Rise, London, N.10. *T.* 01–883 4415; Seymour Press Ltd., 334 Brixton Road, S.W.9.

25p. 13 issues a year.—Articles on general subjects appertaining to opera; reviews; criticisms. *Length:* up to 2000 words. *Payment:* by arrangement. *Illustrations:* photographs and drawings.

OPTICIAN (1891), SHELAGH C. HARDY, M.A., Columbia House, 69 Aldwych, London, W.C.2. *T.* 01–242 5384.

15p. W.—The journal contains authoritative technical and news articles and paragraphs relating to ophthalmic optics and instruments. *Payment:* for accepted contributions by arrangement. Line drawings or photographs.

ORBIS, ROBIN GREGORY, Hub Publications Ltd., Youlgrave, Bakewell, Derbyshire.

25p. Bi-monthly. Covers all topics of interest to the thoughtful reader in Yorks, Derbys., Lancs., Ches., Lincs., Notts., Leics., Staffs., Rutland, Peterborough. *Illustrations:* Photographs and drawings. Study of magazine strongly recommended. *Payment:* £5 per 1000 words.

ORCHID REVIEW (1893), DAVID FEARNLEY SANDER, 27 Portland Road, East Grinstead, Sussex. *T.* 93–25555.

25p. M.—Devoted entirely to orchidology. Contributions and illustrations, by arrangement.

ORGAN (1921), LAURENCE SWINYARD, 87 Wellington Street, Luton, Beds. *T.* Luton 30963.

27½p. Q.—Articles, 4000 to 5000 words, relating to the organ, historical, technical, and artistic. *Payment:* small. *Illustrations:* half-tone and line.

OUTPOSTS (1944), HOWARD SERGEANT (Outposts Publications), 72 Burwood Road, Walton-on-Thames, Surrey. *T.* 40712.

15p. Q.—Poems, essays and critical articles on poets and their work. *Payment:* by arrangement.

OVERSEAS (1915), Editor: TOM IREMONGER, M.P., Over-Seas House, St. James's, London, S.W.1. *T.* 01–493 5051.

Q.—Articles and photographs with a bearing on British Commonwealth and Empire. *Payment:* by arrangement.

PACKAGE REVIEW (1897) TOM TEBBATT, 33–40 Bowling Green Lane, London, E.C.1. *T.* 01–837 1277. *T.A.* Pressimus London E.C.1.

Controlled Circulation. M.—Commercial and technical articles on Packaging materials, pack design, pack production and consumption, packaging technology. *Length:* up to 1500 words. *Payment:* by arrangement. *Illustrations:* line and half-tone.

PAINT MANUFACTURE (1931), L. BILEFIELD, M.A., B.SC., Morgan-Grampian (Publishers) Ltd., 28 Essex Street, Strand, London, W.C.2. *T.* 01–353 6565.

£6 per annum. M.—Articles on paint, varnish, lacquers and all surface coatings. *Length:* 1000 to 5000 words. *Payment:* by arrangement. *Illustrations:* line and half-tone photographs, and diagrams.

PAINT, OIL AND COLOUR JOURNAL (1879), D. E. EDDOWES, John Adam House, John Adam Street, London, E.C.4. *T.* 01–839 6171. *T.A.* Zacetas, London, W.C.2.

£5·20 per annum. W.—Articles of a trade or technical nature of interest to manufacturers of paints, colours, varnishes, high polymers, and oils. *Length:* about 2000 words. *Illustrations:* half-tone or line.

PAINTING & DECORATING JOURNAL, HARRY RYLAND, F.I.O.P., (Managing Editor), 30 Princes Street, Southport, Lancs. *T.* Southport 55368.

15p. M. (1st).—Short articles on all aspects of painting and decorating, up to 2000 words, preferably illustrated; must be sound technically. *Payment:* depends on quality and authority of work. *Illustrations:* line and half-tone.

PAPER MAKER, THE, AND BRITISH PAPER TRADE JOURNAL, J. R. ELLIOTT, 50 Fetter Lane, E.C.4. *T.* 01–353 7076–7.

40p. M.—Technical articles on pulp and paper manufacture and its relative machinery. *Payment:* by arrangement. *Illustrations:* half-tone and line.

PAPER TRADE REVIEW (WORLD'S) (1879), E. F. J. DEAN, Lincoln House, 296–302 High Holborn, WC1V 7JS *T.* 01–405 7055. *T.A.* Stongillis, London, W.C.1. Telex: 887026.

15p. W. (Thursday).—Technical articles on process, new machinery, materials and equipment, relating to the pulp, paper and board making and converting industries. *Length:* 800 to 1600 words. *Payment:* according to merit. *Illustrations:* half-tone and line.

PARADE (1915), ALFRED BROCKMAN, Aldwych House, 81 Aldwych, London, W.C.2. *T.* 01–242 8621.

6p. W. (Saturday).—Short stories (up to 2000 words). Unusual features (400–1000 words). *Payment:* by arrangement. *Illustrations:* line and wash cartoons; photographs.

PARIS (1958), Mme M. MANUSSET-BRIMICOMBE, Brimicombe Publications Ltd., 8 St. John's Park, Blackheath, London, S.E.3. *T.* 01–858 3581.

9p. (6 issues a year.)—Educational magazine for students of French of all ages, printed entirely in that language. Very lively, well-informed articles dealing with France and the French written by French people only. *Length:* 850 to 1000 words. *Payment:* by arrangement. *Illustrations:* photographs and line drawings (on request).

PARISH COUNCILS REVIEW, THE (The Official Journal of the National Association of Parish Councils), CAMPBELL NAIRNE, 100 Great Russell Street, London, W.C.1. *T.* 01–636 4066.

42½p. Q.—Articles on the law and practice of local government especially in relation to rural parishes; on charitable and benevolent activities in the countryside; on co-operation between statutory authorities and voluntary organisations and on any matters which may affect the well-being of the rural elector. *Length:* 400–2500 words. *Payment:* by arrangement. *Illustrations:* line and half-tone.

PARKS AND SPORTS GROUNDS (1935), K. S. H. CLARKE (Clarke & Hunter (London) Ltd.), Armour House, Bridge Street, Guildford, Surrey. *T.* Guildford 76333.

15p. M.—Articles on the design, construction and maintenance of parks and sports grounds. *Length:* 750 to 1500 words. *Payment:* by arrangement. *Illustrations:* line and half-tone.

PAX (1904), The Benedictines, Prinknash Abbey, Gloucester. *T.* Painswick 3224. Subscription 50p. Bi-annual. Chiefly articles connected with Monasticism and the Liturgy.

PEACE NEWS, (1936), IAN DOUGALL, KEVIN McGRATH, ROGER MOODY and PAUL WESLEY. 5 Caledonian Road, London, N.1. *T.* 01–837 4473. *T.A.* Howpa, London, N.1.

5p. W.—Political articles based on non-violence, pacifism, race, religion, socialism etc. *Payment:* None. *Illustrations:* line, half-tone.

PEOPLE, THE (Odhams Newspapers Ltd.), 2–12 Endell Street, London, W.C.2, *T.* 01–836 1200. Editor: ROBERT EDWARDS.

4p. W.—A Sunday paper for all classes of readers. Features, single articles and series, considered. They should be of deep, human interest, with background of romance or adventure or out-of-the-ordinary experiences. Particularly noted for its exposure of social evils, and financial and other rackets, in the public interest. Also strong sports following. Photographs should be supplied if possible. News and news-feature stories also considered, especially if exclusive. Rate of payment high.

PEOPLE'S FRIEND (1869) (D. C. Thomson & Co. Ltd.), Bank Street, Dundee, DD1 9HU, and 186 Fleet Street, London, E.C.4.

2½p. W. (Thursday).—An illustrated weekly appealing to women of all ages and devoted to their personal and home interests. Serial and complete stories of strong romantic and emotional appeal—serials of 60,000–70,000 words, completes of 2000–4000 words. Stories for children considered. Knitting, fashions and cookery are especially featured. *Illustrations:* line and wash. No *preliminary letter* is required. Liberal *payment* on acceptance.

PEOPLE'S JOURNAL (1858) (D. C. Thomson & Co. Ltd.), 7 Bank Street, Dundee DD1 9HU, and 186 Fleet Street, London, E.C.4.

2p. W. (Saturday).—Short serials suitable for family reading. Must have a good plot and develop a strong love interest. Complete stories 2500 words, dealing with Scottish life and character, or having Scottish link. *No preliminary letter required. Payment:* on acceptance.

PERSONNEL MANAGEMENT, Journal of the Institute of Personnel Management, TONY BARRY (Business Publications Ltd.), Mercury House, Waterloo Road, London, S.E.1. *T.* 01–928 3388.

45p; £5 p.a. M.—Features and news items on employee selection, training and wage and salary administration; industrial psychology; industrial relations; welfare schemes, working practices and new practical ideas in personnel management in industry and commerce. *Length:* 850 to 1200 words. *Payment:* from £8·40 per 1000 words. *Illustrations:* good evocative photographs or drawings of people at work in factories or offices.

PETFISH MONTHLY (1966), ANTHONY EVANS, PetFish Publications, 554 Garratt Lane, London, S.W.17. *T.* 01–947 2805.

15p. M.—Practical experiences in fishkeeping and informative interviews with people of special standing in this field. *Payment:* by arrangement. *Illustrations:* line, half-tone, occasional colour.

PETROLEUM TIMES (1899), BART COLLINS (E. C. & M. Press Ltd.), 33–40 Bowling Green Lane, London, E.C.1. *T.* 01–837 1277. *Telex:* 23839.

25p. F. (Friday).—Technical and managerial articles on oil exploration, production, refining transportation and marketing of interest to commercial management and senior technical management in the European oil industry. *Length:* up to 2000 words. *Payment:* by arrangement. *Illustrations:* photographs and line.

PETTICOAT (1966), Editor: TERRY HORNETT, Fleetway House, Farringdon Street, E.C.4. *T.* 01–236 8080.

10p. W.—Aimed at the under thirties, young, easy-going, adaptable, mulls over every new fashion and beauty idea, and every slant on living at that moment. Aims at capturing the readers' interest in 'serious' fiction with classic excerpts, and giving them off-beat stories of situations seen through young eyes. Constantly seeks to give readers in all parts of the British Isles a look in, instead of constantly staying on the London scene. Deals seriously and openly with psychological problems, whether controversial or not. Articles and stories on any situation or subject of particular appeal to the under 30's are judged on merit, content and length, and then paid at top rates. *Illustrations:* in colour and mono, sketches and photographs.

PHARMACEUTICAL JOURNAL, THE (1841), R. BLYTH, F.P.S., 17 Bloomsbury Square, WC1A 2NN *T.* 01–242 9191. *T.A.* Pharmakon, London, W.C.1.

17½p. W.—The official organ of the Pharmaceutical Society of Great Britain. Articles of 1000 words on any aspects of pharmacy may be submitted. *Payment:* by arrangement. *Illustrations:* half-tone and line.

PHILATELIC MAGAZINE, O. W. NEWPORT, F.R.P.S.L., 42 Maiden Lane, London, W.C.2. *T.* 01–836 2684.

15p. M. (15th dated for following month).—Essentially a stamp collectors' journal. Original information about stamps, their designs and artists, but not elementary. Specialised features and articles on postal history. Contributions by those without philatelic knowledge are unlikely to be suitable. *Illustrations:* half-tone (100 screen) and line.

PHILATELY (1946), PETER IBBOTSON, 446 Strand, London, WC2R 0RA *T.* 01–240 0350.

5p. Bi-M.—Organ of the British Philatelic Association. Articles on all aspects of stamp collecting, especially dealing with the detection of forgeries and fakes. *Length:* 500 to 1500 words. *Illustrations:* half-tone and line.

PHOTO FINISHER, 50 Great Russell Street, London, W.C.1. *T.* Holborn 2762.
£2·72½ p.a. M.—News, personality notes and articles on all aspects of the photofinishing industry and allied trades. Area correspondents required at home and abroad. Subjects covered: Laboratory processing techniques, costing, business organisation, staff management and training, etc. *Length:* up to 2500 words. *Illustrations:* line and half-tone. *Payment:* by arrangement.

PHOTOGRAPHY, RICHARD GEE, 46–47 Chancery Lane, London, W.C.2. *T.* 01–242 1411. *T.A.* Nufotog, Holb. London.
17½p. M.—Illustrated articles of 900 to 1400 words on all aspects of photography, pictorial and technical, and how-to-do-it articles, slanted towards the serious amateur and young professional. *Payment:* approximately £5·25 per page black-and-white, £10·50 per page colour, £15·75 front cover (colour). Special features by arrangement. *Illustrations:* line, half-tone and colour.

PHOTOPLAY FILM MONTHLY, KEN FERGUSON, 12–18 Paul Street, London, E.C.2. *T.* 01–247 8233.
15p. M.—1000 word features on film personalities. Stamped addressed envelope to be enclosed for return of MS. if not suitable. *Payment:* by arrangement.

PHYSIOTHERAPY, Journal of the Chartered Society of, PATRICIA YOUNG, 14 Bedford Row, London, WC1R 4ED.
22½p. M.—Articles on physiotherapy and related subjects, news and technical items regarding activities of members of the Society. Contributions welcomed from the medical profession and from physiotherapists. *Length:* 2000 words (average). *Payment:* £5·25 per 1000 words for technical medical articles, £3·15 non-technical. *Illustrations:* photographs and line drawings.

PICTORIAL EDUCATION (1927), MICHAEL POLLARD (Evans Brothers Ltd.), Montague House, Russell Square, WC1B 5BX *T.* 01–636 8521.
20p. M.—Large-scale reproductions in colour and black-and-white of pictures illustrating subjects of the school curricula. First-class photographs of geographical and nature study subjects; historical drawings. Must be sharp and clear. Original drawings usually commissioned. Extra quarterly numbers (17½p. each) contain large pictures in full colour of historical, literary and geographical subjects. *Payment:* by arrangement. Stamps should be enclosed for return of material. No articles required.

PIG FARMING, B. T. HOGLEY, Lloyds Chambers, Ipswich. *T.* Ipswich 54801–3.
10p. M.—Practical, well-illustrated articles on all aspects of pig production required, particularly those dealing with new ideas in pig management, feeding and housing. *Length:* 1000 to 2000 words. *Payment:* £10·50 per 1000 words published. *Illustrations:* half-tone or line.

PIPPIN, G. S. MARLER, Polly Perkins House, 382–386 Edgware Road, London W.2. *T.* 01–723 3022.
3½p. W.—Coloured picture weekly for the very young based on the *Watch with Mother* TV series. *Payment:* variable. *Illustrations:* colour and half-tone.

PLAYHOUR AND ROBIN (1954), New Fleetway House, Farringdon Street, London, EC4A 4AD *T.* 01–634 4444.
3½p. W. (Tuesday).—Age appeal 3–8. All picture. Four colour front, back and centre. Artists invited to submit specimen drawings to the Editor.

PLAYLAND (1968), G. S. MARLER, Polly Perkins House, 382-386 Edgware Road, London, W.2.   *T.* 01–723 3022.
   3½p.   W.—Picture stories, based on television characters, for small children. *Payment:* by arrangement. *Illustrations:* strip work in half-tone and full colour, *payment:* variable.

PLAYS AND PLAYERS, PETER ROBERTS, Hansom Books, Artillery Mansions, 75 Victoria Street, London, S.W.1.   *T.* 01–799 4452 (7 lines).
   25p.   M.—Articles and photos on the professional theatre.

PNEU JOURNAL (1890), JOAN L. MOLYNEUX, Parents' National Educational Union, Murray House, Vandon Street, S.W.1.   *T.* 01–222 7181.
   19p.   Bi-M. (1st).—Journal of the Parents' National Educational Union. Articles on all aspects of education and psychology dealing with children aged from 5 to 16, and consonant with the principles of Charlotte Mason. Also articles of topical interest (e.g. centenaries of distinguished writers, artists, musicians, etc.). *Length:* 1000–1500 words. *Payment:* by arrangement.

POETRY REVIEW, DEREK PARKER, 21 Earls Court Square, London, S.W.5. *T.* 01–373 3556.
   40p.   Q.—Poems of any length.   *Payment:* 52½p. to £8.   Over £200 per annum awarded in prizes for poetry competitions.

POLICY (1902), Mitre House, 44 Fleet Street, E.C.4.   *T.* 01–353 1622.
   35p.   M. (mid-month).—Technical articles from 600 to 4000 words on all classes of insurance. *Payment:* varies.

POLITICAL QUARTERLY (1930), The Political Quarterly Publishing Company Ltd., 49 Park Lane, London, W.1.   *T.* 01–493 2622.   Editors: W. A. ROBSON and BERNARD CRICK.   Literary editor: H. R. G. GREAVES.   Editorial Board: LORD ANNAN, H. L. BEALES, RICHARD M. TITMUSS, BERNARD CRICK, PETER CALVOCORESSI, ESMOND WRIGHT, W. A. ROBSON, H. R. G. GREAVES, KENNETH YOUNGER, R. HARRISON, JOHN P. MACKINTOSH, D. C. WATT.   Editorial Offices: 48 Lanchester Road, N.6.   Books for review to be sent to: H. R. G. Greaves, London School of Economics, Houghton Street, Aldwych, London, W.C.2.
   57½p., £2·10 p.a.   Q.—A progressive review, the function of which is to discuss international social and political questions from a progressive, but not from a party, point of view.   *Average payment:* £5 per 1000 words.   *Average Length:* 3000–5000 words.

PONY (1949), Lt.-Col. C. E. G. HOPE, 19 Charing Cross Road, London, W.C.2. *T.* 01–930 3957.
   15p.   M.—Short stories about children and ponies with original plots up to 1200 words. Technical accuracy essential. Ages catered for 6–16. All other material provided editorially or specially commissioned. *Payment:* by arrangement. *Illustrations:* line. Mostly commissioned.

POPULAR FLYING, Popular Flying Association, Chairman: F. J. PARKER, 2 Waldens Park Road, Horsell, Woking, Surrey.   *T.* Woking 62621.
   15p.   Alt. M.—Topical articles and news paragraphs on ultra-light and light aviation; all aspects of private flying. *Length:* up to 2000 words. *No payment. Illustrations:* photographs and line drawings.

POPULAR GARDENING (1889), FRED WHITSEY, 189 High Holborn, London, WC1V 7BA *T.* 01–242 3344.
 4p. W. (Thursday).—A practical freely-illustrated magazine for the amateur gardener, the specialist and flower arranger, printed in photogravure with full colour covers and containing original and informative articles, photographs and diagrams. *Length:* up to 800 words. *Payment:* by arrangement.

PORT OF LONDON (formerly **THE P.L.A. MONTHLY**) (1925), A. CAMERON, Port of London Authority, London, EC3P 3BX *T.* 01–481 2000 *T.A.* Pola, London. *Telex:* Polaldn 264176.
 10p. M.—The magazine of the Port of London Authority. Articles up to 2000 words considered, semi-technical, historical or having bearing on trade and commerce of London preferred. *Preliminary letter* essential. *Payment:* £5·25 upwards per 1000 words. *Illustrations:* half-tone and line.

POST (1920), H. BURNETT, UPW House, Crescent Lane, Clapham, S.W.4. *T.* 01–622 2291. *T.A.* Postact, London, S.W.4.
 2½p. F. (Saturday).—The journal of the Union of Post Office Workers. The Editor invites articles on postal, telephone and telegraph workers abroad and on other questions of interest to a Trade Union readership. *Length:* 1000 words or less. *Payment:* by arrangement. *Illustrations:* line and half-tone occasionally.

POULTRY INDUSTRY (1935), STUART BANKS, 161–166 Fleet Street, London, E.C.4. *T.* 01–353 5011.
 Controlled circulation.—News, specialist articles. *Length:* 1000-2000 words. *Payment:* by arrangement. *Illustrations:* line and half-tone.

POULTRY WORLD, FRANK BURTON, 161–166 Fleet Street, London E.C.4. *T.* 01–353 5011.
 5p. W. (Thursday).—Practical articles on poultry breeding, marketing and packaging. News of National poultry interest. Articles 600–700 words. *Payment:* by arrangement. Line and photographic illustrations.

POWER FARMING (formerly **POWER FARMER**) (1941), S. F. FARMER, (Agricultural Press Ltd.), 161–166 Fleet Street, London, E.C.4. *T.* 01–353 5011.
 17½p. M.—Articles concerning all aspects of farm equipment in Britain. General engineering in its application to machinery maintenance, etc. *Length:* not exceeding 1500 words. Short practical workshop hints welcomed. *Payment:* by arrangement. *Illustrations:* photographs or drawings.

POWER LAUNDRY + CLEANING NEWS (1903), ANCLIFFE PRINCE, 1 Dorset Buildings, Salisbury Square, London, E.C.4. *T.* 01–353 1555.
 10p. F.—Illustrated news features; authoritative technical articles. Laundries, Cleaneries, Launderettes, Hospital Laundries, Linen Supply firms, etc., covered. *Payment:* £8·40 per 1350 words and upwards. *Illustrations:* half-tone and line.

PRACTICAL BOAT OWNER (1967), DENNY DESOUTTER, Acre House 67–69 Long Acre, London, WC2E 9QF *T.* 01–836 2468.
 20p. M.—Articles of up to 2000 words in length, about practical matters concerning the boating enthusiast. *Payment:* by negotiation. *Illustrations:* photographs or drawings.

PRACTICAL CAMPER, JOHN A. CADE, Haymarket Publishing Group, 5 Winsley Street, London, W1N 7AQ *T.* 01–636 3600.

15p. M.—Practical articles based on picture strip information, subjects arranged with editor. *Payment:* by arrangement. *Illustrations:* top quality bromides.

PRACTICAL ELECTRONICS (1964), F. E. BENNETT, Fleetway House, Farringdon Street, London, EC4A 4AD *T,* 01–236 8080.

15p. M. (14th).—Constructional and theoretical articles. *Length:* 1000–2500 words. *Payment:* £8·40 per 1000 words plus extra for illustrations. *Illustrations:* line and half-tone. Contributors must submit details of qualifications.

PRACTICAL HOME BUILDING & DECORATING (1967), H. KING, Fleetway House, Farringdon Street, London, EC4A 4AD *T.* 01–236 8080.

15p. M.—Articles of up to 1500 words in length, about practical matters and decorating and building problems. *Payment:* by negotiation. *Illustrations:* photographs or drawings.

PRACTICAL HOUSEHOLDER (1955), S. KERNAHAN Fleetway House, Farringdon Street, London, EC4A 4AD *T.* 01–236 8080.

12½p. M. (1st).—Articles, about 1500 words in length, about practical matters concerning the home and its equipment. *Payment:* according to subject. *Illustrations:* photogravure.

PRACTICAL MOTORIST (1954), H. HEYWOOD, Fleetway House, Farringdon Street, London, EC4A 4AD *T.* 01–236 8080.

15p. M. (15th).—Practical articles on upkeep, overhaul and repair of all makes of cars, also practical articles on camping and caravanning. *Payment:* according to subject. *Illustrations:* photogravure.

PRACTICAL TELEVISION (1950), N. STEVENS, Fleetway House, Farringdon Street, London, EC4A 4AD *T.* 01–236 8080.

17½p. M. (22nd).—Illustrated articles of 1000 to 2000 words in length, on all practical aspects of television. Contributors must submit details of qualifications. *Payment:* according to subject. *Illustrations:* half-tone and line.

PRACTICAL WIRELESS (1933), N. STEVENS, Fleetway House, Farringdon Street, London, EC4A 4AD *T.* 01–236 8080.

17½p. M. (7th).—Invites articles of from 1000 to 1500 words from writers well versed in practical aspects of radio, television, audio and electronics. *Illustrations:* half-tone and line. Contributors must submit details of qualifications. *Payment* is made according to subject.

PRACTICAL WOODWORKING, FRANK M. UNDERWOOD, Fleetway House, Farringdon Street, London, EC4A 4AD. *T.* 01–236 8080.

17½p. M.—Articles of a practical nature covering any aspect of woodworking. *Not* articles on tools, joints or timber technology. *Illustrations.*

PRACTITIONER, THE (1868), 5 Bentinck Street, London, W1M 5RN *T.* 01–935 0121. *T.A.* Practilim, London, W.1. Editor: WILLIAM A. R. THOMSON, M.D. £3 p.a. Single copies 25p. (Special numbers 50p.) M. (1st).

PRAM RETAILER (1962), ALICE M. GUPPY, 167 High Holborn, London, W.C.1. *T.* 01–836 9551.

Q.—Articles, news, etc., relating to perambulators, nursery goods, furniture, and toys. *Length:* 1000 words or short items. *Payment:* by arrangement. *Illustrations:* photographs.

PRECAST CONCRETE (1970), 52 Grosvenor Gardens, London, S.W.1. *T.* 01–235 6661.

25p. M.—Articles on concrete products and cast stone, etc., and the uses of precast and prestressed concrete. *Preliminary* letter not necessary. *Illustrations:* photographs and drawings.

PREDICTION (1936), OLIVIA MALTHOUSE, Link House, Dingwall Avenue, Croydon, CR9 2TA *T.* 01–686 2599. *T.A.* Aviculture, Croydon.

12½p. M. (10th of the month, dated for following month).—Articles on all occult subjects. *Length:* 1500 words, maximum. *Payment:* by arrangement. *Illustrations:* half-tone.

PREPARATORY SCHOOLS REVIEW, THE, W. CALDWELL (W. Heffer & Sons Ltd.), Hills Road, Cambridge, CB2 1LW.

85p. p.a. Three times yearly (Februart, June, October.)—The or,gan of the Incorporated Association of Preparatory Schools. Articles dealing with the education of boys in the Association's schools, or of general educational interest. *Length:* 700 to 3000 words. Half-tone and line *illustrations* optional.

PRINCESS TINA (1960), New Fleetway House, Farringdon Street, London, EC4A 4AD *T.* 01–634 4444.

4p. W. (Monday).—For schoolgirls 8–13. Serials and complete stories told in pictures, also written serials and series, *length* 2000. Short illustrated magazine features. Contributors should study paper before submitting ideas to the Editor. *Illustrations:* half-tone and line for web offset.

PRINTING AND BOOKBINDING TRADE REVIEW (1958), GEORGE L. HOWE, George L. Howe Press Service Ltd., 85 Elmhurst Drive, Hornchurch, Essex, RM11 1PB. *T.* Hornchurch 41961.

£1 p.a. M.—Feature articles on printing, bookbinding, book design and production, electrotyping, stereotyping, newspaper production, flexography, process engraving and papermaking. *Length:* 1000 to 3000 words. *Payment:* by arrangement. *Illustrations:* half-tone and line.

PRINTING TRADES JOURNAL AND SALES AND WANTS ADVERTISER (incorporating **GRAPHIC TECHNOLOGY**) (1887), D. G. MUGGLETON (Benn Brothers Ltd.), Bouverie House, 154 Fleet Street, EC4A 2DL *T.* 01–353 3212.

35p., £3·50 p.a. M. (Third Wednesday of each month).—Technical articles, news and features on printing, lithography, bookbinding, stationery, block making, etc. Special features dealing with new machinery and equipment for the printing trade. *Length:* 1000 to 1500 words. *Payment:* Features by arrangement; news items and pictures at standard rates. *Illustrations:* line and half-tone.

PRINTING WORLD (1878), F. T. COLLEY (Stonhill & Gillis Ltd. for Benn Brothers Ltd.), Lincoln House, 296–302 High Holborn, W.C.1. *T.* 01–405 7055. *T.A.* Stongillis, London, W.C.1.

12p. W. (Wednesday).—The features of this journal are current news, technical developments, and commercial information relating to the printing, newspaper production, lithographic, bookbinding, process engraving and screen process trades, and the engineering branches thereof. Outside contributions. *Payment:* from £3·15 a page. *Illustrations:* half-tone and line.

PRIVATE EYE (1962), RICHARD INGRAMS, 34 Greek Street, London, W1V 5LG
T. 01–437 4017.
    10p. F.—Satire. *Payment:* £2·10 cuttings; £12 per cartoon. *Illustrations:*
black-and-white, line.

PRODUCT DESIGN ENGINEERING (1963), CARILL SHARPE, Hermes House, 89
Blackfriars Road, London, S.E.1. T. 01–928 0181.
    Controlled circulation—Free to Senior designers. 62½p. where available—
Articles of specific design and manufacturing content on office, domestic and
light industrial electro-mechanical appliances and applied electronics. *Payment:*
£7. *Illustrations:* line, half-tone and colour.

PRODUCT FINISHING, V. H. FRENCH, 4 Ludgate Circus, London, E.C.4. T.
01–353 4353. *T.A.* Sawells, London, E.C.4.
    37½p., £3 per annum, plus postage (includes **FINISHING HANDBOOK
AND DIRECTORY**). M.—Articles on all subjects connected with finishes
and finishing, having a definite interest for the manufacturer who wants to
know more about improving the finish of his products. *Payment:* £5·25 per
1000 words and upwards according to merit, on publication. *Illustrations:*
line, halftone and occasional colour.

PROGRESS (1881), ALISON E. BROWN, Royal National Institute for the Blind,
224–8 Great Portland Street, W1N 6AA T. 01–387 5251.
    32½p. p.a. M. (7th).—A magazine in braille type for the blind.

PSYCHOLOGIST MAGAZINE (1933), FRANK J. ALLARD, Manfield House,
1 Southampton Street, Strand, W.C.2. T. 01–836 3980.
    7½p. M.—Articles on psychology from a practical and applied point of
view, dealing with the understanding of ourselves, how to face life with courage
and live more effective and happy lives, and the facing and overcoming of the
various problems and difficulties of daily life, through the knowledge of psychology; mental health, mental efficiency; psychology in everyday life and in
dealing with nerves, nervous tension, worry, shyness, self-consciousness and
inferiority feelings, in business, how to make friends, how to get along with
people, the art of conversations, and inspirational. Must be practical and of
real help to the reader. No articles are accepted unless they are based on sound
scientific principles. *Length:* about 1500 words. *Payment:* minimum £2·62½
per 1000 words.

PUBLIC LEDGER, THE (1759), ROBERT HARDAKER (U.K. Publications, Ltd.),
11 Tokenhouse Yard, E.C.2. T. 01–606 7937.
    7½p. Annual subscription £30. D. (Weekly edition, 27½p. Saturdays;
annual subscription £17).—Special news and prices from all the commodity
markets and exchanges. Articles by experts on commodities, industry, and
trade.

PUBLISHER, THE (incorporating **BRITISH BOOKS** and the **PUBLISHERS'
CIRCULAR AND BOOKSELLERS' RECORD**) (1837), A. NORMAN MARSTON,
Whitehall Press Ltd., Wrotham Place, Wrotham, Kent.
    37½p. post free. Bi-M.—Articles and illustrations dealing with all aspects
of the Book and Periodical Publishing Industry, but *preliminary letter* is advisable. *Payment:* by arrangement. *Illustrations:* photographs and line
drawings. Now **BOOK TRADE**.

PULSE, Thomas H. Mapp, Professional Projects Ltd., Ryde House, Chobham Road, Woking, Surrey. *T.* Woking 64321–4.

£1·50 p.a. W. (Saturday).—Articles with a medical flavour or of direct interest to G.P.s. Purely clinical matter cannot be used. *Length:* 150–800 words, average 500. *Payment:* £6·30 to £15·75 average. *Illustrations:* photographs. Cartoons.

PUMPS, POMPES, PUMPEN (Official Journal of Europump), Trade & Technical Press Ltd., Crown House, Morden, Surrey. *T.* 01-540 3897. *T.A.* Tratec, Morden, Surrey. *Telex:* 27526.

£5·50 p.a. post free, UK and overseas. 12 issues p.a.—Technical articles and commercial news on pumping and related applications. *Length:* features up to 3000 words; items up to 250 words. *Payment:* £6·30 to £10·50 per 1000 words. *Illustrations:* line and half-tone.

PUNCH (1841), William Davis, 23–27 Tudor Street, E.C.4. *T.* 01-583 9199.

12½p. W. (Wednesday).—Articles are usually commissioned, and there is no longer any demand for short stories. But Punch is always on the look-out for new talent, and writers are invited to submit, in the first place, a synopsis of intended contributions. Emphasis on public affairs preferred. Cartoons by outside artists welcomed. *Payment:* by arrangement, but not less than £26·25 per 1000 words—usual length 900–1000 words. *Drawings:* line or half-tone: half-pages from £12·60 and small drawings from £7·35.

PURCHASING JOURNAL (incorporating **SUPPLIES**) (1967), Journal of the Institute of Purchasing and Supply. Editor: C. E. Waller, York House, Westminster Bridge Road, London, S.E.1. *T.* 01-928 1851.

£3·15 per year. M.—Authoritative articles on topics connected with purchasing, storage, distribution, accounting, disposal methods, departmental organisation. Authoritative economic, technical and descriptive articles on market trends and movements, goods and supplies of every kind. *Length:* up to 3000 words. *Payment:* £10·50 per 1000 words or by arrangement. *Illustrations:* line and half-tone.

QUAKER MONTHLY (1921), David Firth, Friends House, Euston Road, London, N.W.1. *T.* 01-387 3601.

4p. M.—Mainly commissioned articles.

QUARRY MANAGERS' JOURNAL, THE (1919), Brian G. Fish, 62–64 Baker Street, London, W1M 2BN. *T.* 01-486 2547. *T.A.* Ruspamac, Wesdo, London.

25p., £3 p.a. M.—Technical material directly relevant to the quarrying industry, including the quarrying and processing of roadstone, aggregates and dimension stone; also the preparation of coated materials and other ancillary processes. *Payment:* £7·35 per 1000 words for good, original material. *Illustrations:* photographs and line drawings.

QUARTERLY JOURNAL OF MEDICINE (1907), Clarendon Press, Oxford. *Secretary to Editors:* Dr. C. W. M. Whitty, 3 Lathbury Road, Oxford. *T.* Oxford 57916.

£1·25, £3·75 per annum. Q.—Devoted to the publication of original papers and critical reviews dealing with clinical medicine. *No payment.*

QUEEN (1861), FREDERIC GRUNFELD, 52–53 Fetter Lane, E.C.4. *T.* 01–353 4050. *T.A.* Queenmag London.

25p. F. (Wednesday).—Illustrated magazine containing text and picture features of controversial and topical interest. Regular features cover a wide range of interests including social news, full fashion coverage including men's wear, theatre, film, TV, art and book reviews, travel, motoring, decorating, wine, restaurants and beauty. *Length:* articles not less than 1000 words. *Payment:* by arrangement. All communications to be addressed to the Editor. *Illustrations:* line, wash, or photos.

QUEEN'S HIGHWAY, THE (1931), L. G. WATKINS, 14 Howick Place, S.W.1. *T.* 01–834 2829 and 6477. (The House Journal of the Asphalt & Coated Macadam Association.)

Twice yearly (large gratuitous circulation).—Technical, historical, and biographical articles, dealing directly or indirectly with the Queen's Highway. *Length:* 900 to 1250 words. *Payment:* £5 per 1000 words minimum. Suitable *illustrations* a special feature.

QUESTION (1884), HECTOR HAWTON, 88 Islington High Street, London N.1. *T.* 01–226 7251–2.

25p. Annual.—Articles on a wide range of subjects at a serious level. *Payment:* by arrangement.

QUIET PLEASE (1961), Journal of the Noise Abatement Society, JOHN CONNELL, 6 Old Bond Street, London, W1X 3TA *T.* 01–493 5878.

10p. M.—Articles dealing with any aspect of noise and noise control. If technical should be written in terminology which can be understood by the layman. *Length:* 500–1500 words. *Payment:* by arrangement. *Illustrations:* line and half-tone—cartoons would be welcome.

RADIO CONSTRUCTOR, THE (1947) (Data Publications Ltd.), 57 Maida Vale, W.9. *T.* 01–286 6141.

17½p. M.—Technical articles on radio, television, and electronic subjects. *Payment:* £5·25 per 1000 words plus additional payment for diagrams published. *Illustrations:* line and half-tone.

RADIO CONTROL MODELS AND ELECTRONICS, A. DOWDESWELL, Model & Allied Publications Ltd., 13–35 Bridge Street, Hemel Hempstead, Herts. *T.* Hemel Hempstead 2501–3.

15p., £2·05 p.a. M. (2nd Fiday).—Articles on radio control of all kinds of models and do-it-yourself electronic features. *Length:* 750 to 1500 words or by arrangement. *Payment:* £4·20 to £5·25 per page. *Illustrations:* line and half-tone.

RADIO TIMES (The Journal of the BBC), incorporating World Radio. GEOFFREY CANNON, B.B.C., 35 Marylebone High Street, London, W1M 4AA. *T.* 01–580 5577, Ext. 4555. PETER GILLMAN (Features Editor), Ext. 4991; DAVID DRIVER (Art Editor), Ext. 2293.

5p. W.—Articles supporting and enlarging BBC Television and Radio programmes, which are, therefore, on every subject broadcast. *Length:* from 300 to 2500 words. *Payment:* by arrangement. *Illustrations:* in colour and black and white; photographs, graphic designs, or drawings.

RAILWAY GAZETTE (incorporating **DIESEL RAILWAY TRACTION**), Dorset House, Stamford Street, London, S.E.1. *T.* 01–928 3333.
20p. Twice-monthly.—(Incorporating *Herapath's Railway Journal* (1835); *The Railway News* (1864); *Transport* (1892); and *The Railway Engineer* (1880).) Deals with the management, engineering, operation and finance of railways world wide. Articles of practical interest on these subjects are considered and paid for if accepted. Illustrated articles, of 1000 to 3000 words, are preferred. A *preliminary letter* is desirable.

RAILWAY MAGAZINE (1897), Dorset House, Stamford Street, London, S.E.1. *T.* 01–928 3333.
20p. M.—An illustrated magazine, dealing with all railway subjects; not fiction. Articles from 1500 to 2000 words accompanied by photographs. A *preliminary letter* is desirable. No verse. *Payment:* by arrangement. *Illustrations:* half-tone and line blocks only.

RAILWAY WORLD (founded as **RAILWAYS** 1940), G. M. KICHENSIDE, Ian Allan Ltd., Terminal House, Shepperton, Middlesex. *T.* Walton-on-Thames 28484.
17½p. M.—Articles on railway and allied matters. *Length:* 500 to 3000 words. *Payment:* £3 per 1000 words. *Illustrations:* line and half-tone.

RANGER, THE. Official Organ of The Girl Guides Association, Mrs. J. V. RUSH, 17–19 Buckingham Palace Road, S.W.1. *T.* 01–834 6242.
2½p. M.—Short articles of interest to Ranger Guides (girls aged 14–20 who are members of The Girl Guide Movement). Cartoons. *Payment:* by arrangement. *Illustrations:* line and half-tone.

RATING AND VALUATION REPORTER (1961) (as **Rating and Income Tax,** 1924) (Rating Publishers Ltd.), 2 Paper Buildings Temple, London, E.C.4. *T.* 01–353 4142.
17½p. W.—Articles, etc. on Rating and Valuation. Comprehensive reports by barristers on proceedings on these subjects in the Lands Tribunal and Superior Courts, Scotland and Northern Ireland. (Rating cases in weekly Supplements.)

RAVE (1964), BETTY HALE, Fleetway House, Farringdon Street, London, EC4A 4AD *T.* 01–236 8080.
12½p. M.—Articles and factual personality reporting about leading young entertainers, fashions and the wider general interests of young adults. Humorous articles in this context considered. Fiction involving action or adventure, romance, dialogue, and set among contemporary young people required. *Payment:* by arrangement. *Illustrations:* photographs, mono, or colour, unusual pictures of leading young entertainers.

READER'S DIGEST, MICHAEL RANDOLPH (The Reader's Digest Association Ltd.), 25 Berkeley Square, London, W1X 6AB *T.* 01–629 8144.
20p. M.—Outstanding British articles, up to 5000 words, will be considered; they should conform in theme and style to the very high Reader's Digest standard. Payment, for world rights, is at American rates. Original anecdotes—£75 for up to 300 words—are also required for humorous features.

REALITY (1966), Redemptorist Publications, Orwell Road, Dublin 6. *T.* Dublin 900840 and 903251.
5p. M.—Illustrated Catholic magazine for christian living. Seeks to reflect current thought in the Church at large and with particular reference to the Irish Church. General orientation towards modern human problems especially sociological—poverty, marriage, modern living in all its aspects. Regular features on youth, problems of parents, students. Book reviews. Articles on these and religious and literary topics. Short stories occasionally. *Length:* 1000 to 2000 words. *Payment:* payment for articles at Editor's discretion, average: £5·25 per article.

RECORDS AND RECORDING (1957), ROBERT LESLIE, Hansom Books, Artillery Mansions, 75 Victoria Street, London, S.W.1. *T.* 01–799 4452.

15p. M.—Complete coverage of classical and light music on record. Reviews and articles on every aspect of recording and equipment by leading authorities.

RED LETTER, (D. C. Thomson & Co. Ltd.), Courier Place, Dundee, DD1 9QJ, and Thomson House, 12 Fetter Lane, London, E.C.4.

2½p. W. (Tuesday).—Serials of strong emotion; romantic, with movement and incident. First instalment up to 5000 words. Short stories 1000 to 3000 words. Real-life series. Articles of interest to girls and women. *Payment:* on acceptance. *Illustrations:* line or wash.

RED STAR WEEKLY, (D. C. Thomson & Co., Ltd.), Courier Place, Dundee, DD1 9QJ, and Thomson House, 12 Fetter Lane, London, E.C.4.

2½p. W. (Thursday).—Serials up to 40,000 words with strong emotional dramatic incident. First instalment 5000 words. Short stories 1000 to 3000 words. True life series with strong emotional appeal, told in first-person. Instalments 2000 words. Good romantic interest essential. *Payment:* on acceptance.

RED TAPE (1911), T. J. O'DEA, Civil and Public Services Association, 215 Balham High Road, London, S.W.17. *T.* 01–672 1299.

3p. M. (1st).—The Civil Service Magazine. Well-written articles on Civil Service, trade union and general subjects considered. *Length:* 750 to 1400 words. Also photographs and humorous drawings of interest to Civil Servants. *Illustrations:* line and half-tone.

REFRACTORIES JOURNAL, THE (1925), J. E. ROBERTS, F.R.S.A., Stamford House, 65–66 Turnmill Street, London, E.C.1. *T.* 01–253 8201.

42p. (£4·25 Ann. Sub., £4·75 overseas). M.—Welcomes reviews and notices of current literature, biographical notices, and technical articles, which must be authoritatively written, of interest to the refractories industry. *Length:* 1000 words and upwards. *Payment:* by arrangement.

REFRIGERATION AND AIR CONDITIONING, T. A. O'GORMAN, Davis House, 69–77 High Street, Croydon, CR9 1QH *T.* 01–688 7788. *T.A.* Maclaren, Croydon.

25p. M.—Technical, business, educational and other articles on any aspect of refrigeration or air conditioning. *Length:* by arrangement. *Payment:* by arrangement. *Illustrations:* photographs or diagrams.

RETAIL CHEMIST, THE (1930), DESMOND LANGLEY, 1 Dorset Buildings, Salisbury Square, Fleet Street, London, E.C.4. *T.* 01–353 1555.

W. (Free to registered pharmacies, others £2·60 per annum).—News and business features for the retail chemist. Emphasis on modern marketing and retailing methods. *Payment:* Good for practical case history articles and business news paragraphs. *Illustrations:* photographs and graphics.

RETAIL JEWELLER (1963), ERIC M. BRUNTON, F.B.H.I., F.G.A., Elm House, Elm Street, London, W.C.1. *T.* 01–837 1234.

10p. £2·50 p.a. Fortnightly.—News stories and news features about the jewellery trade and the people in it. *Length:* up to 1200 words. *Payment:* by arrangement. *Illustrations:* line and half-tone.

RETAIL NEWSAGENT, BOOKSELLER AND STATIONER (1889) (official weekly of the National Federation of Retail Newsagents, Booksellers and Stationers), DENNIS C. WARD, 15 Charterhouse Street, E.C.1. *T.* 01–405 9127.
6p. W.—News and features on publishing distributive field, and on news-agency retailing (including marketing of ancillary goods and products). *Length:* articles 600–900 words. *Illustrations:* pictures of shop displays, practical selling methods, etc. *Preliminary letter.*

REVEILLE, K. SIMPSON, 127 Stamford Street, London, S.E.1. *T.* 01–353 0246.
3½p. W. (Monday).—Human interest articles on any subject—topical, scientific, historical. Short stories of action and suspense (800–3000 words). Fiction and non-fiction serials. Amusing and dramatic photographs. Humorous pocket cartoons. *Payment:* good.

REVIEW, THE, IAN HAMILTON, 11 Greek Street, London, W1V 5LE *T.* 01–437 4494.
25p. Q.—poetry, critical essays on modern poetry. *Payment:* £5 per page of verse, £3 per 1000 words of prose.

RIDING: The Horselover's Magazine (1936), E. HARTLEY EDWARDS, 189 High Holborn, London, WC1V 7BA *T.* 01–242 3344.
15p. M.—Instructive and informative articles on breeding, care and schooling of horses and ponies, on riding in general, hunting, racing, polo, shows, on outstanding horses and riders and their history, stories for adults and young people. *Length:* 500 to 2000 words. *Payment:* varies. *Illustrations:* photographs and drawings.

ROADS AND ROAD CONSTRUCTION (1923), J. O. WILLIS, B.SC., A.C.G.I., Blenheim House, Battersea High Street, London, S.W.11. *T.* 01–228 0177.
£1·50 per annum in U.K.—A monthly record of road engineering and development. Acceptance of outside contributions only by arrangement beforehand.

ROD AND LINE (1962), MICHAEL T. SHEPLEY, 38 Barntongate Drive, Edinburgh, EH4 8BY *T.* 031–336 5749.
10p. M.—Articles (600–1200 words) and pictures of special interest to game fishers and sea anglers, mainly Scottish background.

ROMEO (D. C. Thomson & Co. Ltd.), Courier Place, Dundee, DD1 9QJ, and Thomson House, 12 Fetter Lane, London, E.C.4.
2½p. W. (Tuesday).—Romantic teen-age picture-story paper. Complete scripts 25–35 pictures on modern, romantic themes. Serials in script form. Text story. *Length:* up to 2500 words. *Payment:* on acceptance. Promising new writers and artists given special consideration.

ROUND TABLE (1910), MICHAEL HOWARD and ROBERT JACKSON, 18 Northumberland Avenue, London, W.C.2. *T.* 01–930 9993.
£3 p.a. Q.—A non-party quarterly review of world affairs, especially of the politics of the British Commonwealth. All articles commissioned.

ROVER, THE (D. C. Thomson and Co., Ltd.), Courier Place, Dundee, DD1 9QJ, and Thomson House, 12 Fetter Lane, London, E.C.4.
2½p. W. (Monday).—Stories for boys and young men; sport, school, mystery, war, humour, adventure. Serials, series, completes. Instalments of 2000, 3000, 4000 or 5000 words. *Payment:* on acceptance.

ROYAL AIR FORCES QUARTERLY (1961). Founded in 1930. Incorporating **AIR POWER.** Group Captain A. H. STRADLING, O.B.E., R.A.F. (retd.), 4 Parkway, Ratton Manor, Willingdon, Sussex. R.A.F.A. Publishing Co. Ltd., 43 Grove Park Road, Chiswick, W.4. *T.* 01–994 8504.

30p. £1·25 p.a. post free. Q.—Articles concerning military air power of all nations and "light hearted" articles on aviation. *Length:* up to 2000 words. *Payment:* £2·10 per 1000 words. *Illustrations:* photographs, line maps and drawings.

SAFETY AT SEA INTERNATIONAL, RONALD PEARSON, A.I.MAR.E., M.S.E., 54–55 Wilton Road, London, S.W.1. *T.* 01–828 4112.

£2·50 p.a. Bi-M.—Technical and administrative articles dealing with all aspects of safety in the design, construction, management, operation, maintenance and equipping of every class of ship. *Length:* 1000–3000 words. *Payment:* £12·60 per 1000 words. *Illustrations:* line and half-tone.

SATURDAY TIT-BITS (1881), PERROT PHILLIPS, 189 High Holborn, London, WC1V 7BA *T.* 01–242 3344.

3½p. W. (Monday).—Contains crime, adventure and human interest features, big-name profiles, hard-hitting exposure stories, and factual first-person series. *Illustrations:* top-flight glamour, general picture sets and one-shot photographs. *Payment:* by arrangement.

SCHOOL GOVERNMENT CHRONICLE AND EDUCATION REVIEW, W. H. EVANS (1871), Littlefold, South Warnborough, Basingstoke, Hants.

7½p. M.—Outside contributions on administrative educational matters are considered. *Payment:* from £2·10 per 1000 words.

SCHOOL LIBRARIAN (1937), NORMAN FURLONG, 150 Southampton Row, London, WC1B 5AR *T.* 01–837 8114.

75p. Four times a year. £3 per annum, post free.—Official journal of the School Library Assoc., (free to members). *Payment:* by arrangement.

SCIENCE JOURNAL (1965), ROBIN CLARKE, Dorset House, Stamford Street, London, S.E.1. *T.* 01–928 3333. Telex 25137.

30p. M.—Articles on scientific and technological research. *Length:* 4000 words. *Payment:* by arrangement. *Illustrations:* line, half-tone, colour.

SCIENCE PROGRESS, Professor D. LEWIS, F.R.S., Professor J. M. ZIMAN, F.R.S. (Blackwell Scientific Publications Ltd.), 5 Alfred Street, Oxford. *T.* Oxford 40201.

£1·05 Q. (£4 p.a.).—Articles of 5000 to 10,000 words suitably illustrated, on scientific subjects, written so as to be intelligible to workers, in other branches of science. *Payment:* £1·50 per 1000 words. *Illustrations:* line and half-tone.

SCOTLAND (1947), ALWYN JAMES, 1 Castle Street, Edinburgh, EH2 3AJ. *T.* 031–225 7911.

20p. M.—Articles on industry, politics and economics. *Length:* 1500–3000 words. *Payment:* by arrangement. *Illustrations:* photographs and line drawings.

SCOTLAND'S MAGAZINE, 114–116 George Street, Edinburgh EH2 4LX *T.* 226 7491.

10p. M.—Topographical articles of 1000 to 1500 words, with a Scottish background, accompanied by photographs. These may either be purely descriptive or written from a personal standpoint. Articles on Scottish crafts compiled from first-hand information, contributions on modern Scottish life, and nature sketches, all with a Scottish setting, considered. Intending contributors are advised to study the magazine. Books, gramophone records reviewed. *Payment:* by arrangement. *Illustrations:* photographs, black and white and colour, of very high standard, of Scottish landscapes, country scenes and activities, crafts, local industries, etc.

SCOTS MAGAZINE (1739), (D. C. Thomson and Co. Ltd.), Bank Street, Dundee, DD1 9HU.

12½p. M.—Articles on all subjects of Scottish interest. *Payment:* varies according to quality. *Illustrations:* photographs in monochrome and colour.

SCOTSMAN (1817), ALASTAIR M. DUNNETT, 20 North Bridge, Edinburgh. *T.* 031–225 2468. London Office: 200 Gray's Inn Road, W.C.1. *T.* 01–837 1234.

3½p. D.—Independent. Considers articles, 1000–1200 words on political and economic themes, which add substantially to current information. Prepared to commission topical and controversial series from proved authorities. *Illustrations:* outstanding news and scenic pictures.

SCOTTISH EDUCATIONAL JOURNAL, RAYMOND THOMASSON, M.A., F.E.I.S., 46 Moray Place, Edinburgh, EH3 6BH *T.* 031–225 6244.

4p. W.—Professional organ of Educational Institute of Scotland. Articles of 1000 to 1500 words or more on matters of educational interest are considered.

SCOTTISH FARMER, THE (1893), GEORGE MILLAR, 39 York Street, Glasgow, C.2. *T.* 041–221 7911–14. *T.A.* Farming, Glasgow.

4p. W.—Articles on agricultural subjects. *Length:* 1000–1500 words. *Payment:* by arrangement. *Illustrations:* line and half-tone.

SCOTTISH FIELD (1903), COMYN WEBSTER (George Outram & Co. Ltd.), 70 Mitchell Street, Glasgow. *T.* 041–221 9200.

15p. M.—The Editor is prepared to consider articles on all Scottish subjects. These should be 1000–2000 words in *length.* Articles accompanied by first class photographs are preferred. Suitable suggestions by known authors will be commissioned. *Payment:* usually by arrangement, but where articles are submitted direct, payment is according to the merit of the matter. Payment is made after publication.

SCOTTISH FORESTRY (1854 as **SCOTTISH ARBORICULTURAL JOURNAL**), R. MACLAGAN GORRIE, D.SC., 15 Murrayfield Drive, Edinburgh 12. *T.* 031–337 1820.

£1·50 p.a. Q.—Anything having a bearing on forestry. *Illustrations:* line and half-tone.

SCOTTISH HISTORICAL REVIEW (Company of Scottish History Ltd.)—Joint editors: Dr. D. E. R. WATT and Prof. A. A. M. DUNCAN. Distributed by Aberdeen University Press, Farmers Hall, Aberdeen AB9 2XT *T.* 29124.

£2 (£2·50 through booksellers). Twice yearly.—Contributions to the advancement of knowledge in any aspect of Scottish history. *Length:* up to 8000 words. *Payment:* none; contributors are given offprints. *Illustrations:* line and half-tone.

SCOTTISH HOME AND COUNTRY (1924), Miss ISOBEL HORN, 34 West George Street, Glasgow, C.2. *T.* 041–332 2495.

10p. M.—Articles of a practical nature. *Length:* about 800 words. *Payment:* by arrangement. *Illustrations:* must have rural character.

SCOUTER, THE, Ron Jeffries, The Scout Association, 25 Buckingham Palace Road, S.W.1. *T.* 01-834 6005.

10p. M. (1st).—The National Magazine of The Scout Association for Adult members of The Movement, including Venture Scouts. Articles of interest to Leaders and supporters; Training material, accounts of Scouting events and articles of general interest within the field of youth activity. *Illustrations:* photographs of Scouting today, cartoons with a Scout interest. *Payment:* Normal rates for illustrations only.

SEA BREEZES (1919), Craig J. M. Carter, 19 James Street, Liverpool, L2 7PE *T.* 051-236 6415.

12½p. M.—Short factual articles, on the sea, seamen and merchant ships, preferably illustrated. *Payment:* by arrangement. *Illustrations:* half-tone, line.

SEA CADET, G. Wood, The Navy League, Broadway House, Broadway, Wimbledon, London, S.W.19. *T.* 01-540 8222.

5p. M.—Anything to do with the sea, or specifically training of Sea Cadets; articles dealing with various branches of service in the Royal Navy, Royal Marines, Merchant Navy; weather lore; naval custom and tradition; stories of naval engagements, etc. *Length:* 1000 to 1500 words. *Payment:* by arrangement. *Illustrations:* are used.

SECRETS (D. C. Thomson & Co. Ltd.), Courier Place, Dundee, DD1 9QJ, and 186 Fleet Street, London, E.C.4.

2½p. W. (Thursday).—Complete stories of 1000 to 4000 words, long complete stories of 5000–7000 words, with strong dramatic action and love interest, to appeal to working-class young women. Serials, 5000 words instalments. *No preliminary letter* required. *Payment:* on acceptance.

SECRETS STORY LIBRARY (D. C. Thomson & Co., Ltd.), Courier Place, Dundee, DD1 9QJ, and 186 Fleet Street, London, E.C.4.

5p. M. (Last Tuesday of each month)—64 pages. Exciting and romantic stories in text.

SECURITY GAZETTE, 3 Clement's Inn, London, W.C.2.

£2·50 p.a.

SELBORNE MAGAZINE (1888), T. L. Bartlett, Tower Cott, Berrynarbor, North Devon.

50p. p.a. Q.—Articles of not more than 530 words which have a bearing on the aims and work of the Society. *Payment:* £1 per article. *Illustrations:* line and half-tone.

SELF SERVICE & SUPERMARKET (1951), B. E. Moore, 1 Dorset Buildings, Salisbury Square, Fleet Street, London, E.C.4. *T.* 01-353 1555.

5p., £2·60 p.a. W.—News about food stores, openings, promotions, etc. Feature articles on the food retailing industry by prior arrangement with the Editor. *Payment:* news: 50p. per 100 words; features: NUJ rates. *Illustrations:* line and half-tone.

SELLING TODAY (ON THE ROAD) (1883), the organ of the United Commercial Travellers' Association of Great Britain and Ireland (U.K.C.T.A.), Incorporated; Managing Editor: Andrew Lincoln, Bexton Lane, Knutsford, Cheshire. *T.* Knutsford 4136-7.

10p. M.—Articles dealing with the profession of the C.T. and the various fields of salesmanship, e.g., staple goods, selling to industry, specialities, merchandising, export selling, etc.; allied subjects; educational on the techniques and practices of selling. Articles on cars, motoring, marketing, economics, packaging, public speaking. *Length:* average 1000 words. *Payment:* by arrangement, minimum £5·25 per 1000 words.

SERVICE STATION (1925), J. O. Y. BARNES, Service Station Publications Ltd., 3–4 Clement's Inn, London W2CA 2DB *T.* 01–242 1200. Telex: 262568.

£1·50 per annum. M.—A monthly trade journal published in the interests of service station owners and operators. Well-informed trade and technical contributions of about 1000 words in length. *Payment:* based on value of matter accepted. *Illustrations:* trade events, servicing, technical, equipment, etc.

SHE (1955), PAMELA CARMICHAEL, Chestergate House, Vauxhall Bridge Road, London, S.W.1. *T.* 01–834 2331.

15p. M.—Strong action fiction, unusual settings, up to 3000 words, or 1000 word twist-ending stories; no romance. Articles 1000 words on all subjects except fashion and beauty: tough, controversial, factual, general interest rather than "feminine". Picture features especially welcome. *Payment:* from £20 fiction; features by arrangement. *Illustrations:* photos; cartoons.

SHIP & BOAT INTERNATIONAL (1969), KENNETH TROUP, C.ENG., M.R.I.N.A., M.I.MAR.E., Thomas Reed Publications Ltd., 39 St. Andrews Hill, London, E.C.4. *T.* 01–248 8365.

£4 p.a. M.—Technical articles on the design, construction and operation of all types of specialised small ships and workboats. *Length:* 1000 to 3000 words. *Payment:* by arrangement. *Illustrations:* line and half-tone, photographs and diagrams.

SHIPBUILDING & SHIPPING RECORD, BRIAN SINGLETON, 33–39 Bowling Green Lane, London, E.C.1. *T.* 01–837 1277.

15p. W.—A journal devoted to the interests of shipbuilding, marine engineering, docks, harbours, and shipping. Articles of practical interest to shipowners or shipbuilders, with or without drawings or illustrations, are considered and paid for if accepted. These must be written by experts. A *preliminary letter* is desirable. *Illustrations:* line and half-tone.

SHIPPING WORLD AND SHIPBUILDER (incorporating **SYREN AND SHIPPING ILLUSTRATED**) (1896), (A Benn Group Journal), V. A. J. WAKELY, 7–17 Jewry Street, London, EC3N 2HJ *T.* 01–480 5322.

35p., £4·50 p.a. M. (1st Thursday).—Technical articles on building and operation of modern merchant ships, and allied specialist subjects of marine interest. Preliminary contact necessary. *Length:* by arrangement at consultation. *Payment:* by arrangement. *Illustrations:* diagrams, plans and photographs.

SHOOTING TIMES AND COUNTRY MAGAZINE (1882), PHILIP BROWN (Burlington Publishing Co. (1942) Ltd.), Cornwallis Estate, Clivemont Road, Maidenhead, Berks. *T.* Maidenhead 29922.

12½p. W. (Thursday).—Articles on field sports, especially shooting, and natural history not exceeding 1500 words. *Payment:* about £5·25 per 1000 or by arrangement. *Illustrations:* photographs and drawings.

SHOP FITTING INTERNATIONAL (formerly **SHOP REVIEW**) (1955), ALLAN PLOWMAN, 167 High Holborn, London, W.C.1. *T.* 01–836 9551 and 01–836 5816–9.

12½p., £1·50 p.a. post free. M.—Reviews and news, preferably illustrated, of shop, store, and showroom design, planning, construction and fitting, services and lighting. *Length:* 750–1250 words (or longer by arrangement), or short paragraphs; features by arrangement. *Payment:* by arrangement. *Illustrations:* photographs, plans and sketches; colour transparencies.

SHORT WAVE MAGAZINE, THE (1937), AUSTIN FORSYTH, O.B.E., 55 Victoria Street, London, S.W.1. *T.* 01–222 5341–2. *T.A.* Shortwamag, London, S.W.1. Editorial Address: Short Wave Magazine, Buckingham.

20p., £2·25 p.a. M.—Technical and semi-technical articles, 2000 to 10,000 words, dealing with the design, construction and operation of radio amateur short wave receiving and transmitting equipment. *Payment:* from £2·10 to £10·50 per 1000. *Illustrations:* line and half-tone.

SIGHT AND SOUND (1932), PENELOPE HOUSTON (Published by the British Film Institute), 81 Dean Street, W1V 6AA *T.* 01–437 4355.

25p. Q.—Topical and critical articles on the cinema of any country. Highly specialised articles only occasionally. 1000 to 5000 words. *Payment:* by arrangement. *Illustrations:* relevant photographs.

SIGN (1904), The Alden Press, Osney Mead, Oxford. *T.* Oxford 42507.

2p. M.—Religious and devotional matter of definite Church type, 800 to 1000-word Church news stories of national interest, short poems, carefully considered. Special *payment* for special features. All MSS. should bear the author's name and address, and stamps should accompany contributions for return if necessary. *Illustrations:* photos and line drawings.

"600" MAGAZINE (1926), House Journal of The George Cohen 600 Group Limited, Wood Lane, London, W.12. *T.* 01–743 2070.

Q.—High quality satire and humour, or informed and original articles in lively vein likely to interest intelligent business and professional readership. *Length:* 750–2000 words. *Payment:* for full assignment of copyright, dependent on quality and name. Subtle cartoons and anecdotes always welcome for consideration.

SKIER, THE, R. R. BUTCHART, 56–57 Fleet Street, London, E.C.4. *T.* 01–583 5671.

15p. M. (October to January).—Articles, instructive and informative, on ski-ing and winter sports in all parts of the world. Winter travel articles, news items, etc. *Length:* 500 to 3000 words, preferably illustrated. *Payment:* by arrangement. *Illustrations:* Photographs.

SKYTRADER AND AIR MARKETING INTERNATIONAL (1962), PETER HERING, 6 Adam Street, London, W.C.2. *T.* 01–839 7151.

£2·50 p.a. M.—The promotion of air cargo and marketing by air. *Length:* 500–1000 words . *Payment:* by arrangement. *Illustrations:* photographs.

SLR CAMERA (1967), 5 Winsley Street, London, W1N 7AQ. *T.* 01–636 3600.

18p. M.—Technical articles on single lens reflex photography, 1000–2000 words. *Payment:* £5 per page. *Illustrations:* half-tone, colour.

SMALL BOAT (formerly **LIGHT CRAFT**) (1951), PETER JORDAN, Link House, Dingwall Avenue, Croydon, CR9 2TA. *T.* 01–686 2599. *T.A.* Aviculture, Croydon.

15p. M.—News and features on all aspects of small boat activities—power, sail, and canoes, including build-it-yourself. *Length:* 1000 to 1200 average. *Payment:* from £4·20 per 1000 words. *Illustrations:* line and half-tone.

SMASH (1966), J. B. LE GRAND, Fleetway House, Farringdon Street, London, EC4A 4AD *T.* 01–634 4444.

3p. W.—Humorous strip-cartoon drawings. Humorous scripts for established cartoon characters. *Payment:* by arrangement.

SOAP, PERFUMERY AND COSMETICS (established as **SOAP TRADE REVIEW** in 1928). Editor, F. V. WELLS, 9 Gough Square, Fleet Street, London, E.C.4. *T.* 01–353 3172. *T.A.* Markeba, London.

M. (£4 per annum).—Concerned entirely with technical and commercial aspects of the manufacture and marketing of beauty preparations, soaps, perfumes, etc. *Length:* articles 1500 to 4000 words. *Payment:* by arrangement. *Illustrations:* welcomed, and promptly paid for.

SOCIAL SERVICE QUARTERLY (1947), National Council of Social Service, 26 Bedford Square, WC1B 3HU *T.* 01–636 4066.

20p. plus postage. Q.—Authoritative articles on social service subjects up to 2000 words. No *payment.*

SOCIALISM AND HEALTH (incorporating **MEDICINE TODAY AND TO-MORROW**), Mrs. A. THOMAS, Official Organ of the Socialist Medical Association, 3rd floor, Cornwall House, 31 Lionel Street, Birmingham 3. *T.* 021–236 0635.

5p. Bi-M.—"Medical problems in their social setting: social problems in their medical relationship". Most of contents by regular corps of medical contributors. *Length:* not more than 1200 words unless by arrangement. *Payment:* by arrangement. It is advisable for intending contributors to submit suggestions rather than finished articles, so that length, treatment and payment can be mutually arranged.

SOCIALIST COMMENTARY, Dr. RITA HINDEN, 11 Great Russell Street, London, W.C.1. *T.* 01–580 5188.

12½p. M.—Interested in articles, 1200 to 2400 words in *length*, dealing with political subjects from a socialist and democratic point of view; also a section on the arts in our society. Please enclose an s.a.e. *Payment:* £10·50 per 1600 words. *Illustrations:* line drawings and cartoons.

SOCIOLOGICAL REVIEW, Managing Editor: W. M. WILLIAMS, University of Keele, Keele, Staffs, ST5 5BG. *T.* Keele Park 371.

£1·50 (America $4.50). 3 times a year.—Articles of up to 6000 words treating social subjects in a scientific way. No *payment* is made. *Illustrations:* line.

SOFTS DRINKS TRADE JOURNAL, The National Association of Soft Drinks Manufacturers Ltd., The Gatehouse, 2 Holly Road, Twickenham, Middlesex. *T.* 01–892 8082.

20p. M. (7th).—Articles dealing authoritatively with the technical side of soft drinks production and bottling, and with sales and distribution problems. News stories and paragraphs about developments and personalities both in the U.K. and overseas. In the case of articles a preliminary letter is useful, giving particulars of any illustrations available. *Payment:* prompt at customary rates for news items, for articles by arrangement.

SOLDIER (1945), PETER N. WOOD, 433 Holloway Road, London, N.7. *T.* 01–272 4381.

7½p. M.—Cartoons, articles and photographs with military interest. Must have world-wide appeal. No fiction or verse. *Length:* up to 1500 words. *Payment:* minimum £6·30 per 1000 words; minimum £3·15 cartoons. *Illustrations:* preferably whole-plate.

SOLICITORS' JOURNAL, THE (1857) (The Solicitors' Law Stationery Society, Ltd.), Oyez House, Breams Buildings, London, E.C.4. *T.* 01–242 6855. *Telex:* 263579.

10p. W.—Articles, preferably by practising solicitors on subjects of practical interest, are invited. Articles should not generally exceed 2000 words.

SOUND (1967), J. D. HOOD, 105 Gower Street, London, W.C.1. *T.* 01–387 8033.
£1·25 p.a. Q.—High level scientific or professional papers on various aspects of sound, audiology and hearing. *Payment:* by arrangement. *Illustrations:* half-tone and line.

SOUTH ASIAN REVIEW, the journal of the Royal Society for India, Pakistan and Ceylon, JOHN WHITE, 3 Temple Chambers, Temple Avenue, London, E.C.4. *T.* 01–353 8515.
62½p., £2·50 p.a. Q.—Articles on political, economic and social questions concerning India, Pakistan and Ceylon, and on contemporary arts and letters.

SOUTHERN AFRICA (1889), ALAN GRAY, 21 St. Bride Institute, Bride Lane, London, E.C.4. *T.* 01–583 0818.
5p. W. (Friday).—This journal contains articles and detailed news about South Africa and Rhodesia. Articles invariably ordered; no South African "sketches", please. Minimum *payment:* £1·05 for 100 words. *Illustrations:* half-tone.

SPACEFLIGHT (1956), K. W. GATLAND, 10 Brook Mead, Ewell, Epsom, Surrey. *T.* 01–393 1030. Published by The British Interplanetary Society.
Free to members. 50p. to non-members. M.—Articles up to 5000 words dealing with topics of astronomy, rocket engineering and astronautics. *Illustrations:* line and half-tone. *Payment:* none.

SPARKY (D. C. Thomson & Co. Ltd.), Courier Place, Dundee, DD1 9QJ, and Thomson House, 12 Fetter Lane, London, E.C.4.
2½p. W. (Monday).—Picture paper for girls and boys of school age. Bright, cheerful picture-stories; comic strips of fun characters. Encouragement to promising script-writers and artists. *Payment:* on acceptance.

SPEARHEAD (1955), Captain J. SMITH, C.A., The Church Army, P.O. Box 67, 185 Marylebone Road, London, N.W.1. *T.* 01–262 3211.
5p. 4 times a yer.—An Anglican magazine of evangelism, dealing especially with the training and witness of the laity. *Length:* 500 to 2000 words. *Payment:* £1·05 per 500 words. *Illustrations:* photographs and line drawings. *No advertisements or poetry.*

SPECIAL EDUCATION, Official Journal of the Association for Special Education. Education Journal of The Spastics Society. MARGARET PETER, 12 Park Crescent, London, W1N 4EQ *T.* 01–636 5020.
£1 p.a. Q.—Articles by specialists on the education of the physically and mentally handicapped, including the medical, therapeutic and sociological aspects of special education. *Length:* about 2000, 3000 or 4000 words. *Payment:* by arrangement. *Illustrations:* half-tone and line.

SPECIFICATION (1898), DEX HARRISON, F.R.I.B.A., A.M.T.P.I., 9–13 Queen Anne's Gate, Westminster, S.W.1. *T.* 01–930 0611.
£4 Annually.—A reference work for architects, surveyors, civil engineers, contractors, and all engaged in building. It contains a technical résumé of more than 45 branches of the building trade—from site works to painter—together with Specification clauses relating thereto, and numerous copyright articles and illustrations. The volume is revised annually. Authoritative articles in brief technical note form, with diagrams, should be submitted to the Editor for his consideration. *Payment:* by arrangement.

SPECTATOR (1828), G. GALE, 99 Gower Street, W.C.1. *T.* 01–387 3221.
10p. W. (Thursday).—Articles of a suitable character will always be considered. Poetry sometimes is published. The rate of *payment* depends upon the nature and length of the article. A *preliminary letter* is not necessary but may be helpful.

SPEECH AND DRAMA (1951), ARTHUR WISE, 81 Millfield Lane, Nether Poppleton, York, YO2 6NA. *T.* Upper Poppleton 2273.

£1·50 Three issues p.a.—Specialist articles only. *Length:* From 1000 words. The publication covers the field of Speech and Drama in Education. Preliminary letter essential. *Payment:* £3·15 to £5·25. No *illustrations.*

SPORT AND RECREATION (1960), REGINALD MOORE, Central Council of Physical Recreation, 26 Park Crescent, W1N 4AJ. *T.* 01–580 6822–9.

10p. Q.—Articles on various sports, physical education and outdoor activities. *Length:* 1000–2000 words. *Payment:* from £7·50 per 1000 words. *Illustrated.*

SPORTING LIFE, THE, O. W. FLETCHER (Odhams Newspapers Ltd.), 93 Long Acre, London, W.C.2. *T.* 01–836 1200. *T.A.* "Sporting Life", London, W.C.2.

5p. D.—Topical sporting articles.

SPORTS TRADER (incorporating **SPORTS DEALER**) (1907), (Benn Brothers Ltd.), Bouverie House, 154 Fleet Street, London EC4A 2DL *T.* 01–353 3212. *T.A.* Unitrader London E.C.4.

30p., £3·50 p.a. (incl. postage). M. (Last Monday in preceding month).— All matter, including illustrations, commissioned.

SRUTH (1967), F. G. THOMPSON, 92 Academy Street, Inverness. *T.* Inverness 31226.

2½p. Fortnightly—Published by the Highland Association, bi-lingual (Gaelic and English). Articles (maximum 1000 words) specifically related to the Highlands must be topical; in Gaelic or English. *Payment:* by arrangement. *Illustrations:* line, half-tone. *Preliminary letter preferred.*

STAGE AND TELEVISION TODAY, THE (1880), ERIC JOHNS and EDWARD DURHAM TAYLOR, 19–21 Tavistock Street, London, W.C.2. *T.* 01–836 5213–6.

5p. W. (Thursday).—Original and interesting articles on professional stage and television topics may be sent for the Editor's consideration, 500–800 words. *Illustrations:* line and half-tone.

STAMP COLLECTING, KENNETH F. CHAPMAN, Stamp Collecting, Ltd., 42 Maiden Lane, Strand, WC2E 7LL *T.* 01–836 2648 and 7814.

7½p. W.—Articles or notes of interest to stamp collectors, 500 to 2000 words. *Payment:* £3·50 per 1000 words or by arrangement for special commissions. *Illustrations:* half-tone up to 100 screen and line.

STAMP LOVER (1908), Publisher: National Philatelic Society, 44 Fleet Street, London, E.C.4; Editor: PHILIP HALWARD, F.R.P.S.L.

20p. Bi-M.—Organ of the National Philatelic Society and material is mostly contributed by members. Technical articles only. *Length:* up to 4000 words. Rates average £2·10 per 1000. *Illustrations:* half-tone (100 screen) and line.

STAMP MAGAZINE, THE (1934), ARTHUR BLAIR, Link House, Dingwall Avenue, Croydon, CR9 2TA *T.* 01–686 2599. *T.A.* Aviculture, Croydon.

15p. M.—Informative articles and exclusive news items on stamp collecting and postal history. *No preliminary letter. Payment:* by arrangement. *Illustrations:* photographs, half-tone and line.

STAMP MONTHLY, RUSSELL BENNETT, Drury House, Russell Street, London, WC2B 5HD *T.* 01–836 9707.

12½p. Annual postal sub. £1·90. M.—Articles on philatelic topics. Previous reference to the editor advisable. *Length:* 500 to 2500 words. *Payment:* according to value of the contribution, £3·15 per 1000 words and up. *Illustrations:* half-tone and line.

D

STAMP WEEKLY (1967), COLIN NARBETH, Link House Publications Ltd., Link House, Dingwall Avenue, Croydon, CR9 2TA *T.* 01–686 2599. *T.A.* Aviculture, Croydon.

7½p. W. (Thursday).—Articles 200 to 1000 words of general appeal to stamp collectors and investors. Exclusive news items from all areas of the world. *Payment:* by arrangement. *Illustrations:* half-tone and colour.

STAND (1952), JON SILKIN, LORNA TRACY, KEN SMITH and CATHERINE LAMB, 58 Queens Road, Jesmond, Newcastle on Tyne, NE2 2PR. *T.* Newcastle 812614.

£1 p.a., 25p. + 3½p. postage. Q.—Short stories, literary criticism, art criticism, with illustrations, social criticism, poetry, theatre, cinema, and music. *Payment:* £3 per 1000 words of prose; £4 for poetry.

STAR, THE (1887) (formerly YORKSHIRE TELEGRAPH AND STAR), C. T. BRANNIGAN, York Street, Sheffield 1. *T.* 78585. London: 23–27 Tudor Street, E.C.4. *T.* 01–583 9199.

2½p. D.—Well-written articles on topical subjects considered, also short articles of local character. *Length:* about 1000 words. *Payment:* according to value. *Illustrations:* topical photographs, and line drawings.

STAR LOVE STORIES (D. C. Thomson & Co., Ltd.), Courier Place, Dundee, DD1 9QJ, and Thomson House, 12 Fetter Lane, London, E.C.4.

5p. Four each month.—Romantic and emotional stories told in pictures. 63 pages, about 140 pictures, line illustrations. Script writers and promising artists encouraged and given special consideration. *Payment:* on acceptance.

STEAM AND HEATING ENGINEER, THE, COLIN TROUP, B.SC.(ENG.), A.C.G.I., C.ENG., F.I.MECH.E., F.INST.F., F.I.H.V.E., F.I.PLANT.E., Managing Editor, 35 Red Lion Square, WC1R 4SL *T.* 01–242 7856.

Controlled circulation. M.—Practical matter relating to the economics of steam and power generation, heating, air conditioning, ventilation and insulation. *Length:* not exceeding 3000 words, plus illustrations. *Payment:* from £5·25 per 1000 words. *Illustrations:* photographs, line drawings and charts.

STEEL TIMES (1866), PHILIP CARDEN, John Adam House, 17–19 John Adam Street, Adelphi, W.C.2. *T.* 01–839 6171.

£6 per annum (13 issues), single copies 50p., by post 55p. M. (10th).— Iron and steel industries and their ancillary trades and interests, and heavy engineering. Matter of interest to the iron and steel industries from a trade or technical standpoint. Features welcomed. *Payment:* by arrangement. *Illustrations:* line, half-tone and colour.

STONE INDUSTRIES, PHILIP BURTON, 54–55 Wilton Road, London, S.W.1. *T.* 01–828 4112.

40p. Alt. months.—Semi-technical articles on modern uses of natural stone, marble, granite and slate for architecture, sculpture and other purposes. *Payment:* by arrangement. *Illustrations:* line and half tone.

STRAD, THE, E. LAVENDER, 27 Soho Square, London, W1V 6BR *T.* 01–437 1222.

7½p. M.—Technical articles dealing with playing and making the Violin, Viola, Violoncello or Double Bass, also biographical articles on players and famous makers. *Length:* 1000–1500 words. *Payment:* £1·50 per column on publication (£3·75 per 1000 words approx.) or by arrangement. *Illustrations:* rarely used.

STUD & STABLE (1961), Major PETER TOWERS-CLARK, 149 Fleet Street, London, E.C.4. *T.* 01–583 0491.

37½p. £4·50 p.a. M.—Articles and illustrations of interest to the horse racing and breeding world. *Payment:* £10·50 per 1000 words.

STUDIES. An Irish quarterly review, (1912), Rev. PETER M. TRODDYN, S.J., 35 Lower Lesson Street, Dublin 2. *T.* 66785.

40p. Q.—A general review of current affairs, literature, history, the arts, philosophy. Articles written by specialists for the general reader. Critical book reviews. *Length:* 4000 words. *Payment:* by arrangement. *Preliminary letter.*

STUDIES IN COMPARATIVE RELIGION, F. CLIVE-ROSS, Pates Manor, Bedfont, Middlesex. *T.* 01–890 2790.

40p. Q.—Articles on comparative religion, metaphysics, traditional studies, eastern religions, mysticism, holy places, etc. *Length:* 2000–4000 words.

STUDIO INTERNATIONAL (1893), PETER TOWNSEND, 37 Museum Street, London, W.C.1. *T.* 01–405 3956. Editorial: *T.* 01–405 3957 and 3959.

87½p. M.—An international magazine dealing with the contemporary fine arts. *Remarks:* only *illustrated* articles and notes are accepted. A *preliminary letter* is desirable. *Payment:* by arrangement. *Illustrations:* reproductions of paintings, sculpture, drawings, engravings, applied art, etc., in colour and black and white.

STUDIO SOUND (1959), JOHN CRABBE, Link House, Dingwall Avenue, Croydon, CR9 2TA *T.* 01–686 2599. *T.A.* Aviculture, Croydon.

15p. M.—Articles on all aspects of professional or advanced-amateur sound recording and studio affairs. Technical features on the functional and circuit aspects of tape recorders; general features on the various uses of tape recording. *Length:* 2000–3000 words. *Payment:* from £6·30 per 1000 words. *Illustrations:* line and half-tone; cartoons.

STYLE, (1922), RONALD J. MURRAY, Textile Business Press Ltd., 30 Finsbury Square, London, E.C.2. *T.* 01–628 7901–11.

Controlled circulation. W. (Thursday, press day Tuesday).—News and feature articles of interest to men's apparel retailers. *Payment:* on publication. *Illustrations:* line and half-tone.

SUN, THE (1969), LARRY LAMB, 30 Bouverie Street, London, EC4Y 8DE *T.* 01–353 3030. *T.A.* Sunnews, London.

2½p. D.

SUNDAY COMPANION (1894), Mrs. BARBARA JEFFERY, 189 High Holborn, WC1V 7BA *T.* 01–242 3344.

3p. W. (Thursday).—A weekly journal appealing to the whole family with human interest features and strong fiction slant. Serial (4000 words) and complete stories (1500 words) with family or simply romantic interest.

SUNDAY EXPRESS (1918), JOHN JUNOR, Fleet Street, E.C.4. *T.* 01–353 8000.

3½p. W. (Sunday).—Pays highest price in journalism for exclusive news, photographs, and articles by and about the leading thinkers and personalities of the world. Signed articles should be 1000 to 1500 words.

SUNDAY INDEPENDENT, HECTOR G. C. LEGGE, Independent House, 90 Middle Abbey Street, Dublin, 1. *T.* 46121.

5p. W. (Sundays).—Special articles. *Length:* according to subject. *Payment:* at Editor's valuation; good. *Illustrations:* topical or general interest.

SUNDAY MAIL, A. WEBSTER, 67 Hope Street, Glasgow. *T.* City 7000. London Office: 33 Holborn Circus, E.C.1.

3½p. W.—Exclusive stories and pictures of national and Scottish interest. *Payment:* above average.

SUNDAY MERCURY and **WEEKLY POST**, FREDERICK WHITEHEAD, Colmore Circus, Birmingham B4 6AZ. *T.* 021-236 3366.

4p. W.—News specials or features of Midland interest. Any black–and–white *illustrations.* Special rates for special matter.

SUNDAY MIRROR (1915), MICHAEL CHRISTIANSEN, 33 Holborn, London, E.C.1. *T.* 01-353 0246.

4p. W.—Concentrates on first-person human interest news features, social documentaries, dramatic news and feature photographs. As technique is specialised, ideas bought more than articles. Payment high for exclusives.

SUNDAY NEWS, PATRICK J. CARVILLE, 51–59 Donegall Street, Belfast, BT1 2GB *T.* Belfast 44441.

3½p. W.—General topical articles of 500 words. *Payment:* £4·20 to £5·25 per 500 words approx. *Illustrations:* line and half-tone.

SUNDAY POST (D. C. Thomson & Co., Ltd.), 144 Port Dundas Road, Glasgow, Courier Place, Dundee, DD1 9QJ, and Thomson House, 12 Fetter Lane, London, E.C.4. *T.* (Glasgow) 041–332 9933; Dundee 23131; (London) 01–353 2586–8.

3½p. W. (Sunday).—Human interest, topical, domestic, and humorous articles and exclusive news; and short stories up to 3000 words. *Illustrations:* humorous drawings. *Payment:* on acceptance.

SUNDAY PRESS, THE, VINCENT JENNINGS, Burgh Quay, Dublin. *T.* Dublin 757931. *T.A.* Sceala, Dublin.

2½p. W.—Articles of human interest. *Length:* 1000 words. *Payment:* up to £10·50 per article. *Illustrations:* line and half-tone.

SUNDAY SUN, THE (1919), MALCOLM ARMSTRONG, Thomson House, Groat Market, Newcastle, NE99 1BO. *T.* Newcastle 27500.

3p. W.—Immediate topicality and human sidelights on current problems are the keynote of the SUN's requirements. Particularly welcomed are special features of family appeal and news stories of special interest to the North of England. Photographs used to illustrate articles. *Length:* 500 to 1200 words. *Payment:* £4·20 a column; more for special material. *Illustrations:* photographs and line.

SUNDAY TELEGRAPH, BRIAN R. ROBERTS, 135 Fleet Street, London, E.C.4. *T.* 01-353 4242.

3½p. W.

SUNDAY TIMES (1822), HAROLD EVANS, Thomson House, London, W.C.1. *T.* 01-837 1234.

6p. W. (Sunday).—Special articles by authoritative writers on politics, literature, art, drama, music, finance and industry, and topical matters. Top payment for exclusive features. *Illustrations:* first-class photographs of topical interest and pictorial merit very welcome, especially sets in colour.

SUNNY STORIES, Fleetway House, Farringdon Street, London, EC4A 4AD *T.* 01–634 4444.

5p. W.—All literary and art contributions commissioned. Average age of readers, five to eight.

SUPERVISOR, THE (1949), 22 Bore Street, Lichfield, Staffordshire. *T.* 51346.

25p. M.—Technical articles, reports, news items, photographs, cartoons, etc., of interest to foremen, junior managers and supervisors. *Length:* 350 to 1500 words. *Payment:* £5·25 per 1000 words. *Illustrations:* half-tone and line. *No preliminary letter required.*

SURVEYOR—LOCAL GOVERNMENT TECHNOLOGY (1892), ANTHONY HALE (Building & Contract Journals Ltd.), 32 Southwark Bridge Road, London, S.E.1. *T.* 01–928 2060.

15p. W. (Friday).—Civil and municipal engineering, architecture and town planning; highways and bridges, street lighting, traffic engineering, housing and community services building; refuse collection and disposal; water conservation and supply; sewerage and sewage disposal; parks and sports facilities; plant and equipment. *Payment:* by arrangement. Press day, Wednesday. *Illustrations:* photographs and line drawings/plans.

SUSSEX LIFE (1965), H. R. PRATT BOORMAN, C.B.E., D.L., M.A., (Editor-in-Chief), 123 Week Street, Maidstone, Kent. *T.* Maidstone 58444. T, R. SOBEY (News Editor), 207 High Street, Lewes, Sussex. *T.* Lewes 4805.

15p. M.—Historical and geographical articles about Sussex. All MSS. and pictures must have a Sussex connection. *Length:* articles and fiction 750–1250 words. 1 or 2 pictures preferred with articles. *Payment:* £2·10–£5·25. *Illustrations:* half-tone or line drawings.

SWEETS & TOBACCO RETAILING, TERRY HARKNETT, Lennox House, Norfolk Street, London, W.C.2. *T.* 01–836 8111.

40p. p.a. M.—Articles and photographs on all aspects of retailing chocolates, sweets, ice cream, cigarettes, tobacco and smokers' sundries. *Length:* approx. 750 words. *Payment:* £4·20. *Illustrations:* line drawings and half-tones.

SWIMMING POOL REVIEW (1960), K. S. H. CLARKE (Clarke & Hunter (London) Ltd.), Armour House, Bridge Street, Guildford, Surrey. *T.* Guildford 76333.

15p. Q.—Articles on design, construction and maintenance of Swimming Pools for Municipal, School and Private Ownership. *Length:* 750 to 1500 words. *Payment:* by arrangement. *Illustrations:* line and half-tone.

TABLET, THE (1840), T. F. BURNS, 48 Great Peter Street, S.W.1. *T.* 01–799 7146.

10p. W. (Saturday).—The oldest organ of the Roman Catholic Church in England, which contains news of the week, articles on topics of the day, notes, reviews, almost all written by experts. Freelance work welcomed. Articles should not exceed 1500 words. *Payment:* by arrangement.

TABLEWARE INTERNATIONAL + POTTERY GAZETTE (1875), ERIC GIBBINS, 17 John Adam Street, London, WC2N 6JH *T.* 01–839 6171. *T.A.* Topjournals, London, W.C.2.

£2·50 per annum (post free). M.—Articles of interest to pottery and glass retailers. *Length:* about 1500 words. *Illustrations:* essential. Photographs or line drawings. *Payment:* by arrangement.

TAILOR AND CUTTER (1866) (incorporating **WOMEN'S WEAR**), A. A. WHIFE, 42–43 Gerrard Street, W1V 7LP. *T.* 01–437 5353–4 and 4672–4. *T.A.* Tailcutta, Lesquare, London.

7½p., £5 p.a. W. (Friday).—Anything of interest to Bespoke Tailors. *Length:* articles: 1000 to 1500 words. *Payment:* features by arrangement. News, 2½p. per line. *Illustrations:* half-tone and line.

TAIL-WAGGER & FAMILY MAGAZINE (1928), A. S. C. MICHELL, Astral House, Wakering Road, Barking, Essex. *T.* 01–594 7719.

7½p. M.—Short Stories and articles on domestic pets. *Length:* up to 1500 words. *Payment:* by arrangement. *Illustrations:* line and half-tone.

TAPE RECORDING MAGAZINE (1957), DENYS G. KILLICK, 16a Bevis Marks, London, E.C.3. *T.* 01–283 1724.

15p. M.—Articles on all aspects of tape recording, but with special emphasis on the creative and practical use of tape equipment. Must be well written for an intelligent readership, but in non-technical language. *Payment:* by arrangement. *Illustrations:* good photographs with tape themes welcomed.

TAVR MAGAZINE, THE (formerly **THE TERRITORIAL MAGAZINE**), J.HAROLD WATKINS, M.B.E., Centre Block, Duke of York's Headquarters, Chelsea, S.W.3. *T.* 01–730 6122.

12½p. (by post 15p.); £1·80 p.a. (post free). M.—Material required: brightly written articles on Reserve Army subjects. *Length:* 400 to 1500 words. *Payment:* by arrangement. *Illustrations:* original photographs.

TEACHER, THE (1872), MAX WILKINSON, Derbyshire House, St. Chad's Street, London, W.C.1. *T.* 01–837 6331–3.

5p. W. (Friday).—The official journal of the National Union of Teachers; News of current educational events. Features on teaching method and practice, preferably related to the teaching of a particular subject or age-range, and written from personal experience. *Length:* up to 1000 words. *Payment:* by arrangement. *Illustrations:* photographs and line drawings to accompany educational news items and articles. Cartoons.

TEACHERS WORLD (1911), RONALD DEADMAN (Evans Brothers Ltd.), Montague House, Russell Square, London, WC1B 5BX *T.* 01–636 8521.

5p. F.—A paper concerned only with articles from practising teachers, lecturers or educationists. If essential, articles may be accompanied with *illustrations*, both line and half-tone, which are re-drawn by the resident artists when necessary. Number of words per page: 1300. Press days Monday and Tuesday. *Payment:* by arrangement.

TEDDY BEAR (1963), New Fleetway House, Farringdon Street, London, EC4A 4AD *T.* 01–634 4444.

3½p. W. (Monday).—Picture weekly for young children.

TELEVISION MAIL, ROD ALLEN (Television Mail Ltd.), **31 St. George Street,** Hanover Square, London, W1R 9FA *T.* 01–493 3382.

15p. W. (Friday).—News and authoritative articles designed for all concerned with the British television industry and with advertising on television. *Illustrations:* line and half-tone. No cartoons. *Payment:* by arrangement.

TEMPO, COLIN MASON (Boosey & Hawkes, Music Publishers Ltd.), 295 Regen⁺ Street, W1A 1BR. *T.* 01–580 2060.

20p., 80p. p.a. Q.—Articles about 3000 to 5000 words invited which deal authoritatively with contemporary music. *Payment:* by arrangement. *Illustrations:* music type.

TEXTILE MANUFACTURER (1875), A. DAWBER, 31 King Street West, Manchester M3 2PL *T.* 061–834 7086 *T.A.* "Textile", Manchester.

50p. post free. M. (1st).—A journal for mill-owners, spinners, weavers, bleachers, dyers, printers and research workers. Articles on manufacturing practice, textile industrial administration and economics, new machines and processes, cloth design, materials, research and testing, etc., of any length. *Payment:* by arrangement. *Illustrations:* textile machinery drawings, photographs of machinery, plant installations and processes.

TEXTILE MONTH (1968), DEREK T. WARD, Statham House, Talbot Road, Stretford, Manchester, M32 0EP. *T.* 061–872 4211.

£4·50 per annum. M.—Journal deals with everything concerning natural and man-made fibres. Exclusive articles about fibre and yarn production, machinery, manufacture, dyeing, printing, bleaching, finishing, etc. Interest is mainly concentrated on the technological and commercial aspects of the industry, but illustrated historical or semi-historical articles will be considered. *Length:* 1000–1500 words. *Payment:* by arrangement. *Illustrations:* line and half-tone; exclusive photographs preferred.

TEXTILE NEWS, The National Federation of Textile Works Managers' Associations Official Journal, P. G. MIDDLEHURST, Textile Business Press Ltd., Statham House, Talbot Road, Stretford, Manchester, M32 0EP *T.* 061–872 4211.

25p. W.—Industrial or technical articles in textiles, yarn and fabric production (not garments or fashions). *Length:* 1000 to 1500 words. *Payment:* £5 per 1000 words. *Illustrations:* line drawings and photographs of machinery, processes, etc.

THAMES VALLEY COUNTRYSIDE (1961), LESLIE BICHENER, Letchworth Printers Ltd., The Citizen Press, Norton Way North, Letchworth, Herts. *T.* 2501. *T.A.* Citizen, Letchworth.

15p. M.—Articles of interest to Buckinghamshire, Berkshire and Oxfordshire. *Length:* approximately 1000 words. *Illustrations:* half-tone and line.

THEOLOGY (1920), The Revd. Professor G. R. DUNSTAN, King's College, Strand, London, WC2R 2LS.

20p. M.—Articles on theology, ethics, Church and Society. *Length:* not exceeding 3500 words. *Payment:* only by arrangement.

THIS ENGLAND (1968), R. C. F. FAIERS, 1 Brewery Street, Grimsby, Lincolnshire. *T.* Grimsby 56094.

40p. Q.—Non-fiction articles about England's natural beauty, quaint villages, history, traditions, odd customs, legends, folklore, surviving crafts, etc. Stories about famous English People. *Length:* from 250 to 3000 words (maximum). *Payment:* £2 to £4 per 1000 words. *Illustrations:* line, half-tone, colour. S.A.E. required for return of material.

TIGER AND JAG (1954), New Fleetway House, Farringdon Street, London, EC4A 4AD *T.* 01–634 4444.

3p. W. (Monday).—Scripts for picture stories of sport and adventure, suitable for boys of 9 to 15 years of age.

TIMBER TRADES JOURNAL, NORMAN WELCH (Benn Brothers Ltd.), 2nd Floor, Hanover House, 73–78 High Holborn, London, WC1V 7JS.

15p., £7 p.a. W.—News and articles of direct and specific interest to timber and plywood shippers, agents, importers, merchants, sawmillers, and woodworking machinery trades. *Illustrations:* photographs and diagrams.

TIME AND TIDE, WILLIAM J. BRITTAIN, 13 New Bridge Street, London, E.C.4. *T.* 01–353 1751.

15p. M.—Independent. Has now been developed as the British news magazine. Welcomes exclusive, authentic news and photographs of people, and personal stories of business success.

TIMES, THE (1785), WILLIAM REES-MOGG, Printing House Square, E.C.4. *T.* 01–236 2000.

5p. D.—Independent. Outside contributions considered from (1) experts in subjects of current interest; (2) writers who can make first-hand experience or reflection come readably alive. Best *length:* up to 1500 words. *No preliminary letter* is required. *Literary Supplement,* 10p. *q.v.* also *Educational Supplement,* 5p. *q.v.*

TIMES EDUCATIONAL SUPPLEMENT, THE, STUART MACLURE, Printing House Square, E.C.4. *T.* 01–236 2000.

5p. W.—Articles on education (not exceeding 1200 words) written with special knowledge or experience. News items. *Illustrations:* suitable photographs and drawings of educational interest.

TIMES EDUCATIONAL SUPPLEMENT SCOTLAND (1965) COLIN MACLEAN, 56 Hanover Street, Edinburgh, EH2 2DZ. *T.* 031–225 6393.

5p. W.—Articles on education, preferably 1100 words, written with special knowledge or experience. News items about Scottish educational affairs. *Illustrations:* line and half-tone.

TIMES LITERARY SUPPLEMENT, THE, ARTHUR CROOK, Printing House Square, E.C.4. *T.* 01–236 2000.

10p. W.—General articles of literary interest are welcomed.

TOBACCO (1881), VIVIAN RAVEN, 17–19 John Adam Street, London, W.C.2. *T.* 01–839 6171. *T.A.* Topjornals, London, W.C.2.

20p. M.—Matter required: Retail selling and all matters of interest affecting manufacturers, wholesalers, retailers. *Length:* by arrangement. *Payment:* by value as news (or article). *Illustrations:* photographs dealing with trade.

TODAY'S CINEMA, DAVID LEWIN, Editor; C. H. B. WILLIAMSON, Deputy Editor, Film House, 142 Wardour Street, W1V 4BR. *T.* 01–437 5741.

9p. Published Tuesday and Friday.—News only, at usual N.U.J. rates.

TODAY'S GUIDE, Official Weekly Newspaper of the Girl Guides Association, Mrs. J. V. RUSH, 17–19 Buckingham Palace Road, S.W.1. *T.* 01–834 6242.

4p. W.—Articles of interest to Guides (aged 10–15) mostly concerning Guide Training. Serials and short stories with Guiding background (800 words per instalment). Cartoons. *Payment:* by arrangement. *Illustrations:* line, and half-tone.

TOOLING, T. M. RAMSAY GREEN (Sawell Publications Ltd.), 4 Ludgate Circus, London, E.C.4. *T.* 01–353 4353. *T.A.* Sawells, Lud, London.

17½p., post 2½p. (£1·50 p.a. post 30p.). M.—Articles for toolroom management and workers, on all aspects of tool and die making, press tools, gauges, jigs, and kindred subjects. *Length:* 1000 to 3000 words. *Payment:* £4·20 per 1000 words; special rates by arrangement. *Illustrations:* half-tone and line.

TOPPER, THE (D. C. Thomson & Co., Ltd.), Courier Place, Dundee, DD1 9QJ, and Thomson House, 12 Fetter Lane, London, E.C.4.

2½p. W. (Thursday).—All-picture paper for children. Comic strip series, in sets of 6–18 pictures each. Picture stories of 10–20 pictures per instalment. *Payment:* on acceptance.

TOWN AND COUNTRY PLANNING (Review of the Town and Country Planning Association), IAN LYON, 28 King Street, Covent Garden, WC2 8JG *T.* 01–836 5006.

15p. M. (Annual subscription, £1·87½).—Informative articles on town and country planning, regional planning, new towns, green belts, countryside preservation, homes and gardens, and industrial, business and social life in great and small towns. *Length:* 250 to 1500 words. *Payment:* by arrangement. *Illustrations:* photographs and drawings.

TOWNSWOMAN, MICHAEL LESLIE, 2 Cromwell Place, S.W.7. *T.* 01–589 8817/8/9.

5p. M. (20th).—Official organ of the National Union of Townswomen's Guilds. Educational, travel and general articles and reports on work of Townswomen's Guilds. *Length:* 800–1200 words. *Payment:* £5·25 to £10·50, priority to T.G. members. *Illustrations:* half-tone and line.

TRADE UNIONIST (incorporating **PLEBS**) (1969), ROBERT HICKMAN, 350 Gray's Inn Road, London, W.C.1. *T.* 01–837 6484.

15p., £1·75 p.a. M.—2000 word articles on trade union and industrial relations subjects. *Payment:* £12·60 per 1000 words minimum. *Illustrations:* half-tone and line.

TRAFFIC ENGINEERING & CONTROL (1960), ERNEST DAVIES, 34–40 Ludgate Hill, London, E.C.4. *T.* 01–248 4396.

37½p. M.—Technical articles on transportation, traffic planning, traffic engineering and management, street lighting, parking and road safety. *Length:* 1500–2000 words. *Payment:* £8·40 per 1000 words. *Illustrations:* line and half-tone.

TRANSATLANTIC REVIEW, THE, 33 Ennismore Gardens, London, S.W.7. *T.* 01–584 2639.

25p. Q.—Prose fiction, theatre and film interviews, poetry and drawings chiefly by new English and American writers. *Payment:* by arrangement.

TRANSPORT HISTORY (1968), BARON F. DUCKHAM, Department of Economic History, University of Strathclyde, McCance Building, Richmond Street, Glasgow, C.1. *T.* 552 4400. Published by David & Charles, Newton Abbot.

75p., £2·10 p.a. 3 times a year.—Articles on transport history, approx. 3000–5000 words in *length. Payment:* none, but 15 offprints. *Illustrated:* line and half-tone.

TRAVEL WORLD (1950), H. PEARCE SALES, 167 High Holborn, London, W.C.1. *T.* 01–836 9551.

M.—Management and marketing magazine with technical contributions from well known people in the trade. *Payment:* by arrangement.

TREASURE (1963), New Fleetway House, Farringdon Street, London, EC4A 4AD *T.* 01–634 4444.

7½p. W. (Monday).—Educational weekly for boys and girls from 5–9 years. Nature facts in pictures, How and Why things happen, Fairy Tales, Bible Stories, Puzzle pages and other features, are all presented in a style that will teach as well as entertain.

TREFOIL, THE, Miss T. SCARFFE, Official Journal of the Trefoil Guild, C.H.Q. The Girl Guides Association, 17–19 Buckingham Palace Road, London, S.W.1. *T.* 01–828 7610.

5p. Q. (Jan., April, July, Oct.).—Articles on careers for women, on the work of voluntary organisations and on subjects of topical interest. *Length:* not longer than 1400 words. Photographs. No fiction. No *Payment.*

TRIBUNE, RICHARD CLEMENTS, 24 St. John Street, London, E.C.1. *T.* 01–253 2994.

5p. W.—Political, literary, with Socialist outlook. Informative articles (about 800 words), short political notes (250–300 words). *Payment:* by arrangement. *Illustrations:* cartoons and photographs.

TRIDENT (1969), DENNIS WINSTON, IPC Magazines Ltd., 189 High Holborn, London, WC1V 7BA *T.* 01–242 3344.

Distributed free to all passengers on British European Airways. Q.—Very high quality material for an intelligent and affluent readership. Material should be generally upbeat. Short stories, maximum 4000 words by established writers only. Articles about sports, food, industry, art, etc., in Britain and abroad. NOT required are general travel articles, personality articles, cartoons, jokes, poetry. Potential contributors should keep in mind that the magazine's readership is generally well read and sophisticated. *Payment:* by arrangement, but minimum of £31·50 for 1500 words. *Illustrations:* colour, black and white.

TROUT AND SALMON (1955), JACK THORNDIKE, East Midland Allied Press, Oundle Road, Peterborough, PE2 9QR *T.* 61471. *Telex:* 32157.

17½p. M.—Articles of good quality with strong trout or salmon angling interest. *Length:* 400 to 1200 words, accompanied if possible by photographs. *Payment:* good: minimum £6·30 per 1000 words. *Illustrations:* half-tone, four-colour cover.

TRUE LIFE LIBRARY (1954), Fleetway House, Farringdon Street, London, EC4A 4AD *T.* 01–236 8080.

Four issues 5p. monthly.—Designed to appeal to women and girls of all ages who enjoy a deeply emotional or dramatic picture story of romantic character.

TRUE LOVE SERIES (1931) ANNE BRODIE (Wm Stevens Publications, Ltd.), 53 Fetter Lane, London, E.C.4. *T.* 01–583 9027.

4p. Two numbers monthly.—Contains one long novel, 22,000–25,000 words. Sensational, with strong love interest. No sex questions or controversial matter. No illustrations.

TRUE MAGAZINE, Miss S. HARRISON, Fleetway House, Farringdon Street, London, EC4A 4AD *T.* 01–236 8080.

12½p. M.—First-person complete stories and serials reflecting human problems and situations of strong emotional interest; 2000–6000 words. Poetry. *Payment:* by arrangement.

TRUE ROMANCES AND TRUE STORY, Mrs. M. DEAN, 12–18 Paul Street, London, E.C.2. *T.* 01–247 8233. *T.A.* Gigantean, London, E.C.2.

12½p. M.—First-person true stories with strong love interest. *Length:* 1500 to 6000 words. *Payment:* by arrangement, on acceptance.

TV COMIC, R. F. MILLINGTON, Polly Perkins House, 382–386 Edgware Road, London, W.2. *T.* 01–723 3022.

3½p. W.—Strip cartoons. Commissioned work only. *Payment:* £21 per page. *Illustrations:* line and colour.

TV TIMES, PETER JACKSON, 247 Tottenham Court Road, London, W1P 0AU. *T.* 01–636 1599.

4p. W. (Thursday).—Features relevant to ITV programmes and personalities and television generally. *Length:* from 500 words or by arrangement. *Photographs:* only those of outstanding quality and relevant to ITV. *Payment:* by arrangement. Cartoons with television angle, £7.

TWENTIETH CENTURY (1877), Editorial: 3 Clements Inn, London, W.C.1. Accounts: 16 Hawley Square, Margate, Kent. *T.* Thanet 24500.

37½p. Q.—Most articles are specially commissioned. *Average length:* 3000 words. *Payment:* £5·25 per 1000 words. *Illustrations:* line.

TWINKLE (D. C. Thomson & Co. Ltd.), Courier Place, Dundee, DD1 9QJ, and Thomson House, 12 Fetter Lane, London, E.C.4.

3p. W. (Thursday).—Picture stories and feature comics, specially for little girls. Drawings in line or colour for gravure. *Payment:* on acceptance. Special encouragement to promising artists.

UN-COMMON SENSE (1945) (incorporating **PROGRESS** 1956) (formerly **CHRISTIAN PARTY NEWS LETTER** 1943), RONALD S. MALLONE, B.A., F.R.G.S., M.R.S.T., Woolacombe House, 141 Woolacombe Road, Blackheath, S.E.3. *T.* 01–856 6249.

6½p. M.—Published by The Loverseed Press. Factual news articles (450 to 750 words) especially foreign affairs of international significance; cinema, books, art, politics, religion, drama, cricket, opera, ballet, occasional short stories and poems, essays, psychology. New writers considered. *Payment:* £2·10 per 1000 words. *Illustrations:* photographs, line drawings and cartoons.

UNESCO COURIER, THE (1948), S. M. KOFFLER, Unesco, Place de Fontenoy, Paris 7e. *T.* 566 57.57. *T.A.* Unesco, Paris.

10p. (£1 per annum.) M.—Illustrated feature articles on scientific, cultural and educational subjects; promotion of international understanding; mass communication; human rights; first-hand accounts of ways of life—children and adults—in other lands. *Length:* 2000 words. *Payment:* £25–£35. *Illustrations:* photographs, sometimes line drawings.

UNIVERSE, THE (1860), Managing Director and Editor: CHRISTOPHER HENNESSY, Universe House, 21 Fleet Street, E.C.4. *T.* 01–583 8383. *T.A.* Unicredo, London.

4p. W.—A newspaper and review for Catholics. MSS. should not be submitted without stamped envelope. *Payment:* by arrangement. *Illustrations:* colour, features and news pictures.

UNIVERSITIES QUARTERLY (1946), BORIS FORD (Turnstile Press), 10 Great Turnstile, London, W.C.1. *T.* 01–405 8471.

52½p. Q.—Articles on university affairs or special subjects of interest to other graduates. *Length:* 2000 to 5000 words. *No payment:* 25 offprints.

USE OF ENGLISH, THE, FRANK WHITEHEAD (Chatto & Windus), 40 William IV Street, London, W.C.2. *T.* 01–836 0127.

35p. (£1·25 per annum). Q.—Successor to *English in Schools.* For teachers in all fields of English in Great Britain and overseas. *Length:* usually up to 3000 words. *Payment:* £3·50 per 1000 words.

VALENTINE (1957), Fleetway House, Farringdon Street, EC4A 4AD *T.* 01–236 8080.

4p. W. (Monday).—Designed to appeal to a broad, feminine age-group, aged from approx. 13 to 18, though the accent is on the mid-teen area. Requires scripts for complete 1st person romantic real life stories with convincing themes Mechanical contrivances of plot to be avoided. Authors should first submit brief synopses to the Editor.

VALIANT (1962), New Fleetway House, Farringdon Street, London, EC4A 4AD *T.* 01–634 4444.

3p. W. (Monday).—Scripts for picture stories and picture articles, suitable for boys 8–14 years.

VANGUARD, MALCOLM BALE, 101 Queen Victoria Street, London, E.C.4. *T.* 01–236 5222 (Ext. 424).

7p. M.—Two-colour teenage magazine. Stories, features and pictures in harmony with Christian principles for youth; heroic, sport, missionary, etc. *Length:* 1000 to 1500 words. *Payment:* £2·10 to £5·25.

VANITY FAIR, AUDREY SLAUGHTER, Chestergate House, Vauxhall Bridge Road, S.W.1. *T.* 01–834 2331.
15p. 12 issues a year.—A fashion journal dealing with clothes, accessories, beauty, etc. *Payment:* by arrangement. *Illustrations:* photographs and drawings: black-and-white and colour.

VAUXHALL MOTORIST, THE (1933), G. HUGHES (Vauxhall Motors Ltd.), Kimpton Road, Luton, Beds. *T.* Luton 21122. *T.A.* Carvaux, Telex, Luton.
60p. per ann. Alt. M.—Articles of motoring interest up to 1500 words. *Payment:* by arrangement. *Illustrations:* photographs, line and half-tone.

VEHICLE CLEANING NEWS (1967), JOHN A. W. BURROWS, Trade and Technical Press Ltd., Crown House, Morden, Surrey. *T.* 01–540 3897.
£1 p.a. Occasionally. Articles; general, commercial or technical on any aspects of vehicle cleaning or car washing, including trains, tankers, planes, etc. *Length:* 500 to 2500 words. Also interested in Series. *Payment:* £8·40 per 1000 words. *Illustrations:* line and half-tone.

VICTOR, THE (D. C. Thomson & Co. Ltd.), Courier Place, Dundee, DD1 9QJ, and Thomson House, 12 Fetter Lane, London, E.C.4.
2½p. W. (Monday).—Vigorous, well-drawn stories in pictures (line drawings) for boys and young men. War, adventure, western, sport. Instalments 2, 3 or 4 pages; 8 to 10 panels per page. *Payment:* on acceptance.

VOGUE, BEATRIX MILLER, Vogue House, Hanover Square, London, W1R 0AD *T.* 01–499 9080. *T.A.* Volon, London, W.1.
25p. 16 issues yearly.—Fashion, beauty, decorating, art, theatre, films, literature, music, travel, cooking, gardening. Articles from 1000 words.

WAR CRY (1879), Official Organ of The Salvation Army. Lieut-Colonel BERNARD E. McCARTHY, 101 Queen Victoria Street, London, E.C.4. *T.* 01–236 5222.
2½p. (Postage 1p.) Yearly (post free) home and overseas £2·18. W.— Voluntary contributions, mostly by Salvationists. Photographs.

WAR PICTURE LIBRARY (1958), New Fleetway House, Farringdon Street, London, EC4A 4AD *T.* 01–236 8080.
5p. Six each month.—All-picture war stories. Artists and authors invited to submit sample work to the Editor.

WARWICKSHIRE AND WORCESTERSHIRE LIFE, D. J. N. GREEN, 6 Lillington Avenue, Leamington Spa. *T.* Leamington Spa 22003 and 22372. A member of the Whitethorn Press Group.
15p. M.—Articles of interest to the counties concerned based on first-hand experience dealing with work, customs and matters affecting urban and rural welfare. *Length:* 500 to 1200 words. *Payment:* by arrangement. Photographs also by arrangement. *Illustrations:* preference given to articles accompanied by good photographs relating to subject.

WATCHMAKER, JEWELLER AND SILVERSMITH, K. BLAKEMORE (IPC Consumer Industries Press Ltd.), 33–39 Bowling Green Lane, London, E.C.1. *T.* 01–837 1277.
17½p., £2·10 a year, post free. M.—Illustrated articles, of about 750 words and news paragraphs relating to watch and clock-making, jewellery, gold, silver, and cutlery trades.

WATER AND WATER ENGINEERING (1899), D. WILKINSON, John Adam House, 17–19 John Adam Street, Adelphi, London, W.C.2. *T.* 01–839 6171.
25p. M. (15th).—Technical illustrated articles on all aspects of water for public supply, industrial use, irrigation and the generation of electrical power. A *preliminary letter* is advisable. *Payment:* by arrangement.

WATER POWER, (1949), J. Fox, IPC Electrical–Electronic Press Ltd., Dorset House, Stamford Street, S.E.1. *T.* 01–928 3333.
62½p. M.—Technical articles on the development of the world's hydro-electric resources. The journal covers the entire range of the subject, from rainfall to electrical transmission. *Length:* 2000 to 5000 words. *Illustrations:* photographs and line drawings.

WATER SKIER (formerly incorporated in **THE SKIER**) (1963), TONY READER, 52 High Street, Broadstairs, Kent. *T.* Thanet 61765.
12½p. M.—Factual and technical articles including humorous incidents. Accurate information illustrated with photographs on water skiing anywhere in the world. *Length:* 250–3000. *Payment:* by arrangement. *Illustrations:* line and half-tone.

WEEKEND, DAVID HILL, Northcliffe House, London, E.C.4. *T.* 01–353 6000.
2½p. W.—Factual articles appealing to men and women. Occasional short stories (1000 words) with plenty of atmosphere. *Payment:* by arrangement. *Illustrations:* action photographs, pocket cartoons.

WEEKLY NEWS, THE (D. C. Thomson and Co., Ltd.), Courier Place, Dundee, DD1 9QJ. *T.* 23131; 139 Chapel Street, Manchester, M3 6AA. *T.* 061–834 2831–7; 144 Port Dundas Road, Glasgow. *T.* 041–332 9933; and Thomson House, 12 Fetter Lane, London, E.C.4. *T.* 01–353 2586.
2½p. W.—Real-life dramas of around 2000 words told in the first person. Short stories with domestic or emotional slant. Non-fiction series with lively themes or about interesting people. Keynote throughout is strong human interest. Joke sketches. *Payment:* on acceptance.

WELDING AND METAL FABRICATION (1933), R. N. THOMPSON, 33–39 Bowling Green Lane, London, E.C.1. *T.* 01–837 1277.
37½p. £5·10 p.a. M. (1st).—Articles dealing with practical and theoretical aspects of welding and metalworking: detailed descriptions of important welded work. *Length:* 2000 to 5000 words. *Payment:* by arrangement. *Illustrations:* line and half-tone—trade and technical.

WEST AFRICA, D. M. WILLIAMS, Cromwell House, Fulwood Place, London, W.C.1. *T.* 01–242 0661, ext. 31.
10p. W. (Saturday).—A weekly summary of West African news, with articles on political, economic and commercial matters, and on all matters of general interest affecting West Africa. Covers Ghana, Nigeria, Sierra Leone, Gambia, French-speaking West and Equatorial Africa, Portuguese West Africa, Liberia and the Congo. Articles about 1200 words. *Payment:* as arranged. *Illustrations:* photographs, black-and-white.

WESTERN MAIL (1869), JOHN GIDDINGS, Thomson House, Cardiff. *T.* 33022. London Office: Thomson House, London, W.C.1.
2½p. D.—Independent. Articles of political, industrial, literary or general interest are considered. *Payment:* according to value. Special fees for exclusive news. Topical general news and feature pictures.

WESTERN MORNING NEWS, THE (1860), N. A. T. VINSON (Editor), Leicester Harmsworth House, Plymouth PL1 1RE *T.* 66621. London Office: 143–144 Fleet Street, E.C.4. *T.* 01–353 8641.
2p. D.—Articles up to 1500 words accepted on subjects of West Country interest, illustrated when necessary.

WINE MAGAZINE (1958), K. C. BOURKE, B.A., Southbank House, Black Prince Road, London, S.E.1. *T.* 01–735 4953.
15p. Bi-M.—Articles on wine, food, travel, entertaining. *Length:* 1500–2000 words. *Payment:* £3·30 to £21. *Illustrations:* black-and-white drawings, photographs.

WIRE, Enasco Ltd., 177 Fleet Street, London, E.C.4.   *T.* 01–353 8497.
    47½p.   Bi-M.—Technical and special articles on wire industry of highest
standard.   *Illustrations.*

WIRE INDUSTRY, J. WINGFIELD, 33 Furnival Street, E.C.4.   *T.* 01–405 9556.
    £3·50 per annum.   M.—Information on processes and equipment for the
manufacture of wire and its fabrication into wire products.   *Payment:* up to
£12 per 1000 words according to value of technical information.

WIRELESS WORLD (1911), H. W. BARNARD, Dorset House, Stamford Street,
S.E.1.   *T.* 01–928 3333.   *T.A.* Wiworld, Iliffepres 25137, London, Telex.
    17½p.   M. (third Monday of month preceding.)—A journal for those
interested in the technical aspects of radio, television, electronics, audio and
allied techniques.   *Payment:* according to subject.   *Illustrations:* photos, line
and wash.

WIZARD, THE (D. C. Thomson & Co. Ltd.), Courier Place, Dundee, DD1 9QJ,
and Thomson House, 12 Fetter Lane, London, E.C.4.
    2½p.   W. (Monday).—Boys' picture stories—war, adventure, sport, mystery,
but with special emphasis on football.   Line drawings with 9 frames per page,
2–4 pages per instalment.   *Payment:* on acceptance.

(WOLVERHAMPTON) EXPRESS AND STAR (1874), J. CLEMENT JONES, 50
Queen Street, Wolverhampton, WV1 3BU   *T.* 22351.   London: 69 Fleet
Street, E.C.4.
    2p.   D.—Open to consider topical contributions up to 750 words with
or without illustrations.   *Payment:* by arrangement.

WOMAN (1937), BARBARA BUSS, 189 High Holborn, London, WC1V 7BD   *T.* 01–
242 3344.
    5p.   W. (Wednesday).—Practical articles of varying length on all subjects of
interest to women.   Short stories of 2500 to 4000 words, serials and serialisation of book material.   *Payment:* by arrangement.   *Illustrations:* colour
transparencies, photographs, sketches.

WOMAN BRIDE AND HOME (1968), BARBARA BUSS, 189 High Holborn, London,
WC1V 7BD   *T.* 01–242 3344.
    17½p. six times a year. Features—either 500 words or 1300 words, approx-
imately—considered on all topics of house purchase, insurance and household
management.   Also pieces on marriage adjustment and family planning.
Writers should have an expert knowledge on these subjects.

WOMAN AND HOME (1926), ANGELA WYATT, 40 Long Acre, London, WC2E
9QB   *T.* 01–836 2468.
    12p.   M.—Devoted to the personal and home interests of the home-loving
woman.   Articles dealing with interior decorating.   Dress ideas and accessories.   Needlework and knitting.   Things to make for the home.   Poems,
personality features, and memoirs.   Serial stories 4 to 10 instalments, and
complete stories from 2000 to 7000 words in *length*, of strong romantic interest.
Illustrations: photographs and sketches for full-colour and mono reproduction.

WOMAN JOURNALIST, THE, Organ of the Society of Women Writers and
Journalists (1894).   PAT GARROD, 10 Regis Court, Melcombe Place, London,
N.W.1.   *T.* 01–723 7514.
    Free to members.   Q.—Outside contributions accepted, but no *payment* is
made.   Articles of interest to professional writers.   *Length:* 500–1500 words.

WOMAN'S CHOICE (1968), P.O. Box. 320, Botanic Road, Glasnevin, Dublin 9.
T. 303511.
    6p.   W.—Short stories, fashion news, cooking, beauty, serious features.

WOMAN'S JOURNAL (1927), KATHLEEN JONES, Tower House, Southampton Street, London, W.C.2. *T.* 01–836 4363.

20p. M.—A magazine devoted to women's interests. Its contents include serials, short stories of literary merit, biographies and articles (1000–1500 words) dealing with topical subjects, a fashion section, and a house and home section with special features on home-making, other people's houses and cookery. *Illustrations:* full colour, line and wash, first-rate photographs.

WOMAN'S OWN, ROBERT BRUCE, Tower House, Southampton Street, London, WC2E 9QX *T.* 01–836 4363.

5p. W. (Wednesday).—Appealing to modern women of all ages, but with the accent on youth—preferably the young marrieds. There is a first-class opening for short stories of 2000–5000 words. Preference for stories with genuine emotional situations rather than complicated plots—stories with which the reader can identify herself. Crisp, modern technique essential. *Illustrations:* in full colour. Original knitting, crochet, craft designs, interior decorating and furnishing ideas, fashion.

WOMAN'S REALM (1958), JOSY ARGY, 189 High Holborn, London, WC1V 7BA *T.* 01–242 3344.

4p. W. (Saturday).—Practical home magazine specialising in service to women of all ages. Articles on cooking, dressmaking, homemaking. Short stories of 1500 to 4000 words; serials of 40,000–60,000 words. *Payment:* by arrangement. *Illustrations:* four-colour and two-colour drawings; photographs in colour and monotone.

WOMAN'S REALM HOME SEWING AND KNITTING (1966) JOSY ARGY, 189 High Holborn, London, WC1V 7BA *T.* 01–242 3344.

15p. six times a year.—Specialised publication devoted to knitting, crochet, dressmaking, soft furnishings, embroidery and all aspects of handicrafts. All things to make with instructions. *Payment:* by arrangement. *Illustrations:* Photographs in colour and monotone.

WOMAN'S STORY MAGAZINE (1956), Mrs. M. DEAN, 12–18 Paul Street, London, E.C.2. *T.* 01–247 8233. *T.A.* Gigantean, London, E.C.2.

12½p. M.—Short stories with realistic characterisation and strong woman-interest plot. *Length:* 1500–6000 words. *Payment:* by arrangement, on acceptance.

WOMAN'S WAY (1963), CAROLINE MITCHELL, P.O. Box 320, Botanic Road, Glasnevin, Dublin 9. *T.* 303511.

5p. W.—Short stories, light romance, career, holiday, 3500 to 4500 words. *Payment:* £10·50 to £12·60. Articles of interest to women. *Illustrations:* half-tone and colour.

WOMAN'S WEEKLY (1911), JEAN TWIDDY, 40 Long Acre, London, WC2E 9QB *T.* 01–836 2468.

4p. W. (Monday).—A lively, family-interest magazine. Two serials, averaging 6000 words each instalment, and one short story of 3000 to 5000 words of strong romantic interest. Important biographies, and memoirs of celebrities. Poems. *Payment:* by arrangement. *Illustrations:* full colour and mono fiction illustrations, small line sketches and photographs.

WOMAN'S WEEKLY LIBRARY (1962), Fleetway House, Farringdon Street, London, EC4A 4AD *T.* 01–236 8080.

5p. (Eight monthly).—Complete romantic novels of 40,000 words with accent on love interest, to appeal to women of all ages. *Payment:* by arrangement. *Cover:* four colour offset litho.

WOMAN'S WORLD LIBRARY (1913), Fleetway House, Farringdon Street, EC4A 4AD   *T.* 01–236 8080.

5p. (Two monthly).—Complete romantic and family novels of 40,000 words, with accent on love interest, to appeal to women of all ages. *Payment:* by arrangement. *Cover:* three colour half-tone.

WOMEN'S EMPLOYMENT, MARGARET FUGE, 185 Vauxhall Bridge Road, London, S.W.1.   *T.* 01–828 5943 and 01–834 6273.

5p. M. (1st Fri.)—Articles concerning training in women's professions and interests. *Length:* 1500 to 2000 words. *Payment:* £1·05 per 1000 words. No illustrations.

WOOD, NORMAN WELCH (Benn Brothers Ltd.), 2nd Floor, Hanover House, 73–78 High Holborn, London, WC1V 7JS.

30p., £1·50 p.a. 4 times a year.—Emphasis is on the efficient use of wood in industry through modern machining and treating processes to the finished product, with special attention to structural design and the use of timber and wood products in building. *Length:* 1000 to 1800 words. *Payment:* by arrangement. *Illustrations:* photographs or line drawings.

WOODWORKER, V. J. TAYLOR, Model and Allied Publications Ltd., 13–35 Bridge Street, Hemel Hempstead, Herts.   *T.* Hemel Hempstead 2501.

15p. M. (2nd Friday).—For the home and professional woodworker. *Payment:* by arrangement. Practical illustrated articles on cabinet work, carpentry, wood polishing, metal working, plastics. *Illustrations:* line drawings and photographs.

WOODWORKING INDUSTRY Leading Journal of the Timber Using Trades (1944), DEREK HOLLIER, Mercury House, 103–119 Waterloo Road, S.E.1.   *T.* 01–928 3388.   *T.A.* Sysmaga, Souphone, London.

37½p., £4 p.a. M.—Technical articles relating to woodworking processes, machinery and finishing techniques. *Length:* 1000 to 3000 words. *Payment:* £5·25 to £7·35 per 1000 words. *Illustrations:* line and half-tone.

WOOL RECORD AND TEXTILE WORLD, THE (1909), J. H.WILKS, 91 Kirkgate, Bradford, 1.   *T.* 26357–9.   *T.A.* Woolman, Bradford.

Annual subscription £6·50 U.K. and overseas (including postage). W—Little scope for freelances, but topical articles related to any branch of the wool textile industry including clothing and fashion are invited. *Length:* 800 to 1500 words. *Payment:* £5·25 to £12·60 per 1000. *Illustrations:* photographs and line drawings.

WORD, THE (1936), Rev. Brother PAUL HURLEY, S.V.D. (The Word Press, Hadzor, Droitwich), Glena, Rock Road, Booterstown, Dublin, Ireland.   *T.* Dublin 888674.

10p. M.—A Catholic illustrated magazine for the family. Illustrated articles of general interest up to 2000 words and good picture features. *Payment:* by arrangement. *Illustrations:* photographs and large colour transparencies.

WORKSHOP POETRY MAGAZINE (1967), NORMAN HIDDEN, 2 Culham Court Granville Road, London, N.4.   *T.* 01–348 4054.

£1·40 p.a. 6 issues per year.—Poetry only, high quality. *Payment:* by arrangement. *Illustrations:* line and half-tone, black-and-white.

WORK STUDY, T. M. RAMSAY GREEN (Sawell Publications Ltd.), 4 Ludgate Circus, London, E.C.4.   *T.* 01–353 4353.   *T.A.* Sawells, Lud, London.

25p., post 2½p. (£1·80 p.a., post 30p.). M.—Authoritative articles about all aspects of Work Study, i.e. Motion and Time study, methods, engineering, process control, scientific management, incentive schemes, and business efficiency. *Length:* 1000 to 4000 words. *Payment:* £4·20 per 1000 words on publication; special rates for above-average material. *Illustrations:* half-tone, line and colour.

WORKS ENGINEERING AND FACTORY SERVICES, P. MacEwan, 33–39 Bowling Green Lane, London, E.C.1. *T.* 01–837 1277.
Controlled circulation. M.—Technical matter relating to the power and other engineering services, instrumentation and control of industrial plants, textile mills, breweries, gasworks, public utilities, etc., not compilations, should not exceed 2500 words. *Payment:* by arrangement. *Illustrations:* line and half-tone.

WORLD BOWLS (1954), C. M. Jones, Lowlands, Wenhaston, Halesworth, Suffolk, IP19 9DY *T.* 0502–70 264 (Blythburgh 264).
7½p. M.—Unusual features and fiction about lawn bowls, not about current events. *Payment:* NUJ Freelance rates. *Illustrations:* half-tone.

WORLD CROPS (1949), Kenneth Bean, Commercial Exhibitions & Publications Ltd., Riverside House, Hough Street, Woolwich, London, S.E.18. *T.* 01–855 7001.
£4 p.a. Bi-M.—Articles 500–4000 words, dealing with all aspects of tropical sub-tropical and temperate agriculture, agricultural research, land clearance and utilisation, agricultural machinery, agricultural chemicals, plant breeding, agricultural botany, agronomy, ecology and plant nutrition. *Payment:* by arrangement. *Illustrations:* line and half-tone, photographs and diagrams.

WORLD FISHING (1952), H. S. Noel, Commercial Exhibitions & Publications Ltd., Riverside House, Hough Street, Woolwich, London, S.E.18. *T.* 01–855 7001.
£4 p.a. M.—A magazine for those who take their living from commercial fishing. Bright and informative views and articles on methods, design, construction and operation of fishing vessels and gear. *Length:* 500–1500 words. *Payment:* by arrangement. *Illustrations:* line and half-tone, photographs and diagrams.

WORLD OUTLOOK (formerly **THE LAYMAN**), B. W. Amey, 93 Gloucester Place, W1H 4AA. *T.* 01–935 1482.
5p. Q. (20p. per annum, by post 27½ p.).—Articles on world questions from a Christian standpoint. *Length:* from 1500 to 2000 words. *Payment:* £1·05 an article. No illustrations.

WORLD SPORTS, Don Wood, 23–27 Tudor Street, London, E.C.4. *T.* 01–583 9199.
15p. M.—Official magazine of the British Olympic Association. Sporting articles of international interest. *Length:* up to 2500 words. *Payment:* from £2·10 according to value and length. *Illustrations:* colour photographs, half-tone and line.

WORLD SURVEY (incorporating **THE BRITISH SURVEY** 1939), J. Eppstein, published by the Atlantic Education Trust, 23–25 Abbey House, 8 Victoria Street, London, S.W.1. *T.* 01–799 4471.
15p. or £1·75 per annum. M.—The main subject of each number is devoted to a particular country or one subject of international importance. Contributions are considered only from writers with personal knowledge of the country or subject treated. *Illustrations:* maps and photographs. *Length:* 9000–10,000 words. *Payment:* average £30–£40.

WORLD TOBACCO (June 1963), MICHAEL F. BARFORD, 17 John Adam Street, Adelphi, W.C.2. *T.* 01–839 6171.

$10 p.a. Q.—Practical features (1500–2000 words) for guidance or information of readers who are already experts, on any aspect of world tobacco manufacturing, distribution, promotion or production; tobacco news (in depth) from authoritative overseas sources—up to 500 words. *Payment:* by arrangement, from £15·75 per 1000 words. *Illustrations:* photographs, technical and freehand line drawings.

WORLD TODAY, THE (1945), MARGARET CORNELL, The Royal Institute of International Affairs, Chatham House, 10 St. James's Square, London, S.W.1. *T.* 01–930 2233. *T.A.* Areopagus, London.

20p. M.—Objective and factual articles on current questions of international affairs. *Length:* about 3500 words. *Payment:* £12·60 to £15·75 each article.

WORLD'S CHILDREN, THE (1920), the magazine of The Save the Children Fund, FRAN WILLISON, M.I.P.R. (Editorial Director) and JEAN BRAY (Editor), 29 Queen Anne's Gate, S.W.1. *T.* 01–930 2461.

5p. Q.—Articles on child welfare in all its aspects throughout the world, 1000 words. *Payment:* none. Photographs for cover and article illustration.

WORLD'S PAPER TRADE REVIEW (1879) E. F. J. DEAN (Stonhill and Gillis Ltd.), Lincoln House, 296–302, High Holborn, WC1V 7JS *T.* 01–405 7055. *T.A.* Stongillis, London, W.C.1.

15p. W. (Thursday).—Coverage of the pulp, paper and board making and paper converting industries; includes current news, technical and research developments, statistical and marketing information on an international scale. Outside contributions. *Payment:* according to merit. *Illustrations:* half-tone.

WRITER, THE, (1920), A. M. KOAWL, 124 New Bond Street, London, W1A 4LJ *T.* 01–629 4176.

20p. M.—Articles (from 300 to 1200 words) on all subjects of interest to writers, including legal, business and professional problems, news of markets. No fiction, verse, or biographical sketches of living writers. Contributions should be accompanied by brief biographical sketch of writer. Suggestions welcome. *Payment:* according to merit, from £2·10 per 1000 words.

WRITER'S REVIEW (1963), SYDNEY SHEPPARD, United Writers, Trevarren, St. Columb, Cornwall.

25p. Q.—Articles and fiction up to 5000 words. Practical articles on writing for publication. Auto-biographical details of present-day authors and journalists, also photographs of same. *Illustrations:* photographs and line drawings. Contributions from new writers welcomed. *Payment:* varies.

YACHTING AND BOATING WEEKLY, CHARLES E. JONES, Holborn Hall, 100 Gray's Inn Road, London, W.C.1. *T.* 01–242 9700.

7½p. W.—Articles up to 1500 words, illustrated, on practical matters to do with sailing and power boating. *Payment:* by arrangement. *Illustrations:* photos and black-and-white drawings; some colour transparencies, minimum 2¼" square.

YACHTING MONTHLY (1906), J. D. Sleightholme, 63 Long Acre, London, WC2E 9QF *T.* 01–836 2468.
20p.—Technical articles, up to 1500 words, on construction, marine engines, sailing, and general handling of yachts. Well-written accounts, up to 3000 words, of cruises in yachts. *Payment:* quoted on acceptance. *Illustrations:* line and wash drawings, first-class marine photographs.

YACHTING WORLD (1894), IPC Transport Press, Dorset House, Stamford Street, London, S.E.1.
25p. M.—Practical articles of an original nature dealing with sailing or motor-boating. Factual cruising or racing stories, 2000 to 3000 words. *Payment:* varies. *Illustrations:* photographs or drawings.

YACHTS AND YACHTING (1947), Peter Cook, 196 Eastern Esplanade, Southend-on-Sea, Essex. *T.* Southend-on-Sea 82171, 82245 and 82246.
17½p. F.—Short articles which should be technically correct. *Payment:* by arrangement. *Illustrations:* line and half-tone; occasional colour.

YORKSHIRE EVENING POST (1882), 2½p. **FOOTBALL PRESS,** 2½p. John White (York and County Press), 15 Coney Street, York. *T.* York 53051. London Office: Newspaper House, 8–16 Great New Street, E.C.4. *T.* 01–353 1030.
Articles of Yorkshire interest, humour, personal experience of current affairs. *Length:* 500–1500 words. *Payment:* £1–£6. *Illustrations:* half-tone and line.

YORKSHIRE GAZETTE AND HERALD SERIES, N. Railton, 15 Coney Street, York, YO1 1YN. *T.* York 53051.
2½p. W.—Stories and pictures of local interest. *Payment:* varies. *Illustrations:* half-tone and line.

YORKSHIRE LIFE (1947), Maurice Colbeck, 14 Dorrington Street, Leeds, LS2 8AR. *T.* Leeds 27271 and 27585. A publication of the Whitethorn Press, Ltd., Thomson House, Withy Grove, Manchester M60 4BL *T.* 834 1234.
15p. M.—Topics of Yorkshire interest, with or without photographs. Humour and topical subjects treated from a Yorkshire angle especially required. *Payment:* varies. *Illustrations:* half-tone and line; four-colour half-tone on cover. Preliminary letter advisable.

YORKSHIRE POST (1754), John Edwards, Wellington Street, Leeds, LS1 1RF. *T.* 32701. London Office: 23–27 Tudor Street, E.C.4. *T.* 01–583 9199.
2½p. D.—Conservative. Authoritative and well-written articles eludicating new topics or on topical subjects of general, literary or industrial interests are preferred. *Length:* 1200 words. *Payment:* minimum, £8·40 a column; more for authoritative articles. Contributions to *People,* a column about personalities in the news, are welcomed, especially if they have a North Country character. *Payment:* minimum 75p. an item. *Illustrations:* photographs and frequent pocket cartoons (single column width), topical whenever possible.

YORKSHIRE RIDINGS MAGAZINE (1964), Winston Halstead, 33 Beverley Road, Driffield, Yorkshire. *T.* Driffield 3232.
12½p. M.—Articles exclusively about people, life and character of the three Ridings of Yorkshire. *Length:* up to 1000 words. *Payment:* £2·10 per 1000 words minimum. *Illustrations:* line and half-tone.

YOUNG SOLDIER, THE (1881), Gladys Moon, the official gazette of the young people of The Salvation Army; 101 Queen Victoria Street, London, E.C.4. *T.* 01–236 5222. Ext. 216.
2½p. W.—Stories, pictures, and cartoon strips on Christian heroic themes. *Payment:* usual. *Illustrations:* half-tone and line.

RECENT CHANGES

The following changes of title, mergers and terminations of publication have recently taken place.

CHANGES OF NAME AND MERGERS

AEROPLANE   incorporated in FLIGHT INTERNATIONAL

ALL ABOUT CHILDREN   now NURSERY WORLD

THE AMATEUR HISTORIAN   now THE LOCAL HISTORIAN

AMATEUR TAPE RECORDING VIDEO AND HI-FI   see HI FI SOUND

ANGLERS WORLD   now merged with ANGLING

ANTI VIVISECTIONIST   now AV TIMES

ART AND CRAFT EDUCATION   now ART AND CRAFT IN EDUCATION

ASIAN REVIEW   now SOUTH ASIAN REVIEW

AUDIO RECORD REVIEW   incorporated in HI FI NEWS

BIRMINGHAM EVENING MAIL & DESPATCH   now BIRMINGHAM EVENING MAIL

BIRMINGHAM UNIVERSITY HISTORICAL JOURNAL   now MIDLAND HISTORY

BOTTLING   incorporated in BREWING TRADE REVIEW

BREWERS' JOURNAL   now INTERNATIONAL BREWERS JOURNAL

BRITISH SHOEMAN   see FOOTWEAR WEEKLY

BRITISH SURVEY   now incorporated in WORLD SURVEY

BUCKS LIFE   now BUCKS LIFE AND CHILTERN LIFE AND COUNTRYSIDE

BUILDING INDUSTRY NEWS   see CONTRACT JOURNAL

BUS AND COACH   now incorporated in MOTOR TRANSPORT

CAMERA OWNER   now CREATIVE CAMERA

CARWASH AND TRANSPORT CLEANING   now VEHICLE CLEANING NEWS

CATERERS' RECORD   now incorporated in CATERERS' ASSOCIATION BULLETIN

CATERING MANAGEMENT   now CATERING & HOTEL MANAGEMENT

CEMENT AND LIME MANUFACTURE   now CEMENT TECHNOLOGY

CLAYCRAFT   now CLAYCRAFT AND STRUCTURAL CERAMICS

CLIMBER   now CLIMBER AND RAMBLER

COINS AND MEDALS   now COINS

COLLIERY ENGINEERING   merged with MINING AND MINERALS ENGINEERING

COMMEMORATIVE ART   merged with STONE INDUSTRIES

COMMERCE   now COMMERCE INTERNATIONAL

CONCRETE BUILDING AND CONCRETE PRODUCTS   now PRECAST CONCRETE

CYCLING AND SPORTING CYCLIST   now CYCLING

DAILY CINEMA   now TODAYS CINEMA

DAILY WORKER   now MORNING STAR

DANCE AND BINGO NEWS   now LEISURE

DIESEL RAILWAY TRACTION   incorporated in RAILWAY GAZETTE

8MM MAGAZINE   now FILM MAKING

ENGINEERING AND BOILERHOUSE REVIEW   incorporated in WORKS ENGINEERING & FACTORY SERVICES

FAMILY PETS   merged with ANIMALS

FARM IMPLEMENT incorporated in AGRICULTURAL MACHINERY JOURNAL

FARM MECHANIZATION now merged into POWER FARMING

FERTILISER AND FEEDING STUFFS JOURNAL now FEED & FARM SUPPLIES

FISH INDUSTRY incorporated in WORLD FISHING

FURNITURE RECORD incorporated in CABINET MAKER & RETAIL FURNISHER

GIBBONS' STAMP MONTHLY now STAMP MONTHLY

GOLFING incorporated in GOLF WORLD

GOOD PHOTOGRAPHY merged with PHOTOGRAPHY

GRAPHIC TECHNOLOGY see PRINTING TRADES JOURNAL

THE GUIDE now TODAY'S GUIDE

HERDER CORRESPONDENCE incorporated in THE MONTH

HOSPITAL MANAGEMENT PLANNING & EQUIPMENT now HOSPITAL MANAGEMENT

HOTEL & CATERING TIMES now CATERING TIMES

HOTEL & RESTAURANT MANAGEMENT now CATERING & HOTEL MANAGEMENT

HOUSE BEAUTIFUL merged with GOOD HOUSEKEEPING

INDUSTRIAL HANDLING now merged with INDUSTRIAL EQUIPMENT NEWS

JOHN O' LONDON'S merged with BOOKS and BOOKMEN

LAND AND PROPERTY incorporated in THE VALUER

LIFE OF THE SPIRIT incorporated in NEW BLACKFRIARS

LIGHT CRAFT now SMALL BOAT

LION now LION AND EAGLE

LLOYD'S LIST AND SHIPPING GAZETTE now LLOYD'S LIST

LONDON QUARTERLY & HOLBORN REVIEW see CHURCH QUARTERLY

LONDON TEACHER see CENTRE POINT

MACHINE DESIGN ENGINEERING now MACHINE DESIGN & CONTROL

MACHINERY now MACHINERY AND PRODUCTION ENGINEERING

MAN MADE TEXTILES incorporated in TEXTILE MONTH

MEDICAL WORLD NEWSLETTER now incorporated in MEDICAL WORLD

MODEL AIRCRAFT incorporated in AEROMODELLER

MODERN MOTHER & BABYWORLD now MODERN MOTHER

MODERN REFRIGERATION AND AIR CONDITIONING now REFRIGERATION AND AIR CONDITIONING

MUSIC TEACHER AND PIANO STUDENT now MUSIC TEACHER

NATIONAL CHRISTIAN NEWS now COMPASS NEWSPAPERS

NEW CHRISTIAN merged with THE CHRISTIAN CENTURY

NEW EDUCATION now NEW UNIVERSITY AND NEW EDUCATION

NEW YORK TIMES INTERNATIONAL EDITION see INTERNATIONAL HERALD TRIBUNE

OFFICE METHODS AND MACHINES now MANAGEMENT IN ACTION

OUTLOOK merged with CHURCH NEWS

PAPER PACKS now CONVERTING INDUSTRY

PARENT incorporated in MOTHER

PASSENGER TRANSPORT merged with BUSES

PERSONNEL AND TRAINING MANAGEMENT now PERSONNEL MANAGEMENT

P.L.A. MONTHLY now PORT OF LONDON

PLAYHOUR now PLAYHOUR AND ROBIN

POPULAR CAMPING now CAMPING

POPULAR GARDENING AND HOME GARDENING now POPULAR GARDENING

POTTERY GAZETTE AND GLASS TRADE REVIEW now TABLEWARE INTERNATIONAL +
  POTTERY GAZETTE
POWER AND WORKS ENGINEERING now WORKS ENGINEERING AND FACTORY
  SERVICES
PRACTICAL DECORATING & BUILDING now PRACTICAL HOME BUILDING & DECORAT-
  ING
SCHOOL FRIEND merged with JUNE
SCHOOL LIBRARIAN AND SCHOOL LIBRARY REVIEW now SCHOOL LIBRARIAN
S. F. IMPULSE incorporated in NEW WORLDS
SHOP REVIEW now SHOP FITTING INTERNATIONAL
SKINNER'S RECORD incorporated in TEXTILE MONTH
SMALLWARES incorporated in DRAPERY AND FASHION WEEKLY
SOFT DRINKS AND ALLIED TRADES REVIEW now SOFT DRINKS TRADE JOURNAL
SUPPLIES incorporated in PURCHASING JOURNAL
SURVEYOR & MUNICIPAL ENGINEER now SURVEYOR-LOCAL GOVERNMENT
  TECHNOLOGY
SYREN AND SHIPPING incorporated in SHIPPING WORLD AND SHIPBUILDER
TAPE RECORDER now STUDIO SOUND
TECHNICAL EDUCATION AND INDUSTRIAL TRAINING now EDUCATION AND TRAINING
TECHNICAL PUBLICATIONS now INDUSTRIAL AND SCIENTIFIC COMMUNICATION
TERRITORIAL MAGAZINE now TAVR
TEXTILE WEEKLY now TEXTILE NEWS
THEATRE WORLD incorporated in PLAYS AND PLAYERS
TIGER/HURRICANE now TIGER AND JAG
TINA now PRINCESS TINA
TIT BITS now SATURDAY TITBITS
TOBACCO WORLD merged with CONFECTIONERY & TOBACCO NEWS
WINE AND SPIRIT TRADE REVIEW now OFF LICENCE NEWS
WORLD POWER ENGINEERING incorporated in MACHINERY LLOYD
WORLDS PRESS NEWS now CAMPAIGN

MAGAZINES CEASED PUBLICATION

AFRICAN WORLD
AIRPORT AUTHORITY
AMERICAN ABROAD
ANGLICAN WORLD
AU PLAISIR
AUSTIN MAGAZINE
AUTOCAMPING
AVA MAGAZINE
BOOKS
BOYS' WORLD
BRITISH JOURNAL OF MEDICAL
  HYPNOTISM
  BRITISH STATIONER
BRITISH TRADE JOURNAL AND EXPORT
  WORLD

BUILDING INDUSTRIES AND
  SCOTTISH ARCHITECT
CASINO INTERNATIONAL GAMING
  MAGAZINE
CATERING & EQUIPMENT NEWS
CHRISTIAN & CHRISTIANITY TODAY
CHURCH QUARTERLY REVIEW
COUNTRY FAIR
DOGS LIFE
DUBLIN REVIEW
EAGLE
EASY MAGAZINE
EDGAR WALLACE MYSTERY MAGAZINE
ENGINEERING NEWS
FARM NEWS

FASHION
FISHING
FLYING REVIEW INTERNATIONAL
FRONT LINE LIBRARY
FURNITURE DESIGN
GIGGLE
GOOD LIFE
HELP
HOMECARE
HIBBERT JOURNAL
HOSPITAL LAUNDRY NEWS
HOTEL & CATERING REVIEW
HOUSEWIFE
INDUSTRIAL ARCHITECTURE
INDUSTRIAL ELECTRONICS
INTERBUILD
INTERIOR DESIGN
INTERNATIONAL PLASTICS ENGINEERING
INTRO
IRISH ACCOUNTANT AND SECRETARY
IRISH ECCLESIASTICAL RECORD
ISLANDER
JEWISH WOMAN
LA FRANCE
LINK
LOOK WESTWARD
MACHINE SHOP AND ENGINEERING
   MANUFACTURE
MAINTENANCE
MEASUREMENT & CONTROL
MESSENGER OF THE DIVINE CHILD
METALS
METALWORKING EQUIPMENT NEWS
METHODIST MAGAZINE
MIDLAND HAIRDRESSER AND BEAUTY
   SPECIALIST
MINIATURE AUTO
MODEL GIRL, BEAUTY AND HAIRSTYLES
MODERN MOTORING AND TRAVEL
MODERN TRANSPORT
MOTOR CYCLE & CYCLE EXPORT
   TRADER
MOTOR RACING
MOTORING
MUSIC MAKER
MUSIC TRADES REVIEW
NEW DEPARTURES
NEW HEALTH

NOTTINGHAMSHIRE GUARDIAN
NUMBER
OUTDOOR ADVERTISING
OXFORDSHIRE & BERKSHIRE LIFE AND
   COUNTRYSIDE
PERSONNEL MAGAZINE
PLASTICS
PLEBS
POINT OF PURCHASE MARKETING
POULTRY FARMER
POW
PREACHERS QUARTERLY
PRINT IN BRITAIN
PRODUCTION METHODS AND MACHINES
PSYCHOLOGY AND SUCCESSFUL LIVING
QUARTERLY REVIEW
REVIEW OF ENGLISH LITERATURE
RHODESIA AND EASTERN AFRICA
ROBIN
ROSE
SAFETY FAST
SCOOTER AND THREE WHEELER
SECRET AGENT LIBRARY
SERVICE MANAGER
SHOWTIME
SPHERE
SSTA MAGAZINE
STORES & SHOPS
STUPENDOUS LIBRARY
TELEVISION WEEKLY
TEXSTYLE
TEXTILE RECORDER
TIMES REVIEW OF INDUSTRY AND
   TECHNOLOGY
TOBACCONIST AND CONFECTIONER
TOWN
T.V. WORLD
UNDERWATER WORLD
VIEWER
VOICE OF WELSH INDUSTRY
WHAM!
WHOLESALE CONFECTIONER AND YEAR
   BOOK
WINTER SPORTS
WOMAN'S VIEW
YACHTSMAN
YOUNG FARMER
YOUTH

THE COMMONWEALTH,
THE USA AND SOUTH AFRICA

The lists on the following pages contain only a selection of the journals which offer some market for the free-lance. To print, and to keep up-to-date, a complete list for each English-speaking country would increase the extent and cost of the Year Book quite disproportionately to the value of such enlargement. For the overseas market for stories and articles is small, and editors often prefer their fiction to have a local setting.

The larger newspapers and magazines buy many of their stories, as the smaller papers buy general articles, through one or other of the well-known syndicates, and a writer may be well advised to send printed copies of stories he has had published at home to an agent for syndication overseas.

Most of the big newspapers depend for news on their own staffs and the press agencies. The most important papers have permanent representatives in Britain who keep them supplied, not only with news of especial interest to the country concerned, but also with regular summaries of British news and with articles on events of particular importance. While many overseas journals have a London office, it is usual for MSS. from free-lance contributors to be submitted to the head-quarters' editorial office overseas.

There are a good many small magazines and periodicals of an ephemeral nature, especially in India and Pakistan, and would-be contributors must be prepared for disappointment and not infrequently to hear no more of a MS. submitted to some such publications.

When sending MSS, abroad it is important to remember to enclose International Reply Coupons. These cost 6p. each and can be exchanged in any foreign country for stamps representing the minimum postage payable on a letter sent from that country to this country.

Commonwealth Reply Coupons (price 3p. each) are valid only within the Commonwealth and the Irish Republic. They are exchangeable for stamp or stamps representing the minimum postage payable on a letter sent by surface route from that country to this country.

AUSTRALIAN JOURNALS AND MAGAZINES

NOTE.—*Newspapers are listed under the towns in which they are published.*

ADAM (1945), F. C. FOLKARD (The K. G. Murray Publishing Co. Pty. Ltd.), 142 Clarence Street, Sydney, 2000, N.S.W.
   35c. M.—Fiction and general articles. *Length:* 2500 to 5000 words. *Payment:* from $7.00 per 1000 words.

(ADELAIDE) ADVERTISER (1858), B. A. WILLIAMS, Adelaide. London: 110 Fleet Street, E.C.4. *T.* 01–353 5141.
   5c. D.—The only morning daily in S. Australia. Descriptive and news background material, 400–800 words, preferably with pictures. *Payment:* minimum 3c. a line.

(ADELAIDE) CHRONICLE (1858), K. M. Esau, King William and Waymouth Streets, Adelaide, 5001, S. Australia. London: Ludgate House, 110 Fleet Street, E.C.4. *T.* 01-353 3160.

> 10c. W.—Mainly agricultural and horticultural articles with photographs. *Payment:* $4.80 per column of 16 inches minimum. *Illustrations:* line and halftone.

(ADELAIDE) NEWS (SOUTH AUSTRALIA) (1923), Ronald R. Boland, 116 North Terrace, Adelaide. *T.* 51-0351.

> 5c. D.—One feature page open for topical articles. *Length:* preferably 300-600. *Payment:* $10.50—$21. Illustrated articles preferred.

(ADELAIDE) SUNDAY MAIL (1912), Mark Day, 116 North Terrace, Adelaide, 5000. *T.* 51-0351.

> 10 cents. W.

AUSTRALIAN BOOK REVIEW, Max Harris, Rosemary Wighton, 27 Park Road, Kensington Park, South Australia 5068.

> 50c. M.—Literary and general book criticism. *Length:* 600-2000 words. *Payment:* $12 to $40 by arrangement. *Illustrations:* colour and halftone.

AUSTRALIAN FINANCIAL REVIEW, THE, V. J. Carroll, Sydney. London: 85 Fleet Street, E.C.4. *T.* 01-353 5507. New York: 1501 Broadway, N.Y. 10036. *T.* 536-6835.

> 5c. D. (except Saturday & Sunday).—Investment business and economic news and reviews; government and politics, production, banking, commercial, and Stock Exchange statistics; company analysis.

AUSTRALIAN HARNESS SPORT, Paceway Publications, 140 Phillip Street Sydney, 2000, G.P.O. Box 268.

> M.—Anything of interest to followers of trotting and pacing in Australia and New Zealand. Overseas (especially European) news items and photos especially welcome. Special articles also considered up to 3,000 words. *Illustrations:* photograph, line and colour. *Payment:* according to length and general interest to Australian and New Zealand light harness sport patrons.

AUSTRALIAN HOME BEAUTIFUL, THE (1913), Lyle D. Tucker, 44 Flinders Street, Melbourne. London: 110 Fleet Street, E.C.4. *T.* 01-353 5141.

> 30c. M.—Deals with home building, interior decoration, furnishing, gardening, cookery, etc. Short articles with accompanying photographs with Australian slant accepted. *Preliminary letter* advisable. *Payment:* higher than Australian average, with special recognition for outstanding work.

AUSTRALIAN HOME JOURNAL (1894), Australian Consolidated Press, Telegraph House, 54–58 Park Street, Sydney, 2000, N.S.W. London: Australian Consolidated Press Ltd., 107 Fleet Street, London, E.C.4. *T.* 01-353 1040.

> 35c. M.—Homemaker magazine, with strong emphasis on home design, furniture, furnishing, room settings, materials, fabrics etc. Also uses "how to makes", sewing ideas and handyman construction projects. A few light features on home topics but no fiction. Aims to appeal to the young homemaker and housewife. *Illustrations:* sketches and photographs (colour and mono). *Payment:* according to length and merit.

AUSTRALIAN HOT-RODDING REVIEW (1965), M. Dunstan (The K. G. Murray Publishing Co. Pty. Ltd.), 142 Clarence Street, Sydney, 2000, N.S.W.

> 30c. M.—Articles up to 2500 words on hot-rodding subjects, including conversions, technical features. *Payment:* by arrangement. *Illustrations:* half-tone and line.

AUSTRALIAN JOURNAL OF POLITICS AND HISTORY, THE, Prof. GORDON GREENWOOD, University of Queensland Press, St. Lucia, Brisbane, Queensland. $2.00; $5.25 U.K. £2 10s. inc. postage. April, August, December.—Australian, Commonwealth and international articles. *Length:* 9000 words maximum, No *payment.* Necessary line *illustrations* only.

AUSTRALIAN MINING, Thomson Publications Australia Pty. Ltd., 47 Chippen Street, Chippendale 2008, N.S.W. $6 p.a. in Australia; £12 p.a. overseas.

AUSTRALIAN OUTDOORS (1947), D. KELLY (The K. G. Murray Publishing Co. Pty. Ltd.), 142 Clarence Street, Sydney, 2000, N.S.W. 30c. M.—Articles of 1000–3000 words on hunting, shooting, fishing, bush-sciences. *Payment:* from $9.00 per 1000 words. *Illustrations:* half-tone and line.

AUSTRALIAN OUTLOOK, THE, J. L. RICHARDSON, 124–6 Jolimont Road, East Melbourne, Victoria 3002. *T.* 63 6199. $1.35. 3 times p.a.—Scholarly articles on international affairs. *Length:* approx. 5000 words. No *payment.*

AUSTRALIAN QUARTERLY, THE (1929), J. H. MANT, Australian Institute of Political Science, Hosking House, 84½ Pitt Street, Sydney, 2000. *T.* 289544. 75c. Q—Articles of high standard on politics, law, economics, social sciences, international affairs, etc. Book reviews and drama. *Length:* by arrangement with the Editor. No *payment.*

AUSTRALIAN SPORTFISHING, R. B. HUNGERFORD, Managing Editor, Incorporated Press Pty. Ltd., 243 Elizabeth Street, Sydney. *T.* 26 1368. 40c. Stories of up to 3500 words on fishing as a sport. *Illustrations:* line and half-tone. *Payment:* by arrangement.

AUSTRALIAN SPORTING SHOOTER, R. B. HUNGERFORD, Managing Editor, Incorporated Press Pty. Ltd., 243 Elizabeth Street, Sydney. *T.* 26 1368 40c. All aspects of game shooting, collecting, antiques, archery, (associated with hunting), pistol shooting, clay target shooting, reloading, ballistics and articles of a technical nature. *Payment:* by arrangement.

AUSTRALIAN WOMEN'S WEEKLY, THE, Mrs. ESME FENSTON (Australian Consolidated Press Ltd.), 168 Castlereagh Street, Sydney, N.S.W., 2000. London: Australian Consolidated Press Ltd., 107 Fleet Street, E.C.4. *T.* 01-353 1040. 20c. W. (Wednesday).—Short stories and serials. *Length:* short stories, 3000 to 6000 words. *Payment:* according to length and merit. *Illustrations:* sketches by own artists.

(BRISBANE) COURIER MAIL, J. R. ATHERTON (Queensland Newspapers Pty., Ltd.), Campbell Street, Bowen Hills, Brisbane, 4000. 5c. D.—Occasional topical special articles required, 1000 words.

(BRISBANE) SUNDAY MAIL, H. G. TURNER, G.P.O. Box No. 130, Brisbane, Queensland, 4001. London: 110 Fleet Street, E.C.4. 7c. W.—Anything of interest, especially Queensland or Australian. Up to 1500 words. *Illustrations:* line, photographs, black and white, and colour. *Payment:* by arrangement. Rejected MSS. returned if postage enclosed.

(BRISBANE) TELEGRAPH (1872), J. Wakefield, Editor-in-Chief (Telegraph Newspaper Co. Pty. Ltd.), Campbell Street, Bowen Hills, Brisbane, 4006. 4c. D.

CATHOLIC WEEKLY, Kevin Hilferty (Catholic Press Newspaper Co. Ltd.), 104–106 Campbell Street, Surrey Hill 2010, N.S.W. *T.* 2114499.
10c. W.—Articles of general Catholic interest. *Length:* up to 2000 words. *Payment:* standard rates. *Illustrations:* half-tone.

COMMERCIAL FISHING & MARKETING, Keith Bresch Pty. Ltd., 140 Phillip Street, Sydney, 2000; G.P.O. Box 268.
M.—Articles of general interest to the commercial fishing and marketing industries. Photographs of overseas fishing activities etc. Articles on new developments, techniques, processes, by arrangement. *Payment:* according to length and informative interest to Australian and New Zealand fishing and marketing industries. Rejected m.s. and photos returned if postage enclosed.

COUNTRYMAN, THE. Herzel W. Baker, Newspaper House, St. George's Terrace, Perth 6000. *T.* 21–0161. *T.A.* Westralian, Perth. London: 107 Fleet Street, E.C.4.
10c. W. (Thursday).—Agriculture, farming or country interest features and serials. *Payment:* standard rates. *Illustrations:* line and half-tone.

ELECTRICAL ENGINEER, Thomson Publications (Australia) Pty. Ltd., Box 65, P.O., Chippendale, N.S.W., 2008. M.—$6 per year Australia, New Zealand and New Guinea; $12 per year elsewhere.

ELECTRONICS AUSTRALIA (incorporating **RADIO, TELEVISION AND HOBBIES** (1939)), W. N. Williams, 235–243 Jones Street, Broadway, Sydney. London: 85 Fleet Street, E.C.4.
40c. M.—Illustrated magazine devoted to technical television and radio, popular electronics, avionics. *Length:* up to 3000 words. *Payment:* by arrangement. *Illustrations:* line, half-tone.

HISTORICAL STUDIES (formerly Historical Studies—Australia and New Zealand), Melbourne University, Parkville, Melbourne 3052.
$A.3.50; £2 $.U.S.4.50. Twice yearly.—*Length:* 8000 words maximum. No *payment.* No *illustrations.*

INDUSTRIAL MANAGEMENT, Thomson Publications Australia Pty. Ltd., 47 Chippen Street, Chippendale, N.S.W., 2008.
$1. $12 per year. M.—Articles on industrial management.

LABOR NEWS, Laurie Short, 188 George Street, Sydney, 2000, New South Wales. M.—Official Journal Federated Ironworkers' Association of Australia.

(LAUNCESTON) EXAMINER, F. G. N. Ewence, Box 99a P.O. Launceston, Tasmania, 7250. *T.* 22211. *T.A.* Examiner, Launceston, Tasmania. *Telex:* 58511. 5c. D.

(LAUNCESTON) SUNDAY EXAMINER-EXPRESS, Box 99A, P.O. Launceston, Tasmania, 7250. *T.* 22211.
5c. W. (Sunday).

MAN (1936), C. Ruhen (The K. G. Murray Publishing Co. Pty., Ltd.), 142 Clarence Street, Sydney, 2000, N.S.W.
50c. M.—Fiction and general. *Length:* 2500 to 5000 words. *Payment:* from $8 per 1000 words. Photo prints from $3 each. Special rates for special material.

MAN JUNIOR (1937), F. C. Folkard (The K. G. Murray Publishing Co. Pty., Ltd.), 142 Clarence Street, Sydney, 2000, N.S.W.
40c. M.—Fiction and general articles. *Length:* 2000 to 6000 words. *Payment:* from $7.00 per 1000 words.

MEANJIN QUARTERLY (1940), C. B. CHRISTESEN, O.B.E., The University of Melbourne, Parkville, 3052, Victoria. *Subscription;* $A.8 p.a. (post paid).

Authoritative articles and essays (not necessarily Australian) dealing with literature, art, drama, education, the humanities, national and international affairs, of permanent rather than temporary interest. Specialises in short stories and poetry of high quality; book reviews; illustrations. *Length:* 2000–5000 words. *Payment:* on acceptance according to quality and length.

(MELBOURNE) AGE, E. G. PERKIN (David Syme & Co. Ltd.), 250 Spencer Street, Melbourne.   London: The Times Building, Printing House Square, E.C.4. *T.* 01–353 4388.

5c.   D.—Independent liberal morning daily. Room occasionally for outside matter. There are magazine and women's pages daily and a supplement (Junior Age) for children every Friday. An illustrated weekend magazine and literary review is published on Saturday. Accepts articles and photographs of literary interest and popular appeal of 500–1500 words. *Payment:* from $30 per column.

(MELBOURNE) AUSTRALIAN POST, JACK HUGHES, Herald and Weekly Times, 44 Flinders Street, Melbourne.   London: Ludgate House, 110 Fleet Street, E.C.4.

15c.   W.—Opening for casual contributions of factual illustrated articles. All contributions must have Australian interest. Male appeal. *Payment:* average $25 (Aust.) per 800–1000 words plus $10 (minimum) per picture.

(MELBOURNE) HERALD, STUART BROWN, 44–74 Flinders Street, Melbourne. *T.* 63–0211. London: 110 Fleet Street, E.C.4. *T.* 01–353 5786.

4c.   D.—Evening broadsheet with greatest evening circulation in Australia. Articles with or without illustrations. *Length:* up to 750 words. *Payment:* on merit. *Illustrations:* half-tone and line.

(MELBOURNE) SUN NEWS PICTORIAL (1922), H. A. GORDON, 44–74 Flinders Street, Melbourne, 3000.

4c.   D.—Topical articles to 750 words. *Payment:* above standard rates. *Illustrations:* general interest, fashion, sport.

NEW IDEA, THE (1902), JOY HAYES, 32 Walsh, Melbourne, 3001. *T.* 300241.

15c.   W.—Woman's journal of fashions, beauty service, knitting patterns, short stories, and reading matter of general interest to women of all ages. Short stories and articles purchased: stories, 1500 to 4000 words; articles, 1200 to 2000 words. *Payment* (based on $A): on acceptance. Minimum $6.50 per 1000 words. *Illustrations:* good pictures of general interest and fashion.

NEWCASTLE MORNING HERALD AND MINERS' ADVOCATE (1858), E. K. LINGARD, 28–30 Bolton Street, Newcastle, 2300, N.S.W. *T.* 2–0471. 7c.   D.

NEWCASTLE SUN, THE (1918), K. BROCK, 28–30 Bolton Street, Newcastle 2300. *T.* 2–0471.   7c.   D.   (Monday to Friday afternoons).

OVERLAND, S. MURRAY-SMITH, G.P.O. Box 98A, Melbourne, Victoria.

50c.   (Aust.).   Q.—Literary and general, Australian material preferred. *Payment:* by arrangement. *Illustrations:* line blocks.

PEOPLE, K. FINLAY, G.P.O. Box 2728, Sydney, 2001. *T.* 2O 944.

20c.   F.—Informative stories of personal achievement and adventure in all fields of human endeavour, with special emphasis on the Australian scene; all illustrated with photographs and/or artwork.

(PERTH) DAILY NEWS (1840), D. O'SULLIVAN, Newspaper House, St. George's Terrace, Perth 6000.   London: 107 Fleet Street, E.C.4.

5c.   D.   (Evening).—Accepts special articles on subjects of outstanding interest and offers some scope for the free-lance. *Payment:* according to merit, on publication. *Illustrations:* photographs, cartoons, and comics.

(PERTH) SUNDAY TIMES (1897), 34 Stirling Street, Perth 6000, Western Australia. *T.* 28–8000.

8c. W.—Topical articles to 800 words. *Payment:* standard rates on acceptance.

(PERTH) WEST AUSTRALIAN, THE (1833), G. RICHARDS, Newspaper House, St. George's Terrace, Perth 6000. *T.* 21–0161. *T.A.* "Westralian", Perth. London: 107 Fleet Street, E.C.4.

5c. D.—Articles and sketches about people and events in Australia and abroad. *Length:* 300–700 words. *Payment:* Award rates or better. *Illustrations:* line or half-tone.

PIX (National weekly news-pictorial), ROBERT J. NELSON, Sun-Herald Building, Broadway, Sydney, N.S.W. *T.* 20 944. London: 85 Fleet Street, E.C.4. *T.* 01–353 5507.

20c. W.—Mainly pictorial, but good documentary subjects needed. Photographs depicting exciting happenings, candid camera pictures of events affecting Australians, glamour and show business, modern-living features, and complete series of any subject such as unusual industries, rites, customs, etc. *Payment:* on highest Australian scale.

POETRY AUSTRALIA (1964), GRACE PERRY, South Head Press, 350 Lyons Road, Fivedock, Sydney, 2046, N.S.W. *T.* 83. 9754.

$1.00. Bi-M.—Poetry and review articles concerned with new verse, or re-evaluations of verse, or verse criticism. *Payment:* $A.4 a page (minimum).

QUADRANT, JAMES MCAULEY and PETER COLEMAN, 181 Clarence Street, Sydney 2000, New South Wales. *T.* 29 5899.

75c. Bi-M.—Articles, short stories, verse, etc. *Length:* 2000–5000 words. *Payment:* up to $70 per article. *Illustrations:* none.

SEACRAFT (1946), PAUL HOPKINS (The K. G. Murray Publishing Co. Pty., Ltd.), 142 Clarence Street, Sydney, 2000, N.S.W.

35c. M.—Articles up to 2000 words on yachting, seamanship, marine engines, naval design; technical data and high-quality illustrations. *Payment:* from $6.50 (Aust.) per 1000 words. *Illustrations:* half-tone and line.

SPORTS CAR WORLD (1956), K. WOLFE (The K. G. Murray Publishing Co. Pty., Ltd.), 142 Clarence Street, Sydney, 2000, N.S.W.

35c. M.—Articles up to 2500 words on subjects allied to the sports car, motor sport etc. *Payment:* by arrangement. *Illustrations:* half-tone and line.

SUNDAY TRUTH, R. C. JOHNSTON (Mirror Newspapers Limited), Brunswick and McLachlan Streets, Fortitude Valley, Brisbane, 4006. *T.* 50131. London Office: Keystone House, Red Lion Court, Fleet Street, E.C.4. 7c. W. (Sunday).

SUN-HERALD, THE (Sunday edition of *The Sydney Morning Herald* and the *Sun*), F. R. PETERSON, Sydney. London: 85 Fleet Street, E.C.4. *T.* 01–353 5507.

10c. W.—Topical articles to 1000 words; has sections on show business, finance, fashion and other articles of interest to women. Payment as for *The Sydney Morning Herald.*

(SYDNEY) BULLETIN (1880), DONALD HORNE, 54 Park Street, Sydney, N.S.W. *T.* 2–0666. London: Australian Consolidated Press, 107 Fleet Street, E.C.4. *T.* 01–353 1040. New York: Australian Consolidated Press, Room 401, 1501 Broadway, New York, N.Y., 10036. *T.* 212–563 6865.

30c. W. (Wednesday).—Concerned mainly with reporting Australia to Australians, or the world from an Australian aspect. *Payment:* by arrangement.

(SYDNEY) DAILY MIRROR (1941), Chairman of Directors: K. S. MAY, Kippax Street, Sydney. *T.* 2–0924.

5c. D.—Accept modernly written feature articles and series of Australian or world interest. Length: 1000 to 2000 words. *Payment:* according to merit and length.

(SYDNEY) DAILY TELEGRAPH (Australian Consolidated Press Ltd.), J. KING WATSON, 168 Castlereagh Street, Sydney, 2000, N.S.W. *T.* 20–666. London: Australian Consolidated Press, 107 Fleet Street, E.C.4. *T.* 01–353 1040.

5c. D.—Feature articles, based on topical events, 800–1200 words.

SYDNEY MORNING HERALD, THE (1831), J. M. D. PRINGLE, Sydney. London: 85 Fleet Street, E.C.4. *T.* 01–353 5507.

5 cents. D.—Saturday edition has pages of literary criticism and also magazine articles. Topical articles not more than 1200 words. *Payment:* varies, but minimum of $30.00 per 1000 words. All types of illustrations acceptable.

(SYDNEY) NATION, Nation Review Company, Box 112 G.P.O., Sydney, 2001, New South Wales.

(SYDNEY) SUN (1910), B. J. TIER, Jones Street, Broadway, Sydney. *T.* 2O 944. London: 85 Fleet Street, E.C.4. *T.* 01–353 5507. Business: 01–353 1146.

5c. D.—Topical articles, 900 to 1500 words, particularly on international subjects. *Payment:* from $30 according to length and quality. *Illustrations:* line or half-tone.

(SYDNEY) SUNDAY MIRROR (1961), Chairman of Directors: K. S. MAY, Kippax Street, Sydney. *T.* 2–0924.

10c. (Sunday).—Accept illustrated features and series, modernly written feature articles and series of Australian or world interest. *Length:* 1000 to 2000 words. *Payment:* according to merit and length.

TV TIMES (1958), C. N. DAY, 630 George Street, Sydney, 2000. *T.* 31–9211.

10c. W. (Wednesday).—Devoted exclusively to TV stories, programmes and background. *Length:* 800 words. *Payment:* $12 *Illustrations:* Half-tone.

WALKABOUT (1934), Publisher: Australian National Travel Association; Commercial manager: TERENCE YOUNG. Editor: JOHN ROSS, 18 Collins Street, Melbourne, 3000, Australia. *T.* 63–9064. *T.A.* "Antas", Melbourne.

40c. M.—All aspects (illustrated) of life, people and places in Australia and its territories. *Length:* 1000–2500 words. *Payment:* $A.30 to $A.65 per article. *Photographs:* black and white from $A.5.00, colour $A.5.00 to $A.21.00. Pictures should be lively, showing people where possible. Special rates for picture stories and series.

WEEKEND NEWS, F. DEVINE, Newspaper House, St. George's Terrace, Perth 6000. Western Australia. *T.* 21–0161. *T.A.* Westralian, Perth. London: 107 Fleet Street, E.C.4.

8c. W.—Articles, radio and television stories, non-fiction serials. Highly technical articles not required. *Payment:* standard rates. *Illustrations:* line, half-tone.

WHEELS (1953), R. LUCK, (The K. G. Murray Publishing Co. Pty. Ltd.), 142 Clarence Street, Sydney, 2000, N.S.W.

40c. M.—Articles up to 2500 words on motoring, motor sport, history of motoring, technical developments; all strictly authentic, preferably by specialist writers. *Payment:* by agreement. *Illustrations:* half-tone and line.

WOMAN'S DAY WITH WOMAN, JOAN REEDER, Broadway, Sydney. *T.* 20944.

20c. W.—National women's magazine: news, fiction, fashion, general articles, cookery, home economy, T.V. Circulation in excess of 500,000. Printed in gravure.

CANADIAN JOURNALS AND MAGAZINES

NOTE.—*Newspapers are listed under the towns in which they are published.*

BEAVER, MALVINA BOLUS (Hudson's Bay Co.), 77 Main Street, Winnipeg, 1, Manitoba. *T.* WH 3–0881. London: Beaver House, Great Trinity Lane, E.C.4. *T.* 01–236 3223.

24s. p.a. Q.—Articles, historical and modern in the sphere of Hudson's Bay Company's activities. *Length:* 1500 to 3000 words, with illustrations. *Payment:* on acceptance; about 5 cents a word. *Illustrations:* photographs, or drawings. Black-and-white.

CANADIAN AUTHOR AND BOOKMAN, GLADYS TAYLOR, 3 Daleena Drive, Don Mills, Ontario. *T.* 444–7188.

$2.50 ($3 in Great Britain) a year. Q.—The official organ of the Canadian Authors Association. Criticism, articles on the writer's craft and general literary articles 1000 words. Occasional poetry of high quality. The Editor cannot accept responsibility for safe return of unsolicited MSS. No payment, at present.

CANADIAN AVIATION (1927), HUGH WHITTINGTON (Maclean-Hunter Ltd.), 481 University Avenue, Toronto 2, Ontario. *T.* (416) 362–5311. London: Maclean-Hunter Ltd., 30 Old Burlington Street, W1X 3AD.

$12 (Gt. Britain) p.a. M.—Stories with a Canadian angle, on civil or military aviation. *Payment:* $50 per 1000 words minimum. *Photographs:* $5 each minimum.

CANADIAN GEOGRAPHICAL JOURNAL (1930), Major-General W. J. MEGILL, 488 Wilbrod Street, Ottawa, 2, Ontario. *T.* 613–236 7493.

$8 a year the world. M.—Organ of Royal Can. Geog. Soc. Articles 2000 to 3000 words dealing with any part of the world. Preference to Canadian and Commonwealth settings. Must be amply illustrated with photographs. *Preliminary letter* advisable. *Payment:* 3 cent per word. Glossy prints.

CANADIAN MAGAZINE STAR WEEKLY, THE, Fiction to: GWEN COWLEY. Articles to: DICK BROWN, 401 Bay Street, Toronto 103, Ontario. *T.* 363–7151.

20 cents. W.—Complete novel, condensing to 26,000 words for use in one issue. Rates vary, $800 up for novels. Like strongly plotted original manuscript novels, with plenty of action and colour. Novels should appeal to men and women readers. Topical articles of Canadian interest as: new developments in the political, industrial and medical fields; profiles of prominent persons in the news; trends and personalities in sport; entertainment scene; features about controversial subjects. 1500–3000 words. *Payment:* varies, but starts at $250 for full features—on acceptance.

CANADIAN POETRY (1936), ARTHUR S. BOURINOT, P.O. Box 2033, Stn. D., Ottawa.

$2 per annum. Q.—Poems of all kinds. *Payment:* no payment at present; one copy of edition in which poem appears and tear sheet. Accompany all MSS, with s.a.e.

CHATELAINE, 481 University Avenue, Toronto, Canada.
    35 cents.   M.—Articles with woman's slant used; Canadian angle preferred; interested in first short stories and serials, romance, marriage, adventure, children.   *Payment:* on acceptance; from $300 for non-fiction, $400 for fiction. *Illustrations:* by leading artists in Canada and the U.S.

COUNTRY GUIDE, DON BARON, Winnipeg 21, Manitoba, Canada. *T.* 774–1861.
    30 cents., $3 a year outside Canada. M.—Authoritative articles on farming and rural subjects. *Length:* up to 1500 words with good black-and-white pictures. Preferable to query before submitting articles. *Payment:* articles up to $75. Fiction: 2000–3000 words. Wholesome, rural text; first rights up to $125, second rights considered. *Payment:* on acceptance.

DALHOUSIE REVIEW, THE, Editor: C. L. BENNET, Associate Editor: M. G. PARKS. Dalhousie University, Halifax, N.S., Canada.
    $1.00. $4 p.a., or $10.00 for 3 years. Q.—Articles on literary, political, historical, educational and social topics; fiction; verse. *Length:* prose, not more than 5000 words; verse, up to 300 words. *Payment:* $1 per printed page; $3 per printed page for verse. Contributors also receive one copy of issue and 25 offprints of their work. Not more than one story and two or three short poems in any one issue.

MACLEAN'S MAGAZINE, PHILIP SYKES, 481 University Avenue, Toronto 101, Canada.   London: 30 Old Burlington Street, W1X 3AD
    35 cents.   M.—General articles with Canadian interest, 2000 to 2500 words. *Rates:* $400 up.   *Illustrations:* on assignment.

MONTREAL STAR, THE (1869), 241–5 St. James Street W., Montreal 126. 10 cents. Mon.-Fri.; 15 cents Saturday.   D.

QUEBEC CHRONICLE TELEGRAPH (1764), ROBERT TAMITEGAMA (Quebec Newspapers, Ltd.), 255 Avenue St. Sacrement, St. Malo, Quebec. P.O. Box 100.
    10 cents.   D. 15 cents Saturday.—Little or no freelance material published.

SEA HARVEST & OCEAN SCIENCE, A. MUIR (National Business Publications Ltd.), Gardenvale, Quebec.
    $6.00 per annum—in Canada. $12.00 p.a.—in the British Commonwealth and U.S.A.   M.—Short articles, preferably illustrated, on commercial fishing and oceanographic activities; technical developments in instruments and instrumentation for commercial fishing and oceanography. *Length:* up to 1,000 words (longer if article of exceptional interest and importance). *Payment:* 3–5 cents a word. $3.00 per print (minimum).

SPECTATOR, THE (1846), GORDON BULLOCK, 115 King Street East, Hamilton. *T.* 522–8642.
    10 cents Monday to Saturday.—Articles of general interest, analysis and background; interviews, stories of Canadians abroad. *Length:* 800 maximum. *Payment:* rate varies; up to $50 per 800 words.

TORONTO DAILY STAR (1892), 80 King Street West, Toronto. *T.* 367–2000. *L.A.:* The Times Building, Printing House Square, E.C.4. *T.* 01–248 3468. 10 cents.   D.   20 cents Saturday.

(TORONTO) GLOBE AND MAIL, THE (1844), JAMES L. COOPER, Publisher and Editor-in-Chief, 140 King Street West, Toronto.   10 cents.   D.

(VANCOUVER) PROVINCE (1898), PADDY SHERMAN, 2250 Granville Street, Vancouver 9. 15 cents. D.

VANCOUVER SUN, STUART KEATE, Publisher; W. T. GALT, Managing Editor; CLIFF MACKAY, Editor of Editorial Pages; BRUCE HUTCHISON, Editorial Director, 2250 Granville Street, Vancouver, 9, B.C. *T.* 732–2311.
15 cents; Saturday 20 cents. D. (not Sunday). Rates depending on arrangements. Very little outside contribution. Photographs only.

WASCANA REVIEW (1966), ALWYN BERLAND, Wascana Parkway, Regina, Sask.
$1.50 per issue; $2.50 per year; $6 for 3 years. Semi-annual.—Criticism, short stories, poetry, and art. *Length:* prose, not more than 6000 words; verse, up to 100 lines. *Payment:* $3 per page for prose; $10 per printed page for verse. Contributors also receive two free copies of the issue. Manuscripts from freelance writers welcome.

WEEKEND MAGAZINE, FRANK LOWE, 245 St. James Street, Montreal, Canada.
W.—Topical articles of Canadian interest, of 1200–3000 words. *Payment:* on acceptance, varies. First North American serial rights, or, by special arrangement, first Canadian serial rights.

WINNIPEG TRIBUNE (1890), A. RONALD WILLIAMS (Publisher); TOM GREEN (Editor), 257 Smith Street, Winnipeg, 1, Manitoba. *T.* 985–4512.
10 cents. D. (Friday and Saturday, 15 cents.)

E

EAST AND CENTRAL AFRICAN JOURNALS AND MAGAZINES

AFRICAN SCIENTIST, P.O. Box 30571, Nairobi.

BUSARA, P.O. Box 30571, Nairobi.

DAILY NATION, Editor-in-Chief: BOAZ OMORI; Managing Editor: J. RODRIGUES, P.O. Box 9010, Nairobi. *T.* 27691. London: Overseas Newspapers Ltd., Cromwell House, Fulwood Place, W.C.1.
50 cents. D.—News, features, etc. Pictures.

EAST AFRICA JOURNAL, P.O. Box 30571, Nairobi.

EAST AFRICAN AGRICULTURAL & FORESTRY JOURNAL, TECWYN JONES, P.O Box 30148, Nairobi, Kenya.
5s. 15s. p.a. Q.—Papers on agriculture, forestry and applied Sciences. *Length:* 100 to 125 pages.

EAST AFRICAN JOURNAL OF RURAL DEVELOPMENT, P.O. Box 30571, Nairobi.

EAST AFRICAN MEDICAL JOURNAL, Prof. H. M. CAMERON, M.D., F.R.C.PATH. P.O. Box 1632, Nairobi, 50s. p.a. M.

EAST AFRICAN PHARMACEUTICAL JOURNAL, M. A. KEELEY, P.O. Box 3981, Nairobi. *T.* Nairobi 26060 and 23728. *Cables:* Books, Nairobi.
13s. p.a. post free. Q.—Articles of interest to pharmacists and members of the medical and allied professions: in English. Interested in articles on pharmacy. *Payment:* by arrangement.

EAST AFRICAN STANDARD, KENNETH BOLTON, P.O. Box 30080, Nairobi. 40 cents daily; 60 cents Friday. *T.* 57633 and 22953. D. News and topical articles of East African interest.

KENYA DAIRY FARMER, M. A. KEELEY, P.O. Box 3981, Nairobi. *T.* Nairobi 26060 and 23728. *Cables:* Books, Nairobi.
25s. per annum, post free. M.—Dairying articles, especially those of interest to smallholder farmers; in English and Swahili. Interested in articles on dairy farming. *Payment:* by arrangement.

KENYA WEEKLY NEWS, P.O. Box 2768, Nairobi. 1s.

MOMBASA TIMES, W. McATEER, P.O. Box 10, Mombasa.   3d.   D.

POSTGEN, M. A. KEELEY, P.O. Box 3981, Nairobi, Kenya.   T. 26060 and 23728.
Cables: Books Nairobi.
15s. p.a.   Q.—Articles of interest to members of the post office, telecommunications and allied professions: in English.   Interested in technical articles on developments in the telecommunications industry and latest post office equipment and methods.   *Payment:* by agreement.

RHODESIA CALLS,   A. GERRARD ABERMAN, P.O. Box 8045, Salisbury, Rhodesia.
2s.   Alt. months.—Only articles dealing with Rhodesia.   *Payment:* £8 8s. per 1000 words.

RHODESIAN FARMER, THE, published by Rhodesian Farmer Publications (1928), D. H. B. DICKIN, Farmers Mutual House, Moffat Street, P.O. Box 1622, Salisbury, Rhodesia.   T. Salisbury 28515.
Weekly Illustrated.   Official journal of the Rhodesia National Farmers Union, Rhodesia Tobacco Association.   Articles on all aspects of agriculture and kindred subjects.   *Payment:* by arrangement.

STANDARD TANZANIA, THE, FRENE GINWALA, P.O. Box 9033, Dar es Salaam.
T. 22555   6d.   D.

SUNDAY NEWS, FRENE GINWALA, P.O. Box 9033, Dar es Salaam.   T. 22555.
9d.   W.

TANZANIA OPINION, P.O. Box 455, Dar es Salaam.

UGANDA ARGUS, P.O. Box 20081, Kampala.
40 cents.   D.—News, topical features, news pictures.

UGANDA DAIRY FARMER, M. A. KEELEY, P.O. Box 3981, Nairobi, Kenya.
T. 26060 and 23728.   *Cables:* Books Nairobi.
15s. per annum.   M.—Dairying articles, especially those of interest to smallholder farmers; in English.   Interested in articles on dairy farming, cattle breeding, etc.   *Payment:* by agreement.

YOU MAGAZINE, Contemporary Publishers (Pvt.) Ltd., NONIE FOGARTY, P.O. Box 3793, Salisbury, Rhodesia.   T. 22956.
1s.   Monthly magazine for Rhodesian women.   Articles, drawings, photographs, short stories (*length:* up to 3,000 words) and serials (length up to 18,000).   *Payment:* £5 per 1000 words.   *Illustrations:* colour, half-tone and line.

INDIAN JOURNALS AND MAGAZINES

NOTE.—*Newspapers are listed under the towns in which they are published.*

ART IN INDUSTRY, P. SEN, Regional Design Centre, Govt. of India, Ministry of Foreign Trade, All India Handicrafts Board, Park Hotel, 2nd Floor, 17 Park Street, Calcutta 16. *T.* 24–7835.
 2.50 rupees. Q.—Articles on all relevant subjects of industrial and commercial art and craft. *Payment:* £3 3s. to £5 5s. per 1000 words or by arrangement. *Illustrations:* line, half-tone, photographs.

ARYAN PATH (1930), SOPHIA WADIA, Theosophy Hall, 40 New Marine Lines, Bombay 20BR. London: 62 Queen's Gardens, Lancaster Gate, W.2. *T.* Paddington 0688.
 2s. M.—Annual subscription 18s.—An international review of philosophy, mysticism, comparative religion, psychical research, Indian culture and the brotherhood of humanity. Articles of 1000 to 2500 words. *Payment:* on acceptance and by arrangement.

(BOMBAY) EVE'S WEEKLY, Mrs. GULSHAN EWING, Eve's Weekly Private Ltd., Sanj Vartaman Press, Apollo Street, Fort, Bombay 1. *T.* 258004.
 50 paise. W.—Articles and features of feminine interest, such as fashion, cookery, beauty, psychology, stories, handicraft, child-care, mother-craft, social news, women's institutions, organisations and activities, etc. *Illustrations:* pictures, sketches, artwork.

(BOMBAY) ILLUSTRATED WEEKLY OF INDIA, THE, KHUSHWANT SINSH, Bombay. London: 3 Albemarle Street, W1X 3HF *T.* 01–493 0016–7.
 85 paise. W.—First-class photo features and illustrated articles dealing with topical matters by authoritative writers only, for educated Indian public of modern outlook. *Length:* articles from 800–2000 words; fiction up to 2000 words; serials, 60,000 words. *Payment:* on publication. First reproduction rights India, Pakistan, Burma and Ceylon required.

(BOMBAY) THE INDIAN EXPRESS (Daily) (Proprietors: Indian Express Newspapers (Bombay), Private Ltd.), Colaba, Bombay 5. Editor-in-Chief: FRANK MORAES. Also published from Delhi, Madras, Madurai, Vijayawada, Ahmedabad and Bangalore. European and American representative: Sitanshu Das, Morley House, 26–30 Holborn Viaduct, London, E.C.1.
 15 paise. D.—For editorial page articles of current political interest. *Length:* from about 1000–2000. *Payment:* averaging from £2 a column or 750 words.

BOOK BULLETIN (incorporating **INDIAN LITERARY REVIEW**), R. J. H. TARAPOREVALA, Treasure House of Books, 210 Dr. D. Naoroji Road, Bombay 1. *T.* 261433.
 M.—A monthly review of new and forthcoming books in the English language.

CALCUTTA CAPITAL (1888), Dr. B. B. GHOSH, 5 Mission Row, Calcutta. London: 150–153 St. Stephen's House, Westminster, S.W.1.   *T.* Trafalgar 6470.
W. (Thursday)—Subscription in advance. £5 4s. per annum.—Dealing weekly with economic, industrial and public affairs in India.

(CALCUTTA) STATESMAN, N. J. NANPORIA, Statesman House, Chowringhee Square, Calcutta. For Northern India a separate edition is published daily from Statesman House, New Delhi. London: 41–43 Whitehall, London, S.W.1.   *T.* 01–930 1837–8.
18 paise. D. (Sunday Statesman, 18 paise).—Published simultaneously in Calcutta and Delhi. Circulates widely in India and Burma, and generally respected for its reliable news and independent policy. The magazine section is brief because of shortage of newsprint, but there is room for occasional light pieces on the editorial page also. *Rate of payment:* 45 Rs. per column. *Illustrations,* photographs or line drawings according to merit.

THE STATESMAN WEEKLY (Saturday, 1 rupee).   A digest of Indian news and views, market trends and quotations.

COMMERCE (1910). VADILAL DAGLI, Post Box No. 840, Bombay,   *T.* 253505.
Rs. 2.   (Rs. 85 per annum).   W.—Special articles from 1500 to 2200 words, on economic, commercial, financial, and industrial topics with special reference to India and the East generally; matters connected with Indian firms and companies domiciled in the United Kingdom; news paragraphs about new processes and developments. *Payment:* £1 15s. per column (approximately 800 words).

CURRENT EVENTS MAGAZINE (1955), DEVDUTT, 15 Rajpur Road, Dehra Dun, India.   *T.* 3187 and 3785.
Re. 1.25.   30s. or $4.00 p.a.   M.—Coverage: political, social and economic affairs of the world.   Regular features on sports, films, business, law, literature, books reviews, etc.   Articles of about 1500 words on the above subjects invited.   Topical articles on current development in the international political scene.   Asian perspective preferred.   *Payment:* by arrangement.   *Illustrations:* line and half-tone.   Members: Indian and Eastern Newspapers Society, All-Indian Newspaper Editors Conference.   *London Representative:* M/S Publishing & Distributing Co., Ltd., 177 Regent Street, London, W1R 7FB   *T.* 01–734 6534.

(LUCKNOW) NATIONAL HERALD (1938), M. CHALAPATHI RAU (Associated Journals, Ltd.), Bisheshwar Nath Road, Lucknow.   *T.* Lucknow 22173.   London: 165 Strand, W.C.2.   *T.* 01–836 3689.
15 paise.   D.—Articles and illustrations of all kinds, Rs. 20 per column.   No fiction.

(MADRAS) HINDU, THE, 201 Mount Road, Madras 2.   Proprietors: Kasturi & Sons, Ltd.   London: 2–3 Salisbury Court, Fleet Street, E.C.4.   *T.* 01–353 4965.   Washington: National Press Building (Room 537), 14th & "F" Street, N.W., Washington, D.C.20004.   Tokyo: 20 Haramachi, Shibuya-Ku.   Branches at Bombay, Calcutta, New Delhi, Bangalore, Hyderabad, Madurai, Tiruchirapalli, Coimbatore and Trivandrum.
15 paise D.   20 paise S.—Printed in English, having the widest and most influential circulation among the reading public in India.   Accepts contributions on Indian affairs and international topics.   *Payment:* by arrangement.   *Illustrations:* photographs.

(MADRAS) MAIL, P.O. Box 1, 201 Mount Road, Madras. *T.* 83931. London: 55–56 St. James's Street, S.W.1. *T.* 01–629 2476. Managing Editor: T. A. SUBRAMANIAM.

14 paise. D.—Short topical articles, illustrated preferred, principally dealing with some aspect of Indian affairs or India's relations and commerce with other countries. *Length:* about 800 words. Articles, sketches and photographs should be air-mailed direct to Madras. *Payment:* depends upon quality of articles. *Average rate:* Rs. 30 (£2 5s.) per 1000 words for non-syndicated material. *Illustrations:* topical sketches and photographs of Indian interest.

(NEW DELHI) NATIONAL HERALD (1968), M. CHALAPATHI RAU (Associated Journals Ltd.), Herald House, Bahadur Shah, Zafar Marg, New Delhi 1. *T.* New Delhi 271547. London: 165 Strand, W.C.2. *T.* 01–836 3689.

15 paise D. 18 paise Sunday.—Articles and illustrations of all kinds, Rs.20 per column. No fiction.

ONLOOKER, THE (1939), Mrs. FIROZE N. KANGA, 20G Sleater Road, Bombay 1. *T.* 370241. *T.A.* Onlooker.

Re. 1. M.—Articles on travel subjects of unusual interest; big game and sporting stories; personal sketches of well-known figures. *Length:* 1000 words. *Payment:* one shilling per column inch of words published. Special rates according to the author or subject. *Illustrations:* line and half-tone.

THOUGHT (1949), RAM SINGH, 35 Netaji Subhas Marg, Daryaganj, Delhi 6. *T.* 274648.

1s. W. (Saturday).—Deals with political, social and economic affairs from democratic standpoint. Publishes regular literary supplement, short stories, book reviews, etc. Articles of about 1300–1600 words on the above subjects and reviews of about 600–900 words are invited. *Payment:* by arrangement.

TIMES OF INDIA, SHAM LAL, Bombay, Dehli and Ahmedabad. London: 3 Albemarle Street, W1X 3HF. *T.* 01–493 0016–7.

16 p. D.—Topical articles and photographs likely to be of particular interest in India and to Indian readers. Length preferred, 1000–1500 words. *Payment:* Rs. 150 to Rs. 400 per article. Action photographs and line drawings.

UNITED ASIA (1948), Editor-in-Chief: G. S. POHEKAR, Editor: DINKAR SAKRIKAR, 12 Rampart Row, Bombay, 1 *T.* 252158.

Rs. 12 p.a.; 25s. or $4 p.a. outside India. Bi-M.—Articles, short stories, poems of Asian interest. Insistence on an Asian perspective and mood. *Length:* 2000 to 3000 words. *Payment:* by arrangement. *Illustrations:* line, half-tone, colour, photographs, drawings, cartoons of Asian interest.

NEW ZEALAND JOURNALS AND MAGAZINES

NOTE.—*Newspapers are listed under the towns in which they are published.*

ADVERTISING & MARKETING NEWS, S. M. BEVAN, Published by Trade Publications Ltd., P.O. Box 1614, Auckland. *T.* 362–240.
$4.20 (mainly on subscription). M.—New Zealand's only magazine devoted to the interests of advertising agencies and marketing executives. Articles on all aspects of advertising, marketing, sales management, merchandising and publishing. *Payment:* $10.00 per 1000 words on publication.

(AUCKLAND) NEW ZEALAND HERALD (1863), J. F. W. HARDINGHAM, P.O. Box 32, Auckland. *T.* 78–988. London: Ludgate House, 107 Fleet Street, E.C.4. *T.* 01–353 2686.
4c. D.—Literary and informative articles 800 words (one column). *Minimum payment:* $8–$10 a column. Half-tone blocks (65 screen).

AUCKLAND STAR (1870) ROSS SAYERS (New Zealand Newspapers, Ltd.), P.O. Box 3697, Auckland. 4c. D.

(CHRISTCHURCH) PRESS, THE, Christchurch. Editor: A. R. CANT. London: 107 Fleet Street, E.C.4. *T.* 01–353 1814.
4c. D.—Articles of general interest not more than 1200 words. *Payment:* by arrangement. Extra payment for photographs and line drawings.

CHRISTCHURCH STAR (1868), B. A. MAIR (New Zealand Newspapers Ltd.), Kilmore Street, Christchurch.
4c. D.—Topical articles.

CRUCIBLE (1966), WILLIAM WILCOX, P.O. Box 5574, Auckland. *T.* 32–990.
7s. 6d. Q.—Stories and poems of highest calibre only. Stringent, unique literary styles sought. Articles of a commentative controversial nature. *Payment:* by arrangement, but minimum rates: NZ$10 per story or article, NZ$1 per poem. *Illustrated.*

(DUNEDIN) OTAGO DAILY TIMES (1861), Editor: E. ALLAN AUBIN, Dunedin. London: 107 Fleet Street, E.C.4. *T.* 01–353 2686.
4c. D.—Any articles of general interest up to 1000 words, but preference is given to New Zealand writers. Topical illustrations and personalities. *Payment:* Current New Zealand rates.

LANDFALL (1947), ROBIN DUDDING, The Caxton Press, P.O. Box 25–088, Christchurch. *T.* 68516.
$1.00. Q.—All literary and general material by N.Z. writers considered, of any length. Illustrates the work of N.Z. painters, sculptors, architects, photographers, etc. *Payment:* by arrangement.

MANAGEMENT, S. C. NIBLOCK (Modern Productions Ltd.), Box 3159, Auckland. *T.* 768808. *T.A.* Amalmod.

6s. M.—Articles on management, efficiency, topics of general interest to the top businessman. A New Zealand angle or application prefered. *Length:* 500–1200 words. *Payment:* by arrangement. *Illustrations:* photographs, line drawings.

MOTORMAN, Published by Universal Business Directories Ltd., UBD Centre, 360 Dominion Road, Auckland. *T.* 689–959.

3s. 0d. M.—Circulation in New Zealand and Australia. New Zealand's only motoring monthly, devoted mainly to the sporting aspects; also gives coverage to road tests, new products in the automobile field, touring and general motoring. *Illustrations:* photographs, cartoons and line drawings.

NEW ZEALAND BRIDE & HOME, D. S. LUCAS, Published by Lucas-Altman Publishing Co. Ltd., P.O. Box 1849, Auckland. *T.* 362–933.

Published once a year in September. Articles by arrangement—letter required.

NEW ZEALAND FARMER, JOHN CORNWELL, P.O. Box 1409, Shortland Street, Auckland. London: 30–34 New Bridge Street, E.C.4. *T.* Central 4559.

15c. F.—Authoritative, simply-written articles on new developments in livestock husbandry, grassland farming. *Length:* 1000 to 1250 words. *Payment:* according to merit.

NEW ZEALAND GARDENER, (Magazine of Outdoor Living), Wilson and Horton Ltd., P.O. Box 32, Auckland.

25c. M.—Topical articles on gardening, new plants and methods of cultivation, new products of horticultural interest, home workshop project of all kinds for the home and garden. Authoritative articles by specialists only. *Payment:* $14 per 1000 words. *Illustrations:* photographs or line; payment $3 per print on publication; colour transparencies are used.

NEW ZEALAND HOLIDAY, A. P. S. SMITH, Box 1481, Wellington. *T.* 43461.

30c. Q.—Travel in New Zealand and subjects likely to interest tourists and intending travellers. *Payment:* $10 and upwards per 1000 words, on publication. *Illustrations:* photographs, colour transparencies on cover.

NEW ZEALAND HOME JOURNAL (1934), Jo NOBLE, P.O. Box 3697, Auckland. *T.* 74–677.

10c. M.—Articles (preferably illustrated) of homemaking and family interest up to 2500 words. *Payment:* from $6.50 per 1000 words, on acceptance. *Illustrations:* photographs or drawings. Mostly commissioned work.

NEW ZEALAND LISTENER, THE (1939), ALEXANDER MACLEOD, P.O. Box 3140, Wellington. *T.* 48–200.

12 cents. W.—Features and articles on television and sound broadcasting; topical features on non-broadcasting subjects of New Zealand and international interest. Short stories, verse. Length for short stories and articles: up to 2500 words. *Illustrations:* colour transparencies and half-tone. *Payment:* Top New Zealand rates, or by arrangement.

NEW ZEALAND OUTDOOR (1937) (Associated Publications), L. T. MORGAN, P.O. Box 236, Masterton, New Zealand.

25c. M.—Stories or technical type articles up to 2500 words on shooting, fishing, hunting, mountaineering, and other kindred outdoor sports. *Payment:* $5 per 1000 words; photographs $1.00. *Illustrations:* line or half-tone.

NEW ZEALAND WEEKLY NEWS, (1863), R. A. ANDERSON, 149 Queen Street, Auckland.

15c. W.—Topical articles and photographs. *Payment:* best New Zealand rates. *Illustrations:* colour, half-tone and line.

NEW ZEALAND WOMAN'S WEEKLY (1934), JEAN WISHART (New Zealand Newspapers, Ltd.), P.O. Box 1409, Auckland.

10c. W.—Pictorial features. Illustrated articles of general, family, world interest, particularly with a New Zealand slant. *Length:* articles 750–1750. *Payment:* on acceptance. *Illustrations:* photographs.

N.Z. CONCRETE CONSTRUCTION (1957), M. A. CRAVEN, B.E., Technical Publications Ltd., C.P.O. Box 3047, Wellington, C.1. *London Office:* Sawell and Sons Ltd., 4 Ludgate Circus, E.C.4. *T.* 01–353 4353.

3s. M. (except December).—Technical articles, reports, news, etc. Preliminary letter essential. *Payment:* by arrangement.

N.Z. ELECTRICAL JOURNAL (1928), F. N. STACE, B.E., Technical Publications Ltd., C.P.O. Box 3047, Wellington, C.1. *London Office:* Sawell and Sons Ltd., 4 Ludgate Circus, E.C.4. *T.* 01–353 4353.

2s. 6d. M.—Technical and trade news and articles. Preliminary letter essential. *Payment:* by arrangement.

N.Z. ENGINEERING (1946), F. N. STACE, B.E., Technical Publications Ltd., C.P.O. Box 3047, Wellington 1. *London Office:* Sawell and Sons Ltd., 4 Ludgate Circus, E.C.4. *T.* 01–353 4353.

6s. M.—Technical articles of interest to New Zealand engineers. Preliminary letter essential. *Payment:* by arrangement.

N.Z. ENGINEERING NEWS (1970), T. G. EVISON, Technical Publications Ltd., C.P.O. Box 3047, Wellington 1. *London Office:* Sawell & Sons Ltd., 4 Ludgate Circus, E.C.4. *T.* 01–383 4353.

Free M. (not January).—Technical news items of interest to New Zealand engineers and technicians. Preliminary letter essential. *Payment:* by arrangement.

N.Z. TIMBER JOURNAL, CLIVE TIDMARSH, Tidmarsh Publications Ltd., Kingdon House, Kingdon Street, Newmarket, Auckland. *T.A.* Timjer.

4s. M.—Articles, technical and general, dealing with forestry, timber and wood products. *Payment:* by arrangement. *Illustrations:* photographs, and cartoons.

(WELLINGTON) EVENING POST, THE (1865) K. M. POULTON, Willis Street, Wellington. *T.* 47–222. *London Office:* N.Z. Associated Press, 107 Fleet Street, E.C.4. *T.* 01–353 2686.

4c. D.—General topical articles, 800 words. *Payment:* N.Z. current rates or by arrangement. News illustrations.

N.Z. TRUTH (News Media Ownership Ltd.), J. R. N. EDLIN, 23–27 Garrett Street, Wellington, P.O. Box 1122.

10c. W.—Critical articles, on sociological issues, length 500–1000 words, preferably accompanied by photographs. *Payment:* about $10 per column, extra for photographs.

PAKISTANI JOURNALS AND MAGAZINES

(A Preliminary letter is advisable before MSS. are submitted.)

DAILIES:

COMMENT, H. M. ABBASI, Wahid Manzil, 52 Ratan Talao, Karachi. *T.* 71317. 6 paisa. D. (except Sunday).—Informative and interesting stories on all subjects. *Length:* Stories 500–2000 words; preferably of 1000 words.

DAWN, JAMIL ANSARI, Haroon House, Kutchery Road, Karachi. *T.* 516761. 25 paisa. D.—News and features. *Length:* 1200–1800 words. *Payment:* Rs. 30 per column. *Illustrations:* news pictures.

LEADER, SULTAN AHMED, 191 South Napier Road, Karachi.

PAKISTAN OBSERVER, THE, ABDUS SALAM, Motijheel Commercial Area, Dacca 2: *T.* 54115–54117. *T.A.* Observer, Dacca. 25 paisa, 30 paisa on Sunday (including a colour magazine). D. Features, articles on International, Economic, Sociological subjects. *Length:* 1000–2500 words. £5–£10 according to length and Editor's evaluation. *Illustrations:* photographs, drawings including cartoons.

WEEKLIES:

CHITRALI, S. M. PERVEZ, Observer House, Dacca 2. *T.* 254115–6–7. 30 paisa. W.—Film and fashion news and features. *Length:* 1000 words. *Payment:* Rs. 20 per column inch. *Illustrations:* photographs.

FREEDOM, SHER MUHAMMED, 12 Akbar Road, Saddar, P.O. Box 7181, Karachi.

ILLUSTRATED WEEKLY OF PAKISTAN, AJMAL HUSAIN, Haroon Chambers, South Napier Road, Karachi. *T.* 223164. 75 paisa. W.—New pictures, features, scientific articles, short stories, international events and affairs. National social, political and economic news coverage. *Payment:* £2 per 1000 words. *Illustrations:* half-tone and line.

KARACHI COMMERCE, Z. I. ZOBAIRY, P.O. Box 7442, 2/5 Akbar Road, Karachi-3. *T.* 72929. London Rep.; Publishing & Distributing Co. Ltd., 177 Regent Street, W1R 7FB *T.* 01–734 6534–6535 and 2361. 75 paisa. Rs.48 p.a. W.—Articles on economics, trade and industry. *Length:* 1000 to 1500 words. *Payment:* Rs. 25 to 50 per article. No illustrations.

PURBODESH, MAHBUBUL HUQ, Dacca 2. 25 paisa. W.—News, pictures, features and cartoons. *Length:* 1500 words. *Payment:* Rs. 20 per column. *Illustrations:* photographs and drawings.

STATESMAN, THE (Week-end Review), MOHAMMAD OWAIS, 260-c Commercial Area, P.E.C.H.S., Karachi. 25 paisa. W.—Political, social, economic, literary, films. *Length:* 1600 words. *Payment:* Rs. 50 per 1000 words. *Illustrations:* line drawings or exceptional photographs.

WEEKLY AWAM, A. Rauf Siddiqi, Altaf Husain Road, Karachi 2. *T.* 235567.
  25 paisa. W.—Politics, economics, social, sports, etc. Photographs,
  cartoons. *Payment:* Rs. 50 for 1000 word story.

MONTHLIES:

DIPLOMAT, THE, Dr. M. R. Khan and Mahmudul Aziz, 1 Victoria Chambers,
  Victoria Road, Karachi 3. *T.* 54682.
  Rs. 1.50. M.—International, political, economic, and social affairs. *Length:*
  about 1200 words. *Payment:* from Rs. 25 to Rs. 50. *Illustrations:* photographs and maps.

ECONOMIC SURVEY, Board of Economic Inquiry, 59-B Gulberg II, Lahore.
  T. 82302.
  Re. –/75. M.—Economic conditions of the country. Contributions not
  invited. *Illustrations:* Charts and graphs only.

ENTERPRISE, Qayyum Malick, Dr. Billimoria Street, off McLeod Road, Karachi.
  Monthly.

FORWARD, Ahmed Abdulla, PIDC House, Kutchery Road, Karachi.
  Rs. 6 per annum. M.—Industrial and economic articles. *Payment:* Rs. 100
  per article. *Length:* 2000 words. *Illustrations:* photographs and charts.

MIRROR, THE, Begum Zeb-un-Nissa Hamidullah, Eveready Chambers, Burns
  Road/McLeod Road, near Telephone House, Karachi.
  Rs. 2. M.—Social and other articles of a pictorial nature.

PAKISTAN MEDICAL JOURNAL, Dr. M. A. Qureshi, m.b., b.s.(Osmania).
  72 Liaquat Bazar, Bunder Road, Karachi. L.O. Napier House, 24/27 High
  Holborn, London, W.C.1.
  Sub.: £1 6s. Single copies Rs. 1.25.

PAKISTAN REVIEW, Dr. A. Waheed, Editor-in-chief; A. Majeed, Editor, 60
  Shara-e-Quaid-e-Azam, Lahore. *T.* 65196–7–8.
  $6.00. p.a. M.—Articles on political, cultural, social economic affairs of
  Pakistan and the Islamic world. Book reviews. *Length:* 3000 words. *Pay-
  ment:* £3 to £5 per article of 3 pages. *Illustrations:* black-and-white, and colour.

TALIM-O-TARBIAT, Dr. A. Waheed, b.a.(Hons.), ph.d.(Lond.), 60 Shara-i-Quaid-
  i-Azam, Lahore. *T.* 65196–97–98.
  0.75 paisa. M.—Short stories for children, poems, articles on general
  knowledge and of scientific information, comic strips, articles about books, etc.
  Length: approx. 2000 words. *Payment:* Rs. 15 for 1000 words. *Illustrations:*
  black-and-white and colour, line and half-tone.

TRADE CHRONICLE, A. Rauf Siddiqi, Altaf Husain Road, Karachi 2. *T.*
  235567. London Office: 27 Nant Road, N.W.2.
  Rs. 35 p.a. M.—Economic articles. *Payment:* £3 to £5 per article.

WOMAN'S WORLD, Mujeeb M. Akram, 43/4/A, Block 6, P.E.C.H.S., Karachi.
  T. 40864.
  R. 1. M.—Stories and articles on subjects of interest to women. *Length:*
  articles up to 1500 words; stories up to 4000 words. *Payment:* Rs. 15 per
  1000 words for articles; Rs. 25–50 for short stories. *Illustrations:* half-tone
  and line; occasionally colour.

QUARTERLIES:

PAKISTAN HORIZON, K. Sarwar Hasan, Pakistan Institute of International
  Affairs, Karachi. *T.* 512891.
  33s. per annum. Q.—International affairs. *Length:* about 3000 words.
  Payment: Rs. 10 to Rs. 15 per page.

PAKISTAN QUARTERLY (1947), S. Amjad Ali, P.O. Box 183, Karachi. *T.* 510457. *T.A.* Pakinforma.

Rs. 4.—Articles on any aspect of Pakistan—the life of the people, trends of thought, current writing, parts of the country, sociological surveys, philosophical reflection, art, literature, history—of special relevance to Pakistan today. Short stories and poems with Pakistani background. Articles on international affairs also welcomed, but must be directly related to Pakistan. *Average length:* 3000 words. *Payment:* £10 average, extra for pictures. *Illustrations:* drawings, paintings and photographs relevant to the articles.

AMERICAN JOURNALS AND MAGAZINES

Every effort is made to verify each paper in this list, but, in dealing with minor papers, contributors are advised to **communicate by letter, and await reply, before posting MSS.**

This list contains of course only a selection of the several thousand American publications which publish some free-lance material, many of which, however, offer a negligible market for any but the highly specialised writer from outside the United States.

NOTE.—MSS. (with or without illustrations) and their stamped return envelopes, or international postage coupons, should *not* be sent separately, but with the covering letter. It is necessary, when selling to a U.S.A. periodical, to be clear what rights are being sold, for certain Editors like to purchase MSS. outright, thus securing world copyright. MSS. should not be sent to the London office of any U.S.A. publication.

Contributors, who do not retain a specific market in the U.S.A., are recommended to make a careful study of those publications that are preponderantly American in their appeal.

The following survey of the market in America for the free-lance writer has been contributed by Mr. Graham Fisher:

American editors (with which for this purpose may be included Canadian editors), having considerably more space at their disposal, generally require much longer articles than are normally published by magazines in Britain. A few will take articles of around 1500 words, but most are not keen on anything under 2000 words in length (unless it is basically a picture-story, with photographs taking the place of text). Many editors prefer a length of 2500–3000 words, and some of the major magazines even like their articles to run to whatever the subject-matter seems to justify . . . 4000, 5000, even 6000 words.

Generally speaking, U.S. editors prefer their articles to be about people rather than "things", and even articles about "things", as far as possible, should be told through the personalities involved. The story of a new cure for heart trouble, for instance, should be told either through the physician who has developed it or through a patient who has experienced it. U.S. editors prefer the specific to the general, anecdotes instead of explanation. They also like their articles thoroughly researched from every conceivable angle. Articles for the U.S. market should have a lively approach, plenty of anecdotes, lots and lots of facts, and no padding. American magazines have no time for the writer who attempts to conceal a shortage of hard facts behind a mass of high-sounding phrases.

The American market is eager for good adventure articles, unusual experiences, personality profiles of international celebrities, articles about anything new or novel—in industry, in show business for example, controversial articles, and "off-beat" articles which cover entirely new ground. To save time and work, a preliminary letter, enclosing an "outline" is usually advisable. An "outline" is a synopsis of around 500 words which details the basic facts, mentions one or two outstanding anecdotes, and—most important—gives some idea of the treatment and style being afforded the finished article. While most U.S. editors will not usually assign an article even on the basis of an outline—at least, not until you are known to them—most will say whether or not they are interested in seeing the finished product and how they feel it should be handled. It also pays to give the editor your "credits" ... details of some previous articles sold. American editors pay considerable regard to where and when a writer has had work previously published.

Most editors prefer the finished article to be submitted flat and unfolded. If a sale results, it is necessary to be quite clear what rights are being sold, as some U.S. editors prefer to purchase world copyright, at least, until after publication in America. At that stage, many editors, on request, will release subsidiary rights for the writer to dispose of in other countries.

Prices paid for articles—and fiction—in the United States are far above those generally prevailing in Britain. Payment in Canada is higher, too, though not so high as in America. A major series can fetch an astronomical figure. Payment, with very few exceptions, is on acceptance, the cheque arriving by air-mail within 2–4 weeks.

Two useful magazines for those hoping to sell in the United States are *The Writer*, 8 Arlington Street, Boston, Mass. 02116, and *Writer's Digest*, published monthly by the F & W Publishing Corporation, 22 East 12th Street, Cincinnati, Ohio 45210.

AMERICAN ARTIST (1937), STERLING MCILHANY, 165 West 46th Street, New York, N.Y. 10036. *T.* Plaza 7-2800.
$1 ($12 per annum, foreign Sub.). 11 times a year (not July).—Articles on fine arts and commercial illustration, design, ceramics, metal work, pottery, etc. *Length:* 1500–2500 words. *Payment:* $75 to $100. *Illustrations:* (offset) colour, half-tone, line. Free-lance work accepted occasionally; most articles written by contributing editors.

AMERICAN FIELD, WILLIAM F. BROWN, 222 W. Adams Street, Chicago, Illinois 60606. *T.* (Area code 312) FR2–1383.
$9.00 p.a. W.—Short articles, stories and features, principally bird hunting with dogs; breeding, rearing, training, conditioning, etc., of sporting breeds. *Payment:* varies. *Illustrations:* half-tone.

AMERICAN GIRL (1917), PATRICIA DI SERNIA, 830 Third Avenue, New York, N.Y. 10022.
40 cents ($4 a year plus $1.00 foreign postage). M.—Short stories, 2000 to 3000 words; articles, 1500 to 2000 words. Material suitable to teen-age girls—10 to 17, with the average age 14. *Payment:* on acceptance. *Illustrations:* line, half-tone and photographs.

AMERICAN HOME, HUBBARD H. COBB, 641 Lexington Avenue, New York, N.Y. 10022.
50 cents. 10 issues per year.—Articles pertaining to the home; decorating, maintenance, gardening, kitchen planning, home remodelling, food. *Length:* 500–2500 words. *Payment:* depends on value and length; on acceptance. *Illustrations:* colour transparencies, half-tones.

AMERICAN LEGION MAGAZINE, 1345 Avenue of the Americas, New York 10019.
$2 p.a. M.—Major articles on national and international affairs, American history, military history, consumer articles. *Payment:* by arrangement.

AMERICAN MERCURY, LAVONNE D. FURR, (Managing Editor), P.O. Box 1306, Torrance, California 90505.
75 cents. Q.—Articles on the American scene, history, science, humour, travel, biographical sketches, poetry. Length preferred, from 900 to 2000 words. *Payment:* is on publication by arrangement with author. MSS. can only be returned if S.A.E. enclosed.

AMERICAN SCHOLAR, THE (1932), A Quarterly for the Independent Thinker, published by the United Chapters of Phi Beta Kappa; HIRAM HAYDN, Editor, 1811 Q Street, N.W., Washington, D.C. 20009. *T.* Columbia 5–3808.

$1.75. Q.—Articles and essays of permanent rather than temporary interest on science, politics, economics, the humanities, international relations, education, etc. *Length:* preferred: 3000 to 3500 words. No fiction. Pays $150 an article on acceptance. Poems: *payment* $35 to $75, according to length.

AMERICAN SPORTSMAN (1967), ROBERT ELMAN, 17 East 45th Street, New York, N.Y. 10017. *T.* MU 2–4171.

$5.00, $20 p.a. in U.S.; $5.95, $25 p.a. in Europe. Q.—Factual articles on outdoor (non-competitive) sports up to about 6000 words; must be high literary quality. *Payment:* by arrangement. *Illustrations:* Colour photographs.

ANALOG, Science Fact and Fiction, JOHN W. CAMPBELL, 420 Lexington Avenue, New York, N.Y. 10017.

60 cents. M.—Science-fiction short stories up to 7500 words—novelettes up to 20,000 words. Science fact articles with future slant up to 6000 words. Serials to 70,000 words. *Payment:* 5 cents per word on stories under 7500 words; longer material 3 cents per words up, on acceptance plus reader-response determined 1 cent a word bonus.

ARGOSY (Popular), HENRY STEEGER (Publisher), HAL STEEGER (Editor), 205 East 42nd Street, New York 10017.

60 cents. M.—Short stories of colourful, adventurous, vigorous drama, up to 5000 words; novelettes, 12,000–14,000 words; adventure articles, including first-person stories; features, photos and cartoons.

ARTS IN SOCIETY (1958), University Extension, The University of Wisconsin, Madison, Wisconsin 53706. *T.* (Area 608) 262–0646.

$2.00; $5.50 p.a. 3 issues p.a.—A forum for the discussion, interpretation and illustration of the role and function of art in our time; each issue focuses on a particular area of art experience which is explored by authorities from a variety of fields and disciplines; the journal is designed for the art leader, scholar, artist, educator, student, and the layman with broad cultural interests; includes yearly index. Poetry, book reviews. *Honorarium:* for accepted material.

ATLANTIC, THE (1857), ROBERT MANNING, 8 Arlington Street, Boston, Mass. 02116. *T.* Kenmore 6–9500. *T.A.* Lanticmon.

$9.50 per annum. M.—Uses articles on politics, science, art, and literature; sketches, short stories, and poems. Particularly interested in short stories from new writers under Atlantic "First" Competition. Work must be authoritative in matter, not necessarily American, and of distinction in form and style. Discussions, social, literary, economic, political, are particularly welcome. *Length:* from 1700 to 6000 words, exceptionally 15,000. *Illustrations only in special cases. Payment:* on acceptance; $100 per page in print minimum. Deals promptly with MSS.

AVIATION WEEK AND SPACE TECHNOLOGY, ROBERT B. HOTZ (McGraw-Hill Inc.), 330 West 42nd Street, New York, N.Y. 10036. London: HERBERT J. COLEMAN, McGraw-Hill Ltd., 34 Dover Street, London, W1X 3RA *T.* 01–493 1451. $12.00 yearly W.

BETTER HOMES AND GARDENS (1922), JAMES A. RIGGS, Meredith Corporation, 1716 Locust Street, Des Moines, Iowa 50303. *T.* (Area code 515) 284–9011.

50 cents. M.—While over 75% of our material is staff produced, we are in the market for free-lance material in the areas of travel, health, cars, money management, and home and family entertainment. We are also interested in do-it-yourself projects which concern the home and family. Such remodeling or decorating stories should be accompanied by "before" and "after" snapshots and complete data: cost, time, and reason for change. *Length* of articles: 250 to 1000 words. We prefer you query first with an outline. *Payment:* pay top rates, based on estimated space of the published article. Payment is immediate upon acceptance. *Illustrations:* line drawings, half-tone, colour.

BOATING (1956), MOULTON H. FARNHAM, 1 Park Avenue, New York, N.Y. 10016. *T.* (212) 679–7200.

75 cents. $7.00 p.a. in Pan America and Canada, $8.00 p.a. in other countries.—Features boating in America in power and sail. *Length:* 1000 to 1500 words. *Payment:* varies. *Illustrations:* boating photographs in colour or black and white.

BOSTON HERALD TRAVELER (1846), JOHN HERBERT, 300 Harrison Avenue, Boston, Mass. 02112.

10 cents. D. (Sunday 25 cents.)—Ind. Republican

BOYS' LIFE, ROBERT E. HOOD. Published by the Boy Scouts of America, New Brunswick, N.J. 08903. *T.* 201–249 6000, ext. 316.

40 cents. $4 p.a. ($5 abroad). M.—Short stories, 2500 to 3500 words; serials up to 12,000 words. Good stories of adventure, in all parts of the world. Stories that emphasise indirectly the ideals of the Boy Scout Movement. Well stocked. *Payment:* excellent rates on acceptance.

CAROLINA QUARTERLY, GEORGE WOLFE, Box 1117, Chapel Hill, North Carolina 27514.

Poetry and fiction. Competitive *payment*.

CHICAGO REVIEW, HARRY FOSTER, University of Chicago, Chicago, Ill. 60637. $3.50 p.a. Q.—Literary, art work. No *length* limit. No cash *payment*.

CHICAGO SUN-TIMES, JAMES F. HOGE, Jr., 401 N. Wabash, Chicago, Ill. 60611. *T.* 321–2500.

10 cents. D. (Sunday 30 cents).—2000 words or less on topical subjects of interest to Mid-Western U.S. readers. Glossy photos considered, if appropriate. *Payment:* depends on quality.

CHRISTIAN CENTURY, THE, Dr. ALAN GEYER, 407 South Dearborn Street, Chicago, Illinois 60605. European Editor: The Revd. TREVOR BEESON, 56 Woodside Avenue, London, N.6. *T.* 01–883 6040.

9p. W.—An international ecumenical review covering current events as well as religious developments. Articles appealing to radical Christians. A preliminary letter is advisable. *Payment:* by arrangement.

CHRISTIAN SCIENCE MONITOR, THE, DeWITT JOHN, 1 Norway Street, Boston, Massachusetts 02115. London: Africa House, 64–78 Kingsway, W.C.2. *T.* 01–405 0442.

10 cents (8d.) D.—A newspaper publishing, in addition to world news, descriptive articles, essays and poems of literary merit, international or human interest, and constructive purpose. Articles and essays are best prepared by analysing the type of material used by different departments of the paper. *Payment:* subject to arrangement. Contributions, except from the British Isles which should be submitted via the London Office, should be sent direct to Boston. *Illustrations:* artistic pictures, photographs and sketches.

COLUMBIA, ELMER VON FELDT, P.O. Box 1670, New Haven, Conn. 06507. *T.* (203) 772–2130.

20 cents. M.—Articles from 1000 to 3000 words of interest to Catholic layman and family, dealing with current events, social problems, family life, education, literature, science, arts, sports and leisure. *Payment:* from $100 to $300. Articles must be accompanied by photographs. Also fiction up to 3000 words, written from a Christian viewpoint. *Payment:* up to $300.

COMMONWEAL, JAMES O'GARA, 232 Madison Avenue, New York, N.Y. 10016.

$12.00 yearly. Foreign subscription price, $14.00. W.—Articles and essays on political, literary, artistic, scientific, and religious topics. *Commonweal* is edited by a group of Roman Catholic laymen. The rate of *payment* is 2 cents a word, and MSS. should not, as a rule, exceed 2500 words.

COSMOPOLITAN MAGAZINE, HELEN GURLEY BROWN, 224 West 57th Street, New York, N.Y. 10019. *T.* CO 5–7300.

$6.00 per year. M.—Outstanding fiction and timely important articles, geared to the single woman of 18–34 years of age. Short stories, 4000 to 6000 words; also short-shorts, about 2000 words. One short murder mystery in each book. Articles of cosmopolitan interest, about 4000 words. Accept only agent solicitated manuscripts. *Payment:* by arrangement, on acceptance. *Illustrations:* black-and-white and colour.

ELECTRONICS WORLD, W. A. STOCKLIN, 1 Park Avenue, New York, New York 10016. *T.* Oregon 9–7200.

60 cents. M.—Technical articles of 1000–3000 words, with diagrams and photographs of interest to electronic engineers and technicians vocationally in industry, communications, commercial and consumer areas, and avocationally in high fidelity, ham radio, citizens band, etc. *Payment:* on acceptance, 5 cents a word. Diagrams may be only in rough form.

ELLERY QUEEN'S MYSTERY MAGAZINE, ELLERY QUEEN, 229 Park Avenue South, New York 10003.

$7 per year plus $2 postage. M.—Quality writing and quality plots on detection, crime, mystery and suspense. Interested especially in originals, but also use reprints previously published only in non-competitive British periodicals. *Length:* shorts up to 10,000 words; also occasional short-shorts; and novelettes approx. 20,000 words. *Payment:* on acceptance. Good rates.

ESQUIRE, HAROLD HAYES, 488 Madison Avenue, New York City, N.Y. 10022.

$1.00. M.—Masculine viewpoint articles, sophisticated and unsentimental; essays; sketches; short stories; 1500 to 3500 words. *Payment:* on acceptance, according to quality and length. *Illustrations:* only by order, cartoons.

EVERGREEN REVIEW (1957), BARNEY ROSSET, 214 Mercer Street, New York, N.Y. 10012. *T.* 677–2400. *T.A.* Grovepress. Distributors in Great Britain: Transatlantic Book Service Ltd., 43 Essex Street, London, W.C.2.

$1.00. M.—Stories, articles, poems. *Payment:* prose, $45.00 per printed page; poetry, $50.00 per page. *Illustrations:* photographs.

FIELD & STREAM, CLARE CONLEY (Holt Group, C.B.S.), 383 Madison Avenue, New York 10017, U.S.A. *T.* MU. 8–9100.

50 cents. M.—Articles on hunting and fishing. *Length:* 2000 to 2800 words. *Payment:* 12 cents a word up. *Illustrations:* photographs.

FILM QUARTERLY (1958) Successor of **QUARTERLY OF FILM, RADIO AND TELEVISION,** and of **HOLLYWOOD QUARTERLY** (1945), ERNEST CALLENBACH, University of California Press, Berkeley, California 94720. *T.* 415–642–6333. *T.A.* Calpress.

$1.25, $5.00 per year in U.S., Canada and Pan America; $2.50, $9.00 per year elsewhere. Q.—Critical articles and reviews appealing to a highly informed readership. Query editor before submitting. *Payment:* 1.5 cents per word. *Illustrations:* Half-tone.

FLYING, ROBERT B. PARKE, 1 Park Avenue, New York, N.Y. 10016. *T.* OR9–7200.
$7 p.a. M.—Articles up to 2500 words covering all facets of general aviation. *Payment:* according to merit, up to $500; average $200. *Illustrations:* photographs and drawings.

FOREIGN AFFAIRS, H. F. ARMSTRONG, 58 East 68th Street, New York, N.Y. 10021. *T.* 212 Lehigh 5–3300. *Cables:* Foraffairs, New York.
$2.00. Q.—Deals with the international aspects of America's political, economic, and financial problems. *Payment:* on publication at the rate of $250 for an article of 4000 to 5000 words.

FORTUNE, Time and Life Building, New York, N.Y. 10020. London Office: Time and Life Building, New Bond Street, W1Y 0AA
$1.75 outside U.S. M. (except 2 issues in May and August).—American business publication. Prospective contributors advised to study magazine. Little outside matter used. See also under **TIME.**

GLAMOUR MAGAZINE (1939), RUTH WHITNEY, 420 Lexington Avenue, New York, N.Y. 10017. *T.* 212–689–5900. *T.A.* Vonork, New York.
60c. M.—Articles on any subject relevant to young women from 18 to 35. Fashion and beauty copy staff written. *Length:* 3000 to 5000. *Payment:* $700 and up. *Illustrations:* Colour and black and white.

GOOD HOUSEKEEPING, WADE H. NICHOLS, 959 Eighth Avenue, New York 10019. *T.* Columbus 5–7300.
50 cents. M.—Short stories of any length, and novelettes or novels. Short features and articles. Poems. Chief requirement from English writers is fiction, though largely from authors of established reputation. Highest prices paid, on acceptance. *Illustrations:* line, and half-tone; colour.

HARPER'S MAGAZINE, WILLIE MORRIS, 2 Park Avenue, New York, N.Y. 10016. *T.* 212–686 8710.
75 cents (English Edition, 17½p.). M.—Articles on current affairs, military, political, economic, social, scientific, cultural, etc. Short stories, humour, verse, personal experience. Book reviews. Up to 5000 words. *Payment:* is good and is made on acceptance. Limited *illustrations:* in line and photograph. No unsolicited material except through agent.

HOLIDAY, CASKIE STINNETT, 641 Lexington Avenue, New York, N.Y. 10022.
75 cents. $6.00 per annum. On assignment: Well-written articles on travel, entertainment, food.

HUDSON REVIEW, THE, FREDERICK MORGAN, 65 East 55th Street, New York 10022. *T.* PL–5–9040.
$1.75; $6.00 p.a. Q.—Quality fiction, poetry, translations, reviews. *Length:* up to 8000 words. *Payment:* $10 per page. *Illustrations:* Occasional line cuts and reproductions.

INGENUE, JOAN WYNN, 750 Third Avenue, New York, N.Y. 10017.
Fiction and articles of interest to the teenager. *Length:* fiction: 1500 to 6500 words; *payment:* $175 to $500. Articles: 700 to 4500 words; *payment:* $75 to $500.

JEWELERS' CIRCULAR—KEYSTONE, DONALD S. McNEIL, 56th and Chestnut Street, Philadelphia, Pa. 19139. *T.* 215–748 2000.
75 cents. M.—Illustrated feature stories on specific phases of jewellery merchandising, advertising and sales promotion; gem production and processing —from paragraphs to 1000–1500 word articles, illustrated if possible. We pay $25 per published page. Columns 20 picas wide. Type usually 10 point. Photos $5.00. Remitted immediately after publication. *Illustrations:* halftones and line cuts.

LADIES' HOME JOURNAL, JOHN MACK CARTER, 641 Lexington Avenue, New York, N.Y. 10022.
50 cents in the U.S.A.; 50 cents in Canada. M.—No unsolicited MSS. are being considered.

LIFE, Time and Life Building, Rockefeller Center, New York 10020. London Office: Time and Life Building, New Bond Street, W1Y 0AA
35 cents. W.—Articles—about half written by staff writers, the other half by free-lance writers. Articles, other than staff-written ones, are specifically commissioned to outside authors. *Payment:* $500–$750 for short articles (1500 words) and approximately $1250–$1750 (under special circumstances sometimes higher) for long articles (3000 to 5000 words). *Illustrations:* photographs and sometimes drawings or paintings. LIFE INTERNATIONAL, published fortnightly, consists of selected material from the domestic issue of LIFE as well as original articles (*Payment:* $500) and occasional articles adapted from **FORTUNE** and **SPORTS ILLUSTRATED.**

LIVING CHURCH, THE (1878), The Rev. CARROLL E. SIMCOX, 407 East Michigan Street, Milwaukee, Wisconsin 53202. *T.* 276–5420, area code 414.
25 cents. $10.95 annual. W.—Specialised articles on religious and social subjects by authorities in the field. *Length:* 750 to 1500 words. *Payment:* $15–$25 on acceptance, if requested. Occasional short poems; *no payment.* *Illustrations:* line and half-tones.

LOOK (1937) WILLIAM B. ARTHUR, 488 Madison Avenue, New York, N.Y. 10022. *T.* 212–750–7000. *Cable:* Lookmag, New York.
$5 a year. F.—Articles about people. *Illustrations:* half-tone and colour. Picture stories. *Payment:* top American rates.

McCALL'S MAGAZINE, Mrs. S. ALEXANDER, 230 Park Avenue, New York, N.Y. 10017.
50 cents. M.—A leading domestic monthly, using short stories from 3000 to 6000, complete novels. 8000 to 20,000, serials 30,000 to 40,000 words, and articles of 1500 to 5000 words of striking attraction for women and their families, whether in the home or at work. Also practical household feature articles, and miscellaneous matter. *Payment:* top rates and made on acceptance.

MADEMOISELLE, BETSY TALBOT BLACKWELL, 420 Lexington Avenue, New York, N.Y. 10017. *T.* MU 9–5900.
60 cents. M.—$6.00 a year in U.S.A., $6.50 Canada; $9.00 elsewhere. Short stories and articles of interest to young women of 18 to 25. *Length:* up to 3500 words. *Payment:* on acceptance; fiction and articles from $300 poetry from $25. Departmental features to the department editor concerned; general features to Mary Cantwell, Managing Editor; fiction to Ellen A. Stoianoff, Fiction Editor.

MECHANIX ILLUSTRATED, ROBERT G. BEASON, 67 West 44th Street, New York, N.Y. 10036. *T.* 212 661-4000.

35 cents. M.—A popular scientific magazine covering developments in aviation, radio, boats, automobiles, and kindred fields. *Payment:* promptly on acceptance $10 to $25 each for photographs, and $500 or more for unusually good articles which sometimes are as long as 2000 words. A how-to-build section, giving plans for home-workshop and home-improvement projects, is a feature. *Payment* for this is on the basis of interest of the project. Study of the magazine is recommended before submitting material. *Illustrations:* photographs, plans and drawings.

MODERN PHOTOGRAPHY, JULIA SCULLY, 165 West 46th Street, New York, N.Y. 10036. *T.* Plaza 7-2800.

75 cents. M.—Articles 1000 to 3000 words. Instructive, inspirational, technical, movie making. *Payment:* $60 per page text and photographs. *Illustrations:* half-tone and four-colour letterpress, zinc line drawings. Prefer 8 × 10 or 11 × 14 glossy photographs. $10–$35 for black and white photographs; $50–$200 for colour.

MODERN ROMANCES, HENRY P. MALMGREEN, 750 Third Avenue, New York, N.Y. 10017.

50 cents. M.—Strong, dramatic, first-person confession stories, realistically motivated and convincing, with suspense, emotion and true-to-life characterisations. *Story lengths:* up to 7500 words. *Payment:* from 4 to 5 cents per word on acceptance.

NATION, THE (1865), CAREY McWILLIAMS, 333 Avenue of the Americas, New York, N.Y. 10014. *T.* Chelsea 2-8400.

35 cents. ($10 a year; foreign and Canadian $1.00 extra). W.—Non-fiction pieces. *Payment:* 2 cents a word. *Length:* 2000 words.

NATIONAL GEOGRAPHIC (1888), Editor-in-Chief, MELVILLE BELL GROSVENOR (National Geographic Society), 17th & M Streets, N.W., Washington, D.C. 20036. European Office: 4 Curzon Place, Mayfair, London, W1Y 8EN.

$1.10 a copy. M.—Authentic articles and unique photographs of a geographical nature, giving accounts of exploration, adventure, travel, etc., are desired, especially those that bring out the curious and characteristic customs of native life and conditions in distant and out-of-the-way parts of the world. These should be from 2000 to 7500 words, preferably accompanied by a collection (100–150) of original colour transparencies, 35 mm. or larger. Such transparencies unaccompanied by articles on the subject will receive every consideration. Remuneration for articles $1,500 to $3,000, for photographs minimum of $50 for single transparencies or $200 per colour page, upon acceptance, but it is impossible to judge adaptability until careful examination has been made. Unaccepted material returned promptly. Before submitting material prospective contributors are advised to consult several issues of the magazine and then to enquire of the Editor concerning the Society's interest in their chosen subjects.

NEW REPUBLIC, THE, GILBERT HARRISON, 1244 19th Street, N.W., Washington, D.C. 20036.

40 cents. W.—Serious articles on politics, economics, finance and the arts, by outstanding experts who can also write unusually well. *Length:* 2000 words. *Payment:* by arrangement.

NEWSWEEK (1933), OSBORN ELLIOTT, 444 Madison Avenue, New York, N.Y. 10022. *T.* HA 1-1234. *T.A.* Newsweek, New York.

50 cents. W.—No free-lance material solicited.

NEW YORK POST (1801), DOROTHY SCHIFF, Publisher; JAMES A WECHSLER. Editorial Page Editor, 210 South Street, New York, N.Y. 10002. 10 cents. D.

NEW YORK TIMES, Times Square, New York, N.Y. 10036. London Office: Printing House Square, E.C.4. *T.* 01–236 5691.
10 cents. D. (Sunday 50 cents.)

NEW YORK TIMES MAGAZINE, DANIEL SCHWARZ, Times Square, New York, N.Y. 10036. London Office: Printing House Square, E.C.4.
Articles based on the news and current trends from 2500 to 5500 words in length. *Payment:* $750 for 3,500 words. No verse.

NEW YORKER, THE, WILLIAM SHAWN, 25 West 43rd Street, New York, N.Y. 10036.
50 cents. W.—Uses articles, fiction, satirical or humorous prose, light poetry, clever couplets, and quatrains on current affairs, humorous pictures and picture ideas, and anecdotal material for "Talk of the Town" department. Does not buy photographs and pays varying rates on acceptance.

PAGEANT (1945), JACK J. PODELL, 205 East 42nd Street, New York 10017. *T.* Lexington 2–9050.
50 cents. M.—Articles of general interest 1500 to 3000 words. Always query first. *Payment:* averages $300. *Illustrations:* half-tone, black and white. Picture stories.

PARADE, 733 Third Avenue, New York, N.Y. 10017. *T.* 212 867–1100.
Articles with strong family appeal on unusual personalities or giving a fresh angle to a current news story. *Length:* up to 2500 words.

PARENTS' MAGAZINE, Mrs. DOROTHY WHYTE COTTON, 52 Vanderbilt Avenue, New York, N.Y. 10017. *T.* Murray Hill 5–4400.
50 cents. M.—Articles on family relationships, baby care, child development, health, education, 2500 to 3000 words. All material should be written for adults. No juvenile material accepted. Full-length articles and fillers paid for on acceptance, by arrangement. Writers should query article ideas, and enclose an outline and sample opening, before submitting completed MSS.

PLAYBOY, HUGH M. HEFNER, 919 N. Michigan Ave, Chicago, Illinois 60611. *T.* (312) 642–1000.
$10 a year. M.—It is essential to study the type of material used in this magazine before submitting MSS. Good prices for suitable material (e.g. $3000 for leading story in issue, standard length $2,000; short-shorts $1,000).

PLAYS, The Drama Magazine for Young People, A. S. BURACK, 8 Arlington Street, Boston, Mass. 02116. *T.* 617–536 7420.
$1 ($8 per year; $9 per year outside U.S.). M.—One-act plays suitable for production by young people—comedies, farces, mysteries, dramas, fables, holiday plays, etc. *Payment:* $35 upwards per play. No *illustrations*.

POETRY, DARYL HINE, 1228 North Dearborn Parkway, Chicago, Illinois 60610.
$1.25. M.—Long and short poems. Quality alone the test for publication, irrespective of theme. The only requirement for form, whether experimental or more obviously traditional, is that it be genuine. *Payment:* 50 cents a line for verse, $6.00 a page for prose, on publication.

POLITICAL SCIENCE QUARTERLY, Managing Editor, ALDEN T. VAUGHAN (edited for Academy of Political Science by the Faculty of Political Science of Columbia University, New York), 321M Fayerweather Hall, Columbia University, New York, N.Y. 10027. *T.* 280–3651.

$2.50.—Scholarly papers and book reviews: articles on political and legal history, economics, social science, and public law. Articles, 4500 to 7500 words. No payment.

POPULAR ELECTRONICS (1954), OLIVER P. FERRELL, One Park Avenue, New York, N.Y. 10016. *T.* (212)–679 7200.

50c. 12 times a year.—Tutorial and state-of-the-art reports on recent electronic developments, plus detailed construction projects for the advanced electronics experimenter—no minimum or maximum *length. Payment:* 15c. per word. *Illustrations:* line and half-tone.

POPULAR MECHANICS (1902), ROBERT P. CROSSLEY, 224 West 57th Street, New York, N.Y. 10019. *T.* (212) 765–6850.

50 cents, $5.00 per year. M.—Illustrated articles and features on subjects in field of mechanics, science, crafts, hobbies, sports, new products. *Length:* up to 2000 words. *Payment:* $15 for short, illustrated item; minimum rate for typical five-page feature is $300 and may go as high as $600. *Illustrations:* half-tone, line and colour.

POPULAR PHOTOGRAPHY (1937), KEN POLI, 1 Park Avenue, New York, N.Y. 10016. *T.* Oregon 9–7200.

75 cents. M.—Articles of interest to amateur photographers. *Payment:* $20 per black and white picture; $75 per page for pictures and text. *Illustrations:* black and white, and colour.

POPULAR SCIENCE MONTHLY (1872), ERNEST V. HEYN, 355 Lexington Avenue, New York, N.Y. 10017. *T.* Murray Hill 7–3000.

50 cents. $5.00 per year. $8.50 abroad. M.—Timely material on new developments in science and mechanics, well illustrated with photographs, 2000 words or less. Short illustrated articles describing new inventions and scientific discoveries. Photo layouts up to six pages, in black and white. Stories of explorations, new and interesting industrial processes, etc. How-to-make material and "kinks" for the Home and Workshop Department. *Payment:* up to 20 cents a word; $8 and up for shorts, on acceptance.

PUBLISHERS' WEEKLY, CHANDLER B. GRANNIS, 1180 Avenue of the Americas, New York. N.Y. 10036.

$16.50 a year in U.S.; $17.50 a year in Canada and Pan America; $19.50 a year elsewhere.—Articles 1500–3000 words, dealing with general book-trade problems, *not* literary information or comment. *Payment:* by arrangement; within two weeks following publication.

REDBOOK MAGAZINE, SEY CHASSLER, 230 Park Avenue, New York 10017.

50 cents. M.—Short stories and articles, 2500 to 5000 words; short shorts 1200 words; novels of 35,000 to 45,000 words, complete in one issue; articles usually on assignment only. Realistic stories and articles dealing with to-day's problems, with appeal to the 18–34 age group, U.S.A. background preferred. *Payment* on acceptance.

SATURDAY REVIEW, Editor: NORMAN COUSINS, 380 Madison Avenue, New York, N.Y. 10017.

$10 a year. W.—Articles on the arts (with special emphasis on literature and music), education, science, communications, current affairs, etc. Verse. No fiction. *Payment:* on publication.

SPORT MAGAZINE, AL SILVERMAN, Editor (Macfadden-Bartell Corp.), 205 East 42nd Street, New York 10017. *T.* Lexington 2–9050. (See also TRUE Series).
50 cents. M.—Articles—human interest with unusual personalised angles about top personalities in spectator sports or events (preferably in the U.S.), or articles bringing out unusual sports or newly discovered personalities. Adult masculine viewpoint of writer essential. No limit on words, but average 3000 to 4000, with photographs of subject. *Payment:* from $50 for shorts to $1000 for extra-length features. New slant on topical sports controversy always good.

SPORTS AFIELD, LAMAR UNDERWOOD, 575 Lexington Avenue, New York, N.Y. 10022. *T.* Murray Hill 8–8500.
$4.00 p.a., Canada $4.50 p.a., other countries $7.00 p.a. M.—Hunting, fishing, camping type material; stories with a natural history slant on ways and lives of animals. Fiction must pertain to the outdoor field. *Length:* 2000 to 3000 words. *Illustrations:* black and white and colour.

SPORTS ILLUSTRATED, ANDRE LAGUERRE, Rockefeller Center, New York, N.Y. 10020. *T.* Judson 6–1212. *T.A.* Time Inc., New York.
60 cents. U.S., Canada, and U.S. possessions. W.—Non-fiction articles from 250 to 5000 words. *Illustrations:* photographs, duo-tone and four-colour. Sketches or art reproductions up to four-colour.

SUCCESSFUL FARMING (1902), DICK HANSON, 1716 Locust Street, Des Moines, Iowa 50303. *T.* 284–9011.
$2 per year. M.—Farm and farm management material. *Payment:* by arrangement.

SUNDAY DIGEST, L. RICHARD BURNAP, David C. Cook Publishing Co., Elgin, Illinois 60120. *T.* 312–741–2400.
$2.00. W.—Non-fiction articles, to 1800 words; personality profile, personal experiences, application of Christian faith to current problems, missionary, church and ministry needed. Quality photos to illustrate non-fiction articles desired. Little fiction used. Editorial requirements pamphlet available upon request. Good rates on acceptance; 3 cents and up per word. $5–$10 for acceptable photos. Note: 1 year between acceptance and publication.

TIME, Time & Life Building, Rockefeller Center, New York 10020. *T.* Judson 6–1212. London Office: Time and Life Building, New Bond Street, W1Y 0AA
50 cents. W.—All material is staff written, but the London office is glad to be put in touch with reliable sources of information for current news and pictures. The London office is British Headquarters for TIME (all editions), LIFE, LIFE INTERNATIONAL, FORTUNE and SPORTS ILLUSTRATED. TIME LATIN-AMERICA, TIME ATLANTIC, TIME ASIA, TIME SOUTH PACIFIC, TIME CANADA and TIME U.S. have identical editorial content, except that the Canadian edition has extra pages of home news.

TODAY'S HEALTH (formerly HYGEIA), BYRON T. SCOTT, 535 N. Dearborn Street, Chicago, Ill. 60610. *T.* 527–1500.
$4 per year. M.—Popular health articles of 1000 to 2500 words, and series; emphasis on solid material rather than on novel and dramatic. *Payment:* 10 cents a printed word and up. Buys photographs and photo features. Query first. *No unsolicited MSS.*

TRAVEL (1901), MALCOLM MCTEAR DAVIS, Travel Building, Floral Park, New York 11001. *T.* (516) FL 2–9700.

60 cents per copy. M. $6 a year plus $1 for foreign postage.—Articles on travel, exploration, adventure, and significant changes in the post-war world, on areas rather than single cities. Articles from 1000 to 3000 words, preferably 2500; payment on acceptance goes up to $300. Articles should include costs and prices and be accompanied by black and white photographs and/or colour transparencies. Specialises in striking illustrations, and good photographs are always helpful. Contributors should figure at least two illustrations to each 1000 words. No fiction or poetry.

TRAVEL & CAMERA, CRANSTON JONES, 132 West 31st Street, New York, N.Y. 10001. *T.* 868–2600.

75 cents. M.—Articles on travel and photography. *Length:* 500–2000 words. *Payment:* $350–$1,500. *Illustrations:* Photographs. Black and white ($150 per page); colour ($250 per page). Query before submitting. Magazine a wholly-owned subsidiary of American Express Co.

The five following magazines, all but one with similar requirements, are published by the Macfadden-Bartell Corp., 205 East 42nd Street, New York, N.Y. 10017.

TRUE CONFESSIONS MAGAZINE, FLORENCE J. MORIARTY.

50 cents. M.—Is in the market for first-person confession stories from American life, dealing with strong, dramatic problems of young love, romance, marriage, 2000 to 10,000 words. Inspirational, love-problem, self-help fillers, up to 800 words. *Payment:* immediately upon acceptance. 5 cents a word.

TRUE DETECTIVE, A. P. GOVONI.

50 cents. M.—This detective magazine is in the market for true current stories of investigation of crime, by newspaper men, or by professional writers who have examined records and interviewed officers. Material should be written in dramatic story form with good characterisation, suspense, and authentic details of the actual investigation. Stories from 5000–6000 words in length are desired. Photographs of principals, investigating officers, etc., involved in cases are necessary. No fiction. *Payment:* $7 each for photographs used. Preliminary query compulsory.

TRUE LOVE, BRUCE ELLIOTT. 35 cents. M.—First person, true-to-life experiences of to-day; 4000 to 6000 words. 3 cents per word.

TRUE ROMANCE, F. R. GOULD. 35 cents. Stories of family life, courtship, teens, stressing human problems. Stories should be written in first person. Reader must feel these experiences really happened. *Payment:* on acceptance; 3–5 cents per word. *Length:* 2000–11,000 words.

TRUE STORY, SUZANNE HILLIARD. 50 cents. M.

This magazine endeavours to get realism into its stories, not only in themes but in style of writing; all must be first-person. Simple and unfictional, "truth" stories should be developed with the unpredictability of life itself. Problems of today: courtship, young marriage, wife-hood, motherhood, family life dramatically and romantically told. Story *length* ranges from 1,000 to 10,000 words. *Payment:* 5c. per printed word except for short-shorts. Rate for these is based on quality of writing and plot content.

VIRGINIA QUARTERLY REVIEW, CHARLOTTE KOHLER, 1 West Range, Charlottesville, Va. 22903.

$5 p.a. Q.—Poetry. *Length:* of stories and articles 5000 words. *Payment:* $5 a printed page. Please include self-address envelope and postage.

VOGUE, 420 Lexington Avenue, New York, N.Y. 10017. DIANA VREELAND, Editor-in-Chief American **VOGUE.** See also entry in British Journals.

75 cents. F.—20 issues a year. Illustrated publication devoted to fashion, beauty, medicine and health, houses and entertaining, attractive personalities of the moment, travel, theatre, books, movies and the arts. Has an extraordinary list of literary contributors. Designed to interest every woman; and does interest a good many men. Rate of *payment:* varies according to the author and type of material.

VOLTA REVIEW, GEORGE W. FELLENDORF, 1537 35th Street, N.W. Washington, D.C. 20007. *T.* 337–5220.

$1.40, ($12.50 a year domestic, $13.50 a year Canada, $14.00 a year other foreign). M. (except June, July and August).—For parents and teachers of deaf children, and for deaf and hard of hearing adults. Articles on teaching speech and lip reading, on the intellectual welfare of the deaf, elimination of the causes of deafness, etc., and especially suggestions for enabling the deaf child to compete successfully with the hearing child. Personality sketches of successful deaf and hard of hearing persons; hearing aids, lip reading; suggestions for employment for persons with hearing defects. *Length preferred:* about 2000 words maximum. Very courteous in treatment of contributors. No payment. *Illustrations:* any to suit articles. No colour cuts.

WOMAN'S DAY (1937), GERALDINE RHOADS, 67 West 44th Street, New York, N.Y. 10036. *T.* 661–4000.

20 cents. M.—Fiction 3000 to 3500 words; plot; modern settings, subtle humour or satire. Serious and humorous articles 1500–2500 words. *Payment:* on acceptance.

WRITER, THE, A. S. BURACK. Editor, 8 Arlington Street, Boston, Mass. 02116. *T.* 617–536 7420.

60 cents, 75 cents by post. $7.00 a year, $8.00 a year outside U.S. M.— Practical articles on writing for publication, 1000 to 2000 words. Pays for all material. Generally overstocked, however, and advise a query to editor before submitting articles.

YACHTING, WILLIAM W. ROBINSON, 50 West 44 Street, New York, N.Y. 10036. *T.* 212 MU2–3214.

75 cents. M.—Accepts articles relating to yachting in all its phases and variable themes that have to do with pleasure boats. *Rates:* average $50 per 1000 words, paid on acceptance. *Illustrations:* photographs and drawings.

YALE REVIEW, J. E. PALMER, 28 Hillhouse Avenue, New Haven, Conn. 06520.

$6 p.a. $6.50 outside U.S.A. Q.—Limited market for exceptional poetry.

SOUTH AFRICAN JOURNALS AND MAGAZINES

ARGUS SOUTH AFRICAN NEWSPAPERS.

THE ARGUS, Cape Town, 5c. D.; **WEEK-END ARGUS** (Sat.), 5c.; **THE STAR,** Johannesburg, 5c. D.; **THE DAILY NEWS** Durban, 5c. D.; **SUNDAY TRIBUNE,** Durban, 8c.; **THE DIAMOND FIELDS ADVERTISER,** Kimberley, 5c.D.; **THE CHRONICLE,** Bulawayo, 3½c. D.; **THE RHODESIA HERALD** Salisbury, 3½c. D.; **THE SUNDAY MAIL,** Salisbury, 5c.; **THE SUNDAY NEWS,** Bulawayo, 3½c.; **UMTALI POST,** Umtali, 3½c. Accept articles of general, South African and Rhodesian interest. *Payment:* for contributions accepted for publication is made in accordance with an Editor's estimate of the value of the manuscript. Contributions should be addressed to the Managing Editor, Argus South African Newspapers Ltd., 85 Fleet Street, London, E.C.4. (*T.* 01–353 3765), and not direct.

BETHLEHEM EXPRESS (1906), T. C. ROFFE, 10 Muller Street, Bethlehem.
2½ cents (3d.). W.—English and Afrikaans.

(BLOEMFONTEIN) FRIEND, THE, J. R. COLMAN, Editor, P.O. Box 245, Bloemfontein. London: Argus South African Newspapers Ltd., 85 Fleet Street, E.C.4. *T.* 01–353 3765. 5c. D.

(CAPE TOWN) CAPE TIMES, THE (1876), V. NORTON, P.O. Box 11, or 77 Burg Street, Cape Town. *T.* 41–3361. London Editor: W. J. WARD-JACKSON, Room 7d, Daily Telegraph Buildings, Fleet Street, E.C.4. *T.* 01–353 8607.
5c. D.—Contributions must be suitable for daily newspaper and must not exceed a column (about 1000 words). Articles of public, sporting, social, or topical interest, also travel, feminine interest and general articles for **THE CAPE TIMES WEEK-END MAGAZINE.** *Length:* up to 1000 words. *Payment:* minimum £5 5s. per 1000 words. *Illustrations:* photographs of outstanding interest. Payment at minimum rate of £1 10s. per picture.

(DURBAN) NATAL MERCURY (1852), JOHN D. ROBINSON (Robinson & Co., Ltd.), Devonshire Place, Durban. *T.* 24511.
5 cents. D. (except Sundays).—Serious background news and inside details of world events. *Length:* 700 to 900 words. *Payment:* £3 3s. to £7 7s. *Illustrations:* photographs of general interest.

FAIR LADY, JANE RAPHAELY, (National Magazine Company), 42 Keerom Street, Cape Town. *T.* 413181.
10 cents. F.—Articles and stories for women including showbiz, travel, humour. *Length:* articles up to 5000 words, short stories from 3000 to 5000 words; short novels and serialisation of book material. *Payment:* on quality rather than length—by arrangement on acceptance. *Illustrations:* Colour (excluding 35 mm.) and black-and white illustrations for articles and features of general interest—celebrities, royalty, situation pictures. Full colour and black-and-white art illustrations for stories and serials.

FARMERS' WEEKLY (1911), E. C. HAVINGA, P.O. Box 245, Bloemfontein. London: Argus South African Newspapers Ltd., 85 Fleet Street, E.C.4. *T.* 01–353 3765.

  8 cents. Annual subscription R3.50 in South Africa, R8.50 elsewhere. W.—Articles, generally illustrated, up to 2000 words in length dealing with all aspects of practical farming and research with particular reference to conditions in Southern Africa. *Payment:* according to technical merit. *Illustrations:* half-tone and line. Includes women's section which accepts articles suitably illustrated, on subjects of interest to women. *Payment:* according to merit.

FEMINA & WOMAN'S LIFE, Miss MELODY HARLEY (Argus Printing and Publishing Co. Ltd.), P.O. Box 1084, Johannesburg. *T.* 838–6312. London: Argus South African Newspapers Ltd., 85 Fleet Street, E.C.4.

  15 cents. F.—Articles and stories for women. *Length:* 1000 to 4000 words. *Payment:* on quality rather than length; average for stories, £15–£25, for articles, £15–£35. *Illustrations:* line and half-tone; also two-colour and full colour.

(JOHANNESBURG) SUNDAY TIMES, JOEL MERVIS, P.O. Box 1090, Johannesburg. *T.* 28–1700. London: South African Morning Newspapers Ltd., 24 Holborn, E.C.1., or (London Editorial) Room 7d, 135 Fleet Street, E.C.4. *T.* 01–353 8607.

  8 cents. Every Sunday.—Illustrated articles of human interest, from a South African angle if possible. Maximum 1500 words long and two or three photographs. Shorter essays, stories, and articles of a light nature from 750 to 1250 words. *Payment:* average rate R10.50 (£5 5s.) a column. *Illustrations:* photographic and line.

NATAL WITNESS (1846), S. R. ELDRIDGE, 244 Longmarket Street, Pietermaritzburg, Natal. *T.* Maritzburg 22261. London: 85 Fleet Street, E.C.4.

  5c. D.—Accepts topical articles. *Length:* 500 to 1000 words. *Payment:* Average of R10 per 1000 words. *Illustrations:* press photos, occasional line drawings, R2·10 each. All material should be submitted direct to the Editor in Pietermaritzburg.

PERSONALITY, R. A. SHORT (Argus Printing and Publishing Co. Ltd.), P.O. Box 1084, Johannesburg, South Africa. *T.* 838–6312 Johannesburg. London: Argus South African Newspapers Ltd., 85 Fleet Street, E.C.4. *T.* 01–353 3765.

  15 cents. W. Illustrated.—Articles and photo-features, black and white, and colour, about people, preferably with South African angle. Strong news features and/of photojournalism. 1000–4000 words. Limited fiction. Short stories 1500–5000 words. *Illustrations:* usually commissioned. *Payment:* £6 6s.–£9 9s. per 1000 words for the first Southern African serial rights, with special fees for exclusive material. A separate magazine, **TEENAGE PERSONALITY,** covering the pop scene is included as a supplement with each issue of **PERSONALITY.** Same rates and conditions as main magazine.

(PORT ELIZABETH) EASTERN PROVINCE HERALD, P.O. Box 1117, Port Elizabeth, S. Africa. *T.* 2–2331. London: 231 Strand, W.C.2. *T.* City 5906.

  3c. D.—Contributions from 700 to 1500 words considered. *Payment:* £4 4s. per 700 words minimum. *Illustrations:* topical photographs.

RAND DAILY MAIL (1902), R. LOUW, 171 Main Street, Johannesburg, South Africa. *T.* 28–1500. *T.A.* News, Johannesburg. *Telex* 43–7044/7045 JH. *L.A.* South African Morning Newspapers, 135 Fleet Street, E.C.4. *T.* 01–353 4473.

  5c. D. except Sundays. Litho women's supplement, **Eve,** Thursdays. Articles of general and women's interest, current affairs, fiction. *Length:* 1000 words. Special articles 1800 words (discussion beforehand). *Payment:* R15 to R50.

SAUK-SABC BULLETIN, The Weekly Programme Guide of the South African
Broadcasting Corporation (P.O. Box 8606), Johannesburg, South Africa.
T.A. Broadcast.

5c. W.—Contributions about radio and broadcasting considered. *Length:*
from 300 to 1000 words. *Payment:* R1 per 100 words. *Illustrations:* glossy
prints, line or wash drawings. *Payment:* according to value.

SOUTH AFRICAN GARDEN AND HOME, Argus Magazine Division, CHOLE
ROLFES, 5th Floor, Star Buildings, 47 Sauer Street, P.O. Box 1084, Johannesburg.

30c. M.—Gardening articles suitable to Southern Hemisphere, also articles
for Home Section on flower arrangement, furnishings and food. No fiction.
Length: 1000 words. *Illustrations:* half-tone and line.

SOUTHERN CROSS, P.O. Box 2372, Cape Town. *T.* 455007. *T.A.* Catholic.

7c. W. (Wednesday).—The national Catholic weekly. Catholic news
reports, world and South African. 1000-word articles, 1500-word short stories,
poetry, cartoons of Catholic interest acceptable from free-lance contributors.
Payment: £1 10s. to £2 10s. per 1000 words; poems, 10s. 6d. to £1. *Illustrations:* photographs, 10s. 6d. to £1.

WINGS OVER AFRICA, J. K. CHILWELL, P.O. Box 118, Halfway House, Transvaal.

30c. M. (14th).—Aviation news and features with an African angle. *Payment:* £5 5s. per 1000 words. *Illustrations:* photographs, £1 1s. each.

PUBLISHERS

BRITISH AND IRISH PUBLISHERS

Authors are strongly advised not to pay for the publication of their work. If a MS. is worth publishing, a reputable publisher will undertake its publication at his own expense. In this connection attention is called to the paragraphs in the preface on vanity publishing, to the article on Publishers' Agreements, and to Sir Stanley Unwin's article.

Care should be taken to select a suitable publisher. Before submitting a MS. make certain that the firm you have in mind does in fact publish other books of a similar nature. Some publishers, for instance, have no fiction in their list, others publish only fiction. In most cases in the list below publishers have indicated the subjects in which they are interested.

At the present time most publishers' plans are made for a long time ahead, and it is advisable to send a preliminary letter and/or a specimen chapter and synopsis before submitting a MS. In sending a specimen chapter, or a complete MS., the enclosure of stamps for return postage will invariably secure prompter, and sometimes more favourable, consideration.

Publishers are asked to send in notes of the kind of MSS. they chiefly desire so that this list may be made increasingly useful to authors.

*—Membership of the Publishers' Association.
†—Associate Membership of the Publishers' Association.
T.A.—Telegraphic Address. *T.*—Telephone.

*Abelard-Schuman Ltd. (1955), Abelard House, 8 King Street, London, WC2E 8HS *T.* 01-240 1477-9. *Directors:* Klaus Fluegge, Richard Kislik. Associated Companies (*q.v.*) in Canada and U.S.A.
  Archaeology, Art, Belles-Lettres, Biography and Memoirs, Children's Books (Fiction, Non-Fiction, Picture), Current Affairs, General, History, Humour, Mysteries, Philosophy, Science.

*Academic Press Inc. (London) Ltd., Berkeley Square House, Berkeley Square, London, W1X 6BA *T.* 01-493 6436.

†Actinic Press Ltd., 1-5 Portpool Lane, London, E.C.1. *T.* 01-405 7980.
  Medical, Science.

Adlard Coles Ltd. (1933), 3 Upper James Street, Golden Square, London, W1R 4BP. *T.* 01-734 8080. *Directors:* W. R. Carr, J. C. Reynolds (Managing).
  Yachting, shipping and other maritime subjects; outdoor sports and pastimes.

Albyn Press, Raeburn House, 32 York Place, Edinburgh 1. *T.* Waverley 1735 and 50, Alexandra Road, London, S.W.19. *T.* Wimbledon 1009.
  General literature, books on Scottish subjects and Guide Books.

Alden & Mowbray Ltd., The Alden Press, Osney Mead, Oxford, OX2 0EF. *T.* 49071.
  Handbooks and other works relating to Oxford and district; commissioned books.

Allan (Ian) Ltd., Terminal House, Shepperton, Middlesex. *T.* Walton-on-Thames (WT) 28484.
  Transport—Railways, Aircraft, Shipping, Road, Naval, Military; no fiction.

*Allen (George) & Unwin Ltd., Ruskin House, 40 Museum Street, WC1A 1LU. *T.* 01–405 8577. Sales, Distribution, Production and Accounts: Park Lane, Hemel Hempstead, Herts. *T.* Hemel Hempstead 3244. *Directors:* Rayner Unwin (Chairman), Geoffrey Cass (Group Managing Director), Charles Knight (Managing Director, Hemel Hempstead), Charles Furth, Malcolm Barnes, David Knight, Bryan Fuller. Agents for *The Brookings Institution* and *Baedeker Guides.* Publish: Series for *The Royal Institute of Public Administration, Political and Economic Planning, The National Institute for Social Work Training. The School of Oriental and African Studies, St. Anthony's College, Oxford,* etc. Owners of **Thomas Murby & Co.** *q.v.*

Popular and Academic, Secondary School and University level. Philosophy, Psychology, History, Anthropology, Sociology, Economics, Management, Political Theory, Government and Administration, Current Affairs, Natural Sciences and Geology, Oriental Religions, Transport, Travel, Biography, The Arts, Children's Books.

*Allen (J. A.) & Co. Ltd. (1926), 1 Lower Grosvenor Place, Buckingham Palace Road, London, S.W.1. *T.* 01–834 5606–7 and 01–828 8855. *T.A.* Allenbooks, Sowest, London. *Managing Director:* Joseph A. Allen.

Veterinary and Bloodstock Publications, especially those dealing with the Thoroughbred Horse and the Art of Riding, Hunting and Polo, etc.

*Allen (W.H.) & Co. Ltd., 43 Essex Street, Strand, London, WC2R 3JG. *T.* 01–583 0127. *Executives:* J. C. Simmons, Mark Goulden, D. A. Morrison, C. M. Goulden.

Art, Belles-Lettres, Biography and Memoirs, Children's Books (Fiction, Non-Fiction, Rewards), Current Affairs, Educational (Primary, Secondary, Technical), Fiction, Films, General, History, Humour, Practical Handbooks, Reference, Sociology, Television, Theatre and Ballet, Travel.

Allison & Busby Ltd., (1968), 6a Noel Street, London, W1V 3RB *T.* 01–437 2144. *Directors:* Clive Allison, Margaret Grigson, Graham Huntley, John Smith, Malcolm Hill.

Art, Belles-Lettres, Biography and Memoirs, Current Affairs, Economics, Fiction, General, History, Poetry, Politics, Sociology, Translations.

*Allman & Son (Publishers) Ltd. (1800), 17–19 Foley Street, London, W1A 1DR. *T.* 01–580 9074/0. *T.A.* Millsator, London. *Directors:* C. C. Boon, A. W. Boon, J. T. Boon. *Executive Directors:* Mrs. E. J. Bryant, P. Collins, A. T. McKay. *Secretary:* B. C. J. Rogers.

Educational (Primary, Secondary, Technical), Science.

*Angus and Robertson (U.K.) Ltd. 54–58 Bartholomew Close, London, E.C.1. *T.* 01–606 7831.

Biography and Memoirs, Children's Books (Fiction, Non-Fiction), Drama, Fiction, Maps and Atlases, Medical and Technical, Poetry, Sports, Games and Hobbies, Travel.

Anscombe (Robert) & Co. Ltd. (1936), 2 Ellis Street, S.W.1. *T.* 01–730 2229. *Directors:* H. I. Thompson, Reginald Turnor, Christopher Barry.

Commercial and industrial, consultants in print.

Aquin Press, Woodchester Lodge, Woodchester, Stroud, Gloucestershire. *T.* Amberley 2591–2. *Directors:* A. G. Jones, Arthurs Press Ltd.

Sociology, Theology and Religion.

*Architectural Press Ltd., (1902), 9–13 Queen Anne's Gate, S.W.1. *T.* 01–930 0611. *T.A.* Buildable, London, S.W.1. *The Architectural Review* (monthly), *The Architects' Journal* (weekly). Free-lance artists' and designers' work used. Architecture.

†Arco Publications Ltd., 3 Upper James Street, Golden Square, London, W1R 4BP *T.* 01–734 8080. *Trade Counter:* Book Centre Ltd., North Circular Road, Neasden, N.W.10. *T.* 01–459 1222.
   Instructional books, The Fitzroy Editions of Jules Verne and Jack London, Practical Handbooks, Sports, Games and Hobbies.

Armada paperbacks—see William Collins.

Arms and Armour Press, (1966), 677 Finchley Road, London, N.W.2. *T.* 01–794 6300. *Directors:* L. Leventhal, A. Leventhal.
   Books for Collectors on arms, armour and motoring.

*Arnold (E. J.) & Son, Ltd. (1863), Butterley Street, Leeds, LS10 1AX; also Edinburgh. *T.* Leeds 35541; Edinburgh, Caledonian 7134. *T.A.* Arnold, Phone, Leeds. *Book Depot:* Ring Road, Seacroft, Leeds, 14. *T.* Leeds 643171. *Directors:* E. M. Arnold, J. O. Arnold, T. H. Metson, F. H. Harrison, D. C. Hall and D. S. Howard.
   Educational (Primary, Secondary, Technical).

*Arnold (Edward) (Publishers) Ltd., 41 Maddox Street, W1R 0AN *T.* 01–493 8511. *T.A.* Scholarly, London. *Founded* by Edward Arnold in 1890. *Directors:* J. A. T. Morgan, E. A. Hamilton, B. W. Bennett, P. J. Price, M. Husk, J. G. Martyn.
   Educational books in all subjects (secondary, technical, university); advanced works in humanities, pure and applied science, medicine, and business studies.

*Arrow Books Ltd. (1948), 178–202 Great Portland Street, London, W1N 6AQ *T.* (Editorial) 01–580 3020. *Telex:* 261212. (Trade) 062–181 6362. *Telex:* 18130. *T.A.* Literarius, London, W.1. *Directors:* R. A. A. Holt (*Chairman*), Sir Robert Lusty, Noel Holland, Peter M. Taylor. An imprint of the Hutchinson Publishing Group.
   Paperback publications, fiction and non-fiction.

Art Trade Press, Ltd., 23 Wade Court Road, Havant, Hampshire PO9 2SU. *T.* Havant 4943. Publishers of *Who's Who in Art, Art Prices Current.*

*Asia Publishing House, 447 Strand, London, WC2R 0QU *T.* 01–240 3038. (For further details see under Indian Publishers.)

Aslib (1924), 3 Belgrave Square, London, S.W.1. *T.* 01–235 5050 (for further details see entry under Societies and Clubs).

Associated Book Publishers Ltd., the parent company of a group which includes the following firms, *q.v.*:
   Chapman and Hall Ltd., Current Law Publishers Ltd., Eyre & Spottiswoode (Publishers) Ltd., W. Green & Son Ltd. The Law Book Company Ltd., Australia, Methuen and Co. Ltd., Methuen of Canada Ltd., Canada, The Police Review Publishing Co. Ltd., E. & F. N. Spon Ltd., Stevens and Sons Ltd., Sweet & Maxwell Ltd., Sweet & Maxwell (N.Z.) Ltd., New Zealand, Sweet & Maxwell, Spon (Booksellers) Ltd., Tavistock Publications Ltd., Methuen Academic Ltd., Methuen, Eyre & Spottiswoode Ltd. *Directors:* Sir O. Crosthwaite-Eyre, D.L., M.P. (Chairman), Maurice W. Maxwell, John Burke (Joint Vice-Chairman), P. H. B. Allsop, M.A. (Managing Director), Peter L. K. Wait, Dennis W. Alcock, F.C.A. (Deputy Managing Director), F. C. Friend, John D. Cullen, A. S. Forster. *Secretary:* D. P. Wood, A.C.I.S.

*Athlone Press of the University of London, The (1949), 2 Gower Street, London, WC1E 6DR   *T.* 01–580 9535.

Archaeology, Architecture, Art, Belles-Lettres, Biography and Memoirs, Economics, Educational (Secondary, Technical, University), History, Law, Medical, Music, Oriental, Philosophy, Political Economy, Science, Sociology, Theology and Religion.

Atlantic Book Publishing Company Ltd., 3 Upper James Street, Golden Square, London, W1R 4BP   *T.* 01–734 8080.   *Directors:* W. R. Carr, A. R. H. Birch.

Paperback publishers – children's books.

B.P.C. Publishing Ltd., (**British Printing Corporation**), St. Giles House, 49 Poland Street, London, W1A 2LG   *T.* 01–437 0686.   *Directors:* R. G. Holme (Chairman), P. Galliner (Managing, J. Pollock, C. H. Bateson, P. Morrison (Secretary). Associated companies include:

Macdonald & Co. Publishers Ltd., Macdonald Technical, Scientific & Reference Books, Macdonald Educational, Purnell Partworks, Purnell/Bancroft.

Backus (Edgar). *Proprietors:* J. A. Ridge, H. T. H. Taylor, 44–46 Cank Street, Leicester LEI 5GU   *T.* Leicester 58137.   General and Leicestershire literature.

*Bagster (Samuel) & Sons Ltd. (1794), 72 Marylebone Lane, London, W.1.   *T.* 01–486 1320.   *T.A.* Bagster, London, W.1.   *Directors:* G. R. L. Webb, G. H. Fletcher, Miss S. G. Herbert, Mrs. C. Bishop, Mrs. V. M. L. Webb.   *General Manager:* L. A. Dyson.

Theology and Religion.

*Bailey Bros. & Swinfen, Ltd., Warner House, Folkestone, Kent.   *T.* Folkestone 56501–8.   *T.A.* Forenbuks, Folkestone.   *Telex:* 96328.

Dictionaries, Educational, Sports, Games and Hobbies, General.

*Bailliere, Tindall & Cassell, Ltd. (1826), 7 and 8 Henrietta Street, WC2E 8QE   *T.* 01–836 3386–7–8–9.   *Directors:* D. H. Tindall, R. F. West, P. R. West, S. A. Reynolds, B. A. Gentry, W. R. Kramer (*Secretary*), Mrs. Dorothy Poyser. Exclusive agents for the Veterinary books of Lea & Febiger Inc., the Williams & Wilkins Company and the Iowa State Press.

Medical, Veterinary, Nursing, Pharmaceutical.   *Animal Behaviour, Animal Behaviour Monographs, Rheumatology and Physical Medicine,* the *British Journal of Diseases of the Chest,* the *British Veterinary Journal,* and the *International Journal of Psycho-Analysis.*

Baker (Howard) Publishers Ltd., (1967), 47 Museum Street, London, WC1A 1LY   *T.* 01–405 2021–2.   *Directors:* W. Howard Baker, George P. Mann.

General Fiction and Non-Fiction. Library reprints.

*Baker (John), Publishers Ltd. (incorporating **The Unicorn Press** and **The Richards Press**), 5 Royal Opera Arcade, Pall Mall, S.W.1.   *T.* 01–930 4239.   *Directors:* A. A. G. Black, John Baker, J. D. Newth, C.B.E., C. A. A. Black.

Art, Archaeology, Social History, Natural History, Topography and Country Life, young people's non-fiction.

Bancroft & Co. (Publishers) Ltd., now **Purnell/Bancroft,** *q.v.*

Bantam paperbacks—see **Transworld.**

*Barker (Arthur) Ltd., 5 Winsley Street, Oxford Circus, London, W1N 7AQ. *T.* 01–580 7941. *Directors:* Sir George Weidenfeld (Chairman), Robert Anderson, Nicolas Thompson, K. A. Lilley, A. Miles, B. MacLennan.

Biography, History, Military History, Criminology, Sport, Handbooks, Reference Books.

*Barrie and Jenkins (proprietors Barrie Books Ltd.), 2 Clement's Inn, Strand, WC2A 2EP *T.* 01–242 9171. *Directors:* Hon. A. G. Samuel, L. A. Ullstein, John M. Bunting, John G. Pattison, Richard Wadleigh, E. W. Godfrey, C. C. MacLehose.

Antiques and Collecting, Archaeology, Architecture, Art, Belles-Lettres, Biography and Memoirs, Commerce, Current Affairs, Fiction, History, Music, Philosophy, Practical Handbooks, Sports, Games and Hobbies, Television, Theatre and Ballet, Travel, Books for the Hotel and Catering Industry, General.

*Bartholomew (John) & Son, Ltd., (1826), Duncan Street, Edinburgh EH9 1TA. *T.* 031–667 6981. Cartographic printers and publishers.

Maps and Atlases.

*Batsford (B. T.) Ltd. (1843), 4 Fitzhardinge Street, Portman Square, London, W1H 0AH *T.* 01–935 0537. *Directors:* B. C. Batsford, M.P., Samuel Carr, Peter Kemmis Betty, Patrick Connell.

Architecture, Children's Books (Non-Fiction), Education (Secondary, Technical, University), Fine Arts, Crafts and Needlecraft, History, Social Sciences, Technical, Travel, General.

*Bell (G.) & Sons, Ltd. (1838), York House, Portugal Street, WC2A 2HL *T.* 01–405 0805. *T.A.* Bohn, London, W.C.2. *Directors:* R J. B. Glanville (Chairman), S. L. Dennis, W. H. Mills, M. H. Varvill, C.M.G. Publishers of the Merriam-Webster Dictionaries, Pepy's Diary, etc.

Aeronautics, Archaeology, Art, Biography and Memoirs, Children's Books (Non-Fiction), Dictionaries, Economics, Educational (Secondary, Further, University), Geography, History, Medical, Music, Natural History, Oriental, Physical Education, Political Economic, Practical Handbooks, Reference, Science, Sociology, Sports, Games and Hobbies, Travel.

*Benn (Ernest), Ltd. (1923), Bouverie House, 154 Fleet Street, E.C.4. *T.* 01–353 3212. *T.A.* Bentitle, London, E.C.4. *Telex:* 887026. *Directors:* Keon E. Hughes, E. G. Benn, Sir John Benn, Bt., J. R. Denton, Kenneth Day, J. M. Jourdier, Sir Hugh Stephenson, Timothy Benn.

Archaeology, Children's Books (Fiction, Non-Fiction, Toy or Picture), Collectors Books, Directories or Guide Books, Drama, General, History, Music, Printing, Science, Technology.

Bentley's Codes, Ltd. (1939), 11–12 Bury Street, London, E.C.3. *T.* 01–626 5477. *Directors:* P. H. Bentley, H. B. Bentley, M. T. Bentley. Publish only Telegraph Codes and similar works compiled by own staff.

Bernards (Publishers) Ltd., The Grampians, Western Gate, W.6. *T.* 01–603 2581. *Directors:* S. Babani, B. B. Babani, J. S. Assael.

Practical Handbooks on Radio and Electronics.

F

*Black (A. & C.) Ltd. (1807), 4, 5, and 6 Soho Square, W1V 6AD *T.* 01–734 0845. *T.A.* Biblos, London, W.1. *Directors:* A. A. G. Black (Chairman, great-grandson of founder), J. D. Newth, c.b.e., Stewart King, C. A. A. Black, David Gadsby. Proprietors of John Baker (Publishers) Ltd. and The Dacre Press, *q.v.*
Archaeology, Architecture, Art, Ballet, Children's Books (Non-Fiction), Costume, Dictionaries, Economics, Education, Educational Text books (Infants, Primary, Secondary, Technical, University), Fishing, History, Musicology, Natural History, Philosophy, Railway History, Reference, Sailing, Field Sports, Television, Theology and Religion, Year Books. Publishers of *Who's Who* since 1897.

*Blackie & Son, Ltd. (1809), Bishopbriggs, Glasgow. *T.* 041-772 1046. *T.A.* Blackie, Glasgow. 5 Fitzhardinge Street, London, W1H 0DL *T.* 01–935 2910, 2919 and 2152. *T.A.* Glossarium, Wesdo, London. Also Blackie & Son (India) Ltd. All MSS. to Glasgow except for Children's Books. *Directors:* Euan Cooper-Willis, m.a., (Chairman), John Tannahill, G. H. Bisacre, m.a., a.m.i.c.e., George Ogg, J. W. G. Blackie, b.a.
Educational (Infant, Primary, Secondary), Children's Books (Fiction and Non-Fiction for all ages), Scientific and Technical (Mathematics, Engineering and Allied Subjects), General Books (Reference, Dictionaries).

*Blackwell (Basil) & Mott, Ltd. (1879), 49 Broad Street, Oxford OX1 3BP *T.* Oxford 49111. *Directors:* Sir Basil Blackwell, H. L. Schollick, o.b.e., R. Blackwell, J. K. D. Feather, R. H. Sherbourn, J. A. Cutforth, J. Blackwell, J. E. Critchley, P. Saugman, A. T. Hale.
Children's Books, Classical Studies, Economics, Education (Infants, Primary, Secondary, Technical, University), History, Literature and Criticism, Modern Languages and Philology, Philosophy, Politics and Sociology, Theology.

*Blackwell Scientific Publications Ltd. (1939), 5 Alfred Street, Oxford, OX1 4HB and 9 Forrest Road, Edinburgh, EH1 2QH. *T.* Oxford 40201 and Caledonian 4234. *Directors:* Sir Basil Blackwell, Richard Blackwell, J. E. Critchley, P. G. Saugman, H. L. Schollick, o.b.e., Keith Bowker.
Medicine, Veterinary Medicine, Agriculture, Botany, Science and Technology.

Blackwood (James) & Co. Ltd. (1849), Warner House, 22 Baker's Row, E.C.1. *T.* 01–837 8519.
Dictionaries, educational books, trade calculators and Minidex Negative Filing Systems.

*Blackwood (William) & Sons, Ltd. (1804), 45 George Street, Edinburgh EH2 2JA and Buckingham House, Buckingham Street, Adelphi, London, WC2N 6BU. *T.* Edinburgh: 031–225 5835 and London: 01–839 6191. *T.A.* Blackwood's, Edinburgh. *Directors:* G. Douglas Blackwood, Group Captain F. D. Tredrey, c.b.e., J. R. Snowball. *Blackwood's Magazine* (1817).
Biography and Memoirs, General, History, Naval and Military, Travel.

*Blandford Press Ltd., 167 High Holborn, London, WC1V 6PH. *T.* 01–836 9551. *Directors:* G. C. Burt, E. Barnes, N. R. Burt, R. Wenn.
Art, Biography and Memoirs, Children's Books, Commerce, Colour Encyclo-paedias, Educational (Infants, Primary, Secondary, Technical), History, Hobbies, Music, Practical Handbooks, Theology and Religion, Travel.

Bles (Geoffrey), Ltd. (1923), 52 Doughty Street, WC1N 2LZ *T.* 01–405 3591–2, 5005. *T.A.* Astrapeto, London WC1. *Directors:* Sir William Collins, c.b.e. (Chairman), Jocelyn Gibb, c.b.e. (Managing Director), and F. G.Armstrong.
Biography, Autobiography, History, Travel, Adventure, Criticism, Religion, Philosophy, Stage, Farming, Gardening, Countryside, Animals, Humour, Children, General Fiction, Detective Fiction and Thrillers.

*Blond (Anthony), Ltd. (1957), 56 Doughty Street, WC1N 2LS   T. 01–405 2767–8 and 5709. T.A. Literary, London. Telex: 25376. Directors: Ross D. Sackett (USA) (Chairman), Anthony Blond, Desmond Briggs (Joint Managing), J. F. Brauner (USA), K. W. Hoehn (USA).
Biography, Memoirs, Current Affairs, Fiction, General, Humour, Political Economy and handbooks to the Modern World.

†Blond Educational Ltd. (1963), (a division of Anthony Blond Ltd.), 56 Doughty Street, London, WC1N 2LS T. 01–405 2767–8 and 5709. T.A. Literary, London. Telex: 25376. Divisional Directors: Antony Blond, Desmond Briggs, James Kenyon.
Educational (Primary, Secondary).

Bloomsbury Publishing Co., Ltd., Woodchester Lodge, Woodchester, Stroud, Gloucestershire. T. Amberley 2591–2. Directors: A. G. Jones, Arthurs Press Ltd. Catholic publishers.
Educational (Infants, Primary, Secondary), Sociology, Theology and Religion.

*Bodley Head, Ltd., The, (founded by John Lane in 1887), 9 Bow Street, WC2E 7AL. T. 01–836 9081. T.A. Bodleian, Westcent, London. Directors: Sir Hugh Greene, K.C.M.G., O.B.E. (Chairman), Max Reinhardt (Managing), J. B. Blackley, L. A. Hart, J. R. Hews, Sir Francis Meynell R.D.I., D.LITT., James Michie, Anthony Quayle, C.B.E., Sir Ralph Richardson, John Ryder, Judy Taylor.
Belles-Lettres, Biography and Memoirs, Children's Books (Fiction, Non-Fiction, Picture), Current Affairs, Economics, Essays, Fiction, Films, General, History, Photography, Poetry, Practical Handbooks, Sociology, Travel.
Proprietors of Hollis and Carter Ltd., Putnam & Co. Ltd., Bowes & Bowes (Publishers) Ltd., The Nonesuch Library Ltd., T. Werner Laurie Ltd., Nattali & Maurice Ltd.
Distributors for The Nonesuch Press, q.v.

Bowes & Bowes (Publishers) Ltd. (1850), 9 Bow Street, London, WC2E 7AL. T. 01–836 9081. T.A. Bodleian, Westcent, London. Directors: Max Reinhardt (Chairman), J. B. Blackley, J. R. Hews, John Huntingdon, Michael Oakeshott, John Ryder.
Archaeology, Economics, History, Literary Criticism, Philosophy, Reference.

*British and Foreign Bible Society, 146 Queen Victoria Street, E.C.4. T. 01–248 4751. Bibles, Testaments and portions in 885 languages. The sole object of the B.F.B.S. is to encourage the wider circulation of the Holy Scriptures. General Secretaries: Rev. Neville B. Cryer, M.A., B. N. Tattersall, F.I.A.C., Rev. John G. Weller, B.A.

British Broadcasting Corporation (Publications Management), 35 Marylebone High Street, London, W1M 4AA. T. 01–580 5577. T.A. Broadcasts, Telex, London.
Television.

*Brockhampton Press, Ltd., Salisbury Road, Leicester LE1 7QS   T. Leicester 21091. Directors: Paul Hodder-Williams (Chairman), John Attenborough, Ewart Wharmby, Antony Kamm, Clifford Hufton.
Children's Books, General Books.

Brodie (James) Ltd., (1926), 15 Queen Square, Bath, BA1 2HW. T. 22110. Directors: Frank E. Sandy (Chairman and Managing Director), Cecil H. King, F.C.A. (Secretary), Arthur W. Longstaff.
Educational (Secondary), Film Strips and Tape Recordings.

Brown, Son & Ferguson, Ltd. (1860), 52 Darnley Street, Glasgow, S.1.   T. 041–429 1234. T.A. Skipper, Glasgow, S.1.
Nautical books; Scottish books and Scottish plays. Boy Scout, Cub Scout, Girl Guide and Brownie Guide Books.

Brown Watson Ltd., Digit House, Harlesden Road, Willesden Green, London, N.W.10. *T.* 01–459 2184.

Browne & Nolan, Ltd., The Richview Press, Clonskeagh, Dublin 4. *T.* Dublin 693377.

Bruce & Gawthorn Ltd., 146 Holloway Road, London, N.7. *T.* 01–607 5796.
Children's Books (Non-Fiction, Rewards), Educational (Infants, Primary, Secondary, Technical), History, Natural Science, Theology and Religion, Travel.

*Burke Publishing Co., Ltd., 14 John Street, WC1N 2EJ. *T.* 01–242 6724–5 and 01–242 1065. *Directors:* Stanley Rubinstein (Chairman), Harold K. Starke (Managing Director), Peter Stuart-Heaton, Naomi Galinski, Alan J. Walker.
Children's Books (Fiction, Non-Fiction), Educational (Pre-school and Nursery, Primary, Secondary).

Burrow (Ed. J.) & Co. Ltd., (1900), Imperial House, Lypiatt Road, Cheltenham GL50 2QL. *T.* 0242 21616 (3 lines); 41 Streatham Hill, S.W.2. *T.* 01–674 1222. *Chairman:* Bernard Lewis. *Directors:* Paul Lewis (Managing), P. J. Molland.
Guide Books, Street Plans and Maps, Travel, Year Books, etc.

Business Publications Ltd. (1921), Mercury House, Waterloo Road, London, S.E.1. *T.* 01–928 3388.
Business, Advertising, Marketing, Scientific, Technical and Industrial, Reference, Directories.

*Butterworth Group, The (1818) Kingsway, London WC2B 6AB. *T.* 01–405 6900. *T.A.* Butterwort, London, W.C.2. *Directors:* Norman Fisher, Ian C. Dickson, H. Kay Jones, Mrs. S. Carey, Philip Jarvis, Simon Partridge, David Perry, A. B. Vyvyan. *Branches overseas: Australia:* Butterworth & Co. (Australia) Ltd., 20 Loftus Street, Sydney; 343 Little Collins Street, Melbourne; 240 Queen Street, Brisbane. *Canada:* Butterworth & Co. (Canada) Ltd., 14 Curity Avenue, Toronto, 374. *New Zealand:* Butterworth & Co. (New Zealand) Ltd., 49–51 Ballance Street, Wellington; 35 High Street, Auckland. *South Africa:* Butterworth & Co. (South Africa) Ltd., 33–35 Beach Grove, Durban.
Law, Medicine, Science, Technology, Business and Commerce.

Butterworth & Co. (Publishers) Ltd., see The Butterworth Group.

*Calder and Boyars Ltd., 18 Brewer Street, London, W1R 4AS *T.* 01–734 1985. *Directors:* J. M. Calder, Marion Boyars, Michael Hayes.
Belles-Lettres, Biography and Memoirs, Current Affairs, Directories or Guide Books, Drama, Essays, Fiction, Films, General, Music, Poetry, Reference, Sociology, Theatre and Ballet, Theology, Travel, Year Books, Paperbacks: Calder books, and Jupiter Books.

*Cambridge University Press (1521), Cambridge: The Pitt Building, Trumpington Street, Cambridge, CB2 1RP. *T.* Cambridge 58331. *T.A.* Unipress, Cambridge. London: Bentley House, P.O. Box 92, London, N.W.1. *T.* 01–387 5030. *T.A.* Cantabrigia, London, N.W.1. U.S.A.: 32 East 57 Street, New York, N.Y. 10022. Australia: Cambridge University Press (Australia) Pty. Ltd., 296 Beaconsfield Parade, Middle Park, Victoria 3206. Cambridge: *Publisher:* R. W. David, C.B.E., M.A. *Chief Editor:* M. H. Black, M.A.; *Senior Editors* (*Science*): A. K. Parker, M.A., A. Winter, PH.D.; *Senior Editor* (*School Books*): T. F. Wheatley, M.A.; *Production Manager:* P. G. Burbidge, M.A. London: *General Manager:* C. F. Eccleshare, M.A.; *Assistant Manager:* P. J. Tickell, M.A., New York: *Manager:* F. R. Mansbridge, M.A.; *Deputy Manager: and Controller:* J. Schulman, M.A.; *Assistant Manager:* D. Winsor, M.A. Australia: *Manager:* B. W. Harris.
Archaeology, Educational (Secondary, Tertiary), History, Language and Literature, Law, Oriental, Philosophy, Science (Physical and Biological), Social Sciences, Theology and Religion. The Bible and Prayer Book.

*Cape (Jonathan), Ltd. (1921), 30 Bedford Square, WC1B 3EL. *T.* 01–636 5764 (five lines), 01–636 9395 (three lines) and 01–637 2701 (ten lines). *T.A.* and *Cables:* Capajon, London, W.C.1. General Publisher. *Directors:* Tom Maschler (Chairman), Graham C. Greene (Managing), Michael S. Howard, W. Robert Carr, David Machin, Anthony Colwell. *Special Directors:* Norman Askew, John N. Charin.

Archaeology, Biography and Memoirs, Children's Books, Current Affairs, Drama, Economics, Fiction, History, Philosophy, Poetry, Sociology, Travel.

Carruthers (Robt.) & Sons (1817), P.O. Box 13, Bank Lane, Inverness. *T.* Inverness 33059. *T.A.* Courier, Inverness. *Present Proprietor and Editor:* Miss Eveline Barron, M.A. Publishers of *Inverness Courier* and of books concerning the Highlands.

†Cass (Frank) & Co. Ltd. (1958), 67 Great Russell Street, London, WC1B 3BT *T.* 01–405 9405. *Directors:* Frank Cass (Managing), A. E. Cass, J. H. G McMahon, M. P. Zaidner. *T.A.* Simfay, London, WC1B 3BT.

Economics, History, Social Sciences, Politics, African Studies, Literary. Criticism, Art. Also *The Journal of Development Studies, Middle Eastern. Studies* and *African Language Review.*

*Cassell & Co. Ltd. (1848), 35 Red Lion Square, WC1R 4SJ. *T.* 01–242 6281. *T.A.* Caspeg, London, W.C.1. Melbourne, Sydney, Auckland, N.Z., Johannesburg and Toronto. *Directors:* Desmond Flower, M.C., D.LITT. (Chairman), Bryen Gentry, D. Ascoli, Kenneth Parker, Edwin Harper.

General Books of all classes: Biographies, Fiction, Music, Juvenile non-fiction, Dictionaries and Reference Books, Educational (Infant, Primary, Secondary, Technical), Technical.

Catholic Communications Institute of Ireland, Inc., 7–8 Lower Abbey Street, Dublin 1. *T.* 48750. *T.A.* Veritas, Dublin. Will consider well-informed and interesting MSS. for publication in booklet form.

Religion, including social and educational works, and material relating to the media of communication.

Catholic Truth Society (1868), P.O. Box 422, 38–40 Eccleston Square, S.W.1. *T.* 01–834 4392. *T.A.* Apostolic, London, S.W.1. *Chairman:* Rt. Rev. Mgr. Canon C. Collingwood. *Hon. Treasurer:* Michael Dalglish, F.C.A. *General Secretary:* T. H. Rittner, K.S.G.

Bibles, prayer books and pamphlets of doctrinal, historical, devotional, or social interest are published. MSS. of about 5000 words are suitable.

Centaur Press Ltd., Fontwell, Arundel, Sussex. *T.* 024-368 3302. *Directors:* Jon Wynne-Tyson, Jennifer M. Wynne-Tyson. A preliminary letter should be sent before submitting MS.

Philosophy, Biography, the Arts, Dictionaries, Reference, Satire, Guides, *Centaur Classics, The Regency Library, Travellers' Classics.*

*Chambers (W. and R.), Ltd. (1820), 11 Thistle Street, Edinburgh EH2 1DG and 6 Dean Street, W1V 6LD. *T.* 031–225 4463–4; 01–437 1709. *T.A.* Chambers, Edinburgh; Journal, London. *Chairman and Joint Managing Director:* A. S. Chambers. *Joint Managing Director:* I. Gould. *Directors:* A. Turnbull, T. C. Collocott, D. Menzies, Dr. David Dickson.

Biography or Memoirs, Children's Books (Fiction, Non-Fiction, Rewards, Picture Books), Dictionaries, Mathematical Tables, Guide Books, Educational (Infants, Primary, Secondary, Technical, University), General, Reference, Science, Sports, Games and Hobbies.

*Chapman & Hall, Ltd. (1830), 11 New Fetter Lane, London, E.C.4. *T.* 01–583 9855. *T.A.* Pickwick, London, E.C.4. Agents outside U.S.A. and Canada for American Society of Metals, Ohio. *Directors:* Noel Hughes (Chairman and Managing Director), M. R. Turner, Peter Wait, F. B. Walker, D. G. Sampson.
Science, Technology.

*Chapman (Geoffrey), Ltd. (1957), 18 High Street, Wimbledon, London, S.W.19. *T.* 01–946 3047, 01–947 0121 and 01–947 0051. *Directors:* Geoffrey Chapman (*Chairman*), Alexander Tarbett, Patricia de Trafford, Suzanne Chapman, Raymond C. Hagel (*U.S.A.*), Jeremiah Kaplan (*U.S.A.*), Austin J. Farrell (*U.S.A.*), Carl A. Wallen (*U.S.A.*), Robert A. Barton (*U.S.A.*). Allied and Subsidiary Companies: Johnston & Bacon, Duckett Ltd., (*Bookshop*), 140 Strand, London, W.C.2.
General, religious books of interdenominational interest, children's books, educational, specialised African publishing, road maps and atlases and Scottish publications.

*Charles and Son, Ltd. (1890), Woodbridge House. Clerkenwell Green, E.C.1. *T.* 01–253 2411. *Directors:* R. C. Paton, B.L., M. I. Paton, M.A., George Swan.
Educational (Infants).

*Chatto & Windus Ltd. (1855), 40–42 William IV Street, W.C.2. *T.* 01–836 0127. *Directors:* I. M. Parsons, Norah Smallwood, C. Day Lewis, G. W. Trevelyan, Hugo Brunner, John Charlton. Publishers of *The Use of English.* Incorporates the Children's books of Oliver & Boyd Ltd., under imprint Chatto, Boyd & Oliver Ltd.
Archaeology, Art, Belles-Lettres, Biography and Memoirs, Children's Books (Fiction, Non-Fiction), Current Affairs, Drama, Economics, Educational (Infants, Primary, Secondary, Technical, University), Essays, Fiction, History, Poetry, Political Economy, Sociology, Travel.

Christophers (Publishers) Ltd. (1906). Taken over by Chatto & Windus Ltd. *q.v.*

*Church Book Room Press, (1951), 7 Wine Office Court, Fleet Street, London, E.C.4. *T.* 01–583 1484.

Church Missionary Society, 157 Waterloo Road, London, S.E.1. *T.* 01–928 8681. *T.A.* Testimony, London, S.E.1. *General Secretary:* The Rev. Canon John V. Taylor, M.A.
Theology and Religion, Biography and Memoirs, Children's Books (Fiction, Non-Fiction).

Church of Scotland Department of Publicity and Publication, 121 George Street, Edinburgh, EH2 4YN. *T.* 031–225 5722.

*Churchill (J. & A.), (1825), 104 Gloucester Place, W1H 4AE. *T.* 01–935 2902. *T.A.* Churchill, Publishers, London, W.1. A division of Longman Group Ltd.
Medical, Science (Histology, Biology, Microscopy, Food Chemistry, Industrial Chemistry).

Clarendon Press. See Oxford University Press.

*Clark (T. & T.) (1821), 38 George Street, Edinburgh EH2 2LQ. *T.* 031–225 4703. *T.A.* Dictionary, Edinburgh. *Partners:* T. G. Clark, T. G. R. Clark, C.A.
Dictionaries, Philosophy, Theology and Religion.

Clarke (James) & Co., Ltd. (1859), 7 All Saints Passage, Cambridge. *T.* OCA3 50865. *Managing Director:* A. Douglas Millard.
Theology, Religion, Educational, Technical, Reference Books.

Cleaver-Hume Press Ltd. (*See* Macmillan & Co. Ltd.).

Clifton Books (1967), Clifton House, 83 Euston Road, London, NW1 2RE *T.* 01–387 8441. *Directors:* C. H. Burder (Managing) R. M. Kennard, P. A. Sidders.
Politics, Sociology, Economics, Psychology, Cinema, Theatre, Music.

Clowes (W.), & Sons Ltd., Dorland House, 14 and 16 Lower Regent Street, London, S.W.1. *T.* 01–839 3301. Publishers of *Brassey's Annual, The Armed Forces Year Book,* and *The Army Quarterly and Defence Journal.*

Cohen & West Limited (1947), Broadway House, 68–74 Carter Lane, E.C.4. *T.* 01–248 4821. *T.A.* Columnae, London. *Directors:* Norman Franklin, Colin Franklin.
Anthropology, Sociology, Criticism.

Collet's (Publishers), Ltd., *Registered Address and Head Office:* Denington Estate, Wellingborough. *T.* 4351. *Directors:* Mrs. J. Birch, Thomas A. Russell.
Sociology, Economics, Politics, Art, Music and Novels, Technical and Scientific, Language Study materials.

Collie paperbacks—see Transworld.

*Collier-Macmillan Ltd., 10 South Audley Street, London, W1Y 6AE *T.* 01–493 5511. *Cables:* Pachamac, London, W.1.
Directors: Frederick Kobrak (Managing Director), Leo P. Mabel, U.S.A., Joseph F. Bond, U.S.A., Edward Harris, Jr., U.S.A., Carl A. Wallen, U.S.A. *Editorial:* A. R. Evans. *Marketing:* David Cunningham.
Collier-Macmillan Ltd., is the British publishing and distribution subsidiary of Crowell-Collier and Macmillan, New York. Imprints: Macmillan, The Free Press, Collier Books, Crowell Collier Press, Collier-Macmillan.

Collingridge (W. H. & L.) Ltd., books—see The Hamlyn Publishing Group Ltd.

*Collins (William), Sons & Co., Ltd. (1819), General and Children's Book Publishing Offices, and Fontana and Armada Paperback Publishing Offices, 14 St. James's Place, London, S.W.1. *T.* 01–493 5321. Stationery Business Offices and Book Trade Counter, 42–50 York Way, King's Cross, London, N.1. *T.* 01–837 0012–6. Printing Offices and Editorial Offices for Bibles, Educational, Children's and Reference Books, 144 Cathedral Street, Glasgow. C.4. *T.* 041–552 4488. *Branches:* New York, Toronto, Sydney, Melbourne, Auckland, Johannesburg, Salisbury. *Directors:* Sir William Collins, C.B.E. (Chairman and Managing Director), I. G. Collins (Vice-Chairman and Managing Director), W. J. Collins, F. I. Chapman, D. W. Nickson (Managing Directors), W. L. G. Duff, S. A. M. Collins, T. R. Ballard. *Executive Directors:* R. A. Jamieson, R. Knittel, D. Campbell, R. J. Hardingham, A. R. House, C. E. Allen, A. C. Fyfe, J. Garrigan, M. J. S. Hyde, H. McLennan, D. R. Oyler, R. E. Poynton, P. J. Scherer, R. J. Strachan, I. Ure, P. Ziegler.
Archaeology, Architecture, Art, Belles-Lettres, Bibles, Biography and Memoirs, Children's Books (Fiction, Non-Fiction, Rewards, Toy and Picture, Annuals), Current Affairs, Dictionaries, Directories or Guide Books, Educational (Infants, Primary, Secondary, Technical, University), Essays, Fiction, General, History, Humour, Maps and Atlases, Natural History, Naval and Military, Philosophy, Practical Handbooks, Reference, Science (history of), Sports, Games and Hobbies, Travel, Theology and Religion; Crime Club, Fontana, Fontana Library, Fontana Religious paperbacks and Armada Children's paperbacks.

Common Ground Educational Filmstrips, Audio Visual Division, Longman Group Ltd., Longman House, Burnt Mill, Harlow, Essex. *T.* Harlow 26721. *Telex:* 81259.

Condé Nast Publications, Ltd. (1916), Vogue House, Hanover Square, London, W1R 0AD. *T.* 01–499 9080. *T.A.* Volon, Wesdo, London. *Directors:* Daniel Salem (Chairman) John Perry (Managing Director), F. C. Beech, D. P. L. Matthews, R. Britton, R. W. Brook Jones, Beatrix Miller, I. S. V. Patcévitch (U.S.A.). Publishers of *Vogue* and associated magazines. *Brides, House & Garden, Condé Nast Books.* Authors and artists should consult the Editor before submitting MSS.

Connoisseur, The, Chestergate House, Vauxhall Bridge Road, London, S.W.1. *T.* 01–834 2331. (Editor, L. G. G. Ramsey, F.S.A.).
Illustrated monthly on international art, antiques, collecting, etc., also art books.

***Conservative Political Centre** (1945), 32 Smith Square, S.W.1. *T.* 01–222 9000. *Director:* Russell Lewis.
Political Economy, Current Affairs, Sociology.

***Constable & Co. Ltd.** (1890), 10 Orange Street, WC2H 7EG *T.* 01–930 0801–7. *Trade:* 062–181 6362. *T.A.* Dhagoba, London. *Directors:* Benjamin Glazebrook (Chairman and Managing Director), Miles Huddleston, Hon. John Jolliffe, P. N. Marks, Noel Holland, R. A. A. Holt.
Archaeology, Architecture, Art, Belles-Lettres, Biography or Memoirs, Drama, Economics, Educational (Infants, Primary, Secondary, Technical, University), Essays, Fiction, General, History, Humour, Medicine, Music, Naval, Military, Philosophy, Practical Handbooks, Reference, Religion, Science (Anthropology, Biological Sciences, Chemistry; Physics inc. Mathematics, Astronomy, Civil Engineering, Electrical Engineering, Mechanical Engineering, Metallurgy; Materials inc. Powder Science, Chemical Technology, Manufactures), Sports, Games, Hobbies, Travel, Year Books.

†**Cooper (Leo), Ltd.** (1968), 196 Shaftesbury Avenue, London WC2H 8JL *T.* 01–836 5733. *Directors:* Leo Cooper, J. Cooper, T. R. Hartman, J. M. Carew, M.C.
Military History.

Corgi paperbacks—see **Transworld.**

Cornmarket Press Limited, 42–43 Conduit Street, London, W1R 0NL. *T.* 01–734 8282. *T.A.* Graduates, London, W.1. *Telex:* 23282. *Directors:* C. Labovitch, P. Cooper, R. St. G. Cazalet, C. Irving, P. Kogan, J. Pither.

Country Life, books—see **The Hamlyn Publishing Group Ltd.**

Cresset Press, Ltd., The, Incorporated with **Barrie and Jenkins,** *q.v.*

***Crosby Lockwood & Son Ltd.** (1858), 26 Old Brompton Road, S.W.7. *T.* 01–589 0111–2. *Directors:* Humphrey Wilson, A. Candy, Trevor Poyser.
Agriculture, Architecture, Commerce, Dictionaries, Directories, Economics, Practical Handbooks, Science (Physics, Chemistry, Nutrition), Sociology, Hobbies.

Curwen (J.) & Sons, Ltd., 29 Maiden Lane, WC2E 7JX. *T.* 01–240 1666–7–8. *T.A.* Curwen, London, W.C.2. Musical and educational.
Music.

Dacre Press, The (1939). Theological and religious. Business purchased in 1949 by A. & C. Black Ltd., q.v.

Daniel Company (The C. W.), Ltd. (1904), Ashingdon, Rochford, Essex SS4 3JD. *T.* Hockley 3735. *Directors:* W. T. Symons, M. Sweetlove, D. M. Waltham.
Medical, Occult, Philosophy, Theology and Religion.

*Darton, Longman & Todd, Ltd. (1959), 85 Gloucester Road, London, S.W.7. *T.* 01–370 5031. *T.A.* Librabook, London, S.W.7. *Directors:* G. C. Darton, T. M. Longman, J. M. Todd, E. A. C. Russell.
Bibles, Dictionaries, Directories or Guide Books, General, History, Music, Reference, Sports, Games and Hobbies, Theology and Religion, Travel.

Darwen Finlayson Ltd., 50a Bell Street, Henley-on-Thames, Oxfordshire. *T.* Henley 2427. *Directors:* Lord Darwen (Managing Director), M. F. C. Marshall, John Hassell, John Levitt.
General and Educational, History, Practical Handbooks, Sociology, Reference, Reprints; also publishers of Delta paperbacks.

*David & Charles (Publishers) Ltd. (1960), South Devon House, Railway Station, Newton Abbot, Devon. *T.* Newton Abbot 3521–6. *Directors:* David St. John Thomas (Managing), T. Stanhope Sprigg, Eric R. Delderfield, R. J. Shepherd, Eric B. Spencer, P. M. Thomas. Incorporating Raleigh Press (1952). Publishers of *Industrial Archaeology, Maritime History, Studies in Adult Education, Transport History,* and *Textile History.*
Antiques and Collecting, Archaeology, Architecture, Aviation, Canals and Waterways, Economics, Gardening, General, Geography and Cartography, History, Industrial History and Archaeology, Maritime Subjects, Natural History, Practical Subjects, Railway, Regional Studies, Technical, Topography. Ideas welcome, but no Fiction, Belles-Lettres or Memoirs. Authors' guide supplied on request. *European Representatives* for the Smithsonian Institution Press, Washington, and *British Representatives* for Augustus M. Kelley, New York. *Overseas Representatives:* see current catalogue.

Davies, Peter, Ltd. (1925), 15–16 Queen Street, Mayfair, London, W1X 8BE. *T.* 01–493 4141 and The Press at Kingswood, Tadworth, Surrey. *T.* 604 2323. *Directors:* A. Dwye Evans (Chairman), D. E. Priestley (Managing Director), Mark Barty-King, J. W. Dettmer, C. S. Pick, P. W. Mead, A.C.I.S. (Secretary).
Fiction and General, Biography and Memoirs, Travel, Religion, Seafaring, Theatre.

*Davis & Moughton, Ltd. (1883), Ludgate House, 23–25 Waterloo Place, Leamington Spa, Warwickshire. *T.* 092-6 24003.
Educational (Infant, Primary, Secondary)

Dean & Son, Ltd. (The Hamlyn Publishing Group Ltd.), 41–43 Ludgate Hill, London, E.C.4. *T.* 01–236 4674.
Children's Books.

Dean (H. F. W.) & Sons, Ltd., 31 Museum Street, WC1A 1LH. *T.* 01–636 3183.
Plays, drama textbooks, and books on the theatre.

*Delisle Limited, Cromwell House, Long Street, Sherborne, Dorset. *T.* Templecombe 258. *Directors:* Mrs. Vincent Long, Miss Wendy Long.
Biography and Memoirs, Children's Books, Educational (University), General.

Delta paperbacks—see **Darwen Finlayson.**

*Dent (J. M.) & Sons, Ltd. (1888), Aldine House, 10–13 Bedford Street, WC2E 9HG. *T.* 01–836 6211. *T.A.* Malaby, London, W.C.2. *Directors:* F. J. Martin Dent (Chairman and Joint Managing Director), A. E. Pigott (Joint Managing Director), E. C. Brown, J. J. Nelson. *Everyman's Library, Everyman's Encyclopaedia, Everyman's Reference Library.* Proprietors of the Phoenix House imprint.
Architecture, Art, Belles-Lettres, Biography and Memoirs, Children's Books (Fiction, Non-Fiction), Dictionaries, Directories or Guide Books, Drama, Educational (Primary, Secondary, Technical, University), Essays, Fiction, General, History, Humour, Maps and Atlases, Music, Philosophy, Poetry, Political Economy, Reference, Science, Sociology, Sports, Games and Hobbies, Theology and Religion, Travel.

*Deutsch, André, Ltd. (1950), 105 Great Russell Street, London, WC1B 3LJ. *T.* 01–580 2746–9. *T.A.* Adlib, London, W.C.1. *Cables:* Adlib, London, W.C.1. *Directors:* André Deutsch, Nicholas Bentley, Diana Athill, F. P. Kendall, Raimund von Hofmannsthal, Zachary P. Morfogen, Piers Burnett, David Heiman, Clarice Linden. *Secretary:* Philip Tammer.
Art, Belles-Lettres, Biography and Memoirs, Children's Books, Fiction, General, History, Humour, Politics, Poetry, Travel, Grafton Books on Library Science, The Language Library.

*Dobson (Dennis) (1944), 80 Kensington Church Street, London, W.8. *T.* 01–229 0225, and 6022. *Directors:* Dennis Dobson, Margaret Dobson.
Belles-Lettres, Biography and Memoirs, Children's Books (Fiction, Non-Fiction), Current Affairs, Drama, Films, Economics, Educational, Fiction, Science-Fiction, General, History, Humour, Music, Philosophy, Political Economy, Science, Sociology, Theatre and Ballet, Travel.

Dolmen Press, Ltd., 8 Herbert Place, Dublin 2. *T.* Dublin 60587. *Directors:* Liam Miller, Josephine P. Miller, Thomas Kinsella, William C. Browne. Publications distributed outside Ireland by Oxford University Press.
Irish Literature and books of Irish interest.

Dolphin Book Co., Ltd., The (1935), 1A Southmoor Road, Oxford OX2 6RY. *T.* 57877. *T.A.* Dolphin, Oxford. *Directors:* J. L. Gili, E. H. Gili, Spanish Literature and Scholarship.

Drummond Press, The, Drummond House, 41 The Craigs, Stirling, Scotland. *T.* Stirling 3384. *General Manager:* Rev. John Birkbeck, M.C. (see also *Stirling Tract Enterprise*).
Religious and theological.

*Dryad Press, Northgates, Leicester LE1 4QR. *T.* 50405. *T.A.* Dryad, Leicester. *Directors:* D. C. Hackett, S. H. Nichols, R. J. Moore, J. R. Allen, F.C.A.
Art, Educational (Infants, Primary, Secondary, Technical (Craft)), Practical Handbooks.

*Duckworth (Gerald) & Co. Ltd. (1898), 3 Henrietta Street, WC2E 8PY. *T.* 01–836 0576. *T.A.* Ductarius, London, W.C.2. *Directors:* Colin Haycraft, J. Stacey.
Archaeology, Architecture, Art, Belles-Lettres, Biography, Current Affairs, Drama, Economics, Educational (Secondary, University), Fiction, General, History, Humour, Philosophy, Political Economy, Reprints, Science, Sports, Sociology, Theology, Travel.

Duffy (James) & Co., Ltd. (1830), 21 Shaw Street, Dublin, 2. *T.* 778115. Works of a Catholic, Irish, historical or educational nature, and plays.

Ebury Press, Chestergate House, Vauxhall Bridge Road, London, S.W.1. *T.* 01–834 2331.
Food and wine, travel, gardens, general and practical subjects. Publishers of *Good Housekeeping* illustrated books on cookery and household management.

Edinburgh House Press. All enquiries to: **Lutterworth Press,** *q.v.*

*****Edinburgh University Press,** 22 George Square, Edinburgh, EH8 9LF. *T.* 031–667 1011. *T.A.* Edinpress.

Educational Company of Ireland, Ltd. (1910), 89 Talbot Street, Dublin. *T.* Dublin 44361–3. *T.A.* Publish Dublin. *Directors:* M. W. Smurfitt, J. Smurfitt, R. H. Lyon, G. C. M. Thompson, G. E. Hetherington, W. J. Fitzsimmons, G. Browne, G. J. Greene, J. D. Sheridan.
Books for Irish schools and colleges. Irish school stories.

Educational Explorers Ltd. (1962), 40 Silver Street, Reading RG1 2SU. *T.* Reading 83103–4. *Directors:* C. Gattegno, D. M. Gattegno, G. E. Newcomb.
Educational, Mathematics, Language, Languages, Literacy, Reading, Science, Careers.

*****Educational Productions Ltd.,** *Head Office:* East Ardsley, Wakefield, Yorkshire. *T.* Lofthouse Gate 3251; 17 Denbigh Street, London, S.W.1. *T.* 01–834 1067–8. *T.A.* Edpro. High quality illustrated books, including official titles for M.C.C., F.A., A.S.A., etc. Extensive educational publishers specialising in wall charts, filmstrips and illustrated books. Official publishers for U.N.E.S.C.O.
Children's Books (Non-Fiction), Educational (Primary, Secondary, Technical), Practical Handbooks.

*****Elek Books Ltd.,** 2 All Saints Street, London, N1 9RN. *T.* 01–837 0614. *Directors:* Paul Elek, Elizabeth Elek. Associated Company: Paul Elek Productions Ltd. *q.v.*
Archaeology, Architecture, Art, Biography and Memoirs, Current Affairs, Drama, Fiction, General, History, Humour, Philosophy, Travel, *Plays of the Year* series.

Elliot Right Way Books, Kingswood Building, Brighton Road, Lower Kingswood, Surrey. *T.* Mogador 2426. Specialist in instructional and motor books, and publishers of the two series Right Way Books and Paperfronts. Careful consideration for all new ideas, and editorial help can be provided.
Popular Technical, Popular Educational, Popular Medical, Sport, Commerce, General, Humour, Paperbacks.

Emmott & Co., Ltd. (1875), 31 King Street West, Manchester, M3 2PL. *T.* 061–834 7086–7. *Directors:* Alfred Dawber (Chairman and Joint Managing Director), C. Birtles (Joint Managing Director), E. Holland.
Textile and engineering journals and books.

*****Encyclopaedia Britannica International, Ltd.** Dorland House, 18–20 Regent Street, London, S.W.1. *T.* 01–930 7855. *Chairman:* Philip M. Kaiser.

English Theatre Guild, Ltd., Ascot House, 52 Dean Street, London, W1V 6BJ. *T.* 01–437 3822–3. *Directors:* Judith Truman, John E. Hunter, D. M. Sims, Leslie J. Collins.
Drama, Television, Theatre.

*English Universities Press, Ltd., The (1934), St. Paul's House, London, E.C.4. *T.* 01-248 5797. *Directors:* John Attenborough (Chairman), Paul Hodder-Williams, L. M. H. Timmermans, H. S. Foster, B. Steven, Walter Hamilton. Publishers of the "Teach Yourself" series.

Commerce, Dictionaries, Economics, Educational (Secondary, Technical, University), History, Medical, Science, Technology, Sports, Games and Hobbies.

Epworth Press and Methodist Publishing House (1773), 27 Marylebone Road, London, N.W.1. *T.* 01-935 2549-0.

General and Children's Books, Sociology, Theology and Religion.

*Esperanto Publishing Co. Ltd., 120 Heronsgate Road, Chorleywood, Rickmansworth, Herts. WD3 5BP. *T.* Chorleywood 2906.

Books on many subjects in Esperanto. Esperanto textbooks and dictionaries.

*Europa Publications Ltd., 18 Beford Square, WC1B 3JN. *T.* 01-580 8236. *Directors:* W. Simon (Managing), H. T. Higgins, P. G. C. Jackson, J. M. Bacon, H. J. Wombill.

Directors, Economics, International Relations, Reference, Year Books.

*Evans Brothers Ltd. (1905), Montague House, Russell Square, WC1B 5BX. *T.* 01-636 8521. *T.A.* Byronitic, London, W.C.1. *Directors:* L. J. Browning (Chairman and Managing Director), R. P. Hyman (Deputy Managing Director), The Hon. Mrs. A. M. Evans, R. R. S. White, Hugh Buckingham, Edward Hague, O.B.E. Books and periodicals, mainly educational.

Evans Brothers (Books) Ltd. (1969), Montague House, Russell Suare, WC1B 5BX. *Directors:* L. J. Browning (Chairman), R. P. Hyman (Deputy Chairman & Managing Director), The Hon. Mrs. A. M. Evans, Edward Hague, O.B.E., J. M. Thomas, J. Bentley. J. C. Mugliston.

Educational books, particularly infant, primary and secondary; children's books (including Zebra paperbacks), plays (acting editions), dictionaries, practical books. Subsidiary of **Evans Brothers Ltd.**

Evans Brothers (Periodicals) Ltd. (1969), Montague House, Russell Square, WC1B 5BX. *Directors:* L. J. Browning (Chairman), R. P. Hyman (Deputy Chairman), Edward Hague, O.B.E., (Managing Director), J. Bentley.

Publishers of: *Art & Craft in Education, Child Education, Child Education Quarterly, Music Teacher, Pictorial Education, Pictorial Education Quarterly, Teachers World.* Subsidiary of **Evans Brothers Ltd.**

Evelyn (Hugh) Ltd. (1958), 9 Fitzroy Square, London, W1P 5AH...*T.* 01-387 8453. *Directors:* Hugh Evelyn Street (Managing), E. W. Fenton, S. Gorley Putt, O.B.E., M. O. C. Street.

Illustrated books on Architecture, Costume, Military Subjects and Uniforms, History of Land, Sea and Air Transport.

*Eyre & Spottiswoode (Publishers), Ltd., 11 New Fetter Lane, London, E.C.4. *T.* 01-583 9855. *T.A.* Exaltedly, London, E.C.4. Publishers of the Bible and Book of Common Prayer. *Directors:* Sir Oliver Crosthwaite Eyre, F. C. Friend (Vice Chairman), J. Bright-Holmes (Managing), J. D. Cullen.

General; Fiction, Biography and Memoirs, History, Current Affairs, Poetry, Sports and Games, Travel.

*Faber & Faber Ltd. (1929), 3 Queen Square, London, WC1N 3AU. *T*. 01–278 6881. *T.A.* Fabbaf, London, W.C.1. *Directors:* Richard de la Mare (Chairman), Peter du Sautoy (Vice-Chairman), Lady Faber, Charles Montieth, Peter Crawley, Alan Pringle, Rosemary Goad, Giles de la Mare, Matthew Evans. Publishers of *The British Journal of Educational Studies*.

Aeronautics, Agriculture, Archaeology, Architecture, Art, Biography and Memoirs, Children's Books (Fiction, Non-Fiction, Picture), Cookery Books, Current Affairs, Drama, Economics, Educational Books, Fiction, Films, Gardening, History, Humour, Medical and Nursing, Music, Naval and Military, Oriental, Philosophy, Poetry, Politics, Science, Sociology, Sports, Games and Hobbies, Television, Theatre and Ballet, Theology and Religion, Travel. *Faber Paper Covered Editions* cover many of the subjects shown above and *Faber Art Books* include the following series: Faber Monographs on Pottery and Porcelain, Glass, Furniture and Silver, Faber Collectors Library.

Faber & Faber (Publishers) Ltd. (1969), 3 Queen Square, London, WC1N 3AU. *T*. 01–278 6881. *T.A.* Fabbaf London, W.C.1. *Directors:* Richard de la Mare (Chairman), Peter du Sautoy (Vice-Chairman), Charles Montieth, Peter Crawley, Dr. Thomas Faber. Holding company of Faber & Faber Ltd., *q.v.*

Fabian Society (1884), 11 Dartmouth Street, London, S.W.1. *T*. 01–930 3077, (also controls NCLC Publishing Society Ltd.).
Current Affairs, Economics, Educational, Political Economy, Sociology.

*Faith Press Ltd. (1905), 7 Tufton Street, London, S.W.1. *T*. 01–222 3940.
Religious books (Anglican).

*Fallon (C. J.) Ltd. (1927), 77 Marlboro Street, Dublin 1. *T*. 46191. *Directors:* J. J. O'Leary (Chairman), J. H. G. McMahon (Alternate Chairman), M. J. McManus (Deputy Chairman), T. R. Hart (Managing Director), W. J. O'Leary, H. J. McNicholas, E. J. White.
Educational and Religious text books.

Femina Books Ltd. (1967), 1A Montagu Mews North, London, W1H 1AJ. *T*. 01–935 8090. *T.A.* Trifem, London, W.1. *Directors:* Muriel V. Box, F.R.S.A., Anne Edwards, M.A., Carolyn Whitaker, Anona Winn, M.B.E.
Fiction and Non-Fiction, with an angle on women.

Fieldhouse, Arthur, Ltd. (1895), Advertiser Press Ltd., Premier Works, Paddock Head, Huddersfield, HD3 4ES. *T*. Huddersfield 20444.
Commerce, Educational (Technical).

Figgis (Allen) & Co., Ltd., 4 Dawson Street, Dublin. *T*. 776375–8. *Directors:* F. T. Figgis, S. E. Allen Figgis (Managing), G. Stirling.
Books by Irish authors, or of Irish interest: Archaeology, Art, Belles-Lettres, Biography and Memoirs, Children's Books, Fiction, General, History, Humour, Law, Poetry, Travel.

*Focal Press, Ltd. (1938), 31 Fitzroy Square, London, W1P 6BH. *T*. 01–387 4294–5. *T.A.* Focalpres, London, W.1, and New York. *Directors:* R. H. Code Holland, A. Kraszna-Krausz, L. S. Temple. B. G. Brewer, R. W. Dear.
Illustrated technical and scientific books on photography, kinematography, television, sound, and image recording. Practical Handbooks, Reference.

Folens & Co., Ltd. John F. Kennedy Drive, Naas Road, Dublin 12. *T*. Dublin 502932.
Educational (Primary, Secondary, Comprehensive, Technical, in English and Irish).

Fontana paperbacks—see William Collins.

Foulis (G. T.) & Co. Ltd., 50a Bell Street, Henley-on-Thames, Oxon, RG9 2BJ. *T.* Henley 2426–7. *Directors:* H. Marshall (Chairman), M. F. C. Marshall, John Hassell (Joint Managing Directors), Lord Darwen.
Aviation (History of), Motoring (History, Technical, Sport and Touring), General.

*Foulsham (W.) & Co., Ltd. (1819), Yeovil Road, Slough, Bucks. *T.* Slough 26769.
Art, Dictionaries, Do-it-Yourself, Educational, General, Sports, Games and Hobbies, Travel.
Foulsham-Sams Technical Books—electronics and allied subjects.

*Foundational Book Company, Ltd., The, Trade: 77 Beckwith Road, Herne Hill, London, S.E.24. *T.* 01–274 5874.
Philosophy, Theology and Religion.

Fountain Press, Ltd., 46–47 Chancery Lane, London, WC2A 1JU. *T.* 01–242 1411.
Photographic Books.

Four Square paperbacks—see New English Library.

Fowler (L. N.) & Co., Ltd. (1880), 15 New Bridge Street, E.C.4. *T.* 01-353 1668.
Astrology, Health and Healing, Mental Science, Yoga.

*Foyle, W. & G., Ltd., 119–125 Charing Cross Road, London WC2 0EB. *T.* 01–437 5660. For book clubs handled by this firm see pp. 229–230.

*Freeman (W.H.) & Co. Ltd. (1959), 58 Kings Road, Reading, RG1 3AA. *T.* Reading 583250. *Directors:* Sir Jonathan Backhouse, R. Brinckman, A. Kudlacik, S. Schaefer.
Science, Technical.

*French (Samuel), Ltd. (1830), 26 Southampton Street, Strand, London, WC2E 7JE. *T.* 01–836 7513. *Branches:* New York, Hollywood, Toronto, E. Sydney *q.v.* *Directors:* Anthony Wentworth Hogg (Chairman), Harold Francis Dyer (Managing), Noel Norman Hogg, Lionel Noel Woolf (Editorial), Harold Lesley Pumfrett (Secretary). Publishers of plays and agents for the collection of royalties.
Drama.

†Frewin (Leslie) Publishers Ltd., 1 New Quebec Street, Marble Arch, London W1H 8BN. *T.* 01–402 5431–2. *Directors:* Leslie Frewin, E. F. Frewin, M. L. Pirie-Frewin. *General Manager:* Andrew Turvey.
Biography, Autobiography, Current Affairs, Humour, Documentary Books, Poetry, Sport, Politics.

Gairm Publications, incorporating Alex MacLaren & Sons, (1875), 29 Waterloo Street, Glasgow, C.2. *T.* 041–221 1971.
Dictionaries, Novels, Poetry, Music (Gaelic only).

*Gall & Inglis (1810), 13 Henrietta Street, WC2E 8LH. *T.* 01–836 3830. *T.A.* Readyrecks, Rand, London; and 12 Newington Road, Edinburgh, EH9 1RB. *T.* 031–667 2791. *T.A.* "Reckoners", Edinburgh. *Partners:* Robert Inglis, E. Hornsby.
Reference, Science.

Garnstone Press Ltd., The (1965), 59 Brompton Road, London, S.W.3. *T.* 01–589 5578. *Cables:* Balfbooks, London, S.W.3. *Directors:* Michael D. Balfour (Managing), Patrick Balfour, Ralph Yablon, G. A. Yablon, J. Gante.
Non-fiction, guide, travel, business, philosophy, health and information books.

Gee & Co. (Publishers), Ltd. (1874), Head Office and City Library, 151 Strand, London, WC2R 1JJ. *T.* 01–836 0832. *Directors:* Percy F. Hughes (Chairman and Managing Director), T. S. Martin, K. D. Gee, P. Gee-Heaton, Harold P. Kennett (and Secretary), V. M. Snelling, A. E. Webb.
Accountancy, Business Management and taxation.

Gee & Son (1809), Denbigh. *T.* Denbigh 2020. *Partners:* Charles Charman, Morfydd Charman, Edgar Rees, LL.B., Erina M. Rees. Oldest Welsh publishers.
Books of interest to Wales, in Welsh.

*****Geographia Ltd.**, 178–202 Great Portland Street, London, W1N 6AQ *T.* 01–850 3020. *T.A.* Geografo, London, W.1. *Directors:* R. A. A. Holt (Chairman), Noel Holland (Vice-Chairman), Hon. Hugh Astor, Sir Robert Lusty, J. D. Stevenson.
Maps, Atlases, Plans, Guides, Travel, Games, Educational.

Geographical Publications Limited (1933), *E.A.:* The Keep, Berkhamsted Place, Berkhamsted, Herts. *T.* Berkhamsted 2981. *Directors:* A. N. Clark, B. U. D. Stamp. *Secretary:* A. N. Clark. Maps, atlases and geographical works and photographs, both on own account and jointly with other publishers. Publishers and general agents to World Land Use Survey and International Geographical Union. *London Agents:* E. Stanford Ltd., 12–14 Long Acre, W.C.2.

*****Gibbons (Stanley), Ltd.** (1856), 391 Strand, London, WC2R 0LX. *T.* 01–836 9707. *TA.* Philatelic Rand. *Directors:* A. L. Michael (Chairman and Managing Director), A. C. Andrews, N. W. Collet, F. T. Smith, F. S. Wall, J. Webb, S. Zimmerman.

*****Gibson, Robert & Sons Glasgow, Ltd.** (1885), 2 West Regent Street, Glasgow, C.2. *T.* 041–332 6687. *Directors:* Robert Gibson, R. D. C. Gibson, R. G. C. Gibson, George Hirst.
Educational.

Gifford (John), Ltd. (1937), 125 Charing Cross Road, W.C.2. *T.* 01–437 0216. *Telex:* 261107. *Directors:* R. Batty, C. Batty. *Editor:* J. Shillingford.
Gardening, Sport, Natural History, Travel and Practical Books, Art, Collecting Antiques, Marine Aquaria.

*****Gill (George) & Sons, Ltd.** (1862), 67–68 Chandos Place, W.C.2. *T.* 01–836 3278. *T.A.* Gillerva, London. *Directors:* H. J. Lavington, M. E. Forrest (Mrs.), P. Hall (Mrs.), H. D. Milroy.
Educational (Infants, Primary, Secondary, Technical).

Gill & Macmillan, Ltd (1968), 2 Belvedere Place, Dublin 1. *T.* Dublin 49481.
Biography or Memoirs, Educational (Secondary, University), History, Philosophy, Sociology, Theology and Religion, Literature.

*****Ginn and Company, Ltd.**, (1924), 18 Bedford Row, London, WC1R 4EJ. *T.* 01–405 8823. *T.A.* Pedagogy, Westcent, London. *Directors:* N. G. Fisher (Chairman), K. A. Hills (Managing Director), J. D. Bevington, H. C. Baillie, J. Rendall, I. C. Dickson, L. Hall, E. R. Norton.
Educational (Infants, Primary, Secondary).

Globe Book Services Limited, Brunel Road, Basingstoke, Hampshire. *T.* Basingstoke 21002.
Educational (Infants, Primary).

Golden Head Press Ltd., The (1954), 513 Coldham's Lane, Cambridge, CB1 3JS. *T.* 46642. *Directors:* H. Lister, A. K. Astbury, Raymond Lister (Managing Director and Editor), B. H. Lister.

Art, Belles-Lettres, Poetry, Collecting.

Golden Pleasure Books Ltd. (1961), **(The Hamlyn Publishing Group Ltd.),** Hamlyn House, 42 The Centre, Feltham, Middlesex. *T.* 01–751 8400. *T.A.* Pleasbooks, Feltham. *Directors:* P. A. Jarvis, E. S. Birk, John Rendall, R. Haumersen, W. Kidd, H. Johnson, J. Lyle.

Children's Books (Fiction, Non-Fiction, Rewards, Toy or Picture Books, Annuals), Dictionaries, Educational (Infants, Primary, Secondary).

*Gollancz (Victor), Ltd. (1927), 14 Henrietta Street, WC2E 8QJ. *T.* 01–836 2006. *T.A.* Vigollan, London, W.C.2. *Directors:* Livia Gollancz, John Bush, Ruth Gollancz, Mary Brash, Giles Gordon.

Biography and Memoirs, Children's Books (Fiction, Non-Fiction), Current Affairs, Fiction, Science Fiction, General, History, Humour, Music, Philosophy, Sociology, Theology and Religion, Travel.

Gomerian Press (1892), J. D. Lewis & Sons Ltd., Llandysul, Cards. *T.* 2371. *T.A.* Gomerian, Llandysul. *Directors:* J. Huw Lewis, John H. Lewis.

School books in Welsh; biography, fiction, poetry.

Gower Press Ltd. (1968), 140 Great Portland Street, London, W1N 5TA. *T.* 01–580 0521. *Directors:* N. Farrow (Managing), A. J. Merrett, G. R. Cryiax, J. Dening (Editorial).

Industrial and commercial management.

Gramol Publications, Ltd., 60 Broadway, Chesham, Bucks. *T.* 2141–2.

General and children's books.

Grampian Press Ltd. See Morgan-Grampian Publishers Ltd.

Granada Publishing Ltd., 3 Upper James Street, Golden Square, London, W1R 4BP. *T.* 01–734 8080. *Directors:* Lord Bernstein, A. R. H. Birch, W. R. Carr, T. Maschler, J. Pacey, J. C. Reynolds, B. Thompson. Controlling Adlard Coles Ltd., Arco Publications Ltd., Atlantic Book Publishing Co. Ltd., MacGibbon & Kee Ltd., Mayflower Books Ltd., Panther Books Ltd., Rupert Hart-Davis Ltd., Rupert Hart-Davis Educational Publications Ltd., Staples Press Ltd.

*Griffin (Charles) & Co., Ltd. (1820), 42 Drury Lane, WC2B 5RX. *T.* 01–836 4206–7. *T.A.* Explanatus, London, W.C.2.

Scientific and technical, notably statistics.

Grolier Society, Ltd., The, Star House, Potters Bar, Herts. *T.* Potters Bar 58111.

Educational, Technical.

Gryphon Books, Ltd. (1948), 50 Albemarle Street, London, W1X 4BD *Directors:* Mrs. O. L. Farquharson, John Grey Murray.

Fiction.

*Guinness Superlatives, Ltd. (1954), 24 Upper Brook Street, London, W1Y 2NN *T.* Hyde Park 9208.

Reference.

*H. F. L. (Publishers), Ltd. (1884), 9 Bow Street, London, WC2E 7AL. *T.* 01–836 9081. *Directors:* Max Reinhardt (Chairman and Managing Director), J. R. Hews, F.C.A., R. G. Pegler, M.A., F.C.A., Anthony Quayle, C.B.E., D. J. Reinhardt, Sir Ralph Richardson, M.E. Wraith.

Accountancy, Taxation, Commercial Law.

*Hachette (Continental Publishers and Distributors, Ltd., The) (1859), 4 Regent Place, Regent Street, London, W1R 6BH T. 01–734 5259.
Guide Books, Educational (Modern Languages), Travel.

*Hale (Robert), & Co. (1936), 63 Old Brompton Road, London, S.W.7. T. 01–584 4481 (6 lines). T.A. Barabbas, London, S.W.7.
Archaeology, Belles-Lettres, Biography and Memoirs, Current Affairs, Directories or Guide Books, Fiction, General, History, Humour, Medical, Music, Practical Handbooks, Science, Sociology, Sports, Games and Hobbies, Theatre and Ballet, Theology and Religion, Travel, Year Books, Catholic Books.

Hamilton (Edward), 26 Grafton Road, Worthing, Sussex.
Art.

*Hamilton (Hamish), Ltd. (1931), 90 Great Russell Street, London, WC1B 3PT. T. 01–580 4621. T.A. Hamisham, Westcent, London. Cable Address: Hamisham, London. Directors: Hamish Hamilton, M.A., LL.B. (Managing Director), Professor Sir Denis Brogan, M.A., Roger Machell, B.A., Maxwell Martyn, Richard Hough, George Rainbird, T. H. Ancott, J. Glover, C. Sinclair-Stevenson.
Belles-Lettres, Biography and Memoirs, Children's Books (Fiction, Non-Fiction), Current Affairs, Drama, Educational (Primary, Secondary Modern), Fiction, General, History, Humour, Music, Political, Theatre and Ballet, Travel.

*Hamilton (Hamish) Children's Books Ltd., (1970) (formerly the Children's Book Department of Hamish Hamilton), 90 Great Russell Street, London, WC1B 3PT. T. 01–580 4621. T.A. Hamisham, Westcent, London. Directors: Hamish Hamilton (Chairman), Richard Hough (Managing), Julia MacRae (Editorial), Michael Brown (Production), Secretary S. J. Sambels.
Children's Books—fiction, non-fiction and picture books.

Hamlyn, Paul. See The Hamlyn Publishing Group Ltd.

*The Hamlyn Publishing Group Ltd. (1947), Hamlyn House, 42 The Centre, Feltham, Middlesex. T. 01–751 8400. T.A. Pleasbooks, Feltham. Directors: Philip Jarvis (Chairman and Chief Executive), Richard Baldwyn (Managing Director—Music for Pleasure, Director—Prints for Pleasure), Norman Fisher, David Greening (Financial Controller), John Rendall (Marketing Director), Ken Stepehnson.
Associate companies overseas: Paul Hamlyn Pty. Ltd., Australia, The Hamlyn Publishing Group (Canada) Ltd., Paul Hamlyn Inc., U.S.A., Serasia Books, Hong Kong.

*Hammond, Hammond & Co., Ltd. Publications now incorporated with Barrie and Jenkins, q.v.

*Harmsworth Press, Ltd., The, 8 Stratton Street, W1X 6AT T. 01–499 7881. T.A. Field Newspaper, London and Golfirst, Piccy, London, W.1. The Field and Golf Illustrated.

*Harper & Row Ltd., 28 Tavistock Street, London, WC2E 7PN. T. 01–836 4635. T.A. Harprow, London, W.C.2. Directors: M. Arnold, M. Dubois, W. Knowlton, A. J. Rosenthal, Cass Canfield, Jr., R. E. Baensch, Piers Raymond (Managing).
Textbooks, medical, Juveniles, Religious, General, paperbacks.

*Harrap (George G.) & Co., Ltd. (1901), P.O. Box 70, 182–4 High Holborn, London, WC1V 7AX. *T.* 01–405 9935 and 01–405 0941. *T.A.* Butiboox, Westcent, London. *Directors:* R. Olaf Anderson (Chairman and Managing Director), Paull Harrap (Deputy Managing Director), Ian G. Harrap (Director of Future Planning & Training, and Company Secretary), René P. L. Ledésert, Patrick L. Heyworth, G. N. Thompson. *Associate Director:* C. R. Butterworth. (All British.)

Educational (Infants, Primary, Secondary, Technical, University), Fiction, General, History, Naval and Military, Political Economy, Reference, Science, Sociology, Theatre, Travel, Children's Books, and Visual Aids in Modern Languages.

*Hart-Davis (Rupert) Ltd. (1946), 3 Upper James Street, Golden Square, London, W1R 4BP *T.* 01–734 8080. *Directors:* W. R. Carr, J. C. Reynolds (Managing).

Archaeology, Belles-Lettres, Biographies and Memoirs, Children's Books, Fiction, History, Politics and Sociology, Science, Travel and Adventure.

*Hart-Davis (Rupert) Educational Publications Ltd., (1970), 3 Upper James Street, Golden Square, London, W1R 4BP. *T.* 01–734 8080. *Directors:* M. Palmer, (Managing), W. R. Carr, R. N. Cole, J. C. Reynolds.

Primary and Secondary school text and library books.

†Harvill Press Ltd. (Editorial) 30a Pavilion Road, London, S.W.1. *T.* 01–589 1631, 1096 and 4119. (Trade) Wm. Collins, 42–50 York Way, Kings Cross, N.1. *T.* 01–837 0012. *Directors:* W. A. R. Collins, F. T. Smith, P. M. Collins, F. I. Chapman, M. Villiers.

Art, Belles-Lettres, Biography and Memoirs, Current Affairs, Fiction, Humour, Philosophy, Poetry, Theology and Religion, Travel.

*Health for All Publishing Company (1927), Gateway House, Bedford Park, Croydon, CR9 2AT *T.* 01-688 5528. *T.A.* Hygiaward, Croydon.

Books on health, diet, exercise and allied subjects.

*Heffer (W.) & Sons, Ltd. (1876), 20 Trinity Street, Cambridge, CB2 3NG. *T.* Cambridge 58351. *T.A.* Heffer, Cambridge. *Telex:* 81298.

General Academic, Oriental, Science, Linguistics.

Heinemann Group of Publishers Ltd., 15-16 Queen Street, London, W1X 8BE *T.* 01–493 4141. *T.A.* Sunlocks, London, W.1. and Kingswood, Tadworth, Surrey. *T.* Mogador 3511. *T.A.* Sunlocks, Tadworth. *Directors:* Sir Geoffrey Eley, C.B.E. (Chairman), A. Dwye Evans (Managing Director), O. R. Evans, A. J. W. Hill, D. A. J. Manser, C. S. Pick, F. J. Warburg, D. L. Range, F.C.A., (Director and Secretary).

*Heinemann (William) Ltd., 15-16 Queen Street, London, W1X 8BE *T.* 01–493 4141. *T.A.* Sunlocks, London, W.1., and Kingswood, Tadworth, Surrey. *T.* Mogador 3511. *T.A.* Sunlocks, Tadworth. *Directors:* A. Dwye Evans, (Chairman), C. S. Pick (Managing Director), Roland Gant (Editorial Director), Miss E. M. Anderson, J. W. Dettmer, A. J. W. Hill, T. R. Manderson, John St. John, N. M. Viney, P. W. Mead, A.C.I.S., (Secretary).

Art, Biography and Memoirs, Belles-Lettres, Children's Books, Drama, Fiction, General, Poetry, Sports, Games and Hobbies, Technical, Travel.

*Heinemann Educational Books Ltd., 48 Charles Street, London, W1X 8AH *T.* 01–493 9103. *Directors;* A. J. W. Hill (Chairman and Managing Director), A. R. Beal (Deputy Managing Director), A. Dwye Evans, H. MacGibbon, E. D. Thompson, H. K. Sambrook, A. S. McConnell, (Secretary).

Drama, Educational (Primary, Secondary, University), History, Literary Criticism, Music, Political Economy, Science, Sociology, Technical.

†**Heinemann (William) Medical Books Ltd.,** 23 Beford Square, London, WC1B 3HT. *T.* 01–580 4302/9049, and Kingswood, Tadworth, Surrey. *T.* Mogador 3511. *T.A.* Sunlocks, Tadworth. *Directors:* R. Greene, D.M., F.R.C.P., (Chairman), Owen R. Evans (Managing Director), A. Dwye Evans, Selwyn Taylor, D.M., F.R.C.S., R. S. Emery, E. M. Lydon, A.C.I.S. (Secretary).
Medical, Surgical, Dental, Science, Veterinary.

*****World's Work Ltd.,** The Press at Kingswood, Tadworth, Surrey. *T.* Mogador 3511. *T.A.* Sunlocks, Tadworth. *Directors:* A. Dwye Evans, (Chairman), D. A. Elliot (Managing Director), R. A. Aspinall, C. Forster, D. E. Priestley, A. H. Rosenberg (Director and Secretary).
General, religion, practical psychology, children's books.

Heinemann and Zsolnay, Ltd., 15-16 Queen Street, London, W1X 8BE *T.* 01–493 4141. *T.A.* Sunlocks, Audley, London. *Directors:* A. Dwye Evans, (Chairman), J. Beer (Managing Director), A. J. W. Hill, C. S. Pick, H. W. Polak, D. L. Range, F.C.A., E. M. Lydon, A.C.I.S. (Secretary).
Editions in German and French of general books of topical and lasting interest and of novels of literary value.

Hennel Locke, Ltd., 182 High Holborn, W.C.1.
Paperback Outdoor and General books; Seven Dials Library.

Her Majesty's Stationery Office, *Head Office,* Atlantic House, Holborn Viaduct, London, E.C.1. *T.* 01–248 9876. *T.A.* Hemstonery, London, E.C.1. Sovereign House, St. Georges Street, Norwich NOR 76A *T.* 0603 22211. *T.A.* Hemstonery, Norwich. *Government Bookshops* (retail); 49 High Holborn, W.C.1. *T.* 01–928 6977; London Post Orders: P.O. Box 569, London S.E.1; Brazennose Street, Manchester M60 8AS. *T.* 061 834 7201–2; 13A Castle Street, Edinburgh EH2 3AR (wholesale and retail). *T.* 031 225 6333–6; 258–259 Broad Street, Birmingham 1. *T.* 021–643 3740; 109 St. Mary Street, Cardiff CF1 1JW. *T.* 0222 23654–5; 50 Fairfax Street, Bristol BS1 3DE. *T.* 0272 24306–7; 7 Linenhall Street, Belfast BT2 8AY. *T.* 0232–34181. Publications Sale Office (wholesale): Cornwall House, Stamford Street, London, S.E.1. *T.* 01–928 6977, Ext. 202.
Archaeology, Architecture, Art, Current Affairs, Directories or Guide Books, Educational (Infants, Primary, Secondary, Technical, University), General, History, Naval and Military, Practical Handbooks, Reference, Science, Sociology, Year Books.

Herder (B.) (Book Co., Ltd.) (1910), Herder Book Centre, Billingshurst, Sussex. *T.* 040–381 2902.
Catholic works of a serious nature.

Heywood Temple Industrial Publications Limited, see **I.P.C. Business Press Ltd.**

Highway Press, The (Church Missionary Society), 157 Waterloo Road, London, S.E.1. *T.* 01–928 8681. *T.A.* Testimony, London, S.E.1. Books and pamphlets on evangelism and theology: also education, medicine, agriculture, social service with special reference to Christian missionary activity in Africa and the East.

*****Hilger (Adam) Ltd.,** 31 Camden Road, London, N.W.1. *T.* 01–485 5636.
Science (Chemistry, Physics, Optics, Surveying, Engineering, Instruments).

Hinrichsen Edition, Ltd. (1938), "Bach House," 10–12 Baches Street, London, N1 6DN. *T.* 01–253 1638-9. *T.A.* Musipeters, London. *Director:* Carla E. Hinrichsen (Chairman and Managing Director).
Music.

*Hirschfeld Brothers, Ltd. (1885), 205 Great Portland Street, W1N 6LR. *T.* 01–580 6381.
Foreign languages.

Hodder Paperbacks Ltd., St. Paul's House, Warwick Lane, London, E.C.4. *T.* 01–248 5797. *Directors:* John Attenborough (Chairman), Paul Hodder-Williams, Michael Attenborough, Robin Denniston, Philip Attenborough, J. R. McKenzie, Ronald Read.
Paperbacks, Fiction, General non-fiction, Juvenile.

*Hodder & Stoughton, Ltd., St. Paul's House, Warwick Lane, E.C.4. *T.* 01–248 5797. *T.A.* Expositor, London, E.C.4. *Directors:* Paul Hodder-Williams (Chairman), John Attenborough (Deputy Chairman), Robin Denniston (Managing), Philip Attenborough, R. J. Sare (Australia), J. R. McKenzie, Mark Hodder-Williams, M. F. Attenborough, Haydn Stead.
Biography and Memoirs, Current Affairs, Fiction, History, Psychology, Sports, Theology and Religion, Travel.

*Hodge (William) & Co., Ltd. (1872), 12 Bank Street, Edinburgh EH1 2LN and Glasgow. *T.* 031–225 5021. *T.A.* Municipal, Edinburgh; Municipal, Glasgow. *Directors:* James H. Hodge, and Alan G. Hodge.
Law.

Hodges, Figgis & Co., Ltd. (1768), 5–6 Dawson Street, Dublin, 2. *T.* Dublin 76375–8. *Directors:* F. T. Figgis, S. E. Allen Figgis (*Managing*), W. A. N. Figgis, J. F. Murray, G. M. Hodgins. Publishers to Dublin University and the Chester Beatty Library.

Hodgson (Francis) Ltd. (1884), P.O. Box 74, Guernsey, C.I. *T.* 0481–24332.
Scientific and technical reference books.

Hogarth Press, Ltd., The, 40–42 William IV Street, London, WC2N 4DG. *T* 01–836 5549. *Directors:* Ian M. Parsons, Norah Smallwood, G. W. Trevelyan.
Belles-Lettres, Biography and Memoirs, Essays, Fiction, History, Psycho-Analysis, Poetry, Sociology.

Holland Press Ltd., The, 112 Whitefield Street, London, W1P 6DP *T.* 01–387 2466. *Directors:* Martin Orskey, Neville Armstrong.
Bibliography, Arms and Armour, music, travel, reference works of all kinds in limited editions, books of interest to collectors, specialising in reprinting of de-luxe editions, original MSS. also considered.

Hollis & Carter Ltd., 9 Bow Street, London, WC2E 7AL. *T.* 01–836 9081. *T.A.* Bodleian, Westcent, London. *Directors:* Max Reinhardt (Chairman and Managing), L. A. Hart, J. R. Hews, Christopher Hollis, G. Waldman.
Biography and Memoirs, Belles-Lettres, History, Literary Criticism, Nautical, Travel, Current Affairs.

*Holmes McDougall Limited, 30 Royal Terrace, Edinburgh EH7 5AL. *T.* 031–556 1431. *Cables:* Educational Edinburgh. *Directors:* Esmond Wright, (Chairman), Gordon B. Allan, T.D., C.A., Dr. H. Stewart Macintosh, C.B.E., Thomas E. Smith, I. M. Christie, J. W. Macdonald, W. R. Meikle, A. G. Stephen, W. K. Forgie, C.A. (Managing Director). *Secretary:* A. A. Bremner, C.A.
Educational (Infant, Primary and Secondary).

Holt, Rinehart & Winston Ltd. (London 1961; New York 1866), 120 Golden Lane, Barbican, London, E.C.1. *T.* 01–253 0855. *T.A.* Aytcholt, London, E.C.1. *Telex:* 25376. *Directors:* Richard I. Abrams (U.S.A.), Kenneth G. Northrop (U.S.A.), Ross D. Sackett (U.S.A.), William J. Tribe (U.S.A.).
Educational books (School, College, University) in all subjects; trade books.

*Hope (Thomas) and Sankey-Hudson, Ltd. (1947), Ashtons Mill, Chapeltown Street, Manchester, M1 2NH. *T.* 061 3865–6–7. Crusader Works, Chapeltown Street, Ancoats, Manchester, M1 2NH. *T.* Ardwick 1653–4–5. *T.A.* Hudsonian, Manchester. *Chairman:* Alfred Hope. *Managing Directors:* Frank Furniss, J. C. Sant. *Directors:* Richard Hope, Herbert Lewis, D. H. Eglin (Secretary). Contractors for school materials, manufacturing stationers. Educational Books (all levels).

*Hulton Educational Publications Ltd., Raans Road, Amersham, Bucks. *T.* Amersham 4196–7–8. *Directors:* Sir Edward Hulton (Chairman), L. G. Marsh (Managing), Nika Hulton, E. J. Lowman, C. E. Gamborg.
Educational (Infants, Primary, Secondary, Grammar, Technical).

Hurst & Blackett, Ltd. (1812), 178–202 Great Portland Street, London, W1N 6AQ *T.* 01–580 3020. (Trade) 062-181 6362. *Telex:* 18130. *T.A.* Literarius, London, W.1. *Telex:* 261212. *Directors:* R. A. A. Holt (Chairman), Sir Robert Lusty, Dorothy Tomlinson. An imprint of the Hutchinson Publishing Group. Fiction.

*Hutchinson & Co. (Publishers) Ltd. 178–202 Great Portland Street, London, W1N 6AQ *T.* 01–580 3020. *Telex:* 261212. (Trade) 062-181 6362. *Telex:* 18130. *T.A.* Literarius, London, W.1. General Publishers. *Chairman:* R. A. A. Holt. *Managing Director:* Sir Robert Lusty. *Directors:* Noel Holland (*Vice-Chairman*), Harold Harris, Elisabeth Stockwell, David Roy.
Belles-Lettres, Biography and Memoirs, Children's Books (Fiction, Non-Fiction, Rewards, Toy and Picture Books), Current Affairs, Essays, Fiction, General, History, Humour, Music, Poetry, Reference, Travel.
An imprint of the Hutchinson Publishing Group.

*Hutchinson Publishing Group, Ltd. (1887), 178–202 Great Portland Street, London, W1N 6AQ *T.* 01–580 3020. *Telex:* 261212. (Trade) 062-181 6362. *Telex:* 18130. *T.A.* Literarius, London, W.1. General publishers. *Chairman:* R. A. A. Holt. *Managing Director:* Sir Robert Lusty. *Directors:* Noel Holland (*Vice-Chairman*). Hon. Hugh Astor, Harold Harris, John Robinson, Elisabeth Stockwell, David Roy, A. Rudkin, Controls Hutchinson & Co. (Publishers) Ltd., Hurst & Blackett, Ltd.: also Hutchinson Junior Books Ltd., Jarrolds Publishers (London) Ltd., Skeffington & Son, Ltd., Rider & Co., John Long, Ltd., Stanley Paul & Co., Ltd., Arrow Books Ltd., Hutchinson Educational Ltd., New Authors Ltd., Popular Dogs Publishing Co., Ltd.

*Hutchinson Educational Ltd. (1958), 178–202 Great Portland Street, London, W1N 6AQ *T.* 01–580 3020. *Telex:* 261212. (Trade) 062-181 6362. *Telex:* 98130. *T.A.* Literarius, London, W.1.
Directors: R. A. A. Holt (Chairman), Sir Robert Lusty, John R. Stevens. An imprint of the Hutchinson Publishing Group.
Educational (Secondary, Technical, University).

Hutchinson Medical Publications, Ltd., 178–202 Great Portland Street, London, W1N 6AQ *T.* 01–580 3020. *Telex:* 261212. (Trade) 062-181 6362. *Telex:* 18130. *T.A.* Literarius, London, W.1. *Directors:* R. A. A. Holt (Chairman), Sir Robert Lusty, J. R. Stevens. An imprint of the Hutchinson Publishing Group.
Medical, surgical, psychological, and allied subjects.

I.P.C. Books Ltd. (1969), 33 Holborn, London, E.C.1. *T.* 01–353 0246. *T.A.* Intaorbit, London, E.C.4. *Directors:* A. Winspear, P. A. Jarvis, E. S. Birk, N. Fisher. *Associate companies overseas:* The Hamlyn Publishing Group (Canada) Ltd., Paul Hamlyn Inc., U.S.A., IPC Investments Pty. Ltd. (Australia), Paul Hamlyn Pty. Ltd. (Australia), Hamlyn House Pty. Ltd. (Australia), Publishing Associates Pty. Ltd. (Australia), Universal Books Pty. Ltd. (Australia), Butterworth & Co. (Overseas) Ltd., Serasia Books Ltd. (Hong Kong).

I.P.C. Business Press Ltd., 161–166 Fleet Street, London, E.C.4. For a list of journals see end of book.

I.P.C. Magazines Ltd., (International Publishing Corporation) Tower House, Southampton Street, W.C.2. For a list of journals see end of book.

*Iliffe Scientific & Technical Books see The Butterworth Group.

*International Correspondence Schools, Ltd. (1891), Intertext House, Stewart's Road, London, S.W.8. *T.* 01–720 1983; and 2 Norfolk Street, London, W.C.2. *T.* 01–836 3144.
Professional, technical, commercial and general education.

International Learning Systems Corporation Ltd., 72–90 Worship Street, London, E.C.2. *T.* 01–247 8492. *Telex:* 886048.
Educational and Technical.

*International Textbook Co. Ltd., 158 Buckingham Palace Road, London, S.W.1. *T.* 01–730 7216. Imprints: Leonard Hill Books; Morgan Grampian Educational; International Profiles; Leisure Learning; Chemist and Druggist Books.
Technical, Scientific, Educational and Reference Books covering agriculture, chemistry and chemical industries, engineering, architecture and building, biology, botany and food. General Educational Books. International Profiles. The work of young and new authors is given careful consideration.

*Inter-Varsity Press, 39 Bedford Square, London, WC1B 3EY. *T.* 01–636 5113.
Theology and Religion.

Irish University Press (1967), Shannon, Co. Clare, Ireland. *T.* 061–61166. *T.A.* Unipress Shannon. *Directors:* J. J. O'Leary (Chairman), M. J. McManus (Deputy Chairman), R. Hogg, Capt. T. MacGlinchey, Prof. John J. O'Meara.
Scholarly, Technical, Scientific, Religious and Bibliographical books.

Jack (T. C. and E. C.), Ltd. Incorporated with **Thomas Nelson & Sons, Ltd.,** *q.v.*

*Jackdaw Publications Ltd., 24 Tottenham Court Road, London, W1P 9RA. *T.* 01–637 2701. *T.A.* Capajon, London. *Directors:* Graham C. Greene, Tom Maschler, Howard Loxton, Richard Chester, Stephen du Sautoy.
Folders of facsimile documents covering history, geography, science and literature.

James (Arthur), Ltd. (1935), The Drift, Evesham, Worcestershire WR11 4NW. *T.* Evesham 6566. *Directors:* Major R. A. Russell, F. L. Russell, F. A. Russell M. Macqueen.
Religion, Sociology, Psychology, Autobiography.

Jarrolds Publishers (London) Ltd. (1770), 178–202 Great Portland Street, London, W1N 6AQ *T.* 01–580 3020. *T.A.* Literarius, London, W.1. *Telex:* 261212. *T.* (Trade) 062–181 6362. *Telex:* 18130. An imprint of the Hutchinson Publishing Group. R. A. A. Holt (Chairman). *Directors:* Sir Robert Lusty, and Gerald Austin.
Biography and Memoirs, Fiction, General, Travel.

†Jenkins (Herbert), Ltd. Incorporated with **Barrie and Jenkins,** *q.v.*

Jewish Chronicle Publications (1949), 25 Furnival Street, London, E.C.4. *T.* 01–405 9252. *Publishing Manager:* P. G. Mayers.
General, Theology and Religion, Reference, Year Book, Guide Book.

*Johnson Publications Ltd. (1946), 11–14 Stanhope Mews West, London, S.W.7. *T.* Fremantle 8543. *Directors:* Donald McI. Johnson, Ivor R. M. Davies, Norman McI. Johnson.
Belles-Lettres, Biography and Memoirs, Current Affairs, Economics, General, History, Law, Political Economy, Sociology, Travel, Medical, Occult, Philosophy. Return postage should be sent with unsolicited manuscripts.

Johnsons (1846), 10 Stafford Street, Edinburgh EH3 7AZ. *T.* 031–225 4410. *T.A.* Designs, Edinburgh 3. *Principal:* Christopher Yate Johnson, F.R.S.A. Past President, Royal Scottish Society of Arts.
Industrial Designs and Trade Marks.

Johnston and Bacon, see Geoffrey Chapman Ltd.

†Jordan & Sons, Ltd. (1863), 190 Fleet Street, London, E.C.4. *T.* 01–405 9922. *Directors:* D. St. C. Morgan, H. G. M. Leighton, H. Powell, J. J. A. Cowdry, P. R. Milliken-Smith.
Accountancy, Commerce, Economics, Educational (Secondary, Technical, University), Law.

*Joseph (Michael), Ltd. (1935), 52 Bedford Square, WC1B 3EF. *T.* 01–637 0941: *T.A.* Emjaybuks, Westcent, London. Trade Counter and Warehouse: 1 Bloomsbury Street, W.C.1. *Directors:* G. B. Parrack (Chairman), The Hon. Mrs. Michael Joseph (Deputy Chairman), Edmund Fisher (Managing Director), G. C. Brunton, Victor Morrison, Raleigh Trevelyan (Editorial Director), W. Thomas, William Luscombe, T. J. Couper, Richard Douglas-Boyd.
Belles-Lettres, Biography and Memoirs, Children's Books (Fiction, Non-Fiction), Current Affairs, Fiction, General, History, Humour, Sociology.

Jupiter paperbacks—see **Calder & Boyars.**

Justice of the Peace Ltd. (1837), Little London, Chichester, Sussex. *T.* 83637.
Law, Local Government.

*Kaye & Ward Ltd., 194–200 Bishopsgate, London, E.C.2. *T* 01–283 7495-6-7. *Cables:* Kayebooks, Ave, London. *Directors:* G. F. Straker, Stanley Pickard, E. T. L. Marriott, I. F. L. Straker, A. T. Smith.
Sports, Travel, Children's Books, Cookery, Bibliography, Practical Handbooks, Recreations, Physical Education, Hobbies.

Kelly's Directories Ltd., Neville House, Eden Street, Kingston upon Thames, Surrey. *T.* 01–546 7722.
Publishers of Kelly's Post Office London Directory: Kelly's Manufacturers and Merchants Directory including Industrial Services: Handbook to the Titled, Landed, and Official Classes: Debrett's Peerage, Baronetage, Knightage and Companionage; Town, and other Directories.

*Kimber (William) & Co., Ltd. (1950), Godolphin House, 22a Queen Anne's Gate, London, S.W.1. *T.* 01–839 7684. Trade Counter: 72–74 Paul Street, E.C.2. *T.* 01–739 4755. *Directors:* W. T. Kimber, O. J. Colman, Audrey Kimber, F. M. de Salis, Amy Howlett. Freelance artists' and designers' work used.
Aeronautics, Biography and Memoirs, Current Affairs, Fiction, General, History, Travel, Naval and Military.

Kimpton (Henry) (1854) (Medical Book Department of Hirschfeld Brothers, Ltd.), 205 Great Portland Street, London, W1N 6LR   *T.* 01–580 6381.
Medical, Dental.

Knight (Charles) & Co. ,Ltd., 11–12 Bury Street, St Mary Axe, EC3A 5AP   *T.* 01–626 5477.   *Directors:* H. W. Bziley-King, O.B.E. (Chairman), N. Stewart-Pearson, LL.B.
Local Government, Local Government Law, Industrial Law, Government and Politics, Sociology, History, Military, General Non-Fiction.

Lane (John).   See The Bodley Head, Ltd.

Larby (E. J.), Ltd., 15–17 St. Cross Street, Hatton Garden, London, E.C.1.   *T.* 01–242 6428–9.

Larie (T. Werner) Ltd. (1904), 9 Bow Street, WC2E 7AL.   *T.* 01–836 9081.   *T.A.* Bodleian, Westcent, London.   *Directors:* Max Reinhardt (Chairman and Managing), L. A. Hart, J. R. Hews, Joan Reinhardt, M. B. Ormrod.
Biography and Memoirs, Current Affairs, Fiction, General, Sports, Games and Hobbies, Travel.

*Lawrence & Wishart, Ltd., 46 Bedford Row, London, WC1R 4LR.   *T.* 01–405 7565.   *T.A.* Interbook, London, W.C.1.   *Directors:* S. Seifert, R. Simon, N. Green, M. Mynatt, M. Cornforth, M. Costello, J. M. Todd, J. Klugmann, P. Goodwin, I. Walker.
Current Affairs, Economics, History, Philosophy, Political Economy, Sociology.

*Leicester University Press (1951), 2 University Road, Leicester LE1 7RB   *T.* Leicester 20185.   *Secretary:* Peter L. Boulton, M.A.
Academic books, especially in history (including English Local History), History of Science, Archaeology, Transport Studies, Victorian Studies.

Leng (John) & Co., Ltd., Dundee.   See Thomson-Leng Publications.

Letts (Charles) & Co., Ltd. (1796), Diary House, Borough Road, S.E.1.   *T.* 01–407 7871 (10 lines).   *Directors:* L. C. Letts (Chairman), D. N. Letts, R. H. Letts, J. M. Letts, A. A. Letts (Managing), T. R. Letts, N. B. Erskine, D. F. Myers, T. R. Walker.
Diary and book publishers and manufacturers.

Leventhal, Lionel, Ltd.,—see under Arms and Armour Press.

Lewis (A) (Masonic Publishers), Ltd. (1870), 6 Hogarth Place, Earl's Court, London, S.W.5.   *T.* Fremantle 0830.   *Managing Director:* E. N. London.
Masonic books.

Lewis (F.), Publishers, Ltd., The Tithe House, 1461 London Road, Leigh-on-Sea, Essex SS9 2SD   *T.* 0702 78163.   *Directors:* Frank Lewis, Elsie F. Lewis (Governing).
Art, Dictionaries (Art), Reference, Ceramics, Textiles, Illustrated Gift Books.

*Lewis (H. K.) & Co., Ltd. (1844), 136 Gower Street, WC1E 6BS.   *T.* 01–387 4282.   *T.A.* Publicavit, London, W.C.1.   *Directors:* G. W. Edwards, F. Boothby, R. Salter.
Science, Medical.

Linden Press, Fontwell, Arundel, Sussex. *T.* 024–368 3302. *Directors:* Jon Wynne-Tyson, Jennifer M. Wynne-Tyson. A preliminary letter should be sent before submitting MS. Publishers of theses and sociological works, etc. Subsidiary imprint of **Centaur Press Ltd.,** *q.v.*

Lindsey Press, Essex Hall, 1–6 Essex Street, Strand, London, WC2R 3HY *T.* 01-240 2384–5.
Theology and Religion.

Link House Publications, Ltd. Dingwall Avenue, Croydon, CR9 2TA *T.* 01-686 2599. *T.A.* Aviculture, Croydon. *Directors:* F. H. Isaac (Chairman), E. T. Burt, M.B.E. (Vice-Chairman), G. C. Burt (Managing Director), N. R. Burt, R. J. Wenn.
Specialist periodicals; do-it-yourself, caravanning, philately, camping, retailing, occult, small boats, coins, hi-fi, tape recording, motoring. For list of journals published by this firm see end of book.

Literary Services and Production Ltd. (1964), 26 Old Brompton Road, London, S.W.7. *T.* 01–584 9381–2. *T.A.* Litserve. *Directors:* C. P. de Laszlo, C. A. J. Nelson, B. R. Lincoln.
Art, History.

Littlebury & Company, Ltd. (1894), The Worcester Press, Worcester, WR1 2HX. *T.* Worcester 22813 and 23064. *Directors:* H. D. Littlebury, A. F. M. Littlebury. Publishers of agricultural journals.
Science, Maps and Atlases, Guides, Timetables, Directories.

*****Liverpool University Press** (1901), J. G. O'Kane (Secretary), 123 Grove Street, Liverpool 7. *T.* Royal 3630 and 7303. *T.A.* Cormorant, Liverpool.
Architecture, Archaeology and Oriental Studies, Economics, Education, Social Science, Politics, Biography, History, Literature, Philosophy and the Natural Sciences, Languages, and University textbooks.

*****Livingstone, (E. & S.)** (1863), (a division of **Longman Group Ltd.**), 15, 16 and 17 Teviot Place, Edinburgh. *T.* 031–225 6962 (3 lines). *T.A.* Livingstone, Publishers, Edinburgh. London Office: 104 Gloucester Place, W1H 4AE. *T.* 01–935 6164. *Managing Director:* W. G. Henderson.
Medical, Nursing, Dental, Veterinary, Scientific, Dictionaries.

Logos Press Ltd., 2 All Saints Street, London, N.1. *T.* 01–837 0614. *Directors:* E. Elek, P. Elek. *Managing Editor:* J. G. Mordue, M.A.
Science (Physics, Experimental Biology, Chemistry, Mathematics.)

Lomax, Erskine Publications Ltd., 8 Buckingham Street, London, WC2N 6DA. *T.* 01–839 6661. Technical and Engineering.

Long (John), Ltd., 178–202 Great Portland Street, London, W1N 6AQ *T.* 01–580 3020. *Telex:* 261212. Trade Department: 062–181 6362. *Telex;* 18130. *T.A.* Literarius, London. W.1. *Chairman:* R. A. A. Holt. *Directors:* Sir Robert Lusty, Gerald Austin. An imprint of the Hutchinson Publishing Group.
General books on Criminology, Law and the American West. Detective Novels and Thrillers.

Longmans, Browne & Nolan, Ltd., 4 South Great George's Street, Dublin 2. *T.* Dublin 777381. *Directors:* R. Allen Nolan (Chairman), M. W. Smurfit, D. S. Magee, M. F. K. Longman, Sir John Newsom, T. C. Marmion, W. A. H. Beckett, Rosemary Davidson.
Educational MSS. on all subjects in English or Gaelic.

*Longman Group Limited, (1724), 74 Grosvenor Street, London, W1X 0AS. *T.* 01–499 7911. *T.A.* Longman, London, W.1. *Directors:* M. F. K. Longman, (Chairman), R. A. Allan, D.S.O., O.B.E., (Vice-Chairman), W. A. H. Beckett, J. F. G. Chapple, R. P. T. Gibson, D. Meinertzhagen, Sir John Newsom, C.B.E., Lord Robbins, C.H., C.B. *Secretary:* F. W. Tiller. *Exectuive Directors:* W. G. Henderson, P. B. Hepburn, J. A. E. Higham, M. J. A. Hoare, R. A. Hobbs, W. P. Kerr, H. O. A. McWilliam, P. J. Munday, J. Quash, C. J. Rea, J. A. Rivers, T. J. Rix, R. F. Stacey, F. Taylor, P. C. B. Wallis, M. E. Wayte, J. R. C. Yglesias. Associated Companies (*q.v.*) in Canada, India, Australia, New Zealand, Ghana, Uganda, Kenya, Tanzania, Malawi, Rhodesia, Zambia, Hong Kong, Malaysia, Nigeria, The Caribbean and South Africa.

Aeronautics, Architecture, Art, Atlases, Belles-Lettres, Biography and Memoirs, Commerce, Current Affairs, Dictionaries, Drama, Economics, Educational (Infants, Primary, Secondary, Technical, University), Essays, Fiction, General, History, Humour, Law, Medical, Naval and Military, Oriental, Philosophy, Poetry, Political Economy, Reference, Science, Sociology, Sports, Theatre and Ballet, Theology and Religion, Travel, Year Books.

†**Longmans Young Books Ltd.,** 74 Grosvenor Street, W1X 0AS *T.* 01–499 7911. *T.A.* Longmans, London, W.1. *Directors:* P. W. Hardy (Managing Director), M. F. K. Longman (Chairman), Mrs G. Hogarth, Dame Kitty Anderson D.B.E., M. J. A. Hoare. Children's Books.

*Lund Humphries Publishers Ltd., 12 Bedford Square, W.C.1. *T.* 01–636 7676. *T.A.* Lund, 636 7676, London. *Directors:* A. W. Bell, R. Bottomley, E. Moorhouse, H. Spencer, J. A. Taylor.

Architecture, Art, Graphic Art, Dictionaries, Readers, Grammars, Oriental.

*Lutterworth Press (1799), Head Office: 4 Bouverie Street, London, E.C.4. *T.* 01–353 3853-7 (5 lines). *T.A.* Lutteric, Cent, London. M. E. Foxell (General Manager).

Archaeology, Biography and Memoirs, Children's Books (Fiction, Non-Fiction, Rewards), General, Science, Sociology, Theology and Religion, Travel.

Luzac & Company, Ltd. (1890), P.O. Box 157, 46 Great Russell Street, WC1B 3PE. *T.* 01–636 1462. *T.A.* Obfirmate, Westcent, London. *Managing Director:* H. Reynolds.

Archaeology, Architecture, Art Dictionaries, History, Theology and Religion, Travel, Oriental.

*Macdonald & Co. (Publishers), Ltd., 49 Poland Street, London, W1A 2LG, *T.* 01–437 0686. *Directors:* R. G. Holme (Chairman), J. MacGibbon (Managing), P. Galliner, P. Morrison (Secretary). An Associate Company of BPC Publishing Ltd.

Macdonald Educational, 49–50 Poland Street, London, W1A 2LG *T.* 01–437 0686. An Associate Company of BPC Publishing Ltd.

Macdonald Technical, Scientific & Reference Books, 49 Poland Street, London, W1A 2LG *T.* 01–437 0686. An Associate Company of BPC Publishing Ltd.

Macdonald & Evans, Ltd. (1907), 8 John Street, WC1N 2HY. *T.* 01–242 2177-8-9. *T.A.* Evandon, London, W.C.1. *Directors:* J. D. Macdonald, A. L. Rowles, G. B. Davis, R. B. North, M. W. Beevers.

Accountancy and Book-keeping, Banking, Commerce, Economics, Educational (Secondary, Technical, University), Geography, Law, Chemistry and Physics, Dance and Movement Notation.

*MacGibbon & Kee Ltd., Publishers, 3 Upper James Street, Golden Square, London, W1R 4BP *T.* 01–734–8080. Trade Counter: Book Centre, North Circular Road, Neasden, N.W.10. *T.* 01–459 1222. *Directors:* W. R. Carr, D. H. Granger, J. C. Reynolds.

Archaeology, Art, Biography and Memoirs, Current Affairs, Drama, Essays, Fiction, General, History, Hobbies, Instructional, Practical Handbooks, Sociology, Sport, Theatre and Ballet, Travel.

*McGraw-Hill Publishing Co., Ltd., McGraw-Hill House, Shoppenhangers Road, Maidenhead, Berkshire. *T.* Maidenhead 23432. *T.A.* McGraw-Hill, Maidenhead. *Directors:* Ronald R. G. Abbotts, Russell F. Anderson, Edward E. Booher, H. G. Castle, Shelton Fisher, W. Gordon Graham (Managing), Ernest Hunter, John L. McGraw, Charles H. Sweeny, J. K. Van Denburg, George M. Webster, Donald C. McGraw.

Technical, Scientific, Medical, Art and General.

Machinery's Technical Books (1912), Clifton House, 83 Euston Road, London, NW1 2RE *T.* 01–387 8441. *T.A.* Machtool, London, N.W.1. *Directors:* C. H. Burder (Managing) R. M. Kennard, P. A. Sidders.

Engineering (mechanical, production, electrical), Management.

MacLaren (Alex.) & Sons incorporated with **Gairm Publications** *qv.*

*Macmillan & Co. Ltd. (1843), (Subsidiary of Macmillan (Holdings) Ltd.). 4 Little Essex Street, WC2R 3LF. *T.* 01–836 6633. *T.A.* Publish, London, W.C.2. Brunel Road, Basingstoke, Hants. *T.* Basingstoke 5431. *Foreign Cables:* Publish, London. *Chairman:* F. H. Whitehead. *Directors:* N. G. Byam Shaw (*Managing*), R. F. Allen, N. J. Barker, T. M. Farmiloe, M. Hamilton, V. Ivens, W. S. D. Jollands, A. D. Maclean, J. Maddox. *Allied and Subsidiary Companies:* Macmillan(Journals) Ltd., Macmillan (Warehousing) Ltd., Gill & Macmillan Ltd., The Macmillan Company of Canada Ltd., The Macmillan Company of India Ltd., St. Martin's Press Inc., Macmillan & Co. (Nigeria) Ltd., The Macmillan Co. of Australia Pty. Ltd., Macmillan South Africa (Publishers) Pty. Ltd., Macmillan Publishers (H.K.) Ltd., Jamaica Publishing House, Macmillan & Co. (S.) Private Ltd., Singapore.

General Literature, Academic, Biography, Scientific and Technical Works, Fiction and Juvenile Literature, Educational Books and Visual Aids of all grades from Infant to University Level. Publishers of *Grove's Dictionary of Music and Musicians* and *The Statesman's Year-Book.*

Macmillan (Journals) Ltd. *Chairman:* F. H. Whitehead. *Directors:* S. A. Baynton, J. C. N. Hughes, J. Maddox, R. F. Stiff.

Publishers of *Medical Officer, Nature, Nursing Times* (weekly), *British Journal of Pharmacology, Marine Pollution Bulletin, Occupational Health* (monthly), *Brain, Economic Journal, European Studies Review, Minerva, Philosophy, Science Studies, Studies in History and Philosophy of Science* (quarterly), *Russian Mathematical Surveys* (six parts per annual volume).

Macmillan Company, New York, The, see Collier-Macmillan Ltd.

*Manchester University Press (1912), 316–324 Oxford Road, Manchester, M13 9NR. *T.* 061–273 5539/30. Books of value for higher education in all branches.

Archaeology, Architecture, Belles-Lettres, Current Affairs, Drama, Economics, Educational (Secondary Grammar and University), Essays, History, Law, Medicine, Music, Oriental, Philosophy, Political Economy, Science (all branches), Sociology and Theology and Religion.

Map Productions Ltd. (1964), Paulton House, 8 Shepherds Walk, London, N.1. *T.* 01–253 0802. *Directors:* R. J. H. Pollock (Chairman), R. F. A. Edwards (Managing), L. A. Pearce, P. Morrison (Secretary). An Associate Company of B.P.C. Publishing Ltd.

Marlowe (David) Ltd. (1946), 11–14 Stanhope Mews West, London, S.W.7. *T.* Fremantle 8543. *Directors:* Donald McI. Johnson, Betty M. Johnson. General.

*****Marshall, Morgan & Scott, Ltd.,** (1928), 1–5 Portpool Lane, Holborn, E.C.1. *T.* 01–405 7011–6. *T.A.* Grapho, Phone, London. *Directors:* G. S. McKnight (Chairman), S. W. Grant, P. J. Lardi. *Secretary:* T. R. Nicholas. Children's Books, Dictionaries, Theology and Religion, Music.

*****Mason (Kenneth) Publications Ltd.** (1958), 13 and 14 Homewell, Havant, Hampshire. *T.* Havant 6262. *Director:* Kenneth Mason. General and Academic, Directories and Guide Books, Reference. Publishers of the *With BP Series.* Technical Journals.

*****Mayflower Books Ltd.,** 3 Upper James Street, Golden Square, London, W1R 4BP. *T.* 01–734 8080. *Directors:* Lord Bernstein, A. R. H. Birch, W. R. Carr, W. Clare, J. Warton. Paperbacks—originals and reprints. Dragon Books.

*****Medici Society, Ltd.,** 34–42 Pentonville Road, London, N1 9HG. *T.* 01–837 7099. Publishers of the Medici Prints and other colour reproductions of Old Masters and Modern Artists. Art, Children's books, General.

Meiklejohn & Son, Ltd. (1888), now incorporated with **Oliver & Boyd, Ltd.,** *q.v.*

Mellifont Press, Ltd., 60 Russell Square, London. W. C. 1. *T.* 01–637 2541. Children's Books (Fiction and semi-educational for younger children).

Mercier Press, Ltd., The (1945), 4 Bridge Street, Cork, Ireland. *T.* Cork 20292–3. *Directors:* Capt. J. M. Feehan, J. C. O'Connor, M. P. Feehan, P. W. McGrath. Irish Literature, Folklore, History.

†**Merlin Press, Ltd.,** 11 Fitzroy Square, London, W1P 5HQ *T.* 01–387 6073. *Directors:* E. L. Hilton, M. W. Eve. Sociology, Belles-Lettres, History, Philosophy. Publishers of *The Socialist Register.*

*****Merrow Publishing Company Limited** (1951), 276 Hempstead Road, Watford, WD1 3LZ *T.* Watford 34426. *Directors:* J. G. Cook, M. Cook. Textiles, plastics, popular science, scientific.

*****Methodist Youth Department,** 2 Chester House, Pages Lane, Muswell Hill, London, N10 1PR. *T.* 01–444 9845. Theology and Religion.

*****Methuen & Co., Ltd.** (1889), 11 New Fetter Lane, London, E.C.4. *T.* 01–583 9855. *T.A.* Elegiacs, London. *Directors:* Peter L. K. Wait (Chairman), John D. Cullen (Managing Director), John Bright-Holmes, Anthony Forster. Archaeology, Art, Belles-Lettres, Biography and Memoirs, Children's Books (Fiction, Non-Fiction, Picture), Current Affairs, Guide Books, Drama, Educational (University), Essays, Fiction, General and Economic History, Humour, Music, Philosophy, Poetry, Psychology, Sociology, Theatre and Travel.

Methuen Academic Ltd., 11 New Fetter Lane, London, E.C.4. *T.* 01–583 9855. *Directors:* Peter L. K. Wait (Chairman), A. S. Forster (Managing Director), John Naylor, Roger Kirkpatrick, M. R. Turner, Carol Somerset. Academic.

†**Methuen Educational Ltd.** (1967), 11 New Fetter Lane, London, E.C.4. *T.* 01–583 9855. *T.A.* Elegiacs, London. *Directors:* Peter Allsop (Chairman), Julian Hodgson (Managing Director), Anthony Forster, Patricia Hattaway, Ian McKee, Norman Mitchell, Patrick Thornhill.

Educational (Primary, Secondary, Programmed Text Books), Education and Teaching Methods, Educational Materials.

Methuen, Eyre & Spottiswoode Ltd., 11 New Fetter Lane, London, E.C.4. *T.* 01–583 9855. *Directors:* J. D. Cullen (Chairman), J. Bright-Holmes (Managing Director), A. T. J. Burrell, E. Hughesdon, C. H. Shirley, M. R. Turner.

History, Biography, Sport, Drama, Current Affairs, Fiction, Children's (all kinds).

***Miller (J. Garnet) Ltd.** (1951), 1–5 Portpool Lane, London, E.C.1. *T.* 01–405 7980. *Directors:* John G. F. Miller, Mrs. M. J. Miller.

Antiques, Children's Books, Drama, Science, Theatre.

***Mills & Boon, Ltd.** (1909), 17–19 Foley Street, London, W1A 1DR. *T.* 01–580 9074–0. *T.A.* Millsator, Rath, London. *Chairman:* C. C. Boon. *Directors:* J. T. Boon, C.B.E. (Managing), A. W. Boon. *Executive Directors:* Mrs E. J. Bryant, P. Collins, A. T. Mckay, *Secretary:* B. C. J. Rogers.

Fiction, general and educational. Particular interest; general books on handicrafts, social questions, domestic science: educational books in all fields, particularly scientific: fiction, library novels and paperbacks.

Moray Press, c/o W. & R. Chambers Ltd., 11 Thistle Street, Edinburgh EH2 1DG. *T.* 031–225 4463–4; and 6 Dean Street, London, W1V 6LD. *T.* 01–437 1709.

Biography and Memoirs, General, Travel, Scottish.

Morgan Grampian (Publishers) Ltd., 28 Essex Street, London, WC2R 3AZ. *T.* 01–353 6565. For list of periodicals see end of book.

***Mothers' Union, The** (1876), 24 Tufton Street, London, S.W.1. *T.* 01–222 5533. *T.A.* Marisumner, London, S.W.1.

Religious and educational.

***Mowbray (A.R.) & Co., Ltd.,** The Alden Press, Osney Mead, Oxford OX2 0EG. *T.* 0865 42507.

Theology and Religion, Biography, History, Humour, Religious Educational Books, Children's Books.

***Muller (Frederick), Ltd.,** Ludgate House, Fleet Street, E.C.4. *T.* 01–353 1040 and (trade) Earls Court Gardens, Earls Court, S.W.5. *T.* 01–373 7194–5. *T.A.* Efmull, London, E.C.4. *Directors:* L. V. Archer, L. Keith Martin, V. Andrews.

Childrens, Collecting, Creative Hobbies, Educational, History, Metallurgy, Military History, Occult, Technical.

†**Murby (Thomas) & Co.** (1866), 40 Museum Street, WC1A 1LU. *T.* 01–405 8577. *T.A.* Deucalion, London, W.C.1. *Proprietors:* George Allen & Unwin, Ltd. *Chairman:* Rayner Unwin. *Group Managing Director:* Geoffrey Cass.

Science (Geology, Soil Science).

*Murray, John (Publishers), Ltd. (1768), 50 Albemarle Street, London, W1X 4BD
T. 01–493 4361. *T.A.* Guidebook, London, W.1. *Directors*: John G. Murray,
M.B.E., B.A. (Oxon.), Kenneth J. Foster, Leslie A. Miller, Simon B. Young,
Kenneth J. Pinnock, John R. Murray.

Aeronatics, Architecture, Art, Biography and Memoirs, Children's Books
(Fiction, Non-Fiction), Current Affairs, Dictionaries, Educational (Primary,
Secondary, Technical, University), Essays, Fiction, General, History, Humour,
Sports, Games and Hobbies, Theology and Religion, Travel, Oriental, Philo-
sophy.

Cornhill Magazine, School Science Review, Journal of Navigation, etc.

Museum Press, Ltd. (1943), 39 Parker Street, London, WC2B 5PB. *T.* 01–405 9791.
School Library Books, General, Humour, Natural History, Practical Handbooks, Popular Science, Sports, Games and Hobbies.

N.C.L.C. Publishing Society, Ltd., see Fabian Society.

NTP Business Journals Ltd., See I.P.C. Business Press Ltd.

National Adult School Union (1889), Drayton House, Gordon Street, London
WC1H 0BE. *T.* 01–387 5920.
Adult educational handbooks for study groups.

*National Christian Education Council (formerly National Sunday School Union),
Robert Denholm House, Nutfield, Redhill, Surrey. *T.* Nutfield Ridge 2411.
Books on all aspects of Christian education. Material for children's work in
the Church, including youth and mid-week work. Activity and visual material.

*National Magazine Co., Ltd., The, Chestergate House, Vauxhall Bridge Road,
London, S.W.1. *T.* 01–834 2331.
See The Connoisseur and Ebury Press.

National Press, The (1935), 2 Wellington Road, Dublin, 4. *T.* Dublin 689105.
Director: P. Cannon. *Secretary:* M. A. Fortune.
Educational.

Nautical Publishing Company (1967), Nautical House, Lymington, Hants S04 9BA.
T. Lymington 2578. *Partners:* K. Adlard Coles, Commander Erroll Bruce,
R.N.Rtd., Richard Creagh-Osborne. *Associates:* George G. Harrap & Co.
Ltd.

Navarre Society, Ltd. (1921), 1 Grafton Street, London, W1X 3LB. *T.* 01–493
3810. *T.A.* Vespucci, London, W.1. *Director:* C. R. Sawyer.
Reprints of the classics.

*Nelson (Thomas) & Sons, Ltd. (1798), 36 Park Street, London, W1Y 4DE *T.*01–493
8351; Lincoln Way, Windmill Road, Sunbury-on-Thames. *T.* 76–86311.
T.A. Thonelson, London, W.1. *Overseas Houses* at: Johannesburg, Lagos,
Melbourne, Nairobi, New Delhi, Sydney, Toronto. All MSS. should be sent
to the London address.

Archaeology, Art, Belles-Lettres, Bibles, Biography and Memoirs, Children's
Books, Cookery, Dictionaries, Drama, Economics, Educational (Infants,
Primary, Secondary, Technical, University), General, History, Humour, Maps
and Atlases, Music, Naval and Military, Philosophy, Reference, Science, Sports,
Games and Hobbies, Theatre and Ballet, Theology and Religion.

New Authors Ltd. (1957), 178–202 Great Portland Street, London, W1N 6AQ
T. 01–580 3020. *Telex;* 261212. (Trade) 062–181 6362. *Telex:* 98130. *T.A.*
Literarius, London, W.1. R. A. A. Holt (Chairman). *Directors:* Sir Robert
Lusty, M. C. Dempsey. An imprint of the Hutchinson Publishing Group.
First books only. Fiction, Non-Fiction.

New English Library Ltd. (1957), Barnards Inn, Holborn, London, E.C.1. *T.* 01–405 4614. *T.A.* Nelpublish London. *Directors:* Sir John Rodgers, Bart. MP. (Chairman), H. P. Tanner (Managing), C. L. Burr, A. R. Jollye, Martin P. Levin (U.S.A.), T. R. D'Cruz, A.C.A.
Fiction (paperback).

New Left Books Ltd. (1969), 7 Carlisle Street, London, W1V 5RG. *T.* 01–437 3546. *Directors:* Perry Anderson, Robin Blackburn, Ronald Fraser, Quintin Hoare, Nicholas Jacobs, Peter Wollen.
Politics, Biography, Current Affairs, Economics, History, Cultural Criticism.

Newman Neame, Ltd., Maxwell House, 348–350 Gray's Inn Road, London, W.C.1. *T.* 01–837 6484 (for further details see under **Editorial, Literary and Production Services**).

Newnes Technical Books. See The Butterworth Group.

*Nisbet (James) & Co., Ltd. (1810), Digswell Place, Welwyn. Herts. *T.* Welwyn Garden, 25491–2–3. *T.A.* Stebsin, Welwyn Garden City. *Directors:* Mrs. R. M. Mackenzie Wood, W. B. M. Hunter, G. H. B. McLean, Miss E. M. Mackenzie-Wood.
Children's Books, Dictionaries, Economics, Educational (Infants, Primary, Secondary, University), Philosophy, Theology and Religion.

Nonesuch Library, Ltd., The (1951), 9 Bow Street, London, WC2E 7AL. *T.* 01–836 9081. *Directors:* Max Reinhardt (Chairman and Managing Director), L. A. Hart, Sir Francis Meynell, R.D.I. D.LITT., J. R. Hews, F.C.A. New editions of the English classics.
Belles-Lettres.

Nonesuch Press, Ltd., The, *Directors:* Sir Francis Meynell, R.D.I., D.LITT., Max Reinhardt, Benedict Meynell, Pamela Zander. Special Editions designed by Sir Francis Meynell. Distributors: The Bodley Head Ltd., 9 Bow Street, London, WC2E 7AL. *T.* 01–836 9081.

Normal Press, The (1889), 25 Vicarage Lane, Upper Hale, Farnham, Surrey. *Director:* L. W. Cradwick.
Educational.

Odham Books. See The Hamlyn Publishing Group Ltd.

Oliphants Ltd. See Marshall, Morgan & Scott Ltd.

*Oliver & Boyd (1778), A Division of Longman Group Ltd., Tweeddale Court, 14, High Street, Edinburgh, EH1 1YL. *T.* 031–556 4622–4. *T.A.* Almanac, Edinburgh. *Directors:* M. E. Wayte (Divisional Managing Director), M. I. Berrill, A. A. Dunnett.
School Books, Scientific and Technical Text Books, General Publications, including Criticism, History, Social Sciences, Scottish Studies.
See Chatto & Windus Ltd.

Orbis (London), Ltd., 66 Kenway Road, London, S.W.5. *T.* 01–370 2210.

*Oriel Press Ltd. (1962), 32 Ridley Place, Newcastle upon Tyne, NE1 8LH. *T.* Newcastle 20892. *Directors:* Bruce Allsop (Chairman and Joint Managing), R. S. Adams (Joint-Managing), F. C. Allsopp (Secretary), D. M. Bell.
Architecture, Art, Archaeology, Science, Sociology, Geography, History, Technical, Conferences, Symposia, Town Planning, Oriel Academic Publications Series, Oriel Guides Series.

Osprey Publications Ltd., (1968), P.O. Box 25, 707 Oxford Road, Reading, RG3 1JB. *T.* 0734 21914. *T.A.* Osprey, Reading. *Directors:* K. G. Boddington (Managing), M. Garden, T .M. Langdon, Richard Ward, D. E. Provan.
Aircraft, Architecture, Bibliography, General, History, Military.

Outposts Publications (1956), 72 Burwood Road, Walton-on-Thames, Surrey. *T.* Walton-on-Thames 40712. *Directors:* Howard Sergeant, Jean Sergeant. Poetry.

*Owen, Peter, Ltd., 12 Kendrick Mews, Kendrick Place, London, S.W.7. *T.* 01–589 5336 and 01–584 3070. *T.A.* Neocol, London. *Directors:* Peter L. Owen (Managing), Wendy F. J. Owen.
Art, Belles-Lettres, Biography and Memoirs, Fiction, General, Theatre.

*Oxford University Press (1478). *London Publisher and Manager:* J. G. N. Brown, c.b.e., Ely House, 37 Dover Street, London, W1X 4AH *T.* 01–629 8494. *T.A.* Frowde, London, W.1. Trade Dept.: Press Road, Neasden Lane, N.W.10. *T.* 01–450 8080. *T.A.* Oxonian, London, N.W.10. Branches or offices *q.v.* in New York, Toronto, Melbourne, Wellington, Bombay, Calcutta, Madras, Karachi, Lahore, Dacca, Cape Town, Johannesburg, Salisbury, Nairobi, Dar es Salaam, Lusaka, Addis Ababa, Ibadan, Kuala Lumpur, Singapore, Hong Kong, Tokyo.
Aeronautics, Archaeology, Architecture, Art, Belles-Lettres, Bibles, Biography and Memoirs, Cartography, Children's Books (Fiction, Non-Fiction, Picture), Commerce, Current Affairs, Dictionaries, Drama, Economics, Educational (Infants, Primary, Secondary, Technical, University), English Language Teaching, Essays, General, History, Hymn and Service Books, Law, Maps and Atlases, Medical, Music, Naval and Military, Oriental, Philosophy, Poetry, Political Economy, Prayer Books, Reference, Science, Sociology, Sports, Games and Hobbies, Theatre and Ballet, Theology and Religion, Travel, Year Books.

PEP (Political and Economic Planning) (1931), 12 Upper Belgrave Street, London, S.W.1. *T.* 01–235 5271. *Directors:* John Pinder, Richard Davies.
Contemporary Affairs, Economics, Political Economy, Sociology, Industry.

*Pall Mall Press Ltd., 5 Cromwell Place, London, S.W.7. *T.* 01–589 3264. *Managing Director:* Roy Arnold.
Art, Architecture, Archaeology, Politics, Economics, Sociology, Contemporary History.

*Pan Books, Ltd. (1944), 33 Tothill Street, London, S.W.1. *T.* 01–222 7090. *Directors:* R. Vernon-Hunt (Managing), F. I. Chapman, Sir Willian Collins, A. D. Maclean, A. D. Evans, C. A. E. Paget, C. S. Pick, G. V. Risley (*Secretary*), F. H. Whitehead, T. W. V. McMullan. Low-priced reprints of notable novels, detective, fiction, travel, adventure and war books, with a number of original non-fiction works (the *Pan Piper Series*), and a business Management Series in paper covers. Distributor for Coles Notes.
Archaeology, Biography and Memoirs, Current Affairs, Fiction, General, Humour, Practical Handbooks.

*Panther Books Ltd., 3 Upper James Street, Golden Square, London W1R 4BP. *T.* 01–734 8080. *Directors:* Lord Bernstein, K. Banerji, A. R. H. Birch, J. Boothe, W. R. Carr, W. Miller, J. Warton.
Paperback Publishers—Originals and Reprints.

Partridge (S. W.) & Co. (1850), 4, 5 and 6 Soho Square, London, W1V 6AD Business purchased in 1930 by **A. & C. Black, Ltd.,** *q.v.*

*Paternoster Press, The, Paternoster House, 3 Mount Radford Crescent, Exeter, Devon EX4 2JW. *T.* Exeter 58977.
Children's Books (Non-Fiction, Rewards), Educational (University), Theology and Religion.

Paternoster Publications, 15 King Street, Covent Garden, W.C.2. *T.* Temple Bar 2662.
Children's Books (Non-Fiction), Educational (Primary), Theology and Religion, Philosophy.

Paul Elek Ltd. An associated company of Elek Books Ltd. *q.v.*

Paul Elek Productions Ltd. An associated company of Elek Books Ltd. *q.v.*

Paul (Stanley) & Co., Ltd. (1908), 178–202 Great Portland Street, London, W1N 6AQ *T.* 01–580 3020. *Telex:* 261212. Trade Dept.: 062–181 6362. *Telex:* 18130. *T.A.* Literarius, London, W.1. *Directors:* R. A. A. Holt (Chairman), Sir Robert Lusty, R. Bloomfield. An imprint of the Hutchinson Publishing Group.
Sports, Games and Hobbies.

Pearson (C. Arthur); books—See The Hamlyn Publishing Group Ltd.

Pelham Books Ltd. (1959), 52 Bedford Square, London, W.C.1. *T.* 01–637 0941; *T.A.* Emjaybuks, Westcent, London. *Directors:* G. B. Parrack (Chairman), William Luscombe (Managing and Editorial), The Hon. Mrs. Michael Joseph, T. C. Couper, V. Morrison, A. Folly, Edmund Fisher, G. C. Brunton. *Pears Cyclopaedia, Junior Pears Encyclopaedia,* autobiographies of men and women in sport, sports handbooks, hobbies and pastimes and practical handbooks on dogs and other pets.

*****Pemberton Publishing Co. Ltd.** (1954), 88 Islington High Street, London N1 8EN. *T.* 01–226 7251. Dr. David Stewart (Chairman), Hector Hawton (Managing Director), Mrs. G. C. Dowman (Secretary), C. J. G. Macy (Publicity and Sales Director), Dr. Roger Manvell.
Archaeology, Biography and Memoirs, Educational, History, Science, Sociology, Theology and Religion, Humanism, Ethics, Philosophy.

*****Penguin Books Limited** (1936), Harmondsworth, Middlesex. *T.* 01–759 1984 and 5722. *T.A.* Penguinook, West Drayton. *Directors:* R. P. T. Gibson (*Chairman*), M. F. K. Longman (*Vice-Chairman*), R. A. Allan, J. F. G. Chapple, F. Taylor, Lord Boyle, Christopher Dolley, R. J. E. Blass, C. Clark.
PENGUIN BOOKS consist of reprints of novels, detective and science fiction, travel, adventure, and biographical works. PELICAN BOOKS include more serious works on general aspects of the sciences and arts, including many entirely new works. PUFFIN BOOKS are full-length children's stories, often illustrated. PEACOCK BOOKS are for older children. PENGUIN CLASSICS are new translations of the world's greatest books. PENGUIN MODERN CLASSICS consist of reprints of twentieth-century classics. PENGUIN HANDBOOKS are a series of practical handbooks on many subjects of fairly widespread interest. PENGUIN SPECIALS are books on topical subjects, in particular politics and current affairs. PEREGRINE BOOKS are classic works of non-fiction. The PENGUIN ENGLISH LIBRARY consists of some of the English literary masterpieces produced since the fifteenth century. The series of Penguin Educational Books are textbooks at secondary and university level. There are also the PENGUIN AFRICAN LIBRARY, BUILDINGS OF ENGLAND, PENGUIN POETS, PENGUIN PLAYS, PENGUIN REFERENCE BOOKS, PENGUIN SHAKESPEARE, PELICAN HISTORY OF ART.

G

*Pergamon Press Ltd. (1948), Headington Hill Hall, Oxford, OX3 0BW. *T.* Oxford 64881. *T.A.* Pergapress, Oxford. Telex 83177. *Directors:* Sir Henry d'Avigdor-Goldsmid (Chairman), F. A. Kalinski, M.A., PH.D., (Managing), E. J. Buckley (Deputy Managing), Sir Walter Coutts, G.C.M.G., M.B.E., J. G. Salmon, B.SC., B. L. Schwartz, Peter Stevens, A. C. F. Thomson, A. J. Wheaton. *Overseas:* New York, Toronto, Paris, Frankfurt, Tokyo, Mexico City, Sydney, Delhi. Economics, Educational (Secondary, Technical, University), Medical, Research, Science, Technology, Engineering, Sociology, Encyclopaedias.

*Phaidon Press Ltd., 5 Cromwell Place, London, S.W.7. *T.* 01–589 3264. *Managing Director:* Roy Arnold. Books on the fine arts, the history of art and civilization.

*Philip (George) & Son Ltd. (1834), Victoria Road, Willesden, N.W.10. *T.* 01–965 7431–6. *Directors:* G. M. Philip (Joint Managing Director), R. J. Shattock (Joint Managing Director), P. N. Godfrey, H. Fullard, J. A. Bennett. Maps, Atlases, Globes, Guide Books and General Educational Books.

Philip, Son & Nephew, Ltd. (1834), 7 Whitechapel, Liverpool 1. *T.* Liverpool 051–236 0246–8. *T.A.* Philip, Liverpool. English and Foreign Booksellers. *Directors:* John Philip (Chairman and Managing Director), J. Mason Porter, J. S. Smith, J. Waters.

*Pickering & Inglis, Ltd., 26 Bothwell Street, Glasgow, C.2; *T.* 041–552 5044. 29 Ludgate Hill, London, E.C.4. Editorial Department at Glasgow. Children's Books (Rewards), Theology and Religion.

Pitkin, H. A., & W. L., Ltd., (1941), 11 Wyfold Road, London, S.W.6. *T.* 01–385 4351. *T.A.* Pitkins, London, S.W.6. *Directors:* M. Pitkin, R. E. Willson, J. A. Wells, S. Broome, E. M. Goff.

Pitkin Pictorials, Ltd. (1941), 11 Wyfold Road, London, S.W.6. *T.* 01–385 4351. *Directors:* M. Pitkin, R. E. Willson, S. Broome, E. M. Goff, J. A. Wells.

*Pitman (Sir Isaac) & Sons, Ltd. (1845), 39–41 Parker Street, Kingsway, WC2B 5PB. *T.* 01–405 9791 (4 lines). *T.A.* Ipandsons, London, W.C.2. *Chairman:* Sir John Foster, K.B.E., Q.C., M.P. Aeronautics, Architecture, Art, Children's Books (Fiction, Non-Fiction, Rewards), Commerce, Dictionaries, Drama, Economics, Educational (Infants, Primary, Secondary, Technical, University), General, History, Law, Practical Handbooks, Science, Sociology, Sports, Games and Hobbies, Television, Theatre and Ballet, Music, Philosophy.

*Polish Book Depot, 164 Old Brompton Road, London, S.W.5. *T.* Fremantle 1937.

Popular Dogs Publishing Co., Ltd., 178–202 Great Portland Street, London, W.1. *T.* 01–580 3020. (Trade) 062–181 6362. *Telex:* 18130. *T.A.* Literarius, London, W.1. *Telex:* 261212. *Chairman:* R. A. A. Holt. *Directors:* Sir Robert Lusty, Gerald Austin. An imprint of the Hutchinson Publishing Group. Practical handbooks on breeding, care, training, and general management of dogs.

Purnell/Bancroft, 49 Poland Street, London, W1A 2LG *T.* 01–437 0686. *Directors:* R. G. Holme (Chairman), P. Galliner (Managing), P. Morrison (Secretary). An Associate Company of B.P.C. Publishing Ltd.

Purnell Partworks, 49–50 Poland Street, London, W1A 2LG *T.* 01–437 0686. An Associate Company of B.P.C. Publishing Ltd.

*Putnam & Company, Ltd. (1840), 9 Bow Street, WC2E 7AL. *T.* 01-836 9081. *T.A.* Bodleian, Westcent, London. *Directors:* Max Reinhardt (Chairman), J. B. Blackley, L. A. Hart, J. R. Hews, John Huntingdon, John Ryder.
Aeronautics, Fiction, General, History, Humour, Music, Poetry, Autobiography, Naval and Military.

Quaritch (Bernard), Ltd. (1847), 5 Lower John Street, London, W1V 6AB. *T.* 01-734 0562. *T.A.* Quaritch, London, W.1. *Directors:* H. G. Quaritch Wales, PH.D., LITT.D. (Chairman), E. M. Dring, D. C. Quaritch Wales, LL.B., J. A. P. Watson (Managing Director).

Queen Anne Press Ltd., The, National House, 60–66 Wardour Street, London, W1V 3HP *T.* 01-437 0686. *Directors:* R. G. Holme (Chairman), P. Galliner, J. Pollock, L. A. Pearce, P. Morrison (Secretary). An Associate Company of B.P.C. Publishing Ltd.
Industrial, Commercial, Current Affairs, Topography, Home Economics, Sports and Pastimes.

†Rainbird (George), Ltd., Marble Arch House, 44 Edgware Road, London, W.2. *T.* 01-723 9042. *Cables and Telex:* Rainmac, London, 261472. *Directors:* G. M. Rainbird, J. Hadfield, E. Fisher, E. Young, G. V. Speaight, M. Raeburn, G. A. Forbes.
Archaeology, Architecture, Biography, Fine Art, Antiques, History, Natural, History, Travel, Wines and Food.

Rainbird Reference Books Ltd., Marble Arch House, 44 Edgware Road, London, W.2. *T.* 01-723 9042. *Directors:* G. M. Rainbird, J. Hadfield, E. Fisher, E. Young, G. V. Speaight, M. Raeburn, G. A. Forbes.
Reference books and encyclopedias on all subjects.

Raleigh Press—an imprint of David & Charles (Publishers) Ltd., *q.v.*

*Rapp & Whiting Ltd. (1966), 105 Great Russell Street, London, WC1B 3LJ. *T.* 01-580 2746. *T.A.* Rappidly, London, W.C.1. *Directors:* Georg Rapp, B. M. Igra, Miriam Rapp.
Poetry, Science Fiction, Academic and popular non-fiction, serious fiction.

Rationalist Press Association, Ltd. See The Pemberton Publishing Co. Ltd.

*Reader's Digest Association, Ltd., The, 25 Berkeley Square, London, W1X 6AB. *T.* 01-629 8144. *T.A.* Readigest, London, W.1. *Directors:* P. W. Thompson (U.S.A.), T. G. M. Harman, O.B.E., John H. Davenport (Managing Director), M. R. S. Randolph, G. Ravenscroft, V. Ross, G. A. G. Selby-Lowndes, P. Glemser, Peter S. Crane, M.C., A. R. P. Fairlie.

*Redman Books Ltd., 17 Fleet Street, London, E.C.4. *T.* 01-583 8161. *T.A.* Redmanbux, London, E.C.4. *Chairman:* Sidney M. Eagle. *Managing Director:* Geoffrey M. Eagle. *Directors:* S. H. T. Green, T. A. Lines. *Secretary:* S. R. Gibson.
Biography and Memoirs, Guide Books, Fiction, General, History, Technical, Travel.

Reinhardt, Max, Ltd., 9 Bow Street, WC2E 7AL. *T.* 01-836 9081. *Directors:* Max Reinhardt (Chairman and Managing Director), L. A. Hart, J. R. Hews, M. B. Ormrod and Mrs. J. Reinhardt.
Proprietors of the Bodley Head Ltd.
Biography and Memoirs, Drama, Fiction, Films, General, Humour, Sports, Games and Hobbies, Theatre and Ballet, Travel.

Religious Education Press, Headington Hill Hall, Oxford, OX3 0BW. *T.* Oxford 64881. Member of the Pergamon Group.
Educational (Infants, Primary, Secondary, Grammar), Theology and Religion.

Rendel, David, Ltd. (1966), 26 Old Brompton Road, London, S.W.7. *T.* 01–589 5520. *Directors:* David Rendel, Lord Kings Norton, C. P. de Laszlo.
Non-fiction and professional.

*Renwick of Otley, Printerdom, Otley, Yorkshire, LS21 1QH and 151 Fleet Street, London, E.C.4.

Rider & Co. (1892), 178–202 Great Portland Street, London, W1N 6AQ *T.* 01–580 3020. *Telex;* 261212. (Trade) 062–181 6362. *Telex:* 18130. *Proprietors:* Hutchinson Publishing Group Ltd. An imprint of the Hutchinson Publishing Group.
Oriental, Religion and Philosophy, Spiritualism and Occult.

*Rivingtons (Publishers), Ltd., Montague House, Russell Square, WC1B 5BX. *T.* 01–636 8521. *T.A.* Perduro, London, W.C.1. *Directors:* G. C. Rivington (Chairman), J. M. Rivington, L. J. Browning, Hon. Mrs. A. M. Evans, R. P. Hyman.
Educational (Secondary, University).

Roberts & Vinter Ltd., 42–44 Dock Street, London, E.1. *T.* Royal 2232.
Fiction only—science, crime, adventure, historical.

*Ronald (George) (1939), 17–21 Sunbeam Road, London, N.W.10. *T.* 01–965 0433. *Director:* David Hofman. *Talisman books* (paperbacks).
Religion and Philosophy.

Roundwood Press (Publishers), Ltd., The, Kineton, Warwick. *T.* Kineton 400. *Directors:* Gordon Norwood, Ruth Norwood.
Archaeology, architecture, autobiography, biography and memoirs, history (especially local history), travel.

*Routledge & Kegan Paul, Ltd. (1834), Broadway House, 68–74 Carter Lane, EC4V 5EL. *T.* 01–248 4821. *T.A.* Columnae, London, E.C.4. Trade Counter: Broadway House, Reading Road, Henley-on-Thames RG9 1EN. *T.* Henley 3701. *Chairman:* Norman Franklin. *Directors:* David Franklin, R. Locke, R. Bailey, B. Southam, J. Kaplan, Malcolm Crocket.
Archaeology, Art, Belles-Lettres, Dictionaries, Economics, Educational (Secondary, Technical, University), General, History, Political Economy, Reference, Science, Sociology, Music, Occult, Oriental, Philosophy, Psychology, Literary Criticism.

Rowland Ward Ltd., Taxidermists, Publishers and Booksellers, 64–65 Grosvenor Street, London, W1X 0EN *T.* 01–493 4501. *T.A.* Jungle, London, W.1.
Big Game, Field Sports and Natural History.

Royal National Institute for the Blind, The (1868), 224–6–8 Great Portland Street, London, W1N 6AA *T.* 01–387 5251. *T.A.* Pharnib, Wesdo, London. *Director of Publications:* Donald Bell.
Magazines and books for the blind, in Braille and moon embossed types. Also tape-recorded books (Talking Books). For complete list of magazines see Classified Index at end of book.

Runa Press, The (1942), 2 Belgrave Terrace, Monkstown, Dublin. *T.* 801869.
Belles-Lettres, Educational (University), Essays, Poetry, Science, Philosophy.

*Saint Andrew Press, The, 121 George Street, Edinburgh, EH2 4YN. *T.* 031–225 5722. *T.A.* Free, Edinburgh, 2.
Theology and Religion.

*Salvationist Publishing and Supplies, Ltd., 117 Judd Street, London, WC1H 9NN. *T.* 01–387 1656.
Devotional books, Theology, Biography, world-wide Christian and Social service, Children's Books, Music.

Sands & Co. (Publishers), Ltd., 3 Trebeck Street, London, W.1. *T.* 01–499 8525. *Directors:* Hon. G. E. Noel, M.A., (Chairman), G. V. Butler (Managing), A. J. P. Noel.
Ecumenical Theory and General Non-Fiction.

*Saunders (W. B.) Co., Ltd., 12 Dyott Street, London, WC1A 1DB. *T.* 01–836 9241.
Medical and Scientific.

Saville (J.) & Co., Ltd. (1912), Audley House, North Audley Street, London, W1Y 2EU *T.* 01–629 6506.
Educational (Infants), Music.

*Schofield & Sims, Ltd. (1902), 35 St. John's Road, Huddersfield, HD1 5DT. *T.* Huddersfield 30684. *T.A.* Schosims, Huddersfield. *Directors:* H. Cameron Booth, C. Nesbitt, D. Bygott, C. Bygott, J. S. Nesbitt, E. P. Platts, F. R. Lockwood.
Educational (Infants, Primary, Secondary, Technical), Music (for Schools).

Scientific Publishing Co., The, 40 Dalton Street, Manchester, M4 4JP. *T.* 061–205 1514.

Scout Association, The, 25 Buckingham Palace Road, London, S.W.1. *T.* 01–834 6005. *T.A.* Scouting. *General Editor:* R. Jeffries.
Technical books dealing with all subjects relevant to Scouting and monthly journal *Scouting.*

*Scripture Union (1867), 5 Wigmore Street, London, W1H 0AD *T.* 01–486 2561.
Evangelical Publishers and Booksellers. Periodicals listed at end of book.
Music, Theology and Religion and Children's Books.

•Secker (Martin) & Warburg, Ltd. (Founded 1910. Reconstructed and enlarged, 1936), 14 Carlisle Street, London, W1V 6NN *T.* 01–437 2075. *T.A.* Psophidian, London. *Directors:* Frederic J. Warburg, B. D. Farrer, C. Pick, T. R. Manderson, T. G. Rosenthal
Art, Belles-Lettres, Biography and Memoirs, Economics, Fiction, History, Political Economy, Science, Sociology, Theatre and Ballet, Travel.

*Seeley, Service & Co., Ltd., (1744), 196 Shaftesbury Avenue, London, WC2H 8JL *T.* 01–836 5758. I. M. Service, Alastair Service, Leo Cooper, T. R. Hartman.
Coloured illustrations are used.
Art, Biography and Memoirs, General, History, Naval and Military, Sports, Games and Hobbies, Travel.

Shakespeare Head Press (1904), Basil Blackwell & Mott Ltd., 49 Broad Street, Oxford, OX1 3BP.
Finely printed books; scholarly works.

*Sheed & Ward, Ltd. (1926), 33 Maiden Lane, London, WC2E 7LA. *T.* 01–240 1777–8. *T.A.* Stanza, London. *Directors:* M. T. Redfern, E. H. Connor.
Publishers of books, mostly by Catholics.
Biography and Memoirs, History, Philosophy, Politics, Sociology, Theology and Religion.

Sheldon Press, The, Marylebone Road, London, N.W.1. *T.* 01–387 5282. *T.A.* Futurity, London. *General Secretary:* Rev. F. N. Davey, D.D.
School books and handbooks for overseas.

†**Sheppard Press, Ltd.** (1944), P.O. Box, 42, 15 James Street, London, WC2E 8BX. *Directors:* B. N. Rendall Davies and Trefor Rendall Davies.
Directories and Guide Books, General, Practical Handbooks, Reference, Year Books.

Sherratt, John & Son, Ltd, Park Road, Altrincham, Cheshire. *T.* 061–973 5711.
Educational (Primary, Secondary, Technical, University), Medical, Practical Handbooks.

*****Sidgwick & Jackson, Ltd.** (1908), 1 Tavistock Chambers, Bloomsbury Way, WC1A 2SG. *T.* 01–405 7927, and 5364. *T.A.* Watergate, Westcent, London. *Directors:* The Earl of Longford, P.C. (Chairman), J. P. Chancellor (Managing Director), J. S. Knapp-Fisher, Mrs. M. C. Sidwick, R. A. Shadbolt, W. Armstrong.
Archaeology, Belles-Lettres, Current Affairs, Fiction, General, History, Music, Philosophy, Poetry, Political Economy, Science (Biology), Sociology, Theology and Religion, Travel.

Skeffington & Son, Ltd. (1858), 178–202 Great Portland Street, London, W1N 6AQ *T.* (Editorial) 01–580 3020. *Telex:* 261212. (Trade) 062–181 6362. *Telex:* 18130. *T.A.* Literarius, London W.1. R. A. A. Holt (Chairman). *Director:* Sir Robert Lusty. An imprint of the Hutchinson Publishing Group.
Theology and Religion, Philosophy.

*****Skilton (Charles) Ltd.,** 50 Alexandra Road, S.W.19. *T.* Wimbledon 1009. *T.A.* Colophon, Wimble, London. A preliminary letter is desirable.
Art, Biographies, Histories, Reference, Technical (Printing), de Luxe Editions.

Skinner (Thomas) & Co. (Publishers), Ltd. (1866), 30 Finsbury Square, London, E.C.2. *T.* 01–628 4050.
Magazines, Journals, Directories or Guide Books, Reference, Year Books.

Smythe (Colin) Ltd. (1966), Gerrards Cross, Bucks. *T.* Gerrards Cross 86000 and 86575. *T.A.* Smythebooks, Gerrards Cross, Bucks. *Directors:* Sir Robert Mayer (Chairman), Colin Smythe and Peter Bander (Joint Managing), Lady Mayer, Wing Commander C. R. Smythe, Gyles Brandreth.
Publishers of *Youth & Music News* and Robert Mayer Children's Concert Publications.
Education, Religion, Biography, Children's, Current Affairs, Belles-Lettres, Fiction, Histories, and Anglo-Irish Literature.

*****Society for Promoting Christian Knowledge** (1698), Holy Trinity Church, Marylebone Road, N.W.1. *T.* 01–387 5282. *T.A.* Futurity, London.
Children's Books, History, Theology and Religion, Philosophy.

Solicitors' Law Stationery Society, Ltd. (1888), Oyez House, Breams Buildings, Fetter Lane, London, E.C.4. *T.* 01–242 6855. *T.A.* Oyez, London, E.C.4. *Telex:* 263579.
Law, Company and Local Government books.

Soncino Press, Ltd. (1929), Audley House, 9 North Audley Street, London, W1Y 2EU *T.* 01–629 6506. *Cables:* Soncino, London, W.1. *Directors:* P. Bloch, S. M. Bloch, A. Wix. Translations with Commentaries of Jewish Classics.
Theology and Religion.

Southside (Publishers) Ltd. (1968), 6 Sciennes Gardens, Edinburgh, EM9 1NR *T.* 031–667 1225.

*Souvenir Press, Ltd., 95 Mortimer Street, London, W1N 8HP   *T.* 01–580 9307–8.
Executive Directors: Ernest Hecht (*Managing*) and Leslie Smith.
    Archaeology, Biography and Memoirs, Children's Books (Non-Fiction, Rewards), Educational (Secondary, Technical), Fiction, General, Humour, Practical Handbooks, Sports, Games and Hobbies, Travel.

Spearman (Neville) Ltd., 112 Whitfield Street, London, W1P 6DP   *T.* 01–387 2466 and 7506.   *Directors:* Neville Armstrong, M. J. Armstrong.
    Fiction, Reminiscences, Biography, Travel, Music, Autobiography; particularly interested in original, topical and controversial themes on all subjects, especially mysticism.

Spon (E. & F. N.), Ltd (1830), 11 New Fetter Lane, E.C.4.   *T.* 01–583 9855.
    Architecture, Agriculture, Engineering, Science, Mathematical Tables.

*Sporting Handbooks Ltd., (1926), 13 Bedford Square, WC1B 3JE.   *T.* 01–636 4748.
Wisden's Cricketers' Almanack (1864).   *Directors:* Haddon Whitaker, Edmond Segrave, F. H. C. Tatham, David Whitaker.
    Year Books, Sports, Games and Hobbies.

Spring Books. See The Hamlyn Publishing Group Ltd.

Stacey, Tom, Ltd. (1969), 28 Maiden Lane, London, W.C.2.   *T.* 01–240 3974–7.
T.A. Staceybook London.   *Directors:* T. C. G. Stacey (Managing), A. H. Begg (Joint Managing and Marketing), Lord St. Oswald, M.C., (Editorial), Anthony Lejeune (Editorial), Hon. Sir Clive Bossom, B.T., M.P., Victor Goodhew, M.P., Hugh Mitchley, Q.C., M.P., E. A. Fontaine, M.B.E., Robin Jessel.
    General Publishing, Politics, Current Affairs, Ecology, Technical, Fiction.

Stanford (Edward), Ltd. (1852), 12, 13 and 14 Long Acre, London, WC2E 9LP.
T. 01–836 1321.   *T.A.* Estanfomap, Rand, London.   *Directors:* E. G. Godfrey (Chairman), D. P. Woods, C. C. Wilson, R. J. Shattock, P. N. Godfrey.
    Guide Books, Educational (University), Travel, Maps and Atlases.

Stanmore Press Ltd. (1947), 25 Thurloe Street, London, S.W.7.   *T.* 01–589 6807, and 01–743 3278.   *Directors:* G. A. Averill, M. Kahn, C. Kahn, O. M. Averill.
    General non-fiction, music, educational.

†Staples Press Ltd., 3 Upper James Street, Golden Square, London, W1R 4BP   *T.* 01–734 8080. Trade: Book Centre, Ltd., North Circular Road, Neasden, N.W.10.
T. 01–459 1222.
    Business Management, Dental, Economics, Law, Medical, Science, Technical.

Starke (Harold) Ltd., 14 John Street, London, WC1N 2EJ.   *T.* 01–242 6724–5 and 1065.   *Directors:* Stanley Rubinstein (Chairman), Harold K. Starke (Managing), Peter Stuart-Heaton.
    Biography and Memoirs, Referecne.

*Stephens (Patrick) Ltd., (1967), 9 Ely Place, London, E.C.1.   *T.* 01–405 2297.
T.A. Peeselpubs, London, E.C.1.   *Directors:* Patrick J. Stephens, Darryl Reach, E. F. Heaton, A. Guichard, W. J. Germing, F.C.A.
    Motoring, Militaria, Modelling, Aviation, Natural History, Ships and the Sea, Transport History and Railways.

Stevens (Wm.) Ltd., (1842), St. John's House, St. John's Square E.C.1.   *T.* 01–253 6680.   *Managing Director:* Graham Noakes. For lists of periodicals published by this firm see end of book.

†Stevens and Sons, Ltd., (1889), 11 New Fetter Lane, E.C.4.   *T.* 01–583 9855.
Directors: J. Burke, J. S. James, M. W. Maxwell, P. H. B. Allsop.
    Commerce (Law), Current Affairs, Dictionaries (Law), Directories, Law.

†**Stillit Books Ltd.,** 72 New Bond Street, London, W1Y 0QY   *T.* 01-493 1177.
Directors: Gerald B. Stillit, Randolph Vigne.
Programmed books and tests for use with the Stillitron teaching aid.
Primary, Secondary, Industrial Training, Languages.

Stirling Tract Enterprise (1848), (The Drummond Press), 41 The Craigs, Stirling,
Scotland.   *T.* Stirling 3384.   *Director:* Rev. John Birkbeck, M.C.
Religious books for adults and children.

*****Student Christian Movement Press, Ltd.** (1896), 56–58 Bloomsbury Street, WC1B
3QX   *T.* 01-636 3841.   *T.A.* Torchpres, Westcent, London.   *Directors:* Colin
Alves, Kathleen Bliss, John S. Bowden (Managing Director and Editor),
R. A. Chell, Stuart Dalziel, Kenneth Darke, Mark Hammer, David Head,
J. P. Lee-Woolf, R. H. Preston, Alan Richardson, Kenneth Slack.
Educational, Philosophy, Theology and Religion.

*****Studio Vista Ltd.,** Blue Star House, Highgate Hill, London, N.19.   *T.* 01-272
7531.   *T.A.* Studiopub, London, N.19.   *Publishing Director:* David Herbert.
Managing Director: Peter Whiteley.   *Directors:* David Collischon, George
Hiser.
Design, Crafts, Travel, Poetry, History, Gardening, Printing, Architecture,
Applied Art and Fine Art, *Decorative Art in Modern Interiors* (1906), *Modern
Publicity* (1924).

Sumner Press, The (1962), 24 Tufton Street, London, S.W.1.   *T.* 01-222 5533.
T.A. Marisumner, London, S.W.1.
Religious.

Swan (Gerald G.), Ltd., P.O. Box 111, 12 Lever Street, Manchester, M60 1TS.
T. 061-236 4316.   *Telex:* 66 8609.
General, Fiction, and Children's Fiction.

Swedenborg Society, 20–21 Bloomsbury Way, London, WC1A 2TH.   *T.* 01-405
7986.
Theology and Religion.

*****Sweet & Maxwell, Ltd.** (1889), 11 New Fetter Lane, E.C.4.   *T.* 01-583 9855.
Directors: Maurice W. Maxwell, J. S. James, J. Burke, P. H. B. Allsop, D. W.
Alcock, C. D. O. Evans, D. S. Lees, Mrs. K. L. Boyes.
Commerce, Dictionaries, Educational (University), History, Law, Reference.

*****Sylvan Press,** 37 Norfolk Street, Strand, London, W.C.2.   *T.* 01-836 1665.
General, typography, printing, manual crafts (Your Home Crafts Series),
and Sylvan Books on Modern Studies.

Talbot Press, Ltd. (1917), 89 Talbot Street, Dublin.   *T.* 44361-3.   *T.A.* "Publish
Dublin."   *Directors:* R. H. Lyon, W. J. Fitzsimmons.
Publishers of books about Ireland or by Irish authors only.

†**Tavistock Publications Ltd.,** 11 New Fetter Lane, London, E.C.4.   *T.* 01-583 9855.
Directors: Maurice W. Maxwell (Chairman), John Harvard-Watts (Managing),
Diana Burfield, Anthony Forster.
The Social Sciences, Psychology, Medicine, Education, Scientific Manage-
ment.

*****Taylor & Francis, Ltd.,** 10–14 Macklin Street, London, WC2B 5NF.   *T.* 01-405
2237-9.   *Directors:* G. A. Courtney-Coffey (Managing Director), Professor
Sir Nevill Mott, F.R.S., H. Marley, Dr. J. Thomson, G. R. Noakes, S. A. Lewis,
G. F. Lancaster (Secretary), C. W. Wheeler. Publishers of scientific reports and
magazines.
Educational (University), Medical, Science, (Physics, Electronics, Natura
History, Optical, History of Science, Ergonomics).

*Technical Press, Ltd. (1933), 112 Westbourne Grove, London, W.2. *T.* 01–229
7211–2. Sole agents in the U.K. for the publications of *The American Technical
Society of Chicago, U.S.A.*, *C. K. Smoley & Sons, New York.* Distributors for
Agardograph (Nato) Publications and *Mullard Ltd. Directors:* P. Stobart, B.A.
(Oxon), V. A. L. Kirby.
   Aeronautics, Architecture, Commerce, Dictionaries, Law, Practical Hand-
books, Reference, Science (All), Sports and Hobbies, Technology, Educational
(Secondary, Technical, University).

Temple Press, Ltd., see IPC Business Press Ltd.

†Temple Smith, (Maurice) Ltd., (1969), 37 Great Russell Street, London, WC1B 3PP.
T. 01–636 9810. *Directors:* Maurice Temple Smith, Jean Temple Smith,
B. Saklatvala.
   History, Current affairs.

*Thames and Hudson Ltd., 30–34 Bloomsbury Street, London, WC1B 3QP. *T.*
01–636 5488. *T.A.* Thameshuds, London. *Directors:* E. Neurath, T. M.
Neurath, H. J. Jarrold, M.A., H. A. W. Barber, T. Craker, W. Guttmann, S.
Baron.
   Archaeology, Architecture, Art, Travel, History, Sociology.

Thomas (A.) and Co. (1947), 37–38 Margaret Street, Cavendish Square, London,
W1N 8LT. *T.* 01–499 9440.
   Commerce, Dictionaries, General, Humour, Practical Handbooks, Refer-
ence, Sports, Games and Hobbies, Maps and Atlases, Philosophy.

Thomson-Leng Publications, Dundee. *T.* 23131. *T.A.* Courier, Dundee. London:
Thomson House, 12 Fetter Lane, E.C.4. *T.* 01-353 2586. *T.A.* Courier,
London, E.C.4. Publishers of newspapers and periodicals. For list of
newspapers and periodicals see end of book.
   Children's Books (Annuals), Fiction.

*Thorson Publishers Ltd. (1930), 37–38 Margaret Street, London, W1N 8LT. *T.*
01–499 9440. *Directors:* L. H. Woodford (Chairman), J. A. Young (Managing),
S. E. Woodford, M. E. Young.
   Psychology, Hypnosis, Yoga, Physical and Mental Health, Nature Cure,
Physical Culture, Diet Reform, Occult.

Times Newspapers Ltd., Printing House Square, London, E.C.4. *T.* 01–236 2000.
Directors: The Hon. K. R. Thomson (Chairman), C. D. Hamilton (Editor-in-
Chief, and Chief Executive), Sir Donald Anderson, G. C. Brunton, J. M.
Coltart, Sir Kenneth Keith, Sir George Pope, Lord Robens, Sir Eric Roll,
G. C. Rowett (General Manager), Lord Shawcross.
   *Publications: The Times, The Sunday Times, The Times Literary Supplement,
The Times Educational Supplement, The Official Index to The Times.*

*Tiranti (Alec), Ltd. (1895), 72 Charlotte Street, London, W1P 2AJ *T.* 01–636 8565
(3 lines). *Directors:* A. M. and J. Tiranti.
   Architecture, Art, Practical Craft Handbooks, Typography, Design.

Todd Publishing Group (1934), P.O. Box 74, Guernsey, C.I. *T.* 0481–24332.

Tothill Press Ltd., see I.P.C. Business Press Ltd.

*Transworld Publishers Ltd., Cavendish House, 57 Uxbridge Road, London, W.5.
T. 01–579 2652.
   Corgi, Bantam and Collie Books. How and Why Wonder Books.

Triton Publishing Company Ltd. (1964), 1a Montagu Mews North, London, W.1
T. 01–935 8090. *T.A.* Trifem, London, W.1. *Directors*: Muriel V. Box,
Sydney Box, Norman Fisher, M.A., D. G. Trustcott, F.C.A., Carolyn Whitaker.
Fiction and general non-fiction.

Tuck (Raphael) & Sons, Ltd., Pound Street, Warminster, Wilts. *T.* 09852–8251.
Directors: R. Holme (Chairman), F. M. Hudson (Vice-Chairman), E. Turner
(Managing), D. R. Grove, R. S. Persson, M. A. Mitchell.
Fine art and greeting card publishers.

Tufton Press, 15 Tufton Street, London, S.W.1. *T.* 01-799 1701. *T.A.* and
Cables: Gospelize, London, S.W.1.
Theology and Religion.

Tyndale Press, The, 39 Bedford Square, WC1B 3EY. *T.* 01–636 5113.
Theology and Religion, Biblical Archaeology.

United Society for Christian Literature, 4 Bouverie Street, E.C.4. *T.* 01–353
3853-7. *T.A.* Lutteric, Cent., London. Has for over 150 years acted for the
British missionary societies to assist book production in all languages by subsidy
grants. *General Secretaries:* Rev. Canon E. H. Wade, M.A. and Rev. D. Ridley
Chesterton. *Home Secretary:* Col. Arthur Field.
Theology and Religion.

United Society for the Propagation of the Gospel, 15 Tufton Street, London, S.W.1.
T. 01–799 1701. *T.A.* Gospelize, London, S.W.1. Continues the work of
supporting the Church's mission abroad, formerly done by SPG and UMCA.
Publ. *Network, Adventurer,* pamphlets, visual aids, lesson material for Schools
and Sunday Schools.
Theology of mission.

United Trade Press Ltd. (1927), 9 Gough Square, Fleet Street, London, E.C.4. *T.*
01–353 3172. *T.A.* Markeba. *Directors:* Mrs. Marcus H. Smith, A. R. O.
Slater, J. J. Peake, D. M. Broughall, F. Goodridge, F. V. Wells.
Technology, Science, Reference.

Universal-Tandem Publishing Co. Ltd., 14 Gloucester Road, London, S.W.7.
T. 01–584 8766 and 6803. *Chairman:* Arnold E. Abramson (U.S.A.),
Managing Director: Ralph S. Stokes. *Directors:* Robert J. Abramson (U.S.A),
Edwin J. Harragan Snr. (U.S.A.), George Coleman.
Paperbacks.

*****University of London Press, Ltd.**, St. Paul's House, Warwick Lane, London, E.C.4.
T. 01–248 5797. *Directors:* John Attenborough (Chairman), Paul Hodder-
Williams, L. M. H. Timmermans, H. S. Foster, B. Steven, Walter Hamilton.
Art, Children's Books (Non-Fiction), Commerce, Dictionaries, Drama,
Economics, Educational (All Branches for Home and Overseas), English
Language and Literature, Geography, History, Mathematics, Modern
Languages, Physical Education, Science and Technology, Psychology and
Sociology.

University of Wales Press (1922), Merthyr House, James Street, Cardiff, CF1 6EU.
T. Cardiff 31919.
Educational (Welsh and English). Publishers of *Bulletin, Welsh History
Review, Studia Celtica, Llên Cymru, y Gwyddonydd, Efrydian Athronyddol,
Dictionary of the Welsh Language.*

*University Tutorial Press, Ltd. (1901), 9–10 Great Sutton Street, London, E.C.1.
T. 01–253 6992. *T.A.* Tutorial, London, E.C.1. Editorial offices: Bateman
Street, Cambridge.
Commerce, Economics, Educational (Secondary, Technical and University),
History, Philosophy, Poetry, Science (Mathematical Astronomy, Biology,
Botany, Chemistry, Hygiene, Physics, Zoology), Sociology.

Vallancy Research Ltd. (1912), P.O. Box 77, Guernsey C.I. *T.* 0481–24332.

*Vallentine, Mitchell & Co. Ltd. (1949), 31 Furnival Street, London, E.C.4. *T.*
01–405 9252. *Directors:* D. F. Kessler (Managing), M. Epstein, W. Frankel,
J. Gross, Viscount Samuel. *Publishing Manager:* P. G. Mayers.
General, Judaica, Children's Books, Educational.

*Van Nostrand Reinhold Co. Ltd., 46, Victoria Street, S.W.1. *T.* 01–799 6854.
T.A. Denostrand London, *Director:* Ellis Horwood (Managing Director).
Aeronautics, Current Affairs, Dictionaries, Economics, Educational (Secon-
dary, Technical and University), General, History, Mathematics, Medicine,
Philosophy, Political Economy, Psychology, Reference, Science, Sociology,
Sports, Games and Hobbies, Technology, Television. Insights, Momentums,
Anvil Books and Searchlights (original works in paper binding).

Vegetarian Society, (UK) Ltd., The (1969), Parkdale, Dunham Road, Altrincham,
Cheshire. *T.* 061–928 0793. *Secretary:* Geoffrey L. Rudd.
Books on food reform, vegetarianism, dietetics, recipes.

Vernon & Yates Ltd. (1963), 26 Old Brompton Road, London, S.W.7. *T.* 01–589
5520. *Directors:* George Hammer, David Rendel, S. M. H. Vernon, Erica
Watson.
General.

Verschoyle, Derek, Ltd. All books published by Derek Verschoyle have been
taken over by André Deutsch, Ltd., *q.v.*

*Vincent Stuart & John M. Watkins Ltd. (1951), 45 Lower Belgrave Street, London,
S.W.1. *T.* 01–730 9337.
Science, Religion, Philosophy, Psychology, Ecology, General.

Virtue & Co., Ltd. (1819), 25 Breakfield, Coulsdon, Surrey, CR3 2UE. *T.* 01–668
4632. *Directors:* Guy Virtue, M. F. Virtue, E. M. Ottaway, Michael Virtue,
L. J. Vincent.
General, Educational and Religious, by subscription.

*Vision Press Ltd. (1946), 157 Knightsbridge, London, S.W.1. *T.* 01–589 7456.
Directors: Alan Moore, b.a. (Managing), C. A. Rosedale, ll.b.
Psychology, philosophy, history, politics, film, theatre, music, art, literature,
science. General. U.K. distributors for the Peter Pauper Press.

Walker (Wm.) & Sons (Otley), Ltd. (1811), Otley, Yorkshire, LS21 1QH. *T.*
Otley 2375.
Newspapers, children's picture books.

*Walter (Henry E.), Ltd., 26 Grafton Road, Worthing, Sussex.
Religious publishers.

*Warburg Institute, University of London, Woburn Square, London, WC1H 0AB.
T. 01–580 9663.
Archaeology, Art, History, Philosophy.

Ward, Edmund (Publishers) Ltd. See Kaye & Ward Ltd.

*Ward Lock Limited (1854), 116 Baker Street, London, W1M 2BB *T*. 01–486 3271. *T.A.* Warlock, London, W.1. *Directors:* R. E. Dexter, A. A. Shipton, C. J. Lock, P. G. Lock, A. T. Grieve, C. D. Smith. Free-lance artists' and designers' work used.

Cookery, Gardening, Guides, Antiques and Collecting, General Reference, Children's illustrated story books, General Knowledge and Encyclopedias. No fiction.

*Ward Lock Educational Co. Ltd. (1964), 116 Baker Street, London, W1M 2BB. *T*. 01–486 3271. *Directors:* R. E. Dexter, D. C. Bartlett, A. A. Shipton, P. G. Lock.

Educational (Infants, Primary, Secondary Modern), Staffroom Library Books.

*Warne (Frederick) & Co., Ltd. (1865), Chandos House, Bedford Court, Bedford Street, WC2E 9JB. *T*. 01–836 2208. *T.A.* Warne, London, W.C.2.: and New York City. *President:* Frederick Warne Stephens. *Directors:* C. W. Stephens (Chairman and Managing Director), S. R. Smith (Secretary), D. W. Bisacre, R. A. V. Priddle.

Children's Books (Fiction, Non-Fiction, Toy and Picture), Dictionaries, Educational (Infant, Primary, Secondary), General, Natural History, Reference, Religion.

Warren & Son, Ltd. (1835), The Wykeham Press, Winchester. *T*. Winchester 5966. (Associated with **Taylor & Francis Ltd.**, 10–14 Macklin Street, London, W.C.2.) *Directors:* G. A. Courtney-Coffey (Chairman), N. T. Warren, M.B.E., T.D., G. F. Lancaster, A. H. Shergold, F. W. C. Fletcher, C. W. Wheeler.

Educational (Secondary), Science.

*Watts (C. A.) & Co., Ltd. (1885), 39 Parker Street, London, W.C.2. *T*. 01–405 9791. *Directors:* T. M. Schuller, B. G. Brewer.

The New Thinker's Library. Sociology, Philosophy, History, Archaeology, General.

Wayland (Publishers) Ltd. (1969), 101 Gray's Inn Road, London, WC1X 8TX *T*. 01–242 1590/1598/1599. *T.A.* Bookwright, London, W.C.1. *Directors:* Roger Ferneyhough, M.A., John Lewis, B.A., Richard Lewis, M.A.

General History, Biography, Art, Military History, Religious History, Educational and Popular Illustrated Books, Fiction.

*Weidenfeld, George, & Nicolson Ltd., 5 Winsley Street, Oxford Circus, W1N 7AQ *T*. 01–580 7941. *Directors:* Sir George Weidenfeld, (Chairman), Anthony Godwin (Deputy Chairman), D. D. Teasdale (Managing Director), K. A. Lilley (Assistant Managing Director), H. H. Coudenhove, John Curtis, Christopher Falkus, Jeremy Hadfield, Geoffrey Howard, B. J. MacLennan, A. R. Miles, A.C.I.S. (Secretary), Nigel Nicolson, Julian Shuckburgh.

Anthropology, Architecture, Art, Belles-Lettres, Biography and Memoirs, Current Affairs, Economics, Fiction, General, History, Philosophy, Politics, Naval and Military, Science, Sociology, Travel.

Wheaton (A.) & Co., (1780), Headington Hill Hall, Oxford OX3 0BW. *T*. Oxford 64881. Members of the Pergamon Group.

Educational (Infant, Junior and Secondary), Dictionaries, Reference books, Pleasure books for very young children.

Wheldon & Wesley, Ltd., Lytton Lodge, Codicote, Hitchin, Herts. *T*. Codicote 370. Natural history booksellers and publishers. Agency of the British Museum (Natural History).

*Whitaker (J.) & Sons, Ltd., 13 Bedford Square, WC1B 3JE. *T.* 01–636 4748. *Directors:* Haddon Whitaker, M.A., Edmond Seagrave, A.C.E. MUSK, M.V.O., David Whitaker. *Whitaker's Almanack* (1868), *The Bookseller* (1858), *Current Literature, Whitaker's Books of the Month & Books to Come, British Books in Print (The Reference Catalogue of Current Literature)* (1874), *Whitaker's Cumulative Book List* (1924), *Paper Backs in Print, Technical Books in Print, etc.* Reference.

Wilding & Son, Ltd. (1874), 33 Castle Street, Shrewsbury, SY1 2BL. *T.* Shrewsbury 51274.
Histories and Guide Books, Medical, Educational (Magazines, Year Books, Prospectuses), Periodicals (National and Private).

*Wiley (John) & Sons Ltd. (incorporating **Interscience Publishers**), Baffins Lane, Chichester, Sussex. *T.* 84531. *T.A. and Cables:* Wilebook, Chichester. *Telex:* 86290. *Directors:* W. B. Wiley, A. H. Neilly, Jr., R. A. Watson, P. Marriage, Dr. E. S. Proskauer, O. Goulding, H. G. Newman, A.C.A., M. C. Colenso. Scientific, Engineering, Business, Social Science, Mathematics.

*Wills & Hepworth Ltd. (1924), Derby Square, Loughborough, Leicestershire LE11 0AL. *T.* Loughborough 4786 (4 lines). *T.A.* Ladybird, Loughborough. *Directors:* J. S. Clegg (Chairman), T. M. Clark, D. H. Keen, Mrs. M. V. Eales, G. H. Towers, C. W. Hall. Ladybird Children's Books.
Children's Books (Non-Fiction), Educational (Infants, Primary).

Wingate, Allan (Publishers) Ltd., (1969), 14 Gloucester Road, London, S.W.7. *T.* 01–584 6803. *Directors:* Peter Abramson, Anthony Gibbs, David Rowan.
General Fiction and Non-Fiction.

Winsor & Newton Ltd. (1832), Wealdstone, Harrow, Middlesex, HA3 5RH. *T.* 01–427 4343. *T.A.* Sepia, Harrow. Retail Dept.: 51–52 Rathbone Place, W1P 1AB. *T.* 01–636 4231.
Manufacturing artists' colourmen, brushmakers and publishers of books on oil and water-colour painting, etc.

*Witherby (H. F. & G.), Ltd., 15 Nicholas Lane, E.C.4. *T.* 01–248 7373. *Directors:* A. Witherby, R. C. F. Witherby, T. F. Witherby.
Biography and Memoirs, Commerce, Educational (Secondary, University), History, Law, Science (Natural), Sports, Games and Hobbies, Travel.

*Wolff Oswald (Publishers), Ltd., 52 Manchester Street, London, W1M 6DR *T.* 01–935 3441 and 3481. *T.A.* Bookwolff, London. *Directors:* I. R. Wolff, H. S. Wolff.
History, politics, economics, psychology, sociology, biography, literature. Distributed by Interbook Ltd., at the same address.

Women's Employment Publishing Co., Ltd. (1899), 185 Vauxhall Bridge Road, London, S.W.1. *T.* 01–828 5943. Matter connected with the training and employment of educated women. *Payment* £1.05 per 1000 words. Publications: *Women's Employment; Adam's "First-Aid to Verbs".* Managing *Director:* Margaret Fuge.
Educational (Secondary, Technical, University).

*World's Work Ltd., See under **Heinemann Publishers, Ltd.**

*Wright (John) & Sons Ltd. (1825), The Stonebridge Press, Brislington, Bristol, BS4 5NU. *T.* Bristol 75375–6–7. *Directors:* P. J. Wright, L. G. Owens, B.SC., David Brooks, F.C.A. (Secretary), L. J. Slade. They are always pleased to receive for consideration manuscripts of a medical or scientific character, and are glad to arrange an interview at their Bristol office or elsewhere, at any time convenient to authors. Publishers of *The British Journal of Surgery, The Dental Practitioner and Dental Record, Injury, Community, Health, The Medical Annual* and *The Veterinary Annual.*

Medical, Dental, Veterinary, Nursing.

Wyvern paperbacks—see Epworth Press.

*Zwemmer (A.), Ltd. (1951), 33–37 Moreland Street, London, E.C.1. *T.* 01–253 1974.

Architecture, Art, Film.

EDITORIAL, LITERARY AND PRODUCTION SERVICES

Arnott, (Alex S.) Literary Consultants, Box 32, Station J, 685 Danforth Avenue, Toronto 6, Ontario, Canada. *T.* 422–0770. Author's and writer's literary services in reading, appraising, evaluating, reporting, and marketing novels, non-fiction, book-length manuscripts. Short stories, magazine articles and newspaper features. Television plays and motion picture scripts. All for the Canadian and United States markets.

Australian Press Bureau, 49 Rawnsley Street, Dutton Park, Brisbane, Queensland, 4102, Australia. Full editing service for magazines, especially business and cultural publications. Specialist material for salesmen's bulletins available.

Australian Publishing Services, Reay Wilson, J.P., *Editor.* Box 466, G.P.O., Sydney, Australia. *T.* XY 4387. Sydney, Australia. Specialists in press and public relations and editorial publicity. Complete professional supervision, production and distribution facilities for preparation and publication of books, pamphlets, magazines, house journals, brochures, etc., for industry and organisations. Editorial unit supervises all stages of writing, layout, typography, art, photographic work, editing, production, printing and despatch. *Terms:* cost price plus fee. Author's MS. prepared for publication.

Authors' Research Services (1966), Ann Hoffmann, Dolphins, South Street, Rotherfield, Crowborough, Sussex. *T.* Rotherfield (0892 85) 581. Offers comprehensive research service to writers, proof reading, indexing, photocopying and secretarial assistance.

Brymer, James, Chiddingly, nr. Lewes, Sussex. Production of technical or general brochures, handbooks, etc., with or without half-tone or line illustrations, from initial draft to final printed copy. Also all intermediate stages of similar work.

Cagney, Peter (1952), 23 Second Avenue, Hove, BN3 2LN. *T.* Brighton 70788. Press writing, publishing and print-design services. Editorial service for printers, publishers and advertising agencies, using specialised humorous approach.

Cato O'Brien Books, Redan House, 1 Redan Place, London, W.2. *T.* 01–727 2783. *Manager:* Henry Knobil. Specialists in high quality book creation and design.

Ford, Brian J., F.R.M.S., A.B.I.S., A.R.S.H., Mill Park House, 57 Westville Road, Penylan, Cardiff. *T.* Cardiff (0222) 27222. Scientific library, cuttings, information, copy on scientific and medical matters for publications, radio and television. Critical review and correction.

Freelance Presentations Ltd., 155 Queen Victoria Street, London, EC4V 4EL. *T.* 01–236 5781–2–3.

Freelance Press Services (1967), Forestry Chambers, 67 Bridge Street, Manchester, M3 3BS. *T.* 061–832 5079. A Market Research Department for the freelance writer and photographer. Has issued since 1963 a monthly Market News service the *Contributor's Bulletin.* A good rate of pay made for news of editorial requirements. Also published quarterly *Freelance Writing and Photography* (see Journals). An all-in service for editors, and the freelance.

Freelance Services, 20 Manor Mansions, Belsize Grove, London, NW3 4NB *T.* 01–722 9896. Comprehensive editorial, literary and production services. Translations; picture, literary and technical research and abstracting. Jacket design, all art work and typography for books, company histories, brochures, catalogues, annual reports, house styles. Specialists in travel and holiday promotions.

Garnstone Press Ltd, The (1965), 59 Brompton Road, London, S.W.3. *T.* 01–589 5578. *Cables:* Balfbooks, London, S.W.3. *Directors:* Michael D. Balfour (Managing), Patrick Balfour, Ralph Yablon, G. A. Yablon, J. Gante. Books, booklets, journals and all kinds of literature written, edited, designed, produced, distributed, published and promoted. This is a complete specialist publication service offered by an established publishing house with all the necessary facilities.

Hodgkinson Partners Services Ltd., 13–17 New Burlington Place, London, W1X 2LB. *T.* 01–493 1234. *Directors:* Colin Hodgkinson, A. Ellis, D. Jones. Complete supervision from writing to design and production of House Journals, Annual Reports, Brochures and Handbooks.

Holland-Ford Associates (Robert), 3 Ethel Street, Manchester, M10 9BZ. *T.* 061–205 3344. *Director:* Robert Holland-Ford. Impresario, Concert/Lecture Agents.

Illustration Research Service, Mrs. Stuart Rose, 25 Balcombe Street, London, N.W.1. *T.* 01–584 6671 (in association with the **Writer's and Speaker's Research,** *q.v.*). Offers a research service for illustrative material to authors, publishers, art editors and T.V. producers.

Letchworth Publishing Agency Ltd., The Citizen Press, Norton Way North, Letchworth, Herts. *T.* Letchworth 2501–4. *Managing Director:* Leslie Bichener. Undertakes the preparation, editing, illustration, writing and publishing of high-class house magazines, school textbooks, and brochures in any language that is commonly known according to clients' desires, including advertisements if wanted. Terms: cost price plus fee. Estimates beforehand and specimens of work available. Specialists concerning home and overseas industrial, shipping or agricultural trades. Formerly: The House Magazine Publishing Agency.

Literary Services & Production Ltd. (1964), 26 Old Brompton Road, London, S.W.7. *T.* 01–584 9381–2. *Directors:* C. A. J. Nelson, C. P. de Laszlo, B. R. Lincoln. Operates sales force on behalf of British and Overseas publishers throughout the British Isles. Undertakes all aspects of editorial, research, design, typographical work etc., for publishers.

MacLean (Alexander) Press Agency, (1967), Main Street, Tobermory, Isle of Mull. *T.* Tobermory 2099. Supplies reliable information on island history. Photographic service. Will supply details of any Clan and their Septs based on accepted histories.

McWhirter Twins (1950), 24 Upper Brook Street, London, W1Y 1PD. Facts and figures for publishers.

Martin, C. W. Mrs., Ty-newydd, 3 St John's Road, Arlesey, Bedfordshire. Undertakes research and provides information on almost any subject.

Morley Adams, Ltd. (1917), Oldebourne House, 46-47 Chancery Lane, London, WC2A 1JB. *T.* 01-242 8638-9. *Directors:* L. W. Burgess, N. G. Pulsford, A. C. Harris. Specialists in the production of crosswords and other puzzles, quizzes, etc. Experts in handling advertisers' competitions.

Newman Neame Ltd., 348-350 Gray's Inn Road, London, W.C.1. *T.* 01-837 6484. Industrial publishers. Company histories and illustrated anniversary publications, employee newspapers and magazines, export publications in overseas market languages, financial reviews and company reports, house journals marketing products and services.

Oriel Press Ltd. (1962), 32 Ridley Place, Newcastle upon Tyne, NE1 8LH. *T.* Newcastle 20892-3. *Directors:* Bruce Allsopp (Chairman), R. S. Adams, F. C. Allsopp, D. M. Bell. Undertakes the design of books, specialising in the preparation of complete paste-ups ready for camera and production by photo lithography; also jackets and all art work and typography for books, brochures and conference proceedings.

Oriental Languages Bureau, Lakshmi Building, Sir P. Mehta Road, Fort, Bombay 1, India. *T.* 263451. *T.A.* Orientclip. *Proprietor:* K. N. Shah. Undertakes translations and printing in all Indian languages.

Picture Research Agency, Pat Hodgson, Rohan, Hatherley Road, Kew, Richmond, Surrey. *T.* 01-940 5986. Illustrations found for books, films and television. Written research also undertaken particularly on historical subjects, including photographic and film history.

Piggott, Reginald and Marjorie, 3 Kirkdene Grove, Newton Mearns, Renfrewshire. *T.* 041-639 5284. Cartographers to University presses and academic publishers in Britain and overseas.

Publications for Industry Limited, 14 Queen Victoria Street, London, E.C.4. *T.* 01-236 1887. *Directors:* Alan J. Kennard, A. Kennard. Publishers for industrial clients. Complete editorial, design and production of shareholder publications, annual reports, house journals, reviews, brochures, catalogues and company histories.

Queen Anne Press Ltd., The, National House, 60-66 Wardour Street, London, W1V 3HP *T.* 01-437 0686. An associate company of **B.P.C. Publishing Ltd.**

Rainbird (George) Ltd., Marble Arch House, 44 Edgware Road, London, W.2. *T.* 01-723 9042. *Directors:* G. M. Rainbird, E. P. Young, J. Hadfield, G. A. Forbes, E. Fisher, G. V. Speaight, M. Raeburn. Specialists in colour reproduction, fine book design and printing. Editorial services. Free-lance artists' and designers' work used.

Roger Smithells Ltd., Editorial and Publishing Services, 9 Great Chapel Street, W.1. *T.* 01-437 3521. An editorial unit which handles the production of periodical and other publications. Journalistic specialists in everything relating to travel and holidays. Producers of "Sebastian Cash" travel and holiday features and Reader Information Service.

Rutland, Jonathan, Egmont, 7 Sydenham Road South, Cheltenham, Glos. *T.* Cheltenham 52529. Editorial service, design and layout of illustrated books, especially in the educational field. Photographic work on a wide range of subjects—almost anything, almost anywhere.

Science Unit, Mill Park House, 57 Westville Road, Penylan, Cardiff. *T.* Cardiff (0222) 27222. All types of scientific information and research. Special investigations, scripts, papers and articles.

Scriptek Publications Ltd., 25 Kings Road, Reading, Berkshire. *T.* Reading 50496-7. Special handbooks for industrial and research organisations. Complete production including research, writing, illustrating, and printing; or to any intermediate stage.

Vickers, John, 54 Kenway Road, London, S.W.5. *T.* 01-373 3091. Special optical effects for bookjackets and illustration. Consultant on effects for T.V. and commercial films. Archives of British Theatre from 1939–1960.

Writer's & Speaker's Research (1954), Joan St. George Saunders and Joan Bright Astley, 56 Brunswick Gardens, London, W.8. *T.* 01-727 2289. Provides a research service for writers, broadcasters and public speakers.

Writers' Publishing Association, The, John Liggins (Secretary), 2 Park Street, Fleckney, Leicester, LE8 0BB. *T.* Fleckney 579, and BCM/Buildings, London, W.C.1. An old-established firm offering a comprehensive information and research service for journalists, writers, publishers, photographers and artists. Issues the *Free-lance Report,* founded 1931, fortnightly at a subscription rate of £5·25 p.a., supplements extra, providing information on new publications, on their requirements, etc.; *Topical Dates & Facts,* a monthly guide to forthcoming events, centenaries, festivals, etc., at £3 p.a.; a Press Cutting Library dating back some 50 years and offering loan facilities.

AUSTRALIAN PUBLISHERS

* Members of Australian Book Publishers Association

*Angus & Robertson, Ltd. (1884), 221 George Street, Sydney, 2000. *T.* 27 1931. London House: 54 Bartholomew Close, EC1A 7EY. *T.* 01-606 7831. *Directors:* Sir Norman Cowper (Chairman), G. A. Ferguson, A. G. Cousins, E. A. J. Hyde, N. H. Routley, D. F. Hardy, K. Wilder. General fiction and non-fiction, Australiana, poetry, pictorial, practical, educational, medical, technical, children's, paperbacks.

*Australian Council for Educational Research, Frederick Street, Hawthorn, Victoria, 3122. *T.* 81-6870, 81-1271. Educational books.

*Australian Publishing Co., Pty., Ltd., Bradbury House, 55 York Street, Sydney 2000. *T.* 29 3192, 29 1210. *Directors:* A. S. M. Harrap, R. W. Turner, R. J. Sare, G. P. M. Harrap, G. C. Greene, R. S. Unwin. General, fiction, juvenile, education, art and technical.

*Bacon (S. John), Publishing Company Pty., Ltd., 119 Burwood Road, Burwood, Victoria 3125. *T.* 288 1233. *Directors:* John Ferguson Bacon, Joan Diemar. Religious and educational material. Children's books and illustrated gift books. Religious art, greetings cards.

*Cassell Australia Ltd. P.O. Box 32, North Melbourne 3051; 30–36 Curzon Street, North Melbourne 3051. *T.* 329–8577. *Cables:* Caspeg. *Directors:* Dr. Desmond Flower, M.C., J. R. Moad, H. G. Longmuir. Fiction, travel, biography, educational.

*Cheshire Group Publishers, 346 St. Kilda Road, Melbourne 3004. *T.* Melbourne 699 1522. *Managing Director:* Brian Stonier. *Publishing Manager:* J. Curtain. Educational, history, politics, social.

Cochrane, John, Pty., Ltd., 373 Bay Street, Port Melbourne, 3207, Victoria. (Box 2478V., G.P.O., Melbourne 3001). Publishers representative.

*Collins (Wm.) Sons & Co., Ltd., represented by William Collins (Australia) Ltd., 36 Clarence Street, Sydney, N.S.W. 2000. *T.* 29 1388. *Directors:* K. W. Wilder, J. W. Powell, A. S. Rein. Publishers of general literature, fiction, children's books, Bibles and school textbooks. Head Office: 14 St. James's Place, London, S.W.1.

*Currawong Publishing Co. Pty. Ltd., 129 Pitt Street, Sydney, N.S.W. 2000. *T.* 28 3159. Books of general appeal by Australian authors, mainly non-fiction, educational and children's books.

French, Samuel (Australia) Pty. Ltd., represented by Dominie, Drama Department, 405 Victoria Avenue, Chatswood, 2067. *T.* 412 1984. Publishers of plays and agents for the collection of royalties.

*Georgian House Pty. Ltd., 296 Beaconsfield Parade, Middle Park, Victoria 3206. *T.* 94 0457. *Directors:* Brian W. Harris, H. K. Cartledge, Mrs. J. Sullivan. All types of books published.

*Heinemann, William, Ltd., 33 Lonsdale Street, Melbourne. *T.* 6621322. *T.A.* Sunlocks, Melbourne. *Manager:* Dennis Wren. Fiction, travel, biography, history, drama, children's books, technical, medical, educational.

*Hodder & Stoughton, Ltd., 429 Kent Street, Sydney. *T.* 29 6478–9. *Directors:* Paul Hodder-Williams, John Attenborough, Robin Denniston, Philip Attenborough, R. J. Sare (Australia), Eric McKenzie, Mark Hodder-Williams, Michael Attenborough. All types of books.

Holt, Rinehart & Winston (Aust.) Pty. Ltd., 79 Whiting Street, Artarmon, New South Wales. *T.* Sydney 439–1693, 43–4555.

*Horwitz Group Books Pty. Ltd., including **Horwitz Publications, Horwitz Martin, Ure Smith,** 2 Denison Street, North Sydney 2060. *T.* 929–6144: *Cables:* Horbooks Sydney: *Telex:* AA21491. *Directors:* S. D. L. Horwitz (Chairman), L. J. Moore (Managing Director), M. C. Phillips, (Deputy Managing Director), S. Ure Smith, (Director and Publisher). Fiction (Paperback and hardbound) educational (primary, seconday and tertiary) reference books, non-fiction, medical, technical, cookery and children's books. London office: 88 Farringdon Street, E.C.4. (*T.* 01–353–2134).

*Jacaranda Press Pty. Ltd., 46 Douglas Street, Milton, Brisbane. *T.* 36 2755. 142 Victoria Road, Marrickville, Sydney. *T.* 51 5798. 162 Albert Road, South Melbourne. *T.* 69 1169. P.O. Box 97, Glenside, Adelaide. *T.* 79 7375. 136 Victoria Avenue, Dalkeith, Perth. *T.* 86 3463. 57 France Street, Auckland, New Zealand. *T.* 7 3016. P.O. Box 3395, Port Moresby, T.P.N.G. *T.* 5 4551. Itec House, 29–30 Ely Place, London, E.C.1. England. *T.* 01-242 8111. *Cables:* Japress, Brisbane. *Directors:* J. D. Patience, B. Clouston. Fiction, travel, biography, medical, technical, children's books, educational, natural history.

*Lansdowne Press Pty. Ltd., 346 St. Kilda Road, Melbourne 3004. *Cables:* Lansdowne-books. Brian Stonier (Managing Director), John Currey (Managing Editor), Peter Quick (Publishing Manager). Natural history, biography, history, sport, humour, current affairs, children's books.

Law Book Company Ltd, The, 301–305 Kent Street, Sydney, 2000.

*Longman Australia Pty. Ltd., 681 Burke Road, Camberwell, Victoria 3124. *Chairman:* W. P. Kerr. All types of books.

*Lothian Publishing Co. Pty. Ltd., 4–12 Tattersalls Lane, Melbourne, Vic. 3000. *T.* 663–4976. *Directors:* Louis A. Lothian (Managing), L. N. Jupp, K. A. Lothian. Gardening, children's, general literature.

*Macmillan Company of Australia Pty. Ltd., The, 107 Moray Street, South Melbourne 3205. *T.* 69–7491–4. *T.A.* Scriniaire, Melbourne. 155 Miller Street, North Sydney, 2060. *T.* 92–1275. Head Office: London. All types of books.

*Melbourne University Press, 932 Swanston Street, Carlton, Victoria 3053. *T.* 340484. Prepared to consider works of academic, scholastic or cultural interest, educational textbooks and books of reference. Terms of publication are royalty, commission or profit-sharing agreements, according to the nature of the work. Representatives: Britain and Europe and North America, International Scholarly Book Services Inc.; Tokyo, Hong Kong and Singapore, United Publishers Services Ltd.
Chairman of the Board of Management: Professor John Turner. *Director:* P. A. Ryan, M.M. B.A.

*Oxford University Press (Australian Branch), Frank Eyre (Manager), 7 Bowen Crescent, Melbourne. *Postal address:* G.P.O. Box 2784Y, Melbourne, 3001, Victoria. *Cables:* Oxonian, Melbourne. *T.* 26–3748. Australian History, biography, literary criticism, travel and general, including children's books but excluding fiction.

Pacific Publications (Aust.) Pty. Ltd. 27–29 Alberta Street, Sydney N.S.W. 2000. *Postal Address:* G.P.O. Box 3408, Sydney, N.S.W. 2001. General, children's books and reference.

*Pitman (Sir Isaac) (Australia) Pty., Ltd., 158 Bouverie Street, Carlton, Victoria. Technical, educational, general, commercial, medical, legal.

*Reed (A. H. & A. W.) Pty. Ltd. (1964), 51 Whiting Street, Artarmon, N.S.W. 2064. *T.* 439–1566; branch at 357 Little Collins Street, Melbourne 3000. *T.* 674033. Also at Wellington and Auckland, New Zealand. *Directors:* J. H. Richards (Chairman), J. M. Reed (Managing), A. W. Reed, T. O. Kennedy, D. W. Sinclair, A. A. Vercoe, Mrs. E. J. Reed (Associate). General and educational.

*Rigby Ltd., 30 North Terrace, Kent Town, South Australia. *T.* 23 5566. *Cables:* Rigbylim, Adelaide. *Directors:* A. L. Slade (Chairman), V. M. Branson, F.A.I.M., Sir Donald Bradman, W. P. Kerr, J. C. Irwin, O.B.E., E.D. Educational general literature, and useful handbooks.

Shakespeare Head Press, 10–16 Dowling Street, Potts Point, Sydney, 2011. *T.* 355333. Educational and general; fiction, classics, children's books.

*Ure Smith Publishers, 155 Miller Street, North Sydney 2060 (a division of the Horwitz Group Books). *T.* 28 6458. *Cables: T.A.* Imprint, Sydney. *Publishing and Managing Director:* Sam Ure Smith; *Editors:* Barbara Bacon, John Taylor, Ann Ryan (Children's). Fiction, humour, general, art, practical, children's books, historical, sociological, hard-bounds and paperbacks. Representatives for: Phaidon Press, Ariel Press, University of Queensland Press.

Ward Lock Ltd., P.O. Box 34, Brickfield Hill, N.S.W. 2000. *T.* 211–1022, and 211–1480.

*Whitcombe & Tombs Pty. Ltd., 159–163 Victoria Road, Marrickville 2204, N.S.W., and at Melbourne and Perth. *T.* 560–9888. *T.A.* Whitcombes, Sydney. *Directors:* J. K. Simpson, K. G. Davison. Educational and general (except fiction).

CANADIAN PUBLISHERS

NOTE.—The paragraph prefixing "American Publishers" applies to this section also.

Abelard-Schuman Canada Ltd., 228 Yorkland, Boulevard, Willowdale 425, Ontario. *T.* (416) 491–1333.

Bodley Head (Canada) Ltd., The, 17 Prince Arthur Avenue, Toronto. *T.* 924–5761. *President:* Max Reinhardt. *Vice President:* Ann Orford. *Secretary and Treasurer:* Jeanne Kirkpatrick. General, fiction, children's books.

Burns & MacEachern Limited, 62 Railside Road, Don Mills, Ontario. *T.* 447–5131. *President:* B. D. Sandwell, *Vice-Presidents:* G. E. Witmer, Helen M. Sandwell and W. B. Hanna. Publishers of educational books and non-fiction trade books. Agents for a number of British and American publishing companies.

Canada Publishing Co., Ltd., 1500 Birchmount Road, Scarborough 733, Ontario. Publishers of school textbooks.

Clarke Irwin & Company Limited, 791 St. Clair Avenue West, Toronto, 10. *T.* 654–3211. General trade and educational publishers.

Collins (Wm.) Sons & Co. (Canada), Ltd., 100 Lesmill Road, Don Mills, Ontario. Publishers of general literature, fiction, children's books and Bibles. Publishers in Canada for Wm. Collins, Sons & Co., Ltd., Pan Books, Ltd., André Deutsch, Ltd., Geoffrey Bles, Ltd., Harvill Press, Ltd., William Heinemann Ltd., Martin Secker and Warburg Ltd., Peter Davies Ltd., Ladybird books, Corgi Books, Rapp & Whiting.

Copp Clark Publishing Company, The (1841), 495–517 Wellington Street West, Toronto 2–B, Ontario. *T.* 366–4911. *T.A.* Noblecop, Toronto. *President:* M. I. Pitman. *Vice-President:* F. L. Barrett. *Textbook Manager:* Franklin L. Barrett. Educational textbooks for elementary, secondary and college use. Book length juveniles and trade books for adult field, both fiction and non-fiction. Preliminary letter required before submitting manuscript.

Dalhousie University Press Ltd., Dalhousie University, Halifax, N.S. *T.* 424–2541. Publishers of *The Dalhousie Review*.

Dent (J. M.) & Sons (Canada), Ltd., 100 Scarsdale Road, Don Mills 404, Ontario. Textbooks and general publishers. Most textbooks commissioned.

Dodd, Mead & Company (Canada), Ltd., 25 Hollinger Road, Toronto 374. General publishers.

French (Samuel) (Canada), Ltd., 27 Grenville Street, Toronto 5.

Gage Limited, W. J., 1500 Birchmount Road, Scarborough 733, Ontario. Publishers of school and college textbooks.

General Publishing Co. Limited, 30 Lesmill Road, Don Mills, Ontario. *T.* 445–3333.

Hodder & Stoughton, Ltd. 30 Lesmill Road, Don Mills, Ontario. *T.* 445–3333.

Holt, Rinehart & Winston of Canada Ltd., 833 Oxford Street, Toronto, Ontario. *T.* 416–CL5–4493.

Lippincott (J. B.) Company of Canada Ltd., 60 Front Street West, Toronto 1, Ont. Medical, nursing and allied publications only.

Longman Canada Ltd., *Executive Offices:* 55 Barber Greene Road, Don Mills 403, Ontario. *T.* 444–7331. General and educational.

McClelland & Stewart, Limited, 25 Hollinger Road, Toronto 374. General and educational publishers.

McGill-Queen's University Press, 3458 Redpath Street, Montreal 109. London Branch: 70 Great Russell Street, WC1B 3BY. *T.* 01–405–0182–3–4. Academic.

McGraw-Hill Company of Canada, 330 Progress Avenue, Scarboro 707, Ontario.

Maclean-Hunter Ltd. (1887), 418 University Avenue, Toronto 2, Canada. Magazines, financial, business and industrial newspapers. London Office: Maclean-Hunter Ltd., 30 Old Burlington Street, London, W1X 2AE

Macmillan Company of Canada, Limited (1905), St. Martin's House, 70 Bond Street, Toronto. General publishers who pay special attention to what is worth while of Canadian authorship. Agents for: Edward Arnold & Co., London; Baillière, Tindall & Cassell, London: Cambridge University Press, Cambridge and London; Lea & Febiger, Philadelphia; E. & S. Livingstone, Edinburgh; The Viking Press Inc., New York; John Wright & Sons, Ltd., Bristol; Macmillan & Co., Ltd., London; Allyn Bacon Inc., Boston; Studio Books, New York; St. Martin's Press Inc., New York, Gambit, New York.

Musson Book Company, 30 Lesmill Road, Don Mills, Ontario. *T.* 445–3333.

Oberon Press, 555 Maple Lane, Ottawa 2. *T.* 613–746 4098. General.

Oxford University Press (Canadian Branch), 70 Wynford Drive, Don Mills 403, Toronto. *T.* 429–2941. *Cables:* Frowde, Toronto. *Telex:* Frowde-Tor–02–2269. *Manager:* I. M. Owen. General, educational, medicine, music, religious, juvenile and Canadiana.

Review Publishing Co., Ltd., now Dalhousie University Press, Ltd., *q.v.*

Ryerson Press, The, 299 Queen Street West, Toronto 2–B, Canada. *T.* 363–3711. Printers and publishers. Educational, medical, religious and trade books and general printing.

Saunders of Toronto Limited, 1885 Leslie Street, Don Mills. *T.* 445–6121. Publishers and publishers' representative.

Simon & Schuster of Canada Ltd., 225 Yonge Street, N., Richmond Hill, Ontario. *T.* 416–889 7571. Paperbacks.

University of Toronto Press, University of Toronto, Toronto 181. *T.* 928–2011.

INDIAN PUBLISHERS AND AGENTS

Allied Publishers Private Ltd., 15 Graham Road, Ballard Estate, Bombay 1; 17 Chittaranjan Avenue, Calcutta 13; 13/14 Asaf Ali Road, New Delhi 1; Mohan Mansion, 38–C; Mount Road, Madras 6; 39/1 J.C. Road, Bangalore 2. Distrition for A. & C. Black, Ltd., Cassell & Co. Ltd., W. & R. Chambers, Ltd., Routledge & Kegan Paul Ltd., etc.

Asia Publishing House, Calicut Street, Ballard Estate, Bombay 1; 69 Ganesh Chandra Avenue, Calcutta 13; East View, 199 Mount Road, Madras 2; Indra Palace, Connaught Circus, New Delhi 1; Mull Building, Ashok Marg, Lucknow; 621–22 Avenue Road, Bangalore 2; Buena Vista, Bashir Bagh, Hyderabad 29; Chopra House, Sector 15-B, Chandigarh 17; Ashok Rajpath, Patna 4. *London Office:* 447 Strand, W.C.2. *T.* 01–240 3038–9. *New York Office:* 118 East 59th Street, New York, N.Y. 10022. *T.* 759–8955. Literature, general, including art, biography, economics, politics, world affairs, education, history, library science, philosophy and psychology, science and technology.

Atma Ram & Sons (1909), Post Box 1429, Kashmere Gate, Delhi-6. *Managing Proprietor:* Ram Lal Pury and *General Manager:* I. K. Puri. *Branches:* Hauz Khas, New Delhi; Chaura Rasta, Jaipur; University Enclave, Chandigarh; 17 Ashok Marg, Lucknow. Art, Literature, Reference, Biography, Fiction, Economics, Politics, Education, History, Philosophy, Psychology, Science, Technology. Books published in English, Hindi, Punjabi, and Urdu languages. Translations and reprints of foreign books undertaken. Booksellers and importers of foreign books on a large scale.

B.I. Publications, *Proprietor:* British Institute of Engineering Technology (India) Private Ltd. Ucobank Building, Flora Fountain, Bombay 1. *Chairman:* R. D. Bhagat. *General Sales Manager:* K. P. Churamani. Scientific (Pure and Applied), Industrial, Educational, Technical, Reference and other specialised books.

Blackie & Son (India) Ltd., Blackie House, 103–5 Fort Street, Post Box 21, Bombay 1; 285–J Bepin Behari Ganguly Street, Calcutta 12; 1–18 Asaf Ali Road, New Delhi 1; 2–18 Mount Road, Madras 2.

Hind Kitabs Ltd., 32–34 Churchgate House, Veer Nariman Road, Fort, Bombay 1. General publishers and printers.

Hind Pocket Books (P) Ltd., 18–G.T. Road, Shahdara Delhi–32. *T.* 212046. *T.A.* Pocketbook Delhi; Pioneer Publishers of low-priced quality paperbacks in Indian languages and in English under the imprint of Orient Paperbacks. *Managing Director:* D. N. Malhotra.

Imperial Publishing Co., Post Box 1389, Delhi. *T.* 274415. Reference books.

Indian Associated Publishing Co., Private Ltd., 93 Mahatma Gandhi Road, Calcutta 7. *T.* 34–2641. *T.A.* Culture (B). General publishers and booksellers.

Indian Press (Publications) Private Limited, Allahabad (U.P.), India. *T.* 3201. *T.A.* Publikason. Branches and agencies in all principal towns of India. *Overseas Stockists:* Luzac & Co., Ltd., 46 Great Russell Street, London, W.C.1. Stecher Hafner Inc., 31 East 10th Street, New York 10003, N.Y. Publishers of school, college, university and general books in Hindi, Bengali, English; Gurumukhi, Urdu, Marathi, Nepali languages. *Directors:* H. P. Ghosh, S. Ghosh, R. Ghosh, S. P. Ghosh, M. D. D. P. Ghosh, N. N. Mukherjee, K. K. Ghosh and P. K. Ghosh.

Khosla (K. R.) & Sons, Publishers, 3 Netaji Subhash Marg, Daryanganj, Delhi. *T.* 274415.

Khosla Publishing Co. (Post Box 1389), 3 Netaji Subhash Marg, Daryanganj, Delhi. *T.* 274415. Reference books. *Khosla's Industrial & Commercial Directory.*

Kothari Publications, Jute House, 12 India Exchange Place, Calcutta, 1, G.P.O. Box 382. *T.* 22–9563, & 22–6572. *Proprietor:* Ing. H. KOTHARI of Sujangarh, Rajasthan. Publishers of Technical, General and Reference books. Publishers of *Who s Who* series in India. (Controlled by Kothari Organisation.) Agents for many foreign publishers.

Little Flower Co., The (1929), Bhurangam Buildings, 8 Ranganathan Street, Thyagarayanagar, Madras 17 (India). *T.* 441538. *T.A.* LIFCO, Madras, LIFCO books. General, fiction, technical, dictionaries, astrology, medicine, legal, commercial, educational and religious.

Macmillan & Company, Ltd., 276 Dr. Dadabhai Naoroji Road, Bombay; 294 Bow Bazar Street, Calcutta; Patullo Road, Madras. Branches of London House of same name. Publishers of educational, scientific, technical, medical, fiction and general books. Agents in India, Burma, Pakistan and Ceylon for Cambridge University Press, London (*not* Pakistan); J. M. Dent & Sons, Ltd., London (Gallery Press and Phoenix House Publications); W. & A. K. Johnston and G. W. Bacon, Ltd., Edinburgh.

Natraj Publishers, 17 Rajpur Road, Dehra Dun, U.P. *T.* 3382. *Proprietor:* Sohan Lall. Specialists books on military science, forestry, agriculture and geology.

New Book Company, Private Ltd., The (1936), Kitab Mahal, 188–90 Dr. Dadabhai Naoroji Road, Bombay. *T.* 263544–5. *T.A.* Newbook Bombay. *Directors:* F. P. Taraporevala, D. P. Taraporevala, N. F. Taraporevala. Art, technical and general.

Orient Longmans Ltd., Regd. Office: 'A' Block, Hamilton House, Connaught Place, New Delhi 1, and regional offices at 17 Chittaranjan Avenue, Calcutta 13; Nicol Road, Ballard Estate, Bombay 1; 36A Mount Road, Madras 2; 3–5 Asaf Ali Road, New Delhi 1. Publishers educational, scientific, technical, medical, general and children's. Associated with the London House of Longmans, Green & Co. Ltd. Agents and Distributors in India for Longmans, Green & Co., Ltd.; Edward Arnold (Publishers) Ltd.; George Philip & Son. Ltd.; The University of London Press Ltd.; G. Bell & Sons, Ltd.; U.N.E.S.C.O. Paris; Penguin Books Ltd.; Macdonald & Evans Ltd.; Longmans' Young Books Ltd.; Oliver & Boyd; J. & A. Churchill.

Oxford University Press, *General Manager:* C. H. Lewis, Post Box 31, Oxford House, Apollo Bunder, Bombay 1; G.P.O. Box 530, Faraday House, P17 Mission Row Extension, Calcutta 13; Post Box 1079, Oxford House, Mount Road, Madras 6. *Cables;* Oxonian, Bombay, or Oxonian, Calcutta, or Oxonian, Madras. *T.* Bombay 213104; Calcutta 23–1317, 23–2640; Madras 86156 and 86157. Publishers in all lines. Agents in India for the educational books of Geo. G. Harrap & Co. Ltd., University Tutorial Press, Ltd.; for the *Beacon Readers* (Ginn & Co., Ltd.); various American University Presses; Hong Kong University Press.

Palit & Dutt Publishers (1969), 144 Rajpur Road, Dehra Dun (U.P.). *T.* 3792 and 3187. *Directors:* Maj. Gen. D. K. Palit, Dev Dutt Arora. Military Science.

Pustak-Bhandar, Govind Mittra Road, Patna 4. *T.* 50341. *Founder:* Acharya Ramloxhan Saran. *Partners:* M. S. Singh, S. S. Singh, S. Saran, J. B. Saran, Chandramani Devi. Literary, scientific, and educational books in English, Hindi, Nepali, Bengali, Urdu, Mathili, Sanskrit, Santhali, Oriya.

R & K Publishing House, 5 Scindia House, New Delhi-1. Books on and about Indian Art, History, Cookery, Economics, Politics and Travel.

Rajkamal Prakashan Private Ltd., H.O. 8 Faiz Bazar, Delhi–6. *T.* 274463. *T.A.* Prakashak. *Branch:* Opp. Science College, Patna 6. Publishers of original and translated literary and educational books in Hindi and English, magazines (*Alochana, Prakashan Samachar*). Children's books.

Rajpal & Sons, Delhi 6, India. *T.* 226201. *T.A.* Rajpalsons, Delhi: Kashmere Gate, Delhi 6. Publishers of general and textbooks in Hindi and English and also reprints and translations. *Partners:* V. N. Malhotra, D. N. Malhotra, Delhi.

Ram Narain Lal Beni Madho, 2 Katra Road, Allahabad. Publishers of Educational, Legal, books in Hindi, Urdu, Sanskrit, Persian, Bengali, and Technical.

Ranjan Gupta (1966), 22/3–C, Galiff Street, Calcutta–4. *T.* 55–5860. General publishers, specialising in rare books of Indian philosophy, religion, art, literature, history, etc.

Rupa & Co., 15 Bankim Chatterjee Street, College Square, Calcutta 12. *T.* 34–4821. *T.A.* Rupanco, Calcutta-12.

Shiksha Bharati, Madarsa Road, Kashmere Gate, Delhi-6. *T.* 22 6389. Publishers and printers of textbooks in Hindi and English; also juvenile literature. *Partners:* V. Malhotra, S. Malhotra and G. Malhotra.

Taraporevala (D.B.), Sons & Co., Private, Ltd. (Original firm established 1864), Treasure House of Books, 210 Dr. Dadabhai Naoroji Road, Bombay. *T.* 261433. *Directors:* Mrs. Manekbai J. Taraporevala and Miss Sooni J. Taraporevala. *Chief Executive:* Prof. Russi J. Taraporevala. Books on India and of Indian interest, fine arts, handicrafts, pictorial albums, business, economics, education, psychology, cookery, domestic economy, pets, hobbies, reference, languages, religion, philosophy, mysticism, occult sciences, law, history, culture, mythology, sociology, health, medical, sex, science, technology, self-improvement, self-instruction, sport, games, shikar, Indian classics.

Thacker, Spink & Co., (1933), Private Ltd., P.O. Box 54, 3 Esplanade East Calcutta 1. *T.* 23–4214–5. Publishers of books on Indian law, engineering, medicine, anthropology, gardening, agriculture, fiction, domestic economy, sport, shikar, botany, zoology, science, autobiography, religion, history, criminology, philosophy and other subjects relating to India.

Thacker & Co. Ltd., P.O. Box 190, Rampart Row, Bombay. *T.* 252613, 252722 and 373523. *T.A.* Booknotes. *Chairman:* A. N. Kilachand; *Chief Executive:* I. S. Varawala. *Manager Publication Dept:* Z. M. Kadri. Publishers of books on all subjects of special Indian and Asiatic interest. Economics, Sociology, History, Politics, Military Science, Commerce, Law and college level Text Books.

Theosophical Publishing House, The, Adyar, Madras 20, India. *T.* 71904. *T.A.* Theotheca, Madras. Theosophical, mystical and occult literature. Publishers of *The Theosophist*, official organ of the President, Theosophical Society. *Editor:* Mr. N. Sri Ram. *Manager:* K. N. Ramanathan.

Theosophy Co. (India), Private, Ltd., Theosophy Hall, 40 New Marine Lines, Bombay 20. *T.* 299024. *T.A.* Aryahata, Bombay. Publishers: *Theosophical Movement, Aryan Path*, and other Theosophical publications.

United Asia Publications Pvt. Ltd, (1948), 12 Rampart Row, Bombay-1. *T.* 252158. Publishers of Books and Periodicals.

NEW ZEALAND PUBLISHERS

* Membership of the New Zealand Book Publishers' Association

Blackwood and Janet Paul Ltd., now **Longman Paul Ltd**, *q.v.*

*Cassell & Co. Ltd., Box 36–013, Northcote Central, Auckland, 9. *T.* 484–371, and 484–055, and Box 2699, Christchurch. *T.* 30739. *N.Z. Manager:* M. J. T. Earl.

*Caxton Press, The, Ltd., 119 Victoria Street, Christchurch, N.Z., P.O. Box 25–088 *T.A.* Imprint, Christchurch. *Directors:* L. V. Bensemann, D. L. Donovan. Fine printers, and publishers since 1935 of New Zealand books of many kinds, including verse, fiction, biography, history, natural history, travel, and children's books. Publishers of the literary quarterly *Landfall* (q.v.), the fine arts periodical *Ascent* (twice yearly) and the educational quarterly, *Learning*.

*Collins Bros. & Co. Ltd., P.O. Box 1, Auckland, (parent Company William Collins, Sons & Co. Ltd., 14 St. James's Place, London). *Managing Director:* D. L. Bateman. *Editorial Director:* W. E. Forde. *Sales Director:* A. D. Mackie. Publishers of general literature, fiction, Bibles, Children's Books, Reference Books, Educational, Technical, Paperbacks.

*Heinemann, William, Ltd., 46 Lake Road, Northcote, Auckland, N.Z. The Heinemann Group of Publishers consists of William Heinemann Ltd.; Wm. Heinemann Medical Books, Ltd.; Heinemann Educational Books Ltd.; Peter Davies, Ltd; Secker & Warburg, Ltd.; World's Work (1913), Ltd.; and representing also: Epworth Press; A. R. Mowbray & Co., Ltd.; John Murray (Publishers), Ltd., Student Christian Movement Press, Daily Express.

Hicks, Smith & Sons Ltd., 238 Wakefield Street, Wellington.

*Hodder & Stoughton Ltd., 52 Cook Street, Auckland. *T.* 379788/9. *T.A.* Expositor, Auckland.

Kea Press Ltd., *Editorial and Trade:* P.O. Box 2919, Wellington. Premises: Suite 4, Book House, Boulcott Street. Wellington. *T.* 59639. *Directors:* James Milburn, Hugh Price, Isaac Wilson, Arthur Tyers. Specialist publishers of infant readers and other books for reading programmes in junior school.

Longman Paul Ltd., P.O. Box 31–006, Milford Road, Milford, Auckland 9. *T.* 498 595 and 497 292. *Cables* and *T.A.* Freegrove, Auckland. Publishers of New Zealand books of all kinds, including fiction, history, natural history, children's books, books on education and school textbooks. Associated with Longman Group Ltd.

*Minerva Bookshop Ltd. (1946), C.P.O. Box 2597, 13 Commerce Street, Auckland C.1. *T.* 30 863. *T.A.* Minerva. *Managing Director:* Esther Porsolt, *Director:* Nigel Faigan. Books of New Zealand interest, educational.

*New Zealand Council for Educational Research (1933), Box 3237, Education House, 178–182 Willis Street, Wellington 1. *T.* 557–939. *T.A.* Edsearch.

New Zealand University Press, Suite 4, Book House, Boulcott Street, Wellington. *T.* 59–639. Scholarly and educational books.

*Oxford University Press New Zealand Branch, Walton House, 66 Ghuznee Street, Wellington, C.1. *Manager:* R. C. Gooderidge. *Postal Address:* G.P.O. Box 185. *Cables:* Oxonian, Wellington. *T.* 557–413.

*Pegasus Press Ltd. (1948), 14 Oxford Terrace, Christchurch, New Zealand. *T.* 64–509. *Cables:* Royalties, Christchurch. *Directors:* Albion Wright (Managing), M. R. Muir, P. J. Skellerup, P. J. Low. Publishers of high quality fiction and verse, historical works, biographies, art, and other illustrated books on shooting, fishing and mountaineering. Proprietors of the Pegasus Press.

*Price Milburn & Co., Ltd., *Editorial and Trade:* P.O. Box 2919, Wellington. *T.* 59–639. *Warehouse:* 39 Whitemans Valley Road, Silverstream. *T.* UH 85254. *Cables:* MICE Wellington. *Directors:* James Milburn, M.A., DIP. ED., Barbara Milburn, B.A., Hugh Price, M.A., DIP. TCH., Beverly Price, B.A. New Zealand books, particularly Cookery, University Text-books, Literature, quality Children's books and fiction, Primary School Texts especially Reading and Social Studies. *Allied Activities:* New Zealand University Press, Distributors for Kea Press Limited, Bowmar Publishing Corp., PM Records.

*Reed (A. H. & A. W.), (1907), 182 Wakefield Street, Wellington, New Zealand; also at Auckland, Sydney and Melbourne. *T.A.* Reedkiwi, Wellington. *Directors:* A. W. Reed (Chairman), J. H. Richards (Deputy Chairman and Managing Director, publishing), T. O. Kennedy (Managing Director, sales), D. W. Sinclair (art), A. A. Vercoe (music and recordings), G. C. A. Wall (editorial), F. A. Davey (production). Biography, travel, history, art, geography, agriculture, nature, Aboriginal, Maori, music, homecraft, colour pictorials, travel guides, sport, juvenile, educational, general fiction, humour and adventure.

*Sevenseas Publishing Pty., Ltd. (1963), 5–7 Tory Street, P.O. Box 1431, Wellington. *T.* 59–759. *T.A.* Viking. *Managing Director:* M. B. Riley. Travel, music, craft books, Polynesian, general.

*Sweet & Maxwell (N.Z.) Ltd., 238 Wakefield Street, Wellington.

*Whitcombe & Tombs, Ltd., *Head Office* and *Editorial:* P.O. Box 1465, Christchurch, 1. *T.A.* Whitcombes, Christchurch. Branches throughout New Zealand, Australia, and in London. Publishers and printers of New Zealand books of all descriptions, general and educational; booksellers and stationers; trade distributors and publishers' representatives.

OTHER COMMONWEALTH PUBLISHERS

GHANA

Longman Group, Ltd., Ring Road, Industrial Area South, Accra. *T.* 21332. *Postal address:* P.O. Box 2051, Accra.

HONG KONG

Longman Group (Far East) Ltd., P.O. Box 223, Hong Kong. *T.* H–618171–5.

Oxford University Press (East Asian Branch). *Manager:* C. W. Toogood, News Building, 5th floor, 633 King's Road, North Point, Hong Kong. *T.* H–610221–4. *Cables:* Oxonian, Hongkong. *Head Office:* Oxford University Press, Kuala Lumpur.

Vetch and Lee Ltd., (1969), 1035 Man Yee Building, 67–71 Queen's Road Central, Hong Kong. *T.* H–233886, 233585. *Directors:* Sir Lindsay Ride (Chairman), Henri Vetch (Managing Director) and Rupert S. C. Lee. Orientalia of academic and general interest, sinology, natural history, language, arts and crafts.

KENYA

East African Publishing House Ltd., P.O. Box 30571, Nairobi.

Longman Kenya Ltd., P.O. Box 18201, Nairobi. *T.* 58621.

Nelson (Thomas) & Sons Ltd., P.O. Box 25012, Nairobi.

Oxford University Press Eastern Africa Branch, *General Manager:* R. G. Houghton, National and Grindlays Bank Building, Government Road, Nairobi. *Postal Address:* P.O. Box 12532, Nairobi. *Cables:* Oxonian, Nairobi. *T.* Nairobi 23708. Offices also at P.O. Box 2335, Lusaka, P.O. Box 1024, Addis Ababa and P.O. Box 21039, Dar-es-Salaam.

MALAWI

Longman (Malawi) Ltd., P.O. Box 1113, Blantyre. *T.* 2213.

MALAYSIA

Longmans Malaysia Sdn. Berhad, 44 Jalan Ampang, Kuala Lumpur. *T.* 83196–7. *T.A.* Freegrove, Kualalumpur.

Oxford University Press East Asian Branch, *General Manager:* R. E. Brammah, Bangunan Loke Yew, Jalan Belanda, Kuala Lumpur. *Cables:* Oxonian, Kuala Lumpur. *T.* Kuala Lumpur 23101 and 875 Jalan Bukit Timah, Singapore 10. *Cables:* Oxonian Singapore. *T.* 660746/7.

NIGERIA

Evans Brothers (Nigeria Publishers) Ltd., Rational Building, 6 Lagos Bye Pass, P.M.B. 5164, Ibadan.

Longman Nigeria Ltd., Private Mail Bag, 1036, Ikeja. *T.* Lagos 33007.

Macmillan & Co. (Nigeria) Ltd., Mokola-Oyo Road, P.O. Box 1463, Ibadan Western Nigeria. *T.* 24316. *T.A.* Macbooks Ibadan. *Shipping and Warehouse:* Ilupeju Estate, Oshodi, P.O. Box 264, Yaba. *T.* 31188. *Directors:* N. G. Byam Shaw, J. Ashby, Olu Anulopo, Dr. A. Babs Fafunwa. A branch of Macmillan & Co. Ltd., London.

Oxford University Press Nigerian Branch, T. T. Solaru, *Manager*. Oxford House, Iddo Gate, Ibadan. *Postal address:* Private Mail Bag 5095, Ibadan. *Trade Department:* O.U.P., Jericho Reservation, Ibadan. *Postal address:* P.M.B. 5142, Ibadan. *Cables:* Oxonian, Ibadan, or Frowde, Ibadan. *T.* Ibadan 24644. *Trade Department:* 24117.

Pilgrim Books Ltd., 305 Herbert Macaulay Street, P.O. Box 3560, Lagos. *T.* Lagos 45939. *Cables:* Pilgrim, Lagos. London: 18 Bedford Row, W.C.1. *Directors:* K. A. Hills, H. C. Baillie, L. N. Namme, W. T. Shaw. Educational Law, Africana.

PAKISTAN

Ghulam Ali & Sons, Sh. Kashmiri Bazar, Lahore; Chowk Anarkali, Lahore; 17 Hospital Road, Lahore; Bunder Road, Karachi; Hospital Road, Hyderabad. *T.* Lahore 52908 and 64171. Karachi 237203 and 61804, Hyderabad 4433. *Cables:* Kitabman Lahore. Islamic, educational, and general.

Government of Pakistan Press, Karachi. Government Publications.

Malik Din Mohd. & Sons, Ishat Manzil, Bull Road, Lahore. General. *T.* 52621–54315, 54467. *T.A.* Ishatco, Lahore.

Muhammad Ashraf, Sh., Kashmiri Bazar, Lahore. *T.* 53171 (office); 53489 (press) *Cables:* Islamiclit. Islamic books (in English) and *Islamic Literature*, a monthly journal in English.

Orient Longmans Ltd., 36/1 Toynbee Circular Road, Motijheel Commercial Area, Dacca 2. See under India (page 215).

Oxford University Press Pakistan Branch, *General Manager:* D. C. Cunningham, National and Grindlays Bank Building, Merewether Tower, 1.1. Chundrigar Road, Karachi 2. *Postal Address:* P.O. Box 5093, Karachi. Ground Floor, Al-Sarwar Building, Bank Square, Shahrah-i-Qaid-i-Azam, Lahore 3. *Postal address:* P.O. Box 710, G.P.O. Lahore. 1st Floor, Red Cross Building, 114–Motijheel, Dacca 2. *Postal address:* P.O. Box 88, Dacca. *Cables:* Oxonian, Karachi, or Oxonian, Lahore or Oxonian, Dacca. *T.* Karachi 230580; Lahore 68175; Dacca 42457.

Provincial Library, (1919), Victoria Park, Dacca-1, East Pakistan. *T.* 243827. *Proprietor:* K. M. Bashir.

Publishers United Ltd., Anarkali, Lahore.

RHODESIA

Collins, William, (Africa) (Pty) Ltd., P.O. Box 2800, Salisbury.

Longman Rhodesia (Pvt.) Ltd., P.O. Box ST 125, Southerton, Salisbury. *T.* Salisbury 661474 and 660470. *T.A.* Freegrove, Salisbury.

Oxford University Press, Southern African Branch, Jon Stallworthy, *General Manager*, Rms 57–58 Roslin House, Baker Avenue, Salisbury. *Postal address:* Box 3892, Salisbury. *Cables:* Oxonian, Salisbury. *T.* Salisbury 27848.

TANZANIA
Longman Tanzania Ltd., P.O. Box 3164, Dar es Salaam and P.O. Box 3043, Arusha.
T. Dar es Salaam 29748 and Arusha 2217. *T.A.* and *Cables:* Longmans,
Dar es Salaam or Arusha.

UGANDA
Longman Uganda Ltd., P.O. Box 3409, Kampala. *T.* Kampala 42940.

ZAMBIA
Longman Zambia Ltd., P.O. Box 886, Lusaka. *T.* 73746.

Oxford University Press Eastern African Branch, *Manager:* Peter Mackay, Tenzebantu
Road, Lusaka. *Postal address:* P.O. Box 2335, Lusaka. *Cables:* Oxonian,
Lusaka. *T.* Lusaka 74583.

AMERICAN PUBLISHERS

The following is a selected list; it includes few of the very many smaller firms,
and few of the specialist publishers.

The note at the head of British Publishers on p. 157 applies also to American
Publishers.

* Members of the American Book Publishers Council (see page 268).
L.H.: London house.

*Abelard-Schuman, Limited, 257 Park Avenue South, New York, N.Y. 10010.
Biography, science, history, travel, belles-lettres, children's books. *London
House:* Abelard-Schuman Ltd., 8 King Street, W.C.2.

*Abingdon Press, Editorial and Business Offices: 201 Eighth Avenue S., Nashville,
Tennessee 37202. *T.* 615–242–1621. Editor: Emory Stevens Bucke. Religious, general, college and children's books.

*Atheneum Publishers (1960), 122 East 42nd Street, New York 10017. *T.* 212 661–
4500. General, fiction, poetry, drama, juveniles.

*Atlantic Monthly Press, 8 Arlington Street, Boston, Massachusetts, 02116. *Director:*
Peter Davison. (Books are published in association with Little, Brown & Co.,
and appear under joint imprint "Atlantic-Little, Brown.") MSS. of permanent
interest, fiction, biography, autobiography, history, current affairs, social
science, letters, poetry, juveniles. The opportunity of serialising our books in
whole or in part in *The Atlantic* is frequently of assistance in advancing the
interests of the author.

Baker (Walter H.) Company (1845), 100 Summer Street, Boston, Mass. 02110. *President:* M. Abbott Van Nostrand. *Treasurer:* Louis Cooper. Plays and books
on the theatre. Also agents for plays. *London agents:* Samuel French Ltd.,
26 Southampton Street, London, W.C.2.

*Barnes (A. S.) & Co., Forsgate Drive, Cranbury, New Jersey 08512. General
publishers.

*Beacon Press, 25 Beacon Street, Boston, Mass. 02108. *T.* 617–742 2100. Non-
fiction only in fields of religion, ethics, philosophy, current affairs, history,
literary criticism and art.

Better Homes and Gardens Books (Consumer Book Division, Meredith Corporation),
1716 Locust Street, Des Moines, Iowa, 50303. *T.* 515–284 9474. *Editorial
Director:* Don Dooley. Publishes non-fiction in all family and home service
categories including cooking and nutrition, money management, gardening,
home building and improvements, decorating and remodelling, furnishings,
sewing and crafts, health, travel, recreation and entertainment, pets, games,
family legal matters, and other subjects of home service value. Publisher
suggests outline be submitted first. Address manuscripts and/or material to
the above address.

Bobbs-Merrill Company, Inc., The, (a subsidiary of Howard W. Sams & Co. Inc.) 4300 West 62nd Street, Indianapolis, Indiana 46268 and 3 West 57th Street, New York, N.Y. 10019 (trade editorial office). Biographies, history, travel, current affairs, popular science, novels and children's books.

*****Bowker (R. R.) Co.,** 1180 Avenue of the Americas, New York City, N.Y. 10036. *T.* LT1–8800. Bibliographies and tools for the book trade and library world.

*****Braziller, George, Inc.** (1954), 1 Park Avenue, New York, N.Y. 10016. *T.* (212) 889–5900. Philosophy, science, art, architecture, history, fiction, environment, ecology.

*****Cambridge University Press (American branch),** 32 East 57th Street, New York, N.Y. 10022. *T.* (212) 688–8885.

Collier-Macmillan International, 866 Third Avenue, New York, N.Y. 10022. *Cable address:* Pachamac, N.Y. In *London:* Collier-Macmillan Limited, 10 South Audley Street, W.1. *T.* 01–493 5511. *Philippines:* Collier-Macmillan International, P.O. Box 686, Makati, Rizal D-708, Philippines; *Australia:* Collier-Macmillan Australia, 137 Clarence Street, Sydney, N.S.W.; *Canada:* Collier-Macmillan (Canada) Ltd., 1125 B Leslie Street, Don Mills, and Galt, Ontario; *Mexico:* Collier-Macmillan de Mexico, Mariano Escobedo 218, Mexico, D.F. *South Africa:* Collier-Macmillan South Africa (Pty) Ltd., 93 Dekorte, Braamfontein, Johannesburg. Publishers of Collier's Encyclopaedia, Harvard Classics, Collier's Junior Classics, Macmillan text and reference books, paper-backs (Collier Books).

Collins (Wm.), Sons & Co., Ltd., 215 Park Avenue South, New York 10003. *T.* 212–GR3 6110. Bible publishers, general literature, reference books. Head Office: 14 St. James's Place, London, S.W.1.

*****Columbia University Press,** 440 West 110th Street, New York, N.Y. 10025. *T.* (212) UN5 2000. L.H.: 70 Great Russell Street, W.C.1. Scholarly work in all fields and serious non-fiction of more general interest.

*****Concordia Publishing House** (1869), 3558 S. Jefferson Avenue, St. Louis, Mo. 63118. *T.* 314–664 7000. Religious textbooks, prayer books, etc. Stories and articles for *This Day,* a family magazine, used. Free-lance artists' work used.

*****Cornell University Press** (including **Comstock Publishing Associates**) (1869), 124 Roberts Place, Ithaca, New York 14850. *T.* (607) AR3–5155. *University Publisher:* Roger Howley. Text, trade and reference books. *Agents Overseas:* IBEG, 2–4 Brook Street, London W1Y 1AA.

Coward-McCann, Inc., 200 Madison Avenue, New York, N.Y. 10016. *T.* 212-883 5500. *Cables:* Cowmacann, N.Y. *President:* John J. Geoghegan. *Executive Editor:* Ellis Amburn. *Senior Editor:* Patricia Soliman. *Editor:* David S. Hull. *Associate Editor:* Joe Le Sueur. *V.P. Juvenile Dept. & Editorial Director:* Ferdinand N. Monjo, *Secretary and Executive Editor:* Miss Margaret Frith. General publishers. Fiction, juveniles, religion, biography, mystery, history.

Creative Home Library (Consumer Book Division, Meredith Corporation), 250 Park Avenue New York, New York 10017. *T.* 212–YU6–8700. Publishes non-fiction. Publisher suggests outline be submitted first. Address manuscripts and/or materials to the above address, attention: Charles Byrne.

Criterion Books, 257 Park Avenue South, New York, N.Y. 10010. *Editor:* Catherine Reisman. General fiction and juveniles.

*****Crowell, Thomas Y., Co.** (1834), 201 Park Avenue South, New York 10003. *T.* 212–777 2600. Non-fiction, juvenile, reference, college and secondary school texts and audio-visual materials.

*Crown Publishers Inc., 419 Park Avenue South, New York, N.Y. 10016. *T.* MU5–8550. *President:* Nat Wartels. *Editor-in-Chief:* Herbert Michelman. *Senior Editors:* Millen Brand, David McDowell, Nick Lyons. General fiction and non-fiction, illustrated books.

*David McKay Co., Inc., 750 Third Avenue, New York, N.Y. 10017. *T.* MO1–1700. *T.A.* Davmacay. *President and Editor-in-Chief:* Kennett L. Rawson. General fiction, nonfiction, juveniles, reference books, foreign language manuals and dictionaries, educational books.

Dial Press, The, a division of Dell Publishing Co., Inc, 750 Third Avenue, New York 10017. General fiction, non-fiction and juveniles.

*Dodd, Mead & Co. Inc., 79 Madison Avenue, New York, N.Y. 10016. *T.* 685–6464. Fiction, children's books, history, biography, art, belles-lettres, college textbooks, etc. A leaning toward biography, travel, fiction of a permanent kind, mystery stories, and juveniles.

*Doubleday & Company, Inc., 277 Park Avenue, New York 10017. *T.A.* Doubday, New York. L.H.: 100 Wigmore Street, W.1. *T.* 01–935 1269. Trade, juveniles and crime.

*Dutton (E. P.) & Co., Inc., 201 Park Avenue South, New York, N.Y. 10003. *T.* 212 674–5900. General publishers. General non-fiction of all kinds, including biographies, adventure, history, travel; fiction, mysteries, juveniles, paperbacks.

Farrar, Straus & Giroux, Inc. (incorporating Octagon Books and The Noonday Press—paperbacks), 19 Union Square West, New York City, N.Y. 10003. General publishers.

French (Samuel) Inc., 25 West 45th Street, New York, N.Y. 10036. *T.* 212–582–4700, and 7623 Sunset Boulevard, Hollywood, California 90046. Play publishers and author's representatives (dramatic).

*Grosset & Dunlap, Inc., 51 Madison Avenue, New York, N.Y. 10010. *T.* 212 MU9–9200. Adult non-fiction, juveniles, popular reference books, children's picture books, series books, activity books, and religious books.

Harcourt Brace Jovanovich, Inc. (1919), 757 Third Avenue, New York, N.Y. 10017 *T.* 212–572–5000. *President:* William Jovanovich. U.K. office: 7 Ros Crescent, Cambridge. General, textbook and educational tests publishers. Fiction, biography, travel, juveniles, poetry, current events, history.

*Harper & Row, Publishers (1817), 49 East 33rd Street, New York, N.Y. 10016, *T.* 889 7500. *Cable Address:* Harpsam, N.Y. London Office: 28 Tavistock Street, London WC2E 7PN. Fiction, history, biography, poetry, science, travel juveniles, educational, business, technical, medical and religious.

*Harvard University Press, 79 Garden Street, Cambridge, Mass. 02138. *T.* (617) 495–2600.

*Hawthorn Books, Inc., (1952), 70 Fifth Avenue, New York, N.Y. 10011. General non-fiction of permanent value. *Vice-President and Editorial Director:* Paul Fargis. *European Representative:* Feffer and Simons, Inc.

Heath (D.C.) and Co., a division of Raytheon Education Co., 125 Spring Street, Lexington, Mass. 02173. *T.* (617) 862–6650. U.K.: D. C. Heath & Co., c/o 1 Westmead, Farnborough, Hants.

Hewitt House, Old Tappan, New Jersey 07675. *T.* 201–768 8060. Significant family-centered reading.

*Holt, Rinehart and Winston, Inc. (1866), 383 Madison Avenue, New York, N.Y. 10017. *T.* MU8 9100. A subsidiary of **C.B.S.** General publishers. Fiction, history, biography, etc.; college and school textbooks of all kinds; children's; technical; reference; religious; dictionaries. Publishes books formerly published by Dryden Press, Henry Holt & Co., Rinehart & Co., and **The John C. Winston Co.** L.H.: Holt, Rinehart & Winston Ltd., 120 Golden Lane, E.C.1. *T.* 01–253 0855. *Telex:* 25376.

*Houghton Mifflin Company (1832), 2 Park Street, Boston, Mass. 02107. Fiction, biography, history, works of general interest of all kinds, both adult and juvenile, also school and college textbooks in all departments, and standardised tests. Best *length:* 75,000–180,000 words; juveniles, any reasonable length.

*John Day Company, Inc. The, 257 Park Avenue South, New York, N.Y. 10010. *T.* 212–533–9000. *Cable address:* Daypublish, N.Y. Fiction, non-fiction, juveniles.

*Julian Messner, (Division of Simon & Schuster, Inc.), 1 West 39th Street, New York 10018. General non-fiction, fiction, biographies, for ages 8 through the teens.

*Knopf (Alfred A.) Inc. (1915), a division of Random House, Inc., 201 East 50th Street, New York, N.Y. 10022. *T.* 212 751–2600. T.A. Knopf, New York. General literature, fiction, belles-lettres, poetry, drama, sociology, politics, history, etc.

*Lippincott (J. B.) Co. (1792), East Washington Square, Philadelphia, Pa. 19105. *T.* 215–WA5 4100. *Cable:* Lippcott, Phila., and New York office (Adult and Juvenile Trade Editorial Depts.), 521 Fifth Avenue, New York. 10017. *T.* 212 MU7–3980. All classes of literature. Full-length fiction of all descriptions, also biography, juveniles, and other forms of general literature. Religious books, educational textbooks and medical and nursing books and and journals. Bibles published by wholly-owned subsidiary, **A. J. Holman Company** (1801), East Washington Square, Philadelphia, Pa. 19105. *T.* 215 WA5–4100.

*Little, Brown and Company, 34 Beacon Street, Boston, Mass. 02106. *T.* 617 227–0730. *Cable:* Brownlit, Boston. General literature, especially fiction, biography, history, books for boys and girls as well as college, law and medical books. Also publish *Atlantic Monthly Press Books* in association with The Atlantic Monthly Company.

Lothrop, Lee & Shephard Co., Inc. (1859), a division of William Morrow & Co 105 Madison New York, N.Y. 10016. *T.* 212–889–3050. *General Manager:* Mrs. Edna Barth. Children's books only.

*McGraw-Hill Book Co., 330 West 42nd Street, New York, N.Y. 10036. Specialising in textbooks, laboratory manuals and technical and reference books in the fields of pure and applied sciences, technology and engineering, medicine and nursing, economics and business, politics, psychology and sociology, as well as film and film strips. Trade Book Department: specialising in books of interest to the general reader: fiction and non-fiction and juveniles. These materials also available from McGraw-Hill Publishing Co., Ltd., McGraw-Hill House, Maidenhead, England, and McGraw-Hill Company of Canada, 330 Progress Avenue, Scarborough, Ontario.

*Macrae Smith Co., 225 South 15th Street, Philadelphia, Pa. 19102. *T.* KI5–4270. Adult and juvenile ages 6 and up. Fiction and general non-fiction. No poetry or textbooks. Send manuscript.

Morehouse-Barlow Co. Inc., 14 East 41st Street, New York, N.Y. 10017. *T.* 212–532 4350. *President:* Ronald C. Barlow. *Vice-President* and *Editor:* E. Allen Kelley. *Managing Editor:* John Hammond. *Production Editor:* John S. Karpik. *Curriculum Editor:* Margaret L. Sheriff. Religious books, juveniles, secondary level texts.

*Morrow (William) & Co., Inc., 105 Madison Avenue, New York, N.Y. 10016. J. Lawrence Hughes (President), John C. Willey (Editor-in-Chief), Constance Epstein (Juvenile Editor). General literature, fiction, and juveniles. Interested in works dealing with American and foreign life and history. Royalty.

Nelson (Thomas) & Sons (1854), Copewood and Davis Streets, Camden, New Jersey 08103. *T.* 609–365–6550. *New York Office (Juvenile editorial and Promotion):* 250 Park Avenue, New York, N.Y. 10017. *T.* 212–697–5573. Publishers of Bibles, juveniles, religious, non-fiction.

*Norton (W. W.) & Company, Inc., 55 Fifth Avenue, New York 10003. General non-fiction, music, boating, psychiatry, fiction, quality paper backs, college texts, science.

*Oxford University Press, Inc., 200 Madison Avenue, New York, N.Y. 10016. *T.* 212–679 7300. *Cables:* Frowde, New York. *President:* J. R. B. Brett-Smith. All non-fiction, Bibles, college textbooks, religion, medicals, technicals, music.

Pantheon Books, a division of Random House, Inc., 201 East 50th Street, New York, N.Y. 10022. *T.* PL 1–2600. Fiction, belles-lettres, translations, philosophy, history and art, and juvenile books.

*Pitman Publishing Corporation, 6 East 43rd Street, New York, N.Y. 10017. *T.* TN 7–7400. Business education, college, technical, arts and crafts, and general non-fiction.

*Praeger Publishers Inc., 111 Fourth Avenue, New York, N.Y. 10003. *T.* 254–4100. *T.A.* Prabooks, New York. George Aldor (President-Treasurer). International relations, history, military, political and social science, art, archaeology, architecture, reference, college texts. *London Office:* Pall Mall Press Ltd., 5 Cromwell Place, S.W.7.

Prentice-Hall, Inc. (1913), Englewood Cliffs, New Jersey 07632. *Overseas representation:* Prentice-Hall International, Inc., Durrants Hill Road, Hemel Hempstead, Hertfordshire. *T.* 0442–58531. *Cable:* Prenhall, Hemel, England. *Telex.* 82445. Text, technical and general non-fiction, business, selling and management books, juveniles; biographies and autobiographies. Free-lance artists' and designers' work used.

*Putnam's (G. P.) Sons, 200 Madison Avenue, New York, N.Y. 10016. *T.* 212–883–5500. *President:* Walter J. Minton, *Vice President and Treasurer:* Victor C. Thaller, *Secretary and Comptroller:* Robert Copp, *Vice-Presidents:* Arthur C. Fields, William Targ, William Thomas. Publications of books in all divisions of literature. They have a comprehensive list of works in history, economics, political science, natural science, and standard literature. Also an important group of fiction. One of the largest publishers of books for children of all ages.

*Rand McNally & Company, P.O. Box 7600, Chicago, Illinois 60680. *T.* (312) Cornelia 7–6868. Trade, school and college publications including juvenile and adult non-fiction, textbooks, maps, guides, atlases, globes; banking publications. *President:* Andrew McNally III.

*Random House, Inc., 201 East 50th Street, New York, N.Y. 10022. *T.* 212 PL 1–2600. General publishers.

Regnery (Henry) Co. (1947), 114 W. Illinois Street, Chicago, Illinois 60610. *T.* 527–3300. *President:* Harvey Plotnick. Fiction, non-fiction.

Reilly & Lee, a division of Henry Regnery Co., 114 West Illinois Street, Chicago Illinois 60610. *President:* Harvey Plotnick. Juvenile fiction and non-fiction.

Reinhold Publishing Corporation see Van Nostrand Reinhold Co. Inc.

Revell (Fleming H.) Co., Old Tappan, New Jersey 07675. *T.* 201 768–8060. Religious books.

Rinehart & Company, Inc., see Holt, Rinehart and Winston, Inc.

*Roy Publishers, Inc. (1942), 30 East 74th Street, New York 10021. *T.* 212 TR 9–5935. Well known before 1939 as the Warsaw publishing house Rój. General publishers.

*St. Martin's Press Inc., 175 Fifth Avenue, New York, N.Y. 10010. *T.* 674–5151. *T.A.* Saintmart, New York. General. *Associate Company* of Macmillan & Co. of London and representatives of non-medical books on list of Edward Arnold (Publishers) Ltd. in the U.S.A.

Scott (William R.) Inc., 333 Avenue of the Americas, New York, N.Y. 10014. John G. McCullough (Vice-President). Juveniles.

*Scribner's (Charles) Sons (1846), Scribner Building, 597 Fifth Avenue, New York, N.Y. 10017. L.H.: Charles Scribner's Sons, Ltd., 23 Bedford Square, W.C.1. General publishers of standard books in education, biography, history, economics, fiction, belles-lettres, juveniles, etc.

*Seabury Press (1951), 815 2nd Avenue, New York, N.Y. 10017. *T.* TN7-8282. *President:* John C. Goodbody. *Religious Book Editor:* Arthur R. Buckley. *Children's Books Editor:* James C. Giblin. Religious, juveniles, paperbacks.

*Sheed & Ward, Inc. (1933), 64 University Place, New York, N.Y. 10003. *T.* OR 4–8807. *Chairman:* F. J. Sheed. *President:* James F. Kane. Publishing from the Catholic viewpoint.

*Simon and Schuster, Trade Book Division, Simon and Schuster, Inc. (1924), 630 Fifth Avenue, Rockefeller Center, New York, N.Y. 10020. General fiction, biography, detective, humour, occasional novelty books.

*Stanford University Press, Stanford, California 94305. Scholarly non-fiction.

*Theatre Art Books, 333 Avenue of the Americas, New York, N.Y. 10014. *T.* 212–OR5-1815. *Director:* Robert M. MacGregor. *Assistant Directors:* George Zournas and Adelaide Moneta. *Consultant:* Rosamond Gilder. Successor to the book publishing department of Theatre Arts (1921–1948), and controls all books formerly published by the magazine. Theatre, dance and allied books—costume, materials, tailoring, etc., a few plays.

H

Tuttle (Charles E.), Co., Inc. (1949), Rutland, Vermont 05701, and Suido I-chome, 2–6 Bunkyo-ku, Tokyo, Japan. *T.* 811–7106–9. *T.A.* Tuttbooks, Tokyo. *President:* Charles E. Tuttle. Oriental art, culture, history, manners and customs, Americana. *Agents: England:* Prentice-Hall International, Inc., Durrants Hill Road, Hemel Hempstead, Herts. *Continent;* Boxerbooks, Inc., Limmatstrasse 111 Zurich 8031, Switzerland. *Canada:* M. G. Hurtig Booksellers Ltd., 10411 Jasper Avenue, Edmonton, Alberta. *Australia:* Paul Flesch & Co. Pty. Ltd., 259 Collins Street, Melbourne C 1. *New Zealand:* T. C. Lothian Pty. Ltd., 17 Galatos Street, P.O. Box 3661, Auckland. *South Africa, Rhodesia, Basutoland, Bechuanaland, Swaziland, Nyasaland:* Purnell & Sons (SA) Pty Ltd., P.O. Box 4501, Cape Town. *Central and South America, North Africa, Near East:* Feffer and Simons, Inc., 31 Union Square W., New York, N.Y. 1003, U.S.A. *Hong Kong:* M. Graham Brash & Son 105 Wing On Mansion, 26 Hankow Road (I/F), Kowloon, Hong Kong. *Malaysia & Brunei:* M. Graham Brash & Son, 36-C, Prinsep Street, Singapore 7. *The Philippines:* Far East Book Agency, Inc., P.O. Box 4322, Manila, R.P. *Thailand:* Safety Enterprises Co. Ltd., 103 Patpong Road, Bangkok.

*University of California Press, Berkeley, California 94720. Publishes scholarly books, books of general interest, series of scholarly monographs, and twelve scholarly journals. *Agent in England:* IBEG Ltd., 2–4 Brook Street, London W1Y 1AA.

*University of Chicago Press, 5750 Ellis Avenue, Chicago, Ill. 60637. *T.* 312 M1 3–0800. *New York Office:* 31 Union Square West, N.Y. 10003. *T.* (212) 675 3426. *London Office:* 126 Buckingham Palace Road, S.W.1. *T.* 01–730 9208. The Press publishes scholarly books and monographs, college textbooks, religious, medical and scientific books, general trade books and a number of scholarly journals.

*Vanguard Press, Inc., 424 Madison Avenue, New York, N.Y. 10017. *T.* Plaza 3–3906. *Cable:* Vangpress, N.Y. *Director:* Miss Evelyn Shrifte. General trade publishers, fiction, non-fiction and juveniles.

Van Nostrand Reinhold Co. (1848), 450 West 33rd Street, New York 10001. *London:* Van Nostrand Reinhold Co., Windsor House, 46 Victoria Street, S.W.1. Scientific and technical, text, reference, juvenile and non-fiction works in general.

*Viking Press, The (1925), 625 Madison Avenue, New York, N.Y. 10022. *T.* Plaza 5–4330. *President:* Thomas H. Guinzburg. *Financial Vice-President:* Morton Levin. *Editorial Director of Senior Trade Division:* Alan D. Williams. *Senior Consulting Editors:* Marshall Best and Malcolm Cowley. *Senior Editors:* Corlies Smith and Elisabeth N. Sifton. General books, fiction, non-fiction, juveniles, biography, sociology, poetry, art, travel, Studio Books, Viking Portable Library, Viking Compass Books, Viking Junior Books, Seafarer.

*Walck (Henry Z.), Inc. (1958), 19 Union Square, W., New York, N.Y. 10003. *T.* 212-924–7650. *Editor-in-Chief:* Mrs. Patricia Cummings Lord. Juvenile books. *Agents Overseas:* Feffer & Simons Inc., and Oxford University Press, Toronto.

*Walker & Co. (1960), 720 Fifth Avenue, New York, N.Y. 10019. *T.* Columbus 5–3632. Samuel S. Walker Jr. (President). General publishers. Biography, history, religion, philosophy, natural history, travel and adventure, world affairs, criticism, fiction, detective fiction.

Warne (Frederick) & Co., Inc., 101 Fifth Avenue, New York, N.Y. 10003. *T.* 212 675–1151. L.H.: Chandos House, Bedford Street, W.C.2. Juvenile books, coloured picture books. All MSS. to be sent to London House.

Washburn (Ives) Inc., 750 Third Avenue, New York, N.Y. 10017. *T.* 212–661–1700. Fiction and non-fiction; biography, memoirs, politics, travel, juveniles. No textbooks.

*Watts (Franklin), Inc., a subsidiary of **Grolier Inc,** 845 Third Avenue, New York, N.Y. 10022. Adult non-fiction, juveniles.

*Westminster Press, Witherspoon Building, Philadelphia 19107. *T.* PE5–6722. Fiction, non-fiction, juveniles, and religious.

*Wiley (John) & Sons, Inc. (1807), *now incorporates* **Interscience Publishers Inc.,** 605 Third Avenue, New York City, N.Y. 10016. *Directors:* Edward P. Hamilton, W. Bradford Wiley, Charles B. Stoll, Eric S. Proskauer, Francis Lobdell, Andrew H. Neilly, Jr., Martin Matheson, William C. Eiseman, Robert L. Sproull, Kenneth R. Andrews, Charles H. Lieb, Antonie T. Knoppers. Scientific engineering, agricultural, business social science, and chemical books. Royalty basis. *Illustrations:* half-tones and line cuts. L.H.: John Wiley & Sons Ltd., Baffins Lane, Chichester, Sussex.

Winston (The John C.) Company. See Holt, Rinehart and Winston, Inc.

*World Publishing Company, a subsidiary of **Times Mirror Co., Ltd.,** 110 East 59th Street, New York, N.Y. 10022. *T.* 212–759 9500. *President:* Christopher J. H. M. Shaw. Bibles, dictionaries, adult trade, juveniles: informational and reference books, religious books.

SOUTH AFRICAN PUBLISHERS

Central News Agency, Ltd., Head Office: Box 1033, Johannesburg. Wholesale Distributing Depots throughout South Africa and Zambia and Rhodesia. Central News Agency (S.W.A.), Ltd., Windhoek. Swaziland News Agency Ltd., Mbabane. Publishers of books in English and Afrikaans. General and educational booksellers, publishers, stationers, newsagents, and general importers. London Office: Gordon & Gotch, Ltd., 75–79 Farringdon Street, E.C.4.

Collins (William), (Africa) (Pty) Ltd., Pallstate House, 51 Commissioner Street, Johannesburg (P.O. Box 8879). *T.* 838 2147. *Cables:* Fontana, Johannesburg. General publications, fiction, reference books, Bibles, juveniles, and school textbooks.

Heinemann & Cassell S.A. (Pty.) Ltd., P.O. Box 11190, Johannesburg. *T.* 22–0443. *Cables:* Bestbooks.

Juta & Company, Ltd., Cape Town and Johannesburg. Educational and legal publishers. General and educational booksellers and importers. Established 1853.

Longman Southern Africa (Pty.) Ltd., P.O. Box 1616, Vrystaat Street, Paarden Eiland, Cape Town.

Lovedale Press, Lovedale, Cape Province. Missionary and African vernacular publications.

Macmillan South Africa (Publishers) (Pty) Ltd., Total Centre, Jorissen Street, Braamfontein, Johannesburg. (P.O. Box 23134, Joubert Park.) *T.* 724–3364. Publishers of academic educational and general books, as well as those of South African interest.

Maskew Miller Ltd., 7–11 Burg Street, Cape Town. Educational and genera publishers and booksellers; stationers; dealers in prints and artists' materials.

Oxford University Press Southern African Branch, Jon Stallworthy, *General Manager.* Thibault House, Thibault Square, Cape Town. *Postal address:* Box 1141, Cape Town. 69 Walter Wise Building, 50 Joubert Street, Johannesburg. *Postal address:* P.O. Box 10413, Johannesburg. *Cables:* Oxonian, Cape Town, or Oxonian, Johannesburg. *T.:* Cape Town 41–0171; Johannesburg 22–2621.

Purnell & Sons (S.A.) (Pty) Ltd., Head Office: 70 Keerom Street, Cape Town. Branch Office: P.O. Box 10021, Johannesburg. *T.A.* "Purprint." *Chairman:* J. A. F. Wier. *Managing Director:* F. A. Low. General and Juvenile, and stockists for the Purnell Group, England.

Purnell Publications (Pty), Ltd., Head Office: 70 Keerom Street, Cape Town. Branch Office: P.O. Box 10021, Johannesburg. *T.A.* "Purprint." *Chairman:* J. A. F. Wier. *Managing Director:* F. A. Low. Magazine Publishers, books of South African interest and Juveniles.

Shuter and Shooter (Pty.), Ltd. (1925), Church Street, Pietermaritzburg, Natal. *T.* 28121. *T.A.* Shushoo. *Directors:* F. B. Oscroft, D. M. Craib, H. Lanzer, C. A. Roy, K. A. Stewart, W. N. Vorster, R. J. Watkinson, L. E. Wyatt.

Timmins (Howard B.) (Pty.) Ltd., (1937), 68 Shortmarket Street, Cape Town. P.O. Box 94, Cape Town. *T.* 411228, 31485. *T.A.* Composite, Cape Town. General South African interest, travel, biography, gardening, history. Represented by Bailey Bros. & Swinfen.

Van Schaik (J. L.) (1914), Pretoria, South Africa. (P.O. Box 724.) Publishers of books in English, Afrikaans and Bantu languages. Specialists in Afrikaans books.

Winchester Press (1967), P.O. Box 10921, Johannesburg. *T.* 42–8789 and 836–5802. *Directors:* Guy Winchester-Gould, Pamela Winchester-Gould. Travel, Natural history, educational and books of South African interest.

Witwatersrand University Press, Jan Smuts Avenue, Johannesburg, South Africa.

BOOK CLUBS

A book club supplies its subscribing members, usually monthly, with its chosen book at less than the bookshop price of the bookshop edition, and gives the opportunity for this to be exchanged for an alternate choice. Members undertake to purchase a minimum number of books in a club's programme of publication over the period covered by their subscription. The bargain appeal of the clubs is made possible by the guaranteed circulation of their choices, which in the case of a successful club can be very large indeed.

Until 1968 no book club edition could be issued until one year after a book's initial publication; this rule has now been relaxed to allow publication of a club edition at the same time as the publisher's edition for the bookshops, and several *'simultaneous clubs'* have been set up. These are permitted to offer their choices and alternate choices to members at up to 25% less than the published price of the bookshop edition, membership being limited to the United Kingdom and Eire.

The majority of book clubs are still *reprint clubs*, producing for their members reprinted club editions of books which have been published for a year or more, and offering these usually at appreciably lower prices than 25% below the bookshop price.

The author's remuneration is normally in one payment on a royalty basis in respect of the number of copies sold of the club edition, and in some cases the author can obtain before publication a guarantee of a minimum figure.

Adventurers Club, The, Heron Books Ltd., 18 St Ann's Crescent, London, S.W.18.

Book Club, The, W. & G. Foyle Ltd., 121 Charing Cross Road, London, WC2H 0EB. *T.* 01-437 5660.

Bookplan Ltd., 359 Upper Richmond Road West, London, S.W.14. *T.* 01-878 1284.

Business Leaders Book Club, Heron Books Ltd., 18 St. Ann's Crescent, London, S.W.18.

Catholic Book Club, W. & G. Foyle Ltd.

Children's Book Club, W. & G. Foyle Ltd.

Collectors Edition Book Club, Heron Books.

Companion Book Club, Odhams Mail Order Department, 42 The Centre, Feltham, Middx.

Cookery Book Club, The, B.P.C. Publishing Ltd., 49–50 Poland Street, London, W1A 2LG. *T.* 01-437 0686.

Country Book Club, Ltd., Readers Union Ltd., 10 Bedford Street, London, W.C.2.

Garden Book Club, W. & G. Foyle Ltd.

* Publishes the Club Edition simultaneously with the Trade Edition.

*History Book Club, B.P.C. Publishing Ltd.

*Literary Guild, The, Book Club Associates, 9 Grape Street, London WC2H 8DT. *T.* 01-240 1054.

Merlin Book Club, Merlin Press Ltd., 11 Fitzroy Square, London, W1P 5HQ.

Mystery Book Guild, Heron Books Ltd.

Quality Book Club, W. & G. Foyle Ltd.

Readers Union Ltd., David & Charles (Publishers) Ltd., South Devon House, Railway Station, Newton Abbot, Devon.

Romance Book Club, W. & G. Foyle Ltd.

SCM Book Club, Student Christian Movement Press Ltd., 56-58 Bloomsbury Street, London, WC1B 3QX. *T.* 01-636 3841.

Science Fiction Book Club, Readers Union Ltd.

Scientific Book Club, W. & G. Foyle Ltd.

Sophisticated Book Club, Town Bookshop, Enfield, Middlesex.

Sportsman Book Club, Readers Union Ltd.

Subscriber Book Service, Heron Books Ltd.

Thriller Book Club, W. & G. Foyle Ltd.

Travel Book Club, W. & G. Foyle Ltd.

Valentine Romance Club, Heron Books Ltd.

Western Book Club, W. & G. Foyle Ltd.

World Books, Book Club Associates.

* Publishes the Club Edition simultaneously with the Trade Edition.

MUSIC PUBLISHERS

BRITISH MUSIC PUBLISHERS

NOTE.—Copyright in musical compositions comprises: (a) the right of publication in print and sale of printed copies; (b) the right of public performance, and (c) the right to use the work for the purpose of making gramophone records, sound films or other similar contrivances. The musical composer should bear that in mind when entering into an agreement for the publication of his work.

Mr. Rutland Boughton's warning to amateurs given many years ago, still stands. He said that amateurs, "like the more hardened professional composers, find pleasure in seeing their musical thoughts in print. Because of that human weakness they become the prey of tenth-rate publishers, who offer to issue their music for them (however poor and ineffective it may be) *if they will pay for the privilege. If a piece of music is worth publishing a publisher will be willing to pay for it in cash or royalty*." Music publishers requiring work for issue on cash or royalty terms no more advertise in the public press for music and lyrics than a first-class publisher of books advertises for MSS. on that basis.

The Publishers in the following list are all members of the Performing Right Society except those marked†. The list does not include all publisher-members of the Performing Right Society.

Lyrics without a musical setting are not accepted unless stated by individual firms.

Arcadia Music Publishing Co. Ltd., 10 Sherlock Mews, Baker Street, London, W1M 3RH *T.* 01–935 5469. Light orchestral.

†Arnold (E. J.) & Sons, Ltd. (1863), Butterley Street, Leeds LS10 1AX; also Edinburgh. *T.* Leeds 35541; Edinburgh Caledonian 7134. *T.A.* Arnold, Leeds, 10. *Directors:* E. M. Arnold, J. O. Arnold, T. H. Metson, F. H. Harrison, D. S. Howard, D. C. Hall. School music of all types.

Arnold (Edward) (Publishers) Ltd., music series taken over by Novello & Co., 1959.

Ascherberg, Hopwood & Crew, Ltd. (1906), 50 New Bond Street, London, W1A 2BR. *T.* 01–629 7600. Compositions submitted by writers of choral, orchestral, educational, and other music are considered for publication.

Ashdown (Edwin), Ltd. (1860), 19 Hanover Square, London W1A 4DR *T.* 01–629 1184. Educational, ballads, instrumental, pianoforte, organ, choral.

Banks & Son (Music) Ltd., Stonegate, York YO1 2AU. *T.* York 26397. Publishers of choral and educational pianoforte music.

Bayley & Ferguson, Ltd. (1884), 65 Berkeley Street, Glasgow C3. *T.* Central 7240. Accept for publication music, cantatas, sacred and secular, operettas, anthems, part-songs, etc.

Belwin-Mills Music Ltd., 20 Denmark Street, London, WC2H 8ND. *T.* 01–240 1745. Orchestral, instrumental, choral and vocal works by classical and contemporary composers, educational music, light orchestral music, music for military and brass bands and popular music; Music Minus One Records.

Boosey & Hawkes Music Publishers Ltd., 295 Regent Street, London W1A 1BR *T.* 01–580 2060. General and educational.

Bosworth & Co., Ltd. (1889), 14–18 Heddon Street, W.1. *T.* 01–734 4961, 0475. Orchestral, church, educational, pianoforte, violin and part-songs.

Bourne Music Ltd., 34–36 Maddox Street, London, W1R 9PD. *T.* 01–493 6412, 6583. Popular and educational music.

British & Continental Music Agencies Ltd., 8 Horse and Dolphin Yard, London W1V 7LG. *T.* 01–437 3342. Sole agents for Breitkopf & Härtel, Friedrich Hofmeister, Edition Tonos, Verlag Neue Musik, all of Germany. Classical, serious and educational music.

Campbell, Connelly & Co., Ltd., 10 Denmark Street, W.C.2. *T.* 01–836 1653. General and popular.

Cary (L. J.) & Co. Ltd., 50 New Bond Street, London, W1A 2BR. *T.* 01–629 7600. Catholic Church music.

Chappell & Co., Ltd., 50 New Bond Street, London, W.1; New York, Toronto, Sydney, Wellington (N.Z.), Paris, Amsterdam, Hamburg, Brussels, Milan, Zurich, Stockholm, Madrid and Johannesburg. *T.* 01–629 7600. Always willing to consider MSS. Classical, standard and popular music.

Chester (J. & W.), Ltd. (1860), Eagle Court, London, EC1M 5QD. *T.* 01–253 6947–8 and 253 6276–7. *T.A.* Guarnerius, London, E.C.1. Concert and educational works.

Cramer (J. B.) & Co., Ltd. (1824), 99 St. Martin's Lane, London, WC2N 4BA. *T.* 01–240 1612. General and educational.

Curwen (J.) & Sons, Ltd., 29 Maiden Lane, London, WC2E 7JX. *T.* 01–240 1666–7–8. Music for schools. Educational music. English songs, choral, instrumental, orchestra, and Church music. Always glad to consider MSS.

Dash Music Co., Ltd., 10 Denmark Street, London, W.C.2. *T.* 01–836 1653. Popular music.

De Wolfe Ltd., 80–82 Wardour Street, London W1V 3LF. *T.* 01–437 4933–4. Symphonic recorded orchestral (English and foreign). Comprehensive library of recorded music on disc and tape.

Dix, Ltd. (1922), 64 Dean Street, London, W1V 6AU. *T.* 01–437 9336. Principally light music.

Elizabethan Music Co. Ltd., 54 Greek Street, London, W1V 6ED. *T.* 01–734 7111–3. Popular.

Elkin & Co. Ltd. (1903), 27 Soho Square, London W1V 6BR. *T.* 01–437 1222. Publish vocal, choral and instrumental music by contemporary British and classical composers. Specialise in educational music.

Enoch & Sons (1869), 19 Hanover Square, London W1A 4DR *T.* 01–629 1184. Educational, ballads, instrumental, pianoforte, choral, organ.

Faber Music Ltd. (1966), 38 Russell Square, London, WC1B 5DA. (Subsidiary of Faber & Faber Ltd (1929). *T.* 01–636 9543 (6 lines). *T.A.* Fabbaf, London, W.C.1. A general list of the highest quality, comprising both old and new music. Special interest in serious and progressive educational materials.

Fairfield Music Co., Ltd., 27 Soho Square, London W1V 6BR. *T.* 01–437 1222. Contemporary orchestral, instrumental, chamber and film music.

Feldman (B.) & Co., Ltd., 64 Dean Street, London, W1V 6AU. *T.* 01–437 9336. *T.A.* Humfriv, Wesdo, London. Popular and semi-classical.

Forsyth Bros., Ltd. (1873), 190 Grays Inn Road, London, W.C.1. *T.* 01–837 4768. Educational piano and instrumental music. Modern teaching material.

Francis, Day & Hunter, Ltd. (1877), 138–140 Charing Cross Road, WC2H 0LD. *T.* 01–836 9351–5. Publishers of songs, pianoforte, tutors, classical works, solos, tutors, orchestral compositions, musical plays, books of patter stories, humorous recitations, recorded music, etc. Not open to print music for amateurs.

Freeman, H., & Co., 64 Dean Street, London, W1V 6AU. *T.* 01–437 9336. Educational piano music.

Galliard Limited, Queen Anne's Road, Great Yarmouth, Norfolk. *T.* Gt. Yarmouth 4281–2. Editorial Office: *T.* 01–636 2967. Incorporating the catalogues of Augener, Weekes, Joseph Williams, Delrieu (Nice), and Galaxy (New York). General publishers of concert, education, folk and Church music, text-books, etc.

Glocken Verlag Ltd. (1946), 10–16 Rathbone Street, London, W1P 2BJ *T.* 01–580 2827. *Cables:* Operetta, London, W.1. *Directors:* Otto Blau, Francis P. Lehár, F. Benson, R. M. Toeman. Musical works by Franz Lehar.

Goodwin & Tabb, Ltd. (1750), 36–38 Dean Street, London W1V 6LU. *T.* 01–437 1574–5. Vocal, choral and orchestral librarians.

†Gwynn (The) Publishing Co. (1937), Llangollen, North Wales. *T.* Llangollen 2209. Publishers of Welsh Educational and International Choral Music. Official music publishers to The Welsh Folk Song Society, The Welsh Folk Dance Society, the Court of the Welsh National Eisteddfod and the Council of the International Musical Eisteddfod.

Hammond (A.) & Co. (1847), 11 Lancashire Court, New Bond Street, London W1Y 0NJ. *T.* 01–629 1984. Educational.

Harris, The (Frederick) Music Co., Ltd. *Sole Agents:* Alfred Lengnick & Co. Ltd., Purley Oaks Studios, 421A Brighton Road, South Croydon, CR2 6YR. *T.* 01–660 7646; and at Oakville, Ontario. Speciality, artistic songs, piano and educational music.

Hinrichsen Edition, Ltd. (1938), Bach House, 10–12 Baches Street, London, N1 6DN. *T.* 01–253 1638–9. *T.A.* Musipeters, London. Peters Edition, Hinrichsen Edition, Collection Litolff. Classical and modern (piano, organ, other instrumental, vocal, choir and brass band) music. British representatives of American, Dutch, German and Italian music publishers.

Hughes & Son, Publishers, Ltd. (1820), 29 Rivulet Road, Wrexham. T. 4340. Welsh music, school books, and compositions relating to Wales.

Kalmus, Alfred, A., Ltd., 2–3 Fareham Street, Dean Street, London, W1V 4DU *T.* 01–437 5203–4-5. Sole Representatives of Universal Edition A.G., Vienna, Universal Edition (London) Ltd., Universal Edition A.G., Zurich, Universal Edition S.P.A. Milan, Palestrina Complete Edition, Theodore Presser Co., U.S.A., Lea Pocket Scores, U.S.A., Doblinger Edition, Vienna, Edwin Kalmus, U.S.A., Hargail Music Inc., U.S.A. International Music Co., U.S.A., Polish Editions, Cracow (complete Chopin-Paderewsky), Supraphon, Prague, Harmonia Uitgave, Hilversum, Pro-Art, U.S.A. Serious music of all types.

Keith Prowse Music Publishing Co., Ltd., 21 Denmark Street, WC2H 8NE. *T.* 01–836 5501 and 3856. Music by various authors and composers.

Leeds Music Ltd., 139 Piccadilly, London, W1V 9FH *T.* 01–629 7211.

Lengnick (Alfred) & Co., Ltd. (1892), Purley Oaks Studios, 421A Brighton Road, South Croydon, CR2 6YR *T.* 01–660 7646. Music publishers and importers. Publishers of Brahms' and Dvorak's works. Specialise in educational music, leading publishers of English contemporary music. Always ready to consider MSS. of any type. Agents for CeBeDeM (Brussels); Donemus (Amsterdam), and Fredk Harris (Ontario).

Leonard, Gould & Bolttler, 99 St. Martin's Lane, London, W.C.2. *T.* 01–240 1612. General and educational.

Minch Music Ltd., 54 Greek Street, London, W1V 6ED *T.* 01–734 7111–3.

Novello & Co., Ltd. (1811), 27 Soho Square, London W1V 6BR. *T.* 01–437 1222. Classical and modern orchestral, instrumental, vocal and choral music, church music, school and educational music, books and primers.

Octava Music Co. Ltd., (1938), 10–16 Rathbone Street, London, W1P 2BJ *T.* 01–580 2827. *Cables:* Operetta, London, W.1.

Oxford University Press (Oxford University Press established 1478. Music Dept. constituted 1923). Music Department, 44 Conduit Street, London, W1R 0DE. *T.* 01–734 5364–6. Orchestral, instrumental, operatic, choral, vocal works, church and organ music by old and modern composers, educational music, courses, and books on music.

Paterson's Publications, Ltd., 38 Wigmore Street, London, W1H 0EX. *T.* 01–935 3551. Pianoforte, vocal, choral, orchestral, instrumental, educational and bagpipe music.

Paxton (W.) & Co., Ltd., 36–38 Dean Street, London, W1V 6EP. *T.* 01–437 4801–2–3. Branch at 30 Old Compton Street, London, W.1. *T.* 01–437 7042–3. Choral, organ, piano, vocal, orchestral, piano accordion, percussion band, recorder, plays and educational music and records for schools. All publishers' music stocked.

Peter Maurice Music Co. Ltd., The, 21 Denmark Street, London, WC2H 8NE. *T.* 01–836 5501 and 3856. Popular music.

Pickwick Music, Ltd., 139 Piccadilly, London, W1V 9FH. *T.* 01–629 7211.

Reynolds Music, 21 Demark Street, London, WC2H 8NE. *T.* 01–836 5501 and 3856. Songs, musical material and sketches for T.V. and Stage.

Ricordi (G.) & Co. (London), Ltd. (1808), The Bury, Church Street, Chesham, Bucks. *T.* Chesham 3311 and 4427. *T.A.* Ricordi, Chesham. *Professional Dept:* 38 Wigmore Street, London, W1H 9DF. *T.* 01–935 2473. Publishers of Italian operas, music for piano, classical and contemporary, operatic arias, songs, choral large scale works and part songs for all voices, orchestral work, classical and contemporary, instrumental, string, woodwind, brass tutors, exercises, etc., guitar music of all types.

Saville (J.) & Co., Ltd., Audley House, 9 North Audley Street, London, W1Y 2EU. *T.* 01–629 6506. School music.

Schott & Co., Ltd. (1839), 48 Great Marlborough Street, W1V 2BN. *T.* 01–437 1246. Music of a serious and educational nature is considered including music for recorders, percussion and school orchestra.

Smith, R., & Co. Ltd. (1857), 210 Strand, London, WC2R 1AP. *T.* 01–353 1166.

†Sphemusations, Babbacombe Wray, Guestland Road, Cary Park, Torquay, S. Devon. *T.* Torquay 37565. Serious music, brass band, choral, instrumental and educational. Records of modern works.

Stainer & Bell, Ltd., Lesbourne Road, Reigate, Surrey. *T.* Reigate 46791. General music publishers, specialising in English historical music.

Sun Music Publishing Co., Ltd., 138 Charing Cross Road, WC2H 0LD. *T.* 01–836 9351. Light popular music.

Swan & Co. (Music Publishers), Ltd., 10 Sherlock Mews, Baker Street, London W1M 3RH *T.* 01–935 5469. Light orchestral.

Sylvester Music Co., Ltd., 80–82 Wardour Street, London, W1V 3LF. *T.* 01–437 4933–4. Popular and orchestral music. Comprehensive library of recorded music on disc and tape.

United Music Publishers, Ltd. (1932), 1 Montague Street, Russell Square, London, WC1B 5BS *T.* 01–636 5171–2. *General Manager:* Noel Ross Russell, A.M.B.I.M. Agents for the principal French music publishing houses and specialise in the sale of French, Spanish and other foreign music.

Universal Edition (London) Ltd., 2–3 Fareham Street, Dean Street, London, W1V 4DU *T.* 01–437 5203–4–5. Serious music of all types.

Victoria Music Publishing Co., Ltd., 52 Maddox Street, W1R 9PA *T.* 01–629 7600.

Warren & Phillips, Ltd. (1906), 190 Gray's Inn Road, London, WC1X 8EW. *T.* 01–837 4768. Mainly interested in educational music.

Weinberger (Josef), Ltd. (1885), 10–16 Rathbone Street, London, W1P 2BJ *T.* 01–580 2827 (4 lines). *Cables:* Operetta, London, W.1. *Directors:* O. Blau, R. Blau, S. Buchman, F. Benson, R. Toeman. Theatrical and music publishers.

Workers' Music Association, Ltd. (1936), 236 Westbourne Park Road, London, W.11. *T.* 01–727 7005. Music and song emphasising the social aspects of music.

Wright (Lawrence) Music Co., Ltd. (1908), 54 Greek Street, London W1V 6ED. *T.* 01–734 7111–3. Popular, light, orchestral, brass and military band, standard and educational. Ballads. Choral arrangements.

Year Book Press. *Proprietor:* Ascherberg, Hopwood and Crew, Ltd., *q.v.*

AMERICAN MUSIC PUBLISHERS

American Academy of Music, 1790 Broadway, New York, N.Y. 10019.

Ankerford Music Corporation, 1790 Broadway, New York, N.Y. 10019.

Boosey & Hawkes, Inc., 30 West 57th Street, New York, N.Y. 10019. Symphonic, opera, ballet, concert, and educational music.

Bourne Co., 136 West 52nd Street, New York, N.Y. 10019. *T.* CI 7–5500. Publishers of popular, standard, educational, production, and photo-play music.

Chappell & Co., Inc. 609 Fifth Avenue, New York, N.Y. 10017. *T.* (212) Plaza 2–4300. Agents for Chappell & Co., Ltd., London.

Church (John) Company, c/o Theodore Presser Co., Bryn Mawr, Pennsylvania 19010. Established 1854. Considers MSS. from composers of admitted abilities. Does not use or buy songs or lyrics unless with a musical setting. Publication at the firm's expense only.

Ditson (Oliver) Company, c/o Theodore Presser Co., Bryn Mawr, Pennsylvania 19010. Founded 1783: Established 1835. Considers MSS. from composers of admitted abilities. Does not use or buy songs or lyrics unless with a musical setting. Publication at the firm's expense only.

Elkan-Vogel, Inc., c/o Theodore Presser Co., Bryn Mawr, Pennsylvania 19010. Considers suitable MSS. from composers. Does not use or buy songs or lyrics unless with a musical setting. Publication at the firm's expense only.

Gray, H. W., Co., Inc., 159 East 48th Street, New York, N.Y. 10017. *T.* Plaza 5–4323. Choral music of all types and arrangements. Organ music, sacred songs.

Hinrichsen Edition, C. F. Peters Corporation, 373 Park Avenue South, New York, N.Y. 10016. *T.* 212 686–4147. Classical and contemporary music.

Lorenz Publishing Co., 501 East Third Street, Dayton, Ohio 45401. Considers for purchase anthems and church organ voluntaries, for which from £5 to £25 are paid, plus royalty payments based on sales. Accepts lyrics without musical setting; *payment:* from £3 to £5 per lyric.

Marks (Edward B.) Music Corporation (1894), 136 West 52nd Street, New York City, N.Y. 10019. Accepts only musical material from professional writers of reputation on a royalty basis. Publishes every type of music; classic, standard, popular, orchestral, educational, secular, sacred, band, organ, piano, etc. Distributors of many foreign publications.

Mercury Music Corporation, c/o Theodore Presser Co., Bryn Mawr, Pennsylvania 19010. Considers suitable MSS. from composers. Does not use or buy songs or lyrics unless with a musical setting. Publication at the firm's expense only.

Merion Music Company, c/o Theodore Presser Co., Bryn Mawr, Pennsylvania 19010. Established 1953. Considers MSS. from composers of admitted abilities. Does not use or buy songs or lyrics unless with a musical setting. Publication at the firm's expense only.

Mills Music, Inc., 1790 Broadway, New York, N.Y. 10019.

Peters, C. F., Corporation, 373 Park Avenue South, New York, N.Y. 10016. *T.* 212–686–4147. (Peters Edition, Hinrichsen Edition, Eulenburg Pocket Scores, and other European music publications, in U.S.A.)

Presser (Theodore) Co., Bryn Mawr, Pennsylvania 19010. Established 1883. Considers suitable MSS. from composers. Does not use or buy songs or lyrics unless with a musical setting. Publication at the firm's expense only.

Sacred Music Press, The, 501 East Third Street, Dayton, Ohio 45401. Division of Lorenz Publishing Co. *q.v.*

Summy-Birchard Company, 1834 Ridge Ave., Evanston, Illinois, 60204. *T.* 312 869–4700. *President:* David K. Sengstack. Publishers of music textbooks and educational music in the fields of piano, choral, instrumental.

Warner Bros. Music, 488 Madison Avenue, New York, N.Y. 10022. Includes the following companies: WB Music Corp., Warner–Tamerlane Publishing Corp., Harms, M. Witmark, Remick, Advanced, New World Music Corp., Pepamar Music Corp., Shubert Music Publishing Corp., Weill-Brecht-Harms Company Inc.

Wood (B. F.) Music Company, 1790 Broadway, New York, N.Y. 10019.

AGENTS

LITERARY AGENTS

MANY literary agents have a well-deserved reputation for their integrity in dealing with authors and publishers. There are, however, some discreditable and unsatisfactory agents and, in the absence of an established code of practice, a questionnaire has been circulated to agents in the British Isles with a view to providing writers with a more selective and more informative list than hitherto. The literary agents listed below readily completed this questionnaire and it is hoped that such information as the type of work handled and the commission charged will be of value to those who consult the Year Book.

It should be noted that none of the agents charge a fee for marketing or placing manuscripts but certain firms charge a reading fee which is refunded on acceptance of the material. All the agents in this list will suggest revision of worthwhile manuscripts where necessary, suggesting in the first instance that revision should be done by the author. In certain cases, an agency is prepared to recommend a qualified person not connected with their agency to undertake revision. In a few cases where agencies themselves are prepared to undertake revision, this fact is clearly stated. In their own interests writers are strongly recommended to think twice before agreeing to pay for revision. Some agents are prepared to give an author a report and advice on a MS. and they make an appropriate charge for this.

Literary agents exist to sell saleable material. It must be remembered that, while they are always looking for new writers and are often prepared to take immense pains with a writer whose work, in their opinion, shows potential quality or distinctive promise, agents do not exist to teach people how to write.

If a writer of some proven ability is contemplating using an agent, he is advised in his own interests to write a preliminary letter to ascertain whether the agent will consider him as a potential client. He should also enquire the agent's terms if they are not given in the entry in the following pages. Reputable agents do not accept work unless they consider it to be of a marketable standard, an author submitting work to an agent for the first time should therefore enclose return postage.

This list of literary agents does not purport to be exhaustive and, if any who are not included would like to receive a copy of the questionnaire, application should be made to the publishers.

Actac (Theatrical & Cinematic) Ltd. (1946). *Director:* Jimmy Wax. 16 Cadogan Lane, London, S.W.1. *T.* 01–235 2797. *T.A.* Lawax, London, S.W.1.

MSS. for theatre, films, television, sound broadcasting (10%). Will suggest revision if MS. is good enough. Works in conjunction with foreign agencies. No reading fee.

Adamastor Press and Literary Agency Ltd. (1961). *Directors:* Sydney Clouts, Marjorie Clouts. 6 Somerton Road, London, N.W.2. *T.* 01–452 8101. *T.A.* Storsta, London, N.W.2.

Full-length MSS. for book publication, magazine and newspaper offer. Terms on application. No reading fee.

Alpha Book Agency (1967). *Director:* P. H. Hargreaves. 1 Manor Wood Road, Purley, Surrey CR2 4LG. *T.* 01–660 7025.

Educational MSS only (home 10%, overseas 19%). No reading fee.

Stephen Aske (1929). *Proprietor:* A. S. Knight. Chansitor House, Chancery Lane, London, WC2A 1EL. *T.* 01–405 4123. *T.A.* Vigilaske, London, W.C.2.

Full-length MSS. (home 10%, overseas 20%). Short MSS. (home 15%, overseas 25%). Theatre, films, television, sound broadcasting (10%). U.S.A. representative: Jay Garon-Brooke Associates, 415 Central Park West, 17D, New York, N.Y. 10025. Works in conjunction with agents in most European countries, Japan and South America. No reading fee.

Authors' Alliance (1911). Mrs. Deborah Greenep, Hinton Woodlands, Bramdean, Alresford, Hants. *T.* Bramdean 236.

Full-length MSS. (home and overseas 10%). Theatre (10%), Films (10%), Television and sound broadcasting (10%). Represented in Europe and U.S.A. Does not accept MSS. for children's books, articles or short stories. No reading fee.

Curtis Brown Ltd. (1904). *Directors:* Hon. Michael Lambert (Chairman), Graham Watson (Managing), John Cushman (U.S.A.), Richard Odgers, Juliet O'Hea, Richard Simon. 13 King Street, Covent Garden, London, WC2E 8HU. *T.* 01–240 2488. *T.A.* Browncurt, London, W.C.2.

Agents for the negotiation in all markets of novels, general non-fiction and educational books, plays, films, television scripts. Commission – home 10%, U.S.A. 15%, overseas 19% including commission to foreign agent. Wholly owned subsidiaries: John Cushman Associates Inc., Room 1520, 25 West 43rd Street New York, N.Y. 10036. *T.* 212 MU 5–2052, and Curtis Brown (Australia) Pty. Ltd., 186 Liverpool Street, Darlinghurst, New South Wales 2010, Australia. *T.* 31–8301. No reading fee.

Christopher Busby and John Rose Ltd., (1970). *Directors:* Christopher Busby and John Rose. 76 New Oxford Street, London, WC1A 1EU. *T.* 01–580 1538–9. *T.A.* Rosebuz, London, W.C.1.

Full length and short MSS. (home 10%, abroad 20%, in U.S.A. 15% through sub-agents elsewhere, but all commission charges are by arrangement. Films, (15% for new writers, 10% for established writers), television, sound broadcasting (10%). Agency offers a complete range of pre-publication editorial services, coping with all forms of revision from advice to the author on re-writing to offering the services of professional and specialist ghost writers. Charges based on the amount of work required.

U.S.A.: Roslyn Targ Literary Agency, Inc., 325 East 57th Street, New York, N.Y. 10022.

Works with agencies throughout the world. No reading fee.

Miles Byrne (1942). *Directors:* Miles Byrne, Keith Byrne and T. Byrne. Embassy Theatre, Western Road, Hove, BN3 1AE Sussex. *T.* Brighton 735124.

Full-length MSS (home 10%, U.S.A. & other countries 15%, translations 19% of amount received). Theatre, film, television and sound broadcasting (home 10% abroad 19%). No poetry. Represented in most European countries, U.S.A., South America, Israel etc. No reading fee but return S.A.E. essential.

C and B (Theatre), a wholly-owned subsidiary of **Calder & Boyars Ltd., Publishers,** 18 Brewer Street, London W1R 4AS. *T.* 01–734 1985. *Directors:* J. M. Calder, Marion Boyars, Michael Hayes.

An agency handling the sale of dramatic rights to professional and amateur theatre companies, radio, television and film. No reading fee.

Christy & Moore Ltd. (1912). *Directors:* John Smith, E. M. Callaghan. 52 Floral Street, Covent Garden, London, WC2E 9DA. *T.* 01–240 0608. *T.A.* Chrismoore, London, W.C.2.

Full-length MSS. (home 10%, overseas 20%, American 10–15%). U.S.A. Associate: Bill Berger Associates Inc., 535 East 72nd Street, New York, N.Y. 10021. Works in conjunction with agents in most European countries, Japan and South America. No reading fee.

Jonathan Clowes Ltd. (1960). *Directors:* Jonathan Clowes, Veronica Silver, Donald Carroll, Enyd Clowes. 20 New Cavendish Street, London, W1A 3AH. *T.* 01–486 4929–0, 01–935 3969–0. *T.A.* Agenclow, London, W.1.

Full-length MSS. (home and overseas 10%). Theatre, films, television and sound broadcasting (10%). Provides help with revision of promising MS. free of charge. Works in association with agents in France, Italy, Germany and Scandinavia. No reading fee.

Elspeth Cochrane Agency (1967), *Director:* Miss Elspeth Cochrane, 31a Sloane Street, London, S.W.1. *T.* 01–235 5296.

Full-length and short MSS. (home and overseas 10%). Theatre, films, television, sound broadcasting (10%). No reading fee.

Rosica Colin Limited (1949). *Director:* Rosica Colin. 4 Hereford Square, London, S.W.7. *T.* 01–373 7678. *T.A.* Colrep, London, S.W.7.

All full-length MSS. (home 10%; overseas 15%). Theatre, films, television and sound broadcasting (10%). Works in conjunction with several agencies in U.S.A., most European countries and South America. No reading fee.

Donald Copeman Ltd. *Directors:* Donald Copeman, L. G. Turney, F.A.C.C.A., A.C.I.S. 157 Temple Chambers, Temple Avenue, London, EC4Y ODT. *T.* 01–353 1882.

Full-length MSS (home 10%, overseas, 20%). Non-fiction preferred. Film and television. No short stories. Revisions on promising material undertaken by experts. Agents in New York, Paris, etc. No reading fee.

Diana Crawfurd Ltd., (1970). *Directors:* E. W. E. Andrewes, D. Crawfurd. 5 King Street, Covent Garden, London, WC2E 8HN. *T.* 01–836 8653. *T.A.* Dianagram, London, W.C.2.

Full-length and short MSS. (home 10%; overseas 15%–20%). Theatre, films, television, sound broadcasting (10%). If MS. is sufficiently promising, will occasionally suggest revision. Works with agencies in most European countries. No reading fee.

Peter Crouch Plays Ltd. (1967)—in association with **Peter Crouch Ltd.** (1959). *Directors:* P. H. Crouch, S. A. Lemon. 5–6 Coventry Street, London, W.1. *T.* 01–437 0939 and 0930. *T.A.* Croucho London, W.1.

MSS: Films, Theatre, television, sound broadcasting (10%). No articles or short stories. Will advise on MSS if sufficiently promising. Deals through two agencies in U.S.A. and principal continental agencies. No reading fee.

Felix De Wolfe & Associates (1946). *Principal:* Felix de Wolfe. 61 Berkeley House, 15, Hay Hill, London, W1X 7LH *T.* 01–629 5713. *T.A.* Hayhill, London, W.1.

Theatre, films, television, sound broadcasting, fiction and non-fiction. Works in conjunction with many foreign agencies. No reading fee.

T.I.M. Enterprises (Literary). *Directors:* Clive Stanhope, John Satchell. 23 Haymarket, London, S.W.1. *T.* 01–839 6537.

Full-length and short MSS. (home 12½%, overseas 35%). Theatre, films, television, sound broadcasting (12½%). Office in U.S.A., and work is placed through several foreign agents. No reading fee.

Epoque Limited (1960). *Directors:* Noel Barber (Managing), V. J. Bell, Julian Phipps. 12–15 Bouverie Street, London, E.C.4. *T.* 01–353 5000. *Telex.* 23882. *T.A.* Bellepoque, London, E.C.4.

Full-length MSS. (home 15%, overseas 40%). Theatre, films, television, sound broadcasting (15%). Offices in U.S.A. and Paris.

John Farquharson Ltd. (1919). *Directors:* Innes Rose, George Greenfield, June Badcock. 15 Red Lion Square, London, WC1R 4QW. *T.* 01–242 4843–4–5. *T.A.* Jofachad, London, W.C.1.

Full-length and short MSS. (home 10%; overseas 19%, including commission to foreign agents). Films, television, sound broadcasting. U.S.A. Associate: Paul R. Reynolds Inc., 599 Fifth Avenue, New York, N.Y. 10017. Works in conjunction with agents in all European capitals. No reading fee.

Film Rights Ltd. (1932). *Directors:* John E. Hunter, D. M. Sims, Dorothy Mather, Maurice Lambert, Laurence Fitch. 113–117 Wardour Street, London, W1V 4EH. *T.* 01–437 7151.

Theatre, films, television and sound broadcasting (10%). Represented in U.S.A. and abroad. No reading fee.

Laurence Fitch Ltd. (1952) (incorporating The London Play Company) (1922). *Directors:* F. H. L. Fitch, L. Ruscombe-King. 113–117 Wardour Street, London, W.1. *T.* 01–437 7151. *Cables:* Playfitlon, London.

Theatre, films, television and sound broadcasting (10%). Also works with several agencies in New York and in Europe. No reading fee.

Fraser & Dunlop (Scripts) Ltd. (1959)—in association with Fraser & Dunlop Ltd. (1949). Kenneth Ewing, Jill Foster, Richard Wakeley. 91 Regent Street, London, W1R 8RU. *T.* 01–734 7311. *T.A.* Frasanlop, London.

Full-length MSS. (home 10%, overseas 10–20%, including any overseas agent's commission). Theatre, films, television and sound broadcasting (10%). Negotiates with several U.S. agencies. No reading fee.

Freelance Presentations Ltd. (1955). *Directors:* Michael A. Fenton, G. Fenton, John McCorquodale, S. McCorquodale. 155 Queen Victoria Street, London, EC4V 4EL. *T.* 01–236 5781–2–3.

Full-length MSS. (home 10%, overseas 15%), short MSS. (home and overseas 15%). Theatre, films, television, sound broadcasting (10%). If MS. requires revision will suggest someone to do it in special circumstances. Represented in U.S.A., Europe, Scandinavia. No reading fee.

J. F. Gibson's Literary Agency (1950). *Proprietor:* J. F. Gibson. *Secretary:* C. T. P. Hughes. *Editor:* Mrs. Freda Stock. 17 Southampton Place, London, WC1A 2AJ. *T.* 01–242 9637.

Welcomes fiction and non-fiction, short stories and outstanding features. Terms on a commission of sales only. Full-length MSS. (home 10%, overseas 15%). Short stories, features, etc. (home and overseas 15%). Theatre, film, television, sound broadcasting (10–15%). *Represented* throughout the world. No reading fees.

Eric Glass Ltd. (1932). *Directors:* Eric Glass, Blanche Glass, Janet Crowley, Barry J. Glass. 28 Berkeley Square, London, W1X 6HD *T.* 01–629 7162. *T.A.* Blancheric, London, W.1.

Full-length MSS. only (home 10%, overseas 20%). Theatre, films, television, and sound broadcasting (10%). Will occasionally recommend someone for revision of promising material if the author is unable to undertake it. No reading fee. Sole representatives of the French Society of Authors (Societé des Auteurs et Compositeurs Dramatiques).

J.A. Maxtone Graham Literary Agency (1963). 4 Pound Cottages, Streatley, Berkshire, RG8 9JH. *T.* 049–14–2487.

Specialist in articles, up to 5000 words, specifically written for the *American* magazine markets. Representation for established writers only. Commission, 10%. No reading fee.

Elaine Greene Ltd. (1962). *Directors:* Elaine Greene (U.S.A.), Peter Janson-Smith. *Secretary:* Kenneth Thomson. 42 Great Russell Street, London, WC1B 3PN. *T.* 01–636 6561. *T.A.* Peterlaine, London, W.C.1. (See also Peter Janson-Smith Ltd.).

Full-length and short MSS. (home and U.S.A. 10%; translation rights 20%); film, television, sound broadcasting (10%).

U.S.A. Associate: International Famous Agency, Inc., 1301 Avenue of the Americas, New York, N.Y. 10019. Works in conjunction with agencies in most European countries. No reading fees.

Plunket Greene (Writers) Ltd. (1968)—in association with Plunket Greene Ltd. (1952). *Directors:* T. Plunket Greene, Julian Belfrage, P. Rowland. 110 Jermyn Street, St. James's Square, London, S.W.1. *T.* 01–930 0811. *T.A.* Pluver London.

Full-length MSS. only (home 10% overseas maximum 20%, including any overseas agents commission). Theatre, films, television and sound broadcasting (home and overseas 10%). Representation in U.S.A. and Europe. All MSS. and correspondence to be sent to T. Plunkett Greene, Head of Literary Department. No reading fee.

Griffiths & Griffiths (1965). *Partners:* Lt. Col. W. N. Griffiths, E.R.D., Mrs M. M. Griffiths. The Flat, East Lodge, The Green, Frant, Nr. Tunbridge Wells. Kent.

Full length and short MSS (home 15%; overseas 15% to 20%). Will suggest revision of promising MSS. Works in conjunction with agents in Denmark, Italy, France and other countries abroad. No reading fee.

Hamric Literary Agency. See p. 248.

Robert Harben Literary Agency, 3 Church Vale, London, N2 9PD. *T.* 01–883 0141. Specialising in translation arrangements of English works into European languages (particularly German and Dutch), and vice versa.

Alec Harrison and Associates (1954). *Senior Partner:* Alec Harrison. 118 Fleet Street, London, E.C.4. *T.* 01–353 4484–5. *T.A.* Litalic, London, E.C.4. *Telex:* 264461.

Full-length MSS. (home 10%, overseas 19% where another agent is concerned). Short MSS. (home 15%, overseas 15%–25%). Films (10%), television and sound broadcasting (10% for series, 15% for single items).

"In the main, all the people we handle are professional writers who come to us on recommendation. The great bulk of the material we handle is non-fiction, such as educational books and autobiographies, which often have to be ghosted."

"Most of our work is commissioned. For syndication we work with literary agents in almost every country in the world." No reading fee.

Richard Hatton Ltd. (1954). *Directors:* Richard Hatton, Donald Bradley, Henry E. St. L. King. 17a Curzon Street, London, W1Y 7FE. *T.* 01–499 3601. *T.A.* Rephat, Piccy, London.

Theatre, films, television and sound broadcasting (10%). No reading fee.

Michael Hayes Literary Agency Ltd., The (1964). *Directors:* M. P. Hayes, M. C. Hayes. 9 Melbourne Court, 253 Cromwell Road, London, S.W.5. *T.* Fremantle 2634.

Full-length MSS. only (home 10%, overseas 15%). Theatre, films, television, sound broadcasting (10%). Will suggest revision on certain occasions. Scale of reading fees on application.

A. M. Heath & Co. Ltd. (1919). *Directors:* Cyrus Brooks (Chairman), Mark Hamilton (Managing Director), Charles Paul (Secretary), Michael Thomas, Hester Green. 35 Dover Street, London, W1X 4EB *T.* 01–629 7124. *T.A.* Script, London, W.1. *Cables:* Script, London.

Full-length and short MSS. (home and overseas 10%; translations 20%). Theatre, films, television and sound broadcasting (10%). Interested in work of both new and established writers. U.S. Associate: Brandt & Brandt Inc., New York. Agents in all European countries and Japan. No reading fee.

David Higham Associates Ltd. (1935). *Directors:* David Higham (Managing), David Bolt, Sheila Watson, Hilton Ambler, Bruce Hunter, Jacqueline Korn. 5–8 Lower John Street, London, W1R 3PE. *T.* 01–437 7888. *T.A.* Highlit, Wesdo, London. *Cables:* Highlit, London, W.4.

U.S. Associate Agency: Harold Ober Associates Inc., 40 East 49th Street, New York City. Works in conjunction with many foreign agencies in all parts of the world. Terms on application. No reading fee.

Hollander, Vera (1936). 51 Hermitage Lane, London, N.W.2. *T.* 01–435 7272.

10%, principally non-fiction. Please write preliminary letter before sending material and enclose S.A.E.

Hughes Massie Ltd. (over sixty years ago). *Directors:* Edmund Cork, Patricia Cork, J. E. Lunn, N. E. Cork, Joan M. Ling. 69 Great Russell Street, London, WC1B 3DH. *T.* 01–405 8137. *T.A.* Litaribus, London, W.C.1.

Full-length MSS. (home 10%, U.S.A. 15%, translations 20%, including 10% to local agents). Short MSS. (home 10%, or 15%, translations 20%, including 10% to local agents). Theatre, films, television, sound broadcasting (10%). U.S.A. associate: Harold Ober Associates Inc., 40 East 49th Street, New York 10017. Works in conjunction with agents in most European countries, Israel and Japan. No reading fee.

Intercontinental Literary Agency (1965). *Director:* Anthony Gornall. 45–46 Chandos Place, London, WC2N 4HX. *T.* 01–836 6895. *T.A.* Interlitag.

Concerned only with translation rights exclusively for all authors of A.D. Peters & Co., London, Harold Matson Co. Inc. New York and The Sterling Lord Agency, New York.

International Authors Agency (1963). *Partners:* Irfan Orga, Ates Orga, B.MUS. (Dunelm). Member of Royal Musical Association. Margarete D'Arcy Orga. Wadhurst, Sussex. *T.* 0892–88 2040 and 0892–88–2767. *T.A.* Interlit, Wadhurst.

Full-length MSS., films, television and sound broadcasting. The agency also handles books to post-graduate level on natural and social sciences, technology, politics, ancient and modern history, archaeology, music and the arts, and is interested in current researches of value to the scholar and scientist. *U.S.A. Representative:* Shirley Hector and Associates, 29 West 46th Street, New York, N.Y. 10036. Represented by leading agencies throughout the world; also works directly in conjunction with foreign publishers whose books the agency represents in Great Britain. Prospectus and details on application. Preliminary letter essential. No reading fees.

The International Copyright Bureau Ltd. (1903). *Directors:* Dr. Suzanne Czech (Managing Director), Margery Vosper, W. J. Williams. 26 Charing Cross Road, London, WC2H 0D6. *T.* 01–437 5106. *T.A.* Volscius, London.

Selected fiction, full-length MSS. only, (home and overseas 10%). Theatre, films, television, sound broadcasting (10%). Will suggest revision and sometimes suggests someone to do it. Works in conjunction with several agents in U.S.A. and other foreign countries. No reading fee.

International Literary Management (1955). *Directors:* I. M. Thompson, Reginald Turnor, Christopher Barry. 2 Ellis Street, Sloane Street, London, S.W.1. *T.* 01–730 2220 and 01–730 2229. *T.A.* Litfilm, London, S.W.1.

Commission. British Commonwealth and Empire and U.S.A., 10%. Elsewhere overseas, 15%. Representation throughout the world. No reading fees.

Peter Janson-Smith Ltd. (1956). *Directors:* Peter Janson-Smith (Managing), Elaine Greene (U.S.A.), Kenneth Thomson (Secretary). 42 Great Russell Street, London, WC1B 3PN. *T.* 01–636 6561. *T.A.* Peterlaine, London, W.C.1.

Full-length and short MSS. (home and overseas in English language 10%; translation rights 20%); television and sound broadcasting and films (10%).

Short stories, articles and poems handled only for existing authors of full-length works. Agents in Italy, France, Switzerland (for all German language rights), Brazil, Spain and Japan; in all other countries negotiate direct with publishers. No reading fee.

John Johnson (1956). 3 Albemarle Street, London, W1X 3HF *T.* 01–629 4982. *T.A.* Litjohn London.

Full-length and short MSS. (home 10%, overseas 10%, if foreign agent is concerned maximum of 19%), theatre, films, television, sound broadcasting (10%). *U.S.A. associate agency:* Sterling Lord, 660 Madison Avenue, New York, N.Y. 10021. Works in conjunction with agents in many European countries. No reading fee.

Jones Blakey, 14 Monteith Crescent, Boston, Lincolnshire. *T.* Boston 3437.

Book length MSS. only—non-fiction and fiction (10–15%). Theatre, television and sound broadcasting scripts (10–15%). No reading fee, but return postage with all MSS essential.

Josephy, Irene. 35 Craven Street, Strand, London, WC2N 5NG. *T.* 01–930 6936.

Full service for professional writers. Basic commission 10%. Connections in U.S.A. and Europe. Preliminary letter preferred. No reading fee.

Kavanagh Productions Limited (1951). *Directors:* Sonny Zahl, April Young, John Hayes, Denis Norden, Alec Grahame, Alfred Black, Carole Golder. 201 Regent Street, London, W1R 8PB *T.* 01–734 7811/4.

Theatre, films, television, sound broadcasting (10%). World representation. No reading fee.

Charles Lavell Limited (1927). *Directors:* Carl Routledge, Kay Routledge. Mowbray House, Norfolk Street, London, W.C.2. *T.* 01–836 8951. *T.A.* Lavnews, London.

Full-length MSS. (home and overseas 15% on first book by new author, reduced to 10% on second and subsequent books). Short MSS. (home and overseas 15%). Theatre, films, television (10%); sound broadcasting (10% on longer works; 15% on short stories). Works in conjunction with agents in U.S.A., the Commonwealth, and in all European countries. Deals at technical level with scientific and technological authors. No reading fees, but return postage essential with manuscript.

Le Dain Management. *Director:* Yvonne Le Dain. 92 North Road, Highgate, London, N6 4AA.

Full-length MSS. and short MSS. Theatre, films, television, sound broadcasting. Terms on application. Preliminary letter essential.

Hope Leresche & Steele (1960) (successor to Richard Steele & Son, est. 1942; successor to J. B. Pinker est. 1900). Hope Leresche, Tessa Sayle. *Drama Assistant:* Dawn Arnall. 11 Jubilee Place, Chelsea, London, S.W.3. *T.* 01–352 4311, 01–352 2182. *T.A.* Bookishly, London, S.W.3.

Full-length MSS. (home 10%, overseas 20%). Plays, films, television, sound broadcasting (10%). Will suggest revision. *U.S.A. Associate:* Georges Borchardt, 145 East 52nd Street, New York, N.Y. 10022. Represented in all foreign countries. No reading fee.

E. P. S. Lewin & Partners (1936). *Directors:* E. P. S. Lewin, E. T. Lewin, N. S. Lewin. 7 Chelsea Embankment, London, S.W.3. *T.* 01–352 4866. *T.A.* Lewiniwel, London.

Full-length MSS. (home 10%, overseas 10% of amount received). Short MSS. (home and overseas 15%). Films, television, sound broadcasting (10%). No poetry or articles (except in special cases). Works in conjunction with several agents in U.S.A. and in Europe. No reading fee.

Lloyd-George & Coward (1959). *Directors:* W. Lloyd-George, B. G. Coward, D. G. Huddy, A.C.A., 5th Floor, 8 Waterloo Place, London, S.W.1. *T.* 01–839 6571.

Full-length and short MSS. (home and overseas 10%). Theatre, films, television and sound broadcasting (10%). No reading fee.

Lom Associates Ltd. *Director:* Dina Lom. 6A Maddox Street, London, W1R 9PN *T.* 01–493 2801. *T.A.* Lomplay, London, W.1.

Full-length MSS. (home 10%, overseas 10% on net royalty less foreign agents' commission). Theatre, films, television and sound broadcasting (10%). No reading fee.

London Management, 235–241 Regent Street, London, W1A 2IT. *T.* 01–734 4192. Herbert van Thal.

Manuscripts of all kinds of high literary quality only. Basic commission 10%; 20% maximum for overseas rights. *U.S.A. representative:* Kurt Hellmer, 52 Vanderbilt Avenue, New York 10017. Plays, television, film rights: Cecily Ware.

Richard Marsh Ltd. (1943). 11 Gower Street, London, W.C.1. *T.* 01–636 9200. Full-length and short MSS. (home and overseas 15%). No reading fee.

Maurice Michael (1953). *Partners:* M. A. Michael, P. K. Michael. 3–4 Fox Court, London, E.C.1. *T.* 040–371–412. *T.A.* Bartolo, London.

Specializes in books from and for Scandinavia and the Continent. Full-length and short MSS. (home and overseas 10%). Works direct, and in conjunction with several agents, in U.S.A. Negotiates directly with Continental publishers. No reading fee.

Richard Milne Limited (1956). *Directors:* R. M. Sharples, K. N. Sharples. 28 Makepeace Avenue, Highgate, London, N.6. *T.* 01–340 7007.

Full-length and short MSS. (home 10%, overseas 25%). Films, television, sound broadcasting (10%). Unable to represent any additional authors at present. No reading fee.

Observer Books & Features Ltd. (1969), 37A Fleet Lane, London, EC4M 4YA. *T.* 01–236 6824. *T.A.* Obseale, London. *Management:* Patrick Seale (Managing Editor), David Elyan (Commercial Manager), Maureen McConville (Editorial Manager).

Full-length and short MSS. (home 10%, overseas 15–20%, including commission to foreign agents). Theatre, films, television, sound broadcasting, (home 10%). Will suggest revision of promising MSS. Works in conjunction with agents in U.S.A. and Europe. No reading fee.

Penman Literary Agency (1950), *Director:* Leonard G. Stubbs, F.R.S.A., Penman House, 262 London Road, Westcliff-on-Sea, Essex, SS0 7JG. *T.* Southend 40750.

Full-length and short MSS. (home 10%, overseas 15%). Theatre, films, television, sound broadcasting (10%). Revision undertaken by agency at author request; fees depending upon amount of revision required. No reading fee.

A. D. Peters and Company (1924). *Partners:* A. D. Peters, Michael Sissons, Margaret Stephens, Anthony Jones. 10 Buckingham Street, Adelphi, London, WC2N 6BU. *T.* 01–839 2556.

Associated Agencies: Harold Matson, 22 East 40th Street, New York, N.Y. 10016. Sterling Lord, 660 Madison Avenue, New York, N.Y. 10021. Intercontinental Literary Agency, 45–6 Chandos Place, London, W.C.2. Peters and Ramsay, Play Agents, 14A Goodwin's Court, London, W.C.2. Please write before sending. No reading fee.

Laurence Pollinger Limited. *Directors:* Laurence Pollinger, Gerald J. Pollinger, Denis Flack, Rosemary Gould. 18 Maddox Street, London, W1R 0EU. *T.* 01–629 9761. *T.A.* Laupoll, London, W.1.

Authors' agents for all material with the exception of original film stories and poems. Dramatic associate, Margery Vosper, *q.v.* Terms are a commission of 10% of the amounts obtained, except on translation and American sales, where the total commissions of 20% and 15% respectively include the commission to the associate in the territory concerned. No reading fee.

Murray Pollinger (1969), 42 Great Russell Street, London, WC1B 3PN. *T.* 01–636 6561.

Full-length and short MSS. (home 10%, U.S.A. 15%, translations 20%). Theatre, films, television, sound broadcasting (10%). Works in conjunction with agents in many countries abroad. Preliminary letter preferred. No reading fee.

Margaret Ramsay Ltd. (1953). *Director:* M. Ramsey. 14A Goodwin's Court, London, WC2N 4LW. *T.* 01–836 7403 and 01–240 0691. *T.A.* Ramsyplay, London.

MSS. Theatre, films, television, sound broadcasting only (maximum commission 10%). Works in conjunction with agents in U.S.A. and in all foreign countries. Preliminary letter essential. No reading fee.

Deborah Rogers Ltd. (1967). *Directors:* Deborah Rogers, Ann Warnford Davis. 29 Goodge Street, London, W.1. *T.* 01–580 0604. *T.A.* Debrogers, London, W.1.

Full-length and short MSS. (home 10%, overseas 15%, translation 20%). Theatre, films, television sound broadcasting (10%). *U.S.A. Associate:* International Famous Agency, 1301 Avenue of the Americas, New York, N.Y. 10019. No reading fee.

Kay Routledge Associates (1967). *Principal:* Mrs. Kay Routledge. Mowbray House, Norfolk Street, London, W.C.2. *T.* 01–836 8951.

For the professional woman writer of good fiction (book and magazine). Specialises in serials. Full-length MSS. 10%; shorter material 15% (where overseas agent employed additional 10%). Represented overseas. Preliminary letter essential. No reading fees.

Rupert Crew Limites (1927). *Directors:* F. R. Crew, K. A. Crew, D. Montgomery, S. Russell. King's Mews, London, WC1N 2JA. *T.* 01–242 8586–7. *T.A.* Authorship, Holb., London.

International business management for authors and feature writers desiring world representation by a highly geared, personal service, available only to a limited clientele. Preliminary letter. Commission 10%–25% by arrangement, no reading fees except in certain circumstances where optional criticism is offered. Also acts independently as publishers' consultants.

S.C.O.T.T.S., Scottish Casting Office, Television, Theatre, Screen Ltd. (1960). *Managing Director:* Robin Richardson. 21 Woodside Terrace, Glasgow C.3. *T.* 041–332 3566.

Full-length and short MSS. (home 10%, overseas 15% plus postal, telegraphic and telephonic costs). Theatre (10%), films (by arrangement not less than 10%), television and sound broadcasting (10%). Will suggest somebody for revision. Associates in New York, Paris and Hollywood. No reading fee.

Scott Meredith Literary Agency (London) (1946). *Manager:* Victor Briggs. 44 Great Russell Street, London, WC1B 3PA. *T.* 01–636 9177. *T.A.* Esemlond, London, W.C.1.

All MSS. (home 10%, overseas 20%). Theatre, films, television, sound broadcasting (10%). U.S.A. office: Scott Meredith Literary Agency Inc., 580 Fifth Avenue, New York, N.Y. 10036. Works in conjunction with important foreign agencies. No reading fee.

Sheil (Anthony) Associates Ltd. (1962). 47 Dean Street, London, W.1. *T.* 01–734 7792. *T.A.* Novelist. *Directors:* Anthony Sheil (Managing), D. Buckley Sharp, F.C.A., Gillon Aitken.

Full-length MSS. (home 10%; overseas 10%, up to 20% if foreign agent employed); short MSS. (home 10%, overseas 20%). Theatre, films, television, sound broadcasting (10%). Works in conjunction with Julian Bach, Jr., 3 East 48th Street, New York, N.Y. 10017. Strongly represented in all European capitals, and has exceptional facilities for offering suitable material on a world-wide basis. No reading fee.

Robert Somerville Limited (1906). *Directors:* Carl Routledge, Kay Routledge. Mowbray House, Norfolk Street, London, W.C.2. *T.* 01–836 8951. *T.A.* Ertsomvil, London.

Theatre, films, television, sound broadcasting (10%). No reading fees. Preliminary letter essential.

Taylor-Whitehead Agency, The, (1969), 52 Greenend, Bedford Park, London, W.4. *T.* 01–995 3115, and 60 Rue Madame, Paris 6. *T.* BAB 0440. *Partners:* W. J. Taylor Whitehead, M.A., Mrs. J. C. L. Taylor Whitehead.

Full-length and short MSS. (home and overseas 10%). Theatre, films, television, sound broadcasting (10%). Foreign Rights a speciality. No reading fee

Theatrework (London) Ltd. (1957). *Directors:* Warren Tute. 54 Rosemont Road, Richmond, Surrey. *T.* 01–940 3780. *T.A.* Teework.

Full-length and short MSS. Drama and fiction; no short stories. (Home and overseas 10%). Theatre, films, (10%). Occasionally suggests revision, and someone to do it. No reading fees. (Return postage required.)

Campbell Thomson & McLaughlin Ltd. *Directors:* Christine Campbell Thomson and John McLaughlin. Cliffords Inn, Fleet Street, London, E.C.4. *T.* 01–405 8628–9.

Full-length and short MSS. (home 10%, U.S.A. 15%, translations 19% amount received). Theatre, films (not original film material), television and sound broadcasting (home 10%, abroad 19%). No poetry. Revision occasionally arranged with outside experts. U.S. Representation: Ann Elmo Agency Inc., 52 Vanderbilt Avenue, New York 10017; Theron Raines, 224 Madison Avenue, N.Y. 10016. Representatives in most European countries, South America, Israel and South Africa. No reading fee.

United Writers (1962). *Director:* Sydney Sheppard. Trevarren, St. Columb. Cornwall.

Deals almost exclusively with serial stories and romantic fiction for women's magazines, also romantic novels. All MSS (home and overseas 10%). Will provide revision of MS. No reading fee.

Harvey Unna Ltd. (1950). *Directors:* Harvey Unna, Elizabeth Unna, Nina Froud. 14 Beaumont Mews, Marylebone High Street, London, W1N 4HE *T.* 01–935 8589. *Cable:* Harvunna, London, W.1.

Specialise in dramatic works for all media; handle also book MSS. Widely represented in most European and Overseas countries. Commission charged by agency 10% in all instances; where sub-agents are employed overseas, additional commission by arrangement, but not exceeding 9%. No reading fee.

Dr. Jan Van Loewen Ltd. (1944). *Directors:* Jan Van Loewen, LL.D., Elisabeth Van Loewen. 81–83 Shaftesbury Avenue, W1V 8BX. *T.* 01–437 5546–7. *T.A.* Van Loewen, London, W.1.

Full-length and short MSS. (home 10%, overseas 10% except when working with a regional sub-agent—20%). Theatre, films, television, sound broadcasting (10%). Will suggest revision and sometimes suggests somebody to do it. Represented in all major countries. No reading fee.

Margery Vosper Ltd. (1932). 53A Shaftesbury Avenue, London, W1V 8ER *T.* 01–437 5106–7–8. *T.A.* Margevos, Lesquare, London.

Full-length and short MSS. (home and overseas 10%). Theatre, films, television and sound broadcasting (10%). Will suggest revision and sometimes suggests suitable person to do it. Works in conjunction with agents in New York, and in all foreign countries. Reading fee of £2·10 charged only to new and beginning writers, excluding specialists and experts.

S. Walker Literary Agency (1939). *Directors:* S. Walker, E. K. Walker. 199 Hampermill Lane, Oxhey, Watford, WD1 4PJ *T.* Watford 28498.

Full-length and short MSS. (home 10%, overseas 20% including 10% to overseas agent). Theatre, films, television, sound broadcasting (10%). No short topical articles, poetry or stories for juveniles. U.S.A. representative: Howard Moorepark, 444 East 82nd Street, New York, N.Y. 10028. Works in conjunction with agencies in most European countries, and also negotiates directly with foreign publishers. No reading fee.

J. C. Walls (1936). 39 Craven Street, Strand, London, WC2N 5NT. *T.* 01–839 2861.

Full-length and short MSS. (home and overseas 10%). Provides criticism, revision and typing service, from 47½p. per 1000 words. No reading fee.

A. P. Watt & Son (1857). *Partners:* Michael Horniman, Hilary Rubinstein. 26/28 Bedford Row, London, WC1R 4HL. *T.* 01–405 1057. *T.A.* Longevity, London, W.C.1.

Full-length and short MSS. (home 10%, U.S. 15%, foreign 19% including commission to U.S. or foreign agent). Theatre, films, television, sound broadcasting. U.S.A. associate agency: Collins-Knowlton-Wing, Inc., 60 East 56th Street, New York, N.Y. 10022. Works in conjunction with agents in most European countries, Japan and South America. No reading fee.

Winant, Towers Ltd. (1965). *Managing Director:* Ursula R. Winant. *Company Secretary:* Jennifer M. Perkins. 1 Furnival Street, London, E.C.4. *T.* 01–242 3969–0. *T.A.* Towben, London. *Cables:* Towben, London.

Full-length and short MSS. (home 10%, U.S.A. 12½%; elsewhere 20%). Films (10%; U.S.A. 12½%), television and sound broadcasting (10%). Will suggest revision if MS. promising; sometimes suggests outside help. U.S.A. associate agency: International Famous Agency Inc., 1301 Avenue of the Americas, New York, N.Y. 10019. Representatives in all European countries. No reading fee.

Hamric Literary Agency (1967). *Directors:* Joan Dale, Pat Anderson. 2 Frognal Rise, London, N.W.3. *T.* 01–794 8998.

AMERICAN LITERARY AGENTS

* Membership of the Society of Authors' Representatives.

Standard practice in the U.S.A. is a minimum 10 per cent commision on home sales, and a rather higher rate on foreign sales. Some agencies charge a reading fee for unsolicited MSS and for the work of beginners and new writers, such fees sometimes being refunded on the acceptance of the material.

In all cases, and in their own interests, writers are advised to send a preliminary letter and to ascertain terms before submitting MSS.

*Cyrilly Abels, Suite 1410, 119 West 57th Street, New York, N.Y. 10019. *T.* 247–6438.

*Agency for the Performing Arts, Inc., 120 West 57 Street, New York, N.Y. 10019.

American Authors Inc., 342 Madison Avenue, New York, N.Y. 10017. *T.* OX7–2227.

*American Play Company Inc., 52 Vanderbilt Avenue, New York, N.Y. 10017. *T.* 212–MU 6–6333.

*Julian Bach, Jr. Literary Agency, 3 East 48th Street, New York, N.Y. 10017. *T.* PL3–4331. *Cables:* Turtles.

Becker, Maximilian, 115 East 82nd Street, New York, N.Y. 10028. *T.* Yukon 8–3887. *Cable Address:* Becklit, New York.

*Bill Berger Associates Inc., 535 East 72 Street, New York, N.Y. 10021.

*Lurton Blassingame, 60 East 42 Street, New York, N.Y. 10017.

*Brandt & Brandt, 101 Park Avenue, New York, N.Y. 10017. *British representative:* A. M. Heath & Co., Ltd.

*Curtis Brown, Ltd., 60 East 56th Street, New York, N.Y. 10022.

*James Brown Associates Inc., 22 East 60 Street, New York, N.Y. 10022. *T.* 212–EL 5–4182.

*Collins-Knowlton-Wing, Inc. 60 East 56th Street, New York, N.Y. 10022. Representing in N. America A. P. Watt and Son of London.

*Maurice Crain, Inc., 18 East 41st Street, New York City, N.Y. 10017. *T.* MU 5–7566.

*John Cushman Associates Inc., 25 West 43rd Street, New York, N.Y. 10036. *T.A.* Cushcurt, New York. *T.* (212) MU 5–2052. Affiliate and U.S.A. representative of Curtis Brown Ltd. of London.

*Joan Daves, 515 Madison Avenue, New York, N.Y. 10022. *T.* 212–PL9–6250.

*Ann Elmo Agency Inc. (1936), 52 Vanderbilt Avenue, New York, N.Y. 10017. *T.* 686–9282–3.

Hanns Fischer, Literary Agency, 2332 West Farwell Avenue, Chicago, Illinois 60645. *T.* 312–465 1216. *Cables:* Hafis-Chicago.

*Frieda Fishbein, 353 West 57 Street, New York, N.Y. 10019. *T.* 212–247 4398.

Fles, Barthold, 507 Fifth Avenue, New York, N.Y. 10017. *T.* MU 7–7248. *T.A.* Bartflesag, Newyork.

*Harold Freedman, Brandt & Brandt Dramatic Dept., Inc., 101 Park Avenue, New York, N.Y. 10017.

Greenburger (Sanford J.), 595 Madison Avenue, New York, N.Y. 10022. *T.* PL 3–8581–2.

*Gregory (Blanche C.) Inc., 2 Tudor City Place, New York City, N.Y. 10017. *London representative:* Murray Pollinger.

Hellmer, Kurt, 52 Vanderbilt Avenue, New York, N.Y. 10017. *T.* MU 6–2222. *T.A.* Authellmer Newyork. Novels and non-fiction; stage and television plays; films. Represented in Hollywood. *British representative:* London Management (Herbert van Thal).

*International Famous Agency, Inc., 1301 Avenue of the Americas, New York, N.Y. 10019.

Joseph, Nannine, 200 West 54th Street, New York, N.Y. 10019. *T.* Circle 7–4346.

*Lucy Kroll Agency, 119 West 57th Street, New York, N.Y. 10019. *T.* 212 PL 7–4250. *T.A.* Lucykroll, New York.

*Robert Lantz-Candida Donadio Literary Agency, Inc., 111 West 57 Street, New York, N.Y. 10019. *T.* PL 7–5076.

MacCampbell (Donald) Inc., 12 East 41st Street, New York, N.Y. 10017. *T.* Murray Hill 3–5580.

*McIntosh, McKee & Dodds Inc., 22 East 40th Street, New York, N.Y. 10016. *T.* 212–679–4490. *Cables:* Halmatson. See A. D. Peters & Co., London.

*McIntosh & Otis Inc. (1928), 18 East 41st Street, New York, N.Y. 10017.

*Elisabeth Marton, 96 Fifth Avenue, New York, N.Y. 10011. *T.* AL 5–1908.

*Matson Company Inc. (Harold) (1937), 22 East 40th Street, New York, N.Y. 10016. *T.* 212–679–4490. *Cables:* Halmatson. (*See* A. D. Peters & Co., London.)

Moorepark (Howard), 444 East 82nd Street, New York, N.Y. 10028. *T.* 212–737 3961. *T.A.* Homopark, New York.

*Morris (Wm.) Agency, Inc., 1350 Avenue of the Americas, New York, N.Y. 10019.

*Harold Ober Associates Inc., 40 East 49 Street, New York, N.Y. 10017.

PIP Photos Inc., 507 Fifth Avenue, New York, N.Y. 10017. *T.* 212–697 6191. *See* Photographic Agencies.

*Reynolds (Paul R.) Inc. (1893), 599 Fifth Avenue, New York, N.Y. 10017. *Cable address:* Carbonato, New York.

*Rice, Virginia, 301 East 66 Street, New York 10021. *T.* 861–4918. *London:* Curtis Brown Ltd.

*Flora Roberts, Inc., 116 East 59 Street, New York, N.Y. 10022. *T.* 355 4165.

*Marie Rodell, 141 East 55 Street, New York, N.Y. 10022. *T.* PL3–0042. *Cables:* Rodellitag, New York.

*Russell & Volkening, Inc., 551 Fifth Avenue, New York, N.Y. 10017.

*Salisbury (Leah), Inc., 790 Madison Avenue, New York, N.Y. 10021. *T.* 212–628 4404. *T.A.* Leasalis, New York. Play broker.

*Schaffner, John, Suite 6D, 425 East 51st. Street, New York, N.Y. 10022. *T.* Murray Hill 8–4763.

Ad Schulberg Agency, 300 East 57th Street, New York, N.Y. 10022. *T.* Plaza 9–1341.

Scott Meredith Literary Agency, Inc., 580 Fifth Avenue, New York, N.Y. 10036. *T.* Circle 5–5500. *T.A.* Scottmere. *London:* 44 Great Russell Street, W.C.1. *q.v.*

Shuster (H. E.) & Co., 4930 Wynnefield Avenue, Philadelphia, Pa 19131. *T.* 215–Greenwood 3–2195.

Singer, Evelyn. Literary Agency. 41 West 96th Street, New York, N.Y. 10025. *T.A.* Singerage Nyk.

*Sterling Lord Agency, 660 Madison Avenue, New York, N.Y. 10021. *T.* 212 PL 1–2533. *T.A.* Lordage. *British representative:* A. D. Peters, *q.v.*

Strassman, Miss Toni, 130 East 18th Street, New York, N.Y. 10003.

*Tams-Witmark Music Library Inc., 757 Third Avenue, New York, N.Y. 10017.

Roslyn Targ Literary Agency, Inc. (formerly Franz J. Horch Associates Inc.), 325 East 57th Street, New York, N.Y. 10022. Plaza 3–9810.

Austin Wahl Agency, 21 East Van Buren Street, Chicago, Illinois 60605. *T.* 922–3329. Normally requires an author to sign a Power of Attorney.

Watkins (A.), Inc., 77 Park Avenue, New York, N.Y. 10016. *Cables:* Anwat, New-york. *London:* A. P. Watt & Son.

*Max Wilkinson Associates, Shelter Island, N.Y. 11964. *T.* 516–749 0716.

*Williams (Annie Laurie), Inc., 18 East 41st Street, New York 10017. *T.* MU 5–7564.

OTHER LITERARY AGENTS

Most of the agents whose names and addresses are given below work in association with an agent in London.

In all cases, and in their own interests, writers are advised to send a preliminary letter and to ascertain terms before submitting MSS. or books.

ARGENTINA

International Editors Co., Av. Cabildo 1156, Buenos Aires.
Mrs. Catalina W. de Wulff, Cabello 3042, Buenos Aires.
Lawrence Smith, B.A. (1938), Avenida do los Incas 3110, Buenos Aires. *T.* 73–5012. *Cables:* Litagent, Baires.

AUSTRALIA

Greg Branson, Box 1289L G.P.O., Adelaide. Play agent.
Curtis Brown (Australia) Proprietary Ltd., 186 Liverpool Street, Darlinghurst 2010, N.S.W. *T.* 31 8301 and 31 2438. *Cables:* Browncurt.
Alec Harrison, 118 Fleet Street, London, E.C.4.
Yaffa Syndicate Pty. Ltd., Corner Butt and Clisdell Streets, Surrey Hills, N.S.W. *T.* 69–7861.

BELGIUM

Delta Literary Agency, A. van Hageland, 10 Blutsdelle, Alsemberg, B 1641.
Maurice Salenbien, 34 rue du Meiboom, Brussels. Radio and TV only.

BRAZIL

Dr. J. E. Bloch, Rua Oscar Freire 416, Ap. 83, Caixa Postal 8675, São Paulo. *T.* 282-3053.

CANADA

Alex S. Arnott Literary Agent, Box 32, Station J, 685 Danforth Avenue, Toronto 6, Ontario. *T.* 422-0770.

CZECHOSLOVAKIA

Dilia Theatrical and Literary Agency, Vyšehradská 28, Prague—2 Nové Město.
Lita Slovak Literary Agency, ul.Čs. Armády 31, Bratislava.

DENMARK

A/S Bookman, Fiolstraede 12, DK–1171, Copenhagen K.
Preben Jörgensen, 37 Haandvaerkerhaven, 2400 Copenhagen NV. *T.* Söborg 1653.
Edith Kiilerich, Fiolstraede 12, DK–1171, Copenhagen K.
Albrecht Leonhardt, Løvstraede 8, DK–1152, Copenhagen K. *T.* Palae 2523.
Kurt E. Michaels, Jaegersborg Alle 19, DK–2920 Charlottenlund.
Carl Strakosch & Olaf Nordgreen, Nyhavn 5, DK–1051, Copenhagen K.

FINLAND

Charlotte László, Ehrensvàrdintie H/B, Helsinki.

FRANCE

Mrs. W. A. Bradley, 18 Quai de Bethune, 75–Paris IV. *T.* 033–75–14.
Bureau Litteraire D. Clairouin, Mme. Marie Schebeko, 66 rue de Miromesnil, Paris 8ᵉ. *T.* 522 18–06.
Bureau Litteraire International (Ex Marguerite Scialitiel), Mme Josette Hesse, 14 rue Chanoinesse, Paris IV. *T.* ODE 71–16.
Agence Hoffman, 77 Boulevard Saint-Michel, Paris 5. *T.* 033–71–15, 033–23–27.
Mme. Michelle Lapautre, 10 rue de Rémusat, Paris 16. *T.* 525–36–55.
Mme. Alice Le Bayon, 113 Boulevard St. Germain, Paris VI. *T.* 033–50–07.
McKee & Mouche, 14 rue du Regard, Paris VIᵉ. *T.* 548–45–03.
Opera Mundi, 100 Av. Raymond Poincaré, Paris 16.
Agence Quet, Mme. Janine Quet, 20 rue de la Michodière, Paris, 2ᵉ. *T.* 033–38–50.
Maurice Renault, 2 rue de Florence, Paris 8. *T.* 387–44–58.
Mme. Helena Strassova, 4 rue Git-Le-Coeur, Paris 6. *T.* 633–34–57.

GERMANY

Geisenheyner & Crone, Birkenwaldstrasse 155, 7 Stuttgart N. *T.* 293738.
Agence Hoffman, Seestrasse 6, Munich 23.
Dr. Ruth Liepman, Maienburgweg 23, 8044 Zurich, Switzerland. *T.* (051) 47 76 60.
Linder AG, Gerechtigkeitsgasse 22, 8002 Zurich, Switzerland. *T.* (051) 36–16–17.
Mohrbooks Literary Agency, Rainer Heumann, Krummackerstrasse 4, 8700— Itschnach-Zurich, Switzerland. *T.* (051) 90–56–91.
Panorama Literary Agency, Wassergasse 33/3/16 1030 Vienna 3, Austria.

HOLLAND

H. Drijvers, Hilversum, P.O.B. 93.
Alexander Gans, Literair Agent, Witte de Withstraat 20, Noordwijk aan Zee, The Netherlands. *T.* 01719–3133.
Hans Keuls, Internationaal Bureau Voor Auteursrecht N.V., c/o Marius Bauerstraat 30, Amsterdam (Overtoomseveld). *T.* 020–1568 22.
Internationaal Literatuur Bureau, S. Menno, Koninginneweg 2A, Hilversum.
Prins & Prins Literary Agents (Henk Prins), Comeniusstraat 65, P.O. Box 9037, Amsterdam, W.3. *T.* 150 995.

HUNGARY

Artisjus Bureau Hongrois pour la Protection des Droits D'Auteur, Deak Ferenc U.15, Budapest V. *T.* 187–057. *Cables:* Artisjus.

ISRAEL

Bar-David Literary Agency, 41 Montefiore Street, Tel-Aviv, P.O. Box 1104. *T.* 615 365. *Cables:* Davidbarco.
Moadim, Play Publishers and Literary Agents, 144 Hayarkon Street, Tel-Aviv. *T.* 228449.

ITALY

Agenzia Letteraria Internazionale, 3 Corso Matteotti, 20121 Milan. *T.* 79–36–09.
Dais Literary Agency (formerly **Fabio Coen**), Via Nicotera 7, Rome. *T.* 353126.
Transafrica, Via Trieste 34, 25100 Brescia. *T.* 55080–40800.

JAPAN

Orion Press, 55, 1–Chome, Kanda-Jimocho, Chiyoda-ku, Tokyo, 101. *T.A.* Orionserv, Tokyo. *Telex,* TK 4447 Orionprs.
Charles E. Tuttle Co., Inc., 1–2–6 Suido, Bunkyo-ku, Tokyo 112. *T.* 811–7106. *Cables:* Tuttbooks, Tokyo.

NEW ZEALAND

Alec Harrison, 118 Fleet Street, London, E.C.4.
Albion Wright, Ltd., 14 Oxford Terrace, Christchurch. *T.* 64–507. *Cables:* Royalties.

NORWAY

Mrs. Carlota Frahm, Valkyriegaten 17, Oslo 3. *T.* 46–30–02. *Cables:* Frahmbook.
Hanna-Kirsti Koch, P.O.B. 3043, Oslo 2.

PORTUGAL

Ilidio da Fonseca Matos, Rua de S. Bernardo, 68–3, Lisbon 2. *T.* 66 97 80. *Cables:* Ilphoto.

SOUTH AFRICA

International Press Agency (Pty) Ltd., P.O. Box 682, Cape Town.
Shanahan Publications, P.O. Box 3174, Durban. *T.* 65 369.

SPAIN

Miss Carmen Balcells, Urgel 241, Barcelona, 11. *T.* 239–58 44. *Cables:* Copyright, Barcelona.
International Editors Co., Via Layetana 35, Barcelona 3.

SWEDEN

Gösta Dahl & Son, Sveavägen 145, S–11346, Stockholm. *T.* 33 20 96.
Mrs. Lena I. Gedin, Linnégatan 38, 114 47 Stockholm.
Arlecchino Teaterförlag, Strandprom 11, Saltsjö-Duvnäs.

YUGOSLAVIA

Jugoslovenska Autorska Agencija, Dobrinjska 11/IV, Belgrade.

SYNDICATES, NEWS AND PRESS AGENCIES

In their own interests writers and others are strongly advised to make preliminary enquiries before submitting MSS., and to ascertain terms of work. Commission varies. The details given in the following entries should be noted carefully in respect of syndication, as many news and press agencies do not syndicate articles.

Adamastor Press and Literary Agency Ltd. *Directors:* Sydney Clouts, Marjorie Clouts. 6 Somerton Road, London, N.W.2. *T.* 01–452 8101. *T.A.* Storsta, London, N.W.2.
Outstanding newspaper and magazine features for international markets. London representatives of *The International Press Agency (Pty.) Ltd.*, Cape Town, *q.v.*

Anglo-Spanish Press Bureau (1934), 29 Old Bond Street, London, W1X 4LJ. *T.* 01–493 1281. *Director:* J. Ugidos. Theatres, film and book reviews; topical articles; feature articles; fashion features. Also book and film translations into Spanish.

Aries Press Features, P.O. Box 14235, Lyttelton, Transvaal, South Africa. *T.* Pretoria 6–9103. *Director:* Major J. W. Lamb. Well-written features suitable for newspaper reading for world-wide syndication. *Payment:* by arrangement.

Arnott (Alex S.) Syndicate Features, Box 32, Station J, 685 Danforth Avenue, Toronto 6, Ontario, Canada.
Newspaper features and columns dealing with well-known world personalities in the news. A letter of enquiry is requested before submitting the complete manuscript. For Canadian and United States markets. Return postage required for MSS returned to England.

Associated News Service, 30 Fleet Street, E.C.4. *Editorial:* 9 Linthorpe Road, London, N.16. *T.* Stamford Hill 9595. *T.A.* Ansnews, London. General news and photographic agency. Serving U.K. national, provincial, suburban and British Commonwealth and foreign newspapers and periodicals. Feature department supplies London letters, political, sport, fashion, entertainment and general features.

Associated Press (The), Ltd. (News Department), 83–86 Farringdon Street, London, EC4A 4BR. *T.* 01–353 1515. *T.A.* Apworld, London, E.C.4.

Associated Press, The (of America), London office: 83–86 Farringdon Street, London, EC4A 4BR. *T.* 01–353 1515.

Australian News & Press Services (D. J. Varney & Associates 1964), Box T 1834, G.P.O., Perth, W. Australia 6001. *T.* 93–1455 and 21–7027. Australian correspondents for international trade, technical and specialist publications. Airmailed trade news summaries prepared on a weekly, monthly or quarterly basis, generally at normal news rates. Special articles, features or research carried out only when commissioned. Commercial intelligence reports prepared and also special news letters.

Australian Associated Press (1935), R. G. Myerscough (*Chief London Correspondent*), 85 Fleet Street, EC4Y 1EH. *T.* 01–353 0153–4. *T.A.* Austpress, London. News service to the Australian and New Zealand press, radio and television.

Australian Export News Service, Box 466, Sydney, Australia. *T.* XY 4387. *Editor:* Reay Wilson, J.P. Tells the Commonwealth export story overseas. Supplies gratis newsworthy items of latest industrial, commercial and chemical developments to world press on request, on reciprocal, exchange, or straightout basis. Fast Air Mail service for all copy and photos.

Australian General Press, Box 466, G.P.O., Sydney, Australia. *T.* XY 4387. *Editor:* Reay Wilson, J.P. Supplies feature articles, political commentaries, photos, cartoons, comic strips, short and serial stories, book reviews (gratis), to Australian, New Zealand, and Pacific Islands publications and newspapers. Has special interest in latest fashions for Commonwealth readership.

Australian Press Bureau, James M. Dobbie, 49 Rawnsley Street, Dutton Park, Brisbane, Queensland, 4102, Australia. Australian Correspondent for overseas publications. News, humorous topical columns, feature articles every kind although specializing rural, trades, local authority and civic affairs, strong 'people's' interest. Outside contributions seldom accepted. No syndicated material.

Ayrshire Press Agency (1956), Gordon Snead, 37 Ardrossan Road, Saltcoats, Ayrshire. *T.* Saltcoats 2076. Supplies photo news features to daily and weekly papers. Assignments undertaken by own staff photographers. Representatives of the national and provincial press. Photo news articles of particular interest to Scottish readers invited also glamour, fashion and sport. Commission 40%.

Bar-David Photo and Feature Service, 41 Montefiore Street, P.O. Box 1104, Tel Aviv, Israel. *Cables:* Davidbarco. Representing photo and feature syndicates in Israel; supplies photos, features and news articles of the Israel scene upon receipt of firm commission.

Barrow, Ivo (1961), St. Hubert's Road, Glen Huntly, Victoria 3163, Australia. Supplies news, sport and features concerning Ceylon for newspapers, periodicals, syndicates and press agencies, anywhere. Commissions undertaken including photographic assignments.

BIPS—Bernsen's International Press Service Ltd., 25 Garrick Street, London, WC2E 9BG (Head Office). *T.* 01–240 1401. Theo. C. Bernsen, Managing Director-Editor; Onno T. A. Bernsen, Jr., Managing Editor. Specialize in photo-features, both b. & w. and colour. Want human interest, oddity, gimmicky, popular mechanical, scientific, medical, etc., material suitable for marketing through own branches (London, New York, Paris, Hamburg, Milan, Stockholm, Antwerp (for Benelux), Sydney) in many countries. Give full information, well researched. Willing to syndicate, but prefer to assign free-lancers either on BIPS' ideas or photographer's ideas. Buy outright and pay on acceptance. Query with picture story ideas.

BP Singer Features. *Managing Director:* Kurt Singer, 3164 Tyler Avenue, Anaheim, California 92801. Use 15 features every week which are distributed to publications in 35 countries. Current needs for foreign reprint rights (no originals) are the following: Profiles of famous people—1–3 parts; Men's fiction; Women's fiction (high standard only); Adventure features (which are not blood-dripping or over-sexed); Colour transparencies; Westerns—short stories and books; books published by reputable publishers. "We accept only previously published material." Interested in British books for North and Latin America, serial and books rights.

'British-Soviet Friendship' Information Service (1927), 36 St. John's Square, EC1V 4JH. *T.* 01–253 4161. The service is a branch of the British Soviet Friendship Society. British-Soviet friendship, trade, and cultural connections, exchange of delegations, etc. Unpaid except by special arrangement.

Canadian Press, The (1919), Harold Morrison (Chief of Bureau), 83–86 Farringdon Street, EC4A 4BS, *T.* 01–353 6355. *T.A.* Canapress. London Bureau of the national news agency of Canada.

Capel Court Press Agency, Ltd., 20 Copthall Avenue, London, E.C.2. *T.* 01–628 3580. London Financial Editors for daily and weekly newspapers. Supplies syndicated financial and general economic articles.

Capital Press Service, 13 Esher Avenue, Walton-on-Thames, Surrey. *T.* WT 20812. *Cables:* Emespiar. *Directors:* M. Stone, E. W. Stone. *News Editor:* Nicholas Miller. Stories of trade, commerce and industry for trade papers in this country and abroad, and diary paragraphs for the National and provincial press.

Caters News Agency, Ltd., 184 Corporation Street, Birmingham, B4 6QE. *T.* 021–236 9001. *T.A.* Copy, Birmingham. *Joint Managing Directors:* G. Barnwell and J. L. Plant. Collection of news and news features throughout Midlands. Representatives of Overseas, National and Provincial Press.

Central Press Features, Peter L. Davis, M.A. (*Managing Director*), 80 Fleet Street, EC4Y 1ES. *T.* 01–353 7792. *T.A.* Features, London, E.C.4. One of the largest features syndicates in the world, established 1863. Supplies every type of feature to newspapers and other publications in 50 countries. Included in over 100 daily and weekly services are "big-name" columns on international affairs, politics, sports, medicine, law, finance, motoring, science, women's and children's features, strips, crosswords, cartoons and regular 6–12 article illustrated series of international human interest.

Central Press Photos, Ltd., The, 6–7, Gough Square, Fleet Street, EC4A 3DJ. *T.* 01–353 2266-7. *T.A.* Exposure, London, E.C.4. Independent coverage of news events at home and abroad, with special emphasis on sport including Test cricket. Supporting features give all-round picture service, and the particular requirements of Overseas Newspapers are carefully watched. Picture Library dates from 1914.

Coleman, Bruce, Ltd., 70 Vine Lane, Hillingdon, Middlesex. *T.* Uxbridge 32333. Syndication of photos on natural history.

Commonwealth News Service, Box. 466 G.P.O., Sydney, Australia. *T.* XY 4387. *Editor:* Reay Wilson, J.P. Australian feature material, illustrated articles, news stories (by Air Mail or Cable), etc., supplied to World Press. Offers national coverage of Commonwealth political, industrial and agricultural activities. Also interested in overseas short-story writers and cartoonists. Particulars by letter first.

Copley News Service (Australia) Pty. Ltd., 230 Palmer Street, East Sydney, N.S.W. 2010. *T.* 334041. *Cables:* Copley Sydney. *Telex:* AA21632. *Editor:* Gregory Copley. Provides hard news wire coverage for newspapers and broadcast media in Australia and worldwide. Supplies in-depth news features and situationers from world-wide to the Australian press, and from Australia to Asia, U.K. and U.S.A. Write first except when subject is current and urgent. Average rate of commission: 50%.

Crabtree, (J. W.) and Son (1919), 12 Burton Chambers, Kirkgate, Bradford 1. *T.* 32937 (Office); 637312 (Home). News, general, trade and sport; information and research for features undertaken.

Editoriale Aurora TV: Viale delle Belle Arti, 7, 00196 Rome. *T.* 302796/393242. *Director:* Jacopo Rizza, *General Manager:* Vinicio Congiu. TV films, documentaries, educational, industrial and publicity films.

Empire Press Agency, 6 Great James Street, London, WC1N 3DD. *T.* 01–387 7942. British and Commonwealth News and Literary Services. Air Mail Press Service to Commonwealth.

Europa-Press AB, Hälsingegatan 5, Box 6410, S–113 82, Stockholm, Sweden. *T.* 34 94 35. *T.A.* Europress.
Market: Newspapers, magazines and weeklies in Sweden, Denmark, Norway and Finland. Syndicates: High quality features of international appeal such as topical articles, photo-features b/w and colour, women's features, short stories, serial novels, non-fiction stories and serials with strong human interest, cartoons, comic strips etc.

Exchange Telegraph Co., Ltd., Extel House, East Harding Street, EC4P 4HB. *T.* 01–353 1080. Glanvill Benn (*Chairman*), Alan B. Brooker (*Managing Director*), Ernest W. H. Bond (*Secretary*).

Exeter News Features and Photos, P.O. Box 59, Exeter, Devon. *T.* 0392–87 4229. 24 hr. answering service. Presents Cornwall, Devon and the West Country to the world in newspaper/magazine features and photos. Buys tourist and pin-up pictures etc. for conversion into colour slides.

Forum World Features, Kern House Enterprises Ltd., Kern House, 61–62 Lincoln's Inn Fields, London, WC2B 6HP. *T.* 01–406 7911. *T.A.* Formserv London PS4. International features agency which supplies a regular weekly service of articles in English, Spanish and Chinese on World Affairs, Politics, Economics, Science, Technology and other subjects. Articles are commissioned from statesmen, politicians, overseas editors and prominent writers with an international reputation.

Foto-Features (Australia), 230 Palmer Street, East Sydney, N.S.W. 2010. *T.* 33 4041. *Editor:* John Wilson. Complete feature service to magazines, papers from the Australian, N.Z. and South Pacific scene. Available for commission any subject, any time. Will sell submitted overseas material to Australian market at normal commission.

Fox Photos Ltd., 69–71 Farringdon Road, London, EC1M 3JT. *T.* 01–405 6851. Press and commercial photographers.

French Press Agency. Mrs. Barbara Evans, 6 Claremont Street, South Yarra, Victoria, Australia. *T.* 24–6909. *T.A.* Manigo, Melbourne. Syndicates general and pictorial features and fashion material for Australian and New Zealand newspapers and magazines. Represents leading French and Italian newspapers and magazines and children's book publishers. Interested in the purchase of features and pictorial material of highest professional standard only, for syndication.

Gemini News Service, John Carpenter House, John Carpenter Street, London EC4Y 0AU. *T.* 01–353 2567/8. *Telex:* 266879. Derek Ingram (*Managing Editor*). Network of correspondents and specialist writers all over the world. Some opening for freelance. Specialises in news-features; also sport, recreations and human interest stories, wildlife. Preferred *length* 800–900 words. *Illustrations:* monochrome prints.

I

J. F. Gibson's Literary Agency (1950), 17 Southampton Place, London, WC1A 2AJ *T.* 01–242 9637. *Proprietor:* J. F. Gibson. *Secretary:* C. T. P. Hughes. *Editor:* Mrs. Freda Stock. Welcomes all kinds of published works in this country or in any English-speaking country, for translation and publication abroad. Represent both authors and publishers in this direction. Terms for books, stories and features 10%–16%. No reading fees.

Hampton Press (1939), Features Syndicate, Dick Street, Henley, via Gladesville, N.S.W. 2111, Australia. Syndicate features, short stories, serials, novelettes, news photos, book rights, radio plays, cartoons, pin-ups, picture stories, comic strips, comics and T.V. scripts, etc. Established writers only. Represented in all parts of the world. Preliminary letter essential.

Hollywood Informer Syndicate, P.O. Box 3049, Hollywood, California 90028. *T.* 213–465–6743. Specialize in syndication of motion picture and show business features and columns. Furnish columns and features and photographs covering every phase of motion pictures.

Hollywood Press Syndicate, 6605 Hollywood Boulevard, Hollywood, California 90028, U.S.A. *Cable address:* Jopolonsky, Hollywood. Specialise in syndication of topical feature articles (of not more than 3000 words) and unusual photographs. Also plays and stories for film producers, if these have already been published. Furnish photographs and features covering every phase of Hollywood.

India-International News Service, *Head Office:* Jute House, 12 India Exchange Place, Calcutta 1. *Branch & Printing Dept.:* 20 Bepin Bihari, Ganguli Street, Calcutta 12. *T.* 22–9563 and 22–6572. *T.A.* Zeitgeist. *Proprietor:* Ing. H. Kothari, B.SC., D.W.P. (Lon.), A.M.A.I.M. (U.S.A.). "Calcutta Letters" and Air Mail news service from Calcutta. Specialists in Industrial and Technical news. Also acts as public relations and publicity consultants. (Controlled by Kothari Organisation.)

Inter-Prensa, Florida 229, Buenos Aires, Argentina. Picture stories, fashion photos, comics. 40% commission.

Inter-Press Features, 69 Fleet Street, London, E.C.4. *T.* 01–583 8210. Specialists in news-features for newspapers and magazines in Britain and abroad. The main outlet is for top-level series of articles on all subjects of popular interest, especially those whose subject matter makes them of interest to women. Serial rights acquired in biographies, human stories, in fact all stories of a top-level nature. Also needs picture features; especially interested in newsy photographic spreads.

International Feature Service, 99, bd. Em. Jacqmain, 1000 Brussels, Belgium. *Managing Director:* Max S. Kleiter. Feature articles, serial rights, tests, cartoons, comic strips and illustrations. Handles English TV-features.

International Magazine Features, 1 Gough Square, Fleet Street, London, E.C.4. *T.* 01–583 0527. Editor: David Hodgson. Syndicates feature and pictorial material to magazines throughout the world. Interviews, first person series, true life adventures. Photographs from freelance sources are handled on a commission basis.

International Press Agency (Pty), Ltd., The (1932), P.O. Box 682, Cape Town. *Managing Editor:* Mrs. U. A. Barnett (M.A., M.SC.). South African agent for many leading British, American and Continental Press firms. Considers the syndicating of feature articles, short stories, serials, press photos for the South African market. South African feature material, illustrated articles, news stories, etc., supplied to world press.

Irish International News Service, Hardy House, 6 Capel Street, Dublin 1. *T.* 47045–6; and 906183 (night). *Editor:* Barry J. Hardy. News, sport, T.V., radio, photographic department; also equipment for T.V. films, etc.

Jewish Telegraphic Agency, Ltd., 182 Fleet Street, London, EC4A 2HH. *T.* 01–242 8485. *Telex:* 22887. *T.A.* Jewcorrau, London. *European Editor:* S. J. Goldsmith. *London Manager:* S. Malins. Gathering and distributing news of Israel and Jews everywhere. Network of own correspondents in five continents.

Keystone Press Agency, Ltd. (1920), Bert Garai, Keystone House, Red Lion Court, EC4A 3EL. *T.* 01–353 9634 and 6745. *T.A.* Pressillu, Phone, London. News and feature pictures. *Average rate of commission:* 50% to 60%.

Lensmen Ltd; Press & P.R. Photo Agency, Lensmen House, Essex Street, E., Dublin, 2. *T.* Dublin 773447.

London General Press (1926), 1–3 St. Paul's Churchyard, London E.C.4. *T.* 01–248 6229. *Directors:* J. H. Wood, R. L. Rowney, H. R. Williamson. World syndicating agency for series, articles, fiction. Economic department specialises in regular commentaries on finance, industry and trade. *Average rate of commission:* 10–15 per cent U.K.; 33⅓% overseas.

MacLean, Alexanders Press Agency, (1967) (Alexander MacLean sole owner), Main Street, Tobermory, Isle of Mull. *T.* Tobermory 2099. News coverage of isles of Mull, Coll, and Tiree. 24-hour service with phone always attended. Only full time news service operating in Inner Hebrides. Accepts special commissions to cover any of the Western Isles. Supplies reliable information on island history, present conditions and future trends. Photographic service. Will supply details of any Clan and their Septs based on accepted histories.

Maharaja Features, P.O. Box 16769, Bombay 22, India. *Cables:* Mahrajfeat, Bombay 22. *T.* 474945. Syndicates feature and pictorial material to newspapers and magazines in India and abroad. Specialises on well researched articles on India by eminent authorities for publication in prestige journals throughout the world. Also topical features 1000–1500 words. *Illustrations:* Monochrome prints and colour transparencies.

Mermaid Press (Copenhagen), 37 Haandvaerkerhaven, 2400 Copenhagen, NV Denmark. *T.* Soeborg 1653. High quality features on Scandinavian topics. Supplies: Copenhagen-subject-pictures. Handles freelance work on commission. Buy outright in cash on acceptance. No syndicated material.

Monitor Press Features Ltd., 17–27 Old Street, London, E.C.1. *T.* 01–253 7071. *Telex:* 24718. *Directors:* L. Tuppen, S. R. White, F. May, P. G. Mellor. See also under **Photographic Agencies.**

National Press Agency, Ltd. (1873), Newspaper House, 8–16 Great New Street, EC4P 4ER. *T.* 01–353 1030. *T.A.* Typo, Fleet, London. Caters for both daily and weekly papers; supplies leading articles, leader-page articles, Parliamentary notes, topical articles, industrial, motoring, air and medical correspondent's features, crossword puzzles, special matter for women's pages and advertising supplements.

Near and Far East News, Ltd., Buchanan House, 24–30 Holborn, London, EC1N 2HT. *T.* 01–405 1441. *Directors:* Lord Hillingdon, P. H. Knight. News agency.

New Zealand Associated Press, 107 Fleet Street, EC4A 2AN. *T.* 01–353 2686.

New Zealand Press Association, 85 Fleet Street, E.C.4.   *T.* 01-353 7040.

News Blitz International, Via Luigi Canina, 6, 00196 Rome.   *T.* 394787.   *Directors:* Giovanni A. Congiu, Carlo A. Congiu.   Syndicates cartoons, comic strips, humorous books with drawings, feature and pictorial material, especially high quality nudes, throughout the world and Italy.   Material from freelance sources required.   Average rate of commission 60–40%—monthly report of sales, payments every 3 months.   Represents TV films in Italy and all over the world. Brochures and catalogue required.   Average rate of commission: 10–40%.

Newspaper Features, Ltd., 80 Fleet Street, London, E.C.4.   *T.* 01-353 7888.   *T.A.* Newsboy, London, E.C.4.   Established in 1919.   Syndicates to newspapers throughout the world attractively presented daily and weekly features designed for international appeal.   Specialising now in cartoons and strips, the Agency can nevertheless supply regular columns of general interest covering a wide variety of subjects.   Has recently launched a new and very successful service called *Ad-features*, which provides up-to-date articles on numerous subjects, which are especially written for use in conjunction with advertisement features and supplements.   All *Ad-features* are issued with accompanying photographs or illustrations.   *The agency cannot entertain unsolicited articles and series, but is always interested to discuss with top-class writers and artists their ideas for new regular features and special series.*

North West News & Sports Agency Ltd. (1956), 8 Duncan Street, Birkenhead, Cheshire L41 5EX.   *T.* 051-647 7691.   News and sports coverage, Birkenhead, Bebington and Wirral area.

Opera Mundi, 100 Av. Raymond Poincaré, Paris 16.

Orion Press, 55, 1-Chome, Kanda-Jimbocho, Chiyoda-ku, Tokyo, 101.   *T.A.* Orionserv, Tokyo.   *Telex.* TK4447 Orionprs.   International press service.

P. A. Features (the Feature Service of the Press Association Ltd.), 85 Fleet Street, London, E.C.4.   *T.* 01-353 7440.   *T.A.* Profeature, London, Telex.   Peter Norman (*Editor*).   Buys illustrated and unillustrated features, strips and other material.

PIP Photos Inc., 507 Fifth Avenue, New York, N.Y. 10017.   *T.* 212–OX7 6191. Interested in emotion-evoking picture-stories.   Send 5 International Reply Coupons for information materials.

Pictorial Press Ltd., 2-3 Salisbury Court, Fleet Street, E.C.4.   *T.* 01-353–6677/4123. *Directors:* L. W. Gale, A. F. Gale, K. V. Gale.   Established in Fleet Street in 1938, handles photographic features dealing with show business, personalities, animals, children, woman subjects, medical and scientific stories and glamour. Handles freelance work but prefers to commission.   Sells direct to media in every part of the world.

Pixfeatures (Mr. P. G. Wickman), 5 Latimer Road, Barnet, Hertfordshire.   *T.* 01–449 9946 and 01–440 3663.   *Telex:* 27538.   Specialises in London representation of North American, German, Dutch, Belgian and Italian magazines.

Press Alliances, Ltd., 63 Fleet Street, EC4Y 1HU.   *T.* 01-353 5991.   *T.A.* Pressallia, Fleet, London.   Specialises in London representation (advertising) of provincial and overseas newspapers.

Press Association, Ltd. (1868), G. Cromarty Bloom (*General Manager*), D. A. Chipp (*Editor-in-Chief*), J. Purdham (*Secretary and Chief Accountant*), 85 Fleet Street, EC4P 4BE.   *T.* 01-353 7440.   *T.A.* Press Association, London.   Home News Agency: News, photographs, features.   Also distributes world news in British Isles outside London.

Press Photos International Photo News Service, Fleet Street House, 70 Lee Lotts, Great Wakering, Essex. *T.* (24 hours) Great Wakering 538. *Cables:* Press Pixs, Southend. Supplies news, features, statistics, photographs, colour photographs, provides reporters and photographers for special purposes.

Press Trust of Ceylon Ltd., Negris Building, York Street, Colombo 1, Ceylon. *T.* 31163, 31174.

Press Trust of India, 20 2/2 Regent Flats, Colombo 2, Ceylon. *T.* 34480.

Provincial Press Features, 1 Gough Square, Fleet Street, London, E.C.4. *T.* 01–583 0527. *T.A.* Deadline, London, E.C.4. *Editorial Director:* A. Eyre James. Syndicates directly features of all kinds throughout the U.K. and Commonwealth. Agents in the Americas, Far East, Scandinavia and the Common Market countries. Articles (850–1000 words) must be suitable for international readership. Ideas for weekly columns welcomed. Payment by arrangement.

Reportage Bureau Laszlo, Fredrikinkatu 63 A 7, Helsinki-10, Finland. *T.* 640 522.

Reuters Limited, 85 Fleet Street, E.C.4. *T.* 01–353 6060.

Science Features, 69 Fleet Street, London, E.C.4. *T.* 01–583 8210. Specialists in the science news-feature. Interested in features on science as the subjects cut-across the life of the average newspaper reader. Interested, too, in series with a popular scientific basis. Also interested in picture features, including natural history subjects and animals. *Preliminary letter advisable.*

South Bedfordshire News Agency Ltd., 1 Oakley Road, Luton. *T.* Luton 52222.

Space Syndications, Graham Payne, Glenside, London Road, Amersham, Bucks. *T.* Amersham 6000. *Cables:* Pressmen, Amersham. Features from new and established writers welcome. Suitable for the "popular" press: nothing historic or first person. 500–1000 words on bright, breezy, informative subjects. Animals, people, off-beat "well what do you know?" type features in great demand. Send sample selection with S.A.E. for criticism. We take 25 per cent of all gross sales.

Sri Lanka News Agency (formerly **Central Press Agency**), 23 Canal Row, P.O. Box 1208, Colombo—1, Ceylon. *Director:* Gamini Navaratne, B.SC.(ECON.)LOND. Supplies—news, features, photographs and press cuttings to local and overseas newspapers and agencies.

Sunderland News Agency (1948), Ted Elkins, 2 Mary Street, Sunderland. *T.* 57743, 70414. Press, radio and television news and feature writers. Supply general news and features of shipping, industrial and human interest.

Syndication International (1945), IPC Services Ltd., 27 Floral Street, London, WC2E 9DP. *T.* 01–836 8466. Strips, features, cartoons, photography, book serialisations, merchandising, etc.

Tass Agency, Gotch House, 30 St. Bride Street, London, E.C.4. General news service to U.S.S.R. *T.* 01–353 9831; economic and commercial news service to U.S.S.R. *T.* 01–353 2661.

TransAtlantic News Service, 7100 Hillside Avenue, Suite 309, Hollywood, California 90046. News and photo agency serving the British and Foreign press. Staffed by former Fleet Street reporters, TANS supplies entertainment news, features and columns from Hollywood, and topical news in general from California. Covers all Hollywood events and undertakes commissions and assignments in all fields. Candid photos of stars at major Hollywood events a speciality.

United Press International (UK) Ltd., News Division, 8 Bouverie Street, E.C.4. *T.* 01–353 2282.

Universal News Services Ltd., 11 New Fetter Lane, London, EC4P 4DP. *T.* 01–353 5200. *Managing Director:* Alfred Geiringer.

Warwickshire News Agency, 17 Dormer Place, Leamington Spa, Warwickshire. *T.* Leamington Spa 26131, 28345, 20972 and 21463. *Directors:* Bill Price, Barrie Tracey, Tony Tavinor. News and news pictures throughout the administrative county. Representatives of national, provincial and trade press, radio and T.V.

Yaffa Newspaper Service of New Zealand, 31–35 Dixon Street, Wellington, 1, New Zealand. *T.* 555–505. *T.A.* and *Cables:* Yaffaz, Wellington.

Yaffa Syndicate Pty Ltd., Corner Butt and Clisdell Streets, Surrey Hills, N.S.W. Largest and oldest established Australian syndicate and literary agency. *T.* 69–7861.

Van Hallan Photo Features, 57, South Street, Isleworth, Middlesex. *T.* 01–568–0792. Specialists in supplying photographic features of news, current events and society meetings to the world's press, magazines and TV organisations. Agency also photograph for P.R. purposes and has an efficient commercial and industrial photo division. Photo reference library contains over 100,000 negatives of prominent personalities from all over the country.

Zubryn, Emil, Apartado, 540 Cuernavaca, Morelos, Mexico. *T.* 2–50–78. International feature agency interested *only* in blockbusters and top exclusive major impact articles and series with international interest. Anything with potential reader and circulation build up will be seriously considered. Also major need for paperback material, fact and fiction, all categories, but again must be tops. Handle only North American rights.

ART AGENTS & COMMERCIAL ART STUDIOS

In their own interests Artists are advised to make preliminary enquiries before submitting work, and to ascertain terms of work. Commission varies but averages 25 per cent. Special attention is called to *Artists and Designers: Code of Professional Conduct* on later pages of this Year Book.

A.L.I. Press Agency, Ltd., 111–115 Boulevard Anspach, 1000—Brussels. *T.* 02 12.73.94. *Director:* G. Lans. Cartoons, comics, strips, washwork, illustrations for covers posters on order or in syndication. All feature material for newspapers and magazines. The biggest choice in picture stories for children and adults. Art studio with 90 Continental artists. Market for transparencies.

Associated Freelance Artists Limited, 19 Russell Street, London, WC2B 5HP. *T.* 01–836 2507–8. *Directors:* Eva Morris, Rex Moreton and Joan Higgins. General illustrators, graphic designers, photographers, lettering artists, exhibition designers, strip illustrators, technical illustrators, a few writers, and a stock photographic library.

Australian Press Bureau, 49 Rawnsley Street, Dutton Park, Brisbane, Queensland, 4102, Australia. Press, magazine, book and brochure illustration, book jacket designs and magazine covers, advertising layouts, etc. Line, half-tone, colour.

Bardon Press Features Ltd., Bardon Marketing & Merchanding Ltd., 17 Farringdon Street, London, E.C.4. *T.* 01–236 8200. Also Barcelona and Copenhagen. International Artists', Publishers' and Merchandising Agents. Commission by arrangement. Particular interests: newspaper and juvenile picture strips, book jackets and magazine illustration.

Butler, James W., 104–8 Kirkdale, London, S.E.26. *T.* 01–699 0558 (2 lines).

Chelsea Studios Ltd. (1921), 40–41 Upper Thames Street, London, E.C.4. *T.* 01–248 0837–8. General and illustration.

Clement Dane Studio, Ltd., 49 Wellington Street, Covent Garden, W.C.2. *T.* 01–836 9222–5.

Coulthurst, L., 136B Ashley Gardens, London, S.W.1. *T.* 01–828 8982. Christmas fancy and box wrapping paper designs; greeting cards; animals, flowers and children suitable for calendars and box top pictures. Specialising in design for the manufacturing stationers.

Dorien Leigh now Mansell Collection, *q.v.*

Farmer (Joan), 49 George Street, London, W1H 5PG. *T.* 01–486 2697–8.

Francis & Mills (1899), 6 Portman Mews South, London, W1H 9AU. *T.* 01–493 5127. *Directors:* R. G. Francis, R. Attwood, G. C. Attwood. Artists' managers and agents.

Freelance Presentations Ltd., 155 Queen Victoria Street, London EC4V 4EL. *T.* 01–236 5781–2–3. *Directors:* Michael Fenton, G. Fenton, John McCorquodale, S. McCorquodale. Artists' agents undertaking the exclusive representation of artists in every sphere of commercial work with a particular interest in the encouragement of young artists. *Sole rate of commission:* 20 per cent.

Gossop (R. P.) Ltd. (1923), 106 Great Russell Street, W.C.1. *T.* 01–636 8563. *Directors:* Bronson Gossop (Managing Director), Kathleen Wheston. Illustration, book decoration, educational drawings and diagrams, maps, graphic design for publicity, and jackets. *Rate of commission:* 20 to 25 per cent.

Grafton Design Unit, 3-5 Fetter Lane, London, E.C.4. *T.* 01–353 6941–3. Specialists in co-ordinated company styles, packaging and prestige brochures.

Grestock & Marsh Ltd., Gloucester House, 19 Charing Cross Road, London, WC2H 0ES *T.* 01–839 4778–9. *Directors:* J. L. Marsh, K. Berry. Specialising in magazine illustration, features and many other types of artwork.

Helen Jardine Artists Ltd. (1928), Minerva House, 35 Wellington Street, London, W.C.2. *T.* 01–836 6720. *Directors:* F. McLare, L. D. Hamilton. Fashion and commercial illustrations of high standard.

Knight (A. S.), Ltd. (1938), Chansitor House, Chancery Lane, London, W.C.2. *T.* 01–405 6826 (4 lines). *Directors:* A. S. Knight (Managing), E. M. Knight. Every form of painting and graphic art; magazine illustrations; posters, showcards, Press advertising, and three-dimensional display. *Average commission:* 25 per cent.

Link Studios, 21 Charterhouse Street, London. E.C.1. *T.* 01–405 1933. All types of illustrations.

London Art Service, 5–11 Lavington Street, London, S.E.1. *T.* 01–928 3283. Artists, designers, illustrators and photographers.

Martin, John & Artists Ltd., 42 Old Bond Street, London, W1X 3AF. *T.* 01–629 6488. *Directors:* A. E. Bowen-Davies, W. Bowen-Davies, L. L. Kemp. *Production Manager:* W. Bowen-Davies. Illustrations for children (educational and fictional), dust jackets, pocket books, magazines, maps and diagrams, layouts and designs, posters.

Middleton (N. E.), Ltd., 3 Golden Square, London, W1R 3AD. *T.* 01–734 8680. General.

Miller & Lang Ltd., 46–50 Darnley Street, Glasgow, S.1. *T.* 041–429 2094.

Norfolk Studio Ltd. (1906), 43 Gerrard Street, London, W.1. *T.* 01–437 0727. *T.A.* Markeba, London. *Directors:* Mrs. D. Smith, W. E. Chester, E. Silver. Specialists in advertising design.

Rogers & Co., Artists' Agents, Ltd. (1906), 8 Bishop's Court, Chancery Lane, W.C.2. *T.* 01–405 1821 (3 lines). *Directors:* J. W. A. Wall, R. P. H. Wall.

Saxon Artists Ltd., 53 New Oxford Street, London, W.C.2. *T.* 01–240 1481–2. Artists' Agents.

Sheldon Studios, Dominion House, Bartholomew Close, London, E.C.1. *T.* 01-606 2268. Posters, showcards, illustrations, box tops, greeting cards, calendar subjects, strips, book jacket designs, wrapping papers, paper serviette and tablelinen designs.

Temple Art Agency (1939), 93-94 Chancery Lane, W.C.2. *T.* 01-405 8295. Magazine and book illustration; picture strips; book wrapper designs; historical art.

BRITISH PRESS–CUTTING AGENCIES

Note.—In the following section it should be noted that no agency can check every periodical, local paper, etc., and that some agencies cover more than others. Special attention should be given to the time limit specified by certain agencies.

Durrant's Press Cuttings Ltd. (1880), Durrant House, 8 Herbal Hill, London, EC1R 5EL. *T.* 01-278 1733. *T.A.* Durclip, London, E.C.1. *Subscription rates:* 100 cuttings £6·30; 300 cuttings, £17; 500 cuttings, £26; 1000 cuttings, £45; 2000 cuttings £75. *Overseas Cuttings:* £9·50 to £12·50 per 100 cuttings according to country. Subscriptions expire after 12 months.

General Press-Cutting Association, Ltd., 88 Chancery Lane, London, WC2A 1EV. *T.* 01-242 5185. Specialises in Literary notices and the terms are 3 months/100 cuttings, £6·50, 6 months/100 cuttings, £8·00; 6 months/300 cuttings £18·00; 6 months/500 cuttings, £28·00; 6 months/1000 cuttings £53·00.

Holbrook, 22 Peacock Grove, Manchester 18. Subjects A to Z. 75p. for 50 cuttings; £1·50 for 100 cuttings, postage extra.

International Press-Cutting Bureau (1920), 1 Knightsbridge Green, London, S.W.1. *T.* 01-584 8131. *T.A.* Adverburo, London, S.W.1. *Representatives:* Brussels, Copenhagen, Geneva, Madrid, Milan, Paris, Lisbon, Stockhom, Berlin, Helsinki, The Hague.

Newsclip, (incorporating **Apcut Ltd**) 34-35 Norfolk Street, London, WC2R 2BG. *T.* 01-836 0376.

Press Information (Scotland) Ltd., Finlay Chambers, 22A West Nile Street, Glasgow C.1. *T.* 041-221 2868. Comprehensive Scottish cuttings service. Agents for national and international bureaux.

Romeike & Curtice, Ltd. (1851), Hale House, 290-296 Green Lanes, London, N13 5TP. *T.* 01-882 0155. *Subscription rates:* £1·40 month reading fee and 6p. cutting supplied billed monthly in arrears. Minimum charge £6·50.

OVERSEAS PRESS-CUTTING AGENCIES

AMERICA

Literary Clipping Service, Inc., 31 East 28th Street, New York, N.Y. 10016. *T.* 889–1850.

Luce Press Clippings, Inc., 420 Lexington Avenue, New York, N.Y. 10017.

New England Newsclip Agency, Inc., 260 Cochituate Road, Framingham, Mass. 01701. *T.* 617–742 4200 and 617–879 4460.

Reviews on File, Walton, N.Y. 13856. *Owner:* Dorothy M. Brandt. Back clippings on authors. Formerly part of **Literary Clipping Service.**

AUSTRALIA

Australian Press Cutting Agency Reg., Stalbridge Chambers, 443 Little Collins Street, Melbourne, C.1., Victoria 3000. $10 per 100 cuttings; $60 per 1000 cuttings.

Barrow, Ivo (1961), 6 St. Hubert's Road, Glen Huntly, Victoria 3163, Australia. Covers press and all books published in Australia.

CANADA

Canadian Press Clipping Service, 481 University Avenue, Toronto 2.

CEYLON

International Press Cutting Service, 63/21, Bowala, Kandy, Ceylon. *Representatives:* Brussels, Geneva, Berlin, Paris, Stockholm, Helsinki, Calcutta, Karachi, Singapore, Wellington. Undertakes other investigations. *Subscription rates:* 100 cuttings—£5: 300 cuttings—£12·50; 500—£19·50; 1000 cuttings—£35. Subscription expires after 12 months.

INDIA

International Clipping Service, Lakshmi Buildings, Sir P. Mehta Road, Fort, Bombay 1. *T.* 263451 (Telegrams: Orientclip.) Prop. K. N. Shah. Supplies Press Cuttings of news, editorials, articles, advertisements, press releases, etc., from all Indian, Pakistan, Ceylon, Burma and Goa papers. Undertakes compilation of statistical reports on competitive Press advertising pertaining to all products. Member F.I.B.E.P. (Federation Internationale Des Bureaux D'Extraits de Presse), Paris.

PAKISTAN

Orient Press Cuttings Service of Pakistan, Iftikhar Chambers, Altaf Husain Road, Karachi, 2. London office: 27 Nant Road, London, N.W.2. Covering English, Urdu and regional language newspapers of Pakistan.

NEW ZEALAND

Chong's Press Cutting Bureau, P.O. Box 8143, Newton, Auckland. All New Zealand Publications covered. Normal review charge $2.00 per month (up to 10 books) plus 10c. per cutting. (Also accepted $2.00 per book plus 10c. per cutting).

SOUTH AFRICA

S.A. Press Cutting Agency (Pty) Ltd., 36 Point Road, Durban, Natal, South Africa. T. 66403. T.A. Newscut, Durban. English and Afrikaans newspapers and trade journals from Zambia to the Cape. *Rate:* R7.00 per 100 cuttings.

WEST INDIES

Valmor Agency, Lower Westbury Road, St. Michael, Barbados.

SOCIETIES AND CLUBS, ETC.

SOCIETIES AND CLUBS OF INTEREST TO AUTHORS, JOURNALISTS, ARTISTS, AND MUSICIANS

Academi Gymreig, Yr. *President:* Dr. Kate Roberts; *Chairman:* Professor J. E. Caerwyn Williams; *Treasurer:* Bedwyr Lewis Jones, M.A.; *Secretary:* Dr. Gwyn Thomas, 6 Lôn y Meillion, Bangor.

The society was founded in 1959 for the promotion of literature in the Welsh language and to provide a platform for young writers of promise. Membership is open to those who have made some contribution to Welsh literature, members pay a fee, and give their services free to the society. The society's annual Easter Congress, at various centres in Wales, is open to all. The society publishes a literary magazine, *Taliesin*, and awards an annual prize for a Welsh book of special literary merit.

Academi Gymreig, Yr: English Language Section. *Chairman:* Glyn Jones; *Secretary/ Treasurer:* Mrs. Sally Roberts Jones, 3 Crown Street, Port Talbot.

This section was founded in 1968 to provide a meeting-point for writers in the English language who are of Welsh origin and/or take Wales as a main theme of their work. Membership at present is by invitation and members pay an annual subscription. Although it is an autonomous body, members of the English Language Section co-operate with members of the parent body for joint conferences and similar activities.

Academy of Arts, Royal, Burlington House, W1V 0DS. *T.* 01–734 9052. Academicians (R.A.) and Associates (A.R.A.) are elected from the most distinguished artists in the United Kingdom. Women are eligible for membership, and their work is exhibited equally with that of men each year. *Exhibitions:* Summer, May to July; Autumn and Winter, various periods from September to March.

American Book Publishers Council, Inc. (1946), 1 Park Avenue, New York, N.Y. 10016. *T.* Murray Hill 9–8920. *Managing Director:* Richard H. Sullivan. *Senior-Associate Managing Director:* Robert W. Frase. The Council is a non-profit membership corporation supported by major publishers in the United States of books other than textbooks and encyclopedias. Its functions include a general recommendatory service on all matters involving book publishers, including the development of new sales outlets, new and more effective methods of promoting and publicising books, copyright matters, the gathering of industry statistics, and the development of foreign trade. In addition, it maintains a credit information service on domestic retail bookselling accounts, sponsors certain insurance plans for the benefit of its members, and reports on tax legislation. It also acts as an agency of liaison between its members and branches of government and as a clearing house for information from government departments. The ABPC is the largest trade organisation in the book publishing field in the United States.

American Correspondents in London, Association of. *President:* David Nichol, Chicago Daily News, 69 Fleet Street, London E.C.4. *T.* 01–353 7903.

Artists of Chelsea, The Mall Galleries, The Mall, London, S.W.1. *T.* 01–930 6844. *Secretary:* Maurice Bradshaw. To foster appreciation of the arts in the Royal Borough of Chelsea, Kensington. Open Annual Exhibition at the Chenil Gallery, Chelsea.

Arts (1863), 40 Dover Street, London, W.1. *T.* 01–493 4260. *Subs.* £31·50. For men connected with or interested in art, literature, or science.

Arts, Royal Society of, John Adam Street, Adelphi, WC2N 6EZ. *T.* 01–839 2366. Founded in 1754. Sir James Taylor, M.B.E., PH.D., D.SC. (*Chairman of the Council*), G. E. Mercer (*Secretary*). Fellowship (F.R.S.A.) is open to both men and women. The aims of the Society, as indicated by its full title, are, "The encouragement of Arts, Manufactures and Commerce."

Arts Council of Great Britain, 106 Piccadilly, London, W1V 0AU. *T.* 01–629 9495. *Chairman:* The Lord Goodman. *Secretary-General:* Hugh Willatt. To develop and improve the knowledge, understanding and practice of the arts, to increase the accessibility of the arts to the public.

Aslib (1924), 3 Belgrave Square, London, S.W.1. *T.* 01–235 5050. An association of special libraries and information departments. For particulars of membership apply: The Director, Leslie Wilson, M.A.

Association of Assistant Librarians (1895), Central Library, Howard Street, Rotherham, Yorkshire. (Group of the Library Association, *q.v.*) *President:* R. J. Edwards, F.L.A. *Hon. Secretary:* C. C. Williams, D.M.A., A.L.A. Publish library text-books and bibliographical aids.

Association of British Science Writers, 3 Sanctuary Buildings, 20 Great Smith Street, London, S.W.1. *T.* 01–799 7657. *Chairman:* T. Osman. *Secretary:* Miss Mary Lee. An association of science writers, and of editors, and radio, film, and television producers concerned with the presentation of science. Its aims are to improve the standard of science writing and to assist its members in their work. Visits to research establishments, off-the-record luncheon parties for people who are concerned with scientific policy, and receptions for scientific attachés are among its activities.

Australian Book Publishers' Association, c/o H. F. Weston, 163 Clarence Street, Sydney 2000, N.S.W.
    The association aims to foster original publishing in Australia, to help improve Australian book industry as a whole.

Australian Society of Authors, The, 12 Yirra Road, Mount Colah, N.S.W. 2079. *T.* 47 3271. *President:* Dal Stivens. *Executive Secretary:* Jill Hellyer.

Australian Writers, The Society of, Australia House, Strand, London, W.C.2. Formed in 1952 to further the cause of Australian writers and Australian writing wherever possible, and to act as a spokesman and advice and information centre for Australian writers in the United Kingdom. *Subscription:* Writers £1·00 Associates 50p. a year.

Authors (1891), (at the National Liberal Club), Whitehall Place, London, S.W.1. *T.* 01–930 9871. *Secretary:* Michael S. Lindsay.

Authors' Guild of Ireland, Ltd., 1 Clare Street, Dublin, 2. *T.* Dublin 67273–4. *Directors:* John McCann, E. J. Duffy, Frank Carney, John K. Lyons, Thomas Coffey, John O'Donovan. A society for the protection of copyright owned and managed, on a non-profit basis, by Full members who must be owners of copyright in literary or dramatic works by reason of authorship, or who are the personal successors of such authors. Agents for the control of performing rights and collection of royalties in Ireland. *Secretary:* Dermot Guinan.

Authors, The Society of, 84 Drayton Gardens, London, S.W.10. *T.* 01–373 6642. *President:* Sir Alan Herbert. *General Secretary:* M. E. Barber, O.B.E., M.A., Barrister-at-Law.

The Society was founded in 1884 by Sir Walter Besant with the object of representing, assisting, and protecting authors. Since then its scope has been continuously extended until today within the framework of the Society separate associations have been created for playwrights, translators, and writers for radio, details of which will be found elsewhere in this issue. There is also a Children's Writers Group and an Educational Writers Group.

Members are entitled to legal as well as general advice in connection with the marketing of their work, their contracts, their choice of a publisher, etc., and also to have litigation in which their work may involve them in any part of the world conducted by the Society and at the Society's expense provided the Committee of Management is satisfied that the member's case is sound in law and ethics and that the proceedings are justified.

Annual Subscription: £10·50. Full particulars of membership may be obtained from the Society's offices. (See also page viii.)

Authors' Representatives, Inc., Society of (1928), 101 Park Avenue, New York, N.Y. 10017. *T.* Murray Hill 3–5890.

Aviation Artists, Society of, The Mall Galleries, The Mall, London, S.W.1. *T.* 01–930 6844. *Secretary:* Maurice Bradshaw. To promote a greater appreciation of the artistic opportunities of flight, etc.

Bibliographical Society (1892), British Academy, Burlington House, Piccadilly London W1V 0NS. *President:* J. C. T. Oates. *Secretary:* R. J. Roberts. Acquisition and dissemination of information upon subjects connected with bibliography.

Blackpool and Fylde Art Society, The. Founded 1884. *Hon. Secretary:* Marion Rudge, 35 Winchester Drive, Carleton, Poulton-le-Fylde, FY6 7PS. *T.* Poulton 5436. Annual exhibition (members' work only) held in autumn. Studio meetings during week, practice, lectures, etc.; summer: outdoor sketching parties.

Bladon Society of Arts and Crafts, The, Hurstbourne Tarrant, Andover, Hampshire. *T.* Hurstbourne Tarrant 278. *President:* The Lord Moyne. *Founder and Hon. Curator:* Mrs. Doris Bladon-Hawton. To stimulate interest in the arts and crafts by eight annual exhibitions in the Bladon Galleries, and a permanent but changing Crafts sections in the two adjoining cottages. Most exhibits on sale.

Book Association of Ireland (1943), 21 Shaw Street, Dublin 2. *T.* Dublin 778115. Promotion of book reading and wider distribution of books of all kinds, particularly books in Gaelic, books by Irish writers, books published in Ireland and books of Irish interest published anywhere. Book weeks and exhibitions organised. Classified lists of books compiled and circulated. Enquiries concerning books answered if possible.

Books Across the Sea, The English-Speaking Union, Dartmouth House, 37 Charles Street, W1X 8AB. *T.* 01–629 7400. New York: The English-Speaking Union, 16 East 69th Street, New York, N.Y. 10021. Books Across the Sea Society has amalgamated with the English-Speaking Union, and many of its officers continue as members of the Books Across the Sea Committee of the English-Speaking Union. The society still exchanges books with its corresponding Books Across the Sea Committee of the English Speaking Union of New York. The books exchanged are new, not yet published on both sides of the Atlantic, and selected to throw light on each country's daily life, traditions, also heritage and national problems. These books are circulated among members and accredited borrowers to whom new selections are announced by bulletin, and bulk loans are made to schools, colleges, universities and public libraries. Books Across the Sea has now extended its activities with the establishment of committees in Australia and New Zealand, India and Canada. Book exchanges are now in operation between these committees and the committees in London and New York.

Booksellers Association of Great Britain and Ireland (1895), 154 Buckingham Palace Road, London, S.W.1. *T.* 01–730 8214–6. *President:* Eric Bailey. To promote and extend the sale of books and improve educational and technical qualifications of those engaged in it.

Britain in Water-Colours, The Mall Galleries, The Mall, London, S.W.1. *T.* 01–930 6844. *Secretary:* Maurice Bradshaw. An annual exhibition for painters in water-colours illustrating the British character and way of life.

British Academy, Burlington House, Piccadilly, London, W1V 0NS. *T.* 01–734 0457. *President:* Sir Kenneth Wheare, C.M.G. *Treasurer:* Sir Roy Allen, C.B.E. *Secretary:* D. F. Allen, C.B.

British Amateur Press Association (1890), BM/BAPA, London, W.C.1. To promote the Fellowship of Writers, Artists, Editors, Printers and Publishers and other craftsmen, and to encourage them to contribute to, edit and print and publish AS A HOBBY, magazines, books and literary works produced by letterpress and other processes.

British Association of Industrial Editors, The (1949). *President:* Lord St. Oswald, M.C., D.L. *Secretary:* Sidney Charteris, 2A Elm Bank Gardens, Barnes, S.W.13. *T.* 01–876 6283. The objects include development of the qualifications of those engaged in producing house journals in the United Kingdom and the Commonwealth and to work for improved standards in all types of house journals; to maintain an Appointments Bureau and to provide a consultant service on all matters relating to house journals. Membership is open to all men and women engaged in the production of house journals.

British Colour Council (1930), 10A Chandos Street, London, W1M 9DE *T.* 01–580 8946. Co-ordination of colour and design. *Patron:* H.R.H. The Princess Margaret, Countess of Snowdon. *Executive Director:* Hugh H. Muirhead.

British Copyright Council, The, Copyright House, 29–33 Berners Street, London, W1P 3DB. *T.* 01–580 5544. *Chairman:* Sir Alan Herbert, C.H. *Vice-Chairman:* R. E. Barker, O.B.E. *Hon. Treasurer:* Miss M. E. Barber, O.B.E. *Secretary:* Reynell Wreford. Its purposes are to defend and foster the true principles of creators' copyright and their acceptance throughout the world, to bring together bodies representing all who are interested in the protection of such copyright, and to keep watch on any legal or other changes which may require an amendment of the law.

British Council, The, 65 Davies Street, London, W1Y 2AA   *T.* 01–499 8011. *Chairman:* Lord Fulton, LL.D., D.LITT.   *Director-General:* The Hon. Sir John Henniker-Major, K.C.M.G., C.V.O., M.C.

The British Council was established in 1934 to promote a wider knowledge of Britain and the English language abroad and to develop closer cultural relations with other countries.   It received its Royal Charter in 1940.   It has staff in some 75 countries, and some 25 offices and centres in Britain, in university towns which arrange programmes for professional visitors from overseas and provide for overseas students in Britain.

The Council's activities overseas include the promotion of English language teaching and other educational work including science teaching; attention is given to the use of television and radio in this context.   The Council fosters personal contacts between British and overseas people, especially in the educational, professional and scientific fields.   It supports over 200 libraries of British books and periodicals in some 70 Commonwealth and foreign countries; it makes presentations of books and periodicals to appropriate institutions and organizes book and periodical exhibitions overseas.   Its own publications include *Higher Education in the United Kingdom*, *British Medical Bulletin*, *British Medical Booklist*, *British Book News*, a series of specialist booklists and the bimonthly series of essays, *Writers and Their Work*.   It has also produced, in association with the Argo Record Company a complete set of recordings of the works of Shakespeare.   It is now engaged on a recorded anthology of English poetry and on a programme of music recordings.

It sends paintings and sculpture by British artists to international art festivals and on extended tours abroad, and arranges overseas tours by dramatic and musical artists and companies.   Musical scores and records are also provided for loan to musical and educational institutions, radio stations and individual musicians overseas.

British Drama League (1919), 9 Fitzroy Square, London, W1P 6AE.   *T.* 01–387 2666.   *Director:* Walter Lucas.   To assist the development of the art of the theatre.   The largest library in the country devoted essentially to plays and theatrical subjects.

British Film Institute, 81 Dean Street, London, W.1.   *T.* 01–437 4355.   *Telex:* 27624. *Director:* Stanley Reed; *Deputy Director* and *Curator:* Ernest Lindgren, O.B.E.; *Secretary:* Vernon Saunders.   The general object of the British Film Institute is "to encourage the use and development of the cinematograph and television as a medium of entertainment and instruction."   Its departments include the National Film Archive and the National Film Theatre on the South Bank. The emphasis of the Institute is on the entertainment film of quality although its scope embraces other types of film including documentaries and educational films.   Through its information service, its *Monthly Film Bulletin* (which gives credits and reviews of every feature film released in Britain), its quarterly *Sight and Sound* and its Education Department (including lecture and schools service), it is of value to writers dealing with film matters.   The annual subscription is £2·25 (including *Sight and Sound* sent post free).   Associateship (National Film Theatre (London)) £1 (including programmes post free), 75p. to full-time students at recognised educational establishments and film society members).

British Science Fiction Association, Ltd., The (1958).   *Chairman:* Edmund Crispin. *Executive Secretary:* Mrs. A. Walton, 25 Yewdale Crescent, Coventry, Warwickshire, CV2 2FF.   For authors, publishers, booksellers and readers of science fiction, fantasy and allied genres.   Annual convention.   Publishes journal *Vector*, containing news and information.   Membership fees £1·50 per annum, plus 25p. entrance fee.

Brontë Society, Brontë Parsonage Museum, Haworth, nr. Keighley BD22 8DR. *T.* Haworth 2323. *President:* Donald Hopewell. *Chairman of the Council:* W. T. Oliver. *Hon. Secretary:* A. H. Preston. Examination, preservation, illustration of the memoirs and literary remains of the Brontë family; exhibitions of MSS. and other objects. *Publications:* The Transactions of the Brontë Society (Annual).

Canadian Authors' Association, 22 Yorkville Avenue, Toronto 5, Ontario. *President:* Miss M. Carol Wilson. *Secretary:* Mrs. Lyn Harrington.

Canadian Book Publishers' Council. Consists of forty-two educational and trade publishers; maintains offices at 45 Charles Street East, Suite 701, Toronto 285. *T.* 416–964 7231. Interested in advancing the cause of the publishing business by co-operative effort and in encouragement of high standards of workmanship and service. Co-operates with other organizations interested in the reading and study of books. Canadian Book Publishers' Council sponsors two sub-divisions, The Book Publishers' Association concerned with library and general books, and the Canadian Textbook Publishers' Institute, interested in school textbooks. Officers are elected annually. *President:* Campbell B. Hughes.

Children's Writers Group, 84 Drayton Gardens, London, S.W.10. *T.* 01–373 6642. *Secretary:* Mrs. Jeny Patch. A self-governing unit within the network of The Society of Authors.

City of London Art Exhibition, 17 Carlton House Terrace, London, S.W.1. *T.* 01–930 6844. *Secretary:* Maurice Bradshaw. Annual exhibition for artists living or working in the City of London.

Classical Association. *Secretaries:* M. R. F. Gunningham, c/o 11 Fawcett Court, Fawcett Street, S.W.10., Dr. J. G. Landels, The University, Whiteknights, Reading, Berks.

Commonwealth (formerly Empire) Press Union (1909), 154 Fleet Street, E.C.4. *T.* 01–353 6428–9. Organisation of newspapers, periodicals, news agencies throughout the Commonwealth. Lieut.-Colonel Terence Pierce-Goulding, M.B.E., C.D.

Composer's Guild of Great Britain, The, 10 Stratford Place, London, W1N 9AE *T.* 01–499 8567.
    The Composers' Guild was created in June 1945 under the aegis of The Incorporated Society of Authors, Playwrights, and Composers. In 1948 it was formed into an independent body under the title of The Composers' Guild of Great Britain. Its function is to represent and protect the interests of composers of music in this country and to advise and assist its members on problems connected with their work.
    Annual subscription: £2·50. Further particulars may be obtained from the Officers of the Guild.

Confédération Internationale des Sociétés d'Auteurs et Compositeurs-Congrès Mondial des Auteurs et Compositeurs, 11 Rue Keppler, Paris 16ᵉ, France. *T.* 553–5937. *T.A.* Interauteurs, Paris.

Crime Writers' Association (1953). *Secretary:* Mrs. Bonney Harris, c/o National Book League, 7 Albemarle Street, London W.1. For professional writers of crime novels, short stories, plays for stage, television and sound radio, or of serious works on crime. Full membership £3·15 annually; overseas, associate, and country £2·10. Monthly meetings at National Book League.

Critic's Circle, The (1913). *President:* 1970, Cecil Wilson. *Vice-President:* 1970, Andrew Porter. *Hon. General Secretary:* Sidney Charteris, 2A Elm Bank Gardens, Barnes, S.W.13. *T.* 01–876 6283. *Objects:* To promote the art of criticism, to uphold its integrity in practice and to foster and safeguard the professional interests of its members. Membership is by invitation of the Council. Such invitations are issued only to persons engaged professionally, regularly and substantially in the writing or broadcasting of criticism of drama, music, films, ballet, television or radio.

Dickens Fellowship (1902), *Headquarters:* The Dickens House, 48 Doughty Street, WC1N 2LF. *T.* 01–405 2127. *Hon. Secretary:* John Greaves. House occupied by Dickens 1837–9. Relics displayed include manuscripts, furniture, portraits, letters and first editions. Membership £1·75 p.a. including *The Dickensian.*

Dorman (Sean) Manuscript Society, Raffeen Cottage, Union Place, Fowey, Cornwall. For mutual help among part-time writers, whether housewives or in the various professions and trades, as well as those fully professional. Circulating manuscript parcels affording constructive criticism, with Remarks Book and "People and Prejudices" Booklet. Special circulators for advanced writers and overseas members. Technical discussion circulators. Bi-annual magazine *Writing Published* buys verse and articles on journalism, and runs competitions for prizes. *Subscription:* U.K. and Eire: £1·25 p.a.; 75p. six months (after six months' trial period at reduced subscription of 50p.); Overseas £1·50 p.a. only. Further particulars and copy of *Writing Published* supplied on receipt of 25p. and stamped addressed envelope only.

Dramatists, The League of, 84 Drayton Gardens, London, S.W. 10. *T.* 01–373 6642. *President:* St. John Ervine, LL.D. *Secretary:* Julia Jones.

The League was founded in 1931 under the aegis of The Society of Authors. Its primary purpose is to protect and further the interests of British Dramatists at home and abroad. Its activities include the examination and drafting of agreements, the leasing of plays for amateur and repertory performances and the collection of fees. Members are entitled to advice on all questions concerned with their dramatic work. Where legal action is necessary, the costs of a members' case are, with the consent of the Committee, borne by the League.

The annual subscription for Full Membership is £10·50 which includes membership of The Society of Authors. Associate Membership subscription is £5·25 per annum.

Full particulars may be obtained from the offices of the League.

Dunedin Society, The. Founded 1911 for the encouragement of the Scottish creative Arts. *Hon. Secretary:* William MacLellan, 104 Hill Street, Glasgow. *T.* 041–332 1959. The main object of the Society is to provide a focal point through which the creative artist in Scotland can find an interested audience whether in his native country or abroad. Information on all aspects of Scottish culture available on request.

Early English Text Society (1864), Lady Margaret Hall, Oxford. *Hon. Director:* Professor Norman Davis, M.B.E. *Executive Secretary:* Dr. Anne Hudson. To bring unprinted early English literature within the reach of students in sound texts. Annual subscription, £3·15.

East Anglian Writers, *President:* Correlli Barnett, F.R.S.L. *Hon Secretary:* Hilda Nickson, Artilda, The Street, Dilham, North Walsham, Norfolk. *Object:* To stimulate a greater public interest in books and those who write them and to provide a meeting ground for writers. Membership open to writers who have had at least one book published or one play professionally acted and produced and who were born or who live in the region. Members' meetings by arrangement. Two public literary functions per year: a Spring Lunch and an Autumn Dinner. Annual subscription, 60p.

Edinburgh Bibliographical Society (1890), c/o National Library of Scotland, Edinburgh EH1 1EW. *Secretary:* J. R. Seaton. *Treasurer:* M. A. Begg.

Educational Writers Group, 84 Drayton Gardens, London, S.W.10. *T.* 01–373 6642. *Secretary:* Philippa MacLiesh. A self-governing unit within the network of The Society of Authors.

Empire Art Loan Exhibitions Society, The Mall Galleries, The Mall, London, S.W.1. *T.* 01–930 6844. *Organising Director:* Maurice Bradshaw. To arrange, from public or private sources, exhibitions for loan within the British Commonwealth.

English Association, 29 Exhibition Road, London, S.W.7. *T.* 01–589 8480. *President:* Professor Nevill Coghill. *Secretary:* Mrs. K. Sales.

English Speaking Board, 32 Roe Lane, Southport, Lancashire. *T.* Southport 55510. *President:* Sir Michael Redgrave. *Aim:* to foster all activities concerned with English speech. It conducts examinations where stress is on individual oral expression. The examination auditions include talks, prepared and unprepared. Examinations are also held for those engaged in technical or industrial concerns, and in spoken English for foreign students. Three times a year, in January, May and September, members receive the English Speaking Board Journal, *Spoken English.* Articles are invited by the editor on any special aspect of spoken English. Members can also purchase other publications at reduced rates. Adult membership £2 per annum (£20 Life membership). Residential summer conference held annually, July–August.

Folklore Society, The (1878), c/o The Library, University College, Gower Street, London, WC1E 6BT. *T.* 01–387 5894. *Hon. Secretary:* Venetia J. Newall, M.A., F.R.G.S., F.R.S.A. Collection, recording and study of folklore.

Foreign Press Association in London (1888). *President:* H. G. Alexander. *Hon. Secretary:* Carlos Forsberg. Registered office: 11 Carlton House Terrace, London, S.W.1. *T.* 01–930 0445. *Objects:* The promotion of the professional interests of its members. Membership open to foreign professional journalists men or women, residing in the United Kingdom. Entrance fee, £5·25; annual subscription, £7·35.

Freelance Photographers, Bureau of, (1965), 59 Tottenham Lane, London, N.8. *T.* 01–348 4463. *Head of Administration:* John Tracy. To help the freelance photographer by providing information on markets, legal service, free criticism service. Membership fee: £3·15 per annum.

Graphic Artists, Society of (1919), The Mall Galleries, The Mall, London, S.W.1. *T.* 01–930 6844. *Secretary:* Maurice Bradshaw. Membership open to both men and women. Exhibitions open to all artists. Drawings and prints in any medium, including collages and constructions.

Green Room (1877), 8–9 Adam Street, W.C.2. *T.* 01–240 2844–5. *Subs.* £20. *Entrance fee:* £5. Dramatic, musical, literary, artistic. The Club is instituted to promote the association of members of the dramatic profession.

Greeting Card and Calendar Association, The, 6 Wimpole Street, London, W1M 8AS. *T.* 01–580 3121–2.

Guild of Agricultural Journalists, Agriculture House, Knightsbridge, London, S.W.1. *T.* 01–235 5077. *President:* Ernest Jay. *Chairman:* Alexander Kenworthy. *Hon. General Secretary:* Peter Bell. Established to promote a high standard among journalists who specialise in agricultural matters and to assist them to increase their sources of information and technical knowledge. Membership is open to those earning their livelihood wholly or mainly from agricultural journalism.

Guild of Motoring Writers, The, 35 Alwyne Road, London, N.1. *T.* 01–359 0755. *General Secretary:* Mrs. Jenny Brittan. To raise the standard of motoring journalism. For writers, broadcasters, photographers on matters of motoring, but who are not connected with the motor industry.

Guild of Travel Writers, The, 23 Linden Lea, London, N2 0RF. *T.* 01–455 9570. *Information Officer.* Mrs. Lorna Braithwaite. To assist members by arranging meetings and discussions to extend the range of their knowledge and experience and by writing seriously and conscientiously about travel to contribute to the growth of public interest in and knowledge of the subject. Entrance fee £2, annual subscription £5.

Hakluyt Society (1846), c/o British Museum, WC1B 3DG. *T.* 01–580 6622. *President:* Professor Charles F. Beckingham, M.A., PH.D. *Hon. Secretaries:* Professor E. M. J. Campbell, M.A., F.S.A., and T. E. Armstrong, M.A., PH.D. Publication of original narratives of voyages, travels, naval expeditions, and other geographical records.

Harleian Society (1869), Ardon House, Mill Lane, Godalming, Surrey. *Chairman:* Sir Anthony Wagner, K.C.V.O., D.LITT., F.S.A., Garter King of Arms. *Secretary:* J. P. Heming, B.A. Instituted for transcribing, printing and publishing the heraldic visitations of Counties, Parish Registers and any manuscripts relating to genealogy, family history and heraldry.

Imperial Arts League, The (Incorporated) (1909). R.W.S. Galleries, 26 Conduit Street, London, W1R 9TA. *T.* 01–629 8300. *Secretary:* Malcolm Fry. Run by Artists for Artists and renders advice and assistance in every difficulty met with in their professional capacity. *Annual Subscription,* £1·05 (minimum), (52½p. if under 25); Life membership, £15·75 Entrance Fee: £1·05.

Indexers, The Society of. Objects: (1) to improve the standard of indexing; (2) to maintain a panel of indexers from which authors, editors and publishers may be furnished with suitable names; (3) to act as an advisory body on the qualifications and remuneration of indexers; (4) to publish or communicate books, papers and notes on the subject of indexing; (5) to raise the status of indexers and to safeguard their interests.

Membership is open to those who do indexing of books and periodicals, and others interested in promoting its objects and is of two kinds: Individual and Institutional. There is no entrance fee. *Annual subscription:* Individual members and non-profit-making organizations: £2·10; Other institutional members: £4·20. Copies of the Society's journal, *The Indexer,* are sent free to members. *Chairman:* Richard F. L. Bancroft, M.A., *Secretary:* Miss P. M. Trew, B.A., A.C.I.S., c/o Barclays Bank, 1 Pall Mall East, London, S.W.1.

Industrial Painters' Group, 17 Carlton House Terrace, London, S.W.1. *T.* 01–930 6844. *Secretary:* Maurice Bradshaw. To introduce industrial patrons to artists.

Institute of Contemporary Arts, Nash House, The Mall, S.W.1. *T.* 01–839 5344. *President:* Sir Roland Penrose, C.B.E. A centre which aims at encouraging collaboration between the various arts, the promotion of experimental work and the mutual interchange of ideas. Exhibitions, readings of contemporary poetry, lectures and discussions on the arts, play readings, concerts, etc.

Institute of Incorporated Photographers, Amwell End, Ware, Hertfordshire. *T.* Ware 4011–3. *Secretary:* J. L. A. Hunt, F.C.I.S. (Founded 1901, Incorporated 1921.) *Principal Objects:* To represent all who practise photography as a profession in any field; to improve the quality of photography; establish recognised examination qualifications and a high standard of conduct; to safeguard the interests of the public and the profession. *Membership:* Exceeding 3,500. Admission can be obtained either via the Intermediate and Final examinations, or by submission of work and other information to the appropriate examining board. *Designatory Letters:* F.I.I.P. and A.I.I.P. Fellows, Associates and Licentiates are entitled to the designation Incorporated Photographer. *Meetings:* The Institute organises numerous meetings and conferences in various parts of the country throughout the year. *Publications:* A monthly journal, the *Photographer.*

Institute of Journalists. The. R. F. Farmer (*General Secretary*), 2–4 Tudor Street, EC4Y 2AB. *T.* 01–353 3376 (2 lines). The senior organisation of the profession, founded in 1883 and incorporated by Royal Charter 1890. Men and women are equally eligible for Fellowship (F.J.I.) and Membership (M.J.I.). Qualified members are entitled to automatic membership of National Union of Journalists without extra subscription; Institute now serves professional—as distinct from trade union—interests of total joint membership of both bodies. Maintains a successful Employment Register and has considerable accumulated funds for the assistance of members; offers a service of free legal advice to members in matters relating to their professional activities. A Free-lance Section maintains close co-operation between editors and publishers and free-lances. A panel of free-lance writers on special subjects is available for the use of editorial publishers. There are also Special Sections for Trade, Technical, periodical and Book Journalists and for Public Relations Officers. Subscriptions, £11·50; £8·50 below age of 24.

International Bureau for Cultural Exchange. *Hon. Secretary:* William MacLellan, 104 Hill Street, Glasgow C2. *T.* 041–332 1959. The function of the Bureau is to assist artists in travelling abroad on the basis of mutual exchange between artists of different countries. Those working in the arts who wish to present their talents overseas and are prepared to assist in presenting the work of foreign artists in their own country, are invited to write to the Bureau.

Johnson Society of London (1928). *President:* Dr. L. F. Powell. *Secretary:* A. G. Dowdeswell, 92 St. Paul's Road, Canonbury, N.1. To study the life and works of Doctor Johnson, and to perpetuate his memory in the city of his adoption.

Keats-Shelley Memorial Association (1903). *Chairman:* Lord Abinger. *Patron:* H.M. Queen Elizabeth the Queen Mother. *Hon. Secretary:* Norman Kilgour, Longfield Cottage, Longfield Drive, London, S.W.14. *T.* 01–876 8136. Occasional meetings; annual *Bulletin* and progress reports. Supports house in Rome where John Keats died, and celebrates the poets Keats, Shelley, Byron, and Leigh Hunt. Subscription to "Friends of the Keats-Shelley Memorial" minimum £1·50 per annum.

Kent and Sussex Poetry Society, centre Tunbridge Wells, has been formed to create a greater interest in Poetry. *President:* Richard Church, C.B.E., F.R.S.L. *Vice-President:* Patric Dickinson. *Chairman:* Elliot Gorst, Q.C. *Hon. Secretary:* Mrs. E. Harmer, 82A Grosvenor Road, Tunbridge Wells, Kent. *T.* 31398. *Annual Subscription:* adults, £1·05; under 21, 37½p. Prominent poets address the Society, a Folio of members' work is published, and a full programme of recitals, discussions and readings is provided. The lives of poets and their work are intensively studied by means of lectures, readings and discussions.

Lancashire Authors' Association .The (1909), "for writers and lovers of Lancashire literature." *President:* Dr. Geoffrey Handley-Taylor, F.R.S.L. *General Secretary:* Miss M. J. Webster, 44 Lonsdale Street, Accrington, Lancashire BB5 0HL. *T.* 33374. *Subscription:* £1 p.a. *Publications: The Record.*

Liaison of Actors, Managements & Playwrights (LAMP). *Secretary:* Edgar Bates, 13 Wolseley Road, London, N.8. Has been formed by members of the theatrical profession with the aim of producing rehearsed stage-readings of new plays in order to bring actors and playwrights into closer contact. Services are given voluntarily and authors are helped to assess their own work. Meetings are held first Thursday in the month at Lamb & Flag, Rose Street, off Garrick Street, London, W.C.2. at 7.30 p.m.

Library Association, 7 Ridgmount Street, Store Street, London, WC1E 7AE. *T.* 01–636 7543. *President:* D. T. Richnell, B.A., F.L.A. *Secretary:* H. D. Barry, D.P.A. Barrister at Law. Founded in 1877 to promote bibliographical study and research and the better administration of libraries, and to unite all persons interested in library work. Conferences and meetings are held, publications issued and a library and information bureau maintained. The monthly journal, *The Library Association Record*, is distributed free to all members. Standard subscription: £15, but varies according to income, etc.

London Writer Circle. For mutual help among writers of all grades. Lectures, study groups, MS. clubs, discussions, competitions. *Subs.:* £1·50 (town). 62½p. (country). Entrance fee, 25p. Full particulars from the *Hon. Secretary*, Miss M. E. Harris, 308 Lewisham Road, London, S.E.13.

Marine Artists, Royal Society of, 17 Carlton House Terrace, London, S.W.1. *T.* 01–930 6844. *Secretary:* Maurice Bradshaw. To promote and encourage marine art. Open Annual Exhibition: October.

Master Photographers Association of Great Britain, 80 Rochester Row, London S.W.1. *T.* 01–828 9174. To promote and protect professional photography in all its applications. *Entrance fee:* 50p. *Subscription:* £3·50 a year. Members can qualify for awards of Associateship and Fellowship.

Miniature Painters, Sculptors and Gravers, Royal Society of (1895), The Mall Galleries, The Mall, London, S.W.1. *T.* 01–930 6844. *Secretary:* Carl de Winter. Open Annual Exhibition.

Miniaturists, Society of (1895), R.W.S. Galleries, 26 Conduit Street, W1R 9TA. *T.* 01–629 8300. Malcolm Fry (Secretary). Members only (both men and women). Annual Exhibition.

Mural Painters, Society of, The Mall Galleries, The Mall, London, S.W.1. *T.* 01–930 6844. *Secretary:* Maurice Bradshaw. To promote and encourage the art of mural painting.

National Book League, 7 Albemarle Street, London, W.1. *T.* 01–493 9001–5, 01–493 3501. Founded in 1925 as the National Book Council, and incorporated as a non-profit-making association. *President:* H.R.H. Prince Philip, Duke of Edinburgh. *Director:* Martyn Goff. *Deputy Director:* Clifford Simmons. The League's principal aim is to foster the growth of a wider and more discriminating interest in books. The membership now exceeds 8,000. Among the League's services free to its members are a lending library of books about books, and the use of the Book Information Bureau. Book lists and Readers' Guides on many subjects are published at intervals and circulated or sold at special rates to members. The League organises book exhibitions throughout the year at its London headquarters, 7 Albemarle Street, and touring exhibitions are shown in many parts of the country. It also takes part in Trade Fairs and numerous research projects. Lectures are held at the headquarters, which is a meeting-place for members, with reading and writing rooms, and a buffet and bar. Membership is open to all. Annual subscription: £4·20 for members living within 30 miles of Piccadilly, £2·10 for country members, entrance fee £1·05. Life membership available. Special facilities and subscriptions for libraries, schools and other corporate bodies. Full details may be had on application to the League.

National Society (1930), The Mall Galleries, The Mall, London, S.W.1. *T.* 01–930 6844. *President:* Ben Mathews; *Secretary:* Maurice Bradshaw. For artists of every creed and outlook for an annual Exhibition representing all aspects of art.

National Society for Art Education (1888), 37A East Street, Havant, Hants. *President:* S. Spedding, DIP. F.A., *Secretary:* W. J. L. Gaydon, A.R.C.A. The recognised professional body for specialist Art and Design staff in general, further and higher education. Through the Society members are represented on the National Advisory Council for Art Education, the Burnham Committee and other National and Regional bodies which are of concern to those engaged in Art and Design education.

National Union of Journalists. *Gen. Secretary:* Kenneth Morgan. Head Office: Acorn House, 314 Gray's Inn Road, London, WC1X 8DP. *T.* 01–278 7916. A trade union for working journalists, with 23,000 members and 175 branches throughout the British Isles and Ireland. Its wages and conditions agreements cover the whole of the newpaper press, the major part of periodical publishing, the news and public relations departments of radio and T.V. services and a number of public relations departments and consultancies. Administers unemployment, benevolent, and widow and orphan benefits. N.U.J. Superannuation Fund, a separate society, provide pensions. Official publications: *The Journalist* (contributions are not usually paid for), *Freelance Directory.*

New English Art Club, The Mall Galleries, The Mall, London, S.W.1. *T.* 01–930 6844. *Secretary:* Maurice Bradshaw. For persons interested in the art of painting, and the promotion of the fine arts. Annual Exhibition.

Newspaper Press Fund, Bouverie House, Fleet Street, EC4A 2DR. *T.* 01–353 8864. *Secretary:* S. C. Reynolds. For the relief of necessitous newspaper journalists who are members of the fund, their widows, and other dependants. Some small help is available for non-members.

Newspaper Publishers Association, Ltd., The, 6 Bouverie Street, EC4Y 8AY. *T.* 01–583 8132.

Newspaper Society, Whitefriars House, Carmelite Street, London, EC4Y 0BL. *T.* 01–353 4722. *Director:* Douglas Lowndes.

Oil-Painters, Royal Institute of (1883), The Mall Galleries, The Mall, London, S.W.1. *T.* 01–930 6844. *Secretary:* Maurice Bradshaw. Membership (R.O.I.) open to both men and women. Annual Exhibition is open to all artists.

P.E.N., International. A world association of writers. *International Secretary:* David Carver, O.B.E., D.LITT. (Hon) (*also Secretary of English Centre*). Headquarters: 62–63 Glebe Place, London, S.W.3. *T.* 01–352 9549 and 6303. *Cables:* Lonpenclub—London—S.W.3. *Membership:* approximately 8000.

P.E.N. was founded in 1921 by C. A. Dawson Scott under the presidency of John Galsworthy, to promote friendship and understanding between writers and defend freedom of expression within and between all nations. The initials P.E.N. stand for Poets, Playwrights, Editors, Essayists, Novelists—but membership is open to all writers of standing (including translators), whether men or women, without distinctions of creed or race, who subscribe to these fundamental principles. P.E.N. takes no part in state or party politics; it has given care to, and raised funds for, refugee writers, and also administers the P.E.N. Writers In Prison Committee which works on behalf of writers imprisoned for exercising their right to freedom of expression, a right implicit in the P.E.N. Charter to which all members subscribe. Through the P.E.N.–UNESCO Translations' Scheme the two bodies co-operate to promote the translation of works by writers in the lesser-known languages. International Congresses are held in most years. In 1970 the Korean Centre were hosts to the 37th Congress, and in 1971 the Congress to mark P.E.N.'s Jubilee Year will be held in Dublin.

Membership of the English Centre is £4·20 per annum for country members, £5·25 for London members. Fellows pay a minimum of £7·35 annually. Entrance fee, £1·05. Associate membership for those interested in literature, but are not themselves writers is available with an annual subscription of £3·15. Membership of any one Centre implies membership of all Centres: at present 81 autonomous Centres exist throughout the world. The English Centre holds frequent discussions and other meetings and has organised several large-scale conferences; distinguished writers are entertained. The Hermon Ould Memorial Lecture (in memory of the International Secretary from 1921–1951) is given in London.

Publications: P.E.N. News; P.E.N. Bulletin of Selected Books (bi-lingual, Fr-Eng., reviews of books in languages of limited currency; sponsored by UNESCO); News Bulletins published by various Centres; English Centre edits a series of annual anthologies of contemporary poetry; *New Poems*—1952–62; from 1965 the volume has appeared biennially. *Translation and Translators*, a report on a P.E.N. conference in Rome and *Translation and the Theatre* the report of the Rheims Conference, were published in *Arena*, also a report on the June 1964 Oslo Congress, *The Writer and Semantics—Literature as Concept, Meaning and Expression*. A report on the 1966 New York Congress, *The Writer as Independent Spirit* was published late in 1968.

Painter-Etchers and Engravers, Royal Society of (1880), 26–27 Conduit Street, W1R 9TA. *T.* 01–493 5436. *President:* Paul Drury. *Secretary:* Malcolm Fry. Fellows (R.E.) and Associates (A.R.E.) may be either men or women. Annual Exhibition: February/March, normally open to non-members. Particulars from the Secretary.

Painters in Water Colours, Royal Institute of (1831), The Mall Galleries, The Mall, London, S.W.1. *President:* Rowland Hilder, *Secretary General:* Maurice Bradshaw. Membership (R.I.) open to both men and women. Exhibitions are open to all artists.

Painters in Water-Colours, Royal Society of (founded 1804), 26–27 Conduit Street, W1R 9TA. *T.* 01–629 8300. Robert Austin, R.A. (*President*): Malcolm Fry (*Secretary*). Membership (R.W.S.) open to both men and women. An election of Associates is held usually in January of each year, and applications for the necessary forms and particulars should be addressed to the Secretary in November. Exhibitions: April and September.

Pastel Society, The (1899), The Mall Galleries, The Mall, London, S.W.1. *President:* Aubrey Sykes, V.P.R.I. *Secretary:* Maurice Bradshaw. Membership open to both men and women. Exhibitions are open to all artists. Pastel and drawings in pencil or chalk.

Penman Club, The, Penman House, 262 London Road, Westcliff-on-Sea, Essex, SS0 7JG. *T.* Southend 40750. *President:* Trevor J. Douglas. *General Secretary:* Leonard G. Stubbs, F.R.S.A. Literary Society for writers throughout the World, published and unpublished. Members in almost every country. Benefits of membership include criticism of all MSS. without additional charge, Monthly News Letter by Trevor J. Douglas, Quarterly Magazine and use of large writers' library. *Subscription:* Home six months 75p., one year £1·25; Overseas 6 months 87½p., one year £1·50. Prospectus available on application to the General Secretary.

Performing Right Society Ltd., (1914), 29–33 Berners Street, London, W1P 4AA *T.* 01-580 5544. See reference section of *Year Book*.

Periodical Publishers Association Ltd., Imperial House, Kingsway, WC2B 6UN. *T.* 01-836 9204 and 7111. *Secretary:* H. MacDougall, F.C.I.S.

Personal Managers' Association Ltd., The, see p. 287.

Philosophical Society of England, The (1913). *President:* The Rev. Dr. F. H. Cleobury, B.A., F.PH.S. *Chairman of the Council:* The Rev. J. W. Griffiths, A.K.C., PH.D., F.PH.S., F.R.S.A. (London). Membership open to all interested in Philosophy. Associate and Fellowship status by examination and Thesis. Open lectures by leading Philosophers. Study groups. Journals: *The Philosopher* and *The Quest*. All details from *General Secretary:* Rev. Dr. Edgar J. Ford, M.A., PH.D., F.PH.S., 7 Cholmley Gardens, Aldred Road, London, N.W.6. *T.* 01-435 7691. *Branches:* Manchester, London, Glasgow, Edinburgh and U.S.A.

Player-Playwrights (1948), 1 Hawthorndene Road, Hayes, Bromley, Kent. Weekly meetings in Central London. A society for the benefit of newcomers to Play and T.V. writing. Members' plays tried out on well-equipped stage, followed by discussion and friendly criticism. Annual subscription: 52½p. Meetings: 12½p. each. *Patrons:* Dame Sybil Thorndike, Hon. William Douglas Home, Sir Michael Redgrave.

Playwrights Workshop, (1949). A meeting place where those people in the Manchester Area interested in drama can meet to discuss playwriting in general and their own plays in particular. Details of places and times of meetings from *Hon. Secretary:* Albert Dobson, 15 Sealand Road, Wythenshawe, Manchester, M23 0JF.

Poetry Lovers' Fellowship. *President:* Oliver C. de C. Ellis. *Office:* Unicorn Meadow, Clee Saint Margaret, Craven Arms, Salop, SY7 9DT. *Hon. Director:* D. M. Gibbons Turner, Barrister at-Law. *Hon. Sec. General:* Marjorie Dawson, M.A. In connection with its campaign against the debasement of English manners, morals, ethics, language and speech by sound-film, wireless, press, state schools and public libraries, it runs examinations in (1) Reading Aloud, (2) Dramatic Speech, (3) Poetry-Speaking, (4) Choral Speaking (5) Public Speaking, (6) Mime, (7) Storytelling, (8) Shakespeare, (9) Handwriting, etc.; and issues handbooks of technical instruction. Syllabus and regulations 7½p. post free. Personal membership (per annum), £2·10, conditional on pledge to work for Fellowship's aims. Open to "all persons not in receipt of any grant or allowance from funds raised by taxation, nor engaged in any State-authorised interference with the private lives of well-conducted citizens and their families." The Fellowship also awards an annual prize of £5 for the best essay of 5000 words (general subject: Our Struggle against the Cad) contributed to the winter annual "Harvest and Horizons," before 31st March.

Poetry Society, The (1909) Incorporated, 21 Earls Court Square, London, S.W.5. *T.* 01–373 3556 and 2551. *Chairman:* Norman Hidden, M.A. *General Secretary:* Michael S. Mackenzie, B.A. *Treasurer:* May Ivimy. This Society is the national Society for the encouragement of the art. It provides a forum for all poets and poetry lovers. It has information and library services and competitions. It conducts verse speaking examinations leading to the Society's Gold Medal. Its Centres and Affiliations cover the United Kingdom and other countries. The official organ of the Society is *The Poetry Review* edited by Derek Parker.

Poets' Workshop, The, *Secretary:* Roy Bennett, 79 Tonfield Road, Sutton, Surrey. *Chairman:* Alan Brownjohn. The Workshop is a poetry discussion group whose members consist of published poets, critics, and people with a professional interest in poetry. Members meet fortnightly in the Poetry Society, 21 Earls Court Square, S.W.5. to discuss the new unpublished work of a fellow member which is circulated in book form, obtainable only by members, before the meeting. Membership: £3 p.a., associate membership: £1 p.a.

Portrait Painters, Royal Society of (1891), The Mall Galleries, The Mall, London, S.W.1. *T.* 01–930 6844. *Secretary:* Maurice Bradshaw. Annual Exhibition is arranged in the Galleries, when work may be submitted by non-members with a view to exhibition.

Portrait Sculptors, Society of (1952), *President:* Michael Rizzello, F.R.B.S., A.R.C.A. *Secretary:* Maurice Bradshaw, The Mall Galleries, The Mall, London, S.W.1 *T.* 01–930 6844. Membership open to men and women. Open Exhibition held annually.

Press (1882), St. Bride's House, Salisbury Square, EC4Y 8EN. Sir Max Aitken (*President*), Thomas H. McArthur (*Secretary*). *Subs.:* £15·75 town, £5·00 country and foreign £2·00. Entrance fees, £3·15 and £1·05 respectively. Strictly journalistic. *T.* 01–353 2644.

Press Council, The (1953), Independent. *Chairman:* Rt. Hon. The Lord Pearce, P.C. *Secretary:* Noël S. Paul, New Mercury House, 81 Farringdon Street, London, E.C.4. *T.* 01–353 1248.

Private Libraries Association (1956), 41 Cuckoo Hill Road, Pinner, Middlesex. *President:* Sir Arthur Elton, Bt. *Hon. Editor:* John Cotton. *Subscriptions:* £3·15 per annum. International society of book collectors and private libraries. Publications include the quarterly *Private Library*, annual *Private Press Books*, and other books on book collecting.

Publishers Association, 19 Bedford Square, London, WC1B 3HJ. Established 1896. *T.* 01–580 6321–5. *President:* Mark Longman. *Secretary:* R. E. Barker, O.B.E. The national association of British publishers whose membership represents some 355 firms (starred in the list of British Publishers given earlier in this book).

Radiowriters Association, The (1947), 84 Drayton Gardens, London, S.W.10. *T.* 01–373 6642. *Secretary:* John Coleby. A self-governing unit within the general network of the Society of Authors exclusively concerned with the interests and special problems of radiowriters. Members are entitled to advice on all questions connected with their work for broadcasting, and free access to the legal Secretariat of the Society should they require legal advice. The annual subscription is £10·50. which includes membership of the Society of Authors. Full particulars may be obtained from the offices of the Association.

Robert Louis Stevenson Club (London), The (1923). *President:* Miss Lettice Cooper. *Vice-Presidents:* Baroness Elliot of Harwood, Miss G. B. Stern, E. G. Crowsley, *Chairman:* E. G. Crowsley. *Hon. Sec.* and *Treasurer:* N. D. Nash, 37 St. Olam's Close, Luton, Bedfordshire LU3 2LD.

Romantic Novelists' Association, The. *Chairman:* Dorothy Mackie Low. *Hon. Secretary:* Miss R. Viveash, 1 Guinness Court, St. Edmunds Terrace, London, N.W.8. To raise the prestige of Romantic Authorship. Open to romantic and historical novelists.
See also under Literary Awards.

Royal Birmingham Society of Artists, 69A New Street, Birmingham 2. *T.* 643 3768. *President:* Douglas Perry, A.T.D., R.B.S.A *Hon. Secretary:* James Priddey, R.B.S.A., F.R.S.A. The Society has its own galleries and rooms prominently placed in the city centre. Members (R.B.S.A.) and Associates (A.R.B.S.A.) are elected annually. There are two annual Spring Exhibitions open to all artists and an Autumn Exhibition of Members' and Associates' works. *Annual Subscription:* £1·50. entitles subscribers to season ticket for exhibitions and lectures organised by the Society. Further details from the Hon. Secretary.

Royal British Colonial Society of Artists, 17 Carlton House Terrace, London, S.W.1. *T.* 01–930 6844. *Secretary:* Maurice Bradshaw. To unite in one body artists of the Commonwealth for the advancement of the arts.

Royal Literary Fund, The (1790), 11 Ludgate Hill, E.C.4. *T.* 01–248 4138. Grants made to necessitous authors of some published work of approved literary merit or their dependants. *President:* John Lehmann, C.B.E. *Secretary:* Victor Bonham-Carter.

Royal Musical Association, The, 44 Philip Victor Road, Birmingham, B20 2QD. *T.* 021–554 4633.

Royal Societies Club, 100 Piccadilly, W.1. *T.* 01–499 3535. *Subs.,* £21, £9·45 and £6·30. Literature, science, and art, etc.

Royal Society, The (1660), 6 Carlton House Terrace, London, S.W.1. *President:* Lord Blackett, O.M., C.H. *Secretaries:* Sir Bernard Katz, Sir Harrie Massey. Improving natural knowledge.

Royal Society for India, Pakistan & Ceylon, The, 2–3 Temple Chambers, Temple Avenue, London, E.C.4. *T.* 01–353 8515. For the promotion of friendship and understanding between the peoples of Great Britain and of India, Pakistan and Ceylon. Publication: *South Asian Review,* quarterly journal (contemporary South Asian economic and social affairs, and arts and letters) free to members. *Subscription:* £1·58 per annum, £2·10 for husband and wife; *Life:* £15·75 and *Corporate:* £10·50.

Royal Society of Arts. See Arts, Royal Society of.

Royal Society of British Artists, The Mall Galleries, The Mall, London, S.W.1. *T.* 01–930 6844. *Keeper:* Maurice Bradshaw. Incorporated by Royal Charter for the purpose of encouraging the study and practice of the arts of painting, sculpture and architectural designs. Open Exhibition.

Royal Society of British Sculptors, 8 Chesham Place, London, S.W.1. *T.* 01–235 1467. *President:* A. E. Sean Crampton, M.C., G.M. *Vice-President:* M. Clark. *Hon. Treasurer:* G. Davien. *Secretary:* Mrs. O. H. D. Churchill. The object for which the Society is established is the promotion and advancement of the Art of Sculpture; to diffuse among the members of the Society and others information on matters relating to the Art of Sculpture and the practice of that Art.

Royal Society of Literature (1823), 1 Hyde Park Gardens, W.2. Fellows and Members. Men and women. *President:* The Rt. Hon. Lord Butler, C.H.; *Chairman of Council:* the Rt. Hon. the Earl of Birkenhead; *Secretary:* Mrs. J. M. Patterson. For the advancement of literature by the holding of lectures, discussions, readings, and by publications. Administrators of the Dr. Richards' Fund and the Royal Society of Literature Award, under the W. H. Heinemann Bequest and the Winifred Holtby Memorial Prize.

Scottish Academy, Royal (1826), Princes Street, Edinburgh. *T.* 031–225 6671. *President:* William H. Kininmonth, P.R.S.A., F.R.I.B.A. *Secretary:* Robin Philipson, R.S.A. *Treasurer:* Hew Lorimer, R.S.A., F.R.B.S. *Assistant Secretary:* W. Keith. Academicians (R.S.A.) and Associates (A.R.S.A.) and non-members may exhibit in the Annual Exhibition of Painting, Sculpture and Architecture. Annual Exhibition dates approximately April 13 to August 4; Festival Exhibition August 17 to September 15; Royal Scottish Academy Diploma Collection, October to January. Royal Scottish Academy of Painting Competition held in March.

Scottish Arts, 24 Rutland Square, Edinburgh, EH1. *T.* 031–229 1076. *Secretary:* Thomas R. Moffat, C.A., 6 Rutland Square, Edinburgh, EH1 2AU. Entrance fee £5·25. *Subs.:* £16 and £7. Art, literature, music.

Scottish History Society (1886), National Library of Scotland, George IV Bridge, Edinburgh, EH1 1EW. *Hon. Secretary:* T. I. Rae, PH.D. The Society exists to discover and print unpublished documents illustrating the history of Scotland.

Scottish Newspaper Proprietors Association, 10 York Place, Edinburgh. *T.* 031–556 6787. *President and Chairman:* H. Livingston. *Secretary:* W. Barrie Abbott, B.L., C.A. To promote and safeguard newspaper interests, and to assist members who are involved in legal proceedings arising out of matter published in their newspapers.

Senefelder Group of Artist Lithographers, The Mall Galleries, The Mall, London, S.W.1. *T.* 01–930 6844. *Secretary:* Maurice Bradshaw. To display original work of lithographers.

Sesame Pioneer & Lyceum Club, 49 Grosvenor Street, W.1. *T.* 01–629 4473. *Subs.,* Town £15 ·75; Country £12·60. Literary and social. Men and women.

Shakespearean Authorship Society. *President:* Sir John Russell, Q.C. *Hon. Secretary:* Miss Gwynneth Bowen, 25 Montagu Square, London, W1H 1RE. *T.* 01–486 3764. *Assistant Hon. Secretary:* Miss N. Loosely, 167 Holland Park Avenue, W.11. Object of the Society is to seek, and if possible establish the truth concerning the authorship of the 'Shakespeare' plays and poems. Programme of monthly meetings, catalogue and rules of Library available from the Assistant Hon. Secretary. *Annual Subscription:* London £1·50., country £1, students 50p, Life Membership £10. Members receive *Shakespearean Authorship Review* published twice yearly by the Society.

Shaw Society, 3 Chestnut Court, Middle Lane, London, N.8. *T.* 01–340 8331. *President:* Ellen Pollock. *Hon. Gen. Secretary:* Miss Toni Block. *Editor:* T. F. Evans, 45 Manor Road, Ashford, Middlesex. The Society seeks to promote a wider and clearer understanding of Bernard Shaw's life and work, but its lectures and discussions cover a wide range of interests. Publishes *The Shavian* 3 times a year; £1 p.a.

Society for Theatre Research, The. *Hon. Secretaries:* Kathleen Barker and Jack Reading, 14 Woronzow Road, London, N.W.8. *T.* 01–722 1199.

Society of Authors, The. See Authors, The Society of.

Society of Civil Service Authors. *Secretary:* Sydney Dobson, 17 Abbotsford Road, Goodmayes, Ilford, Essex. Aims of the Society are to encourage authorship both by present and past members of the Civil Service and to provide opportunities for social and cultural relationships between civil servants who are authors or aspirant authors. Literary competitions are held annually for members only. *Subscriptions:* £1·05 per annum for London members and 75p. for provincial members. S.A.E. for enquiries.

Society of Industrial'Artists and Designers Ltd. *Secretary:* William L. Dickson, 12 Carlton House Terrace, London, S.W.1. *T.* 01–930 1911. Membership of the Society is open to graphic and industrial designers. The Society's Code of Conduct is included in later pages. Schedules of fees and conditions of engagement can be obtained from the Society's offices.

Somerset Guild of Playwrights. Organises original play competitions and festivals and looks after the interests of Somerset playwrights. *Hon. Secretary:* D. C. Kuhn, Dorion Cottage, Catcott, Bridgwater, Somerset. *T.* Chilton Polden 410.

Sussex Playwrights' Club. Founded in 1935 by a group of playwrights to encourage the art of playwriting and an interest in the theatre. Annual subscription: 62½p Further particulars from the *Hon. Secretary:* Neil McKellar, 52 Greenfield Cresent, Patcham, Brighton.

Syndicat des Representants Litteraires Français, 117 Boulevard St. Germain, Paris VI.

Syndicat National des Editeurs (the French publishers' association), 117 Boulevard St. Germain, Paris VI. *T.* 326 56 01.

Technical Authors and Illustrators, Institution of, 17 Bluebridge Avenue, Brookmans Park, Hatfield, Herts. *T.* Potters Bar 55392. A professional body for those engaged in the communication of technical information by the printed word, illustrations, or other means. *Objects:* to promote the advancement and improvement of technical publications techniques, and to provide a centre from which information and advice are available to all interested persons.

Television and Screen Writers Guild, The. See Writers' Guild of Great Britain, The.

Francis Thompson Society, The (1963), 3 Kemplay Road, Hampstead, London, N.W.3. *President:* Henry Williamson. Collates research done on the life and work of Francis Thompson in various parts of the world. A review of such material is published occasionally in the Society's own journal, *The Journal of the Francis Thompson Society.* This periodical also contains articles specially contributed by scholars and other serious students of Thompson. The Society arranges lectures, poetry readings, and exhibitions, at intervals. *Annual Subscription:* £1·50. Student membership 75p.

Translators Association, The (1958), 84 Drayton Gardens, London, S.W.10. *T.* 01–373 6642. *Secretary:* George Astley. A self-governing unit within the network of the Society of Authors, exclusively concerned with the interests and special problems of writers who translate foreign literary, dramatic or technical work into English for publication or performance in Great Britain or English-speaking countries overseas. Members are entitled to general and legal advice on all questions connected with the marketing of their work, such as rates of remuneration, contractual arrangements with publishers, editors, broadcasting organisations, etc. The annual subscription is £10·50 and includes membership of the Society of Authors. Full particulars may be obtained from the offices of the Association.

Translators' Guild, of The Institute of Linguists, 91 Newington Causeway, London S.E.1.   *T.* 01–407 4755–.6   *Secretary of the Guild:* B. R. Walters, M.A. (Oxon).
The Translators' Guild is the specialist body within the Institute comprising those members of the Institute who have satisfied its requirements as to experience and competence in particular fields of technical, scientific, commercial and literary translation work.   Members of the Guild, with full particulars of their languages and the subjects they can handle, appear in the Translators' Index which is kept up-to-date by means of quarterly supplements.   Translating and interpreting fee lists are also published by the Institute of Linguists.

United Society for Christian Literature (1799), 4 Bouverie Street, E.C.4.   *T.* 01–353 3853.   *President:* Lord Luke.   *Chairman:* The Hon. H. Lawson Johnston. To aid and undertake Christian publishing at home and overseas.

United Society of Artists, The Mall Galleries, The Mall, London, S.W.1.   *T.* 01–930 6844.   *Secretary:* R. P. Underwood.   An exhibiting Society open to all artists.

H. G. Wells Society, 21 Fawe Park Road, London, S.W.15.   *T.* 01–874 4956.   Exists to encourage an interest in the works and ideas of H. G. Wells.   The society runs an information service for writers, journalists and students, and is currently re-printing a number of Well's non-fiction works.

Wildlife Artists, Society of, The Mall Galleries, The Mall, London, S.W.1.   *T.* 01–930 6844.   *Secretary:* Maurice Bradshaw.   To promote and encourage the art of Wildlife painting and sculpture.   Open Annual Exhibition.

Women-Artists, Society of (1855), The Mall Galleries, The Mall, London, S.W.1. *President:* Lady Muriel Wheeler,   *Secretary:* Maurice Bradshaw.   Annual Exhibition, pictures, sculpture and crafts.   Open to all women.

Women Musicians, Society of (1911), 45 Wolseley Road, London, N.8.   *T.* 01–340 5025.

Women Writers and Journalists, Society of, c/o The Royal Scottish Corporation Hall, Fleur-de-Lys Court, Fetter Lane, London, E.C.4.   Founded in 1894 for women writers and artists.   Lectures, monthly lunch-time meetings.   Free literary advice for members.   Quarterly journal: *The Woman Journalist.* Subscription: Town £2·25; Country and Associate members, £1·37½; Overseas, £1·05.

Women's Press Club of London Ltd.   Now meets at the Arts Theatre Club, 6/7 Great Newport Street, London, W.C.2.   *T.* 01–836–7541.   Open to men and women journalists.   *Objects:* To provide the amenities of a club for journalists and writers and those engaged in creative work, to enhance the status of the profession, and to promote international understanding and goodwill among journalists.   Applications for membership will be considered from journalists and others who work in this field.   *Subscription:* £5·25.

Worshipful Company of Musicians (1500), 4 St. Paul's Churchyard, London, E.C.4. *Clerk:* W. R. I. Crewdson.

Worshipful Company of Stationers and Newspaper Makers (1403), Stationers' Hall, E.C.4.   *T.* 01–248 2934.   *Master:* Major E. H. Burt.   *Clerk:* D. St. P. Wells. One of the Livery Companies of the City of London.   Connected with the printing, publishing, bookselling and allied trades.

Writers' Guild of Great Britain, The, 430 Edgware Road, London, W.2. *T.* 01-723 8074-5-6. *President:* Carl Foreman. *Chairman:* Norman Crisp. *General Secretary:* Alan Griffiths.

The Guild was formed on 13th May 1959. It is affiliated to the TUC and with the Writers Guild of America. The Guild's function is to represent and protect the interests of Screen, Television, Radio and Advertising Writers in this country and to advise its members on problems connected with their work.

Particulars of membership and associate membership may be obtained from the offices of the Guild.

Yorkshire Bookmen, The Association of (1943). *President:* Lettice Cooper. *Hon. General Secretary:* Miss M. E. Scoffield, 9 Hawkstone View, Guiseley, Nr. Leeds LS20 8ER. *T.* Guiseley 4347. Branches at Rotherham, Harrogate, Brighouse, Leeds, Dewsbury and Batley, Spenborough, Wakefield, Morley, Aireborough, Pudsey, Skipton. *Object:* To further the interests of book lovers throughout the county.

Yorkshire Dialect Society, The (1897). The aims of the Society are to encourage interest in: (1) Dialect speech; (2) the writing of dialect verse, prose and drama; (3) the publication and circulation of dialect literature and the performance of dialect plays; (4) the study of the origins and the history of dialect and kindred subjects—all dialects, not only of Yorkshire origin. *Annual subscription:* 50p.; life membership, £10·50. *Meetings:* the Society organises a number of meetings during the year—details from the Hon. Secretary. *Annual Publications: Transactions* and *The Summer Bulletin* free to members, list of other publications on request. *Hon. Secretary:* Ian Dewhirst, B.A., A.L.A., 14 Raglan Avenue, Fell Lane, Keighley, Yorks, BD22 6BJ. *T.* Keighley 2915.

Personal Managers' Association Ltd., The, 50 Mount Street, Park Lane, London, W1Y 5RE. *Chairman:* Felix de Wolfe. *Secretary:* James Sharkey. *Treasurer:* Frederick A. Joachim. An association of personal managers, primarily in the theatre, film and entertainment world generally, but including also a number of literary agents.

PRIZES AND AWARDS

LITERARY PRIZES AND AWARDS

IN the past year many special awards and prizes have been offered for novels, short stories and works of non-fiction. Details of these awards, as they are offered, will be found in such journals as *The Author*. The number of permanent literary prizes in Great Britain is small compared with America, where there are scores of literary awards.

THE ALEXANDER PRIZE

Candidates for the Alexander Prize may choose their own subject for an Essay, but they must submit their choice for approval to the Literary Director, Royal Historical Society, University College London, Gower Street, London, W.C.1. *T.* 01–387 7532.

AUTHORS' CLUB FIRST NOVEL AWARD

The award was instituted in 1954 and is made to the author of the most promising first novel published in the United Kingdom during each year. The award takes the form of a silver mounted and inscribed quill and is presented to the winner at a House Dinner held in the Club. Entries for the award are accepted from publishers (up to a maximum of three titles from each publisher), and must be full length novels—short stories are not eligible—written and published in the United Kingdom during the year.

THE ALICE HUNT BARTLETT PRIZE

The Poetry Society announces that this prize of not less than £200 is awarded annually to the author of a volume of poetry comprising not less than 20 poems or 400 lines published in English and presented in duplicate to the Society's library in the year of publication. The closing date for 1971 is 1st October. In judging the entries the adjudicators give special consideration to newly emerging poets so far as merit warrants. In the event of the poems translated into English the prize is divided equally between the poet and the translator. This is the most important award made for poetry during the year.

THE DAVID BERRY PRIZE

Candidates for the David Berry Prize of a Gold Medal and £50 may select any subject dealing with Scottish History within the reigns of James I to James VI inclusive, provided such subject has been previously submitted to and approved by the Council of the Royal Historical Society, University College London, Gower Street, London, W.C.1. *T.* 01–387 7532.

THE JAMES TAIT BLACK MEMORIAL PRIZES

The James Tait Black Memorial Prizes were inaugurated by the late Mrs. Black in memory of her husband, James Tait Black, a partner in the publishing house of A. & C. Black Ltd. A sum, which some years ago totalled £12,430, was set aside to be used for providing two prizes of whatever income the fund should produce after paying expenses, including a fee to the judge, for (First) the best biography or literary work of that nature of each year, and (Second) the best novel of each year, the choice to be made by the Regius Professor of Literature in Edinburgh University (Old College, South Bridge, Edinburgh, EH8 9YL. *T.* 031–667 1011), or failing him, the Professor of Literature in the University of Glasgow. No formal entry of books for consideration is required. The awards are generally made in the year following publication of the books selected. The first awards were made in 1919. Publishers may submit works for the consideration of the Professor.

THE BLACKWELL PRIZE FOR ENGLISH ESSAY

Founded in 1793, in Marischal College, by Mrs. Barbara Blackwell, widow of Thomas Blackwell, M.A., Marischal College, 1718; LL.D., King's College, 1752, eleventh Principal of Marischal College. The value of the Prize, which is open to unrestricted competition, is £150 for the best English Essay on a prescribed subject, and is awarded as far as possible every alternate year. The last award was made in 1971, and the subject of the Essay was *Colonial Legacies and the Prospects of Developing Countries.* Candidates were advised that their Essays, which must be typewritten, should approximate from 10,000 to 20,000 words and must have been lodged with the Secretary to the University of Aberdeen on or before 1st January, 1971. Each Essay must bear a motto only and be accompanied by a sealed envelope bearing the same motto and containing the full name and address of the writer. The successful Essays are preserved in the University Library. Full details are available from the Secretary, the University of Aberdeen, AB9 1AS.

THE BOOKER PRIZE

This annual prize for fiction of £5,000 is given by Booker McConnell Ltd. in co-operation with the Publisher's Association. The Prize will be awarded to the best novel in the opinion of the judges, published between 1st December and the following 30th November each year. The Prize is open to novels written in English by citizens of the British Commonwealth, the Republic of Ireland and the Republic of South Africa and published for the first time in the U.K. by a British publisher. Entries are to be submitted only by U.K. publishers who may each submit not more than two novels. The judges may also ask for other eligible novels to be submitted to them. The 1970 prize was awarded to Bernice Rubens for her novel *The Elected Member,* published by Eyre & Spottiswoode Ltd. Entry forms are available from the Publishers' Association, 19 Bedford Square, London WC1B 3HJ.

THE CHILDREN'S BOOK CIRCLE ELEANOR FARJEON AWARD

In 1965 the Children's Book Circle instituted an award to be given annually for distinguished services to children's books and to be known as the Children's Book Circle Eleanor Farjeon Award in memory of the much-loved children's writer. The award carries with it a prize of 50 guineas and may be given to a librarian, teacher, author, artist, publisher, reviewer, television producer or any other person working with, or for children through books who has made an outstanding contribution during the previous year.

The winner of the 1969 award was Miss Kaye Webb, editor of Puffin Books and founder of the Puffin Club.

K

CHOLMONDELEY AWARDS

In 1965, the Marchioness of Cholmondeley established these awards for the benefit and encouragement of poets of any age, sex or nationality. In 1970 the awards
went to Kathleen Raine, Edward Brathwaite, Douglas Livingstone. The
prize amounted to £1050. The Scheme is administered by the Society of Authors.

THE DUFF COOPER MEMORIAL PRIZE

Friends and admirers of Duff Cooper, first Viscount Norwich (1890–1954),
contributed a sum of money which has been invested in a Trust Fund. The interest
will be devoted to an annual prize for a literary work in the field of biography,
history, politics or poetry published in English or French during the previous
twenty-four months. There are two permanent judges (the present Lord Norwich,
and the Warden of New College, Oxford) and three others who will change every
five years. The present judges are Mr. Cyril Connolly, Mr. John Fuller and Mr.
V. S. Naipaul.

THE ROSE MARY CRAWSHAY PRIZE

The Rose Mary Crawshay Prize is of the value of £100. It was originally founded
in 1888, by the late Rose Mary Crawshay, for yearly prizes on Byron, Shelley, and
Keats. In 1915 the Scheme passed into the administration of a body of Trustees
consisting of the President and Secretary of the British Academy, and others.
The Prize may be awarded annually to a woman of any nationality who, in the
judgment of the Council of the British Academy, has written or published within
three calendar years next preceding the date of the Award an historical or critical
work of sufficient value on any subject connected with English Literature, preference
being given to a work regarding one of the poets Byron, Shelley, or Keats. Communications may be addressed to the Secretary of the British Academy, Burlington
House, Piccadilly, London, W1V 0NS. The latest award was made in 1970 to
Miss Barbara E. Rooke, for her edition of Coleridge's *The Friend*.

THE CROMER GREEK PRIZE

The Cromer Greek Prize was founded by the first Earl of Cromer with the view
of encouraging the study of Greek. The Prize, which is competitive, is administered
by the British Academy, and awarded for the best Essay on any subject connected
with the language, history, art, literature, or philosophy of Ancient Greece. The
Prize, which is ordinarily a sum of £150, is awarded every second year in May.
The next award will be in 1971. Copies of the rules governing the Cromer Prize may
be obtained from the Secretary of the British Academy, Burlington House, Piccadilly,
W1V 0NS

DENIS DEVLIN MEMORIAL AWARD FOR POETRY

This award, value £300, is awarded triennially for the best book of poetry by an
Irish citizen published in the preceding three years. The next award will be made in
1973. The award is administered by The Irish Arts Council, 70 Merrion Square,
Dublin 2.

THE GEOFFREY FABER MEMORIAL PRIZE

As a memorial to the founder and first Chairman of the firm, Messrs. Faber &
Faber Limited established in 1963 the Geoffrey Faber Memorial Prize.

This prize of £250 is awarded annually: and it is given, in alternate years, for a
volume of verse and for a volume of prose fiction.

Subject to the qualifications set out below, it is given to that volume of verse or
prose fiction first published originally in this country during the two years preceding
the year in which the award is given which is, in the opinion of the judges, of the
greatest literary merit.

To be eligible for the prize the volume of verse or prose fiction in question must
be by a writer who is:

(a) not more than 40 years old at the date of publication of the book; and

(b) a citizen of the United Kingdom and Colonies, of any other Commonwealth state, of the Republic of Ireland or of the Republic of South Africa.

There are three judges. The judges are reviewers of poetry or of fiction as the case may be; and they are nominated each year by the editors or literary editors of newspapers and magazines which regularly publish such reviews.

Messrs. Faber & Faber invite nominations from such editors and literary editors. No submissions for the prize are to be made.

The 1970 Geoffrey Faber Memorial Prize was awarded to Geoffrey Hill for his volume of verse *King Log*.

The three judges for the 1971 prize are: Julian Symons (nominated by *The Sunday Times*); Terence Kilmartin (nominated by *The Observer*); Francis King (nominated by *The Sunday Telegraph*.

FARMER'S POETRY PRIZE

A competition for which all poets are elegible to enter every two years. Full details from Farmer's Poetry Prize, 350 Lyons Road, Five Dock, N.S.W. 2046, Australia.

SIR BANISTER FLETCHER PRIZE TRUST

The late Sir Banister Fletcher, who was President of the Authors' Club for many years, left the Authors' Club a sum of money to be held upon trust:—

"to apply the income thereof in or towards the provision of an annual prize for the book on architecture or the arts which, in the opinion of the Committee . . . shall be most deserving of it, such prize to be known as the Sir Banister Fletcher Prize."

The Committee of the Club decided that the prize be awarded annually for a period of two years ending on December 31st, alternately for the best book on architecture and the best book on the fine arts, excluding architecture. A sub-Committee of the Club examines eligible works and submits a short list to a person distinguished in architecture or the fine arts, as may be appropriate, for final judgment. The award, which is at present £50, is presented to the winner by the person making the final selection, at a House Dinner held in the Club.

THE JOHN FLORIO PRIZE

An annual prize of £200 for the best translation into English of a twentieth century Italian work of literary merit and general interest published by a British publisher during the preceding year was instituted in 1963 under the auspices of the Italian Institute and the British-Italian Society, and named after John Florio, a language teacher and lexicographer of Italian parentage who made Italian literature known in Elizabethan Society.

The 1969 award from a Prize fund contributed by the British and Italian publishers and Literary Associations was won by Angus Davidson for his translation of *On Neoclassicism* by Mario Praz, published by Thames & Hudson Ltd.

There is also a bi-annual Classical Prize of £200 for any new translation of works of fiction and criticism, poetry, history or belles-lettres, biographical studies and travel books written prior to 1900.

Details may be obtained from The Secretary, The Translators Association, 84 Drayton Gardens, London, S.W.10.

THE GREENWOOD PRIZE FOR 1971

The Poetry Society is empowered by the executors of the late Mrs. Julia Wickham Greenwood to offer the sum of £20 as the Shirley Carter Greenwood Prize for 1971 for the best single poem in open competition addressed "The Greenwood Prize, 21 Earls Court Square, London, S.W.5," before July 31st, 1971, only one poem to be submitted by any one competitor, length not exceeding 250 lines; no previously published poem may be entered. A nom-de-plume must be adopted and the name and address of the sender must be given in a closed envelope bearing the pseudonym. Copies should be kept as no poems can be returned. The winning poem shall be printed in THE POETRY REVIEW and may be reprinted at the discretion of the Poetry Society and the adjudicator may reserve near winners for publication in THE POETRY REVIEW. This annual prize is one of high authority and significance.

E. C. GREGORY TRUST FUND

Awards are made annually from this Fund for the encouragement of young poets who can show that they are likely to benefit from an opportunity to give more time to writing. A candidate for an Award must: (a) be a British subject by birth but *not* a national of Eire or any of the British dominions or colonies and be ordinarily resident in the United Kingdom or Northern Ireland; (b) be under the age of thirty at 31st March 1972; (c) submit for the consideration of the Judges a published or unpublished work of belles-lettres, poetry or drama (not more than 30 poems). Entries for the Award should be sent not later than 31st October 1971 to the Society of Authors, 84 Drayton Gardens, London, S.W.10.

GUARDIAN FICTION PRIZE

The *Guardian's* annual 200 guinea prize for a novel published by a British or Commonwealth writer. The winning novel will be chosen by the Literary Editor in conjunction with the *Guardian's* regular reviewers of new fiction. In 1969 the prize was awarded to Maurice Leitch for his novel *Poor Lazarus* published by MacGibbon & Kee.

GUARDIAN AWARD FOR CHILDREN'S FICTION

The *Guardian's* annual prize of 100 guineas for an outstanding work of fiction for children by a British of Commonwealth writer, instituted in 1967. In 1970 the award went to K.M. Peyton for her *Flambards* trilogy, published by Oxford University Press.

THE HAWTHORNDEN PRIZE

The Hawthornden Prize, for which books do not have to be specially submitted, may be awarded annually to the author of what, in the opinion of the Committee, is the best work of imaginative literature published during the preceding calendar year by a British author under forty-one years of age. The Prize is £100. It was founded by the late Miss Alice Warrender in 1919. Awards in 1970 have been to Mr. Geoffrey Hill for his book *King Log* published in 1968 and to Mr. Peirs Paul Read for his book *Monk Dawson* published in 1969.

THE FELICIA HEMANS PRIZE FOR LYRICAL POETRY

The Felicia Hemans Prize consists of a bronze medal together with a sum of money (about £4·43 less the cost of the medal). It is awarded annually for a lyrical poem, the subject of which may be chosen by the competitor. Open to past and present members of University College or of the University of Liverpool. The prize shall not be awarded more than once to the same competitor. Poems endorsed "Hemans Prize", must be sent in to the Registrar of Liverpool University, P.O. Box 147, Liverpool L69 3BX. *T.* 051–709 6022, on or before May 1st. Competitors may submit either published or unpublished verse, but no competitor may submit more than one poem.

RICHARD HILLARY MEMORIAL PRIZE

The Richard Hillary Memorial Prize, valued £750, for a work of the imagination, prose or poetry, published in the current year. Chairman of the Trustees: Hon. Michael Astor, 1 Swan Walk, London, S.W.3.

WINIFRED HOLTBY MEMORIAL PRIZE

Miss Vera Brittain has given to the Royal Society of Literature a sum of money to provide an annual prize of £100 in honour of the late Winifred Holtby who died at the age of thirty-seven.

The prize will be for the best regional novel of the year written in the English language. The writer must be of British or Irish nationality, or a citizen of the Commonwealth. Translations, unless made by the author himself of his own work, are not eligible for consideration.

Publishers are invited to submit novels published during the current year to The Royal Society of Literature, 1 Hyde Park Gardens, London, W.2. The closing date for submissions will be December 31st.

The award for 1969 was made to Ian McDonald for his book *The Humming Bird Tree*.

THE MARTIN LUTHER KING MEMORIAL PRIZE

A prize of £100 is awarded for a literary work reflecting the ideals to which Dr. Martin Luther King dedicated his life: viz. a novel, story, poem, essay, play, TV, radio or motion picture script, first published or performed in the United Kingdom during the calendar year preceding the date of the award. Full details of the award can be obtained from John Brunner c/o Midland Bank Ltd., 122 Finchley Road, London, N.W.3.

THE LIBRARY ASSOCIATION CARNEGIE MEDAL

The Library Association Carnegie Medal is awarded annually for an outstanding book for children written in English and receiving its first publication in the United Kingdom during the preceding year. It was instituted by the Library Association, whose work owes so much to the benefactors of the Carnegie Trust, to commemorate the centenary of Andrew Carnegie's birth in 1835.

Recommendations for the award are made by members of the Library Association and the final decision rests with a Committee of the Library Association. Consideration is given not only to the literary quality and suitability of the work, but also to the type, paper, illustrations and binding. It should be added that the award is not necessarily restricted to books of an imaginative nature.

The award was made for 1969 to Kathleen Peyton for *The Edge of the Cloud* (O.U.P.).

THE LIBRARY ASSOCIATION KATE GREENAWAY MEDAL

The Kate Greenaway Medal is intended to recognise the importance of illustrations in children's books. It will be awarded to the artist, who, in the opinion of the Library Association, has produced the most distinguished work in the illustration of children's books first published in the United Kingdom during the preceding year. Books intended for younger as well as older children are included and reproduction will be taken into account. The award was made, for 1969 to Helen Oxenbury for her illustration to *The Quangle Wangle's Hat* and *The Dragon of an Ordinary Family*.

THE LIBRARY ASSOCIATION WHEATLEY MEDAL

The Wheatley Medal is awarded annually for an outstanding index published during the preceding year. It is awarded to indexes compiled by individuals and not by corporate bodies although any type of publication is considered. Recommendations for the award are invited from members of the Library Association and the Society of Indexers. The compiler of the index must be British and the book must have been published in the United Kindgom. The award was made for 1969 to James Thornton for the index to *The Letters of Charles Dickens, Vol. 2.*

MACAULAY FOUNDATION

Fellowships value £1,000 are awarded once every five years in both Prose Fiction and in Playwriting to writers under 30 years of age (or in exceptional circumstances under 35 years) in order to enable them to further their liberal education. An award in Prose Fiction was made in 1969 and the next award in Playwriting will be in 1973. Candidates must be Irish-born (Northern Ireland included). The Foundation is administered by The Irish Arts Council, 70 Merrion Square, Dublin 2

KATHERINE MANSFIELD MENTON SHORT STORY PRIZE

The municipality of Menton offers a triennial prize in tribute to Katherine Mansfield and in memory of her stay in the Villa Isola Bella.

Two prizes are offered for short stories, one English and one French, selected independently by a panel of English and a panel of French judges respectively. At the invitation of the Municipality of Menton, judges are appointed by the English Centre and the French Centre of International P.E.N., and prizes were awarded for the first time in 1959.

Further details can be obtained from the English P.E.N. Centre, 62 Glebe Place, London, S.W.3. (Menton Prize.)

ARTHUR MARKHAM MEMORIAL PRIZE

A prize for a short story, essay or poems on a given subject is offered annually as a memorial to the late Sir Arthur Markham. Candidates must be manual workers in or about a coal mine, or have been injured when so employed. Full details can be obtained from The Registrar, The University, Sheffield S10 2TN.

THE SOMERSET MAUGHAM TRUST FUND

The purpose of these annual awards, which consist of two sums of £500 each, is to encourage young writers to travel, to acquaint themselves with the manners and customs of foreign countries, and, by widening their own experience, to extend both the basis and the influence of contemporary English literature. Mr. Maugham has urged that, in the selection of prize-winners, originality and promise should be the touchstones: he did not wish the judges to "play for safety" in their choice.

A candidate for the award must be a British subject by birth and ordinarily resident in the United Kingdom or Northern Ireland. He or she must, at the time of the award, be under thirty-five years of age, and must submit a published literary work in volume form in the English language, of which he or she is the sole author. The term "literary work" includes poetry, fiction, criticism, history and biography, belles-lettres, or philosophy, but does not include a dramatic work. A candidate who wins an award must undertake to spend not less than three months outside Great Britain and Ireland, and to devote the prize to the expenses of this sojourn.

Any questions relating to the terms of the award should be addressed to The Society of Authors, 84 Drayton Gardens, S.W.10, to which candidates should send the literary work they wish to submit for an award. Three copies of one published work should be submitted by a candidate, and it must be accompanied by a statement of his or her age, place of birth, and other published works.

The closing date for the submission of books to be considered is December 31st of the preceding year.

The 1970 awards went to Jane Gaskell for *A Sweet Sweet Summer*, and Piers Paul Read for *Monk Dawson*.

THE NEW ENGLISH LIBRARY YOUNG WRITERS AWARD, see p. 298.

THE FREDERICK NIVEN LITERARY AWARD

In memory of Frederick Niven, the Scottish novelist, who died in 1944, his widow has inaugurated a prize of £50 awarded every 3 years, for the most outstanding contribution to the novel by a Scotsman or Scotswoman. The prize will not be awarded more than once to the same person, and if on occasion the judges consider that no work submitted reaches a high enough standard, the award may be withheld. The 1965–68 award was won by Mr. Archie Hind for his novel *The Dear Green Place* (Hutchinson). Next Award covers years 1968–71.

Inquiries to Miss M. Baxter, Hon. Secretary, P.E.N. Scottish Centre, 20 Canninesburn Road, Bearsden, Glasgow. *T.* 041–942 0594.

THE NOBEL PRIZE

The Nobel Prize in Literature is one of the awards stipulated in the will of the late Alfred Nobel, the Swedish scientist who invented dynamite. The awarding authority is the Swedish Academy (for Literature), and particulars concerning conditions, etc., can be obtained from Nobelstiftelsen, Sturegatan 14, S–11436 Stockholm. No direct application for a prize will, however, be taken into consideration. For authors writing in English it was bestowed upon Rudyard Kipling in 1907, upon W. B. Yeats in 1923, upon George Bernard Shaw in 1925, upon Sinclair Lewis in 1930, upon John Galsworthy in 1932, upon Eugene O'Neill in 1936, upon Pearl Buck in 1938, upon T. S. Eliot in 1948, upon William Faulkner in 1949, upon Bertrand Russell in 1950, upon Sir Winston Churchill in 1953, upon Ernest Hemingway in 1954, upon John Steinbeck in 1962, and upon Samuel Beckett in 1969. The Nobel Prizes are understood to be worth about £32,000 each. They number five: (*a*) Physics, (*b*) Chemistry, (*c*) Physiology or Medicine (*d*) Literature, and (*e*) the, Promotion of Peace.

POETRY LOVERS' FELLOWSHIP

For details of the prize awarded annually by the Fellowship see page 281.

POETRY REVIEW QUARTERLY PREMIUM

A premium prize is offered for the best poem submitted to the Premium Editor during the quarter (without limitation of subject). Not more than two lyrics or one long poem should be submitted. MSS. should reach "The Premium Editor, THE POETRY SOCIETY, 21 Earls Court Square, London, S.W.5," typewritten if possible. It is essential that entrants to this competition be members of The Poetry Society and that each poem bears the name and address of the author marked "For Premium Competition," *Entrance fee:* 12½p.

THE JOHN LLEWELYN RHYS MEMORIAL PRIZE

The Prize, inaugurated by the late Mrs. Rhys in memory of her husband who was killed in 1940, and administered jointly by the trustees and the National Book League is offered annually to the author of the most memorable literary work of any kind which shall have been published for the first time during the *previous* calendar year. The only conditions are that such an author shall be a citizen of this country or the Commonwelath, and shall not have passed his or her thirtieth birthday by the date of the publication of the work submitted.

Books should be sent to: the Selection Committee, John Llewelyn Rhys Memorial Prize, c/o The National Book League, 7 Albemarle Street, London, W1X 4BB. Three copies of each entry should be submitted, and should be received by December 31st of the year of publication. Publishers only may submit books.

In 1970 the Prize was awarded to Angus Calder for *The People's War*.

ROMANTIC NOVELISTS' ASSOCIATION AWARD

The Annual Award for the best Romantic Novel of the Year is open to members and non-members of the Romantic Novelists' Association. Requirements: Novels published between 1st January and 31st December. Authors may obtain entry forms from *Hon. Treasurer*, Miss B. Taylor, Bell's Farm House, Spurriers Lane, Melling, Maghull, Lancashire L31 1BA. Entry fee—Non-members £1·05. The Netta Muskett Award is an annual award for probationary members only, for the best unpublished work and the winning novel in this competition may be published in book form by one of the associated publishers. Information from the Hon. Treasurer.

ROYAL NATIONAL EISTEDDFOD OF WALES, 1971

Details of prizes for Drama, Poetry, Literature, etc., in the Welsh language, can be obtained from The Organiser, Eisteddfod Office, Bangor, Caerns.

THE ROYAL SOCIETY OF LITERATURE AWARD UNDER THE W. H. HEINEMANN BEQUEST

The purpose of this foundation is to encourage the production of literary works of real worth. The prize shall be deemed a reward for actual achievement. Works in any branch of literature may be submitted by their publishers to the verdict of the Royal Society of Literature which shall be final and without appeal. Prose fiction shall not be excluded from competition, but the Testator's intention is primarily to reward less remunerative classes of literature: poetry, criticism, biography, history, etc. Any work originally written in the English language, shall be eligible. The recipient of a Prize shall not again be eligible for five years. The awards for 1969 were made to Brian Fothergill for his book *Sir William Hamilton*, to Ronald Blythe for his book *Akenfield*, and to Nicholas Wollaston for his book *Pharoah's Chicken*.

THE SCHLEGEL-TIECK PRIZE

A prize was established in 1964 under the auspices of the Society of Authors and the Translators Association to be awarded annually for the best translation published by a British publisher during the previous year. Only translations of German twentieth-century works of literary merit and general interest will be considered. The work should be entered by the publisher and not the individual translator. The 1969 award was won by Eric Mosbacher for his translation of Alexander Mitschelich's *Society Without the Father* published by Tavistock Publications.

Details may be obtained from The Secretary, The Translators Association, 84 Drayton Gardens, S.W.10.

THE SCOTT-MONCRIEFF PRIZE

A prize established in 1964 under the auspices of the Society of Authors and the Translators Association to be awarded annually for the best translation published by a British publisher during the previous year. Only translations of French twentieth century works of literary merit and general interest will be considered. The work should be entered by the publisher and not the individual translator. The award for works published in 1969 was won jointly by W. G. Corp, Richard Barry and Elaine P. Halperin for their translations respectively of Bernard Clavel's *The Spaniard* published by Harrap, Andre Beaufre's *The Suez Expedition 1956* published by Faber and Faber and Michel Bernanos' *The Other Side of the Mountain* published by Victor Gollancz. The value of the prize is £400. Details may be obtained from The Secretary, The Translators Association, 84 Drayton Gardens, London, S.W.10.

SILVER PEN AWARDS

Instituted in 1969 by the English Centre of International P.E.N. and administered by their Executive Committee. At an annual dinner held in the Café Royal in November a "Silver Pen" emblem and a silver Parker pen are presented to each of the authors of the three books, published during the preceding twelve months, which are adjudged best, one in each of three categories of writing. *"The Novel"* is always one of the three categories, and the other two vary. For 1970 they were *Biography/Autobiography* and *Children's Book*. In May each year letters are sent to publishers requesting them to submit one entry in each category. Full details are available from International P.E.N., 62–63 Glebe Place, London, S.W.3.

THE W. H. SMITH & SON ANNUAL LITERARY AWARD

A prize of £1,000 is awarded annually to a Commonwealth author (including a citizen of the United Kingdom) whose book, written in English and published in the United Kingdom, within 12 months ending on December 31 preceding the date of the Award, in the opinion of the judges makes the most outstanding contribution to literature. Further details are available from W. H. Smith & Sons, Ltd., Strand House, Portugal Street, London, W.C.2.

THE BERTRAND STEWART PRIZE

At least £80 is given annually under the will of the late Captain Bertrand Stewart, a London Solicitor, who was killed in the Battle of the Marne in September 1914, for the best essay on some military problem, the study or discussion of which would tend to increase the efficiency of the Armed Forces.

The right to compete is limited to British subjects who have served, or who are serving, as officers or in other ranks or ratings of the Armed Forces of the Commonwealth.

Full particulars are published in the *Army Quarterly and Defence Journal*.

E. REGINALD TAYLOR ESSAY COMPETITION

An annual prize of twenty-five guineas and a medal in instituted memory of the late E. Reginald Taylor, F.S.A., and awarded for the best essay on an antiquarian or historical subject prior to 1830. The essays must show original research and must not be longer than 7,500 words. Subjects must be approved by the Editor, British Archaeological Association, 67 Victoria Road, Kensington, W.8.

THE TOM-GALLON TRUST

This Trust was founded by the late Miss Nellie Tom-Gallon and is administered by the Society of Authors. Awards amounting to about £100 a year for two years are made biennially from this Fund to fiction writers of limited means who have had at least one short story accepted for publication. Authors wishing to enter should send to the Society of Authors, 84 Drayton Gardens, S.W.10: (i) a list of their already published fiction, giving the name of the publisher or periodical in each case and the approximate date of publication, (ii) one short story, published or unpublished; (iii) a brief statement of their financial position; (iv) an undertaking that they intend to devote a substantial amount of time to the writing of fiction as soon as they are financially able to do so; (v) a stamped addressed envelope for the return of the work submitted. The closing date for the next award is September 1971.

The adjudicators bear in mind Miss Tom-Gallon's expressed preference for work of a traditional rather than of an experimental character.

Any author wishing to compete for the award must have had at least one short story accepted for publication.

SIR THOMAS WHITE MEMORIAL PRIZE

Details of this prize are available from The Secretary, The Society of Australian Writers, Australia House, London, W.C.2. The 1970 prize, worth £200 is for a crime novel by an Australian or New Zealand writer, published during 1970.

YORKSHIRE POST BOOK OF THE YEAR

Prizes totalling £460 are awarded annually for the best works of fiction and non-fiction published during the year. In 1969 the first prize went to Elizabeth Longford for *Wellington, The Years of The Sword* and the fiction prize to Iris Murdoch for *Bruno's Dream*.

The Best First Work award of £100 went to Spike Mays for *Reuben's Corner* and the runner-up award of £60 to Eithne Wilkins for *The Rose-Garden Game*. A special award of £50 was made to James Plunkett whose *Strumpet City* was adjudged as one of the two finest works of fiction published during 1969. All correspondence to Richard Douro, 24 Fearnville Mount, Leeds, LS8 3DL.

THE NEW ENGLISH LIBRARY YOUNG WRITERS AWARD

New English Library Ltd., Barnards Inn, Holborn, London, E.C.1, is to award an annual prize of £2,500 for a new and previously unpublished novel, in English, by a writer aged 25 or under. The award is open to all residents of the United Kingdom, Eire and the British Commonwealth, and manuscripts should be submitted before 10th May 1971. The judges are Lady Antonia Fraser, Martyn Goff, H. P. Tanner and Laurence James.

MARKETS SECTION

MARKETS FOR WRITERS

MORE than a thousand journals are included in the British Journals section of the *Year Book*, almost all of them offering opportunities to the writer. Some 350 leading Commonwealth and American journals are also included, and while some of these have little space for free-lance contributions, many of them will always consider outstanding work.

Over 500 British publishers are included, as well as some 200 overseas publishers, all of them ready to consider work by new writers.

The advice we would offer to all writers is to study their market carefully. Many publishers include no fiction in their list, yet numerous manuscripts are submitted to them by writers who have not taken sufficient trouble to ascertain: (*a*) do Messrs. Blank publish fiction? (*b*) and equally important, do they publish the sort of fiction I have written? A novel suitable for Mills and Boon is unlikely to be acceptable to Macmillans, and *vice versa*. Similarly an article or short story suitable for *Woman's Own* is unlikely to appeal to the readers of *The New Statesman*. The importance of studying the market cannot be over-emphasised. It is an editor's job to know what his readers want, and to see that they get it. Thus free-lance contributions must be tailored to fit a specific market; subject, theme, treatment, length, etc., must meet the editor's requirements.

The Classified Indexes at the end of the *Year Book* provide a rough guide to markets. They must be used with discrimination, and it is always desirable to examine a copy of a journal if you are not familiar with it, and are submitting a MS. to the editor for the first time.

Most publishers have a full programme, with a long list of books awaiting reprinting. Even so, first class MSS. of almost every category will find a publisher. Here it must again be emphasised: take care to choose a suitable publisher, and remember that a reputable publisher will undertake all financial risk of publication, except possibly for works of an academic nature.

MARKETS FOR PLAYS

It is not easy for a new or comparatively unknown writer to find a management willing to present his play. The Royal Court Theatre and one or two similarly enterprising organisations present a number of plays by new authors. The new and inexperienced writer may find it easier to persuade amateur drama groups or provincial repertory theatres to present his work.

It is probable that competitions for full-length and one-act plays and other special opportunities for new plays will be announced after the *Year Book* has gone to press, and writers with plays on the stocks would do well to watch carefully for announcements in the Press. *The Observer, The Author, Plays and Players, Drama, Amateur Stage*, and *The Stage*, are the journals in which announcements are most likely to appear.

Sketches for revues, concert parties, and broadcasting, and plays for youth organisations are in demand. Sketches are usually bought outright, but in any case authors should make quite certain of what rights they will be disposing before accepting any offer.

In every case it is advisable to send a preliminary letter before submitting a manuscript. Suggestions for the preparation of manuscripts will be found on page 403 of the *Year Book*.

Writers of plays are also referred to Marketing a Play on page 360, and to the section on Television on pages 305, 313 and 355, a medium which provides a very big market for the writers of plays

LONDON

Albery, Donald, New Theatre, St. Martin's Lane, W.C.2.

Bridge, Peter, 16 Red Lion Square, London, WC1R 4QB.

Codron, Michael, Ltd., 117 Regent Street, London, W1R 8JY. *T.* 01–437 3577.

English Stage Company Ltd., Royal Court Theatre, Sloane Square, London, S.W.1.

Caryl Jenner Productions Ltd., Arts Theatre, 6–7 Gt. Newport Street, London, W. C. 2. (Plays for children only).

Lewenstein, Oscar, Plays Ltd., 5 Goodwin's Court, St. Martin's Lane, London, WC2N 4LL. *T.* 01–836 4792.

Linnit & Dunfee Ltd., 7 Goodwin's Court, St. Martin's Lane, London, WC2N 4LL. *T.* 01–836 4822.

Lister, Laurier, Productions Ltd., 7 Goodwin's Court, St. Martin's Lane, London, WC2N 4LL

Littler, Emile, Palace Theatre, London, W1V 8AY.

Macdonald, Murray, and John Stevens Ltd., 7 Goodwin's Court, St. Martin's Lane, London, WC2N 4LL *T.* 01–836 4822.

Mermaid Theatre (Sir Bernard Miles), Puddle Dock, Upper Thames Street, London, E.C.4.

Mitchell, Stephen (Theatrical Productions) Ltd., 84 Albion Gate, London, W.2.

O'Brien, Barry (1968), Ltd., 18 Charing Cross Road, London, W.C.2. *T.* 01–836 6447.

Pilbrow, Richard, Theatre Projects, 10 Long Acre, London, WC2E 9LH. *T.* 01–836 7877.

Questors Theatre, Mattock Lane, Ealing, London, W.5.

Rix, Brian, Enterprises, 131–132 Grand Buildings, Trafalgar Square, London, WC2N 5EP.

Rowland, Toby, Ltd., Cranbourn Mansions, Cranbourn Street, London, W.C.2.

Saunders, Peter, Ltd., 350 Grand Buildings, Trafalgar Square, London, W.C.2.

Tennent, H. M., Ltd., Globe Theatre, Shaftesbury Avenue, London, W.1. *T.* 01–437 3647.

PROVINCIAL

Abbey Theatre, Lower Abbey Street, Dublin 1. *T.* 48741. The Abbey Theatre is mainly restricted to the production of plays in Irish or English written by Irish authors or on Irish subjects. Foreign plays are however regularly produced.

Alexandra Theatre (Birmingham) Ltd., Station Street, Birmingham B5 4DS. *T.* 021–643 5536.

The Arthur Brough Players Ltd., Leas Pavilion, Folkestone.

Belgrade Theatre, Corporation Street, Coventry CV1 1GS. *T.* 56431/7.

Birmingham Repertory Theatre Ltd., Station Street, Birmingham 5. *T.* 021–643 2472.

Bristol Old Vic Company, Theatre Royal, Bristol, BS1 4ED.

Bromley Theatre Trust Ltd., New Theatre, High Street, Bromley, Kent BR1 1HA.

Canterbury Theatre Trust Ltd., Marlowe Theatre, Canterbury, Kent.

Chesterfield Civic Theatre Ltd., Civic Theatre, Corporation Street, Chesterfield. *T.* 0246–4633.

Chester Gateway Theatre Ltd., Gateway Theatre, Chester. *T.* 0244–40392.

Colchester Repertory Company Ltd., High Street, Colchester, Essex. *T.* 0206–77006.

Derby Playhouse Ltd., The Playhouse, Sacheverel Street, Derby.

Farnham Repertory Company Ltd., Castle Theatre, Farnham, Surrey. *T.* Farnham 5301.

Glasgow Citizens' Theatre Ltd., Gorbals Street, Glasgow, C.5.

The Hornchurch Theatre Trust Ltd., The Queen's Theatre, Hornchurch, Essex RM12 6JS. *T.* Hornchurch 43772.

Ipswich Arts Theatre, Tower Street, Ipswich, IP1 3BE. *T.* 0473–52717.

Lincoln Theatre Royal, Clasketgate, Lincoln.

Liverpool Repertory Theatre Ltd., The Playhouse, Williamson Square, Liverpool L1 1EL. *T.* 051–709 8478.

Manchester Library Theatre, Manchester M2 5PD.

Northampton Repertory Players Ltd., Royal Theatre and Opera House, Guildhall Road, Northampton NN1 1EA. *T.* Northampton 38343.

Nottingham Theatre Trust Ltd., The Playhouse, Wellington Circus, Nottingham NG1 6AF. *T.* 0602–44361.

Oldham Repertory Theatre Club, The Coliseum, Oldham. *T.* 061–624 1731.

Oxford Playhouse, Meadow Plays Ltd., Beaumont Street, Oxford.

Peacock Theatre, The Abbey Theatre, Lower Abbey Street, Dublin 1.

Perth Repertory Theatre Ltd., Perth Theatre, Perth.

Richmond Theatre, The Green, Richmond, Surrey. *T.* 01–940 0220.

St. Andrews Byre Theatre, Abbey Street, St. Andrews, Fife. (Small cast plays only.)

Salisbury Arts Theatre Ltd., The Playhouse, Fisherton Street, Salisbury.

Sheffield Repertory Company Ltd., The Playhouse, Townhead Street, Sheffield S1 1YD. (Until August 1971).

Sheffield Theatre Trust, New, Townhead Street, Sheffield. (from November 1971).

Stoke on Trent & N. Staffs. Theatre Trust Ltd., Victoria Theatre, Stoke-on-Trent ST4 6AE. *T.* 63954. (Theatre in the round.)

Theatre South-East, (Richard Burnett), De La Warr Pavilion, Bexhill, Sussex.

Thorndike Theatre, Church Street, Leatherhead, Surrey. *T.* 6211.

Windsor Theatre Company (Capoco Ltd.), Theatre Royal, Windsor.

Worthing and District Connaught Theatre Trust Ltd., Connaught Theatre, Worthing, Sussex.

York Citizens' Theatre Trust Ltd., Theatre Royal, York.

The Stage reports productions of most new plays first produced by repertory theatres and a study of this journal may reveal other potential new markets for plays.

AGENTS SPECIALISING IN PLAYS, FILMS, TELEVISION AND RADIO

Further particulars about Agents and a Note to which special attention is called will be found on page 238.

Actac

Aske (Stephen)

Author's Alliance

Curtis Brown, Ltd.

Busby, Christopher and John Rose Ltd.

Clowes, Jonathan

Cochrane (Elspeth) Agency

Colin (Rosica) Ltd.

Copeman Donald Ltd.

Crawfurd, Diana, Ltd.

Crouch (Peter) Plays Ltd.

Felix De Wolfe & Associates

Enterprises, T.I.M.

Epoque Limited

Farquharson (John) Ltd.

Film Rights Ltd.

Fitch, Laurence, Ltd.

Frazer & Dunlop (Scripts) Ltd.

Freelance Presentations Ltd.

Gibson's (J. F.) Literary Agency

Glass (Eric).

Greene (Elaine) Ltd.

Greene (Plunket) (Writers) Ltd.

Alec Harrison and Associates.

Hatton, Richard, Ltd.

Hayes (Michael) Literary Agency Ltd.

Heath (A. M.) & Co., Ltd.

Higham (David) Associates Ltd.

Hughes Massie Ltd.

International Authors Agency.

International Copyright Bureau Ltd.

International Literary Management

Janson-Smith, Peter, Ltd.

Johnson, John

Jones Blakey

Kavanagh Productions Ltd.

Le Dain Management Ltd.

Leresche (Hope) & Steele

Lewin (E. P. S. and Partners

Lloyd-George & Coward

Lom Associates Ltd.

London Management

Richard Milne

Observer Books & Features Ltd.

Penman Literary Agency

Peters (A. D.) & Company

Pollinger (Laurence) Ltd.

Pollinger, Murray

Margaret Ramsay Ltd.

Rogers (Deborah), Ltd.

S.C.O.T.T.S. Ltd.

Scott Meredith Literary Agency (London)

Sheil (Anthony) Associates Ltd.

Somerville (Robert) Ltd.

Steele's Play Bureau, 13 Tottenham Street, W.1.

Taylor-Whitehead Agency

Theatrework (London) Ltd.

Thomson (Campbell) & McLaughlin Ltd.

Unna (Harvey) Ltd.

Van Loewen (Dr. Jan) Ltd.

Vosper (Margery) Ltd.

Walker, Samuel

Watt (A. P.) & Son

Winant, Towers Ltd.

PUBLISHERS SPECIALISING IN THE PUBLICATION OF PLAYS

(For other particulars regarding Publishers, see under "British Publishers," page 157.)

Calder and Boyars Ltd., 18 Brewer Street, London, W1R 4AS

Cape (Jonathan), Ltd., 30 Bedford Square, WC1B 3EL.

Dean (H. F. W.) & Sons, Ltd., 31 Museum Street, W.C.1.

English Theatre Guild Ltd., Ascot House, 52 Dean Street, London, W1V 6BJ.

Evans Bros., Ltd. (Evans Plays), Montague House, Russell Square, London, WC1B 5BX.

French (Samuel), Ltd., 26 Southampton Street, Strand, WC2E 7JE.

Heinemann (William), Ltd., 15–16 Queen Street, Mayfair, W1X 8BE.

Methuen & Co. Ltd., 11 New Fetter Lane, London, EC4P 4EE.

Miller (J. Garnet) Ltd., 1–5 Portpool Lane, London, EC1N 7SL.

(For a list of periodicals dealing with the Theatre see the Classified Index.)

MARKETS FOR SCENARIOS

Markets for scenarios are extremely limited. Most of the larger film companies maintain editorial departments, whose job is to search out literary material suitable for the cinema. They are usually in close touch with publishers and agents and little that is outstanding escapes their notice. Nevertheless there may be occasional openings for the free-lance writer in the general market, and more frequent opportunities for children's and documentary films.

† *Film Companies which read stories submitted through recognised Literary Agents only.*

†British Lion Films, Ltd., Broadwick House, Broadwick Street, London, W1V 2AH *T.* 01–437 8676.

†EMI Film Productions, Ltd. (Scenario Dept.), EMI–MGM Elstree Studios, Boreham Wood, Herts. *T.* 01–953 1600. Work accepted only through an accredited agent.

†M.C.A. (Universal) Ltd., 139 Piccadilly, London, W.1. *T.* 01–629 7211. Read stories for both their American and British productions. Synopses are not wanted. Unpublished material accepted only through accredited agent.

†Metro-Goldwyn-Mayer, Story Department, 3 Queen Street, Mayfair, London, W1X 7PH. *T.* 01–499 9671–6
Read stories for both their American and British productions. Synopses are not wanted. Unpublished material accepted only through an accredited agent.

†Paramount British Pictures, Ltd., 162–170 Wardour Street, London, W.1. *T.* 01–437 7700.
Read stories for Paramount's *American* and *European* productions. Synopses are not wanted. Unpublished material accepted only through the medium of an accredited agent.

†Walt Disney Productions Ltd., 68 Pall Mall, London, S.W.1. *T.* 01–839 8010.

FILM SCENARIOS

PREPARING THE MS.

1. A title page is essential. This should be made out in the same way as when sending a story or article to an editor, except that it is not necessary to mention the number of words.
2. A list of characters should be given. Some writers include short character sketches and mention the types of player or the particular player they have in mind (do not do this unless you know that the cast you suggest is at least feasible and not an impossibility for the company to whom the MS. is submitted). Other writers simply give the names of the characters and a two- to five-word note about each.
3. If you have written your story out to more than about 5000 words, it is not a bad idea to preface it with a shorter version—provided you can write such a version in a manner calculated to interest and arouse curiosity.
4. It is essential to have the MS. typed. Double-spacing is to be recommended, with a wide margin on the left-hand side. Quarto or A4 paper is probably the most convenient size.
5. It is advisable to bind the MS. in some form of simple cardboard cover.

SUBMISSION

It is obviously useless to submit your story to one of the companies who refuse to read stories unless they are sent in through a recognised literary agent. It is advisable therefore, to find out which these companies are before sending it in.

When submitting a film story direct to a film company it is usual to address the envelope to "The Scenario Editor." There is no necessity to write a covering letter. An adequately stamped return envelope must of course be enclosed. If you do write a covering letter, make it as brief as possible. If you think the story might be suitable for one or more of the company's long-contract artists, that is worth mentioning. Remember that the scenario editor and his assistants are busy men and completely indifferent either to your private problems or personal achievements. If your story involves detailed knowledge about a subject upon which you are specially qualified to write, a brief reference to the fact that you have lived for ten years with Bedouin Arabs or in a steel works, or whatever it is, might be advisable.

AGENTS WHO HANDLE FILM STORIES

See page 302

(For a list of periodicals dealing with the Cinema see the Classified Index.)

BROADCASTING: RADIO AND TELEVISION

BRITISH BROADCASTING CORPORATION

For fuller information see *Writing for the BBC*—a guide for writers on possible markets for their work within the BBC. Published by the BBC, price 25p (by post 29p) obtainable through booksellers or from BBC Publications, 35 Marylebone High Street, London, W1M 4AA.

TELEVISION

Drama.—Original plays dealing with contemporary problems are most wanted. Plays needing only a few sets and characters start at an advantage. Specially-shot film sequences should only be written into a script if essential for the story. No standardised layout is expected in unsolicited scripts. Dialogue should be set out in a way that makes it clearly distinguishable from "stage directions" and sound/ visual effects. Further details about length and type of plays currently required are available from Script Unit.

All scripts should be clearly typed and sent to Head of Script Unit, BBC Television Centre, London, W.12.

RADIO

Short Stories.—Short stories specially written for broadcasting will be considered. A short story written for a fifteen-minute broadcasting space should be between 2150 and 2250 words in length.

Plays.—Approximately five hundred new plays are broadcast each year on the basic services, and several hundreds more in the Regions. Many of these are written specially for radio, some are stage plays, and there is a wide field for adaptations of short stories and novels. *Before starting on an adaptation*, it is essential to find out from the BBC Drama Department if such an adaptation would be acceptable. (There might, for example, be copyright difficulties, or the book might have been previously adapted.)

If an adaptation is agreed in principle, a short synopsis, accompanied by a few pages of dialogue, enables the BBC to judge whether it is worthwhile to encourage the writer to proceed. This also applies in the case of original radio plays. It should be remembered that the standard of writing required is a high one and demands real distinction in dramatic writing and also considerable concentrated study of the radio medium. A preliminary letter should be addressed to the Script Editor, Drama (Radio), BBC, 1AA, Broadcasting House, London, W1A 1AA, or to the Drama Producer in any of the Regional studios. *Manuscripts must be clearly typed.*

Music.—The music policy of the BBC, dedicated to the encouragement of the best music old and new, continues to enlarge its range. Audition sessions for professional soloists and ensembles are held every week, except in July and August, with an outside professional assessor on the listening panel.

A Music Panel of distinguished musicians meets regularly to advise on the suitability for performance of the large number of MSS. constantly submitted. The BBC also commissions from British composers works of various kinds. These have included opera and works for special occasions. Incidental music is also commissioned for features and drama. In the case of music commissioned by the BBC the original score is now returned to the composer at his request and not as in the past automatically retained by the BBC.

Light Entertainment.—Careful consideration is given to new ideas for Light Entertainment programmes by the Script Editor and senior members of the Light Entertainment Department. The chief requirement is originality; the vast majority of scripts sent in are merely variations of existing programmes. In general it is inadvisable to write scripts for a particular star artist unless the writer has a really intimate knowledge of the artist's work; and even then material for "solo" performances (as distinct from scripts for comedy series) is almost invariably provided by the artists themselves. No real decision can be reached on a new proposition until the complete script is seen: but the Script Editor is prepared to look at detailed synopses and specimen dialogue and offer opinions if requested. Fees are a matter for negotiation with the Corporation's Copyright Department. Typewritten scripts should be addressed to the Script Editor (Light Entertainment), BBC, Aeolian Hall, New Bond Street, London, W.1.

Talks.—The BBC welcomes manuscripts either from experts or from people with a personal experience to describe: suggestions for single talks are more acceptable than for series. Manuscripts should be written to be spoken aloud, and timed for either 2–5 minutes or, 10, 15 or 20 minutes, allowing one minute for every 120 words. Talks are normally read at the microphone by their authors, and writers submitting manuscripts may be asked before final acceptance to attend an audition, either in London or in one of the Regional Studios.

All typewritten manuscripts should be addressed to the Organiser Talks and Current Affairs Group, (Radio), BBC, P.O. Box 1AA, Broadcasting House, London, W1A 1AA.

BROADCASTING RIGHTS AND TERMS

Specially written material for television: Fees for one performance of a 60-minute original television play range from a minimum of £400 for a play broadcast by one region only and £475 for a network production, or *pro rata* for shorter or long timings. Authors of established status or with experience of writing for television can get considerably more. Half the fee is paid on a work being commissioned and half on its acceptance as being suitable for television. If the work is submitted it is paid for on acceptance. Fees for a 50-minute episode in a series range from £440.

Specially written material for radio: Fees are assessed on the basis of the type of material, its length, the author's status and experience in writing for radio. Minimum fees for one performance of specially written radio dramas in English (other than educational programmes) are £2·25 a minute for beginners and £2·75 a minute for established writers.

Higher rates are paid to very well-known contributors or to those with very great experience of writing for radio programmes. For Light Entertainment programmes rates are higher, the fee for a 30-minute programme by a beginner being from £75, and by an established writer £110 or more for one performance. Fees for submitted material are paid on acceptance, and for commissioned material half on commissioning and half on acceptance as being suitable for broadcasting.

Short stories specially written for radio: fees range from £18 for 15 minutes.

Stage plays for television: Fees for one television performance of a full-length stage play range between £400 and £750 or more in special cases.

Stage plays and published material for radio (domestic services):

Dramatic works: £2 per minute up to 60 minutes; thereafter £1·50 per minute.

Prose works: £1·50 per minute up to 20 minutes: thereafter £1·25 per minute.

Prose works required for adaptation into dramatic form: £1·25 per minute up to 60 minutes; thereafter £1 per minute.

Poems: £2 per half minute up to 2 minutes; thereafter £1·50 per half minute.

Rather lower rates than those set out above are paid for broadcasts in the BBC's external services.

Repeats in BBC programmes: Further proportionate fees are payable for repeats.

Use abroad of recordings of BBC programmes: If the BBC sends abroad recordings of its programmes for use by overseas broadcasting organisations on their own networks or stations, further payments accrue to the author, usually in the form of additional percentages of the basic fee paid for the initial performance. This can apply to both sound and television programmes.

TALKS FOR TELEVISION

The standard Television Talks contract provides that the BBC shall have the following rights of broadcasting mechanical reproduction and publication.

(1) Without further payment the Corporation shall be entitled to edit or abridge the contribution(s) and to make or authorise the making of translations and recordings thereof in any language and:

(i) to broadcast the contribution(s) once only;

(ii) to broadcast extract(s) from the contribution(s) provided that such extracts do not amount to a substantial part of the contribution(s) within the meaning of Section 49 (1) of the Copyright Act 1956;

(iii) to use extracts from the contribution(s) for the purpose of fair dealing within the meaning of Section 6 (1) (2) and (3) of the Copyright Act 1956;

(iv) to use the contribution(s) for its private purposes; and in addition (but without prejudice to the generality of the rights conferred by sub-paragraphs (ii) and (iii) of this clause);

(v) to broadcast extracts from the contribution(s) in programmes of an historic or reminiscent nature;

(vi) to broadcast extracts from the contribution(s) of up to two minutes duration in the Corporation's News Bulletins and News Magazines of every kind whether for television or sound;

(vii) to make and supply recordings of the contribution(s) and extracts therefrom to third parties for the sole purpose of private study on condition that the Corporation makes no charge beyond the actual cost of making and supplying the same;

(viii) to exhibit or authorise the exhibition of the contribution(s) to paying and non-paying audiences in theatres, cinemas, halls and elsewhere at television or film or other festivals in all countries.

(2) (i) The Corporation and its assigns shall have the right without payment to broadcast as required in trailer programmes:

(a) extracts from the contribution(s) or from recordings of any rehearsal thereof;

(b) recordings of material specially contributed by the Broadcaster for trailer programmes;

(ii) If the provision of any specially contributed material involves a separate attendance the Broadcaster shall receive a payment of five guineas.

(3) On payment of additional fees as below the contribution(s) may be rebroadcast:
  (i) in the Corporation's Television Services for the United Kingdom:
    (a) for the first rebroadcast a fee equal to three-quarters of the original fee;
    (b) for each subsequent rebroadcast a fee equal to one-tenth of the original fee;
  (ii) in the Corporation's Sound Services only for the United Kingdom:
    (a) for the first rebroadcast a fee equal to one-quarter of the original fee;
    (b) for each subsequent rebroadcast a fee equal to one-twentieth of the original fee;
  (iii) in the Corporation's External Services only:
    (a) on payment of a fee equal to one-quarter of the original fee which shall cover the first period of twenty-eight days during which any rebroadcast(s) are actually given;
    (b) for each such subsequent period of twenty-eight days on payment of a fee equal to one-twentieth of the original fee.

(4) (a) Recordings of the contribution(s) may be distributed by the Corporation to overseas broadcasting organisations for the sole purpose of broadcasting from transmitters outside the United Kingdom on payment of additional fees in accordance with the following scale:

Territory	% of original fee
All territories throughout the World	100
British Commonwealth and South Africa	50
U.S.A. and its territorial possessions	25
Rest of World	25

(b) Payment of the fees mentioned above permits unlimited use of the recording(s) by the appropriate overseas broadcasting organisation for Television and Sound;
(c) If the overseas broadcasting organisation requires to use the recording(s) for Sound only then all payments shall be at half the rates mentioned above.

(5) The Corporation and its assigns shall in addition be entitled to sell or hire recordings of the contribution(s) and of translation(s) thereof:
  (i) for showing to non-paying audiences on payment of a fee equal to one-tenth of the original fee; and
  (ii) for showing to paying audiences on terms to be mutually agreed.

(6) In the case of rebroadcasts by the Corporation in Television or Sound, distribution to overseas broadcasting organisations or sale or hire to non-paying audiences of abridgement(s) or excerpt(s) from the contribution(s) (other than an abridgement or excerpt which may be broadcast or used without further payment – See Clause (1) above) a proportionate fee based on the length of the abridgement or excerpt shall be paid, but no such payment shall be less than one guinea. Abridgement(s) or excerpts(s) shall be so described unless the Broadcaster agrees on request that such a description may be omitted.

(7) The Corporation shall have exclusive publication rights in the contribution(s) or any translation(s) from the date of the Agreement until twenty-eight days after the date of the first broadcast but such rights shall only be exercised in respect of its own journals excluding the *Radio Times:*
  (i) if the contribution(s) is/are published as a whole or in part in *The Listener* the Broadcaster will be entitled to a fee to be settled by mutual agreement, or failing agreement, by an arbitrator under the Arbitration Act 1950. Abridgements or excerpts will be so described unless the Broadcaster agrees on request that such a description may be omitted;
  (ii) *unless at the time of acceptance of this contract the Broadcaster directs that this sub-clause shall be struck out,* the Corporation shall have the non-exclusive right to publish or authorise the publication of the contribution(s) or any translation(s) thereof anywhere in the World (excluding Europe and the U.S.A.). The Corporation will account to the Broadcaster for any fees which it may charge for such rights.

(8) A right to "broadcast" or "rebroadcast" shall include the following rights:-
  (a) in relation to any broadcast or rebroadcast in the Corporation's Television Services the right to disseminate it once throughout each Region either simultaneously or at different times;
  (b) in relation to any broadcast in the Corporation's Sound Radio Services for the United Kingdom only the right to disseminate it once throughout each Region either simultaneously or at different times;
  (c) the right to give or authorise the giving of simultaneous television and sound relays throughout the United Kingdom and overseas;
  (d) the right to disseminate or authorise dissemination by means of transmitters and/or any system of wire broadcasting;
  (e) the right for the Corporation to authorise recordings of the contribution(s) to be made by or on behalf of Broadcasting Stations Overseas for the sole purpose of broadcasting the recordings once within thirty days of the Corporation's broadcast or rebroadcast in lieu of a simultaneous relay.

In addition recordings of the contribution(s) may without payment be used by the British Film Institute and made and used by the British Institute of Recorded Sound for their respective private purposes.

TALKS FOR RADIO

The standard BBC contracts for contributing Talks to Sound Radio provide that the BBC shall have the following rights of broadcasting mechanical reproduction and publication.

(1) The Corporation shall be entitled to make or to authorise the making of translations and records of the talk(s) in any language and without further payment.
  (i) to use the talk(s) or translations or records thereof for its private purposes;
  (ii) to broadcast extracts from the talk(s) or from translations or records thereof provided that such extracts do not amount to a substantial part of the talk(s) within the meaning of Section 49 (1) of the Copyright Act 1956;
  (iii) to broadcast the records once only in substitution for an actual performance;
  (iv) to use extracts from the talk(s) or from translations or records thereof for the purposes of fair dealing within the meaning of Section 6 (1), (2) and (3) of the Copyright Act 1956.

(2) The talk(s) or translations or records thereof may be rebroadcast in the Corporation's Services for the United Kingdom irrespective of the Service in which the original broadcast was given on payment for each rebroadcast of a fee equal to three-quarters of the original fee.

(3) The talk(s) or translations or records thereof may be rebroadcast in the Corporation's External Services on the following terms:
  (i) If the original broadcast was given in the External Services
    (a) as required during a period of three months from the date of the original broadcast without further payment;
    (b) thereafter as required on payment of a fee equal to one-half of the original fee in respect of each period of 28 days during which any rebroadcasts are actually given.
  (ii) If the original broadcast was given in the Services for the United Kingdom as required on payment of a fee equal to one-half of the original fee in respect of each period of 28 days during which any rebroadcasts are actually given.

(4) (i) The Corporation shall have exclusive publication rights in the talk(s) or any translation from the date of the agreement until 28 days after the date of the first broadcast but such rights shall only be exercised in respect of its

own journals excluding the *Radio Times*. If the talk(s) is published in full in *The Listener*, the Corporation will pay a fee equal to 50 per cent of the original broadcasting fee. If only excerpts or abridgements are published a proportionately smaller fee to be assessed by the Corporation will be paid, but the fee shall not be less than 52½ p. Abridgements or excerpts will be so described unless the Broadcaster agrees on request that such a description may be omitted.

(ii) *Unless at the time of acceptance of the contract the Broadcaster directs that this sub-clause shall be struck out* the Corporation shall have the non-exclusive right to publish or authorise the publication of the talk(s) or any translation thereof anywhere in the world (excluding Europe and U.S.A.). The Corporation will account to the Broadcaster for any fees which it may charge for such rights.

(5) (i) Any broadcast of the talk(s) may be simultaneously relayed by the Corporation and its assigns in the United Kingdom and overseas by means of transmitters and any system of live broadcasting.

(ii) Broadcasting Stations overseas may be authorised by the Corporation to record any broadcast of the talk(s) for the sole purpose of broadcasting the record once within 7 days of the Corporation's broadcast in lieu of a simultaneous relay.

(6) The talk(s) or translations or records thereof may be used for the purposes of the BBC Transcription Service on payment of an additional fee equal to the original fee in return for the right to use the whole of the talk(s) in all territories throughout the world or if the whole of the talk(s) is used in certain territories only (as the Corporation may decide) on payment of a proportion of the original fee in accordance with the following scale:

British Commonwealth and South Africa—one half of the original fee.

U.S.A. and its territorial possessions—one-quarter of the original fee.

All other territories—one-quarter of the original fee.

(7) If there shall be a rebroadcast in the Corporation's services for the United Kingdom or in the External Services or a use for the purposes of the BBC Transcription Service of

(i) a translation of the talk(s) which is not read by the Broadcaster the additional fee payable shall not be based on the original fee but on the script element thereof which shall be deemed to be three-quarters of the original fee;

(ii) an abridgement or excerpt(s) from the talks or translations or records thereof (other than an abridgement or excerpt(s) which may be broadcast or used without further payment) a proportion of the rebroadcast fee based on the length of the abridgement or excerpt(s) shall be paid but no such payment shall be less than one guinea. Abridgements or excerpts shall be so described unless the Broadcaster agrees on request that such a description may be omitted.

(8) The word "records" shall include any contrivance whereby the talk(s) as delivered may be mechanically reproduced. The right to broadcast or rebroadcast in the Corporation's services for the United Kingdom shall include the right to broadcast or rebroadcast once throughout each Region either simultaneously or at different times within a period of one year from the date of the original broadcast or rebroadcast in the Corporation's services for the United Kingdom.

In addition The British Institute of Recorded Sound is entitled to the right to make and use records of the broadcast talk(s) for its private purposes.

ADDRESSES

Letters addressed to speakers c/o the BBC will be forwarded, but for statistical purposes the letters may be opened before being forwarded unless the BBC are notified of any objection. Letters marked "Personal" are forwarded unopened.

LONDON

Head Office: P.O. Box 1AA, Broadcasting House, London W1A 1AA
Telegrams Broadcasts, London, Telex
Cables Broadcasts, London, W.1.
Telephone 01–580 4468
Television: Television Centre, Wood Lane, London, W.12.
Telegrams Broadcasts, London, Telex
Telephone 01–743 8000
Publications: 35 Marylebone High Street, London, W1M 4AA
Telegrams Broadcasts, London, Telex
Telephone 01–580 5577

NORTH WEST REGION

Broadcasting House, Piccadilly, Manchester M60 1SJ.
Telephone 061–236 8444

NORTH EAST

Broadcasting House, New Bridge Street, Newcastle upon Tyne, NE1 8AA
Telephone 0632–20961

NORTH

Broadcasting House, Woodhouse Lane, Leeds 2.
Telephone 0532–31516

SOUTH

South Western House, Canute Road, Southampton.
Telephone 0703–26201

SOUTH WEST

Broadcasting House, Seymour Road, Mannamead, Plymouth.
Telephone 0752–62283

WEST

Broadcasting House, Whiteladies Road, Clifton, Bristol, BS8 2LR.
Telephone 0272–32211

MIDLANDS

Broadcasting House, 52 Carpenter Road, Edgbaston, Birmingham, B15 2JU.
Telephone 021–454 4888

EAST ANGLIA

St. Catherine's Close, All Saints' Green, Norwich, NOR 88B.
Telephone 6003–28841/2

NORTHERN IRELAND

Broadcasting House, Ormeau Avenue, Belfast, BT2 8HQ
Telephone 0231 27411

SCOTLAND

Glasgow Office
Broadcasting House, Queen Margaret Drive, Glasgow, W.2.
Telephone 041–339 8844
Edinburgh Office
Broadcasting House, 456 Queen Street, Edinburgh 2.
Telephone 031–225 3131
Aberdeen Office
Broadcasting House, Beechgrove Terrace, Aberdeen.
Telephone 0224 25233

WALES

Cardiff Office
Broadcasting House, Llandaff, Cardiff.
Telephone 0222 74888
Bangor Office
Bron Castell, High Street, Bangor.
Telephone 0248 2214
Swansea Office
Broadcasting House, 32 Alexandra Road, Swansea.
Telephone Swansea 54986

OVERSEAS OFFICES

U.S.A.

630 Fifth Avenue, New York 10020, N.Y. U.S.A.
Cables Broadcasts, New York City
Telephone 212–581–7100

CANADA

135 Maitland Street, Toronto 5, Ontario, Canada.
Postal Address: P.O. Box 500, Terminal A. Toronto, Ontario, Canada.
Cables Loncalling, Toronto
Telephone Toronto 925 3311

MIDDLE EAST

P.O. Box 3609, B.B.C., Beirut, Lebanon.
Cables Broadcasts, Beirut
Telephone Beirut 225658, 223102

SOUTH EAST ASIA

B.B.C. Representative, L2, 11th Floor International Building, 360 Orchard Road, Singapore 9.
Cables Loncalling, Singapore
Telephone Singapore 372937

AUSTRALIA AND NEW ZEALAND

177 Elizabeth Street, Sydney, N.S.W., Australia.
Cables Loncalling, Sydney
Telephone Sydney 61–9059

FRANCE
155 rue du Faubourg Saint-Honoré, Paris 8e.
Cables Broadbrit, Paris
Telephone 225, 3900/3901/3902
Telex 65341

GERMANY
B.B.C. German Service Representative, Savignyplatz 6, West Berlin, 12
Telephone West Berlin 316773, 316263

LATIN AMERICA
Piso 14, Avenida Cordoba 657, Piso 14, Buenos Aires, Argentina.
Telephone Buenos Aires 31–3786, 32 5553

BBC LOCAL RADIO STATIONS

Material should be submitted to the Programme Organiser.

FT=First Transmission.
* =First Transmission dates to be announced.

Birmingham, BBC Radio Birmingham, Pebble Mill Road, Birmingham B5 750. *T.* 021 472 5141. *Telex:* 33921. *F.T.* 9th November 1970.

Blackburn, BBC Radio Blackburn, King Street, Blackburn, Lancashire BB2 2EA *T.* 0254 62411. *Telex:* 63491. *F.T.**

Brighton, BBC Radio Brighton, Marlborough Place, Brighton BN1 1TU. *T.* 0273 680231. *Telex:* 87313. *F.T.* 14th February 1968.

Bristol, BBC Radio Bristol, 3 Tyndalls Park Road, Bristol BS8 1PP. *T.* 0272 311111. *Telex:* 449170. *F.T.* 4th September 1970.

Derby, 56 St. Helen's Street, Derby DE1 3HY. *T.* 0332 361111. *Telex:* 37257. *F.T.**

Durham, BBC Radio Durham, Park House, Merry Oaks, Durham. *T.* 0385 62611. *Telex:* 53619. *F.T.* 3rd July 1968.

Humberside, BBC Radio Humberside, 9 Chapel Street, Hull HU1 3NU. *T.* 0482 23232. *Telex:* 527031. *F.T.**

Leeds, BBC Radio Leeds, Merrion Centre, Leeds LS2 8NJ. *T.* 0532 29637. *Telex:* 57230. *F.T.* 24th June 1968.

Leicester, BBC Radio Leicester, Epic House, Charles Street, Leicester LE1 3SH. *T.* 0533 27113. *Telex:* 34401. *F.T.* 8th November 1967.

London, BBC Radio London, Harewood House, Hanover Square, London W1R 0JD. *T.* 01-493 5401. *Telex:* 267223. *F.T.* 6th October 1970.

Manchester, BBC Radio Manchester, 33 Piccadilly, Manchester M60 7BB. *T.* 061 228 1991. *Telex:* 668708. *F.T.* 10th September 1970.

Medway, BBC Radio Medway, 30 High Street, Chatham, Kent. *T.* 0634 46284. *Telex:* 965011. *F.T.**

Merseyside, BBC Radio Merseyside, Commerce House, 13–17 Sir Thomas Street, Liverpool L16 BS. *T.* 051 236 3355. *Telex:* 62364. *F.T.* 22nd November 1967.

Newcastle, BBC Radio Newcastle, Crestina House, Archbold Terrace, Newcastle-upon-Tyne, NE2 1DZ. *T.* 0632 812253. *Telex:* 537007. *F.T.**

Nottingham, BBC Nottingham, York House, Mansfield Road, Nottingham NG1 3JB. *T.* 0602 47643. *Telex:* 37464. *F.T.* 31st January 1968.

Oxford, BBC Radio Oxford, 242–254 Banbury Road, Oxford OX2 7DW. *T.* 0865 53411. *Telex:* 83571. *F.T.**

Sheffield, BBC Radio Sheffield, Ashdell Grove, 60 Westbourne Road, Sheffield S10 2QU. *T.* 0742 66185. *Telex:* 54400. *F.T.* 15th November 1967.

Solent, BBC Radio Solent, South Western House, Canute Road, Southampton SO9 4PJ. *T.* 0703 31311. *Telex:* 47420. *F.T.**

Stoke-on-Trent, BBC Radio Stoke-on-Trent, Conway House, Cheapside, Hanley, Stoke-on-Trent, Staffordshire ST1 1JJ. *T.* 0782 24827. *Telex:* 36104. *F.T.* 14th March 1968.

Teesside, BBC Radio Teesside, 91–93 Linthorpe Road, Middlesbrough, Teesside TS1 5DG. *T.* 0642 48491. *Telex:* 58203. *F.T.**

COMMERCIAL TELEVISION

Independent Television Authority, 70 Brompton Road, London, S.W.3. *T.* 01–584 7011. The Authority does not produce programmes, and material intended for broadcasting on the Authority's service should be addressed to the programme contractors, who are responsible for supplying programmes for transmission.

Material required by the Programme Contractors as listed below depends upon the contract held by the Company, i.e. London mid-week programmes will obviously differ from those for the Midlands. In all cases complete scripts are preferred to synopses. Programmes should be planned with natural breaks for the insertion of commercials.

Contracts are held by the following companies:

Anglia Television, Anglia House, Norwich, NOR 07A   *T.* Norwich 28366. London: Brook House, Park Lane, W1Y 4OX   *T.* 01–493 8331. Provides programmes in the East of England during the whole week and drama and natural history programmes. 60 and 80 minute original dramas are welcomed. Writers should contact the Head of Anglia Drama Dept.

ATV Network Ltd., 150 Edmund Street, Birmingham, B3 2JL. *T.* 021–236 5191. 7 days a week Midlands. As ATV Network's requirements are constantly changing, interested professional writers are asked, in the first instance, to communicate with Miss Renée Goddard, Head of the Script Department, who will be able to give the latest information.

Border Television Ltd., Carlisle, CA1 3NT. *T.* 0228–25101. London: 14 Curzon Street, W1Y 7FH. *T.* 01–499 7541. Provides programmes for South Scotland, North-West England, and the Isle of Man during the whole week.

Channel Television. The Television Centre, Rouge Bouillon, St. Helier, Jersey, C.I. *T.* 0534 23451. To provide programmes in the Channel Islands the whole week.

Grampian Television Limited, Queens Cross, Aberdeen. *T.* 0224 53553. 103–105 Marketgait, Dundee. *T.* Dundee 21777. 10 Wardour Street, London, W1V 4JQ. *T.* 01–734 7779. Provides programmes in North and East Scotland during whole week.

Granada Television Limited, TV Centre, Manchester 3. *T.* 061–832 7211 and 36 Golden Square, London, W1R 4AH. *T.* 01–734 8080. (North West New Granadaland Region 7 days). Granada has for some time largely pursued a policy of initiating its own dramatic material, e.g. MURDER, SPINDOE, MR. ROSE and THE CAESARS or adaptations of established works like the stories of D. H. LAWRENCE and INHERITANCE. It is, therefore, advisable for writers to make their approach through agents who would have some knowledge of Granada's current requirements.

Harlech Television Ltd., Pontcanna Studios, Cardiff, Glam. *T.* 0222 26633. London: 99 Baker Street, W1M 2AJ. *T.* 01–486 4311. Wales and West of England.

London Weekend Television Ltd., Station House, Harrow Road, Wembley, Middlesex. *T.* 01–902 8846. (London: Friday 7 p.m. to Sunday Close Down). Scripts through agents only. Professional writers please get in touch first with Miss Margaret Morris, Head of Scripts, for latest information.

Scottish Television Ltd., Theatre Royal, Glasgow, C.2. *T.* 041–332 9999. Gateway Theatre, Edinburgh. *T.* 031–556 5372. (Scottish Station, whole week.) *Material:* Ideas and formats for programmes *other than* one shot plays, particularly with European or international flavour. Approach in the first instance to Controller of Programme's Office.

Southern Television Ltd., Southern Independent Television Centre, Northam, Southampton SO9 4YQ. *T.* 28582. London Office: Glen House, Stag Place. London, S.W.1. *T.* 01–834 4404, Dover Studios, Russell Street, Dover, *T.* 2715. (Southern England—7 days a week.) *Material required:* No scripts will be considered unless submitted through an accredited literary, dramatic or variety agency. No regular demand for television material, but outstanding scripts and programme ideas—through agencies—will be given the fullest consideration. All material should be addressed to the Controller of Programmes, Southern Television Ltd.

Thames Television Ltd., Teddington Lock, Teddington, Middlesex. *T.* 01–977 3252 (Drama/Light Entertainment). Thames Television Ltd., Television House, Kingsway, London W.C.2. *T.* 01–405 7888 (Features). (London weekday contractor Monday to Friday). *Material required:* Drama Department: 60-minute plays, suspense thrillers, comedies, strong social and psychological dramas utilising contemporary themes, written for television will be considered. Scripts should be addressed to George Markstein, Story Supervisor, Drama. A preliminary letter is usually advisable. Light Entertainment: invite ideas and synopses for 30-minute situation comedies, also material for sketch shows. Manuscripts to be addressed to Light Entertainment Script Editors.

Tyne Tees Television Ltd., The Television Centre, City Road, Newcastle upon Tyne NE1 2AL. *T.* 0632 610181. London: 29–30 Old Burlington Street, W1X 2PU. *T.* 01–734 4070. *Material required:* Scripts of first-class quality should be submitted to the Programme Controller. Provides programmes in North-East, whole week.

Ulster Television Ltd., Havelock House, Ormeau Road, Belfast BT7 1EB. *T.* Belfast 28122. London: 19 Marylebone Road, N.W.1. *T.* 01–486 5211. Provides programmes in Northern Ireland, whole week. Programme suggestions welcomed, and should be sent to the Head of Production.

Westward Television Ltd., Derry's Cross, Plymouth PL1 2SP. *T.* Plymouth 69311. P.O. Box 2LE, 4–7 Woodstock Street,, New Bond Street, London, W1A 2LE. *T.* 01–493 8262. Dominions House, 23–25 St. Augustine's Parade, The Centre, Bristol BS1 4UG. *T.* Bristol 292240. Provides programmes in the West country during the whole week.

Yorkshire Television Ltd., The Television Centre, Leeds, LS3 1JS. *T.* 0532 38283. London: Yorkshire House, 7 Portland Place, W1N 3AA. *T.* 01–636 8622. Yorkshire.

Independent Television News Ltd., ITN House, 48 Wells Street, London, W1P 3FE. *T.* 01–637 2424. (All news programmes.)

COMMONWEALTH, AMERICAN AND OTHER BROADCASTING AND TELEVISION COMPANIES

RADIO TELEFÍS EIREANN

R.T.E., Donnybrook, Dublin, 4: the Irish national Broadcasting service operating radio and television. *Television headquarters:* Donnybrook, Dublin, 4. *T.* 693111. Telex. 5268. *Radio:* Henry Street, Dublin, 1. *T.* 42981.

Television: script requirements: original television plays preferably set in Ireland or of strong Irish interest. Plays should be sent to the Head of Drama. Before submitting material to Public Affairs, Features or Children's programmes, authors are advised to write to the department in question.

Radio: talks and short stories (length 14 minutes) in Irish or English suitable for broadcasting: features, dramatic or narrative and plays are welcomed and paid for according to merit. Plays should run 30, 45, 60, 75 or 90 minutes. MSS. should be addressed as follows: R.T.E. (Sound programmes) Henry Street, Dublin, 1.

AUSTRALIAN BROADCASTING COMMISSION

THE Australian Broadcasting Commission controls, under the authority of the Federal Government of Australia, the national broadcasting system. The ABC has two nation-wide networks radiating from the capital cities of the six States, thus serving both metropolitan and country listeners, and, while its programmes range through the whole spectrum of broadcasting, it regards itself as possessing a special responsibility to exert a cultural influence. Accordingly, the Commission needs literary material, much of it similar to that used by the BBC but with the essential difference that the public to be catered for is the Australian public, a public, that is to say, with its own environment, needs, outlook, ideas, opinions, and tastes.

Plays, Radio and Television.—Some plays broadcast by the BBC are used by the ABC. But apart from these, many other plays are required. Most types of play are in regular production—the classic drama of the greatest writers, every variety of modern drama and comedy, radio plays, stage plays adapted for radio, adaptations of stories, etc. The average length of plays is from sixty minutes to seventy-five minutes.

Light Entertainment.—Variety material, scripts of topical or of fanciful humour, scripts of light-entertainment type with music, and so forth, may be submitted.

Short Stories.—Occasional openings for short stories of about 1750 words, although most available periods are used for local writers.

Talks.—News Commentaries and talks on international affairs are all commissioned so there is no market for submitted scripts. Limited openings for general interest talks. Scripts should be of 4½ or 8½ minutes' length.

(Matter coming under any of these headings may be addressed to the European Representative, Australian Broadcasting Commission, 54 Portland Place, London, W1N 4DY, who will also be glad to give any further information required. Head Office: Box 487, G.P.O., Sydney, N.S.W., 2001 Australia.)

CANADIAN BROADCASTING CORPORATION

ENGLISH SERVICES DIVISION

The CBC's interest in plays for television and radio has a natural emphasis on Canadian writers and Canadian themes. There is also a smaller market for plays from abroad which should be submitted in complete script form. Release forms are not required, nor is submission through an agent.

The right to a single broadcast on each station of the network within a three-year period is usually bought, and the fees refer to these terms. Fees are by individual negotiation and are according to ACTRA rates.

Television

A limited number of ninety-minute productions are considered for special programmes. Must be of wide interest and top quality.

One Hour—these scripts are mainly commissioned for both series and anthology productions. Ideas are considered also. The series traditionally are based on Canadian themes.

Half Hour—both the series and anthology programmes in this length are similar in concept to the one-hours.

Radio

Very small market for superior ninety-minute scripts.

One Hour—originals preferred but adaptations considered. All types of drama used.

Half Hour—daily evening serial of five thirty-minute episodes. Every type of story considered.

Requirements for scripts other than drama, such as children's, schools, documentary, etc., are mainly met locally on commission, after discussion. Ideas can be forwarded, however, on speculation.

All scripts and inquiries should be addressed to the CBC National Script Department, P.O. Box 500, Station "A", Toronto 116, Ontario, Canada.

ALL INDIA RADIO

All India Radio, Broadcasting House, Parliament Street, New Delhi, is the department of the Government of India which operates the broadcasting network in the country. There are 36 stations now at Delhi, Bombay, Madras, Calcutta, Lucknow, Tiruchirapalli, Patna, Ranchi, Cuttack, Gauhati, Nagpur, Vijayawada, Allahabad, Jullundur, Ahmedabad-Baroda, Dharwar, Hyderabad, Bangalore, Trivandrum, Kozhikode, Jaipur, Simla, Poona, Rajkot, Indore, Bhopal, Jammu, Srinagar, Kurseong, Kohima, Port Blair, Imphal, Goa, Mathura, Bhuj and Pondchery.

Programmes are planned by Station Directors and are drawn up well in advance of their scheduled dates. The regional station is a self-contained unit in charge of a Station Director who has under him expert staff for administration, engineering, programme planning and production. Except in matters of co-ordination with other stations, its programme plans are drawn up independently. Each centre has its own studios, offices, transmitters and receiving centres. Programmes are arranged and produced locally and consist of music, talks, plays, special programmes for women and children, school broadcasts and rural broadcasts for community listening. Programmes are broadcast in seventeen languages: English, Sanskrit, Hindi, Bengali, Tamil, Telugu, Marathi, Konkani, Sindhi, Gujarati, Kannada, Malayalam, Oriya, Kashmiri, Punjabi, Assamese and Urdu. In its broadcasts, AIR emphasis the instructional, cultural and entertainment items. It avoids politics of a controversial nature and does not accept sponsored broadcasts or any matter that would amount to commercial advertising. It does not include in its programmes any appeal for funds or contributions. It strives to maintain and uphold canons of good taste.

The External Services of All India Radio broadcast programmes in 21 langues for a duration of 43 hours 5 minutes every day. Some of the important languages are English, French, Burmese, Indonesian, Chinese, Tibetan, Nepali, Thai, Sinhala, Arabic, Persian, Pushtu, Swahili, Hindi, Tamil and Gujarati. These programmes are beamed to North and South East Asia, Australia, New Zealand, East, West and North Africa, Western Europe, U.K. and West Asia.

In each language service a composite programme is presented consisting of News, Commentaries, Press Reviews, Talks on matters of general and cultural interest, feature programmes, documentaries, Indian classical and light classical music, film songs, folk songs, orchestral music as well as music of the area concerned.

Listeners are invited to send Reception Reports and comments on the programmes to the Director of External Services, All India Radio, Post Box No. 500, New Delhi (India).

NEW ZEALAND BROADCASTING CORPORATION

The New Zealand Broadcasting Corporation controls all National and Commercial sound and television broadcasting in the country. It also controls the short wave service which is directed primarily to the Pacific Islands and Australia.

Plays.—The New Zealand Broadcasting Corporation considers plays of all types up to 90 minutes' duration. Serious plays may exceed this length.

Serials.—Serials of 13 or 26 quarter- or half-hour episodes.

Talks.—There is a limited demand for general-interest talks. Duration of talks or actualities designed for entertainment Magazine programmes must not exceed 6 minutes. Others may range up to 15 minutes.

Documentaries and Features.—Scripts or taped programmes of interest to a New Zealand audience are purchased, generally of 30 minutes' duration.

Light Entertainment.—Variety material, sketches, musical comedy and continuities are purchased.

Short Stories.—Short stories of up to 1800 words approximately or 15 minutes' duration.

Children's Sessions.—Plays, stories and serials are used. These should not normally exceed 7 minutes' duration.

Enquiries and submission to: The Director-General, New Zealand Broadcasting Corporation, P.O. Box 98, Wellington, C.1, N.Z.

SOUTH AFRICAN BROADCASTING CORPORATION

The South African Broadcasting Corporation, established in terms of the Broadcasting Act No. 22 of 1936 as amended, operates three national networks: the English, Afrikaans, and Springbok Radio and three regional services, Radio High Veld, Radio Port Natal and Radio Good Hope. The Bantu Service operates seven regional services in seven languages, viz. Zulu, Xhosa, Southern Sotho, Northern Sotho, Tswana and Venda, Tsona. Services in four languages are broadcast to the native people of South-west Africa. The SABC introduced an External Service on May 1st 1966 known as Radio RSA, *The Voice of South Africa* which will eventually transmit programmes to all corners of the world except the unpopulated "Cold South". This service echoes around the world in nine languages to carry a positive and objective message about South Africa, its peoples and their achievements, their culture, tradition and ideals. The languages used are English, Afrikaans, Portuguese, French, German, Dutch, Tsonga, Chichewa and kiSwahili.

Plays.—Most types are produced—classical and modern dramas, comedies and thrillers, original radio plays and adaptations of stories, etc. Contributions are welcomed in all sections. The most convenient lengths are 30, 60 and 90 minutes. The Afrikaans network also accepts high quality material for translation. Programmes on the Commercial Service (Springbok Radio) are typical of modern commercial radio, and serials of 15-minute episodes are widely used. Series of self-contained episodes of 15, 30 or 60 minutes are also acceptable. Variety programmes of 30 minutes' duration are always in demand.

Feature Programmes.—Material of topical, scientific and historical interest of 30 to 60 minutes' duration is welcomed.

Talks.—Most are commissioned locally, but outstanding material of particular interest may be submitted. Most suitable length is 5, 10 and 15 minutes.

Short Stories.—There are occasional openings for short stories of 1500–1800 words.

Light Entertainment.—Variety material, light entertainment scripts, and light plays with music may be submitted. The SABC particularly needs first-class variety material.

Youth and Children's Programmes.—Plays, talks, stories, and serials may be submitted. Lengths: plays, up to 15 minutes, and 30 minutes for youth; stories, from 5 to 10 minutes.

It should be stressed that all outside contributors should take into consideration the fact that Radio South Africa caters for a South African public, a public, that is to say, with its own needs, ideas, and tastes.

Enquiries and submissions may be made to SABC, P.O. Box 8606, Johannesburg, South Africa.

AMERICAN BROADCASTING COMPANY	I.T.N. House, 48 Wells Street, London, W1P 3FE	*T.* 01–637 0972–6
NATIONAL BROADCASTING COMPANY INC.	25 St. James's Street, London, S.W.1	*T.* 01–839 4571
CBS NEWS	100 Brompton Rd., S.W.3.	*T.* 01–584 3366
IBC SOUND RECORDING STUDIOS LTD.	35 Portland Place, W1N 3AG	*T.* 01–580 2000

MARKETS FOR ARTISTS, DESIGNERS, ETC.

MOST of the advice given to writers on page 299 applies equally to artists, illustrators and designers. Most book publishers are glad to see artists' work, either by post or appointment, and maintain a file of artists whose work they hope to use when suitable opportunities occur. It is not always easy to secure appointments with editors of journals and magazines, and it is often more advantageous to send a small selection of work by registered post (enclosing stamps for return). It is, however, a waste of time to submit, shall we say, illustrations for boys' adventure stories to Messrs. Batsford: markets must be studied carefully.

The attention of artists is called to the article of special interest to them on pages 383–6.

FIRMS WHICH ARE PREPARED TO CONSIDER DRAWINGS, DESIGNS AND VERSES FOR CARDS, ETC.

Arnold (Joseph) & Co. Ltd., Church Bridge Works, Accrington, Lancashire BB5 4EL. *T*. Accrington 31313. Designs and paintings suitable for reproduction as Christmas Cards.

Brent Press Ltd., Brent Building, Western Ave., London, W.3. Designs and verses of a high standard for all types of Greeting Cards considered. Address to the Art Manager.

Clark (David J.) Ltd., 34–38 Cadogan Street, Glasgow, C.2. *T*. 041–221 9186. Sketches suitable for reproduction as Christmas Cards.

Delgado & Mowbray Ltd., 53–55 East Road, London, N1 6AJ. *T*. 01–253 5651. Publishers of Christmas cards, calendars, and all other kinds of greeting cards. Pleased to receive and consider original paintings, drawings and designs, suitable for the purpose. *Verses* not required.

Fairservice (Geo. C.) Ltd., 42 Bain Street, Glasgow S.E. *T*. Bell 1649. Designs suitable for reproduction by line for high class personal Christmas greeting cards.

Felix Rosentiel's Widow & Son Ltd., Picture Publishers, 13 Queen's Road, Wimbledon, London, S.W.19. *T*. 01–947 1321. Invite offers of Originals of a professional standard for reproduction as colourful Picture Prints for the Picture Framing, Calendar and Box Trades, etc. Oil paintings and strong Water-colours not smaller than 14×10. Also colour transparencies not smaller than 2¼″ square. Any type of subject considered. Verses or cards are *not* required.

Greeting Cards by ilo Ltd., Station Road, Didcot, Berks. *T*. Didcot 3291.

Mansell (A. Vivian) & Co. Ltd., Vicarage Road, Croydon, Surrey, CR9 4AQ. *T*. 01–688 2656. Prepared to consider drawings, etc.

Mason (A.) & Co. Ltd., St. James's Works, Croydon, Surrey, CR9 2HU. *T.* 01–684 1167. *Art Director;* D. W. H. Bostock. Colour rough designs from freelance professional artists required for greeting cards suitable for the general market.

Medici Society, Ltd., The, 34–42 Pentonville Road, N1 9HG. *T.* 01–837 7099. Requirements: paintings and colour drawings suitable for reproduction as large prints or greeting cards.

Millar & Lang, Ltd., 46, 48, and 50 Darnley Street, Glasgow, S.1. *T.* 041–429 2094–5–6. Christmas card, calendar, birthday card and local view postcard publishers.

Newton Mill Ltd., Newton Mill, P.O. Box No. 2, Hyde, SK14 4BG. *T.* 061–368 2601. Greeting cards, notelets, stationary, party invitations.

Philmar Ltd., St. Giles House, 49–50 Poland Street, London, W1A 2LG. *T.* 01–437 0686. Popular children's toys, games, cardboard and wooden jigsaws. Ideas for toys and novelties considered.

Photo Production Ltd., Featherby Road, Gillingham, Kent. *T.* 0634 33241. Colour transparencies.

Royle Publications, Ltd., Royle House, Wenlock Road, London, N1 7ST. *T.* 01–253 7654. Greeting cards, postcards, calendars, prints and gift wrap.

Rust Craft Greeting Cards (U.K.) Ltd., Mill Street East, Dewsbury, Yorkshire. *T.* Dewsbury 67171–8.

Scriptek Publications Ltd., 25 Kings Road, Reading, RG1 3AR. *T.* Reading 50496–7.

Studio ISP of High Wycombe (Industrial and Scientific Photo-services, Limited), 93 West Wycombe Road, High Wycombe. *T.* High Wycombe 30341–2. Printers, Photographers, designers and artists of sales promotion materials.

Taraporevala (D. B.) Sons & Co. Private Ltd., "Treasure House of Books," 210 Dr. Dadabhai Naoroji Road, Bombay 1. Indian art, architecture, natural history, botany, horticultural, musical instruments, dances, handicrafts, sculpture, paintings, technical and scientific subjects.

Thomas Leach Limited, Ock Street, Abingdon-on-Thames, Berks. *T.* Abingdon 444. (Address to J. F. Leeson.) Sketches of religious subjects suitable for reproduction as Christmas or Easter Cards. *T.* 444.

Tuck (Raphael) & Sons Ltd., Pound Street, Warminster, Wilts. *T.* 8251–4. Fine art and greeting card publishers. *Directors:* R. Holme (Chairman), E. Turner (Managing), F. M. Hudson, D. R. Grove, R. S. Persson, M. A. Mitchell.

Valentine & Sons, Ltd., Balgray Place, Dundee, DD1 9NQ. *T.* 89291. Christmas, and everyday greeting cards, and gift wraps. Address to *The Publishing Manager.*

Webb Ivory Limited, Queensbridge Works, Queen Street, Burton upon Trent, Staffs. *T.* 66311–8. Everyday and Christmas greetings cards.

Wilson Bros. Greeting Cards Ltd., Academy House, 45 Uxbridge Road, Hayes, Middlesex. *T.* 01–573 3877.

MARKETS FOR PHOTOGRAPHERS

Photographers are advised to study carefully the Classified Index of requirements on page 415 in conjunction with the detailed requirements of journals at the beginning of the *Year Book*. Book publishers, especially those issuing technical books and school books, will be glad to know the range of subjects covered by a photographer.

FIRMS PREPARED TO CONSIDER PHOTOGRAPHS FOR CALENDARS, GREETING CARDS, ETC.

* Membership of the Greeting Card and Calendar Association
A preliminary letter to ascertain requirements is advisable.

So far as colour is concerned, and most of the firms mentioned below are concerned with colour, usually colour transparencies are required. Very few firms will consider 35 mm. frames; 5 in. × 4 in. is preferred, and 3¼ × 2¼ is acceptable. 2¼ in. square is the minimum size acceptable to film libraries and agencies. Only top quality transparencies should be submitted; inferior work is never accepted. Postage for return of photographs should be enclosed.

GREETINGS, VIEWCARD, CALENDAR AND COLOUR SLIDES

Arnold (Joseph) & Co. Ltd., Church Bridge Works, Accrington, Lancashire BB5 4EL. *T.* Accrington 31313. Greeting Cards and Calendars.

*Bamforth & Co. Ltd., Holmfirth, Yorkshire. *T.* Holmfirth 3107. Pictorial and view postcards, calendars, greeting cards. Use nothing less than 5 in. × 4 in. transparencies for reproduction purposes.

Cardall Ltd., 8 Cope Street, Dublin 2. *T.* Dublin 775540. Natural colour postcards, real photographic postcards, photographic view albums.

*Clark (David J.) Ltd., 34–38 Cadogan Street, Glasgow C.2. *T.* 041–221 9186. Christmas Cards only.

*Delgado & Mowbray Ltd., 53–55 East Road, London, N1 6AJ. *T.* 01–253 5651. 35 mm. not acceptable.

*Dennis (E. T. W.) & Sons Ltd., Printing House Square, Melrose Street, Scarborough, Yorks. *T.* Scarborough 61317. Especially interested in first class transparencies for reproduction as fancy postcards and local view cards. 5 in. × 4 in. or 3¼ in. × 2¼ in. transparencies ideal for postcard reproduction.

L

*Dixon (J. Arthur) Ltd., Forest Side, Newport, Isle of Wight. *T.* Newport 3381. Greeting cards, postcards and calendars.

Exeter News Features and Photos, P.O. Box 59, Exeter, Devon EX4 6BN. *T.* 0392-87 4229. Tourist and pin-up pictures for calendars, picture post-cards and colour slides.

Felix Rosenstiel's Widow & Son Ltd., 13 Queen's Road, Wimbledon, London, S.W.19. *T.* 01-947 1321. Colour transparencies not less than $2\frac{1}{4}''$ square, any type of subject considered.

Forman (Thomas) & Sons Ltd., Hucknall Road, Nottingham NG5 1FE. *T.* Nottingham 65573. Nothing less than 5 in. × 4 in. acceptable.

*Greeting Cards by ilo Ltd., Station Road, Didcot, Berks. *T.* Didcot 3291-2-3.

Jarrold & Sons Ltd., (Printers & Publishers) Cowgate, Norwich, NOR 50P. *T.* Norwich 25261.

*Kardonia Ltd., Barnsbury Street, London, N.1. *T.* 01-607 4641.

Lilywhite Ltd., Brighouse, Yorkshire. *T.* Brighouse 5241. Postcard publishers.

Lowe Aston Calendars Ltd., Saltash, Cornwall PL12 4HL. *T.* Saltash 2233. Calendar printers.

*Mansell (A. Vivian) & Co. Ltd., 224–236 Walworth Road, London S.E.17. Interested in colour transparencies.

*Mason (A.) & Co. Ltd., St. James's Works, Croydon, Surrey, CR9 2HU *T.* 01-684 1167. Greeting Cards.

Medici Society Ltd., The, 34–42 Pentonville Road, London, N1 9HG. *T.* 01-837 7099. Greeting cards.

*Millar & Lang Ltd., 46–50 Darnley Street, Glasgow, S.1. *T.* 041-429 2094.

Mowbray (A. R.), & Co., Ltd., The Alden Press, Osney Mead, Oxford. $2\frac{1}{4}''$ square colour transparencies for parish magazine covers. Seasonal scenes, human interest subjects.

*Newton Mill Ltd., Newton Mill, P.O. Box No. 2, Hyde, SK14 4BG. *T.* 061-368 2601. Greeting Cards, stationary, notelets, party invitations.

Philmar Ltd., St. Giles House, 49–50 Poland Street, London, W1A 2LG. *T.* 01-437 0686. Popular children's toys, games, cardboard and wooden jigsaws. Ideas for toys and novelties considered.

Photo Precision, Ltd., Somersham Road, St. Ives, Hunts. *T.* St. Ives (Hunts.) 4121.

*Photo Production Ltd., Featherby Road, Gillingham, Kent. *T.* 0643-33241.

Pictorial Press Ltd., 2–3 Salisbury Court, Fleet Street, London, EC4Y 8AA. *T.* 01-353 6677 and 4123.

Pillans & Wilson Ltd., 20 Bernard Terrace, Edinburgh, EH8 9NY.

*Royle Publications Ltd., Royle House, Wenlock Road, London, N1 7ST. *T.* 01-253 7654.

Rust Craft Greeting Cards (U.K.) Ltd., Mill Street East, Dewsbury, Yorkshire. *T.* Dewsbury 67171-8.

*Salmon (J.) Ltd., 100 London Road, Sevenoaks, Kent. *T.* Sevenoaks 52381. Picture postcards, calendars and greeting cards.

Scott, Walter (Bradford) Ltd., Ivanhoe Studios, Thorncliffe Road, Bradford BD8 7DJ *T.* Bradford 41193.   Local view postcards, greeting cards and calendars.

Walton Sound and Film Services, 87 Richford Street, London, W.6. *T.* 01-743 9421.

Webb Ivory Limited, Queensbridge Works, Queen Street, Burton upon Trent, Staffs. *T.* 66311-8.   Everyday and Christmas greeting cards.

Whitethorn Press Ltd., The, P.O. Box 237 Thomson House, Withy Grove, Manchester M60 4BL.   *T.* 061-834 1234.   Transparencies not smaller than 2¼in. × 2¼in.   Pictures required relevant to Cheshire, Lancashire, Yorkshire, Warwickshire, Worcestershire, and Gloucestershire only.

*Wilson Bros. Greeting Cards Ltd., Academy House, 45 Uxbridge Road, Hayes Middlesex.   *T.* 01-573 3877.

PHOTOGRAPHIC AGENCIES AND PICTURE LIBRARIES

PHOTOGRAPHIC AGENCIES—THEIR USE AND ABUSE

PHOTOGRAPHIC agencies can be useful to the photographer who wants to get his work into the newspapers. Their methods of working can be understood by comparison with news agencies rather than literary agencies; they look for *news value* rather than style or technical perfection, and they do not make the placing of freelances' work their sole occupation. Rather—in most cases—they look upon the unattached photographer as somebody who can supplement the activities of their staff men.

With news pictures to appear in that night's or next morning's national papers there must be no delay. You cannot send them round from paper to paper seeking the highest bidder. If you send them to one paper and state that they are *Exclusive*, you may be paid more than if they were not. But it will probably pay you better still to sell them to seven or eight different papers. This is where the agencies help. It is generally worth your while to allow them to take the forty or fifty per cent commission they require, for a good agency can multiply your sales manifold.

If your pictures are really "hot" news, waste no time in developing, but (from the provinces) send undeveloped negatives by passenger train from your nearest railway station to the London terminus, addressed to the agency and marked "to be called for."   Include with the negatives your name and address and description of what the pictures represent. If you have to write this by hand, write proper names in CAPITAL LETTERS. Having put your packet on the train, telephone or send a telegram to the agency to which it is despatched, stating station and time of arrival in London. Less urgent negatives can go by special delivery or 1st class post.

If you have taken your pictures in London, you can take them yourself, or send them by messenger.

A few exceptionally good "feature" pictures are accepted by agencies from freelances, but it must be remembered they are not likely to be used by as many papers as newspictures (it would look rather silly if all the dailies came out the same morning with the same picture of, say, Highland sheep), so you may do better by submitting direct to one or two likely editors and saving agency commission. When you *know* the *best* market for your picture, send it straight there; do not bother an agency with it, but save time and commission.

A-Z Botanical Collection Ltd., 54 The Grove, Ealing, London, W.5. *T.* 01–567 2796. Colour transparencies, minimum size 2¼ in. square, of all subjects of a botanical nature.

Actualit, 89 Rue de la Consolation, Brussels 3. *T.* 16.58.98. *T.A.* Actualit, Brussels. Colour transparencies of the world. Landscapes and human interest. Minimum 2¼ in. sq. Rate of commission 60%.

Aerofilms Limited, 4 Albemarle Street, London, W1X 4HR. *T.* 01–493 5211. Library of Aerial and Ground Photographs. The most comprehensive collection of its kind in the United Kingdom, also agents for Associated Companies in many parts of the world.

Associated Freelance Artists Limited, 19 Russell Street, London, WC2B 7HP. *T.* 01–836 2507–8. Photographic library.

Associated News Photos, 30 Fleet Street, EC4Y 1AA. *Editorial:* 9 Linthorpe Road, N16 5RE. *T.* Stamford Hill 9595. *T.A.* Ansfotos, London. News photos and feature pictures; animal and human interest. Good rates for exclusive material. Pin-ups (black and white) and colour transparencies must be exclusive.

Associated Press (The), Ltd., (News Photo Department), 83–86 Farringdon Street, London, EC4A 4BR. *T.* 01–583 1691. *T.A.* Appho, Telex, London. News and feature pictures. Negatives preferred. Terms fixed by mutual agreement.

Barnaby's Picture Library, 19 Rathbone Street, London, W1P 1AF. *T.* 01–636 6128–9. Requires photographs for advertising and editorial publication and always interested to see new work of outstanding quality in black-and-white and colour, of all subjects, British and foreign.

Beard (Harry R.) Theatre Collection, Little Eversden, Cambridge. Prints, drawings, playbills and other theatre documents; portraits of actors, musicians, etc.; pictures of theatres. Italian, French, and other foreign material as well as English. Arrangements for photographs can be made.

BIPS-Bernsen's International Press Service Ltd., 25 Garrick Street, London, WC2E 9BG. *T.* 01–240 1401. (For full details see under **Syndicates, News and Press Agencies**).

British Tourist Authority Photographic Library, 239 Old Marylebone Road, London, N.W.1. *T.* 01–262 0141.

Carr (James) (1937), c/o National Provincial Bank, Cromwell Road, London, S.W.7. Foreign, dominion and colonial subjects, natural history and documentary photographs. Photographs of animals in action. Speciality: "picture stories" from all parts of the world. Especially interested in natural history colour transparencies. Fifty per cent royalty on gross sales to contributor who will retain copyright.

Central Japan Photo Service Ltd., P.O. Box Mizuho 32, Nagoya, Japan. *T.* 841–5506. *Cables:* Centphotos. Colour transparencies, black and white photographs for books, magazines, television, calendars. Terms: 60 to 40 per cent.

Central Press Photos Ltd., The, 6 & 7 Gough Square, Fleet Street, London, EC4A 3DJ *T.* 01–353 2266–7.

Coleman, Bruce, Ltd., 70 Vine Lane, Hillingdon, Middlesex. *T.* Uxbridge 32333. Photographs of natural history. Colour transparencies must be 2¼ sq. or larger. Interested in top quality only and photographers must have extensive coverage. Limited number of new photographers accepted by us each year. Write for details first.

Evans, Mary, Picture Library, 11 Granville Park, London, S.E.13.   *T.* 01–852 5040. Library containing some 250,000 prints and engravings on all subjects, up to 1914.

Exclusive News Agency, *see* **Popperfoto (Paul Popper Ltd.)**

Exeter News Features and Photos, P.O. Box 59, Exeter, EX4 6BN.   *T.* 0392–87 4229. 24 hr. answering service.   Presents Cornwall, Devon and the West Country to the world in newspaper magazine features and photos.   Buys tourist and pin-up pictures etc., for conversion into colour slides and post-cards, magazines and other media.

Fleetway Photographic Library, Fleetway Publications, Ltd., Fleetway House, London, E.C.4.   *T.* 01–236 8080.   *Manager:* Peter Ward.

Fox Photos, Ltd., 69–71 Farringdon Road, EC1M 3JT.   *T.* 01–405 6851.   *T.A.* Foxfotopic, Cent, London.   Pictures of news or topical interest; "live" feature pictures of good quality technically.   **Terms:** 50 per cent.   Payment on 20th of month following publication.

Greater London Council Photograph Library, County Hall, London, S.E.1. 01–633 5000 ext. 255.   150,000 photographs of London and the London area from *c.* 1890 to present day.   Especially strong on Council projects— schools, housing, open spaces, etc.

Horticultural Photo Supply Service, The International Horticultural Advisory Bureau, Arkley, Barnet, Herts.   *T.* 01–449 3031 and 2177.

Independent Features, 1 Electric Parade, Seven Kings Road, Ilford, Essex. *T.* 01–989 2529.   Human interest and other unusual features for syndication on 50–50 basis.

Indian Foto News Features, 44-East Avenue, Punjab Bagh, Delhi–26.   India.   *T.* 564545.   News and feature assignments for newspapers, magazines; black and white, colour.   Also Calendar and Advertisement Pictures.

International News Service Ltd., Tokyo Central P.O. Box 1651, Tokyo, Japan. *T.* 571–0245 and 572–3598.   *Cables:* Newsinter, Tokyo.   News items, features, black and white photographs, colour transparencies, cartoons.   *Terms:* 30–70.

Inter-Prensa Features, Florida 229, Buenos Aires, Argentina.   *T.A.* Interprensa Baires.   Picture-stories, fashion photographs, hair styles, men's fashions, etc. Good market for colour transparencies.   Terms: 40 per cent.

Irish International News Service, Hardy House, 6 Capel Street, Dublin, 1.   *T.* 47045– 6; and 906183 (night).   *Editor:* Barry J. Hardy.

Kevin Court Universal, P.O. Box 11, Camberley, Surrey.   *T.* Yateley 3602.   Particularly interested in children and glamour subjects.   No 35 mm transparencies. Terms: 50 per cent.

Keystone Press Agency, Ltd., (1920), Keystone House, Red Lion Court, EC4A 3EL. *T.* 01–353 9634.   *T.A.* Pressillu, Phone, London.   Mainly "hot" news pictures; feature pictures; colour; studio for creative photography; publicity; industrial.   Global service.   Terms: When negatives are supplied, 60–40 per cent.   When prints are supplied, 50–50 per cent.   Payment and reports of sales, 15th–20th of month.

Lane, Frank W., Drummoyne, Southill Lane, Pinner, Middlesex HA5 2EQ. *T.* 01–866 2336. Natural history.

Lensmen Ltd; Press P.R. Photo Agency, Lensmen House, Essex Street, E., Dublin, 2. *T.* Dublin 773447.

Mansell Collection, 42 Linden Gardens, London W.2. *T.* 01–229 5475.

Monitor Press Features Ltd., 17–27 Old Street, London EC1V 9HL. *T.* 01–253 7071. *Directors:* L. Tuppen, S. R. White.
 Over 40,000 current personalities from the political, sporting and entertainment worlds, mostly portraits. Plus a World picture library in colour and monochrome. Considers good quality material in B/W and colour on any country and almost any subject for documentary and travel library. For international service require feature sets in colour and/or B/W of glamour, pop, human interest, animal subjects and 'at home' type series on well-known personalities. Also single pictures of a 'timeless' variety and a limited number of news pictures. Mainly 60% colour, 50% B/W commission to the photographer.

Mustograph Agency, The, 19 Rathbone Street, London, W1P 1AF. *T.* 01–636 6128–9. Photographs and colour transparencies of Britain only. General subjects of countryside life, work, history and scenery. No topical or hot news pictures. Photographs not purchased: sender retains copyright. Terms: 50 per cent, payable on receipt of client's cheque. Applicants *must* first write for particulars.

Newman (L. Hugh), Natural History Photographic Agency, The Studios, Betsoms, Westerham, Kent. *T.* Westerham 2193. Representing 50 of the leading natural history photographers specialising in colour transparencies.

Orion Press, 55, 1-Chome, Kanda Jimbocho, Chiyoda-ku, Tokyo, 101. *Cable:* Orionserv, Tokyo. *Telex:* TK4447 Orionprs.

PAF International Press Service Ltd., 20 Dover Street, London W1X 3PA. *T.* 01–493 0707. *Cables:* Interfoto, London. International press service organisation specialising in high quality colour and black and white photographs for editorial, advertising, travel and commercial markets. Comprehensive stock of all subjects, as well as unlimited resources abroad. *Management:* J. L. M. Crick.

PIP Photos, Inc., 507 Fifth Avenue, New York, N.Y. 10017. *T.* 212 OX7-6191. Represents leading photographers around the world. Particular interest in movie fan material, gossip materials, exposes, sets of nudes,—men's adventure stories, great exploits, and dramatic emotion evoking picture series. Send 5 Postal reply coupons and large self addressed envelope for particulars. Also has a literary agency division, primarily for photo books.

Photo-Masters, 23 Hamam Street, Fort, Bombay 1. *T.* 251381. *T.A.* Fotomaster. Require: Black and White and colour transparencies of children, girls and ladies in fashion, people in fields and Industries, Indian monuments, architecture and landscape for Calendar and illustrated feature articles for Indian Press. Terms: 50% commission on gross sales.

Photo Precision, Ltd., Somersham Road, St. Ives, Hunts. *T.* St. Ives (Hunts.) 4121.

Pictorial Press Ltd., 2–3 Salisbury Court, Fleet Street, London, EC4Y 8AA. *T.* 01–353 6677 & 4123. *Directors:* L. W. Gale, A. F. Gale, K. V. Gale. Established in Fleet Street in 1938, handles photographic features dealing with show business, personalities, animals, children, woman subjects, medical and scientific stories and glamour. Handles freelance work but prefers to commission. Sells direct to media in every part of the world.

Picturepoint Ltd., 120, Holland Park Avenue, London, W.11. *T.* 01–727 3131 and 01–727 3113. Have ready markets for high quality colour transparencies $2\frac{1}{4}''$ sq. or preferably larger. Any subject other than *news.* Send transparencies by registered post. *Terms:* 55% to photographer.

Pixfeatures (Mr. P. G. Wickman), 5 Latimer Road, Barnet, Herts. Picture-features, preferably topical. Especially for sale to German, Dutch, Swiss, Belgian and Italian magazines. 40% of all sales, unless otherwise arranged.

Popperfoto (Paul Popper Ltd.), 24 Bride Lane, London, EC4Y 8DR. *T.* 01–353 9665–6. *Telex:* 21202. Offer and require documentary photos (black and-white and colour) from all countries of the world showing geographical features, principal towns, architecture, village life, native people, their work and customs, industries, agriculture, communications, education, religion, history, archaeology, fauna and flora. Also topical pictures for News Photo Department. Act as photographers' agents on commission basis.

Press Association Photos (the news picture service of **The Press Association.**), 85 Fleet Street, EC4P 4BE. *T.* 01–353 7440.
P.A. Studios division (colour and black and white industrial), 371 Euston Road, London, N.W.1. *T.* 01–387 5262.

Press Photos International Photo News Service, Fleet Street House, 70 Lee Lotts, Great Wakering, Essex. *T.* (24 hours) Great Wakering 538. *Cables:* Press-pixs, Southend. *Registration fee:* £3 3s. for which photographers receive Agency press pass, quarterly news letter *News Flash* and a photo market sheet. *Terms:* 75% to photographer if registered with agency, otherwise 50%. Features, news, black and white and colour, cine film 16 mm and 35mm, world-wide service.

Radio Times Hulton Picture Library, 35 Marylebone High Street, London, W1M 4AA. *T.* 01–580 5577.

Ronan Picture Library, Ballards Place, Cowlinge, Newmarket, Suffolk. *T.* Wickhambrook 328 (0440–82 328). Woodcuts, engravings, photographs of history of science and technology.

Ruck (Peter) & Associates, 72 Furlong Road, Westcott, Dorking, Surrey. *T.* Dorking 5361. Require photo-stories of human interest, black-and-white or colour which must not be smaller than $2\frac{1}{4}''$ sq. No "hot" news required. Preliminary letter essential.

Rudeni Photographers, 161 Preston New Road, Blackburn, Lancashire BB2 6BN. *T.* Blackburn 59368. Consider exclusive feature series, photographs with copy, or copy which requires illustrating, devoted to women's interests. Outright purchase or on percentage sale basis by arrangement. No "hot" news. Integrated service with **Europa Press AB,** Stockholm, Sweden.

Sene, Etulgama, 63/21 Bowala, Kandy, Ceylon. Feature pictures, historical feature subjects a speciality; colour creative photography; wild life photography. Acts as photographic agent on commission basis. Terms 60–40 per cent.

Skyport Fotos, Norman Tomalin, 227 Sipson Lane, Sipson, West Drayton, Middle-sex. *T.* 01–897 8947. Specialists in travel and landscapes. Interested in work of photographers who can produce first-class colour transparencies (6×6cm or larger).

Spectrum Colour Library, 44 Berners Street, London W1P 3AB. *T.* 01–637–1587. Require high quality B/W prints and colour transparencies (35 mm. or larger) for advertising and editorial publication. Need all subjects except topical or hot news pictures—list of requirements available on request. *Terms:* 60% to photographer.

Sport & General Press Agency, 2–3 Gough Square, Fleet Street, EC4A 3DH. *T.* 01–353 1161. *T.A.* Sportangen, London, E.C.4. Press photographs. Send photographs, but negatives preferred.

Sutcliffe Gallery, 1 Flowergate, Whitby, Yorkshire. *T.* Whitby 2239. Collection of 19th-century photography all by Frank M. Sutcliffe, HON. F.R.P.S. (1853–1941). Especially inshore fishing boats and fishing community, also farming interests. Period covered 1872 to 1910.

Syndication International, 27 Floral Street London, WC2E 9DP. *T.* 01–836 8466.

Taraporevala (D. B.) Sons & Co. Private Ltd., "Treasure House of Books," 210 Dr. Dadabhai Naoroji Road, Bombay 1. Indian art, architecture, natural history, botany, horticulture, musical instruments. dances, handicrafts, sculpture, paintings, technical and scientific subjects.

Topix, The Picture Service of Thomson Newspapers Ltd., 200 Gray's Inn Road, London, W.C.1. *T.* 01–837 1234. Produces topical news and feature pictures covering the British Isles and Europe, and has a Photographic Library of over one million pictures covering news and sporting events, royal activities, people and places over the last fifty years.

Tourist Photo Library Ltd., 54 The Grove, Ealing, London, W.5. *T.* 01–567 2796. Colour transparencies, preferably 5×4 of domestic pets, floral arrange-ments, children and glamour subjects. Also posed beach scenes suitable for Travel Brochure covers. Terms 50%, payable on receipt of our clients' cheque. Please write first.

Transafrica, via Trieste 34, 25100 Brescia, Italy. *T.* 55080–40800. *T.A.* Trans-africa-Brescia. Folklore, zoology, botany, geology, industry and agriculture of Africa, Asia and South America. Seek skilled contributors from all parts of the world. Act as agents on commission basis.

Transatlantic Photo Service, 7100 Hillside Avenue, Suite 309, Hollywood, California, 90046. Supplies candid pictures of Hollywood stars at all social events. Staffed by former Fleet Street photographers. Assignments undertaken.

United Press International (UK) Limited 8 Bouverie Street, Fleet Street, EC4Y 8BB. *T.* 01–353 3671–3. *T.A.* Unipix London. Any pictures suitable for press generally on spot news and features, both black and white and colour. Terms: on application.

Universal Pictorial Press & Agency Ltd. (1929), New Bridge Street House, 30–34 New Bridge Street, London EC4Y 6BN. *T.* 01–236 6730 and 01–236–5840. Suppliers of a daily press and library service of black & white photographs and colour transparencies to the national and provincial press, periodicals and television companies throughout the British Isles and overseas. The library contains over 200,000 black & white photographs and 25,000 colour transparencies of notable Political, Company, Academic, Legal, Diplomatic, Church, Military, Pop, Arts, Entertaining and Sports personalities and well-known views and buildings.

Van Hallan Photo Features, 57 South Street, Isleworth, Middlesex. *T.* 01–568–0792. Agency issues a regular photographic service of news, society and current events to the world's press, magazines and television organisations. The commercial division specialise in P.R. and industrial photography. Picture reference library section contains over 100,000 negatives of prominent personalities including, business, company, diplomatic, political, sporting executives and the aristocracy.

REFERENCE SECTION

COPYRIGHT

By the late F. E. SKONE JAMES, B.A., B.C.L., and E. P. SKONE JAMES, M.A.

GENERALLY

It is not possible, in a short article such as this must be, to examine the law of copyright in detail. The general principles are explained, and attention is drawn to many points of special interest. Expert legal advice should be sought in case of practical difficulty.

The Copyright Act, 1956 ("the Act") which substantially replaces the Copyright Act, 1911 ("the Act of 1911"), received the Royal Assent on November 5, 1956, and came into operation on the 1st June 1957. The Act has been amended by the Design Copyright Act 1968, which came into operation on the 25th October 1968, and which deals with the relationships between copyright under the Act and copyright under the Registered Designs Act 1949.

The Act, though more complicated, will not, it is thought, be found to have made substantial changes affecting the rights of writers and artists. The Act provides (Section 45(5)) that no copyright shall subsist otherwise than by virtue thereof, and the Seventh Schedule to the Act contains lengthy transitional provisions which assume that the provisions of the Act have always been in force, but then proceed to modify its provisions in respect of works which were in existence before its commencement. Thus, devolutions of title to copyright works valid under the Act of 1911 are to be treated as remaining valid, and, in general, copyright which subsisted in works under the Act of 1911, will continue to subsist under the Act. Again, the proviso to Section 3, and Section 4 of the Act of 1911, which dealt respectively with the right, 25 years after the death of the author of a published work, to reproduce the work without infringement of the copyright therein if the necessary notice had been given, and, the right to apply to the Judicial Committee of the Privy Council for a compulsory licence in certain circumstances, and the proviso to Section 5(2) of the Act of 1911 are repealed by the Act: but, if the necessary notice has been given under such proviso before Section 3 is repealed, then, as respects reproductions of that work by the person who gave the notice, after the repeal of Section 3, such proviso is to have effect as if re-enacted in the Act (Paragraph 9, 7th Schedule of the Act), and in the case of an assignment before 1957 under the Act of 1911 there will still be a reverter to the personal representatives of the author at the end of twenty-five years from his death.

The Act also made the necessary changes in the law to enable this country to ratify the Brussels Convention and the Universal Copyright Convention.

NATURE OF COPYRIGHT

Copyright protection is not given to ideas or systems, plots or themes, however original; it is aimed solely to prevent the copying of literary, musical, dramatic or artistic works, sound recordings, films, television and sound broadcasts and published editions of works. The idea, theme or plot must therefore be reduced into concrete form before protection can be claimed, and then the protection given is to the form and not to the idea. If the idea is reproduced in a quite different form, this is not an infringement of copyright.

Another basic principle of copyright law is that it does not give a monopoly even to the form selected, since it is directed to preventing copying, and not to giving an absolute title to any particular form of words, or of artistic production. Copyright protection is given to dictionaries and directories and to photographs, but this does not mean that another may not lawfully produce independently an almost identical work; he is only guilty of infringement if he copies the earlier work.

A further important matter in regard to copyright protection is that, in the United Kingdom and most European countries at least (see *post* "Works protected abroad"), no formalities are required. Copyright protection is afforded as soon as the page of manuscript is written, the sketch is drawn or the melody is composed. The work does not need to be printed or published, no form of registration is needed, no "copyright reserved" or other copyright notice is required. Publishers are required to deliver certain copies of published books to libraries (Section 15 of the Act of 1911, which is not repealed by the Act), but failure to do this does not affect the copyright, though it may give rise to liability for penalties (sub-section (6)). Copies of scripts of certain new plays are required to be delivered to the British Museum under the Theatres Act 1968.

KIND OF WORKS PROTECTED

Literary, dramatic and artistic works are defined in the Act (Sections 48(1) and 3(1); see also definitions of "sculpture," "engraving," "photograph," "building," "construction," "drawing," "manuscript," "writing").

It has been decided that the expression "literary" does not involve any qualification of style, but covers any work expressed in print, or writing, so long as it is substantial enough to involve some literary skill and labour of composition. And a similarly slight degree of skill and labour is imposed in regard to other classes of works.

Thus, selections of poems, abridgements, notes to school textbooks, arrangements of music, football championship fixtures list and other compilations are protected, provided that it is established that the production has involved a certain amount of intellectual endeavour, and is not merely mechanical.

Under the Act of 1911 (Section 22), artistic works intended for use as industrial designs were not protected under such Act, but could be protected under the Patents and Designs Acts, 1907–31. If the author of such a work failed to register the work as a design he lost both his artistic and designs copyright. Under the Act (Section 10) the author was not required to register his design until it was actually about to be licensed for industrial use, and, even if so licensed without registration, its artistic copyright was preserved, except in regard to industrial use (see Dorling v. Honnor Marine Ltd. 1964, 2 W.L.R. 195). On the other hand, the protection against industrial use would endure only for the period of fifteen years provided by its registration. This position has been changed by the Design Copyright Act 1968 in respect of works created after its coming into force. The 1968 Act amends section 10 of the Act in such a way that industrial use will not affect copyright under the Act except to limit the period of protection against industrial use. The position as to pre-1968 works is not made clear by the 1968 Act.

Protection under the Registered Designs Act, 1949, requires certain formalities of registration, and a Patent Agent should be consulted.

Sound recordings, films, television and sound broadcasts are defined in the Act (Sections 12 (9), 13 (10) and 14 (10); and see *post* "Sound recordings," "Films," "Broadcasting and Television," "Published Editions").

PUBLISHED EDITIONS

The Act provides for the first time that a separate copyright is to subsist in every published edition of any literary, dramatic or musical work first published in the United Kingdom, or of which the publisher was a qualified person at the date of first publication. The publisher is entitled to such copyright (Section 15 of the Act).

Copyright in published editions subsists until the end of the period of twenty-five years from the end of the calendar year in which the edition was first published, and such copyright is infringed by making by any photographic or similar process a reproduction of the typographical arrangement of the edition.

TITLES AND PSEUDONYMS

The title of a book or story is normally not protected under the Act since it is too short to be treated as a literary work.   If, however, a title is taken and used in such a way as to cause confusion, a "passing off" action can often be brought successfully.

A similar ground of action arises if an author's pseudonym is used by another in such a way as to cause the public to believe that the second work is by the first author.

Apart from agreement, if an author has been writing for a periodical under a particular pen name, and ceases to contribute, he is entitled to use the pen name elsewhere, and the periodical is not entitled to continue to use it (and see *post* "Anonymous and Pseudonymous works").

TO WHOM COPYRIGHT PROTECTION IS GIVEN

In general the person to be protected is the author.   This means the person who has actually written the book or drawn the picture; a person who has merely suggested a theme, or supplied information, is not an author; this follows from the general principle stated above that protection is given to form and not ideas; it is the author of a form with whom copyright law is concerned.

However, where a literary, dramatic or artistic work is made by an author in the course of his employment by the proprietor of a newspaper, magazine or similar periodical under a contract of service or apprenticeship, and is so made for the purpose of publication in a newspaper, etc., such proprietor is entitled to the copyright in the work, but only in so far as the copyright relates to such publication: the remainder of the copyright remains in the author (Section 4 (2) of the Act).   Subject to this, in the case of photographs and portraits, engravings and sound recordings (Section 4 (3) and 12 (4) of the Act), if the original is ordered, and paid for, the copyright vests in the client, and not in the artist, photographer or maker.

But, if in a case not falling within either Section 4 (2) or Section 4 (3), a work is made in the course of the author's employment by another person under a contract of service or apprenticeship, that other person, and not the author, is entitled to the copyright in the work (Section 4 (4) of the Act).   Where the author or artist is merely employed to provide a certain work, and is not a servant liable to detailed control as to the manner of production, the copyright vests in him, and not the employer.   And, even in the case of a full-time employee, work done for the employer out of hours will remain the copyright of the servant.

ANONYMOUS AND PSEUDONYMOUS WORKS

Copyright in published literary, dramatic or musical works, and artistic works other than photographs, which are anonymous or pseudonymous, subsists until the end of the period of fifty years from the end of the calendar year in which the work was first published, unless, at any time before the end of that period, it is possible for a person, without previous knowledge of the facts, to ascertain the identity of the author (or one or more of the authors in the case of joint works), by reasonable enquiry (Second Schedule to the Act).   However, publication of a work under two or more names is not pseudonymous unless all the names are pseudonyms.

The normal period of copyright is fifty years from the end of the calendar year in which the author died.   In certain circumstances, therefore, a shorter period of protection only is obtained (see also "Duration of copyright protection" *post*).

JOINT AUTHORS

Joint authorship involves that two or more persons must have collaborated to produce a single work. Each must have taken some part in producing jointly the work protected; as has been seen, a man who merely suggests the idea or theme is not an author at all. Again, if the parts produced by each are easily separable, it is not a case of joint authorship, but each owns a separate copyright in each part (Section 11 (3) of the Act). The Act provides that, with certain exceptions, references therein to the author of a work are to be construed in relation to a work of joint authorship as a reference to all the authors of the work (Third Schedule to the Act). The more important exceptions are that, for the purposes of establishing copyright in literary, dramatic, musical and artistic works, it is sufficient if only one of the joint authors satisfies the necessary conditions. Further if one or more of the joint authors does not satisfy the necessary conditions to establish copyright in the joint work, then the remaining author or authors are to be considered the person or persons entitled to the copyright in such work. In the case of a work of joint authorship, neither can deal with the copyright without the consent of the other or others, but, on the other hand, each can bring actions against the other or third parties for any infringement. Other matters of importance to joint authors are referred to under "Duration of copyright protection."

ASSIGNMENT OF COPYRIGHT

An assignment of copyright must be in writing and signed by or on behalf of the assignor (Section 36 (3) of the Act), but no other formality is required. Copyright may be assigned for certain areas, or for a certain period, or the right may be assigned to do certain of the acts which the copyright owner has the exclusive right to do (e.g. the right to make adaptations, the right to perform, and publishing rights). The right to do acts not separately mentioned in the Act may now be assigned separately.

Future copyright (that is, copyright which will, or may, come into existence in respect of any future work, or on the coming into operation of any of the provisions of the Act, or in any other future event), will vest, on the coming into existence of the copyright, in the assignee under a purported assignment of such copyright, without any further document: such assignment must, however, be in writing, and signed by or on behalf of the prospective owner of such copyright (Section 37 (1) of the Act). In drafting publishing agreements and other transactions, authors will therefore have carefully to consider these provisions.

LICENCES

A mere licence to publish or perform or to do other acts which the copyright owner has the exclusive right to do does not require to be in writing unless exclusive but may be implied from conduct, and licences in writing may be granted by a prospective owner of copyright in relation to his prospective interest therein (Section 37 (3) of the Act). The principal distinction between the position of an assignee and a licensee is that the former can, but the latter cannot, except in the case of an exclusive licence, in writing, sue third parties for the infringement of the right. Other distinctions are referred to under "Publishing Agreements." However, if a licence (in the Act called an "exclusive licence") is made in writing, and signed by or on behalf of the owner or prospective owner of copyright, authorising the licensee exclusively to do any of the acts which the copyright owner has the exclusive right to do, then the licensee has (except against the owner of the copyright) the same remedies for damages, etc., as if the licence had been an assignment, subject to the owner of the copyright, either being joined as Plaintiff or added as Defendant in certain circumstances (Section 19 of the Act). A licensee, like an assignee, may make alterations in the work unless the terms of the licence expressly or impliedly forbid alterations being made and the courts will readily imply such a term (Frisby v. BBC 1967 2 W.L.R. 1204).

WHAT CONSTITUTES INFRINGEMENT

Copyright is infringed by the reproduction, or colourable imitation, of any substantial part of a copyright work without permission. Such infringements are proved by a detailed comparison of similarities, and proof is often difficult in the case of compilations which, of necessity, resemble one another; in such cases, copying may be proved from the coincidence of trifling errors. In considering whether the part taken is substantial, more regard is had to the importance than to the quantity of what is taken; Ladbroke (Football) Ltd. v. William Hill (Football) Ltd. 1964 1 W.L.R. 273. Thus, to take a few bars of the essential melody of a tune may constitute an infringement. An infringement is committed whether the copying has been directly from the original, or through an intervening copy and may be committed where the copying is from memory; Francis Day & Hunter Ltd; v. Bron 1963 2 W.L.R. 868.

Other modes of infringement are: to publish an unpublished work, to make an adaptation of a work, which latter includes making a version of the work in which the story or action is conveyed wholly, or mainly, by means of pictures in a form suitable for reproduction in a book or newspaper, magazine or similar periodical, making a translation, dramatising a book and making a novel of a play. (See also "Performance," "Films," "Records," "Broadcasting and Television" *post*, and "Publishing Editions" *ante*.) It is to be noted that to parody a work such as a picture or a play may not be an infringement if the parody amounts to an original work (Joy Music Ltd. v. Sunday Pictorial Newspapers (1920) Ltd. 1960 2 W.L.R. 645).

In addition to the direct infringements above described, an actionable wrong is committed by anyone who knowingly sells, exhibits in public, distributes or imports (otherwise than for private and domestic use) copies unlawfully made (Section 5 of the Act). It is to be noted that in these cases proof of knowledge is essential, and, in practice, it may be difficult to establish these offences, except by giving express notice, and taking action if the offence is committed hereafter.

PERFORMANCE IN PUBLIC

It is an infringement to perform any substantial part of a literary, dramatic or musical work in public, and to permit a place of public entertainment to be used for private profit for such a performance. A performance is in public unless it is purely private and domestic. It is not necessary that every member of the public shall have access, or that a charge shall be made for admission. Performances at clubs or institutes with limited membership are therefore generally in public for this purpose, and a place of public entertainment is defined by the Act (Section 5 (6)), as including any premises which are occupied mainly for other purposes, but are from time to time made available for hire to persons desiring to hire them for purposes of public entertainment (see also "Sound Recordings" and "Broadcasting and Television" *post*).

EXCEPTIONS TO LIABILITY FOR INFRINGEMENT

It cannot of course be an infringement if the consent of the owner of the copyright has been given or is to be implied. Where, however, a consent has been given without payment, such consent may be withdrawn at any time.

No fair dealing with literary, dramatic, musical and artistic works for purposes of research or private study is an infringement of the copyright therein. Nor is a fair dealing with such works an infringement if it is for the purposes of criticism or review of the work itself or another work, if accompanied by a sufficient acknowledgment. "Sufficient acknowledgment" is defined by the Act (Section 6 (10)), and the test of fairness is whether the purpose of the use made is reasonable in the interests of criticism, etc., or whether what is produced is in substance a competing publication.

Some other exceptions in Section 6 of the Act are: reporting current events in newspapers, etc., if accompanied by a sufficient acknowledgment, or by means of broadcasting, or in a film; reproduction for the purposes of judicial proceedings (this applies equally to films and sound and television broadcasts); reading or reciting in public extracts of works, if accompanied by a sufficient acknowledgment; including passages in collections intended for schools, if accompanied by a sufficient acknowledgment. In Section 9 of the Act: copying works exhibited in public; copying works of architecture; including artistic works as backgrounds to films or television broadcasts; reconstructing buildings which are works of architecture. In Section 15 of the Act, making reproductions by or on behalf of librarians of the typographical arrangement of a published edition. In Section 41 of the Act, reproducing the work, or an adaptation thereof, in the course of instruction for schools, or as part of examination questions and answers. In Section 42 of the Act, making or supplying reproductions of public records.

Section 7 of the Act provides that the making or supplying of copies of articles contained in periodical publications, and of parts of published literary, dramatic, and musical works (not being such articles), and any illustrations thereof, by, or on behalf of, the librarian of a library of a class prescribed by Board of Trade Regulations, is not an infringement. (1957, S.1. No. 868.)

It should be observed, however, that ignorance was no defence even if reasonable in the circumstances; printers ran considerable risks in this connection since they had often no means of knowing that an infringement was being committed but they were nevertheless liable. However, now, in proceedings for conversion of infringing copies, damages cannot be recovered from an innocent defendant.

WHO IS LIABLE FOR INFRINGEMENT

In the case of an infringement by the publication of a copy or imitation, the author, publisher and printer of the infringing work are equally liable.

Where an infringement is committed by performance in public, not only the actual performers but the firm or company by whom they are employed are liable.

Greater difficulty arises in the determination of the liability of hirers of films, owners of halls, and other persons who have not infringed either personally or by their actual servants. It is an infringement, however, to "authorise" any infringing act so that, if it is proved that any person, by supplying the material or otherwise, made the infringement possible, he will generally be held liable. Section 5 (5) of the Act, however, provides that a person who permits a place of public entertainment to be used for a performance in public of a work, does not infringe the copyright in the work, if he was not aware, and had no reasonable grounds for suspecting, that the performance would be an infringement or, if he gave his permission gratuitously, or for a nominal consideration, or for a consideration not exceeding his estimated expenses consequential from the use of the place for the performance.

THE REMEDIES FOR INFRINGEMENT

A copyright owner whose right is infringed is, in general, entitled as of right to an injunction, i.e. an Order of the Court restraining the Defendant from repeating the infringement, and can insist upon such an Order, although offered a personal undertaking first. It is to be noted however that such an Order will be directed only to repetition of the actual infringement; i.e. an Order cannot be obtained to restrain copying of future parts of a serial story because earlier parts had been copied.

A second remedy is damages for infringement. These are usually based upon evidence of loss suffered by the Plaintiff, i.e. that if the infringing book had not been published, he would have been able to publish more copies of his own book or that he otherwise has lost a market for his material. Damages for infringement, may, however, be increased, in effect, by way of an award of exemplary damages if the Court, having regard to the flagrancy of the infringement, and any benefit shown to have accrued to the Defendant by reason of the infringement, is satisfied that effective relief is not otherwise available to the Plaintiff (Section 17 (3) of the Act). It is permissible, in assessing damages, to have regard to the sort of fee which would have been asked if a licence had been requested. However, if it is proved or admitted that the Defendant was not aware, and had no reasonable grounds for suspecting, that copyright subsisted in the work, the Plaintiff cannot recover damages from the Defendant (Section 17 (2) of the Act). In view of the fact that every work enjoys copyright without formality, such ignorance is difficult to establish, except in special circumstances where it might be reasonably thought that the work was out of copyright, or not protected in this country.

Damages, however, can alternatively be based upon a claim for conversion, upon the principle that the infringing material is deemed the property of the copyright owner. Under this head, regard is had, not to the loss to the copyright owner, but to the value of the infringing work. Where only a portion of the work containing the infringement represents infringing material, it is necessary, first to assess the value of the infringing work as a whole by reference to the sale price of each copy multiplied by the number of copies, and then to assess the damages at that fraction of this figure which the infringing material bears to the whole. Where the portion of the whole which is infringing is relatively slight, e.g. in the case of an infringing article in a newspaper, this calculation is difficult. However, a plaintiff is not now entitled to damages for conversion if it is proved or admitted that at the time of conversion, the defendant believed, and had reasonable grounds for believing, that the articles were not infringing copies (Section 18 (2) of the Act).

A further alternative remedy is an account of profits. Here the claim is based, not upon the value of the infringing material, but upon the amount of profit made by the defendant in respect of the infringement, and the plaintiff is entitled to this relief even where the defendant's ignorance of the subsistence of copyright in the work is proved or admitted.

In addition to the foregoing remedies a successful plaintiff is entitled to have delivered up to him all infringing material in the defendant's possession.

The Act, unlike the Act of 1911, does not specifically provide for any period during which a copyright action may be brought, so that presumably the Limitation Act of 1939 will apply (see Section 18 (1) proviso of the Act). Therefore the period for bringing actions in respect of infringements of copyright will be six years from the infringement, and in respect of actions for conversion of infringing copies, will be six years from the conversion whether there is only one conversion, or a succession of conversions. Under the Act of 1911 the period in each case was three years.

There are further restrictions on the remedies obtainable in the case of exclusive licensees (Section 19 of the Act) and in relation to buildings (Section 17 (4) of the Act).

Section 20 of the Act provides for various presumptions of facts in copyright actions. These deal with the subsistence of copyright in a work, the owner of the copyright, the author of the work, the originality of the work, the first publication of the work, and the maker and date and place of first publication of records. These presumptions can greatly simplify the evidence which would be required in a copyright action.

The above remedies are enforceable by civil action.

OTHER REMEDIES

In addition to the remedies above mentioned there are certain special forms of procedure open to persons whose rights are infringed.

Certain infringements of copyright constitute a criminal offence rendering the offender liable to fines or imprisonment (Section 21 of the Act). It should be noted, however, that proof of knowledge that an infringement is being committed is essential in all these cases.

It is a breach of statutory duty, but not a criminal offence, in relation to literary, dramatic, musical and artistic works without licence: (1) to affix another person's name on a work of which that person is not the author, so as to imply that the other person is the author; (2) to publish, or sell, a work, or reproduction thereof, on which the other person's name has been affixed, knowing that person is not the author; (3) to perform in public, or broadcast, a work, as being a work of which another person is the author, knowing that other person is not the author; (4) to publish or sell an altered artistic work, or reproduction of the altered artistic work, as being the unaltered work, or reproduction of the unaltered work, knowing that is not the case, and (5) to publish, sell, or distribute reproductions of an artistic work as reproductions made by the author, knowing that is not the case (Section 43 of the Act). Damages are recoverable where such an offence has been committed. "Name" includes initials or a monogram.

Provision is also made (Section 22 of the Act), for the detention by the Customs authorities of infringing copies of copyright works made abroad to be imported into the United Kingdom.

THE DURATION OF COPYRIGHT PROTECTION

The normal period of copyright protection is during the life of the author and fifty years from the end of the calendar year in which he died (Sections 2 (3) and 3 (4) of the Act). In the case of a work of joint authorship, the protection, if it has not expired before the commencement of the Act (see below), extends during the life of the author who dies last and fifty years from the end of the calendar year in which he died (paragraph 2, third Schedule to the Act).

The Act contains special provisions for determining the period of copyright in relation to works of joint authorship, which are first published under two or more names, of which one or more of the names, or all the names, are pseudonyms (paragraph 3, third Schedule to the Act).

In the case of literary, dramatic or musical works which have not been published, performed in public, or broadcast before the death of the author, the period is fifty years from the end of the calendar year which includes the earliest occasion on which one of these acts is done (Section 2 (3) of the Act). In the case of engravings not published before the death of the author, the period is fifty years from the end of the calendar year in which they are first published (Section 3 (4) of the Act). For photographs, except those made before the commencement of the Act (see below), the period is fifty years from the end of the calendar year in which the photograph is first published (Section 3 (4) of the Act). For Government publications the period for literary, dramatic and musical works, if published, is until fifty years from the end of the calendar year in which it is first published, and for artistic works fifty years from the end of the calendar year in which the work was made; but, if the artistic work is an engraving or photograph, the period is fifty years from the end of the calendar year in which the engraving or photograph is first published (Section 39 (3) and (4) of the Act). (See as to duration of copyright in "Published Editions" and "Anonymous and Pseudonymous works" *ante* and in "Films," "Sound Recordings" and "Television and Sound Broadcasts" *post*).

In the case of works which were in existence before the commencement of the Act of 1911 (July 1, 1912) the terms of copyright above described apply if the work enjoyed copyright at such date (paragraph 35, seventh Schedule to the Act). This involves an examination of the terms of copyright subsisting under the various Acts in force before 1912. In general, protection under these Acts was the life of the author and seven years, or forty-two years from publication (whichever was the longer), but different terms of copyright were given by the various Acts dealing with artistic works.

Where the copyright in a pre-Act of 1911 work has been assigned before 1912, and copyright subsists therein by virtue of any provisions of the Act, such copyright reverts to the author or his assigns at the expiration of the old term of copyright applicable to the work (paragraph 38, seventh Schedule to the Act), but subject to various options in favour of the assignee.

In the case of records and photographs coming into existence after July 1, 1912, but before the commencement of the Act, the seventh Schedule to the Act provides that the period of copyright under the Act of 1911 shall apply; further, copyright is not to subsist under the Act in a joint work first published after July 1, 1912, but before the commencement of the Act, if the period of copyright under the Act of

1911 in that work expired before the commencement of the Act. This is because the Act provides different periods for these works from those under the Act of 1911.

FILMS

(1) Under the Act copyright now subsists in films as such (Section 13 of the Act) but without prejudice to the copyright in any literary, dramatic, musical or artistic works from which the subject-matter is derived (Section 16 (6) of the Act). Thus, there is now copyright in the film itself, and a separate copyright in its subject-matter, whereas, under the Act of 1911, films were protected only as photographs, and, in most cases, as dramatic works. The new film copyright is not to subsist in films made before the commencement of the Act, but the Act provides for the protection of such films if they were dramatic works, and of the photographs forming part of such films (paragraphs 14–16, seventh Schedule to the Act).

(2) "Film" is defined by the Act (Section 13 (10)), and includes the sounds embodied in any sound track associated with the film. Copyright subsists in every film of which the maker was a qualified person for the whole, or a substantial part, of the period during which the film was made, or which is first published in the United Kingdom. The "maker" of a film is defined as the person by whom the arrangements necessary for the making of the film are undertaken, and he is entitled to the copyright in the film. Film copyright subsists, if the film is registrable under Part II of the Films Act, 1960, until registration, and thereafter until fifty years from the end of the calendar year in which it is so registered. If not so registrable, then until the film is published and fifty years from the end of the year in which it is first published; if copyright only subsists in such a film by virtue of its place of publication, then until fifty years from the end of the calendar year in which it was first published.

A form of infringement peculiar to film copyright is to cause the film, in so far as it consists of visual images, to be seen in public, or, in so far as it consists of sounds, to be heard in public, except in the case of newsreel films where fifty years have elapsed from the end of the calendar year in which the principal events depicted in the film occurred.

(3) It is an infringement of the copyright in a novel, or story, to convert it into a film, whether the actual language of the literary work is taken or not. But something more than a mere plot or idea must be taken; it must be proved that the film adopts a substantial part of the incidents used in the story to work out the plot.

There is no copyright in a scene in actual life, e.g. sporting events, so that the organiser has no remedy in the case of the filming of such events provided that the film can be taken without trespass, and the passer-by cannot complain if he is filmed in the street.

(4) Under the Act of 1911, the making of a film involved the creation of an artistic work, i.e. a series of photographs, and, unless it was merely a record of passing events, the creation of a dramatic work. The first owner of the artistic copyright was the owner of the negative at the time it was made, whereas the first owner of the dramatic work might have been difficult to determine. In fact a commercial film used to involve the exercise of a number of separate copyrights since, at each stage of its inception, a separate copyright work might have been produced, e.g. story, screen dialogue and the film as finally cut, and the ownership of copyright would depend upon the agreements of the various parties concerned with the film company.

SOUND RECORDINGS

The Act provides that copyright subsists in every sound recording of which the maker was a qualified person at the time the recording was made, or which has been first published in the United Kingdom (Section 12 of the Act). "Sound recording" is defined by the Act as meaning the aggregate of the sounds embodied in, and capable of being reproduced by means of, a record of any description other than a film sound track.

The maker of the sound recording is entitled to the copyright therein, except where sound recordings are commissioned, and the "maker" is defined as the person who owns the record at the time the recording is made. Copyright in sound recordings subsists for a period of fifty years from the end of the calendar year in which the record is first published.

Such copyright can be infringed by making a record of the recording, or causing the recording to be heard in public, but it is not an infringement to allow the recording to be heard in public (i) as part of the amenities for the residents of any premises where persons reside or sleep unless a special charge for admission is made, or (ii) as part of the activities of a club or other non-profit-making organisation whose main objects are charitable, unless a charge is made for admission, and any of the proceeds are not applied for the purposes of the organisation. In *Phonographic Performance Ltd.* v. *Pontins Ltd.*, 1967 3 W.L.R. 1622 it was held that the holiday camp there in question constituted premises where persons reside or sleep and that, on the facts of that case, records were caused to be heard in public as part of the amenities provided exclusively or mainly for residents or inmates of that camp. If a record of music is performed in public, a licence to perform is required in respect of the record as well as in respect of the music itself. But see below as to broadcast performances.

The seventh Schedule to the Act contains provisions relating to the subsistence of copyright under the Act in records made before July 1, 1912.

A literary, dramatic or musical work is infringed by making a record of it or including it in the sound track of a film (Sections 2(5)(a) and 48(1) of the Act). The right to record such a work is therefore a valuable right and is quite distinct from the publishing right and performing right.

There are, however, a complicated series of provisions (Section 8 of the Act) under which when a musical work has been once recorded with the consent of the copyright owner, it can be recorded thereafter by anyone else on payment of a fixed royalty, the payment whereof is in general secured by the issue of adhesive stamps to be attached to the record. The normal royalty is 6¼ per cent of the ordinary retail selling price of the record with the minimum of three farthings for each work reproduced on a single record. Where the retail selling price was partly cash and partly three chocolate wrappers, it was held by the House of Lords in Chappell & Co. Ltd. v. The Nestle Co. Ltd. 1959 3 W.L.R. 168 that the section did not apply.

BROADCASTING AND TELEVISION

(1) The Act for the first time establishes copyright in television and sound broadcasts as such, if made by the B.B.C. or the I.T.A., and from a place in the United Kingdom (Section 14 of the Act). This right is therefore limited in this country to broadcasts by these two bodies and the copyright in their broadcasts vests in them. Further, copyright does not so subsist by virtue of the Act in television and sound broadcasts made before the commencement of the Act. "Television broadcast" means visual images broadcast by way of television together with any sounds broadcast for reception with those images, and "sound broadcast" means sounds broadcast otherwise than as part of a television broadcast. "Broadcasting" is defined by the Act (Section 48(2)). By reason of 1959 S.I. No. 2215 1960 S.I. No. 847 1961 S.I. Nos. 60, 2460, 2462 and 2463 1962 S.I. Nos. 1642, 1643, 2184 and 2185 1963 S.I. Nos. 1037, 1038, 1039 and 1147 1964 S.I. No. 689 1965 S.I. Nos. 1858, 1859, 2009, 2010, and 2158, 1966 S.I. Nos. 79 and 685 and 1967 S.I. No. 974, copyright now subsists in broadcasts made in the Isle of Man, Sarawak, Gibraltar, Fiji, Uganda, Zanzibar, Bermuda, North Borneo, Bahamas, Virgin Islands, Falkland Islands, St. Helena, Seychelles, Kenya, Mauritius, Montserrat, St. Lucia, Botswana, Cayman Islands, Grenada, Guyana, British Honduras and St. Vincent. By reason of 1964 S.I. No. 690 (as amended) copyright now subsists in sound broadcasts made in Brazil, Congo (Brazzaville), Czechoslovakia, Denmark, Ecuador, Mexico, Niger, Sweden, Federal Republic of Germany and Paraguay, and in television broadcasts made in Belgium, Czechoslovakia, Denmark, France, Norway, Sweden, Congo

(Brazzaville), Ecuador, Mexico, Niger, Federal Republic of Germany, Brazil, Cyprus and Paraguay; see as to protection in Gibraltar 1966 S.I. Nos. 945 and 1409, 1968 S.I. No. 1858 and 1970 S.I. Nos. 290 and 637, and in Bermuda 1969 S.I. No. 743 and 1970 S.I. Nos. 290 and 637.

Copyright in television and sound broadcasts subsists until the end of fifty years from the end of the calendar year in which the broadcast is made. Such copyright is infringed (a) in the case of television broadcasts in so far as it consists of visual images, by making a film of it otherwise than for private purposes, or by causing it to be seen in public by a paying audience: in so far as it consists of sounds, by making a record of it otherwise than for private purposes, or by causing it to be heard in public by a paying audience, and (b) in the case of a sound broadcast, by making a record of it otherwise than for private purposes. Where the alleged infringement is of the visual images of a television broadcast, it is only necessary to prove that the act in question extended to a sequence of images sufficient to be seen as a moving picture. Further, the Act provides that television broadcasts are seen or heard by a paying audience, if seen or heard by persons who either (i) have been admitted for payment to the place where the broadcast is seen or heard and are not (a) residents of such place nor (b) members of a club or society where the payment is only for membership and the provision of facilities for seeing or hearing television broadcasts is only incidental to the main purposes of the club or society, or (ii) have been admitted to such place in circumstances where goods or services are supplied at prices which exceed the price usually charged at that place, and are partly attributable to the facilities afforded for seeing or hearing the broadcast.

(2) Literary, dramatic and musical works, records and films are infringed by broadcasting them, and artistic works are infringed by including such works in a television broadcast: since this right to broadcast is now additional to the right to perform in public, authors will need to consider this when drafting agreements. If broadcast performances, for instance, in the case of sound broadcasts, are played from a loud-speaker in a public place, this in general involves a separate public performance not covered by any licence to perform given to the broadcasting body, but if the broadcast is from a record, the performance of the broadcast does not, as under the Act of 1911, infringe the copyright in the record as well (Section 40 (1) of the Act). And, dramatising a literary work for the purposes of a broadcast would infringe the right to make adaptations thereof, unless the necessary licence had been given.

PERFORMING RIGHT TRIBUNAL

The Act (Sections 23–30), for the first time establishes a Tribunal, in particular to control licence fees, but it is concerned only with disputes between licensing bodies and persons, or organisations, concerned in the public performance of works. By definition, licensing body excludes organisations whose objects only include negotiation or granting of individual licences each relating to a single work, or works of a single author, where such licences are to do acts with which a writer is most concerned, e.g. licences to perform in public, or broadcast, literary, dramatic and musical works, or adaptations thereof. Writers, other than perhaps songwriters, are not likely therefore to be concerned with the Tribunal, and, where necessary, expert advice should be taken.

The Tribunal consists of a chairman, who can be either a barrister or solicitor, or a person who has held judicial office, and not less than two, nor more than four other members appointed by the Board of Trade. The fourth Schedule to the Act contains provisions relative to the functions of the Tribunal. Questions of law may be referred to the High Court before, and in some circumstances, after, the Tribunal has given its decision. Rules relating to the Tribunal came into operation on 1st June 1957 (1957 S.I. No. 924 as amended) and have been revoked and replaced by other rules (1965 S.I. No. 1506). Upon a reference to the Tribunal under Section 25 of the Act by the Scottish Ballroom Association, the Tribunal varied a 1957 fee tariff and upon an application under Section 27 of the Act by Southern Television Limited the Tribunal held that a clause in a draft licence to perform was unreasonable.

During 1960 references were made to the Tribunal in respect of the *Juke Box* tariffs both of the P.R.S. for music and the P.P. Ltd. for records, in each case the tariffs were in substance confirmed. In 1965 the tribunal determined the terms and charges on which the Isle of Man Broadcasting Company Limited could broadcast records, and in 1967 the tribunal determined the terms and charges on which the BBC could broadcast music. Decisions of the Tribunal are referred to in *Current Law*.

PUBLISHING AGREEMENTS

The simplest form of publishing agreement is a mere licence to publish in a newspaper or periodical for a single payment. The terms of such agreements usually depend upon implication, or trade custom. Where an article is sent to a periodical without a covering letter, there will be implied, on the one hand a licence to publish, and on the other, an agreement to pay such remuneration as is normal and reasonable. If the article is kept, and the author is sent a proof for revision, the author is entitled to a fee, even if the work is not actually published.

Where a work is to be published on royalty terms, it is important from the point of view of the author that he does not assign his copyright, but only grants a licence. If he assigns, he will not be able to prevent the publisher from selling the rights in the work. He may be seriously prejudiced if the publisher gets into financial difficulties. Some protection is given to authors under Section 60 of the Bankruptcy Act 1914, but this is not available where the publisher is a limited company. A licence, however, is generally personal to the publisher, even if this is not expressly stated, and provision can be made to protect the author in the case of insolvency of the publisher. A difficult question concerns the extent to which works may be altered, the most important consideration being whether the author has assigned his copyright, or merely granted a licence to publish. If the former, then the assignee may freely alter, subject to possible proceedings by the author for defamation, malicious falsehood or under section 43 of the Act. If the latter, then alterations may be freely made by the publisher unless the licence expressly or implicitly forbids it, but subject to defamation and so on as before. However the courts will be very willing to imply a term limiting the right to make alterations; Frisby v. BBC 1967 2 W.L.R. 1204. There may be cases, however, where it could be established to the satisfaction of the court that custom permits reasonable alterations, at least of unsigned articles.

It is often difficult to determine whether the words used involve an assignment, or a licence, and this should be clearly expressed. However, an exclusive licensee now has, under the Act, the same rights of action and remedies as if the licence had been an assignment (see "Licences," *ante*).

The publishing agreement, in the interests of the author, should require publication within some fixed time, should deal with the style and price of publication, the method of advertising, the number of free copies allowed, and provide for proper accounts.

Publishing agreements often provide options to the publisher to acquire other rights in a work such as rights to make adaptations, including translations and dramatisation rights and rights to broadcast (see "Broadcasting and Television," *ante*), film rights, and rights to publish abroad. From the author's point of view it is usually preferable that such rights shall be granted on royalty terms rather than for a single payment. The publisher may also take an option on subsequent works of the author; such an option is enforceable by injunction to restrain the author from publishing elsewhere and in view of the provisions of the Act as to future copyright, care should be taken when drafting an agreement (see "Assignment of Copyright," *ante*).

Apart from express agreement a publisher is entitled to dispose of stock in hand after the licence is determined, since such stock, having been lawfully made, does not constitute infringing copies.

WORKS ORIGINATING ABROAD

The Act, except as extended by Order in Council, applies only within the United

Kingdom, including Northern Ireland (Sections 31, 32 and 51 of the Act), whereas the Act of 1911, in practice, applied throughout the British Commonwealth. Therefore, there will now be one code for the United Kingdom and other codes for other parts of the Commonwealth, unless the Act, or similar legislation, is in force there: this may not necessarily occur.

Orders in Council under the Act may direct that any of the provisions of the Act shall (a) extend to the Channel Islands, the Colonies and Dependencies and (b) apply to any other countries to which those provisions do not extend. By an Order (1957 S.I. No. 1523) which came into operation on the 27th September, 1957 (the date at which the Universal Copyright Convention came into effect between the U.K. and other members), as amended, the Act was applied to works originating in Universal Copyright or Berne Convention countries. This in effect included most of the world except the U.S.S.R. This Order for the first time protected works first published in the U.S.A. which was not a member of the Berne Union. The Order and its ancillary orders have been largely revoked and replaced by a further Order (1964, S.I No. 690), which has itself been amended. By an Order (1959 S.I. No. 861) which came into operation on 31st May, 1959, the Act was extended to the Isle of Man; by further Orders (1959 S.I. No. 2215, 1960 S.I. No. 847, 1961 S.I. Nos. 60, 2462 and 2463, 1962 S.I. Nos. 629, 1642, 1643, 2184 and 2185, 1963 S.I. Nos. 1037, 1038, 1039, and 1147, 1964 S.I. No. 689 1965 S.I. Nos. 1858, 1859, 2009, 2010 and 2158, 1966 S.I. Nos. 79 and 685 and 1967 S.I. No. 974) which came into operation on 1st January, 1960, 1st June, 1960, 1st February, 1961, 1st January, 1962, 1st January 1962, 1st May, 1962, 6th August, 1962, 6th August, 1962, 11th October, 1962, 11th October, 1962, 10th June, 1963, 10th June, 1963, 10th June, 1963, 4th July, 1963, 21st May, 1964, 5th November, 1965, 5th November, 1965, 4th December, 1965, 4th December, 1965, 1st January, 1966, 5th February, 1966, 16th June, 1966 and 5th July 1967 respectively, the Act was extended to Sarawak, Gibraltar, Fiji, Uganda, Zanzibar, Bermuda, North Borneo, Bahamas, Virgin Islands, Falkland Islands, St. Helena, Seychelles, Kenya, Mauritius, Monserrat, St. Lucia, Botswana, Cayman Islands, Grenada, Guyana, British Honduras and St. Vincent, respectively. Works originating in British Colonies other than Sarawak, Gibraltar, Fiji, Uganda, Zanzibar, Bermuda, North Borneo, Bahamas, Virgin Islands, Falkland Islands, St. Helena, Seychelles, Kenya, Mauritius, Monserrat, St. Lucia, Botswana, Cayman Islands, Grenada, Guyana, British Honduras and St. Vincent, are still protected under the old law as no new Orders have yet been made, as are existing works of foreign origin. In those cases the place of first publication remains of substantial importance. A work is deemed first published within the United Kingdom, or in any other country, if published there within thirty days (or 14 days in the case of existing works) after first publication elsewhere (Section 49 (2) (d) of the Act), and a work is published if reproductions are issued to the public in such quantities as are reasonably necessary to meet the public demand.

Copyright throughout the British Empire extended, prior to the commencement of the Act, to works first published in countries of the Copyright Union, and unpublished works of authors who were nationals of, or resident at the time of the making of the work in, such countries.

HOW FAR BRITISH WORKS ARE PROTECTED ABROAD

Works first published in the United Kingdom, and unpublished works of British subjects, are protected in all Berne and Universal Copyright Convention countries though it should be noted that "first publication" in this case has not necessarily quite the same meaning in all countries. Some countries do not accept the mere issue of copies as constituting publication in a country, and require that copies shall be issued from a distributing centre in the nature of a publishing house in the country, and the simultaneous publication period which, under the Act, will be thirty days is not universal.

As regards other foreign countries, copyright can only be secured by complying with the formalities prescribed by the law of the country. In the U.S.A. copyright, prior to the 27th September, 1957, was secured by registration and deposit of copies. Copyright could not be acquired unless a "Copyright Reserved" notice was affixed to all copies sold in the U.S.A. Application for registration had to be made promptly or the right to protection was lost, but an interim protection could be obtained which enabled the position to be preserved pending publication in the U.S.A. Books, or periodicals, in the English language, could not secure permanent protection in the U.S.A. unless an edition was printed in the U.S.A. from type set up there. However, after the 27th September, 1957, British authors are relieved of most of the formalities connected with obtaining U.S.A. copyright in published works. including the "Copyright Reserved" notice, registration, deposit of copies, and printing of editions from type set up in the U.S.A. The only formality required is that, after first publication, all copies of the work whether sold in the U.S.A. or elsewhere will have to bear the symbol ©, together with the name of the copyright proprietor, and the year of publication (see p. 344, *post*, "U.S. Copyright").

In some South American countries copyright can only be secured by some form of local registration.

THE COPYRIGHT ACTS 1956* AND 1911†

A SELECTION OF CLAUSES OF INTEREST TO WRITERS AND ARTISTS

THE COPYRIGHT ACT 1956

Nature of Copyright (Section 1), *Copyright in Literary, Dramatic, Musical and Artistic Works* (Sections 2, 3 and 4); *Infringement of Copyright in Literary, Dramatic, Musical and Artistic Works* (Sections 5, 6, 7, 8 and 9); *Provisions as to Designs* (Section 10), *Copyright in Sound Recordings, Films, Broadcasts and Published Editions* (Sections 12, 13, 14, 15 and 16); *Remedies for Infringement* (Sections 17, 18, 19, 20, 21 and 22), *The Performing Rights Tribunal* (Sections 23, 24 and 30); *Application of the Act to other Countries* (Sections 31, 32, 34 and 35), *Assignments and Licences* (Sections 36, 37 and 38); *Crown Copyright* (Section 39), *Educational Material and Public Records* (Sections 41 and 42); *False Attribution of Authorship* (Section 43), *Savings* (Section 46), *Interpretation* (Sections 48 and 49); *General* (Section 51); *Anonymous and Pseudonymous Works* (the second Schedule), *Joint Works* (the third Schedule).

* Published by H.M. Stationery Office, price 36p. net
† Published by H.M. Stationery Office, price 12½p. net

THE COPYRIGHT ACT 1911

(*Note:* the following Section is not repealed by the Act of 1956)—

Section 15

U.S. COPYRIGHT

Revised by ALBERT H. ROBBINS, PH.B., J.D.
American Attorney and Counsellor-at-Law
and R. H. GRAVESON, LL.D., S.J.D. (Harvard)
Barrister-at-Law

THE UNIVERSAL COPYRIGHT CONVENTION

U.S. Copyright Law was changed in important respects for British authors when the Universal Copyright Convention came into force in both Great Britain ("G.B.") and the U.S. *These changes resulted in great advantages to British authors.*

A. *The Universal Copyright Convention* ("the Convention") was signed by G.B. and U.S. and many other nations on September 8, 1952, at an Intergovernmental Conference on Copyright at Geneva. The necessary U.S. legislation to implement the Convention was enacted on August 31, 1954. The Convention came into force in the U.S. in September 1955, and in G.B. in September 1957.

B. *The basic concept of the Convention* is the reciprocal extension of national treatment in each Contracting State to works of the other Contracting States. Article II provides that *published and unpublished works of nationals* of any Contracting State and *works first published in that State* shall enjoy in other Contracting States the same protection the latter accord to works of their own authors.

    i. *Unpublished works.*—Thus unpublished works of British authors will continue to have the same protection in U.S., without any formalities, which is accorded to American authors. U.S. Law protects the author of an unpublished work at Common Law or in Equity, and he can prevent the copying, publication, or use of such unpublished work, without his consent, and obtain damages therefor.

    ii. *Published works.—The only formality now required from a British author (not domiciled in the U.S.) is that from the time of first publication (outside the U.S.) all copies of his work must bear the symbol C, in a circle, accompanied by the name of the copyright proprietor and year of publication,* placed in such a manner and location to give reasonable notice of claim of copyright. Consequently, *British authors (not domiciled in U.S.) wherever they first publish their works (except in the U.S.,* and works of authors of any nationality, excepting U.S. authors, first published in G.B.) *who comply with this formality obtain automatic copyright in U.S.* (See below for summary of benefits granted under U.S. Copyright.) *Notes: (a) British authors domiciled in U.S. are treated in the same way as are U.S. authors. (b) Works of U.S. or British (whether domiciled or not in the U.S.) or any other foreign authors first published in U.S., must still comply with U.S. laws and regulations for obtaining Copyright.*

    iii. *Definition of "publication."*—Article VI of the Convention states: " 'Publication' . . . means the reproduction in tangible form and the general distribution to the public of copies of a work from which it can be read or otherwise visually perceived."

C. Thus for British authors (not domiciled in U.S., *unless their works are first published in the U.S.) the following, former requirements are now eliminated:* (1) *The necessity of printing and binding in U.S., books and periodicals in the English language of foreign origin.* This is the most important benefit the British author obtains under the new Copyright Law in the U.S. (2) *All of the formalities previously necessary to obtain copyright.* [These formalities were listed in previous editions.] As stated above, the only formality now required is the copyright notice of C in a circle with its accompanying information.   (3) *"Ad Interim" Copyright*. [Explained in previous editions.]   *British authors who had "Ad Interim" Copyright before the Convention came into force in G.B. automatically receive full U.S. Copyright in its place from the date of first publication abroad.*

D.   *The Convention has no retroactive effect.*—U.S. publishers will be able to continue publication without any liability of works by British authors which did not have copyright protection in U.S. before the Convention came into force in G.B.

E.   *U.S. Copyright Law protects the works covered in Article I of the Convention* which provides that: "Each Contracting State undertakes to provide for the adequate and effective protection of the rights of authors and other copyright proprietors in literary, scientific and artistic works, including writings, musical, dramatic and cinematographic works, and paintings, engravings and sculpture."   Thus *all writings* of a British author secure copyright, in accordance with B. ii., above, including books, composite and cyclopaedic works, Directories, Gazettes and other compilations, and periodicals including newspapers.

SYNOPSIS OF U.S. COPYRIGHT

The objective of the Convention was to harmonise existing national systems of copyright on the basis of simplified reciprocal national treatment rather than create a new substantive international copyright law or code. Hence, once a British author obtains U.S. Copyright in accordance with B. ii., above, U.S. Copyright Law applies to him as well as to American authors. It is thus of importance to a British author to have some idea of the basic provisions of U.S. Copyright Law.

A new Copyright Revision Bill has been before the American legislature since February 1965, but there is still no clear indication when this is likely to become law. The following are among the various changes proposed in the Bill: (*a*) that the term of copyright protection be for the life of the author and fifty years thereafter; (*b*) that the author may terminate any grant of his copyright after the first thirty-five years; (*c*) that the term for anonymous or pseudonymous works shall be a minimum of seventy-five years from first publication; (*d*) that the "divisibility" of copyright shall be recognized; (*e*) that certain new "fair dealing" provisions shall be introduced, particularly in the field of education; and (*f*) that the manufacturing requirements shall not apply to the works of U.S. citizens living abroad more than twelve months, nor to works of which "any substantial part" is by a "non-American author". It remains, of course, to see whether these and other proposals in the Bill will be passed into law.

I.   The copyright proprietor is entitled:

(*a*) To print, reprint, publish, copy, or vend the copyrighted work.

(*b*) To translate, etc., to dramatise a non-dramatic work; to convert into a novel, etc., a dramatic work.

(*c*) To deliver or authorise the delivery of the work *in public for profit* if it be an address, sermon, lecture or similar production.

(*d*) To perform or represent the work publicly, if it is a dramatic work, *and not reproduced in copies for sale*, to vend any MS. or any record whatsoever thereof. To make or to procure the making of any transcription or record thereof by or from which in whole or in part it may in any manner or by any method be exhibited, performed, etc., and to exhibit, perform, and represent, etc., in any manner or by any method.

(*e*) To perform the copyrighted work publicly for profit if it be a musical composition; and for the purpose of public performance for profit and for the purposes set forth in subsection (*a*) hereof, to make any arrangement or setting of it or of the melody of it in any system of notation or any form of record in which the thought of an author may be recorded and from which it may be read or reproduced.

II. *Duration of Copyright.*—Copyright endures for twenty-eight years from date of first publication, with an extension of another twenty-eight years, subject to the right being exercised during the twenty-eighth year by application to the Register of Copyrights, Washington, D.C., accompanied by a small fee, for such renewal. Pending the introduction of a new copyright law the copyright in works whose second term of 28 years would have expired is being extended automatically so that they may enjoy the new term of copyright when it is introduced.

III. *Assignment of Copyright.*—Under U.S. Law, copyright is distinct from the property in the material object copyrighted or in which it is embodied and *is indivisible.* What therefore under British Law would be the assignment of a portion of the copyright, e.g. the assignment of the right to publish in book form, merely amounts to the guarantee of a licence in the U.S. But the assignment of Copyright covers *everything* that is copyright under U.S. Law. *Licences, however, are divisible*; thus, they may be exclusive or non-exclusive, and may be limited as to person, territory, time or place, etc. They may be expressed or implied, written or oral. But such licences which are partial assignments of copyright have to be registered under the Statute as assignments.

(*a*) *Copyright may be "assigned,* granted or mortgaged by an instrument in writing signed by the proprietor of the copyright." (Section 28 of the Copyright Act of 1947, and as since amended.) *Copyright may also be bequeathed by will.* (Section 28).

(*b*) "*Every assignment of copyright executed in a foreign country* shall be acknowledged by the assignor before a consular officer or secretary of legation of the United States authorised by law to administer oaths or perform notarial acts." (Section 29.)

(*c*) "*Every assignment of copyright shall be recorded in the Copyright Office* within three calendar months after its execution in the United States or *within six months after its execution without the limits of the United States*, in default of which it shall be void as against any subsequent purchaser or mortgagee for a valuable consideration, without notice, whose assignment has been duly recorded." (Section 30.)

IV. *Infringement.*—Although not defined by statute, infringement of copyright is a tort. Intention to infringe is immaterial. *An infringer may be liable to one or more of the following remedies:*

(*a*) *Injunction.* The Court may grant a temporary as well as a permanent injunction restraining future infringement. Ordinarily, a temporary injunction will not be granted unless a strong case is made out. Injunctions are granted on the basis of established general equitable principles. Under new rules of federal procedure whether the plaintiff had an adequate remedy at law is immaterial in a suit for injunction and damages.

(*b*) *Actual damages and profits.* Section 101 (*b*) of the Copyright Act of 1947 provides for recovery of damages as well as profits made by the infringer. In practice, the Courts construe this provision as meaning that the copyright proprietor may have one or the other, whichever is the greater. The Section also provides that "in proving profits the plaintiff shall be required to prove sales only, and the defendant shall be required to prove every element of cost which he claims."

(*c*) *Statutory Damages.* Section 101 (*b*) also provides that "in lieu of actual damages and profits," the Court has discretion to award damages "as shall appear to be just," but such statutory damages must not exceed $5,000 nor be less than $250 (except in certain cases, e.g. a newspaper reproducing a copyrighted photograph when statutory damages cannot exceed $200, etc.). Statutory damages are awarded by the Court in its complete discretion, regardless of whether or not the plaintiff can prove any actual damage. This type of damages is of considerable importance in cases involving small performing uses of the copyright without licence. However, Section 101 (b) also provides that the maximum limitation does not apply "to infringements occurring after the actual notice to a defendant, either by service of process in a suit or other written notice served upon him."

(d) *Impounding during action.* Section 101 (c) empowers the Court to order the defendant "to deliver up on oath, to be impounded during the pendency of the action, upon such terms and conditions as the Court may prescribe, all articles alleged to infringe a copyright."

(e) *Destruction of infringing copies and plates.* The Court can also order a defendant "to deliver up on oath for destruction all the infringing copies or devices, as well as all plates, moulds, matrices or other means for making such infringing copies, . . ." (Section 101 (d).)

(f) *Royalties for use of mechanical reproduction of musical works* may be ordered by the Court in certain cases. (Section 101 (e).)

(g) *Criminal penalties for wilful infringement for profit.* Section 104 provides that, "Any person who wilfully and for profit shall infringe any copyright . . . or who shall knowingly and wilfully aid or abet such infringement, shall be deemed guilty of a misdemeanor, and upon conviction thereof shall be punished by imprisonment for not exceeding one year or by a fine of not less than $100 nor more than $1,000, or both, in the discretion of the Court." However, no criminal proceedings can be maintained unless commenced within three years after the cause of action arose. (Section 115.)

(h) *Period of limitation for civil actions.* The Copyright Act of 1947 does not provide for any period of limitation for civil actions under the Act. The legal situation is complicated and in general depends on the nearest applicable type of limitation period provided by the State (e.g. New York, California) statutes in which the case is brought.

(i) *Costs and attorney's fees.* Section 116 provides that "In all actions, suits or proceedings . . . except when brought by or against the United States or any officer thereof, full costs shall be allowed, and the Court *may* award to the prevailing party, a *reasonable* attorney's fee as part of the costs." Attorney's fees in the U.S., unlike in England, do not ordinarily constitute part of costs and the victorious litigant must pay his own attorney's fees himself—hence the concession in Section 116 is not only an unusual one but also a valuable one, especially as lawyers' fees in the U.S. are generally higher than in England.

THE FLORENCE AGREEMENT

THIS Agreement, sponsored by Unesco and signed in Florence in 1950, is concerned with the free flow of books and the removal of tariff and trade obstacles. The principle undertaking of the signatories is the exemption of books and other educational, scientific and cultural imports from customs duties, and the granting of licenses and foreign exchange as far as possible for their importation. Books of every sort are included in the Agreement, not excepting those printed abroad from the work of an author in the importing country. Unbound sheets do not come under the Agreement.

The following is an up-to-date list of the States adhering to the Agreement: Afghanistan, Austria, Belgium, Cambodia, Cameroon, Ceylon, Congo (Leopoldville), Cuba, Cyprus, Denmark, El Salvador, Finland, France, Gabon, Germany (Federal Republic of), Ghana, Greece, Guatemala, Haiti, Iran, Israel, Italy, Ivory Coast, Jordan, Laos, Luxembourg, Malagasy Republic, Malaya (Federation of), Malawi, Monaco, Netherlands, New Zealand, Nicaragua, Nigeria, Norway, Pakistan, Philippines, Ruanda, Sierra Leone, Spain, Sweden, Switzerland, Tanzania, Thailand, Uganda, United Arab Republic (Egypt), United Kingdom, United States of America, Upper Volta, Viet-Nam, Yugoslavia.

SUBSIDIARY RIGHTS

By E. P. SKONE JAMES, M.A.

GENERALLY

The Copyright Act 1956 ("the Act of 1956") in Section 1(1) defines "copyright" in relation to a work as the exclusive right to do, and to authorise other persons to do, certain acts in relation to that work in the United Kingdom or in any other country to which the relevant provisions of that Act extend. Such acts in relation to a work of any description, being those acts which in the relevant provision of that Act are designated as the acts restricted by the copyright in a work of that description.

The "copyright" in respect of any work therefore consists of several different "restricted acts," or rights, which are not the same in respect of all works, and each of which may be the subject of a separate licence. It follows therefore, that great care should be taken in drafting and signing agreements concerned with copyright, that such an agreement expressly refers to the rights in respect of which a licence is intended to be granted. For instance, an agreement to print and publish would not normally vest in the publisher any other rights of the author such as film rights, nor would an agreement granting a publisher the right to convert a literary work into a dramatic work vest in the publisher the film or broadcasting rights. However, such an agreement could expressly give a publisher an option to acquire additional rights, or specify who was to exploit such other rights, and, if the publisher, then specifying whether the author was to receive a percentage of the publisher's receipts. If the author is to receive a percentage, then such percentage should vary with the different rights since some rights will be obviously more valuable than others.

It should be noted also that, since, under the Act of 1956, it is now possible to assign future copyright (e.g. copyright which will, or may come into existence in respect of any future work or class of works or other subject-matter), care should be taken that any such agreement expressly excludes future copyright if so desired.

The Act of 1956 contains special provisions as to libraries, permitting copying for special purposes unless the librarian knows the name and address of a person entitled to authorise the making of the copy, or could, by reasonable enquiry, ascertain the name and address of such a person. For this reason, an author should give his publisher power to grant such authorisation so that the publisher may be entitled to demand a fee, a percentage of which should be payable to the author.

It is not possible in this article to deal with all the rights restricted by copyright in a work but some of those of the greatest importance to writers and artists will be considered, either because they are rights conferred by the Act of 1956, or because they form part of such rights. It should be noted that a parody of a work such as a painting or a song is not an infringement if the parody amounts to an original work and no licence need be asked for or given (Joy Music Ltd. v. Sunday Pictorial Newspapers (1920) Ltd. 1960 2 W.L.R. 645).

RIGHT TO REPRODUCE THE WORK BY RECORDS OR FILMS

It is a restricted act in relation to literary, dramatic, musical and artistic works (*inter alia*), to make a record or film thereof. Separate licences for each of these acts would therefore be necessary, though not in the case of a film of an artistic work if such work was included in the film only by way of background or was otherwise only incidental to the principal matters represented in the film.

Film companies will usually require to have the right to broadcast the film of the work, but this is not of course the same as the right to broadcast the work itself using live actors, which right an author should be sure to retain.

RIGHT TO BROADCAST THE WORK

The Act of 1956 for the first time makes "broadcasting" (e.g. by sound or television), a separate right in respect of literary, dramatic and musical works, and "including the work in a television broadcast" a separate right in the case of an artistic work, so that a separate licence to broadcast by sound or to broadcast by television is required, except where an artistic work is included in a television broadcast, if its inclusion therein was only by way of background, etc., as mentioned above in respect of a film.

RIGHT TO MAKE ADAPTATIONS OF THE WORK

An "adaptation" is a new expression in the Act of 1956 the making of which is a restricted act applicable only to literary, dramatic and musical works. An "adaptation" is defined by the Act of 1956 and means (i) An arrangement or transcription of a musical work, (ii) Converting a non-dramatic work into a dramatic work or vice versa, (iii) Translations of literary or dramatic works. The person making a translation will acquire a copyright in his work if he had a right to translate. (iv) Versions of literary or dramatic works in which the story or action is conveyed wholly or mainly by means of pictures in a form suitable for reproduction in a book or in a newspaper, magazine or similar periodical, e.g. comic strips. This is a new right granted by the Act of 1956.

The Copyright Act 1911 contained certain similar rights but not classed under the one heading and care should be taken to limit a licence to the particular "adaptation" intended as a licence to make "adaptations" would confer all such rights.

RIGHT TO SERIALISE

The Act of 1956 does not define "serial rights" though, by reason of common usage, its meaning is well known. In the case of *Jonathan Cape Ltd.* v. *Consolidated Press Ltd.*, 1954, 1 W.L.R. 3013, by Clause 1 of an Agreement between the author of an original work and the plaintiff publishers, the author agreed to grant to the publishers the exclusive right to print and publish the work "in volume form." Clause 12 of the Agreement referred, *inter alia*, to the first serial rights in the work in the terms "publication of instalments in several issues of a newspaper, magazine or periodical prior to publication in volume form" and Clause 13 referred, *inter alia*, to "all rights of serialisation subsequent to publication in volume form." It was held that Clauses 12 and 13 of the Agreement were concerned with serial rights in regard to the work, and they indicated that the transfer of rights effected by the Agreement was not to include, in the terms contained in Clause 1, the rights as regards the publication of the work in serial form; further, looking at the Agreement, the real point was that the distinction was made between the publication of the work as a whole, which was meant by the word "volume", and the publication of the work by instalments, which was publication in a serial form, and was dealt with by the Agreement in a separate way.

In that case, the defendants published a story in a single edition of a periodical, and it was held that there was an infringement of the plaintiffs' rights to publish in volume form. It would, of course, be possible to licence specifically publication in a single edition of a periodical.

It must be noted that serial rights are not limited to one serialisation since there can be first, second and third, etc., serial rights. Thus the licence should specify in respect of which serial rights it is granted.

Other matters which the licence should specify are: (i) the price to be paid; (ii) the date of payment; (iii) the date of publication; (iv) the place of publication. The last two are most important. The date of publication is important because the article may be a topical article: therefore, in order to preserve the value of the first serial rights, these should be sold on terms that they will be published by a prescribed date.

The place of publication is important, and should always be stipulated, because serial rights, like other rights, may be separately sold for publication in different countries.

RIGHT TO HAVE THE WORK, OR PART THEREOF, INCLUDED IN AN ANTHOLOGY

An anthology, strictly a collection of poems, but also extended to include collections of short passages from various authors, is itself the subject of copyright protection. This was decided in an Indian case dealing with Palgrave's *The Golden Treasury of Songs and Lyrics*. The inclusion of a work, or part of it, in an anthology would be an infringement of the author's right to reproduce the work and to publish it, if unpublished, and would require a separate licence. Such a licence would not normally be included in a licence to print and publish (see also "Quotations" below).

RIGHT TO HAVE THE WORK ABRIDGED

The usual form of abridgment, or digest, of a work consists of a statement designed to be complete and accurate of the thoughts, opinions and ideas expressed in the work by the author but set forth much more concisely in the compressed language of the abridger (per Lord Atkinson in *MacMillan & Co. Ltd.* v. *Cooper*, 1923, 40 T.L.R. 186), and is itself the subject of copyright protection. Again, to make a digest of a work would be an infringement of the author's right to reproduce the work and to publish it, if unpublished, and would require a separate licence. A digest which consisted merely of a synopsis of the plot of a work might not be an infringement of that work, though an offence might be committed if the name of the original author was put on such digest in such a way as to imply that the original author was the author of the digest (Section 43 of the Act of 1956).

RIGHT TO HAVE THE WORK QUOTED

Quotation in the wide sense, by including part of the work in an anthology, has been referred to above, and, as a general rule, quotations from works are only permissible if licensed. But it is generally more convenient if the publisher is given a right to license quotations so that the author does not have to be sought on each occasion.

However, the Act of 1956 provides various exceptions to this rule. Thus, no fair dealing with the work for the purposes of research, private study, criticism or review is an infringement of the copyright therein, if, in the last two cases, the work and the author are identified.

Similarly no fair dealing with the work for the purpose of reporting current events in newspapers, etc., or by broadcasting, or in a film, is an infringement if, in the last two cases, the work and author are identified.

Further, the reading or recitation in public (other than for the purposes of broadcasting), by one person of any reasonable extract from a published, literary or dramatic work, is not an infringement if the work and author are identified. Again, in certain circumstances, the inclusion of a short passage from a published literary or dramatic work in a collection intended for the use of schools is not an infringement.

All these exceptions apply to adaptations of the work as well as to the work itself (as to the meaning of "adaptation" see above).

RIGHT TO HAVE THE WORK REPRINTED

A licence to print and publish may be expressly confined to one edition only, with a right for the author to require further editions to be published when the first edition has gone out of print. If the publisher, on receipt of a notice from the author requesting the publication of a further edition, will not do so, the author should be entitled to go to another publisher.

RIGHT TO HAVE THE WORK PRINTED BY BOOK CLUBS

Book Clubs normally produce a special edition of the work at a cheaper price, and therefore the author's licence to the publisher should contain express provisions as to whether, and on what terms, such editions may be printed.

THE PERFORMING RIGHT SOCIETY, LTD.

THE Performing Right Society is an Association of Composers, Authors and Publishers of copyright musical works, established to collect royalties for the public performance and broadcasting of such works and their use by diffusion services; also to restrain unauthorised use thereof.

The Society's operations do not extend to the performance of plays, sketches or other works of a non-musical character; nor to operas, musical plays or other dramatico-musical works when performed by living persons on the stage.

Licences are granted which convey the necessary permission for the public performance of any of the works of its members and those of the affiliated national societies of more than 30 other countries. The combined membership thus represented by the Society is over 175,000. Over 100,000 premises where music is publicly performed are covered by the Society's licence in the British Isles alone.

The constitution of the Society is that of a Company limited by guarantee, having no share capital. The General Council is unpaid and consists of twelve composers and authors and twelve music publishers elected by the members from among their own number. The Society is not a profit-making organisation, the whole of the royalties it collects being distributed amongst its members and the affiliated societies after deduction of administration expenses and contributions to the P.R.S. Members' Fund, established for the benefit of necessitous members and their dependants. The Society's official journal is issued to members gratis.

There are two distributions of general performing fees each year, and two distributions of broadcasting fees. The Annual General Meeting is usually held in June or July. Every full member has one vote at General Meetings.

Applicants for membership are not required to pay an entrance fee, nor is any membership subscription or agency commission payable. Composers of musical works, and authors of lyrics or poems which have been set to music, are eligible to apply for membership, provided that their works are such as could be controlled by the Society and that they are performed in public to an appreciable extent.

Authors and composers desiring further information should communicate with the Secretary at the Society's offices, 29 Berners Street, London, W1P 4AA. *T.* 01–850 5544. *T.A.* Perforight, London, W.1.

PUBLISHERS' AGREEMENTS

Royalty Agreements

The royalty agreement is now the most usual arrangement between author and publisher, and almost invariably the most satisfactory for the author. It provides for the payment to the author of a royalty of an agreed percentage on the published price of all copies of his book which are sold. The rate of royalty varies with circumstances: for general books it rarely commences at less than ten per cent and provision is usually made for it to increase after the sale of a certain number of copies. An established author of proved selling-power will command a higher commencing royalty and a more attractive rising scale. Similarly, most authors

can secure in their contracts provision for an advance from the publisher in antici-
pation and on account of the specified royalties, and the amount of this advance will
depend largely upon the publisher's estimate of the book's prospect of sales.

Most publishing houses nowadays have printed agreement forms in which blanks
are left for the insertion of the proposed royalty rates, the sum payable in advance,
and so on.   The terms are usually agreed between author and publisher before the
form is completed, but the fact that a printed form has been signed by the publisher
does not mean that an author, before signing it himself, cannot discuss any of its
clauses with the publisher.   The majority of publishers value the establishment of
confidence and understanding between themselves and their authors and are willing
to make reasonable amendments.

It is impossible to set out in detail here the numerous provisions of publishing
agreements or to comment on the differing effects of these upon different sorts of
book.   Every sensible author will scrutinize his agreement carefully before signing
it, will not hesitate to ask his publisher to explain any point in it which is not clear
to him, and if he still has doubts will seek professional advice from a reliable literary
agent, or the Society of Authors, or one of the few firms of solicitors who specialize
in authors' business.   The careful author will see that the contract contains an
undertaking to publish the book by a certain date (just as the publisher may require
the author to deliver his MS. by a certain date); he will look for a comprehensive
clause setting out the contingencies in which it is to terminate; he will examine the
clauses covering the handling of overseas sales, American rights and subsidiary rights
(film, serial, broadcasting, etc.) which for some books may well bring in more than
the book publication rights, clauses giving the publisher an option to publish his
future work, and clauses which may restrict a specialist author's future output by
preventing him from writing other books on the same subject.   The author should
also satisfy himself that he understands what the contract proposes in relation to
cheap editions, "remainders", sheet sales, reprints and new editions, and the indem-
nification of the publisher against actions for libel and infringement of copyright.

Outright Sale

Outright sale of copyright for an agreed sum is rarely—perhaps never—to be
recommended, though it may be justified in special cases, as for example the supplying of a small amount of text as commentary for a book which consists primarily of
illustrations.   It is a survival from the days when copyright meant for all practical
purposes, merely the exclusive right of publication in book form.   So long as it was
possible to gauge approximately a book's potential sales and the profit to be antici-
pated, the value of a copyright could be fairly accurately estimated.   But to-day,
anything from 1,000 to a million copies of a book may be sold and when the various
subsidiary rights—the film rights in particular—may prove either valueless or worth
thousands of pounds, any arrangement for an outright sale of copyright must be a
gamble in which the author is almost certain to be the loser.

Profit-Sharing and Commission Agreements

Under a profit-sharing agreement the publisher bears the cost of production, but
the author makes no money until the book shows a profit, at which point the profit
is divided in agreed proportions between author and publisher.   In theory this
sounds fair, but it is rarely satisfactory in practice.   Such agreements can lend
themselves readily to abuse, largely because of the difficulty of defining the term
"profit".

Under a commission agreement the author bears the cost of production and pays
the publisher a commission for marketing the book.   If no publisher is prepared to
publish a work on the normal royalty basis, the chances are that if the author finances
the publication himself he will lose most, if not all, of his outlay.   In consequence
commission agreements, save in exceptional circumstances, are to be discouraged.
Many good publishers refuse to handle books on commission in any circumstances
whatsoever; others confine their commission publishing to authoritative books of a
highly specialised or scholarly nature.   The specialist author who decides that

commission publishing is justified by special circumstances should make sure that the firm with which he is negotiating is reputable and able to market his book efficiently.

No firm of standing will publish fiction on commission and publishers offering to do so should be given a wide berth. There are quite a few firms ready to exploit the vanity of a would-be author. Such firms ask the author for a large sum as "a contribution towards the cost" of producing his book. Too often in fact it more than covers the cost of bringing out a small and shoddy edition, which the "publisher" makes no effort to distribute.

Publishing agreements are lucidly discussed at considerable length in Sir Stanley Unwin's *The Truth About Publishing* (Seventh Edition) (George Allen and Unwin, 90p).

A GUIDE TO AUTHORS*

By the late SIR STANLEY UNWIN, K.C.M.G., LL.D.

PUBLISHERS are not necessarily either philanthropists or rogues. Likewise they are usually neither lordly magnates nor cringing beggars. As a working hypothesis, regard them as ordinary human beings trying to earn their living at an unusually difficult occupation. (It is easy to become a publisher, but difficult to remain one; the mortality in infancy is higher than in any other trade or profession.)

Remember that it is in your work that the publisher is primarily interested. Let your manuscript therefore be your ambassador and do not mar its chances by insisting upon a quite unnecessary interview. The publisher will request you to call fast enough if he finds your work attractive.

Your manuscript may be a masterpiece, but do not suggest that to the publisher, because many of the most hopeless manuscripts that have come his way have probably been so described by their authors. The works of genius are apt to arrive unheralded, and it is for those that the publisher is looking.

Your manuscript is your baby, maybe your only child, but the publisher finds a dozen or so new babies on his doorstep every morning and has several thousand older children over-running his warehouse and his entire establishment, all of them calling simultaneously for his undivided attention.

With the best will in the world, therefore, there is a definite limit to the time he can spend on yours. Every moment of the publisher's time you waste on needless interviews may be a moment less for the more important task of attending to your offspring.

If you want your manuscript to make a good impression, bestow some care upon it and don't ask the publisher to look at it in instalments. Outward appearances do not matter, but slovenliness and inconsistency do. The fact that a manuscript is dog-eared does not distress a publisher, but the fact that a proper name is seldom spelt twice running in the same way; that a word capitalized on one page is not capitalized on the next; that the first and third chapters have headings, but the second none; that quotations are inaccurately given; that, in brief, the author has skimped his job, makes the worst possible impression upon the publisher as well as upon the publisher's reader. A little extra time spent on the preparation of the MS. is worth more to the author than the longest interview with a publisher, or any letter of introduction.

Bear in mind that in common with all human beings, publishers are fallible. They all, I imagine, wish they were not, but they all know (and admit) that they are. "Publishing fallibility" is too expensive an item in his trading account for any publisher to be in danger of overlooking it. If a publisher declines your manuscript, remember it is merely the decision of one fallible human being, and try another.

*Reproduced, in a slightly abridged form, by permission of the author, from, *The Truth About Publishing*, by Sir Stanley Unwin, K.C.M.G., LL.D. (Seventh Edition) (Allen & Unwin, Ltd.).

M

Don't try to bully the first publisher into telling you why he declined it. He would, in most cases, be a fool to tell you, because, despite fervid assurances to the contrary, not one author in a hundred wants aught but praise of his offspring. One common error may be worth mentioning—the failure of the author to make up his mind at what public he is aiming. Consistency in this matter is essential.

If a publisher accepts your manuscript, remember that in the long run it is the public which decides what the reward of authorship shall be: that the public is a fickle paymaster, and that if it decides to reward handsomely some disher-up of scandal, and to grant the learned historian or philosopher nothing, the publisher is not to blame. If the public will not buy your book the publisher cannot make money either for you or himself. The source of profit, strange as it is to be compelled to reiterate the fact, is the difference between what a book costs to manufacture and what the booksellers pay the publisher for it. A profit cannot be made out of selling a book for what it costs to produce. It is astonishing how many authors think it can; who assume, in fact, that the laws of arithmetic do not apply to publishers.

All is not gold that glitters. The most effective advertiser is not usually the most showy, just as the most efficient doctor is not often the one with the largest doorplate. The widespread distribution of a book in every corner of the globe does not begin and end with advertisements in two Sunday papers. It is a process laboriously built up brick by brick. It is one thing to be able to sell a book for ten or twelve weeks—quite another to do so for ten or twelve years. These are points to bear in mind when choosing your publisher, but there are others. Does he *really* know his job? If he does, trust him to get on with it; if he does not, do not go to him. Is he financially sound—beyond a peradventure? If he is, the hardest bargain he may drive is likely to prove more profitable to you than the most alluring contract with an insolvent firm. A 10 per cent royalty that arrives the day it is due is better than a 20 per cent royalty that is never forthcoming.

The most stable firms are usually those which have a strong back list of publications with a continuous and profitable sale and who therefore have no need to gamble to secure new business.

Having chosen your publisher, co-operate with him, but do not start out to teach him his job. It is not co-operating, but positively hindering him, to ring him up on the telephone when a postcard or a letter would be equally or probably more effective. Never bother the head of a firm with a departmental job. If lengthy instructions must be given over the telephone (they should in any case be confirmed in writing), ask a shorthand-typist to take them down.

Just as you can take a horse to the water but cannot make it drink, a publisher can take a new book to a bookseller, but cannot make him buy. Over twenty thousand new books are published every year, and booksellers can of necessity only stock a selection of them. Because your friends affect surprise that your book is not in stock at the local newsagent, there is no need for you to do so.

The fact that a best seller or a cheap reprint is on a railway bookstall is no reason why your book should be. It will not become a best seller just because it is put on a bookstall; it is much more likely to become soiled stock. The railway bookstall proprietors, who see all the new books, know better than anyone else what they can and cannot sell, and if they decide against yours, the chances are at least a hundred to one upon their being right.

Every new book issued by a well-established publisher is shown before publication to the London booksellers and either before publication or shortly thereafter to all the principal booksellers in the provinces. This process takes time which is most unwise to curtail. The fact that the particular bookseller's assistant you interviewed had never heard of your book is no evidence that your publisher was negligent. On the contrary, it may merely mean on the other hand that when the book was "subscribed" the bookseller declined it, or on the other that the assistant is not following the lists of new publications in the book trade papers as carefully as he might. But any bookseller or bookstall ought to be able to execute an order for your book promptly, and if any difficulty is experienced your publisher should be immediately informed.

Despite all impressions to the contrary, the selling of new books is seldom a lucrative business; too few people *buy* them. Possibly you have observed that even your own friends and acquaintances unblushingly try to "cadge" copies of your books. Pocket your pride (or your snobbery!) and tell them boldly that if they don't think the book worth buying, you would rather they did not read it; and do your part in educating the public into a deeper appreciation of books by joining the National Book League and working for it.

The growing commercialisation of literature—inevitable though it may be—does not tend to promote more harmonious relations between authors and publishers. It is based on the assumption that manuscripts and books are mere commodities; dead, not living things. Such an assumption ignores the peculiar and indeed parental relationship of the author to his work, the realisation of which is the beginning of wisdom in a publisher.

Two last points: If a publisher has had enough faith in you to go on losing money over the publication of your early and possibly immature work, it is not cricket either to take your first readily saleable MS. elsewhere without submitting it to him or to expect him to bid for it in competition with others who have not spent a penny in helping to establish your reputation. It is even more unsporting to ask a literary agent to kick away on your behalf the ladder which has enabled you to climb.

Finally, read your contract and remember that your publisher is just as much entitled to expect you to honour your signature as you are to insist upon his honouring his.

WRITING FOR TELEVISION

ARTHUR SWINSON

ANYONE writing, or hoping to write, for television today must recognise two factors: the first, that every weekly programme "spot" makes specific demands, and the second, that these demands are frequently changing. Accurate and up-to-date information is therefore vital. The position regarding straight drama is now very little different in this respect from that of other output, plays being grouped into weekly series. These vary in aim, length and scope but each works to a specific brief, which may be varied or changed completely at short notice. The emphasis may be on entertainment, suspense or social themes. The film allocation may be generous, meagre or non-existent.

This situation inevitably demands a policy of "horses for courses". The writer should submit to the script editor concerned only those ideas which naturally fit the brief, or can be developed to fit it. It is certainly no use merely offering a play with the hope that it will somehow find its own market.

But how, it may be asked, can the writer cope with the fickleness of the demand and obtain up-to-date information? If he has an agent there is no problem, as all agents receive on request the information bulletins from the B.B.C. and I.T.V. companies. If the writer works without an agent, he should write for the information direct. (Writers belonging to the *Writers Guild of Great Britain* receive market information as it becomes available.) He should also obtain a copy of the booklet *Writing for the BBC* (Price 25p.) which contains an excellent summary of the Corporation's requirements in the field of both television and radio.

Having decided on the correct play "spot" for his idea, the writer's next task is to decide how to submit it. Here the best advice—for any writer who is in range—is to make an appointment with the script editor and discuss the idea face to face. It does not matter whether the writer has worked for television before: writers in other fields are enormously respected in television studios, especially novelists. The fact that a writer is coming fresh to the medium may even be an advantage; his style and potentialities are still unknown quantities. Once seated with the script editor, the writer should expound briefly:

    (a) The general theme of his play.
    (b) The main characters.
    (c) The plot, and climax.

He should not speak for more than three or four minutes. And he should be prepared to answer questions as to how his play differs from any other play in the same field, and why it is much better. The personal approach may take courage; but it undoubtedly provides the best chance of selling an idea.

However, preceded by an interview or not, the synopsis of the play must be completed. *This should occupy not more than one foolscap page—between 300 and 400 words.* Any script editors demanding 2,000 or 3,000 word synopses should be courteously refused. The synopsis should bear:

    (a) The author's name, address, and phone number.
    (b) The type and length of the play (i.e. 60-minute comedy).
    (c) The title.

It does not matter if the title is merely a "working title"; it must be included for identification and copyright reasons. The synopsis should be acknowledged by the company within two weeks; and a decision should be taken on it in four weeks. If these limits are exceeded the writer should begin harassing the company.

A writer who has not written for television before may be asked to submit 'the first few scenes' before a contract is issued, so that the quality of his dialogue can be seen. In this case, he should write five pages only; and if a request comes for more he should refuse. Once a writer has any credits he should never write a line of dialogue before the contract is signed.

A short note on the lay-out of the script. There are a number of books on this subject, which should present little difficulty. Any writer in doubt should write to the B.B.C. or I.T.V. company concerned and ask for a specimen lay-out. Usually this will be supplied.

The above points apply to drama. A good deal of television output, however, is in the form of series (*Dr. Finlay's Casebook, Softly, Softly,* etc.). It is very unusual for a writer without experience in the medium to be commissioned to write for these, as the manipulation of 'running characters' requires a good deal of professional skill. New writers do, however, succeed in breaking into television via series, and there is no reason why stories should not be submitted if they exactly fit the pattern. Here, though, up-to-date information is vital, as series editors usually contract known writers the moment a further batch of programmes is decided on. Ideas for new series, however, are always welcome, and writers should submit fairly detailed descriptions of:

    (a) The background.
    (b) The main characters.
    (c) The story reservoir.

The latter is most important, as television companies will not consider a subject unless it has a potential yield of 26 programmes.

Apart from plays and series, the field of television has narrowed: there is little demand at the moment for children's plays and serials, and comedy shows are firmly tied to specific comedians. A developing field lies in educational programmes, but, here again, a writer should obtain detailed information as to requirements.

Contracts are now fairly standardised though the method of payment varies from company to company. A common pattern is for the writer to be paid the first half of his fee on commissioning, and the balance on acceptance. Sometimes, however, the fee is split into three, one-third being paid on delivery of the MS. In general, the writer should not accept any contract which guarantees him less than one-third of the fee before he starts writing the script. Contracts cover not only the original transmission of the work, but repeats, and foreign sales. The clauses governing these are standard, however, and it is seldom that a writer can vary them. He need have no worry about payment of the fees, which will be dealt with meticulously. All contracts specify that the writer will carry out such re-writing as may be required. There is also a clause which gives the company the right to bring in a new writer if the original writer does not complete the script to its satisfaction. In this case he is usually paid three-quarters of his fee (with a right to half the residual rights) and has the option of either taking a joint credit or having his name removed. With series such an eventuality happens quite often. With plays, very rarely.

A list of independent television organisations with their addresses is given on pages 313–4, and of the B.B.C. on pages 311–2. Writers should communicate with script editors at these addresses individually (if their name is known) or otherwise write to the Head of Drama. In the case of the B.B.C. unsolicited scripts should be sent to the Head of Television Script Unit.

THE MARKET FOR VERSE

DOUGLAS GIBSON*

No true poet writes for money, but having completed his poem, he naturally wants an audience for it and, if possible, payment. He cannot hope to earn his living from verse alone, but he may get a small income from his work in periodicals in Britain and the U.S.A., and possibly, but far less likely, from book publication.

For many years now poetry has been, from a financial viewpoint, the Cinderella of literature; and the market for it today is considerably more restricted than it was before and during the last war.

Many poetry magazines and literary periodicals which opened their pages to new poets have, unfortunately, gone out of existence, changed their character, or been swallowed up by larger publications. Today there are no national newspapers which publish poetry, but during the last ten years several new literary and poetry magazines have appeared, the leading ones being *The London Magazine* and *Encounter*. Others include *Ambit, Stand, Transatlantic Review*; and two with a Welsh accent: *Anglo-Welsh Review*, and *London Welshman*. Two long-established poetry magazines open to most types of good verse are *Poetry Review* and *Outposts*.

Established literary periodicals which still publish poetry, though less frequently than formerly, include *Cornhill, English, Listener, New Statesman, Spectator, Sunday Times* and *Times Literary Supplement*.

Magazines devoted mostly to the open-air and that regularly publish poetry with a country flavour are *Country Life, Countryman* and *The Field*.

There is very little scope for humorous or satirical verse; *Punch*, which also, occasionally uses serious poems, and *She* and *Reveille* sometimes use short humorous verse.

The periodicals listed on page 417 comprise almost every possible market for poetry in Great Britain, but many of them only occasionally use verse, and are frequently over-stocked. It will, therefore, be obvious that a most careful study of the periodicals is essential if the poet wishes to appear in them.

Payment varies so widely between periodicals, length of poem and reputation of the poet, that to quote any regular fees, based on my own experience would be misleading.

In America, the market for verse is wider but the competition is keener. However, the British poet would be well advised to try America, especially as, in my experience, American periodicals on the whole are more sympathetic to traditional verse than are their British counterparts and, of course, they pay more highly.

The *New York Times* publishes about 2 poems each week and pays 25 dollars for each. The *Christian Science Monitor* publishes verse regularly in its Home Page Forum at 20 dollars a poem.

Leading literary periodicals which regularly publish verse include *American Scholar, The Atlantic, Harpers Magazine* and *Saturday Review*.

Leading mass-circulation women's magazines pay extremely generously but they are generally over-stocked with verse and the prospects of breaking in are very limited.

There are a few American magazines that like very short, humorous or epigrammatic verse, some of only two lines: the leading one is *New Yorker*, which also prints serious poetry.

The U.S.A. has over twenty magazines devoted exclusively to verse. The major one is *Poetry* which pays 50 cents a line. The majority of the verse magazines make little or no payment, except in free copies or small prizes.

* Author of *Winter Journey and other Poems* (Cape), *The Singing Earth* (Heinemann), etc.

For the British poet, the study of the American verse market is even more essential than the periodicals of his own country.

Poems sent to America should normally be addressed to The Poetry Editor, enclosing an International Reply Coupon costing 6p.

In addition to publication in British and American periodicals, the poet has opportunities in anthologies and the occasional B.B.C. broadcasts of new poetry. There are also a number of poetry competitions details of which appear in this Year Book, and others are from time to time announced in the *Poetry Review* and *Outposts*.

In the past year or two an increasing number of Local Authorities have presented Arts Festivals, which have included the reading of poetry. Naturally, most of the poets who have been invited have already achieved considerable success in publication, or are known to the general public through television or other mass media. These can earn considerable fees from such appearances, and even higher fees if they are selected to recite or lecture in America.

Once his name has become known through regular appearance in the periodicals, the poet will begin to look forward eagerly to book publication. Unless he is very gifted, or is prepared to subsidise the cost of production himself, he is likely to be disappointed. The fact is that publishers lose money on most books of poetry and with some exceptions, a volume of poetry published today is not likely to sell more than a few hundred copies.

Publishers are, therefore, reluctant to risk almost certain loss, unless the poetry is of such quality as to enhance their reputation, or the author is already on their lists with more profitable books, or if young, shows exceptional promise for the future. Most poets find the road to success long and arduous. They have to market the poems themselves: literary agents are unlikely to be interested. They will receive many more rejections than acceptances. Yet the occasional poem on the printed page and a modest cheque will be ample reward for all the disappointments. And one day, if the poems are original and of permanent value, will come the unequalled pleasure of seeing a volume brought out by a reputable publisher. Meanwhile, the real joy will continue to be in the creation of the poems themselves.

MARKETING A PLAY

JULIA JONES

As soon as a play is written, it is protected under the Copyright laws of this country (see p. 330). No formalities are necessary here to secure copyright protection but it is a good plan to deposit a copy with the bank and take a dated receipt for it, so as to be able to prove the date of its completion, if this should be necessary at some time either, for example, to enforce a claim for infringement of copyright or to rebut such a claim. The copyright belongs to the author unless and until he parts with it and this he should never do, since the copyright is in effect the sum total of all his rights in his work. He should, so far as possible, deal separately with the component rights which go to make up the copyright and grant limited licences for the principal rights with, where customary or necessary, limited interests in the ancillary rights. A West End production agreement (see below) illustrates this principle.

The author can try to market the play himself, but once a play is accepted, it is wise to have professional assistance. There is no standard author's contract in this country; all points are, therefore, open for negotiation and the contractual complications are best handled by a reputable literary agent.

Although most ambitious young playwrights visualise a West End opening for their plays, the first step, except for the established dramatist, is usually to try to place the play with a repertory company known to be interested in presenting new plays. It is wise to write to the company first, giving salient details, such as type of play, size of cast, number of sets, etc., and ask if the management would be willing to read it. This saves the frustration and expense of copies of the play being kept for long periods by managements who have no interest in it. (Do not send your only copy of the play away—this seems obvious, but many authors have suffered the torment of having to rewrite from memory when the only copy has been lost.) It is also possible to get a first production by entering the play for the various competitions which appear from time to time, but in this case great care should be taken to study the rules and ensure that the organisers of the competition do not acquire unreasonably wide rights and interests in the entries.

Many repertory companies will give a new play a try-out production in the hope that it will be seen by London managements and transfer to the West End. For the run at the repertory company's own theatre the company will receive a licence for a given period from a fixed date and pay the author a royalty of between 6 per cent and 10 per cent calculated on the gross box office receipts. In return for the risk involved in presenting a new play, the repertory company will expect a share in the author's earnings from subsequent professional stage productions of the play during a limited period (usually two years). Sometimes on transfer the West End management will agree to take over responsibility for part or all of this payment.

The contract, for repertory or West End production, or for the use of any other rights in the play, should specify precisely the rights to which it refers, the territory covered, the period of time covered, the payments involved and make it clear that all other rights remain the property of the author.

For a first-class production in the West End of London, usually preceded by a short provincial tour, the author's contract will include clauses dealing with the following main heads of agreement. The substance, as well as the phrasing of these clauses will vary considerably, but those given below probably represent the average, as do the figures in brackets, which must not be assumed to be standard:

1. *U.K. Option.* In consideration of a specified minimum sum (between £100 and £250) as a non-returnable advance against royalties, the Manager shall have the exclusive option for a specified period (usually six months) to produce

the play in a first-class theatre in the West End of London (preceded possibly by a tour of a specified number of weeks) with an extension for a further period upon payment of a further similar sum.

2. *U.K. Licence.* When the Manager exercises his option he shall have the U.K. Licence for a specified period (three or five years) from the date of the first performance under the licence such licence to terminate before the expiry of the specified period if

(*a*) the play is not produced before a specified date;

(*b*) (i) less than a specified number (between 50 and 75) of consecutive professional performances are given and paid for in any one year; or

(ii) the Manager has not paid at the beginning of any year a non-returnable advance against royalties. This variant on clause (*b*) (i) prevents the rights being tied up for a year while waiting to check if the qualifying performances have been given and is thus desirable from the author's point of view.

3. *U.S. Option.* If the Manager gives a specified number (usually 24) of consecutive performances in the West End he shall have an option exercisable within a specified period of the first West End performance (six weeks) to produce the play on Broadway on payment of a specified non-returnable advance on royalties (between £200 and £350).

4. *U.S. Licence.* When the Manager exercises his option the Broadway licence shall be for a specified period (3 years) on terms not less favourable than those specified in the U.S. Minimum Basic Agreement.

5. *Other Rights.* Provided the play has run for the qualifying period (usually 24 performances) the Manager acquires interests in some of the other rights as follows:

(i) *Repertory.* The author should reserve these rights paying the Manager a share (one-third) of his royalties for a specified period (two years after the end of the West End run or the expiry of the West End licence whichever is the shorter.) The author agrees not to release these rights until after the end of the West End run without the Manager's consent, this consent not to be unreasonably withheld. It is recommended that a play should be released to theatres on the A* list immediately after the end of the West End run, and to theatres on the B* list within three months from the end of the West End run, if an option for a tour has not been taken up by then, otherwise at the end of the tour.

(ii) *Amateur.* The author should reserve these rights and pay the Manager no share in his royalties, but should undertake not to release these rights for an agreed period, to allow the repertory theatres to have the maximum clear run.

(iii) *Radio and Television.* The author should reserve these rights but it may well be in his interest not to release them until some time after the end of the West End run. During the run of the play in the West End, however, the Manager may arrange for an extract from the play to be broadcast or televised for publicity purposes, the author's fee for such broadcast or television performances being paid to him in full without any part of it going to the Manager.

(iv) *Film.* If the Manager has produced the play for the qualifying period it is expected that the author will pay him a percentage (often 20 per cent) of the author's net receipts from the disposal of the film rights, if these rights are disposed of within a specified period (one year) from the last West End performance. If the Manager has also produced the play on Broadway for the qualifying period the author is expected to allow him a further percentage

* These are the theatres recommended by the Theatres' National Committee for immediate and early release of plays to repertory.

(20 per cent) of the author's net receipts from the disposal of the film rights if the rights are disposed of within a specified time (one year) of the last Broadway performance. This is a field where the established dramatist can, not unnaturally, strike a much better bargain than the beginner. In no case, however, should the total percentage payable to the Manager exceed 40 per cent.

(v) *Foreign Language.* These rights should be reserved to the author, the Manager receiving no share of the proceeds.

Other clauses which should appear include:

(a) *A royalty clause* setting out the royalties which the author shall receive from West End and touring performances of the play—usually a scale rising from 5 per cent through 7½ per cent to 10 per cent.

(b) *Cast approval, etc.* The author should be consulted about the casting and the director of the play, and in some cases may be able to insist on approval of the casting of a particular part.

(c) *Rehearsals, scripts, etc.* The author should be entitled to attend all rehearsals of the play and no alteration in the title or script should be made without the author's consent. All approved alterations in or suggestions for the script should become the author's property. In this clause also should appear details about supply of tickets for the author for opening performances and any arrangements for tickets throughout the West End run.

(d) *Credits.* Details of billing of the author's name on posters, programmes and advertising matter should be included.

(e) *Lord Chamberlain's Licence.* The Theatres Act 1968 abolishes the power of the Lord Chamberlain to censor stage plays and play licences are no longer required. However, it is obligatory for managers to deposit a copy of the script on which the public performance of any new play is based with the Keeper of Manuscripts, British Museum, London, W.C.1. within one month of the performance.

(f) The author will normally warrant that the play contains nothing that is obscene or defamatory or that infringes copyright.

There must also be:

(g) An accounting clause giving details of payment and requiring a certified statement of box office receipts.

(h) A clause giving the conditions under which the agreement may be assigned or sub-leased.

(i) A termination clause, stating the conditions under which the agreement shall terminate.

Arrangements for Other Rights
After the First-class Run of the Play

Repertory. The author or his representative will license repertory performances for a fixed royalty on the gross box office receipts—usually 10 per cent for a new play immediately after its West End run, dropping perhaps to 7½ per cent in later years.

Amateur. The author or his representative will license amateur performances of the play for a flat fee (normally £7 for a new play, £5 or £6 later).

Publication. A firm specialising in acting editions of plays may offer to publish the play in which case it will expect to license amateur performances and collect the fees on a commission basis (20 per cent to 50 per cent). The publication contract will also usually provide for the author to receive a royalty of 10 per cent of the published price of every copy sold.

Radio and Television. Careful negotiation is required and care should be taken that repeat fees for repeat performances are included in the contract in addition to the initial fee for the first broadcast.

Film Rights. Professional advice is absolutely necessary when dealing with a film contract as there are many complications. The rights may be sold outright or licensed for a number of years—usually not less than 7 or 10 or more than 15. The film company normally acquires the right of distribution throughout the world in all languages and expects a completely free hand in making the adaptation of the play into a film.

Foreign Rights. It is usual to grant exclusive foreign language rights for the professional stage to an agent or translator who will arrange for a translation to be prepared and produced—it is wise to ask for evidence of the quality of the translator's work unless the translator is very well known. The financial arrangement is usually an advance against royalties for a given period to enable a translation to be prepared and then a licence to exploit the translation for a further period after production (usually five years).

INDEXING

The Society of Indexers (for details see the entry under "Societies of Interest to Authors, etc.,") maintains a Register of Indexers, members of which may be reached through the Secretary of the Society from whom further particulars may be obtained. The Register at present lists over 150 names and addresses of indexers qualified in most subjects. While it provides this information for authors, publishers and others, the Society takes no direct responsibility for the work of its members. At the same time it maintains standards by making it a condition for inclusion on the Register that a member must submit an index of adequate standard for inspection by the Council. Also a short training course on indexing is held at the North-Western Polytechnic.

TRANSLATION

THE role of the translator in enabling literature to pass beyond its national frontiers is receiving growing recognition, partly as a result of the intervention of UNESCO, which has initiated a series of translations from lesser known languages, published the *Index Translationum*, an annual bibliography of translations, and sponsored the Fédération Internationale des Traducteurs, an international organisation for the promotion of all aspects of translating. In view of the general increase of activity in this field, it is not surprising that many people with literary interests and a knowledge of languages should think of adopting free-lance translating as a full- or part-time occupation. Some advice may be usefully given to such would-be translators.

The first difficulty the beginner will encounter is the unwillingness of publishers to entrust a translation to anyone who has not already established a reputation for sound work. The least the publisher will demand before commissioning a translation is a fairly lengthy specimen of the applicants' work, even if unpublished. The publisher cannot be expected to pay for a specimen sent in by a translator seeking work. If, on the other hand, a publisher specifically asks for a lengthy specimen of a commissioned book the firm will usually pay for this specimen at the current rate. Perhaps the best way the would-be translator can begin is to select some book of the type which he feels competent and anxious to translate, ascertain from the foreign author or publisher that the English-language rights are still free, translate a substantial section of the book and then submit the book and his specimen translation to an appropriate publisher. If he is extremely lucky, this may result in a commission to translate the book. More probably, however—since publishers are generally very well informed about foreign books likely to interest them and rarely open to a chance introduction—the publisher will reject the book as such. But if he is favourably impressed by the translation, he may very possibly commission some other book of a similar nature which he already has in mind.

In this connection it is important to stress that the translator should rigidly confine himself to subjects of which he possesses an expert knowledge. In the case of non-fiction, he may have to cope with technical expressions not to be found in the dictionary and disaster may ensue if he is not fully conversant with the subject. The translation of fiction, on the other hand, demands a special gift for the writing of dialogue and the translator should be certain he is able to cope successfully with dialogue before taking steps to secure work of this nature.

Having obtained a commission to translate a book, the translator will be faced with the question of fees. These vary considerably from publisher to publisher but for the commoner European languages they range from £5·00 to £8·00 a thousand words. In some cases translators are able to obtain a royalty of $2\frac{1}{2}\%$ after a sale of five thousand copies of the first edition of their work, but this is by no means a general practice. More frequently, however, some publishers are willing to pay the translator $2\frac{1}{2}\%$ or 3% royalties on the second and subsequent editions, if any, over and above his initial fee. In the case of plays a proportion of the author's royalties (up to 50%) is the usual method of payment. Translators are now, in some cases, able to secure *licence* rather than *assignment* agreements with their publishers.

Advice regarding fees and other matters may be obtained from the Translators' Association of the Society of Authors (see page 285).

Technical translators are catered for by the Translators' Guild of the Institute of Linguists (see page 286). Annual prizes are awarded for translations from the German, the Italian and the French languages (see LITERARY PRIZES AND AWARDS).

LIBEL

By JAMES EVANS

WHAT follows is an outline of the main principles of the law of Libel, with special reference to points which appear most frequently to be misunderstood. But it is no more than that and specific legal advice should be taken when practical problems arise. The law discussed is the law in England and Wales. Scotland has its own, albeit somewhat similar rules.

LIBEL: LIABILITY TO PAY DAMAGES

English Law draws a distinction between defamation published in permanent form and that which is not. The former is Libel, the latter Slander. "Permanent form" includes writing, printing, drawings and photographs and radio and television broadcasts. It follows that it is the law of Libel rather than Slander which most concerns writers and artists professionally, and the slightly differing rules applicable to Slander will not be mentioned in this article.

Publication of a libel can result in a civil action for damages and/or in certain cases a criminal prosecution against those responsible, who include the writer (or artist or photographer), the printers, the publishers, and the editor, if any, of the publication in which the libel appeared. Prosecutions are rare. Certain special rules apply to them and these will be explained below after a discussion of the question of civil liability, which in practice arises much more frequently.

In an action for damages for libel, it is for the plaintiff to establish that the matter he complains of (1) has been published by the defendant, (2) refers to himself, (3) is defamatory. If he does so, the plaintiff establishes a *prima facie* case. However, the defendant will escape liability if he can show he has a good defence. There are five defences to a libel action. They are (*a*) Justification, (*b*) Fair Comment, (*c*) Privilege, (*d*) S.4 of the Defamation Act, 1952, (*e*) Apology, etc., under the Libel Acts, 1843 and 1845. These matters must now be examined in detail.

THE PLAINTIFF'S CASE

(1) "Published" in the legal sense means communicated to a person other than the plaintiff. Thus the legal sense is wider than the lay sense but includes it. It follows that the contents of a book is published in the legal sense when the manuscript is first sent to the publishing firm just as much as it is when the book is later placed on sale to the public. Both types of publication are sufficient for the purpose of establishing liability for libel, but the law differentiates between them, since the scope of publication can properly be taken into account by the jury in considering the actual amount of damages to award. On this point, it should be noted that it is not necessary for the plaintiff in a libel action to prove that he has actually suffered any loss. The law presumes damage.

(2) The plaintiff must also establish that the matter complained of refers to himself. It is of course by no means necessary to mention a person's name before it is clear that he is referred to. Nicknames by which he is known or corruptions of his name are just two ways in which his identity can be indicated. There are more subtle methods. The sole question is whether the plaintiff is indicated to those who read the matter complained of. In some cases he will not be unless it is read in the light of facts known to the reader from other sources, but this is sufficient for the plaintiff's purpose. The test is purely objective and does not depend at all on whether the writer intended to refer to the plaintiff.

It is because it is impossible to establish reference to any individual that generalisations, broadly speaking, are not successfully actionable. To say boldly "All lawyers are crooks" does not give any single lawyer a cause of action, because the statement does not point a finger at any individual. However, if anyone is named in conjunction with a generalisation, then it may lose its general character and become particular from the context. Again if one says "One of the X Committee has been convicted of murder" and the X Committee consists of, say, four persons, it cannot be said that the statement is not actionable because no individual is indicated and it could be referring to any of the committee. This is precisely why it is actionable at the suit of each of them as suspicion has been cast on them all.

(3) It is for the plaintiff to show that the matter complained of is defamatory. What is defamatory is decided by the jury except in the extreme cases where the judge rules that the words cannot bear a defamatory meaning. Various tests have been laid down for determining this. It is sufficient that any one test is satisfied. The basic tests are: (i) Does the matter complained of tend to lower the plaintiff in the estimation of society? (ii) Does it tend to bring him into hatred, ridicule, contempt, dislike or disesteem with society? (iii) Does it tend to make him shunned or avoided or cut off from society?

"Society" means right-thinking members of society generally. It is by reference to such people that the above tests must be applied. A libel action against a newspaper which had stated that the police had taken a statement from the plaintiff failed, notwithstanding that the plaintiff gave evidence that his apparent assistance to the police (which he denied) had brought him into grave disrepute with the underworld. It was not by their wrongheaded standards that the matter fell to be judged.

Further, it is not necessary to imply that the plaintiff is at fault in some way in order to defame him. To say of a woman that she has been raped or of someone that he is insane imputes to them no degree of blame but nonetheless both statements are defamatory.

Sometimes a defamatory meaning is conveyed by words which on the face of them have no such meaning. "But Brutus is an honourable man" is an example. If a jury finds that words are meant ironically they will consider this ironical sense when determining whether the words are defamatory. In deciding therefore whether or not words are defamatory, the jury seek to discover what, without straining the words or putting a perverse construction on them, they will be understood to mean. In some cases this may differ substantially from their literal meaning.

Matter may also be defamatory by innuendo. Strictly so called, an innuendo is a meaning that words acquire by virtue of facts known to the reader but not stated in the passage complained of. Words, quite innocent on the face of them, may acquire a defamatory meaning when read in the light of these facts. For example, where a newspaper published a photograph of a man and a woman, with the caption that they had just announced their engagement, it was held to be defamatory of the man's wife since those who knew that she had cohabited with him were led to the belief that she had done so only as his mistress. The newspaper was unaware that the man was already married, but some of its readers were not.

DEFENCES TO A LIBEL ACTION

(a) Justification:

English law does not protect the reputation that a person either does not or should not possess. Stating the truth therefore does not incur liability and the plea of justification namely, that what is complained of is true in substance and in fact, is a complete answer to an action for damages. However, this defence is by no means to be undertaken lightly. For instance, to prove one instance of using bad language will be insufficient to justify the allegation that a person is "foulmouthed". It would be necessary to prove several instances and the defendant is obliged in most cases to particularise in his pleadings giving details, dates and places. However, if there are two or more distinct charges against the plaintiff the defence will not fail by reason only that the truth of every charge is not proved, if the words not proved to be true do not materially injure the plaintiff's reputation having regard to the truth of the remaining charges. It is for the defendant to prove that what he has published is true, not for the plaintiff to disprove it, though if he can do so, so much the better for him.

One point requires special mention. It is insufficient for the defendant to prove that he has accurately repeated what a third person has written or said. If X writes "Y told me that Z is a liar," it is no defence to an action against X merely to prove that Y did say that. X has given currency to a defamatory statement concerning Z and has so made it his own. His only defence is to prove that Z is a liar by establishing a number of instances of Z's untruthfulness. Nor is it a defence to prove that the defendant genuinely believed what he published to be true. This might well be a complete answer in an action, other than a libel action, based on a false but non-defamatory statement. For such statements do not incur liability in the absence of fraud or malice, which, in this context, means a dishonest or otherwise improper motive. Bona fide belief, however, may be relevant to the assessment of damages, even in a libel action.

(b) Fair Comment:

It is a defence to prove that what is complained of is fair comment made in good faith and without malice on a matter of public interest.

"Fair" in this context means "honest". "Fair comment" means therefore the expression of the writer's genuinely held opinion. It does not necessarily mean opinion with which the jury agree. Comment may therefore be quite extreme and still be "fair" in the legal sense. However, if it is utterly perverse the jury may be led to think that no one could have genuinely held such views. In such a case the defence would fail, for the comment could not be honest. "Malice" here includes the popular sense of personal spite, but covers any dishonest or improper motive.

The defence only applies when what is complained of is comment as distinct from a statement of fact. The line between comment and fact is notoriously difficult to draw in some cases. Comment means a statement of opinion. The facts on which comment is made must be stated together with the comment or be sufficiently indicated with it. This is merely another way of saying that it must be clear that the defamatory statement is one of opinion and not of fact, for which the only defence would be the onerous one of justification. The exact extent to which the facts commented on must be stated or referred is a difficult question but some help may be derived in answering it by considering the purpose of the rule, which is to enable the reader to exercise his own judgement and to agree or disagree with the comment. It is quite plain that it is not necessary to state every single detail of the facts. In one case it was sufficient merely to mention the name of one of the Press lords in an article about a newspaper though not one owned by him. He was so well known that to mention his name indicated the substratum of fact commented upon, namely his control of his group of newspapers. No general rule can be laid down, save that, in general, the fuller the facts set out or referred to with the comment the better. These facts must always be true, except that in an action for libel partly in respect of allegations of fact and partly of expressions of opinion, a defence of fair comment will not fail by reason only that the truth of every allegation of fact is not proved, if the expression of opinion is fair comment, having regard to such of the facts alleged or referred to in the matter complained of as are proved.

The defence only applies where the matters commented on are of public interest, i.e. of legitimate concern to the public or a substantial section of it. Thus the conduct of national and local government, international affairs, the administration of justice, etc., are all matters of public interest, whereas other people's private affairs may very well not be, although they undoubtedly interest the public.

In addition matters of which criticism has been expressly or impliedly invited, such as publicly performed plays and published books, are a legitimate subject of comment. Criticism need not be confined merely to their artistic merit but equally may deal with the attitudes to life and the opinions therein expressed.

It is sometimes said that a man's moral character is never a proper subject of comment for the purpose of this defence. This is certainly true where it is a private individual who is concerned and some authorities say it is the same in the case of a public figure even though his character may be relevant to his public life. Again, it may in some cases be exceeding the bounds of Fair Comment to impute a dishonourable motive to a person, as is frequently done by way of inference from facts. In general, the imputation is a dangerous and potentially expensive practice.

(c) Privilege:

In the public interest, certain occasions are privileged so that to make defamatory statements upon them does not incur liability. The following are privileged in any event: (i) Fair, accurate and contemporaneous reports of public judicial proceedings in England published in a newspaper, (ii) Parliamentary papers published by the direction of either House, or full republications thereof. The following are privileged provided publication is made only for the reason that the privilege is given and not for some wrongful or indirect motive: (i) Fair and accurate but non-contemporaneous reports of public judicial proceedings in England, whether in a newspaper or not, (ii) Extracts of Parliamentary papers, (iii) Fair and accurate reports of Parliamentary proceedings, (iv) A fair and accurate report in a newspaper of the proceedings at any public meeting held in the United Kingdom. The meeting must be bona fide and lawfully held for a lawful purpose and for the furtherance or discussion of any matter of public concern. Admission to the meeting may be general or restricted. In the case of public meetings, the defence is not available, if it is proved that the defendant has been requested by the plaintiff to publish in the newspaper in which the original publication was made a reasonable letter or statement by way of explanation or contradiction, and has refused or neglected to do so, or has done so in a manner not adequate or not reasonable having regard to all the circumstances. This list of privileged occasions is by no means exhaustive, but they are those most commonly utilised.

(d) S.4 of the Defamation Act, 1952:

The defence provided by the above section is only available where the defamation is "innocent". As has been seen, liability for libel is in no way dependent on the existence of an intention to defame on the part of the defendant and the absence of such an intention does not mean that the defamation is "innocent".

Defamation is innocent if the publisher did not intend to publish the matter complained of about the plaintiff and did not know of circumstances by virtue of which it might be understood to refer to him, or, if the matter published was not defamatory on the face of it, if the publisher did not know of circumstances by virtue of which it might be understood to be defamatory. Further the publisher must have exercised all reasonable care in relation to the publication. If the publisher has published matter innocently, he should make an "offer of amends" to the party aggrieved. This consists of an offer to publish a correction and apology and as far as practicable to inform others to whom the alleged libel has been distributed that the matter is said to be defamatory. If the offer of amends is accepted, it is a bar to further proceedings against the person making the offer. If rejected, the making of the offer affords a defence provided the defendant can prove that he did publish innocently and made the offer as soon as practicable after learning that the matter published was or might be defamatory. The offer must not have been withdrawn and must have been expressed to be for the purposes of the defence under S.4 and have been accompanied by an affidavit. It is vital that the offer should be made swiftly, but it is inadvisable to make it without professional advice owing to its technicality. An example of the first type of innocent publication is where a reference to a person by name has been understood to refer to another person of the same name and this could not reasonably have been foreseen.

An example of the other type of innocent publication is the case referred to earlier in this article of the man pictured with "his fiancée". The publishers did not know that he was already married and that accordingly the picture and caption could be understood to be defamatory of his wife.

In practice all the conditions for a successful defence under this section are infrequently fulfilled.

(e) *Apology under the Libel Acts, 1843 and* 1845:

This defence is rarely utilised, since if any condition of it is not fulfilled, the plaintiff must succeed and the only question is the actual amount of damages. It only applies to actions in respect of libels in newspapers and periodicals. The defendant pleads that the libel was inserted without actual malice and without gross negligence and that before the action commenced or as soon afterwards as possible he inserted a full apology in the same newspaper, etc., or had offered to publish it in a newspaper, etc., of the plaintiff's choice, where the original newspaper is published at intervals greater than a week. Further a sum must be paid into court with this defence to compensate the plaintiff.

CRIMINAL LIBEL

Whereas the object of a civil action is to obtain compensation for the wrong done, the object of criminal proceedings is to punish the wrongdoer by fine or imprisonment or both. There are four main types of writing which may provoke a prosecution and can be collectively described as "Criminal Libels". They are:—

(i) Defamatory Libel;
(ii) Obscene Libel;
(iii) Seditious Libel;
(iv) Blasphemous Libel.

(i) The publication of defamatory matter is in certain circumstances a crime as well as a civil wrong. The following differences from a civil action should be specially noted. In a prosecution, it must be proved that the matter published had a tendency to cause a breach of the peace. Secondly, the libel is "published" even though only communicated to the person defamed. Thirdly, though no civil action lies for defamation of a dead man or where only a group of persons and no individual is defamed, a prosecution may do so. Fourthly, truth, by itself is no defence to a prosecution. It must also be proved that publication of the defamatory matter was for the public benefit.

(ii) It is an offence to publish obscene matter. By the Obscene Publications Act, 1959, matter is obscene if its effect is such as to tend to deprave and corrupt persons who are likely, having regard to all relevant circumstances, to read, see or hear it. "To deprave and corrupt" is to be distinguished from "to shock and disgust". It is a defence to a prosecution to prove that publication of the matter in question is justified as being for the public good, on the ground that it is in the interests of science, literature, art or learning, or of other objects of general concern. Expert evidence may be given as to its literary, artistic, scientific or other merits. Playwrights, in particular, should note the Theatres Act, 1968.

(iii) Writings which tend to destroy the peace of the Realm are seditious and may be the subject of a prosecution. Seditious writings include those which advocate reform by unconstitutional or violent means or incite contempt or hatred for the Monarch or Parliament. These institutions may be criticised stringently, but not in a manner which is likely to lead to insurrection or civil commotion or indeed any physical force. Prosecutions are a rarity, but it should be remembered that writers of matter contemptuous of the House of Commons, though not prosecuted for seditious libel, are, from time to time punished, by that House for breach of its Privileges, although, if a full apology is made, it is often an end of the matter.

(iv) Blasphemous libel consists in the vilification of the Christian religion or its ceremonies. The offence lies not so much in what is said concerning, for instance, God, Christ, the Bible, the Book of Common Prayer, etc., but how it is said. Temperate and sober writings on religious topics however anti-Christian in sentiment will not involve liability. But if the discussion is "so scurrilous and offensive as to pass the limit of decent controversy and to outrage any Christian feeling," it will.

THE WRITER AND INCOME TAX LIABILITY

By J. H. BURTON, F.C.A.

Fellow of the Institute of Chartered Accountants,
Fellow of the Chartered Institute of Secretaries;
Fellow of the Institute of Taxation, Fellow of the Royal Economic Society.

MOST authors have at least two interests in their work, the literary and the financial. Few, indeed, wish to write purely as a hobby without monetary reward. With income tax at 39p. (which with surtax can rise to 89p.) in the £ and an additional impost termed a special charge on the investment income of an individual in excess of £3000 plus his personal allowances deducted for surtax assessment for that year, together with a short-term capital gains tax and a long-term capital gains tax, it is well to know something about the taxation of income from authorship. Profit tax is not imposed on authors; instead they are liable to pay surtax if their earnings bring them in the prescribed category.

Both royalties and the proceeds of outright sales arising from writing—whether professionally, for a livelihood or as a spare-time hobby, for pleasure and pocket-money—when received by a person resident in this country are, as a rule, paid "gross".

A writer, whether of fiction, educational, or general matter may, for present purposes, be classified as either a salaried person or a free-lance. If the former, he is assessed under Schedule E, the tax being deducted from the remuneration by the employer under the pay-as-you-earn scheme and he is only entitled to the very restricted deductions allowable under the rules relating to that Schedule, and these are limited to expenses incurred wholly, exclusively and necessarily in the performance of the duties of the office. And so, as the employer bears most of the expenditure incurred, comparatively little has to be met out of the salary.

The free-lance is assessable under Schedule D, and it is with such that this contribution mainly deals. If the writer practises the art more or less habitually he is assessed under Case II of Schedule D. If his writings are casual, infrequent, or perhaps a single work, he may be taxed under Case VI of Schedule D, or he may be immune from the impost.

An isolated sale of a manuscript such as happens when one writes a single contribution either by request (because one is an acknowledged expert on the subject-matter) or spontaneously, may not be taxed if it can be regarded as a casual transaction, but it is likely that the Inspector of Taxes, if he knows of the affair, will try to get tax on the fee earned. More will be said about that point later.

A frequent contributor of articles, stories, news paragraphs, etc., to newspapers, magazines or other publications, or a writer of books for publication, is entitled by law to be regarded as carrying on the occupation or profession of an author. (Note—this income need not be the only means of his livelihood; in fact, it may be only a small part of the author's total income.)

An author should not submit to an assessment on the full amount of his fees earned. He is entitled to deduct therefrom all expenses necessarily incurred in the execution of his business or profession of author. The items of allowable expenditure are more numerous and costly than one is apt to imagine until they are examined, and they include the following:

(1) Press Agents' fees.

(2) Secretarial fees (if any).

(3) Wages paid to typists and others employed direct.

(4) Typewriting charges where the work is done by others, outside.

(5) Repairs to and renewals of typewriting machines. (In the latter circumstance the allowance is the amount paid for the new machine, less whatever is received for the old one.)

(6) Stationery (including printing).

(7) Postages, telegrams and telephone charges.

(8) Rent, rates, lighting, heating, water, repairs to building, cleaning, etc., of the rooms used by the author (being either the full cost, where the rooms are separate from the residence and are used solely for the purpose of literary work, or a proportion of the total cost of those items in regard to his house, flat or rooms, where the author works at home).

(9) Travelling, where necessary to see agents, editors, or publishers, or to get "local colour" or information for one's work. If the travelling is done in one's own motor car a proportion of the cost of upkeep should be claimed as an expense of authorship.

(10) Renewal (but not original cost) of reference books, etc.

(11) Hotel expenses in so far as necessary and additional to normal cost of living.

(12) Subscriptions to journalists', authors', playwrights', composers' or other relevant societies, libraries, and news-cuttings services.

(13) Periodicals, if reasonably necessary *in the performance* of the work of authorship, but not those which merely train or prepare a person for that profession.

(14) The cost of photographs, etc., where they form part of the published work.

(15) National Insurance contributions paid by an (author) employer in respect of his (the employer's) proportion of the cost of insurance stamps placed on the cards of his employees (if any) in the business of authorship. Also the payroll tax where applicable.

(16) The proportion of payments (if any), made by an author to publishers as part of the cost of publishing his work, which sales in a year bear to the total number of copies printed.

(17) Regularly recurring accountancy, auditing and legal expenses incurred in connection with the preparation of accounts for Inland Revenue purposes, but not any such items as are occasioned by appealing against tax assessments.

(18) Premiums to secure a life annuity in old age are allowed as deductions from earned income. Maximum relief is the lesser of one-tenth of the taxpayer's net relevant earnings of £750 (or more according to age and other conditions). (Annuities so acquired, when received as income in so far as it ranks as *income*, will be treated as *earned income*, the balance of the annuity (ranking as capital) is not now taxable). Several new conditions have been imposed by recent Finance Acts both as regards allowances for income tax and surtax and as to the proceeds of life assurance policies.

(19) Allowable deductions for the purposes of assessment for surtax involve some variations embracing the writing back of certain allowances for income tax. (e.g. interest on deposits in the Post Office or a Trustee Savings Bank and even their being 'grossed-up'). A deduction to be claimed arises where under a settlement payments are made to a named individual (or child thereof). Further information can be obtained from the clerk to the Special Commissioners of Income Tax, Lynwood Road, Thames Ditton, Surrey.

(20) Possibly the cost of attending (for business purposes) a conference or congress (see under CASE LAW).

An official concession giving double taxation relief applies to receipts from abroad for copyrights, etc. These may be treated as income arising outside the United Kingdom except to the extent that they represent consideration for services (other than merely incidental services) rendered in this country by the recipient to the payer.

From time to time correspondents state that they cannot get an allowance under No. (8) (and others) and conclude that the advice therein is unsound. These people do not approach the Inspector of Taxes or the Appeal Commissioners with a properly made case and are, to use the words of one such author, "flatly refused" and contend that "the Tax Inspector has the last word". The information in the article is quite correct but, one fears, is not carefully studied and acted upon by those who are disappointed. If an application be turned down by the Revenue Officer the author should within thirty days of the date on the notice of assessment send to the Inspector of Taxes a written notice of intention to appeal to the Commissioners. They will hear him personally or through an accredited agent. If he is fortified by facts, puts them forcefully to the Inspector and firmly insists on an appropriate allowance, intimating that he will appeal if his request be not acceded to, he should, in most cases gain his point without an appeal to the Commissioners. The Inspector of Taxes definitely has *not* the last word. (More advice on this and many other points can be had from the book: *How to Appeal Against Tax Assessments*, by J. H. Burton, and published by Messrs. Jordan and Sons Ltd.)

Cash benefits received under the National Insurance Scheme (except sickness benefits and the maternity and death grants), are taxable income.

Losses (excess of expenditure over income) in one year from authorship can be deducted from or set against taxable income from other sources in the same year, or carried forward and set against profits of subsequent years.

Occasionally, a question arises whether literary prizes, awards and rewards are taxable. While, to an author, words denote the meaning conveyed to readers, wrong usage cannot affect an income tax assessment to one's advantage (though possibly the reverse may happen).

An *award* is a document or a decision; a *reward* is the return or consideration for service. For present purposes it is assumed that an award is made on the basis of relative merits while a reward is compensation more or less expected, and a *prize* signifies that which is given as compensation. It is the nature of the consideration that is the determining factor for tax purposes. There is more expectation about a reward than an award the gift in which is more particularly something which could not, in any way, be demanded and is nothing more than a hope.

If an established writer or even one who has had only a few acceptances is operating for money (reward) an earning or whatever may be received from a voluntary donor, e.g. a prize in a competition, is most probably taxable income, especially if it is money or something capable of being converted into cash. An isolated receipt of that kind by one who is not a writer, is probably not assessable since it is not an earning in the course of trading, business or occupation. It is not wise to place much importance on the term "lump sum payment" in an attempt to distinguish between an outright sale for cash and remuneration by instalments, since the fee for each single article is virtually a settlement by a lump sum.

In deciding in which category a prize, an award or a reward (or whatever term be used) should be placed for income tax purposes, one should examine the facts carefully and label them on the basis of the fundamental principle above briefly mentioned.

SOME SPECIAL POINTS

A taxpayer who suffers P.A.Y.E. or other deductions under the coding system can demand a formal assessment within five years of the year in question. It is recommended that such a demand be made in order to verify the accuracy of the amounts deducted and to secure repayment of tax over deducted.

It has been held (*Daphne* v. *Shaw*, 1927, 11 T.C. 265) that for the purposes of income tax assessments, books are not "plant and machinery" and therefore no wear-and-tear allowance may be claimed on the cost of the books where such outlay is not wholly allowable as an expense in the year in which it is incurred. Expenditure on renewals may, however, be claimed, as and when incurred.

A proper record should be kept of expenditure on travelling, hotels, etc., incurred in search of information, "colour," interviews, and the like, in order to support a claim for its allowance against profits.

The following excerpt from the judgment of Macnaghten, J., in *Beare* v. *Carter* (1940, 23 T.C. 353), is helpful:

" 'Copyright is property and a price paid for an out-and-out purchase of copyright is capital' are propositions which are not disputed by the Crown. On the other hand, royalties are income and that is not disputed by the respondent."

It must be borne in mind that this case embodies some unusual features, and, as stated later, the decision should not be regarded as applying where the circumstances are not identical. An author who sells a copyright is normally required to bring in the amount received as income for tax purposes, as stated later in reference to the cases of *Glasson* v. *Rougier*, *Howson* v. *Monsell* and *Mackenzie* v. *Arnold*.

No less important is it to bear in mind the dictum of Lawrence, J., in *Billam* v. *Griffith* (1941, 23 T.C. 757), since it helps indicate the distinction between fixed capital (non-taxable) and circulating capital (taxable). He said:

"His brain being his fixed capital and his circulating capital being the plays which, no doubt, may for certain purposes be regarded as property but, at the same time, may be realised in the course of the business which he carried on."

And in *Glasson* v. *Rougier* (1944, 26 T.C. 86) Macnaghten, J., held that a sum received by a novelist for selling copyrights is as much assessable to income tax as are sums received as royalties.

Another case dealing with the question of lump sums received for the copyright in literary, etc., work is that of *Howson* v. *Monsell* (Ch. Nov. 7, 1950, T.R. 333) wherein the General Commissioners had held that lump sums received were capital in their nature and not, therefore, taxable. But that decision was later reversed by the High Court. The reason for the reversal was, the Judge said, that Mrs. Monsell received the money by reason of the fact that she was carrying on the vocation of authoress and that such money came to her in the course of such vocation. He applied the decision in *Glasson* v. *Rougier*. But if the money had come in after the authoress had ceased to exercise her vocation it would not have been taxable and the ruling in *Nethersole* v. *Withers* would have applied.

In a recent case *C.I.R.* v. *Innes* the Revenue unsuccessfully sought to tax the author of a book the copyright of which he had assigned as a gift to his father (see later under Case Law).

The Finance Act 1956 provides that an Inspector of Taxes can demand a return as to periodical or lump sum payments made in respect of any copyright except where income tax is deductible before payment or where the total payments to any one person do not exceed £15 in the year.

ROYALTIES PAID LESS TAX

Royalties and payments to persons whose place of abode is outside Great Britain and Northern Ireland are distributed "net," that is, after deduction of income tax at the standard rate in force at the time. These provisions do not, however, extend to royalties on copies of works shown to the satisfaction of the Special Commissioners of Income Tax to have been exported from the United Kingdom for distribution elsewhere. Where the royalties are paid to a person resident abroad through an appointed agent in this country, the assessment is made on the income after deduction of the agent's commission. Should the royalty be paid over without deduction of such commission, the latter being paid subsequently, any tax overpaid will be refunded to the agent for remittance to the copyright owner. Agreements which provide for the payment of royalties in full to authors resident abroad are regarded as null and void and the recipient of the income renders himself liable to a penalty of £50 for refusing to allow the proper deduction of income tax at the source. The ordinary rules of residence apply and publishers have to use their discretion in determining whether or not, for the purpose in question, an author is resident abroad. If there is doubt, it is the safer plan to deduct tax before paying the royalties or fees.

SPREADING EXPENDITURE OVER PERIOD OF PRODUCTION

Arising out of agitation made to the Chancellor of the Exchequer that in the United States of America writers who have been engaged on a particular piece of work for some years and then sell it for a lump sum are allowed, for tax purposes, to spread the figure over the period of production instead, as in Great Britain, of having to treat it as income wholly of the year of receipt, the Finance Act, 1944 (Section 24), provided a somewhat similar concession to persons in Britain. (This is now regulated by Section 471 of the Income Tax Act, 1952.) As amended (extended) by Section 22 of the Finance Act 1953 and the Finance Act 1968 it applies to any payment of or on account of royalties or sums payable periodically as it applies to a lump sum payment. But this does not apply to payments in respect of the copyright in any work which only becomes receivable more than two years after its publication. The concession deals with assignments of copyright in whole or in part, or grants of any interest in a copyright by licence in respect of literary, dramatic, musical and artistic works for a lump sum by providing that where the author has been engaged in the making of a work for a period of more than twelve months, on his making a claim for the purpose, the lump sum may be dealt with as follows. If the period does not exceed 24 months the lump sum payment may be treated as receivable to the extent of one-half only, on the date when it was actually receivable, and the other half shall be treated as having become receivable a year before that date. If the period in question exceeds 24 months, one-third of the sum may be regarded as receivable when it was actually receivable, one-third a year before that date and one-third two years before. A claim under this section must be made to the Commissioners of Inland Revenue not later than twelve months after the end of the year of assessment for which the lump sum would normally have fallen to have been included in assessment.

The provisions as to spreading therefore now apply also to advance payments to authors by publishers, and to grants of interest in a copyright.

The term "author" includes a "joint author" and the expression "lump sum payment" includes a non-returnable advance on account of royalties. There is a right of appeal on these points to the Special Commissioners. These provisions are extended to payments of or on account of copyright royalties and similar periodical payments except such as do not become receivable until more than two years after the first publication of the work. All sums relating to the same work must be included in the claim for relief and the claim should be made not later than the 5th April next following the expiration of three years after the first publication of the work. In deciding whether to make a claim the effect of its application to all the years involved should be taken into consideration.

An author may produce a highly successful work—a best-seller, perhaps, and though making a big income in a single year, his earnings may dwindle very considerably, perhaps to next to nothing in the lean years that so soon follow. Were it not for these concessions he might have to pay tax at the standard rate and possibly surtax at a high poundage too, in his peak period, and thus his actual profit retainable for himself may be very little indeed.

OTHER AMENDMENTS

Further amendments are provided by recent Finance Acts in regard to a number of other minor matters. One of benefit to some authors and creative artists is that where the copyright in a work is assigned or a grant of an interest in it by Licence for a period of two of more years is effected not less than ten years after the first publication of the work, the sum received therefor may be spread over a period of up to six future years instead of its being taxed in the year of receipt.

Where assessments are made by reference to records kept on a *cash* (as distinct from *earnings*) basis, sums received after discontinuence of one's business or profession (which were not previously taxable) are now chargeable. There is however tapering relief for persons over 50 years of age. Personal reliefs are slightly increased by The Finance Act 1970, which Act abolishes reduced rate relief on certain parts of one's income.

APPEALING AGAINST ASSESSMENTS

Any assessment with which the taxpayer is not satisfied as to its accuracy may be appealed against if he gives notice of such intention within 30 days after the date on the demand note. The Finance Act, 1949 (now by Sec. 510 of the Income Tax Act, 1952), makes provision for appeals to be settled (if both sides are agreeable) between the Inspector of Taxes and the taxpayer, thus avoiding a hearing by the Appeal Commission. Such an agreement is binding on both parties. (A comprehensive treatment of the subject of appealing against assessments appears in the present writer's book *How to Appeal Against Tax Assessments* already mentioned in this article.)

AVOIDANCE OF DOUBLE TAXATION

The standard rate of income tax is 39p. and in certain circumstances surtax, surcharge and 'wealth tax' (special charge) on incomes in the higher ranges. This burden, when borne alone, is heavy, yet income from literary, etc., work sold in the United States of America—and that market offers scope for writers in this country—has had to bear American tax too. Urge for immunity from double taxation was made for some time, and a Convention resulted in an agreement between the Governments of Great Britain and Northern Ireland and the Government of the United States of America for "the avoidance of double taxation and the prevention of fiscal evasion with respect to taxes on income." It was signed in Washington on the 16th April, 1945, and, while dealing with income of various kinds, so far as concerns that from royalties and the amounts paid as consideration for copyrights from sources in the United States by residents in the United Kingdom who are subject to United Kingdom tax on such royalties or other amounts and who are not engaged in trade or business in the United States, it is, by the Treaty referred to (Article VIII thereof), to be exempt from United States tax. Para. 2 of the same Article gives identical treatment in the reverse direction, i.e. exemption from United Kingdom tax on similar income derived from the United Kingdom by residents of the United States who are subject to the taxes of that country on such income, provided they are not engaged in trade or business in the United Kingdom.

Para. 3 of Article VIII prescribes that the term "royalties" shall be deemed to include rentals in respect of motion picture films.

Since the foregoing Convention the problem of double taxation has been the subject of statutory provision in Sections 51 to 56 of the Finance (No. 2) Act, 1945 (and continued in Sec. 350 of the Income Tax Act, 1952), which enacted that agreements for relief from double taxation (declared by His Majesty by Order of Council) made with the Government of any territory outside the United Kingdom shall have effect in relation to income tax and surtax but the provisions for Dominion income tax relief under the Finance Act, 1920, Section 27, shall cease to have effect. The provisions are difficult to understand. Briefly stated they are regarded as providing relief from double taxation by the allowance as a credit against tax payable in the United Kingdom of the figure payable in the country of origin.

Arrangements have already been made with a number of countries to give effect to this. Other countries are from time to time added to or deleted from the list.

The problem of double taxation and its avoidance is very complex. Readers who have income from overseas are advised to obtain the 32-page booklet (No. 420) entitled *Double Taxation Relief—Explanatory Notes* issued free of charge on application to the Board of Inland Revenue. Double taxation relief applies to capital gains tax.

CASE LAW

Some further cases of importance to authors are the following:

In *Hooley* v. *Bladon* it was held that royalties received from a book of memoirs, though an isolated literary effort by a person not an author by profession, was taxable. (It is possible that an outright sale of the copyright of the book would have been exempt from taxation.)

In *Jarvis* v. *Curtis Brown Ltd.* (1929, 14 T.C. 744) the same principle was held to apply.

In *Commissioners of Inland Revenue* v. *Longmans, Green & Co., Ltd.* (1932, 17 T.C. 272) the decision showed that the results of the above-mentioned cases is not free from doubt in regard to future appellants, since in that case a lump sum payment was held to have been made on account of royalties and not for an assignment of copyright.

In *Billam* v. *Griffith* (1940, 23 T.C. 757), a person not being a professional playwright, sold the motion-picture rights in a play and was held to be taxable thereon.

In *Beare* v. *Carter* (1940, 23 T.C. 353) a sum received for the licence to publish the sixth edition of a single book was held *not* to be taxable. The copyright remained with the author. This dictum is difficult to understand. While it held in the case named it is doubtful if it would apply in full measure in any other case unless the circumstances were identical. See *Glasson* v. *Rougier* and *Howson* v. *Monsell* explained later.

In *Hobbs* v. *Hussey* (1942, 24 T.C. 531) the appellant had, for years, been preparing an account of episodes in his life and received £1500 from a Sunday paper for the serial rights thereof. It was his sole literary effort, but he was held to be taxable on his net profit therefrom.

In *Glasson* v. *Rougier* (1944, 26 T.C. 86) an authoress who had granted limited publishing rights in respect of three works in consideration for payment varying with the number of books sold, was held to be taxable.

In a still later case *Mackenzie* v. *Arnold*, (1952, 33 T.C. 363) it was held that while a writer continues to exercise his vocation any sums received by him on the sale of copyright in his works are to be treated, for tax purposes, as profits from that vocation and not as capital sales. The author had spent twenty or more years abroad and now had returned to Britain. During his residence abroad he had written a number of books, the copyright in which he recently disposed of for £20,000. He continues his vocation as an author. The Commissioners of Income Tax assessed him on the receipts named and Mackenzie appealed against the assessment on the ground that the money arose from the sale of capital assets. Alternatively, if the proceeds were to be regarded as revenue income, he claimed to be allowed to deduct therefrom, before assessment, the sum of £19,000 in respect of his estimated expenses incurred in executing his work. The appeal was, however, dismissed, the Judge holding that neither contention could succeed on the facts stated. The assessment was confirmed.

The case of *Nethersole* v. *Withers* (1948, 28 T.C. 514) concerned sums received for a grant of film rights. The appellant had dramatised one of the late Rudyard Kipling's novels and had agreed to dispose of the film rights, her share of the proceeds being one-third. Agreements with film producers yielded £8000 over a period of years, the dramatist's share being £2666. The Special Commissioners had upheld an assessment on her in this sum, under Case VI of Schedule D. The dramatist took the matter to the High Court where Macnaghten, J., upheld the assessment. The taxpayer then took the case to the Court of Appeal where the High Court decision was reversed, it being held that the transaction diminished the appellant's rights under the agreement and that the sums received were capital in character, no part being distinguishable as representing income. The Crown then appealed to the House of Lords unsuccessfully.

Another case *Tennent Plays Ltd.* v. *Commissioners of Inland Revenue* (1948, 30 T.C. 107) decided in the Court of Appeal has an indirect interest for the author and playwright. The company was formed to produce stage plays in collaboration with C.E.M.A. It had no share capital; its income and property had to be applied to the provision of its objects and its members were not entitled to receive any profits. It was claimed that the company had the right to be regarded as a charity for tax purposes under provision of Section 30 (1) of the Finance Act, 1921, since, although it numbered among its objects the carrying on of business as theatre, cinema, etc., proprietors and managers those objects were subsidiary and ancillary, merely to enable the company to raise the necessary finance for its main object. The Special Commissioners rejected that contention and the High Court saw no reason to reverse that decision and so dismissed the appeal. Later the Court of Appeal dismissed the Company's appeal with costs, and refused leave to appeal to the House of Lords.

A more recent case, similar in most respects to that of Miss Nethersole (*supra*), is one heard in the High Court on the 7th November, 1950 (*Howson* v. *Monsell*), wherein the last-named was a writer of historical works who sold the film rights in two of her books for a lump sum. She was assessed under Case II of Schedule D on the money received and appealed against the assessment to the General Commissioners successfully. But later, the point was taken to the High Court by the Revenue Authorities, where it was held that the lady was carrying on the profession or vocation of authoress and that the sum received for the disposal of her film rights in the two works was properly assessable as earnings of her occupation. Distinguishing from *Beare* v. *Carter* (where the author retained the copyright in his work but gave a limited licence to print a certain number of copies of the book) and *Nethersole* v. *Withers* (where the sum received for a grant of film rights was unsuccessfully sought to be taxed), the authoress (Monsell) was held to be taxable.

A still later case of importance to authors who write for the films is that of *Household* v. *Grimshaw* (1953, T.R. 147). An author was under contract to render exclusive services to a film company as a writer of stories for the films, for three years, the company to pay him £200 per week for not fewer than twelve weeks each year. The company also had an option to acquire at stated prices the motion picture, etc., rights in the author's novels published after the date of the contract and prior to the expiration of the contract period. The contract was cancelled by agreement under which the company paid the author £3000 and received a new option similar to the previous one on the film rights of the work. The Revenue contended that the compensation for cancellation was taxable as income, it being a receipt from his profession, whereas the author contended that it was for the premature termination of his contract. The Special Commissioners and the High Court held that the money was not a capital receipt but was taxable as arising out of the author's profession.

A further case of importance to readers is that of *Mitchell* v. *Rosay* (1954 T.R. 87). It arose out of contracts which the respondent obtained for the exploitation of a film in which she had played the leading part. For £1000 she acquired exclusive rights to exploit the film in the United Kingdom, Eire, Channel Islands and Isle of Man, including the right of alteration. The agreement provided that receipts (less expenses) should be shared with the other party to the contract. Later the artist agreed to give the exclusive rights to a company in consideration of its paying her £1000 plus 70% of the profits from the film. The latter yielded her £2848 of which she paid a half (£1424) under her first contract. The Revenue Authorities assessed her portion (£1424) of the £2848 but not the £1000 and she appealed against such assessment.

The Special Commissioners decided that no part of the net receipts (the £1000 or the £1424) was assessable, the case not being sufficiently distinguishable from that of *Nethersole* v. *Withers* (*supra*), but the court later reversed that decision which was favourable to the respondent, holding that the sums she received were a portion of the profits from exploiting the film and were accordingly assessable to tax under

Case III. His Lordship said the respondent had had complete choice in the manner of exploitation—either to receive a capital sum or to receive an income profit and she had chosen the latter, since her share was not to be a specified figure but a sum calculated according to the rise or fall in the receipts of the firm to whom she had assigned her rights in the film.

The case of *Carson* (H.M. Inspector of Taxes) v. *Peter Cheyney's Executor* was decided in the House of Lords (1958 T.R. 349) in favour of the taxpayer who had been an author receiving during his lifetime royalties taxed under Case II of Schedule D. The Revenue sought to assess the executor under Case III or IV of Schedule D, on royalties received after Cheyney's death. It was held that the decision in *Purchase* v. *Stainer's Executors* (1952, 32 T.C. 367) applied in these circumstances and accordingly the sums received were remuneration in respect of professional activities and as they were received after the profession had ceased, they were not taxable. The Court of Appeal affirmed this judgment in the Chancery Division on 21st October, 1957, and in the House of Lords on 25th November, 1958. The Finance Act, 1960, by Sec. 32, nullifies these two decisions in respect of sums received after 5th April, 1960, and causes them to be assessable under Case VI of Schedule D.

Another case of note is that of *Housden* v. *Marshall* (1958, T.R. 337), wherein the Chancery Division of the High Court reversed the decision of the Special Commissioners. Marshall, a jockey, provided a newspaper with material (reminiscences of his life and experience on the turf, photographs and newspaper cuttings) for their "ghost" writer to prepare four articles therefrom. He was assessed under Case VI of Schedule D and on appeal against that assessment the Special Commissioners decided that Marshall had primarily sold publication rights rather than that he had performed services and discharged the assessment. Reversing this, the Court, decided that Marshall was assessable to tax on the fee received from the newspaper company.

An unusual turn arose in a case in 1955 (*Sharpey-Schafer* v. *Venn*) wherein the appellant had appealed in the Chancery Division against an assessment which the Special Commissioners had already determined in his favour. Apparently he wished to air some grievances in regard to the conduct of the Inspector of Taxes. Mr. Justice Danckwerts said it was not the method for following up any such allegation and ruled that there was no case for him to consider or decide.

Compared with *Nethersole* v. *Withers*, where profits from the sale of film rights in a novel were held by the Court to be non-taxable and *Mitchell* v. *Rosay* (*supra*) wherein it was held that such income was taxable a recent case *Shiner* v. *Lindblom* (3. AER 832), adds some new features to a somewhat similar problem. While in *Mitchell* v. *Rosay* the taxpayer chose to receive as income profit, rather than a capital sum, and in consequence was taxable thereon although there was no question of her having carried on a business assessable (on profits) under Case 1 of Sched. D. Mr. Shiner had bought film rights in a book and had obtained a contract to play the leading part in the film, which contract provided for the sale of the film rights to the company. This latter showed a profit of £2300. Details are somewhat complicated for treatment in an article such as this, but the case is worthy of study by those interested, since the taxpayer was held not to be trading in copyrights and therefore not taxable on the profit made.

Still another case has come before the Courts (*C.I.R.* v. *Hammond Innes*). Mr. Innes wrote a book and before offering it to a publisher assigned the copyright to his father as a gift. The copyright was at that date valued at £15,425. The Revenue raised an additional assessment in that sum under Case II of Schedule D on the author who contended that it was not a taxable receipt. The High Court decided in his favour as also did the Court of Appeal in May 1967.

A case decided in the High Court in favour of the taxpayer may interest authors, though not necessarily settling the point in regard to other than the taxpayer in this case (*Edwards* v. *Warmsley, Henshall & Co.* 21st December 1967). A partner in a firm of chartered accountants attended a congress in New York. His firm claimed to charge the cost against their profits. The Revenue unsuccessfully contested the claim.

A recent case *Hume* v. *Asquith* (1968 T.R. 369) dealt with some complex points, determining that some sums received from copyright in plays were taxable while others were not.   The royalties were classified in three groups those under one heading being taxable while those in the other two categories were exempt.

SURTAX

Certain amendments were made by the Finance Act 1970.   The Board of Inland Revenue has issued a booklet of explanatory notes on surtax (No. 700—free).

CAPITAL GAINS TAX, SHORT TERM GAINS TAX, WEALTH TAX (termed SPECIAL CHARGE) AND SELECTIVE EMPLOYMENT TAX

These recently imposed taxes are not peculiar to authors and artists, but are equally applicable to them.   The Board of Inland Revenue has also issued explanatory notes on these imposts—free.

THE WRITER AND ARTIST AND NATIONAL INSURANCE

SOME IMPORTANT POINTS TO REMEMBER

By J. H. BURTON, F.C.A.

1. All persons must contribute to the National Insurance Scheme unless they are self- or non-employed and can show that their total income, taking cash and kind together (i.e. including the value of board, lodging, free meals, etc.) is under the currently prescribed figure, in which case they *may apply* for exception from liability to pay contributions.   The necessary form on which to make the application can be obtained from the local Social Security Office. Entitlement to the benefits named later in this article are affected by a period of exception from liability to contribute.

2. The insured population are divided into three classes:—

CLASS 1   Those who work for an employer under a contract of service.   (The employer is responsible for stamping the cards in this class.)

CLASS 2   Persons engaged in business on their own account from which they ordinarily earn at least £2 per week are regarded as self-employed and are responsible for stamping their own cards.

CLASS 3   Persons who fall into neither of the first two classes are regarded as non-employed and are also responsible for stamping their own cards.

3. An author who is insurable may have some difficulty in determining in which class he comes.   He knows, of course, whether he is in salaried (or other form of remunerated) employment, or if he is a free-lance without any control as to how and when he does his writing.   But that is not the extent of the test to be applied.   If he is free-lance, he is *self-employed.*

4. A writer's classification can change from week to week; for instance, if an otherwise self-employed person performs eight or more hours' work for an employer under a contract of service in any week, for that week he ranks as an employed person.   His employer must stamp the card at the higher rate; the writer is not liable to do it himself.

5. An employed person is one who is employed under a "contract of service" which would be distinguished from a "contract for services" which latter does not make one an employed person.   The former embodies an element of

relationship of master and servant, the one having power to control the way in which the other performs his tasks. Those under "contract for services" are regarded as self-employed persons whereas those under a "contract of service" are deemed to be employed persons. Careful distinction should be made as to the category in which one should rightly be placed, bearing in mind what was once stated by a Master of Rolls when he remarked that "it would be absurd to hold that a skilled music master who gives lessons to a pupil . . . is to be regarded as the 'workman' and the pupil as the employer." That illustrates what is a "contract for services" and there may be circumstances, similar in principle, in which an author may be treated as self-employed rather than employed, as, for instance if he contracted with a pupil to teach authorship. Employment of an author under a contract of service by his wife is treated as self-employment. Employment of a woman by her husband is also treated as self-employment provided the employment is in a "trade or business" and she ordinarily works therein for not fewer than 24 hours a week, earning not less than £2 a week; otherwise the employment is disregarded for insurance purposes.

6. A married woman in employment under contract of service in respect of which she would ordinarily be treated as an employed person may elect whether to pay National Insurance contributions but she must pay Industrial Injury Contributions. A married woman who works as a self-employed person (Class 2) is not under any obligation to pay contributions, but, if she wishes, she may choose to contribute at either the self-employed or non-employed rate.

7. Employed persons (Class 1) pay their quota by deduction from their remuneration, self-employed and non-employed persons must buy their stamps from a Post Office and put them on their cards weekly, cancelling them in ink by writing the date on them. The card must be sent to the local branch of the National Insurance Office within six days after the end of the last week for which provision is made on the card. A new card will be received in exchange.

8. The graduated pension contributions entitle a contributor to a deduction from the amount of income tax chargeable, equal to tax at the standard rate on the figure appropriate to his category (see Finance Act, 1960, Sec. 19 and Schedule 3). The figures are varied from time to time. Wherever changes are possible current figures should be ascertained from the Social Security office. The question of graduated contributions and retirement pensions and the contracting-out provisions is too big to deal with fully in an article such as this.

9. Rates of contributions and benefits can be varied by authority under statute. The current figures can be ascertained from one's local office of the Department of Health and Social Security. The amount which may be earned without any reduction of the pension of a retired man under 70 (woman 65) is varied from time to time; above such figure a reduction is made according to scale.

10. Contributions are not usually payable during whole weeks of notified sickness. Credits are usually given if medical certificates are furnished.

11. Contributions are not compulsorily payable abroad unless a person works abroad in certain circumstances, for a British employer. But a person may be entitled to pay Class 2 or Class 3 contributions voluntarily to retain title to certain benefits. The general conditions may be modified by reciprocal agreements on social security with a number of countries. Details can be obtained from the local office of the Department of Health and Social Security.

SELECTIVE EMPLOYMENT TAX

Though described as a tax, it is an impost payable by employers (no part chargeable to employees) along with National Insurance Contributions. This is included in one combined stamp. In certain circumstances repayment may be claimed, e.g. where domestic or nursing assistance is employed in a private household.

BENEFITS

The following information sets out briefly and in a form easy for reference the benefits obtainable from National Insurance.

Sickness Benefit

1. Flat-rate sickness benefit is payable for an unlimited period (up to pensionable age) once 156 contributions as an employed (Class 1) or self-employed (Class 2) person have been paid between date of entry into insurance and date of beginning of the incapacity, provided all the qualifying conditions are satisfied.
2. Flat-rate sickness benefit is limited to 312 days (one year excluding Sundays) if at least 26 but fewer than 156 contributions as an employed or self-employed person have been paid. To requalify for sickness benefit a person who has received benefit for the 312 days period has to resume employment and pay 13, Class 1 (employed) or Class 2 (self-employed) contributions (unless a total of 156 is reached before 13 have been paid).

In either case the rate of benefit payable depends on the contributions paid or credited in the contribution year immediately preceding the benefit year in which the claim is made (the contribution year is the period covered by the contribution card and the benefit year starts five months after the end of the contribution year). To be entitled to flat-rate sickness benefit at the full rate at least 50 contributions must be paid or credited in the relevant contribution year. Benefit is payable at a reduced rate if there are fewer than 50 but at least 26 contributions paid or credited. Increases of benefits may be made for the claimant's dependants.

In addition to flat-rate benefit an earnings-related supplement may be payable if the claimant's reckonable earnings were at least £450 in the relevant income tax year. Reckonable earnings are those on which income tax is assessable under Schedule E and payable through P.A.Y.E. The supplement is payable for a maximum of 156 days in a period of interruption of employment and is not payable for the first twelve days of such a period.

Maternity Benefit

1. Maternity grant payable up to nine weeks before the expected week of confinement. If two or more children are born a grant is payable for each additional child.
2. Maternity allowance (while not working) for 18 weeks commencing 11 weeks before the expected week of confinement, payable to women who have been paying full flat-rate contributions as employed or self-employed persons.

Widow's Benefit

1. The relevant contribution conditions must be satisfied on the late husband's insurance.
2. Widow's allowance which is at a higher rate than other widow's benefits is payable for the first 26 weeks of widowhood if the husband was not entitled to a retirement pension or the widow is under 60 years of age. An earnings-related supplementary allowance may also be payable for the same period if the husband had earnings on which income tax was assessable under Schedule E and payable through P.A.Y.E.
3. After first 26 weeks:
   (*a*) if the widow has one or more children under the age of 19 years she will

usually become entitled to a widowed mother's allowance which can continue in payment until the child or youngest child reaches 19.

(b) When the widowed mother's allowance ends a widow's pension will be payable if the widow is then over 50 but under 65 years of age and at least three years have passed since her marriage.

(c) If there is no title to widowed mother's allowance a widow's pension will be payable if at the date of her husband's death the widow was over 50 but under 65 and had been married for three years or more.

(d) Special arrangements give immediate cover for sickness and unemployment benefits for the widow who is unable to qualify for a widow's pension under (b) or (c) and is either unable to work because of ill-health or finds difficulty in obtaining employment when her widow's allowance or widowed mother's allowance ends.

4. From April 1971 there will be two easements in the qualifying conditions for a widow's pension. The three-year-length-of-marriage condition will cease to apply and a widow who is between the ages of 40 and 50 when widowed or when her entitlement to widowed mother's allowance ends, will be able to qualify for a widow's pension, scaled down according to her age at that time.

Guardian's Allowance

A weekly allowance payable to a person who has in his or her "family" a child whose parents are dead and one of whom has been an insured person. The child must be under the age limits (15 in general but 16 for certain handicapped children and 19 for those continuing in full-time education).

Family Allowances

These allowances are payable for families with two or more children below the age limits (which are the same as for Guardian's Allowances). Details can be obtained from the local office of the Department of Health and Social Security.

Retirement Pension

The currently prescribed sums. At the time of writing these are £5 per week for life from 65 years of age (if man) or 60 (if woman); £8·10—for a married couple if sufficient contributions have been paid (i.e. 156) and an average yearly number of 50 or more contributions or credits in respect of each year of insurance. People who were of the age of 16 or over on 5th July 1948 and entered insurance then or later, have their yearly contribution average for pension purposes calculated from 1948. Increased rate of pension may be had by deferring retirement (see leaflet NI 15 obtainable from local Social Security offices). The amounts of the benefits are amended from time to time.

Death Grant

A lump sum of up to £30 payable on the death of an insured person or of the wife, husband or child of an insured person. The amount depends both on the age of the deceased person and on the extent to which the contribution conditions are satisfied. No grant is payable for the death of a person who was over pension age at 5th July 1948.

Supplementary Pensions and Allowances

Supplementary benefit can be claimed by anyone in Great Britain who has reached the age of 16 years, who is not in full-time employment, and whose income, including National Insurance pensions and benefits is below the minimum level laid down by Parliament. For persons under pension age benefit is payable only on condition of registration for employment at the Employment Exchange (unless they are sick). In working out entitlement the value of an owner-occupied house is ignored and the first £800 of savings can normally be disregarded. Up to £1 per week of certain forms of other income, e.g. charitable payments, may be ignored, and for persons over pension age the first £2 per week of part-time earnings can be ignored.

Explanatory leaflets (S1 for persons under pension age and SP1 for persons over pension age) are available at local offices of the Department and at Post Offices.

Miscellaneous Points

1. Amounts receivable as benefits are obtainable by cashing Giro Orders at the Post Office.

2. Treatment under the Health Service is available for all persons normally resident in the United Kingdom whether insured or not.

3. As a general rule only Retirement Pensions and Widow's Benefit can be paid abroad, but there are reciprocal agreements on Social Security with a number of countries which may modify the general conditions. Details can be obtained from the local office of the Department of Health and Social Security.

4. In his capacity of employer of others an author's or artist's contributions are allowable in full for income tax purposes as a business expense.

5. Title to benefit and relative matters are decided by independent statutory authorities, the first of these is the Insurance Officer. A claimant who disagrees with a decision can appeal to a Local Tribunal. The decision of such Tribunal can be the subject of a further appeal by either the claimant or the Insurance Officer, to the Commissioner. Disputes as to classification of insured persons, contribution records, etc. are questions for decision by the Secretary of State.

6. A self-employed or non-employed person whose income is small (see the first paragraph of this article) can claim exception from payment of National Insurance Contributions.

7. Employed or self-employed persons who do not retire at 65 (men) or 60 (women) can increase their ultimate rate of pension on retirement by continuing to pay contributions.

8. A person who retires from employment or self-employment before reaching retirement pension age (65, men; 60, women) will normally have to continue to pay contributions as a non-employed person until such age is reached. Provided sufficient contributions were paid before retirement there would be entitlement to Sickness Benefit for the relevant benefit year following such retirement.

9. Under the Collection of Contributions Regulations an insured person in Class 2 (self-employed) or Class 3 (non-employed) is required to stamp his or her card in respect of each week for which a contribution is *due*; failure to stamp for any such week is an offence under the Act.

10. When applying for a Retirement Pension one is required to obtain and to fill in and send to the local office of the Department of Health and Social Security, the necessary form, not earlier than four months before the date on which one becomes entitled to receive the pension and not later than one month after the date of retirement. If only a day too soon the form will be returned and if much less than four months in advance, delay in receiving the money and perhaps loss may be caused. A pension cannot be paid for any period which is more than one month before the date of retirement specified in the application unless the person shows that there was good cause for the delay in giving notice of retirement. Separate notice is required in respect of one's wife, if she, too, claims a Retirement Pension. Notices must state that the claimant has retired or is to retire on the specified date, is of the prescribed age and claims his or her pension.

Pensions for the Older and the Not-insured Persons

The Department of Health and Social Security have recently announced what they describe as "New Pensions for Old People". These are allowances to those who were too old to contribute to the normal scheme which began in 1948 and for certain of their dependants, as from 2nd November 1970. To qualify one must:

(1) not be receiving a National Insurance Pension *or* receiving one of less than £3 per week in the case of a man (£1·85 married woman);

(2) on 5th July 1970 have been 87 (man) or over, (82 woman);

(3) be a married woman under 82 but not less than 60 on 2nd November 1970 whose husband qualifies for the new pension;

(4) be a widow under 82 whose husband was alive and 65 or over on 5th July 1948 and herself was over 50 when her husband died;

(5) be a woman under 82 whose marriage to a man who was alive and 65 or over on 5th July 1948 ended in divorce or annulment after she was 60;

(6) be subject to certain residential conditions.

The pension is £1·85 per week for a married woman or £3 for all other persons. If, however, one is receiving any other pension from public funds, the new pension figures, just named, may be affected. (There is a (free) leaflet NI 177.)

ARTISTS AND DESIGNERS
CODE OF PROFESSIONAL CONDUCT
Issued by the Society of Industrial Artists and Designers Ltd. (see p. 285)

THE observance of this Code is a condition of membership of the Society. The Council may reprimand, suspend or expel any member* who infringes this Code, or who, in its opinion, conducts himself in any manner which discredits the profession. Any questions which may arise as to the interpretation of the Code are to be referred to the Council whose decision is final. Members conducting *a design practice* in partnership or association with non-members shall be responsible for the observance of this Code by all members of their organisation. Members working or seeking work in a country other than their own shall however observe the relevant Code of Conduct of the national society concerned.

1. A member shall not divulge confidential information of his clients' or employers' intentions, production methods and business organisation. It is the designer's responsibility to ensure that all members of his staff are similarly bound to secrecy.

2. A member shall not release for publication any information about work he is doing or has completed unless his client or employer has given express consent.

3. A member shall not work simultaneously on assignments which are in direct commercial competition without the agreement of the clients or employers concerned.

4. A member who is financially concerned with any company, firm or business which may benefit from any recommendations made by him in the course of his work shall inform his client or employer of this fact.

5. A member shall work only for a fee, a royalty or a salary. A member shall not retain any discounts, commission or allowances from contractors or suppliers. Where necessary separate charges shall be made for contracting or supply services provided for the client.

6. A member shall not undertake any work at the invitation of a client or employer without payment of an appropriate fee. A member may, however, undertake work without fee or at a reduced rate for charitable or non-profit-making organisations.

7. A member shall not attempt, directly or indirectly, to supplant another designer, nor shall he compete with another designer by means of a reduction of fees or by other inducements.

8. A member shall not knowingly accept any professional assignment on which another designer has been or is working except with the agreement of the other designer or until he is satisfied that the former appointment has been properly terminated.

Fellow, Member, Associate, Licentiate or registered student of the Society.

9. A member shall not knowingly plagiarise any design.
10. A member who is asked to advise on the selection of designers shall not accept payment in any form from the designer recommended.
11. A member shall not enter or act as an assessor in any open or limited competition whose terms are at variance with the regulations for design competitions published by the Society.
12. A member may not take advertising space in any medium in which to advertise his professional services.
13. A member may approach a potential client or employer only in the following manner:

   (a) By means of a letter in the form prescribed by the Council.
   (b) By the presentation of specimens of work in those fields only where by custom an open invitation to do so already exists; e.g. to advertising agencies, publishers, textile and wallpaper manufacturers, etc. Specimens, which may be originals or reproductions, may be left with the client at the discretion of the designer.
   (c) By applications for a salaried appointment, whether advertised or not.
   (d) By insertion of an advertisement for a salaried appointment in the classified columns of appropriate magazines or newspapers.
   (e) By answer to an advertisement or invitation asking for names from which the advertiser may select a designer for a particular project, provided that the response to such an advertisement does not contravene this Code or the Society's Regulations for the Conduct of Open or Limited Competitions.

14. A member may notify his change of address or form of practice by:

   (a) An announcement which may appear once in the appropriate professional and trade publications.
   (b) One communication through the post to his correspondents.

15. A member may advertise a vacancy in his organisation in the classified columns of appropriate publications.
16. A member may issue to the Press illustrations, factual descriptions of his work and biographical material for publication provided he does not pay for such insertions and provided such action does not contravene Clause 1, 2, 12, or 13 of this Code.
17. A member may allow his name to be used by clients, employers, agents or others in advertisements only in connection with factual statements of goods or services offered and provided the statements in such advertisements are not harmful to other members or detrimental to the dignity of the profession.

Conditions of Engagement

These conditions may be varied according to the circumstances of a particular contract.

Commissions for design services shall always be confirmed in writing, the form of service and fees being stated, with conditions appropriate to the commission. Exclusive services in a particular field of design may be secured by agreement between client and designer.

Copyright

There should be complete understanding between the designer and client as to the ownership and the extent of copyright in any design. In the case of a rejected, cancelled or uncompleted commission the copyright is retained by the designer and the sketches, drawings or models remain his property.

Design Registration

When the ownership of a design is acquired by the client the designer shall, where desired, assist in any application for design registration. The costs shall be borne by the client.

N

Patents

All patentable material that may be originated by the designer during the development of a project shall remain his property unless, or until, a separate agreement is entered into assigning patent rights in part or in full, as may be desired.

Additional Instructions and/or Change of Brief

If the client's original instructions be subsequently varied or augmented during the course of a commission, a fee "pro rata" for the additional work is chargeable.

Alteration

A design shall not be altered or adapted by the client without the designer's consent.

Design Credits

The designer shall be entitled to claim authorship of a design for which he has been responsible, and his consent shall be obtained before his name or signature is reproduced on any finished product or otherwise published by the client.

Miscellaneous Expenses

These are charged at cost. They include travelling, hotel and out-of-pocket expenses, long distance telephone calls, typesetting costs and copies of photographs and prints; and the cost of models or prototypes furnished at the client's request or with his approval (except where they comprise part of the initial design proposals).

Payments

Accounts may be rendered on completion of the commission or at intermediate stages to be agreed with the client.

Renewal of Contract

Where a contract is on an annual basis it will be deemed to be automatically renewed unless three months' prior notice is given by either party of revised terms being required or of the contract being terminated.

Termination of Project or Appointment

Upon the premature cancellation of any agreement by the client, the designer is entitled to payment for the services rendered in relation to the time and expenses involved.

Arbitration

Any dispute or differences arising out of the contract shall be referred under the provisions of the Arbitration Act of 1950 or any statutory modification or re-enactment thereof for the time being in force to the arbitration of a single arbitrator to be mutually agreed upon or failing agreement to an arbitrator to be appointed jointly by the President of the Society of Industrial Artists and Designers Ltd. and the President of the appropriate trade association or chamber of commerce.

This document is subject to revision as the Council of the Society may determine.

JOURNALISTS' CALENDAR

1971-1972

For general events and publications, the anniversaries of which fall in 1971, see 1970 edition of *Year Book*, pages 384–387.

1971

MAY

1 Padstow Hobby-horse, Cornwall.
Bank of England resumed cash payments, 1821.
2 Mrs. Piozzi, Dr. Johnson's friend, d. 1821.
3 Impeachment of Sir Francis Bacon, 1621.
4 Battle of Tewkesbury, 1471.
5 Edward Montagu, Earl of Manchester, d. 1671.
Napoleon d. 1821.
William Friese Greene, cinematograph pioneer, d. 1921.
London ultimatum of Allies, 1921.
6 Thomas Tresham, Speaker, beheaded, 1471.
Congress of Laibach ended, 1821.
7 St. John of Beverley d. 721.
Asa Briggs, historian, Vice-Chancellor of the University of Sussex, b. 1921.
8 Innocent XIII became Pope, 1721.
W. H. Vanderbilt b. 1821.
Charlotte Maria Tucker, writer ("A.L.O.E."), b. 1821.
Treaty of Washington, 1871.
Louis Madelin, French historian, b. 1871.
10 Sebastian Brant d. 1521.
Treaty between France and Germany, 1871.
11 Beginning of the Tichborne case, 1871.
Sir John Herschel, astronomer, d. 1871.
12 Emilia Pardo-Bazan, Spanish authoress, d. 1921.
13 Abbotsbury Garland Day, Dorset.
Auber, composer, d. 1871.
14 Robert Owen, reformer, b. 1771.
Thomas Wedgwood, photography experimenter, b. 1771.
Fascists elected to Italian assembly at general election, 1921.
15 J. W. Callcott, composer, d. 1821.
16 Sir Frederick Mappin, benefactor, b. 1821.
17 Dennis Brain, horn player, b. 1921.
19 Rahel b. 1771.
20 Loyola wounded, 1521.
21 Henry VI assassinated, 1471.
Dürer b. 1471.
Christopher Smart, poet, d. 1771.
22 Karl Elze, German scholar, b. 1821.

Baron Royden, shipping magnate, b. 1871.
Versailles army entered Paris, 1871.
24 Archbishop of Paris shot, 1871.
25 Delescluze, French communist, d. 1871.
Admiral A. K. Wilson d. 1921.
Dublin Custom House burnt down, 1921.
27 Georges Rouault, French artist, b. 1871.
28 End of French insurrection, 1871.
29 Garland Day, Castleton, Derbyshire.
Frederick Locker-Lampson, poet, b. 1821.
G. H. Thayer, American artist, d. 1921.

JUNE

— Joan, Queen of Scotland, b. 1321.
1 John Story martyred at Tyburn, 1571.
3 Sydney Smith, writer and divine, b. 1771.
5 Ernest Augustus, Duke of Cumberland and King of Hanover, b. 1771.
William Crooks, politician, d. 1921.
6 First issue of *Corante*, pioneer English newspaper, 1621.
Sir E. Denison Ross, orientalist, b. 1871.
7 R. C. Bosanquet, cricketer, b. 1871.
10 Duke of Edinburgh b. 1921.
11 Sir Walter Henry Cowan, naval officer, b. 1871.
13 Stephen Joseph, theatrical producer, b. 1921.
14 First performance of Weber's *Preciosa*, 1821.
W. W. Fowler, scholar, d. 1921.
16 John Ballantyne, printer, d. 1821.
17 J. H. Pepper, inventor of "Pepper's Ghost," b. 1821.
18 First performance of Weber's *Der Freischütz*, 1821.
George Grote d. 1871.
C. L. Fraser, artist, d. 1921.
19 Mayor of Ock Street ceremony, Abingdon, Berkshire.
G. J. Whyte-Melville, novelist, b. 1821.
20 Magna Carta commemoration ceremony, London.

21 Alliance between England, France, and Spain, 1721.
22 William McDougall, psychologist, b. 1871.
24 Melrose Festival.
    Lucie Duff Gordon, writer, b. 1821.
27 Wall Pulpit Sermon, Magdalen College, Oxford.
    August Conradi, composer, b. 1821.
29 Madame Tetrazzini, prima donna, b. 1871.
    Trade Unions declared legal, 1871.
30 W. H. Dixon, author, b. 1821.

JULY
— Despensers exiled, 1321.
1 Safeguarding Industries Act, 1921.
2 Sir Charles Tupper, colonial statesman, b. 1821.
   Rome became the capital of Italy, 1871.
   Sir Evan Williams, industrialist, b. 1871.
   United States officially at peace with Germany and Austria, 1921.
3 W. H. Davies, poet, b. 1871.
4 Richard Cosway, miniaturist, d. 1821.
7 John Britton, antiquary, b. 1771.
   Benjamin Seebohm Rowntree b. 1871.
8 Vintners' Company Procession, London.
   La Fontaine, French poet, b. 1621.
   Prussia began "Kulturkampf" against the Roman Catholic Church, 1871.
10 Taddiport Tub Race, Devon.
    Marcel Proust b. 1871.
11 John Rodgers, American naval officer, b. 1771.
12 Padley Martyrs Commemoration, Derbyshire.
13 Sarah Emily Davies, educationalist, d. 1921.
14 Sir Robert Strange, engraver, b. 1721.
    Enwonwu, Nigerian sculptor, b. 1921.
15 Translation of St. Swithin's remains, Winchester Cathedral, 971.
16 Mary Baker Eddy, founder of Christian Science, b. 1821.
17 Carl Tausig, Polish pianist and composer, d. 1871.
18 Watteau, artist, d. 1721.
19 Coronation of George IV, 1821.
    Sir Jonathan Trelawny d. 1721.
20 End of Purchase System, British army, 1871.
21 Paul Reuter b. 1821 (prob.).
22 Earl Shaftesbury b. 1621.
25 Belgium–Luxemburg trade agreement, 1921.
26 Pope Paul II d. 1471.
28 Independence of Peru proclaimed, 1821.
30 Thomas Gray, poet, d. 1771.
31 William Wood (of "Wood's halfpence") b. 1671.

AUGUST
— Henry VIII's *Golden Book*, 1521.
— Turks took Cyprus, 1571.
1 Elizabeth Inchbald, writer, d. 1821.
2 Marquis of Granby, soldier, b. 1721.
   Sir Edward Robert Peacock, Canadian financier, b. 1871.
   Caruso d. 1921.
3 Grinling Gibbons d. 1721.
6 Dominic d. 1221.
7 Queen Caroline d. 1821.
8 Thomas à Kempis d. 1471.
   Arthur Pougin, French musicologist, d. 1921.
10 Missouri became a member of the United States, 1821.
11 Octave Feuillet, novelist, b. 1821.
12 Mary Gibson legacy ceremony, Sutton, Surrey.
14 Local Government Boards created, 1871.
15 Sir Walter Scott b. 1771.
    Sir Arthur George Tansley, botanist, b. 1871.
16 Arthur Cayley, mathematician, b. 1821.
19 Orville Wright, pioneer aviator, b 1871.
22 Coracle Races, River Teifi, Cardiganshire.
    Irvine Marymas Fair, Ayrshire.
23 J. B. Yeats, artist, b. 1871.
24 Blessing the Mead, Guval, Cornwall.
    Sir Sam Hughes, Canadian soldier and politician, d. 1921.
25 Treaty between Charles V and Wolsey at Bruges, 1521.
26 Matthias Erzberger assassinated, 1921.
29 Eyam Plague Memorial Service, Derbyshire.
    Suleiman captured Belgrade, 1521.
30 Baron Rutherford, scientist, b. 1871.
31 Hermann von Helmholtz b. 1821.
    Thiers became President of France, 1871.

SEPTEMBER
2 Henry Austin Dobson, poet, d. 1921.
4 Lennox killed, 1571.
5 John, Earl of Mar, succeeded as Regent, 1571.
6 M. C. Norman, financier, b. 1871.
7 George Hirst, Yorkshire cricketer, b. 1871.
8 Harry Secombe b. 1921.
9 Ralph Hodgson, poet, b. 1871.
10 Treaty of Nystad, 1721.
    Champfleury, French author, b. 1821.
    Richard Bentley, publisher, d. 1871.
11 Louis Alexander Mountbatten d. 1921.
13 Bishop Frank Weston b. 1871.
14 Dante, Italian poet, d. 1321.
17 Bellarmine d. 1621.
    Tobias Smollett d. 1771.

Mount Cenis Tunnel opened, 1871.

18 Dr. Johnson birthday celebrations, Lichfield.
Matthew Prior, poet, d. 1721.

19 William Robertson, Scottish historian, b. 1721.

20 Mungo Park, explorer, b. 1771.
John Coleridge Patteson, bishop, assassinated in Santa Cruz, 1871.

21 St. Matthew. Christ's Hospital Bluecoat ceremony at Mansion House, London.
Thomas Doggett, actor and founder of rowing race, d. 1721.

22 Selim I, Sultan, d. 1521.
Charlotte Elliott, hymn writer, d. 1871.

23 John Jewel, divine, d. 1571.

24 Louis Joseph Papineau, Canadian politician, d. 1871.

25 Mary Herbert, Countess of Pembroke, d. 1621.
Henry Jackson, classical scholar, d. 1921.

27 Slave emancipation bill, Brazil, 1871.
Engelbert Humperdinck, German composer, d. 1921.

28 Admission of Sheriffs, Guildhall, London.
Pietro Badoglio, Italian officer, b. 1871.

OCTOBER

— Sir Edward Poynings, Lord Deputy of Ireland, d. 1521.

— Albert Richard Holcombe, newspaper proprietor, b. 1871.

2 Cordell Hull, American statesman, b. 1871.

3 Frederick-William, Duke of Brunswick, b. 1771.

4 John Rennie, engineer, d. 1821.

7 Battle of Lepanto, 1571.
Friedrich Kiel, German composer, b. 1821.
Field Marshal Sir John Fox Burgoyne d. 1871.

8 Fire of Chicago, 1871.

10 Wickham Steed, journalist, b. 1871.

11 Edward Colston, Bristol benefactor, d. 1721.
Sir George Williams, reformer, b. 1821.

12 Drobny, tennis player, b. 1921.

13 Rudolf Virchow, German surgeon, b. 1821.

14 Heligoland fortresses demolished, 1921.

16 Lion Sermon, Church of St. Katherine Kree, London.
Henry II landed in Ireland, 1171.
J. P. Sweelinck, composer, d. 1621.

18 Charles Babbage, mathematician, d. 1871.

21 Trafalgar Day ceremonies in Portsmouth, London, and elsewhere.

22 Peter the Great proclaimed Emperor of All Russia, 1721.
Sir Roderick Murchison, geologist, d. 1871.

23 Marshal Junot b. 1771.
J. B. Dunlop, inventor of pneumatic tyres, d. 1921.

24 Big mail robbery in America, 1921.
Sena Jurinac, Austrian singer, b. 1921.

26 Sir Robert Bruce, journalist, b. 1871.

27 Britain annexed diamond fields at Kimberley, 1871.

28 U.S.A. treaty with Liberia, 1921.

30 Dostoievsky, great Russian writer, b. 1821.
Paul Valéry, French poet, b. 1871.

NOVEMBER

— Sir Francis Bacon pardoned, 1621.

3 Francis Place, reformer, b. 1771.

4 James Montgomery, poet, b. 1771.
Sir Charles Lucas, Irish doctor and statesman, d. 1771.

5 Turning the Devil's Stone, Shebbear, Devon.
Oscar Montelius, Swedish archaeologist, d. 1921.

6 Colley Cibber, actor and playwright, b. 1671.
Hapsburgs exiled from Hungary, 1921.

8 Charles Francis Hall, explorer, d. 1871 (b. 1821).

9 Mark Akenside, poet, b. 1721.

10 Stanley met Livingstone at Ujiji, 1871.

11 American Unknown Soldier honoured, Arlington National Cemetery, Washington, 1921.

12 Henry II proclaimed King of Ireland, 1171.
Fairfax d. 1671.
Washington Disarmament Conference, 1921.

14 M. F. Bichat, French anatomist, b. 1771.

18 R. H. Benson, divine, b. 1871.

19 Edward Thring, great headmaster, b. 1821.

21 Baron Kindersley, banker, b. 1871.
Etienne Boutroux, French philosopher, d. 1921.

22 St. Cecilia Festival, Church of the Holy Sepulchre, High Holborn, London.
H. M. Hyndman, early socialist, d. 1921.

23 Alfonso X, "the Astronomer", b. 1221.

24 H. T. Buckle, historian, b. 1821.

26 Don Luigi Sturzo, Italian political thinker, b. 1871.

27 Hercules Brabazon, artist, b. 1821.

28 Panama declared itself independent of Spain, 1821.

30 Archbishop Frederick Temple b. 1821.

George Stephen, Baron Mount Stephen, financier, d. 1921.

DECEMBER
— Sir James Yorke Scarlett, soldier, d. 1871.
— Vladimir Korolenko, Russian writer, d. 1921.
— First performance of *Love for Three Oranges*, by Prokofiev, 1921.
1 Pope Leo X d. 1521.
4 Germany adopted the gold standard, 1871.
6 Henry VI b. 1421.
  Morgagni, Italian anatomist, d. 1771.
  Dora Greenwell, poet, b. 1821.
7 St. Columba b. 521.
9 Sir Arthur Pearson, newspaper proprietor, d. 1921.
  Baron Lindley, judge, d. 1921.
11 G. G. Bradley, English divine, b. 1821.
   Earl of Halsbury, Lord Chancellor, d. 1921.
12 Alexander Selkirk, prototype of "Robinson Crusoe", d. 1721.
   Flaubert, French novelist, b. 1821.
   Phoebe Hessel, Brighton character, d. 1821.
13 Sir Noel Paton, artist, b. 1821.
   Four-power Pacific Treaty signed at Washington, 1921.

14 George Hudson, the "Railway King", d. 1871.
15 *Alabama* arbitration commission met, Geneva, 1871.
19 English Commons claimed freedom, 1621.
20 Sir Guy Marshall, entomologist, b. 1871.
21 Laurence Irving, actor, b. 1871.
22 Edward Law, Earl of Ellenborough, d. 1871.
23 Sir Edmund Berry Godfrey b. 1621.
   Heneage Finch, statesman, b. 1621.
24 Tolling the Devil's Knell, Dewsbury, Yorkshire.
   First performance of Verdi's *Aïda*, 1871.
25 William Collins, poet, b. 1721.
   Dorothy Wordsworth b. 1771.
26 Long-sword dancing, Sheffield.
   Helvetius d. 1771.
27 Kepler b. 1571.
28 Baron Pethick-Lawrence, socialist statesman, b. 1871.
   Sir John Hare, actor, d. 1921.
29 Madame Pompadour b. 1721.
   Mackenzie King became Premier of Canada, 1921.
30 Joseph Farington, artist, d. 1821.
31 Swinging the fireballs, Stonehaven, Scotland.

1971

ANNIVERSARIES AND CENTENARIES

122 c. Hadrian's Wall begun.
222 Heliogabalus, Roman boy emperor, d.
422 c. St. Geneviève b.
672 c. First church at Ripon; eventually to become the Cathedral.
872 Harald Fairhair established King of Norway.
922 c. Liuprand, Italian historian, b. (d. 972).
1022 c. Harold II b.
1072 Hereward the Wake subdued by the Normans.
     Edgar, King of Scotland, b.
1122 Concordat of Worms.
     c. "Barbarossa," Frederick I, b.
     c. Queen Eleanor of Aquitaine, b.
1172 Henry the Lion made a pilgrimage to Palestine.
1222 Padua University founded.
     The Golden Bull, basis of Hungarian liberties.
1422 c. Willam Caxton b.
1472 Ingolstadt University founded.
1522 Lamoral, Count of Egmont, b.
     Joachim du Bellay b.
     Completion of Magellan circumnavigation.
     Complutensian Polyglot Bible.

Rhodes taken by the Turks: Knights of St. John moved to Malta.
1572 c. John Donne, poet, b.
     Society of Antiquaries, London, founded.
1622 Francisco Lobo, Portuguese author, d.
1672 Pondicherry and Coromandel coast occupied by the French.
     English Guinea and Royal African Companies combined, giving a monopoly of the slave trade.
     Lord Blakeney, defender of Minorca, b.
1722 Flora Macdonald b.
     Atterbury Plot.
1772 Royal Marriage Act.
     Beginning of enquiry into Clive's administration.
     Pierce Egan b.
     James Ballantyne, publisher, b.
1822 "Unfinished" Symphony: Schubert.
     Caledonian Canal finished.
     British Anti-slavery Society founded.
1872 University College, Aberystwyth, founded.
     National Union of Agricultural Workers founded.

Union for Social Politics begun in Germany.

Secret ballot introduced in Great Britain.

PUBLICATIONS (Books)

1522 Luther's Bible (–1534).

1572 Os Lusiados: Camoens.
La Françiade: Ronsard.

1622 History of the Reign of Henry VII: Bacon.
Polyolbion, part 2: Drayton.
Virgin Martyr: Massinger and Dekker.

1672 The Conquest of Granada: Dryden.
The Character of Holland: Marvell.
The Rehearsal Transposed: Marvell.
The Gentleman Dancing Master: Wycherley.
The Country Wife: Wycherley.

1722 Moll Flanders: Defoe.
Journal of the Plague Year: Defoe.
History of Colonel Jack: Defoe.

1772 Poems: Akenside.
Execution of Sir Charles Bawdin: Chatterton.
The Fashionable Lover: Cumberland.
Poems, chiefly translations from the Asiatic Languages: Jones.
Emilia Galotti: Lessing.

1822 Werner: Byron.
The Provost: Galt.
Sir Andrew Wylie: Galt.
Poems: Heine.
Welsh Melodies: Hemans.
Bracebridge Hall: Washington Irving.
Adam Blair: Lockhart.
Maid Marian: Peacock.
Fortunes of Nigel: Scott.
The Pirate: Scott.
Peveril of the Peak: Scott.
Hellas: Shelley.
Memorials of a Tour on the Continent: Wordsworth.
Ecclesiastical Sketches: Wordsworth.

1872 Fifine at the Fair: Browning.
Erewhon: Butler.
Tartarin de Tarascon: Daudet.
Life of Dickens: Forster.
Under the Greenwood Tree: Hardy.
Memorials of a Quiet Life: Hare.
Poet at the Breakfast Table: Holmes.
L'Année Terrible: Hugo.
The Martyrdom of Man: W. W. Reade.
Principles of Psychology (completed): Spencer.
How I Found Livingstone: Stanley.
The Old Faith and the New: D. F. Strauss.
Under the Microscope: Swinburne.
History of English Literature (English translation): Taine.

Gareth and Lynette: Tennyson.
Roughing It: Mark Twain.

1922 Shall We Join the Ladies? Barrie.
The Love Match: Bennett.
The Shepherd and Other Poems: Blunden.
Mary Stuart: Drinkwater.
The Waste Land: Eliot.
The Forsyte Saga (in one volume): Galsworthy.
Loyalties: Galsworthy.
Late Lyrics and Earlier: Hardy.
Little Plays of St. Francis: Housman.
Angels and Ministers: Housman.
Dethronements: Housman.
A Hind in Richmond Park: Hudson.
Mortal Coils: Aldous Huxley.
Outspoken Essays, vol. 2: Inge.
Ulysses: Joyce.
Aaron's Rod: Lawrence.
Babbitt: Sinclair Lewis.
On a Chinese Screen: Maugham.
Façade: Edith Sitwell.
More Trivia: L. P. Smith.
The Cathedral: Walpole.
Jacob's Room: Woolf.

PUBLICATIONS (Journals)

1722 Gloucester Journal.
Worcester Post or Western Journal.

1772 Derry Journal.
Devon and Exeter Gazette (now incorporated with the Western Times and Gazette).
Hampshire Chronicle.
Hertfordshire Mercury.
Shrewsbury Chronicle.
Yorkshire Gazette and Herald.

1822 Dysgedydd.
Fife Herald and Journal.
Law Journal.
Stockport Advertiser.
Sunday Times.

1872 Barmouth Advertiser.
Bognor Regis Observer.
Bondholders' Register.
Cambridgeshire Times.
Chatteris Advertiser.
Chichester and Southdown Observer.
Christian Irishman.
Electrical Review.
Guy's Hospital Gazette.
Irvine and Fullarton Times.
Kent and Sussex Courier.
Newmarket Journal.
Peterborough Standard.
Pudsey and Stanningley News.
Quarterly Journal of the Royal Meteorological Society.
Schoolmaster and Woman Teacher's Chronicle.
Shetland Times.
Soham Advertiser.
Sydenham, Forest Hill, and Penge Gazette.

West Lothian Courier.
Yorkshire Evening News.
1922 *Animals' Magazine.*
Annotated Tax Cases.
Ashton Guardian.
Bognor Regis Post.
Borough Record.
Cenhadwr.
Chichester and Southern Post.
C.M.S. Outlook.
Coates's Herd Book.
Colliery Year Book.
Dublin Opinion.
Earlestown and Newton News.
Felixstowe Times.
Fuel in Science and Practice.
Geophysical Journal.
Golborne, Culcheth, and Glazebury Guardian and Star.
Good Housekeeping.
Guernsey Football Press.
Haydock Guardian.
Industrial Welfare.
International Affairs.
Iris Oifigiuil.
Irish Nursing News.
Journal of the Association of Local Government Financial Officers.
Labour Press Service.
Littlehampton Post.
Louth Standard.
Magistrate.
Music Teacher.
Norbury and Thornton Heath News.
Portadown Times.
Review of Applied Mycology.
Rover.
Royal Dental Hospital Magazine.
Scottish Decorators' Quarterly Review.
Scottish Drapery Journal.
Scottish Temperance Reformer (now *Scotia Quarterly*).
Scottish Tobacco News.
Skegness Standard.
Southend Times.
Style for Men.
Sutton Times and Cheam Mail.
Taxes.
Toc H Journal.
Tutors' Bulletin.
Wayfarer.
Weekly Bulletin (Glasgow).
Weekly Sporting Review.
West African Review.
Wizard.
Year's Photography.

JANUARY
— Molière, great French playwright, b. 1622.
2 Stop of Exchequer, 1672.
4 First performance of Racine's *Bajazet*, 1672.
  Conference of Cannes; German war payments postponed, 1922.

5 Sir Ernest Shackleton d. 1922.
6 Epiphany Service, Chapel Royal, St. James's Palace, London.
  Heinrich Schliemann, archaeologist, b. 1822.
8 Hussites defeated Sigmund at Deutschbrod, 1422.
  Samuel Bough, artist, b. 1822.
  Alfredo Piatti, musician, b. 1822.
9 Henry Wager Halleck, American general, d. 1872.
10 Building of Empire Exhibition, Wembley, inaugurated, 1922.
11 Burning the Clavie, Burghead, Scotland.
12 Poincaré became Premier of France, 1922.
15 Sir Walter de Manny, founder of the Charterhouse, d. 1372.
  Bishop John Cosin d. 1672.
  Formation of HM Coastguard Service, 1822.
16 Henri Eugène, Duc d'Aumale, son of Louis Philippe, b. 1822.
  Edward Gordon Craig, theatrical designer, b. 1872.
21 Grillparzer, Austrian playwright, d. 1872.
  Paul Schofield, actor, b. 1922.
22 First mail steamer, Dover–Calais, 1822.
  Pope Benedict XV d. 1922.
  Sir W. H. M. Christie, astronomer royal, d. 1922.
  Viscount Bryce, statesman, d. 1922.
23 William Baffin, explorer, killed, 1622.
  Boulainvilliers, French political writer, d. 1722.
24 Krzhizhanovski, Russian engineer, b. 1872.
25 Burns Night celebrations.
26 Alexander Carlyle, Scottish divine, b. 1722.
27 Declaration of Greek Independence, 1822.
  Learned Hand, U.S. judge, b. 1872.
28 Dean Kipling of Peterborough d. 1822.
  Alexander Mackenzie, Prime Minister of Canada, b. 1822.
29 Sir William Rothenstein, artist, b. 1872.
30 General Chesney, explorer, d. 1872.

FEBRUARY
1 Viscountess Milner b. 1872.
2 Title of *Fidei Defensor* given to Henry VIII, 1522.
  Gold Coast ceded to Great Britain from Holland, 1872.
3 J. E. D. Esquirol, French physician, b. 1772.
  Christian de Wet d. 1922.
5 Ali Pasha executed, 1822.
  Sir William Nicholson, artist, b. 1872.

6 End of Anglo-Japanese alliance, 1922. Independence of China secured, 1922. Washington Naval agreement, 1922. Pius XI became Pope, 1922.
8 Lord Mayo, Viceroy of India, assassinated in Andaman Islands, 1872.
9 Jim Laker, cricketer, b. 1922.
10 Leofric, first bishop of Exeter, d. 1072.
11 Habeas Corpus suspended, 1822.
14 Blessing the salmon nets, River Tweed, Norham, Northumberland.
15 Court of International Justice, The Hague, opened, 1922.
16 Sir Francis Galton, anthropologist, b. 1822.
Viceroy held a durbar to honour the Prince of Wales, 1922.
20 "Walking Stewart" d. 1822.
22 Lord Northbrook appointed Viceroy of India, 1872.
Lady Feodora Gleichen, sculptor, d. 1922.
24 John Burgoyne, soldier, b. 1722.
Thomas Coutts, banker, d. 1822.
"Geddes Axe" Report, 1922.
Viscount Harcourt, politician, d. 1922.
26 Augustin Calmet, French monk and theologian, b. 1672.
28 Boston Assembly threatened secession, 1772.
1st Viscount Hailsham b. 1872.
Princess Mary married Viscount Lascelles, 1922.

MARCH
— Cadwaladr, Welsh prince, d. 1172.
— William Lily, grammarian, d. 1522.
— Anglo-French War on the Dutch, 1672.
— Sir C. W. Dilke's bill for the reform of the Civil List, 1872.
1 "Whuppity Scoorie," Lanark,Scotland.
2 St. Chad (d. 672).
7 Lionel George Curtis, publicist, b. 1872.
9 Edward Daniel Clarke, traveller, d. 1822.
10 J. L. Clark, engineer and inventor, b. 1822.
Mazzini d. 1872.
11 First performance of Molière's "Les Femmes Savantes," 1672.
John Toland, deist, d. 1722.
Mahatma Gandhi arrested, 1922.
12 Sir Richard Steele b. 1672.
Jack Kerouac, American author, b. 1922.
13 First air crossing of the South Atlantic, 1922.
15 Declaration of Indulgence to Nonconformists, 1672.
Independence of Egypt recognised, 1922.
16 Vernon Hartshorn, miners' leader, b. 1872.

N*

Baron Wedgwood, politician, b. 1872.
19 Diaghilev b. 1872.
20 W. C. Wentworth, "the Australian patriot," d. 1872.
21 Loyola vowed to devote his life to the Church, 1522.
Waterloo Station opened by Queen Mary, 1922.
22 Thomas, Earl of Lancaster, beheaded, 1322.
Rosa Bonheur, French painter, b. 1822.
24 Four-power Pacific Treaty ratified by U.S. Senate, 1922.
25 Tichborne Dole, Alresford, Hants.
27 Alexander Boswell d. 1822.
28 Oranges and Lemons Service, St. Clement Danes, London.
29 Swedenborg d. 1772.
Sir William Fettes Douglas, artist, b. 1822.
30 Arthur Griffith, Irish politician, b. 1872 (d. 12th August, 1922).

APRIL
— Don Carlos made King of Spain as Charles VII, 1872.
1 Archibald Armstrong, court jester, buried, 1672.
Hobart Pasha b. 1822.
J. F. D. Maurice, divine, d. 1872.
Emperor Charles d. 1922.
William Manchester, American author, b. 1922.
2 Richard, Earl of Cornwall and King of the Romans, d. 1272.
S. F. B. Morse, inventor of the Morse Code, d. 1872.
3 Hugh Bourne, founder of the Primitive Methodists, b. 1772.
Olivia Serres, "Princess Olive," pretender, b. 1772.
5 Paolo Ferrari, Italian playwright, b. 1822.
Laveleye, Belgian economist, b. 1822.
7 François Fourier, French writer, b. 1772.
9 Tom Shaw, labour leader, b. 1872.
Léon Blum, French statesman, b. 1872.
Sir Patrick Marten, physician, d. 1922.
10 Conference of Genoa, 1922.
13 Warren Hastings became Governor of Bengal, 1772.
Lady Georgiana Bloomfield, writer, b. 1822.
Sir Ross Macpherson Smith killed at Brooklands, 1922.
15 Geoffrey Saint-Hilaire, zoologist, b. 1772.
16 Treaty of Rapallo between Russia and Germany, 1922.
17 French Huguenots under Royal Commissioners, 1622.

17 Henry Vaughan, "the Silurist", poet,
    b. 1622.
19 Charles Spencer, Earl of Sunderland,
    d. 1722.
    David Ricardo, economist, b. 1772.
22 Joseph Warton baptised, 1722.

23 St. George's Court, Lichfield.
24 Great eruption of Vesuvius, 1872.
25 Leone Battista Alberti d. 1472.
    C. B. Fry b. 1872.
27 General Grant b. 1822.

TYPEWRITING SERVICES

A NUMBER of the agencies listed below do not state their terms because these vary for the many different varieties of work which they undertake. They are willing to quote their terms for work submitted to them or to give a provisional indication of their rates on receiving a description of MS to be submitted.

It is wise to enclose a stamped, addressed envelope when making a preliminary enquiry.

Further typewriting offices or agencies may be added to this list in subsequent editions if they apply to the publishers with a note of their charges.

London

MISS JOAN GRANT, 17 Park Gate, Park Road, London, N.2. *T.* 01-883 9770. 42½p. per 1000 words, 2½p. per carbon copy.

FREELANCE SERVICES, 20 Manor Mansions, Belsize Grove, NW3 4NB. *T.* 01-722 9896. Manuscripts, Scripts and duplicating from 62½p. per hour.

MISS JUNE TAYLOR, The Green Door, 12 Finchley Road, London, N.W.8. *T.* 01-586 1350; 01-624 8239.

BETTY NUNN (OFFICE SERVICES), 14 Grecian Cresent, Upper Norwood, S.E.19. *T.* 01-670 0922. 30p. per 1000 words, 1½p. per carbon copy. 20p. per copy for binding.

MISS G. E. L. CONSENTIUS, 58 St. George's Square, S.W.1. *T.* 01-828 2305. Charges according to subject-matter. Translations.

PETER COXSON TYPING SERVICE, 56 Draycott Place, London, S.W.3. *T.* 01-584 5566. From 30p. per 1000 words, plus 2½p. per carbon copy. For theses from 42½p. per 1000 words, plus 2½p. per carbon copy. Minimum charge £1·05.

MISS DORIS E. GREGORY, 42 Triangle Place, London, S.W.4. 20p. per 1000 words, including one carbon copy. Additional carbon copies 2½p per 1000 words.

PETER JOHN, 67 Sedlescombe Road, London, S.W.6. *T.* 01-385 6093. Scripts from 20p. per 1000 words. Tape-recording transcription 47½p. per hour; speeds 1, 3 and 7, single, double-track and four-track, and Stenorette. Postage extra at cost.

MRS. M. CHAN, 13 Badminton Road, S.W.12. *T.* 01-673 2657. 50p. per 1000 words, plus one carbon copy; additional carbons 2½p. per 1000 words.

SHIRLEY DEWIS TYPING SERVICE, 4 Florian Road, Putney, S.W.15. *T.* 01-870 3223. 27½p. per 1000 words inclusive, no extras.

MRS. M. CROOKS, 40 Hatch Road, Norbury S.W.16. 35p. per 1000 words, plus 1½p. per carbon copy.

MAUREEN MARRS SECRETARIAL SERVICES, 89–90 Turnmill Street, London, EC1M 5QP. *T.* 01-253 8318. 40p. per 1000 words of MS, carbon copies 1p. per page. Plays 10p. per quarto page, 12½p. per foolscap page, carbon copies 1p. per page.

TYPO SERVICE, 45b Blandford Street, London, W1H 3AF. *T.* 01–486 4002. 42p. per 1000 words and one carbon copy, additional carbon copies 1½p. extra.

MRS SHEILA MARTLAND, 8 Airedale Avenue, Chiswick, W.4. *T.* 01–995 3540. 30p. per 1000 words, plus 1 carbon; extra carbon copies 2½p. each.

MRS. JOLLY, 5 Newport House, Gt. Newport Street, WC2H 7JG. *T.* 01–836 5588.

STELLA FISHER SECRETARIAT LTD., 430 Strand, London, WC2R 0QN. *T.* 01–836 6644.

MRS. AUDREY TESTER, 72 Berrylands, Surbiton, Surrey. *T.* 01–399 6990. Work collected in London.

Bedfordshire
MRS. E. M. PICKERING, 121 Highbury Grove, Clapham. 20p. per 1000 words including 1 carbon. Extra carbons 1p. each. Postage extra.

Berkshire
MRS. J. B. SMITH, 28 Woodford Close, Caversham, Reading, RG4 7HN. *T.* Reading 76490. 25p. per 1000 words.

MRS. IDA BAKER, TYPING AND DUPLICATING SERVICE, 56 Perrycroft, Windsor. *T.* Windsor 60154.

TYPEWRITING SERVICES, 64 Frances Road, Windsor. *T.* 62743. 25p. per 1000 words, plus 2½p. per carbon copy.

Buckinghamshire
AUTO SECRETARIES, Amberley, Hollow Way Lane, Amersham. *T.* 4768, and 22 Treachers Close, Chesham. *T.* 6106.

HELEN A. BULLOCK, 9 The Braid, Chesham. *T.* 3557. 12½p. per 1000 words, plus 1p. per carbon per 1000 words. Scripts, verse, technical by arrangement.

MRS. I. TURNBULL, Secretarial service, 39 Northern Woods, Flackwell Heath, High Wycombe. *T.* Bourne End 24216.

FREELANCE SECRETARIES, 4 Westhorpe Road, Marlow. *T.* Marlow 4901. Manuscript copying: from 25p. per 1000 words+4p. per carbon. Typescript copying 22½p. per 1000 words+2½p. per carbon. Quarto stencils: 12½p. to 15p. each. Foolscap stencils: 15p. to 17½p. each.

Cambridgeshire
MRS. C. A. CLARK, 3 Lansdowne Close, Ely, 20p. per 1000 words, plus 1p. per carbon per 1000 words.

MISS S. MANN, 27 County Road, March. *T.* March 2876. 25p. per 1000 words, carbon copies 2½p. extra.

MRS. A. TINKLEY, Thatch End, Mill Green, Shudy Camps, Cambridge. *T.* Ashdon (Essex) 277. 30p. per hour or by arrangement, up to 3 carbon copies included. Extra carbon copies 1p. each.

Cheshire
MRS. GWEN M. BUDDEN, Aigh Vie, Daleford Lane, Whitegate, nr. Northwich. *T.* Sandiway 2030.

MRS. MAVIS E. JOHNSTONE, 24 Glen Park Road, Wallasey L45 5JG. *T.* 051–639 2500. 20p. per 1000 words.

MISS LAURA MOSELEY, Iconhurst, 93 Penkett Road, Wallasey. 15p. per 1000 words including carbon, postage extra.

MRS. VERONICA O'NEILL, F.S.C.T., 61 Townfield Lane, Bebington, Wirral, L63 7NL. 17½p. per 1000 words including one carbon copy.

Cornwall
D. J. COCKING, 14 Trelawney Road, St. Agnes. *T*. 625. From 15p. per 1000 words plus 2½p. per carbon copy. Quotations for stencils, plays, verse, etc.

Derbyshire
MRS YVONNE J. HAGGETT, B.A., 103 Station New Road, Tupton, Chesterfield. *T*. Clay Cross 862294. From 25p. per 1000 words, including 1 carbon copy, stationery, postage; extra carbons 1p. per 1000 words. Plays from 5p. per page. Translations from French; typing from French and German.

MRS. W. LOCKER, 47 Brackens Lane, Alvaston, Derby. *T*. 72017. 37½p. per 1000 words including up to 3 carbon copies.

MRS. A. M. HAWKINS, 34 Church Street, Swanwick, Derby, DE5 4AN. *T*. Leabrooks 2572. Terms negotiable.

Devonshire
W. CORNECK, 3 Higher Penn, Brixham. 12½p. per 1000 words.

MRS. B. E. STEWART, 123 North Boundary Road, Brixham TQ5 8LA. *T*. Brixham 3171. 25p. per 1000 words plus 2½p. per carbon copy.

MRS. S. CAIRNS, The Acorns, 40 Okefield Road, Crediton, EX17 2DL. 20p. per 1000 words.

MRS. M. MAXWELL, 10 Hill Drive, Exmouth. *T*. Exmouth 3226. Manuscripts, theses, terms by arrangement.

MRS. A. HEBBARD, 45 Outland Road, Milehouse, Plymouth. Quotations on request.

Dorset
MRS. ROSAMOND M. R. DUFFERIN, 27 North Street, Beaminster. *T*. Beaminster 521. 17½p. per 1000 words, plus paper and carbons. Any kind of audio. Shorthand, if within driving distance.

MRS. M. J. CANNELL, 19 Fernlea Avenue, Ferndown, BH22 8HG. *T*. Ferndown 3261. 22½p. per 1000 words, including carbon copy.

Durham
MRS. J. MCARTHUR, 26 Kingsmere, Chester-le-Street. *T*. Chester-le-Street 3622. 25p. per 1000 words.

MRS. J. C. HOWELL, 16 Weardale Avenue, South Bents, Sunderland, SR6 8AS. *T* Whitburn 2436. 17½p. per 1000 words, plus 1p. per carbon copy.

Essex
MRS. D. GRAY, 2 The Chase, Woodman Road, Brentwood. 12½p. per 1000 words, plus 1½p. per 1000 words carbon copy.

CHELMER TYPING, 35 Butterfield Road, Boreham, Chelmsford, CM3 3BS. *T*. Boreham 509. All classes of work undertaken at reasonable charges.

MRS IRENE WAY, 122 Bodmin Road, Chelmsford, CM1 5LL. *T*. Chelmsford 50770. 20p. per 1000 words including 1 carbon copy. Postage extra.

MRS. M. E. RANSOME, The Paddock, Spring Road, St. Osyth, Clacton-on-Sea. *T*. St. Osyth 775. MS, Plays, tapes, stencils etc. (Charges vary according to technicality of work).

MRS. E. DEEKS, Field Bungalow, Stoke Road, Leavenheath, Colchester. *T.* Boxford 553. 20p. per 1000 plus 1p. per carbon copy.

MRS. J. P. KEEVIL, 95 Monkwick Avenue, Colchester. 2½p. per 100 words. *T.* Colchester 82040.

MRS. B. SPIERS, Somerhayes, Fountain Lane, Hockley, SS5 4ST. *T.* Hockley 3217. From 16p. per 1000 words including one carbon copy; stationery and postage extra.

SOUTH OFFICE SERVICES, Osborne Cottage, Little Chesterford, Saffron Walden. *T.* Great Chesterford 462. 12½p. per 1000 plus 1p. per carbon. Also duplicating, tape transcripts and shorthand notes.

MRS. M. PUTNAM, 4 Manor Road, Wivenhoe, nr. Colchester. *T.* Wivenhoe 3450. Rate to be negotiated.

Gloucestershire

MRS. D. M. NEWTON, 19 Ridgeway Road, Long Ashton, Bristol BS18 9EY. *T.* Long Ashton 3216. 20p. per 1000 words, plus 2½p. per 1000 words carbon copy.

MRS. DOREEN SAMMELS, 16 Battledown Close, Cheltenham. *T.* Cheltenham 53614. 25p. per 1000 words, plus 1p. per carbon copy.

Hampshire

MISS I. H. ANDRADE, 4 Southwood Avenue, West Southbourne, Bournemouth BH6 3QA. *T.* Bournemouth 46135. 22½p. per 1000 words. 2½p. per 1000 words per cardon copy. Postage extra.

MRS. M. HAITE, 18, Gudge Heath Lane, Fareham. *T.* Fareham 82996. 20p. per 1000 words plus 1p. per carbon copy. Postage extra.

MRS. J. ALEXANDER, 90 Everton Road, Hordle, Lymington. *T.* New Milton 80407. Photo-copying.

MRS. DOROTHY ARNOT, 17 Ashdown Road, Fawlay, Southampton SO4 1EF. *T.* Fawley 474. 12½p. per 1000 words, plus 1p. per 1000 words carbon copy. Quotations for plays and verse.

MRS. D. POW, A.F.T.COM., 27 Broadlands Avenue, Waterlooville. Books, stories, plays, etc., 25p. per 1000 words.

MRS. EVELYN THORNTON, 6 Coastguard Cottages, Totland Bay, Isle of Wight. 22½p. per 1000 words plus 1p. per carbon copy.

MRS. B. WESTMORE, 9 Meadowside, Pan Estate, Newport, Isle of Wight. 20p. per 1000 words.

Hertfordshire

MRS. P. BRODY, 18 Ashurst Road, Cockfosters. *T.* 01–440 1931. From 22½p. per 1000 words; 2½p. per 1000 words per carbon copy.

RICKMANSWORTH TYPING SERVICE, 74 High Street, Rickmansworth. *T.* Rickmansworth 76991.

SWIFT TYPING SERVICE, 31 Orchard Drive, Park Street, St. Albans. *T.* Park Street 2181. 23½p. per 1000 words, including 1 carbon copy. Extra carbon copies: 1p. each.

MRS. S. GORDON, 14 Easington Road, Dane End, Ware. *T.* Dane End 403. Charges by arrangement.

Kent

JEAN PALMER (The Swift Typing & Duplicating Service), 53 Queens Road, Broadstairs. *T.* Thanet 63652. 25p. per 1000 words including one carbon copy. Duplicating charges on request.

MRS. CHRISTINE SEAGER, 1 Merton Cottages, Stuppington Lane, Canterbury. 20p. per 1000 words, plus 1p. per carbon copy.

Lancashire

H. Cox, 9 Lowerhouse Lane, Rosegrove, Burnley. Reasonable rates, quotations on request.

Heaton Typing Services, 647 Stockport Road, Longsight, Manchester, M12 40A. T. 061-224 0269. 9s. per 1000 words inclusive of 1 carbon.

Mrs. C. I. Holbrook, m.f.t. comm., and Mrs. Harrison, m.f.t. comm., 22 Peacock Grove, Hyde Road, Manchester 18 and 15 Ballard Street, off Hengist Street, Hyde Road, Manchester 18. 16p. per 1000 words, inc. 1 copy; paper, postage, packing extra.

Mrs. K. Taylor, 29 Rossall Road, Rochdale. T. Rochdale 47185. 42½p. per hour including carbon copy. Estimates given for all types of work.

Leicestershire

Mrs. S. M. Humby, 47 Romway Road, Evington, Leicester, LE5 5SD. T. 737844. 27½p. including 1 carbon copy. Extra copies 1p. each.

Mrs. M. Austin, 20 Appleton Avenue, Stocking Farm, Leicester, LE4 2GA. 25p. per 1000 words including one carbon copy. Extra carbons 2½p. each per 1000 words. Postage extra.

Mrs. Audrey Curtis, 115 Fosse Way, Syston, Leicester. T. Syston 5215. 25p. per 1000 words, including 1 carbon copy. Extra copies 1p. per sheet. Paper, postage extra. Quotations for plays, verses, theses on application.

Lincolnshire

Jones Blakey, 14 Monteith Crescent, Boston. T. Boston 3437.

Miss Paula Hempsall, Dunsby Dale, 120 Pinchbeck Road, Spalding, PE11 1QN. T. Spalding 3162. 12½p. per 1000 words, 1p. each 1000 word carbon copy.

Middlesex

Mrs. R. Barnett, 22 Monastery Gardens, Enfield. T. 01-363 8677. 30p. per 1000 words, including carbon copies.

Mrs. Doreen Aumonier, 54 Albury Drive, Pinner. T. 01-866 3418. 25p. per 1000 words, plus 1p. per carbon copy.

Mrs. Margaret King, 8 Evelyn Avenue, Ruislip, HA4 8AS. T. Ruislip 35610. 25p. per 1000 words plus 1p. per carbon copy.

Norfolk

Miss M. M. Shaw, Lawn Farm, Fressingfield, Nr. Diss. T. Fressingfield 267. 17½p. per 1000 words plus 1½p. per 1000 words carbon copy. Also translation/ typing from French and German.

Mrs. Temple, 10 Valleyside Road, Norwich, NOR 97R. T. Norwich 33137. 25p. per 1000 words.

Mrs. T. M. Warden, 10 Barford Road, Marlingford, Norwich, NOR 40X. 25p. per 1000 words plus 2p. per 1000 words carbon copy. Tape/Cassette transcription. Binding 10p. per copy.

Northamptonshire

Mrs. F. Meadowcroft, 51 Mays Way, Pottersbury, Towcester, NN12 7PP. T. Moor End 242. 37½p. per 1000 words plus 1 carbon copy.

Nottinghamshire

Mrs. Phyllis Breddy, 79 Ordall Road, Retford. *T.* Retford 3863. Authors MSS. 20p. per 1000 words, 1 carbon included. Quotations for plays, novels, etc. Postage extra.

Mrs. R. J. Cumberland, 80 Elms Park, Ruddington, Nottingham, NG11 6NQ. *T.* 211010. From 22½p. per 1000 words plus 1p. per 1000 words carbon copy. Postage extra.

Mrs. J. A. Mitson, 82 Walcote Drive, West Bridgford, Nottingham, NG2 7GS. *T.* 233804. From 37½p. per 1000 words.

Rutland

Mrs. M. Bonny, 18 Chestnut Road, Oakham. 15p. per 1000 words, plus 1p. per carbon copy.

Somerset

Miss D. J. Tucker, 51 Warminster Road, Bath. *T.* Bath 60787.

Miss J. Watson, 5 Dene Close, Keynsham, Bristol, BS18 1RL. From 25p. per 1000 words, plus 3p. per carbon copy. Also duplicating.

Staffordshire

Mrs. Gillian Baillie, 36 Hartlands Road, Eccleshall. 22½p. per 1000 words, 1p. per carbon copy. 1p. per sheet.

Mrs. Eileen Beg, 44 Avon Crescent, Heath End, Pelsall, Nr. Walsall. 19p. per 1000 words. Carbon copies 1p. each. Plays 5p. per page. Special rate for express service. Postage extra.

Miss Harris, 17 The Crescent, Tettenhall Wood, Wolverhampton, WV6 8LA. 9p. per quarto page, including 1 carbon copy. Literary and Scientific.

Suffolk

Mrs. Collett, 7 Rembrandt Way, Bury St. Edmunds. 17½p. per 1000 words, 1p. per carbon copy.

Mrs. Irene Hone, 65 Normanston Drive, Lowestoft, 0502. *T.* 62819, 5082 after 6 p.m. 50p. per A4 page, 62½p. per hour. First carbon free, 2½p. per carbon thereafter.

Surrey

Mrs. Jean Turner, 109 Tollers Lane, Old Coulsdon, CR3 1BG. *T.* Downland 53341. From 30p. per 1000 words, including 1 carbon copy.

Ellenor Handley, 42 Lime Tree Grove, Shirley Croydon, CR0 8AW. *T.* 01-777 3781. From 50p. per 1000 words.

Miss A. B. Reid, 22 Adecroft Way, East Molesey. *T.* 01-979 4567. Manuscript copying from 20p. per 1000 words, carbon copy ½p. per sheet. Plays 30p. per 1000 words. Tape transcripts. Translation/Typing from French language. Postage extra.

Miss Dallas Fry, 20 Gloucester Road, Kingston Hill. Tapes.

Miss F. Sandell, 83 Fleetwood Road, Kingston-upon-Thames. 37½p. per 1000 words, plus 1½p. per carbon copy.

Mrs. M. Priestley, Rose Bank, Town Hill, Lingfield. *T.* Lingfield 3579. 25p. per 1000 words, plus 7½p. for complete carbon copy.

Miss B. R. Haines, 5 Sussex Lodge, 25 Hook Road, Surbiton. *T.* 01–399 3278.

Mrs. Q. Smith, 2 Kingslee Court, Worcester Road, Sutton. *T.* 01–643 3259. 25p. per 1000 words, plus 1p. per 1000 words carbon copy. For theses from 27½p. per 1000 words, plus 1p. per carbon copy.

Mrs. J. F. Jackson, Rose Cottage, Barnett Lane, Wonersh, Nr. Guildford. *T.* Bramley 2017. 25p. per 1000 words; 40p. per hour, 1p. per carbon copy.

Sussex
Mrs. S. Webb, 19 Hazel Close, Langley Green, Crawley. 20p. per 1000 words including carbon copy. Collection within 25 mile radius Crawley (extra).

Miss E. Stevens, Ley Spring, Ansty, Haywards Heath. *T.* Haywards Heath 4003. 22p. per 1000 words plus 1½p. per 1000 for carbon copies.

Bell Typewriting Bureau, 25 West Parade, Worthing. *T.* 39381. 24 hour tapes. Electronic (illustrated) books, plays, theses, duplicating, indexing, editing.

Mary Courtney, 110 Balcombe Avenue, Worthing. 14p. per 1000 words, plus 1p. per 1000 words carbon copy.

Multijob Enterprises, 144 Lyndhurst Road, Worthing. *T.* 34788. From 17½p. per 1000 words, including one carbon copy; postage extra.

Warwickshire
Mrs. C. Spindler, 275 Broad Lane, Kings Heath, Birmingham, B14 5AF. 5p. per quarto page, including carbon copy.

Mrs. A. Goodchild, 223 Church Road, Sheldon, Birmingham, B26 3YG. 25p. per 1000 words, plus 2½p. per 1000 words for each carbon copy.

Mrs. J. Blezard, 51 Faraday Road, Rugby. 30p. per 1000 words, inclusive of one carbon copy.

Mrs. S. Gaskell, 24 Melford Hall Road, Solihull. *T.* 021–705 2509. From 25p. per 1000 words.

Mrs. Olive Williams, 89 Rawlings Road, Smethwick, Warley, nr. Birmingham. 42½p. per hour including carbon copies but excluding postage.

Wiltshire
Mrs. M. J. Newell, 5 Longcroft Crescent, Devizes. 20p. per 1000 words. Copies and postage extra.

Worcestershire
Gertrude Young, Chantreys, Danes Green, Claines, nr. Worcester, WR3 7RU. *T.* Worcester 51521.

Mary Carter, 33 St. Peter's Close, Durcott Estate, Evesham. 25p. per 1000 words, plus 1 carbon copy. Extra copies 1½p. each. Theses 27½p. per 1000 words.

Mrs. Carole Sanders, 139 Coningsby Drive, Ferndale Estate, Kidderminster. *T.* 62409. 20p. per 1000 words, plus 1p. per 1000 words per carbon copy.

Yorkshire
Mrs. Audrey Barr, 216 Moore Avenue, Bradford, 7. 35p. per 1000 words plus 1p. per carbon copy. Postage extra. Plays 7½p. per page.

MRS. V. HEALD, Flat 3 Colston House, Moor Lane, Burley-in-Wharfedale, Nr. Ilkley. *T.* Burley-in-Wharfedale 2411. 35p. per 1000 words including 1 carbon copy; extra carbon copies 2½p.

MRS. I. MORGAN, 165 Radcliffe Road, Golcar, Huddersfield, HD7 4EZ. *T.* Slaithwaite 2924. 19p. per 1000 words, plus 1½p. per 1000 words per carbon copy.

V. BROOMHEAD, 66 Wolsey Croft, Sherburn-in-Elmet, Leeds. *T.* South Milford 3213. 22½p. per 1000 words; carbon copies 1p. per 1000 words. Plays 6p. per page.

MRS. J. M. SMITH, 14 Mill Rise, Swanland, North Ferriby, Yorks. HU14 3PW. *T.* Hull 633185. 20p. per 1000 words.

MRS. D. MARCZINKE, Sunnyside, Burras Avenue, Otley. 15p. per 1000 words, plus 1p. per carbon copy.

VICTORIA HEALD LTD., (Typing and Duplicating), Barclays Bank Chambers, Manor Square, Otley. *T.* Otley 3567. 41p. per 1000 words, including 1 original, 1 copy. Extra copies 1½p. each.

SKIPTON OFFICE SERVICES (Duplicating and Typing), Central Chambers, 2 Otley Street, Skipton, BD23 1DZ. *T.* Skipton 3153. 40p. per 1000 words including 1 original and 1 copy. Extra copies 1½p. each. Tape transcription.

Wales
Caernarvonshire
MRS. N. M. BANFIELD, 77 Bryniau Road, Llandudno. From 13½p. per 1000 words, plus 1½p. per 1000 words carbon copy.

S. MASTERSON, 1 Boston Terrace, Port Dinorwic. *T.* 457. 2½p. per page, plus 1½p. per page carbon copy.

Denbighshire
ARTHUR GREGSON, Westhome, Borthyn, Ruthin. 14p. per 1000 words including one carbon copy.

Glamorganshire
DAVIES & BIDDLE, 76 Mackintosh Place, Cardiff. *T.* 30189. Typing of all descriptions, including Welsh MSS.

MISS M. L. FRY, Horton, Swansea SA3 1LQ. 25p. per 1000 words, plus 1p. per carbon copy.

Monmouthshire
MISS IVY SANDERS, 12 Fields Park Road, Newport. *T.* 64783. 22½p. per 1000 words; 1p. per page carbon copies. Plays, 10p. per foolscap page, 1p. per page carbon copies.

Scotland
MRS. JEANNE MARSHALL, 50 Grange Road, Edinburgh, EH9 1TU. 32½p. per 1000 words, each set of carbon copies 10p. extra.

MRS. M. M. BROWN, Top Flat, 18 Montague Street, Glasgow, C.4. *T.* 041-339 4118.

MISS JOAN EDWARDS, 107 Anderson Street, Kelloholm, Dumfriesshire. 20p. per 1000 words, plus 1 carbon copy.

PREPARATION AND SUBMISSION
OF MANUSCRIPTS

Neatness of a manuscript is of the utmost importance: the first impression made on an editor or publisher's reader is vital. MSS. should be *typed* on one side of the paper only, and not handwritten. Do not let the typewriter become dirty: a little petrol and an old toothbrush cleans characters quickly and effectively.

Paper should be neither flimsy nor too thick, and quarto in size (about 10 by 8 inches), or the new standard size A4 ($11\frac{7}{10} \times 8\frac{3}{10}$ inches).

Black typewriter ribbon is preferable, except for plays when *red* and *black* should be used:

Red for names of characters, stage directions, etc. *Black* for dialogue. If a black-red ribbon is not available, characters' names should be in capitals and stage directions underlined in red.

Double-spacing is always preferable. Each page should have the same number of lines and width of line.

Good margins are essential, particularly on the left-hand side. If left-hand margins are not adequate, it is impossible to read the MS. when it is in a file or holder.

Corrections should be kept to a minimum on the final typed copy.

Pages should be *numbered* throughout.

Fastening should be firm. Pages should be clipped together: in a long MS. each section or chapter should be secured separately.

Tired-looking MSS. should not be sent. This can be cured by retyping the first and last sheets.

Protection of MSS.—This can be achieved by a stiffer and slightly larger sheet at back and front.

On the first page give the title of the MS., and at the top or bottom the name and address of the author, and the approximate number of words. Repeat name and address elsewhere, e.g. at end, in case the front page becomes detached.

Submission of MSS.—(1) Stamps to cover return of MSS. should *always* be sent. Many authors always send MSS. by recorded delivery or registered post. It is not necessary to do so for short MSS., but it is worthwhile for MSS. of book length. If an exact copy is kept of the submission, so that the loss of one copy is not a disaster, it is cheaper to send MSS. by second class rate, in a sealed envelope with a stamped addressed gummed label enclosed for return of the manuscript. Few packets and parcels if well packed are lost in the post, by whichever rate they are sent.

(2) Keep a copy of MS. in case of loss.

(3) Maintain a record of all MSS. sent out. (A suggested layout for a register is given below.)

Date	Name of MS.	Where sent	Accepted or rejected	Date	Payment made

Estimating.—To estimate the length of a MS., calculate the average number of words on a page—take the average of say eight pages; multiply the average by the total number of pages in the MS., making allowance for half-pages, etc., at the ends of chapters.

Indexing.—There is no quick method. It is advisable to leave the preparation of an index until the book is in page form. The words to be indexed can be under-lined and then typed out with the page references against them. The typed pages of entries can then be cut up and arranged in alphabetical order; and the whole re-typed. An alternative method is to write each word and page reference on a separate slip of paper, and from these slips to type out a final copy.

Approach to Publisher, Agent or Editor.—(1) *Editor.* A preliminary letter is *not* necessary before submitting a short article to an editor.

(2) *Publisher.* In submitting a long MS. to a publisher it is worth while telling him in advance what the book is about and finding out if he is interested. DO NOT SEEK A PERSONAL INTERVIEW. A good MS. will make its own way.

(3) *Agent.* Preliminaries should be arranged with literary agents before forward-ing MS.

After despatch of MSS.—There may be a considerable interval before a MS. is returned by the publisher whether accepted finally or not, but most publishers acknowledge receipt of MSS. There is no need to remind him within a reasonable period (say 2 or 3 months), as he may wish to get more than one person's opinion before coming to a decision. In the case of a topical book it would be necessary to ask for a decision considerably earlier. Even in the best firms it has been known for MSS. to be lost or mislaid; for this reason it is advisable to keep a copy.

Illustrations.—If the main feature of a proposed book lies in its illustrations (as is often the case with travel books and books for children), they should be submitted with the MS. It should be remembered that good illustrations cannot make up for a bad text, nor will a good text make up for bad illustrations. Travel manuscripts in particular should always be accompanied by a map, however rough, if the area covered is too small to be shown in detail in a large-scale atlas; i.e. Jamaica usually appears only as a blob in the ocean, and any manuscript which refers to places on the island is unintelligible without a detailed map of some sort.

Quotations from Copyright Material.—Authors using quotations from copyright material must ensure that they or their publishers obtain permission for the right of reproduction. It is often costly, and authors should consider this before embark-ing on a work inviting extensive quotation from modern authors.

Correction.—It cannot be too strongly emphasised that correction, once a book is in type, should be kept to a minimum: if corrections have to be made, the new matter should *exactly* fit into the space made by removing something on the same page to make room for it.   This cannot always be done, but is of special importance when the book is in page proof: the cost of rearranging subsequent pages to incorporate the new matter is considerable.   Most publishers include a clause in their contracts to the effect that the cost of corrections exceeding 20 per cent of the cost of composition must be borne by the author.   This may appear to be a generous allowance, but in point of fact allows for little to be done, since the cost of correcting type is out of all proportion to the original cost of setting it up.

It is a common weakness on the part of writers to make corrections in their manuscript up to a certain point and then to leave final polishing up to be done on the proofs when the book is set up in type.

Even experienced authors are guilty of this to a large extent, and as it greatly increases the cost of the production of a magazine or book, most publishers insert a clause in their agreements stipulating that the cost of all corrections beyond a certain percentage shall be borne by the author.

This unfortunately leads to constant friction, for an author does not realise that when he, perhaps, deletes or adds two or three words at the beginning of a paragraph, this necessitates the overrunning of every line to the end of that paragraph, and what looks to the author to be the work of a moment to correct probably takes a compositor half an hour to put right.

After such emendation in galley form the publisher should surely be entitled to expect that the book is then ready to be printed off when it is made up into page, apart from the rectification of any printer's errors that may occur (such as letters dropped or transposed) in the make-up into page; it is not, however, uncommon for an author, when he gets the page proofs, to continue amending sentences or paragraphs almost as heavily as in the galley proofs.

The result of all this is unsatisfactory to both the author and publisher, for when the invoice is rendered for the cost of the excess corrections the author becomes indignant and thinks that the amount charged is an imposition on the part of the publisher.   He writes protesting, and the publisher takes up the matter with the printer again, upon which the printer gets out all the corrected proofs, spends much time in getting out his working dockets and proves that instead of the charge being excessive it is really much more moderate than was justified by the time and trouble spent.   So it must be seen how unsatisfactory the whole matter is, and from the point of view of both the publisher and the printer there should have been no necessity for any such friction if the author had attended to editing his typescript before submitting it for the printer.

SIGNS USED IN CORRECTING PROOFS

The following notes and table are extracted from B.S. 1219: 1958 Recommendations for proof correction and copy preparation (This extract is B.S. 1219C Table of Symbols for Printers' and Authors' Proof Corrections), and are reproduced by permission of the British Standards Institution, 2 Park Street, London, W1Y 4AA, from whom copies of the complete Standard may be obtained. The information given below is available on a card (B.S. 1219C) from B.S.I.

NOTES ON THE USE OF THE SYMBOLS

All corrections should be distinct and made in ink in the margins; marks made in the text should be those indicating the place to which the correction refers.

Where several corrections occur in one line, they should be divided between the left and right margins, the order being from left to right in both margins, and the individual marks should be separated by a concluding mark.

When an alteration is desired in a character, word or words, the existing character, word or words should be struck through, and the character to be substituted written in the margin followed by a /.

Where it is desired to change one character only to a capital letter, the word "cap" should be written in the margin. Where, however, it is desired to change more than one character, or a word or words, in a particular line to capitals, then one marginal reference, "caps", should suffice, with the appropriate symbols made in the text as required.

Three periods or full stops (constituting an ellipsis, see No. 61) should be used to indicate an omission, except where the preceding sentence has been concluded, in which case *four* full stops should be inserted, the first of which should be close up to the preceding word.

Normally, only matter actually to be inserted or added to the existing text should be written on the proof. If, however, any comments or instructions are written on the proof, they should be encircled, and preceded by the word PRINTER (in capitals and underlined).

(Words printed in italics in the marginal marks column below are instructions and not part of the marks).

SYMBOLS FOR CORRECTING PROOFS

No.	Instruction	Textual mark	Marginal mark
1	Correction is concluded	None	/
2	Insert in text the matter indicated in margin	λ	*New matter* / *followed by* /
3	Delete	Strike through characters to be deleted	∂
4	Delete and close up	Strike through characters to be deleted and use mark 21	∂
5	Leave as printed	. . . . under characters to remain	*stet*
6	Change to italic	——— under characters to be altered	*ital*

No.	Instruction	Textual mark	Marginal mark
7	Change to even small capitals	☰ under characters to be altered	*s.c.*
8	Change to capital letters	☰ under characters to be altered	*caps*
9	Use capital letters for initial letters and small capitals for rest of words	☰ under initial letters and ☰ under the rest of the words	*c. & s.c.*
10	Change to bold type	⌇ under characters to be altered	*bold*
11	Change to lower case	Encircle characters to be altered	*l.c.*
12	Change to roman type	Encircle characters to be altered	*rom*
13	Wrong fount. Replace by letter of correct fount	Encircle character to be altered	*w.f.*
14	Invert type	Encircle character to be altered	⑨
15	Change damaged character(s)	Encircle character(s) to be altered	X
16	Substitute or insert character(s) under which this mark is placed, in ' superior ' position	/ through character or ⋀ where required	*under character* (e.g. ⤳)
17	Substitute or insert character(s) over which this mark is placed, in ' inferior ' position	/ through character or ⋀ where required	*over character* (e.g. ⤳)
18	Underline word or words	——— under words affected	*underline*
19	Use ligature (e.g. ffi) or diphthong (e.g. œ)	⌒ enclosing letters to be altered	*enclosing ligature or diphthong required*

No.	Instruction	Textual mark	Marginal mark
20	Substitute separate letters for ligature or diphthong	/ through ligature or diphthong to be altered	*write out separate letters followed by* /
21	Close up—delete space between characters	⌒ linking characters	⌒
22	Insert space*	⅄	#
23	Insert space between lines or paragraphs*	> between lines to be spaced	#
24	Reduce space between lines*	(connecting lines to be closed up	*less* #
25	Make space appear equal between words	| between words	*eq* #
26	Reduce space between words*	| between words	*less* #
27	Add space between letters*	ⅠⅠⅠⅠⅠⅠ between tops of letters requiring space	*letter* #
28	Transpose	⌐⌐ between characters or words, numbered when necessary	*trs*
29	Place in centre of line	Indicate position with ⌐ ⌐	*centre*
30	Indent one em	⊐	☐
31	Indent two ems	⊐	☐☐
32	Move matter to right	⊐ at left side of group to be moved	⊐
33	Move matter to left	⊏ at right side of group to be moved	⊏

* Amount of space and/or length of re-spaced line may be indicated.

No.	Instruction	Textual mark	Marginal mark
34	Move matter to position indicated	[ ] at limits of required position	*move*
35	Take over character(s) or line to next line, column or page	⊏	*take over*
36	Take back character(s) or line to previous line, column or page	⊐	*take back*
37	Raise lines*	⌃ over lines to be moved / ⌐⌐ under lines to be moved	*raise*
38	Lower lines*	⌐⌐ over lines to be moved / ⌄ under lines to be moved	*lower*
39	Correct the vertical alignment	‖	‖
40	Straighten lines	═══ through lines to be straightened	═══
41	Push down space	Encircle space affected	⊥
42	Begin a new paragraph	⌐ before first word of new paragraph	*n.p.*
43	No fresh paragraph here	⌐ between paragraphs	*run on*
44	Spell out the abbreviation or figure in full	Encircle words or figures to be altered	*spell out*
45	Insert omitted portion of copy NOTE. The relevant section of the copy should be returned with the proof, the omitted portion being clearly indicated.	⋏	*out see copy*
46	Substitute or insert comma	/ through character or ⋏ where required	,/
47	Substitute or insert semi-colon	/ through character or ⋏ where required	;/

* Amount of space and/or length of line may be included.

No.	Instruction	Textual mark	Marginal mark
48	Substitute or insert full stop	/ through character or ⋏ where required	⊙
49	Substitute or insert colon	/ through character or ⋏ where required	⊙
50	Substitute or insert interrogation mark	/ through character or ⋏ where required	?/
51	Substitute or insert exclamation mark	/ through character or ⋏ where required	!/
52	Insert parentheses	⋏ or ⋏ ⋏	(/)/
53	Insert (square) brackets	⋏ or ⋏ ⋏	[/]/
54	Insert hyphen	⋏	|-|
55	Insert en (half-em) rule	⋏	en
56	Insert one-em rule	⋏	em
57	Insert two-em rule	⋏	2 em
58	Insert apostrophe	⋏	ᶜ/
59	Insert single quotation marks	⋏ or ⋏ ⋏	ᶜ/ ᶜ/
60	Insert double quotation marks	⋏ or ⋏ ⋏	ᶜᶜ/ ᵗᵗ/
61	Insert ellipsis	⋏	.../
62	Insert leader	⋏	⊙
63	Insert shilling stroke	⋏	∅
64	Refer to appropriate authority anything of doubtful accuracy	Encircle words, etc. affected	⊘

For examples of the use of these marks see B.S. 1219.

BOOK PAGE SIZES

Book sizes hitherto have been as follows:

Sheet	Size of Page Untrimmed		
	Sixteenmo (16mo)	Octavo (8vo)	Quarto (4to)
	inches	inches	inches
Foolscap	$4\frac{1}{4} \times 3\frac{3}{8}$	$6\frac{3}{4} \times 4\frac{1}{4}$	$8\frac{1}{2} \times 6\frac{3}{4}$
Crown	$5 \times 3\frac{3}{4}$	$7\frac{1}{2} \times 5$	$10 \times 7\frac{1}{2}$
Large Post	$5\frac{1}{4} \times 4\frac{1}{8}$	$8\frac{1}{4} \times 5\frac{1}{4}$	$10\frac{1}{2} \times 8\frac{1}{4}$
Demy	$5\frac{5}{8} \times 4\frac{3}{8}$	$8\frac{3}{4} \times 5\frac{5}{8}$	$11\frac{1}{4} \times 8\frac{3}{4}$
Medium	$5\frac{3}{4} \times 4\frac{1}{2}$	$9 \times 5\frac{3}{4}$	$11\frac{1}{2} \times 9$
Royal	$6\frac{1}{4} \times 5$	$10 \times 6\frac{1}{4}$	$12\frac{1}{2} \times 10$
Super Royal	$6\frac{3}{4} \times 5$	$10 \times 6\frac{3}{4}$	$13\frac{1}{2} \times 10$
Imperial	$7\frac{3}{4} \times 5\frac{1}{4}$	$11\frac{1}{2} \times 7\frac{3}{4}$	$15\frac{1}{2} \times 11\frac{1}{2}$

Five standard metric sizes are now recommended jointly by the Publishers' Association and the British Federation of Master Printers. It is expected that these recommended sizes will now become the general practice. The five recommended standard book sizes are:

	Trimmed sizes	Untrimmed sizes	"Quad" Paper sizes
	mm	mm	mm
Metric Cr. 8vo	186×123	192×126	768×1008
Metric Large Cr. 8vo	198×129	204×132	816×1056
Metric Demy 8vo	216×138	222×141	888×1128
Metric Royal 8vo	234×156	240×159	960×1272
A5	$210 \times 148^*$	215×152.5	RAO$860 \times 1220^*$

These measurements are ISO sizes.

GOVERNMENT OFFICES AND PUBLIC SERVICES

Enquiries, accompanied by a stamped addressed envelope, should be sent to the Public Relations Officer.

Agriculture, Fisheries and Food, Ministry of, Whitehall Place, S.W.1. *T.* 01–839 7711.

Arts Council of Great Britain, 105 Piccadilly, W1V 0AU. *T.* 01–629 9495.

Bodleian Library, Oxford, OX1 3BG *T.* Oxford 44675.

British Broadcasting Corporation, Broadcasting House, W1A 1AA. *T.* 01–580 4468.

British Council, The, 65 Davies Street, London, W1Y 2AA *T.* 01–499 8011.

British European Airways, Bealine House, Ruislip, Middlesex. *T.* 01–845 1234.

British Film Institute, 81 Dean Street, London, W1V 6AA *T.*01–437 4355. *Telex.* 27624.

British Museum, Bloomsbury, WC1B 3DG. *T.* 01–636 1555.

British Museum Newspaper Library, Colindale Avenue, N.W.9. *T.* 01–205 6039 & 4788.

British Overseas Airways Corporation, B.O.A.C. Head Office, Heathrow Airport, London. *T.* 01–759 5511; Air Terminal, Buckingham Palace Road, S.W.1. *T.* 01–834 2323; 75 Regent Street, W1A 2HX *T.* 01–834 2323. 107 New Bond Street, W.1. *T.* 01–834 2323, 62–63 Cheapside, E.C.2. *T.* 01–834 2323.

British Railways Board, 222 Marylebone Road, N.W.1. *T.* 01–262 3232.

British Theatre Centre, 9 Fitzroy Square, London, W.1.

British Tourist Authority, 64 St. James's Street, London, S.W.1. *T.* 01–629 9191.

Canada, High Commissioner for, Canada House, Trafalgar Square, S.W.1. *T.* 01–930 9741.

Central Electricity Generating Board, Sudbury House, 15 Newgate Street, London, EC1A 7AU. *T.* 01–248 1202.

Central Office of Information, Hercules Road, Westminster Bridge Road, London, S.E.1. *T.* 01–928 2345.

Ceylon, High Commissioner for, 13 Hyde Park Gardens, W.2. *T.* 01–262 1841.

College of Arms or **Heralds' College,** Queen Victoria Street, E.C.4. *T.* 01–248 2762.

Commonwealth Institute, Kensington High Street, London, W.8. *T.* 01–602 3252–6. Educational publicity about the Commonwealth. Exhibition galleries, cinema, art gallery, licensed restaurant, bookstall, film strips, etc. Contemporary reference library for use by general public, of books and periodicals.

Commonwealth of Australia, High Commissioner for, Australia House, Strand, WC2B 4LA. *T.* 01–836 2435, also Canberra House, Maltravers Street, Strand, WC2R 3EH. *T.* 01–836 2435.

Cyprus High Commission, 93 Park Street, W1Y 4ET *T.* 01–499 8272.

Defence, Ministry of, (Press and P.R. Depts.) (General, Navy, Army and Air Force Departments), Main Building, Whitehall, London, S.W.1. *T.* 01–839 8070.

Education and Science, Department of, Curzon Street, London, W1Y 8AA. *T.* 01–493 7070.

Electricity Council, 30 Millbank, London, S.W.1. *T.* 01–834 2333.

Employment and Productivity, Department of, 8 St. James's Square, S.W.1. *T.* 01–930 6200.

English Tourist Board, 4 Grosvenor Gardens, London, S.W.1.

Foreign and Commonwealth Office, Downing Street, S.W.1. *T.* 01–930 8440 and 2323.

Forestry Commission, 25 Savile Row, W1X 2AY *T.* 01–734 0221.

Gambia High Commission, 28 Kensington Court, London, W.8. *T.* 01–937 0800.

Gas Council, 59 Bryanston Street, Marble Arch, London, W1A 2AZ *T.* 01–723 7030.

General Register Office, now Office of Population Censuses and Surveys, *qv.*

Ghana, High Commissioner for, 13 Belgrave Square, S.W.1. *T.* 01–235 4142–5.

Health and Social Security, Department of, Alexander Fleming House, Elephant and Castle, London, S.E.1. *T.* 01–407 5522.

Home Office, Whitehall, S.W.1. *T.* 01–930 8100. *Public Relations Branch:* Chief Information Officer: T. D. McCaffrey

Housing and Local Government, Ministry of, Whitehall, S.W.1. *T.* 01–930 4300.

Independent Television Authority, 70 Brompton Road, S.W.3. *T.* 01–584 7011.

India, High Commissioner for, India House, Aldwych, WC2B 4NA. *T.* 01–836 8484.

Industrial Design, Council of, The Design Centre, 28 Haymarket, London, S.W.1. *T.* 01–839 8000.

Ireland, Ambassador of, 17 Grosvenor Place, S.W.1. *T.* 01–235 2171.

Kenya High Commissioner, 45 Portland Place, London, W1N 4AS. *T.* 01–636 2371.

London Museum, Kensington Palace, W.8 (office and exhibition galleries). *T.* 01–937 9816.

London Transport Executive, 55 Broadway, S.W.1. *T.* 01–222 5600.

National Central Library, Store Street, London, WC1E 7DG. *T.* 01–636 0755. *Telex:* 25816.

National Coal Board, Hobart House, Grosvenor Place, S.W.1. *T.* 01–235 2020.

National Library of Scotland, George IV Bridge, Edinburgh, EH1 1EW. *T.* 031–225 4104. *Telex:* Natlibscot 72638.

National Library of Wales, Aberystwyth SY23 3BU. *T.* 3816–7. *Telex* 35165.

National Maritime Museum, Greenwich, S.E.10, including the Old Royal Observatory. *T.* 01–858 4422.

National Savings Committee, Alexandra House, Kingsway, WC2B 6TS. *T.* 01–836 1599.

New Zealand, High Commissioner for, New Zealand House, Haymarket, S.W.1. *T.* 01–930 8422.

Northern Ireland Tourist Board, 10 Royal Avenue Belfast, BT1 1DQ.

Office of Population Censuses and Surveys, Somerset House, London, WC2R 1LR. *T.* 01–836 2407.

Pakistan, High Commissioner for, 35 Lowndes Square, London, S.W.1. *T.* 01–235 2044.

Patent Office (Board of Trade), 25 Southampton Buildings, WC2A 1AY. *T.* 01–405 8721. *Sale Branch* (for information retrieval services), Patent Office Orpington, Kent, BR5 3RD.

Post Office Central Headquarters, 23

Howland Street, London, W1P 6HQ. *T.* 01–631 2345.

Public Buildings and Works, Ministry of, Lambeth Bridge House, Albert Embankment, S.E.1. *T.* 01–735 7611. *Press Office:* Ext. 1450/52/53/60.

Public Record Office, Chancery Lane, WC2A 1LR *T.* 01–405 0741.

Science Museum, South Kensington, S.W.7. *T.* 01–589 6371. Enquiries to Information Office.

Scottish Home and Health Department, St. Andrews House, Edinburgh, EH1 3DE. *T.* 031–556 8501.

Scottish Office, Dover House, Whitehall, London, S.W.1. *T.* 01–930 6151.

Scottish Tourist Board, 2 Rutland Place, West End, Edinburgh, EH1 2YU. *T.* 031–229 1561.

Sierra Leone, High Commissioner for, 33 Portland Place, London, W1N 3AG *T.* 01–636 6483–6.

South Africa, Republic of, South African Embassy, Trafalgar Square, WC2N 5DP *T.* 01–930 4488.

Stationery Office, Her Majesty's, Atlantic House, Holborn Viaduct, London, EC1P 1BN. *T.* 01–248 9876 and Sovereign House, St. Georges Street, Norwich, NOR 76A. *T.* 0603–22211.

Technology, Ministry of, Millbank Tower, Millbank, S.W.1. *T.* 01–834 2255.

Trade, Board of, 1 Victoria Street, S.W.1. *T.* 01–222 7877.

Transport, Ministry of, St. Christopher House, Southwark Street, S.E.1. *T.* 01–928 7999.

Treasury, H.M., Treasury Chambers, Gt. George St., S.W.1. *T.* 01–930 1234.

United Kingdom Atomic Energy Authority, 11 Charles II Street, S.W.1. *T.* 01–930 6262.

Victoria and Albert Museum, South Kensington, S.W.7. *T.* 01–589 6371.

Wales Tourist Board, 7 Park Place, Cardiff, CF1 3UJ. *T.* Cardiff 27281.

Wellington Museum, Apsley House, Hyde Park Corner, W1V 9FA *T.* 01–499 5676.

West India Committee (The West Indies, British Honduras (Belize), British Virgin Islands, Cayman Islands, Turks and Caicos Islands), 40 Norfolk Street, WC2R 2LD. *T.* 01–836 8922.

West London Air Terminal, Cromwell Road, London, S.W.7. *T.* 01–370 4255.

In *Whitaker's Almanack* will be found names and addresses of many other public bodies In *The Year Book of Technical Education* will be found details of many scientific technical and similar organisations.

INDEXES, ETC.

CLASSIFIED INDEX OF SUBJECTS LISTED ON PAGES 419–428

CLASSIFIED INDEX OF JOURNALS AND MAGAZINES

American Journals   *Commonwealth and South African Journals* †

This Index is necessarily only a broad classification. It should be regarded as only a pointer to possible markets, and should be used with discrimination.

SHORT STORIES

This list does not include the many women's journals requiring short stories, for which *see under* FEMININE

†Adam (Aus.)
*Analog
Anglo-Welsh Review
Argosy
*Argosy
*Atlantic
Blackwood's Magazine
†(Bombay) Illustrated
  Weekly (In.)
Caritas
Catholic Fireside
Christian Herald
Cork Weekly Examiner
Cornhill Magazine
*Cosmopolitan Magazine
†Country Guide (Can.)
Dalesman
*Ellery Queen's Mystery
  Magazine
Encounter
*Esquire
Evening News
*Evergreen Review
Family Star
Glasgow Evening Citizen

Good Housekeeping
Harper's Bazaar
*Harper's Magazine
Ireland's Own
†(Johannesburg) Sunday
  Times (S.A.)
Listener
*McCall's Magazine
*Mademoiselle
†Man (Aus.)
†Man Junior (Aus.)
Men Only
*Modern Romances
†New Idea (Aus.)
New Worlds
*New Yorker
†Onlooker (In.)
Parade
People's Friend
†Personality (S.A.)
*Ranch Romances
*Redbook Magazine
Reveille
She
Sign

Spectator
Stand
Sunday Companion
*Sunday Digest
Sunday Sun
†Sun-Herald (Aus.)
†(Sydney) Bulletin (Aus.)
†(Sydney) Morning Herald
  (Aus.)
*This Week
Transatlantic Review
True Magazine
True Romance
*True *Series*
Un-common Sense
Weekend
Yachting World

DETECTIVE SHORT STORIES

Ellery Queen's Mystery Magazine	Family Star London Mystery	Reveille Weekend

THRILLER SHORT STORIES

*Ellery Queen's Mystery Magazine	Family Star London Mystery	Reveille Weekend

LONG COMPLETE STORIES

From 8000 words upwards. (*See also under* FEMININE)

*Analog
*Argosy
†Canadian Magazine
Star Weekly
Christian Novels
*Ellery Queen's Mystery
Magazine

Love Story Library
*McCall's Magazine
*Modern Romances
New Moon
*Ranch Romances
*Redbook Magazine

True Love Series
True Magazine
*True *Series*
Woman's Weekly Library
Woman's World Library

SERIALS

(*See also entries under* FEMININE)

*Analog
†Australian Woman's
Weekly (Aus.)
†(Bombay) Illustrated
Weekly (In.
*Boys' Life

Christian Herald
Cross, The
Family Star
Ireland's Own
*McCall's Magazine

People's Friend
People's Journal
*Redbook Magazine
Sunday Companion
Weekly News

POETRY AND VERSE

Children's Verse is not included under this heading.

Agenda
Ambit
*American Scholar
Anglo-Welsh Review
Animal Ways
Atlantic
†Australian Letters
†Canadian Poetry (Can.)
*Carolina Quarterly
*Christian Science Monitor
Cornhill Magazine
Country Life
Countryman
†Dalhousie Review (Can.)
Encounter
English
Envoi

*Evergreen Review
Field
Good Housekeeping
*Harper's Magazine
Home Words
*Hudson Review
Lady
Listener
London Magazine
London Welshman
New Statesman
*New Yorker
*Northwest Review
Outposts
*Poetry
†Poetry Australia
Poetry Review

Punch
Reveille
Review, The
*Saturday Review
She
Spectator
Stand
Sunday Times
Times Literary
Supplement
Transatlantic Review
*Virginia Quarterly
*Yale Review
Workshop Poetry Maga-
zine

CARTOONS

(*See also* FOR YOUNG PEOPLE: HUMOROUS AND PICTURE PAPERS)

Anglers Mail
Animal Ways
*Argosy
Civil Service Opinion
Countryman
Daily Sketch
Elizabethan
*Esquire
Film & Television
Technician
Good Life
Guider
Hi-fi News
Ireland's Own
Men Only

Morning Star
†Motorman (N.Z.)
†NZ Timber Journal
†Pakistan Observer
Parade
†Perth Daily News (Aus.)
Private Eye
Punch
Quiet Please
Ranger
Red Tape
Reveille
Scouter, The
She
600 Magazine

Socialist Commentary
Soldier
†Southern Cross (S.A.)
Studio Sound
Sunday Post
Today's Guide
Tribune
TV Comic
TV Times
Un-Common Sense
†United Asia (Ind.)
Weekend
Yorkshire Post
Young Soldier, The

O

HUMOUR

*American Mercury
Civil Service Opinion
Cycling
Dundee Evening Tele-
    graph and Post

*Esquire
Men Only
*New Yorker
Private Eye

Punch
600 Magazine
Weekend

FEMININE

Fiction, Home, Fashions, Children, Beauty Culture.

Annabel
†Australian Women's
    Weekly (Aus.)
†(Bombay) Eve's Weekly(In.)
†Chatelaine Can.)
Family Circle
†Femina (S.A.)
Flair
*Glamour Magazine
Good Housekeeping
*Good Housekeeping
Good Life
Harper's Bazaar
Hers
Home and Country
Home Words
Homes and Gardens
Honey
Ideal Home
Junior Age
Lady
*Ladies' Home Journal
Love Story Library

*McCall's Magazine
*Mademoiselle
Millinery and Boutique
Mother
Mother and Baby
My Home and Family
My Weekly
†New Idea (Aus.)
New Moon
†New Zealand Home
    Journal (N.Z.)
†New Zealand Woman's
    Weekly (N.Z.)
Nova
Nursery World
*Parents Magazine
People's Friend
People's Journal
Pram Retailer
Queen
Red Letter
Red Star Weekly
Scottish Home and Country

Secrets
She
Townswoman
*True Confessions
Vanity Fair
Vogue
*Vogue
Woman
Woman and Home
Woman Bride and Home
Woman's Choice
*Woman's Day
†Woman's Day with
    Woman (Aus.)
Woman's Journal
Woman's Own
Woman's Realm
Woman's Story Magazine
Woman's Way
Woman's Weekly
Women's Employment
World's Children

MEN

(See also AVIATION, MOTORING, SPORT, etc.)

*Esquire
Men Only

Men's Wear
Style Weekly

Tailor and Cutter

FOR YOUNG PEOPLE

PERIODICALS

Boys and Girls
*American Girl
Animal Ways
Beezer
*Boys' Life
Brownie
Busy Bees News
Elizabethan
Fabulous
Hornet
Hotspur
*Impact

Junior Bookshelf
Lion and Eagle
*Plays
Pony
Princess Tina
Ranger
Rover
*Sunday Digest
Sunny Stories
Tiger and Jag
Today's Guide
Topper

Treasure
Valiant
Vanguard

Young Children
Lucie Attwell's Annual
Pippin
Playhour and Robin
Teddy Bear

HUMOROUS AND PICTURE PAPERS

Beano, The
Beezer
Bimbo
Bunty
Buster
Dandy, The
Hotspur

Jack and Jill
Judy
June and School Friend
Mandy
Playhour and Robin
Playland
Princess Tina

Smash
Sparky
Tiger and Jag
Topper
TV Comic
Twinkle
Valiant

SOME JOURNALS WHICH CONTAIN A CHILDREN'S PAGE OR COLUMN

Church Times
Ireland's Own
Jewish Chronicle

†Melbourne Age (Aus.)
Nursery World

People's Friend
Woman

SUBJECT ARTICLES

ADMINISTRATION AND LAW

Chartered Secretary
Civil Service Opinion
Country Gentlemen's
    Magazine
Criminologist
Data Systems
Export Management
*Fortune
Justice of the Peace and
    Local Government
    Review

Local Government
    Chronicle
†Management (N.Z.)
Management in Action
Municipal Engineering
Municipal and Public Ser-
    vices Journal
Municipal Review
New Law Journal
New Society
Parish Councils Review
Personnel Management

Political Quarterly
Post
Rating and Valuation
    Reporter
Red Tape
Social Service
Sociological Review
Solicitors' Journal
Supervisor
Surveyor-Local Govern-
    ment Technology
Work Study

ADVERTISING AND SALESMANSHIP

Advertisers' Weekly
†Advertising and Marketing
    (N.Z.)

Campaign
Design
Display

Selling Today

AGRICULTURE AND GARDENING

Agricultural Machinery
    Journal
Amateur Gardening
British Farmer
Commercial Grower
Country Gentlemen's
    Magazine
Country Life
Countryman
†Country Guide (Can.)
†Countryman (Aus.)
Country-side
Dairy Farmer
Dairy Industries
Farm and Country

Farmer and Stock-
    Breeder
Farmer's Weekly
†Farmer's Weekly (S.A.)
Feed & Farm Supplies
Field
Fruit, Flower, etc.,
    Journal
Garden News
Gardeners Chronicle
Grower
Guild Gardener
Journal of Park Adminis-
    tration
Milk Industry
†New Zealand Farmer

†New Zealand Gardener
Orchid Review
Parks and Sports
    Grounds
Pig Farming
Popular Gardening
Power Farming
†Rhodesian Farmer
Rose, The
Scottish Farmer
Scottish Forestry
*Successful Farming
Timber Trades Journal
Town and Country
    Planning
World Crops

ANIMALS, ETC.

Animal Ways
Animals
Animals' Defender and
  Anti-Vivisection News
Animals' Magazine
AV Times
British Racehorse
Cage and Aviary Birds

Country-side
Dog's Life
Gamekeeper
Guild News
Horse and Hound
Light Horse
Petfish Monthly
Pig Farming

Pony
Poultry Industry
Poultry World
Riding
Stud and Stable
Tail-Wagger

ARCHITECTURE AND BUILDING

Architect and Building
  News
Architect and Surveyor
Architects' Journal
Architectural Design
Architectural Review
†Art in Industry (In.)
Building
Building Materials
Building Societies'
  Gazette

Contract Journal
Contractor
Decorating Contractor
Education
House Builder and Estate
  Developer
Illustrated Carpenter and
  Builder
Industrialised Building
Irish Builder
National Builder

Official Architecture
Parks and Sports Grounds
Specification
Town and Country
  Planning

ART AND COLLECTING

*American Artist
Antique Collector
Apollo
Art and Artists
Art and Craft in Education
†Art in Industry (In.)
Arts Review
Artist

*Atlantic
Book Collector
Burlington Magazine
Canvas
Ceramics
Collectors Weekly
*Commonweal
Connoisseur

Country Life
Design
Illustrated London News
Museum
Museums Journal
Numismatic Chronicle
Pottery Quarterly
Studio International

AVIATION

Aeromodeller
Air-Cushion Vehicles
Air Pictorial
Aircraft Engineering
*Aviation Week & Space

Technology
†Canadian Aviation (Can.)
Flight International
*Flying
*Mechanix Illustrated

Popular Flying
Skytrader International
Trident
†Wings over Africa (S.A.)

BLIND AND DEAF-BLIND

(Published by the Royal National Institute for the Blind, see page 196)

Braille Chess Magazine
Braille Digest
Braille Journal of Physio-
  therapy
Braille Musical Magazine
Braille News Summary
Braille Radio Times
Braille Rainbow
Channels of Blessing
Crusade Messenger
Diane
Fleur de Lys

Gleanings
"Law Notes" Extracts
Light of the Moon
Moon Magazine
Moon Messenger
Moon Newspaper
Moon Rainbow
National Braille Mail
New Beacon (in Braille
  and letterpress)
Nuggets
Physiotherapists' Quarterly

Piano Tuners' Quarterly
Portland Magazine
Progress
Roundabout
School Magazine
Scripture Union Daily
  Notes
Tape Record
Theological Times
Torch
Trefoil Trail

CINEMA AND FILMS

Film and Television
    Technician
Film Quarterly

Film User
Films and Filming
Kine Weekly

Movie Maker
Sight and Sound
Today's Cinema

DIGESTS

English Digest. 223 Shaftesbury Avenue, W.C.2
Irish Digest. 43 Pargate Street, Dublin.
Reader's Digest. 25 Berkley Square, London, W.1. *T*. 01-629 8144 (see page 87).

Science Digest. 200 East Ontario Street, Chicago 11, Illinois, U.S.A. *London*, 109 Jermyn Street, S.W.1. *T*. Whitehall 4856.

ECONOMICS, ACCOUNTANCY AND FINANCE

Accountancy
Accountant
Accountant's Magazine
*American Scholar
†Australian Financial
    Review (Aus.)
Banker
Bankers' Magazine
British Trade Journal
Building Societies Gazette
†(Calcutta) Capital (In.)
Certified Accountants
    Journal
Chartered Secretary

City Press
Commerce
†Commerce (In.)
Eastern World
Economic Journal
Economica
Economist
Far East Trade
Financial Times
Financial World
*Foreign Affairs
*Harper's Magazine
Insurance Brokers
    Monthly

Investors Chronicle and
    Stock Exchange Gazette
Irish Accountant and
    Secretary
*New Republic
New Statesman
Policy
*Political Science
    Quarterly
Public Ledger
South Asian Review
Time and Tide
Trade Unionist

EDUCATION

A.M.A.
*American Scholar
Art and Craft in Education
Britannia
Britannica
British Esperantist
Catholic Education To-day
Centre Point
Child Education
Church Teacher
Education
Education and Training
English
Esperanto Teacher
Guider
Health Education Journal
Housecraft

Incorporated Linguist
Junior Bookshelf
Modern Language Review
Modern Languages
Month
Music in Education
Music Teacher
New Era
New University and New
    Education
Occupational Psychology
*Parents' Magazine
Paris
Pictorial Education
PNEU Journal
Preparatory Schools
    Review

School Government
    Chronicle
School Librarian
Scottish Educational
    Journal
Scouter
Special Education
Speech and Drama
Teacher
Teachers' World
Times Educational
    Supplement
Unesco Courier
Universities Quarterly
Use of English
*Volta Review
World's Children

ENGINEERING AND MECHANICS

(*Not included under* AGRICULTURE, ARCHITECTURE, AVIATION, MOTORING, NAUTICAL,
RADIO, SCIENCE, TRADE AND COMMERCE, q.v.)

Assembly and Fastener
Engineering
†Australian Mining
Automobile Engineer
Automotive Design
Engineering
British Engineer
British Steelmaker
Buses
Car Mechanics
Civil Engineering
Colliery Guardian
Computer Survey
Computer Weekly
Concrete
Concrete Building
Control and Instrumenta-
tion
Cranes
Design and Components
in Engineering
Design Electronics
Electrical Age
Electrical and Electronics
Manufacturer
Electrical & Radio Trading
†Electrical Engineer (Aus.)
Electrical Equipment
Electrical Review
Electrical Times
Electronic Components
Electronic Equipment News
Electronics Weekly
Electroplating
Engineer
Engineering
Engineering Materials
and Design
Engineering Production
Fire Protection Review
Fluid Power International

Foundry Trade Journal
Gas and Oil Power
Gas Journal
Gas Service
Gas Showroom
Gas World
Heating and Ventilating
Engineer
Hydraulic Pneumatic
Power
Industrial and Scientific
Communication
Industrial Equipment News
Industrial Finishing
Industrial Gas
†Industrial Management
(Aus.)
Insulation
International
Construction
Irish Builder
Journal of Fuel and Heat
Technology
Journal of Refrigeration
Light and Lighting
Machine Design & Control
Machinery and Production
Engineering
Machinery Lloyd
Machinery Market
Maintenance
Marine Engineer
Mechanical Handling
Metal Forming
Metalworking Production
Mining and Minerals
Engineering
Mining Journal
Mining Magazine
Mining World
Model Engineer

Model Railway News
Modern Railways
Municipal Engineering
Nuclear Engineering
†N.Z. Concrete Construc-
tion
†N.Z. Electrical Journal
†N.Z. Engineering
†N.Z. Timber Journal
Petroleum Times
*Popular Electronics
*Popular Mechanics
Practical Woodworking
Pumps
Queen's Highway
Railway Gazette
Railway Magazine
Railway World
Refrigeration and Air
Conditioning
Roads and Road Con-
struction
Spaceflight
Steam and Heating
Engineer
Steel Times
Surveyor - Local Govern-
ment Technology
Traffic Engineering
Water and Water En-
gineering
Water Power
Welding
Wire
Works Engineering & Fac-
tory Services.

HEALTH, MEDICINE AND NURSING

Bio-Medical Engineering
British Food Journal
British Journal of
Chiropody
British Medical Journal
British Vegetarian
Caritas
Chemist and Druggist
European Chemical News
Good Health
Health
Health Education Journal
Health for All
Heredity
Here's Health

Hospital
Hospital Management
Irish Journal of Medical
Science
Lancet
Medical News
Medical News Tribune
Medical Officer
Medical World
Mental Health
Modern Mother
Mother and Baby
Municipal Engineering
Nursery World
Nursing Mirror

Nursing Times
Nutrition
Occupational Health
Occupational Psychology
Optician
Pharmaceutical Journal
Physiotherapy
Practitioner, The
Pulse
Quarterly Journal of
Medicine
Retail Chemist
Socialism and Health
*Today's Health

HISTORY AND ARCHAEOLOGY

Antiquity
Contemporary Review
English Historical Review
Folklore
Geographical Magazine

History
History Today
Illustrated London News
Industrial Archaeology
Local Historian

Midland History
Scottish Historical
   Review
South Asian Review
*Travel

HOME
(See also FEMININE)

*American Home
†Australian Home
   Beautiful (Aus.)
*Better Homes and
   Gardens
Caritas
Do It Yourself

Domestic Science
Electrical Age
Embroidery
Homemaker
Homes and Gardens
House & Garden
Housecraft

Ideal Home
*Mechanix Illustrated
*Parents' Magazine
Practical Householder
†South African Garden
   and Home (S.A.)

LITERARY

*American Mercury
*American Scholar
Anglo-Welsh Review
*Atlantic
†Australian Letters
Author
Blackwood's Magazine
Book Collecting & Library
   Monthly
Book Trade
Books and Bookmen
Bookseller
†Canadian Author (Can.)
*Commonweal

Contemporary Review
Cornhill Magazine
Critical Quarterly
†Dalhousie Review (Can.)
Dickensian
Encounter
English
*Harper's Magazine
Journalist
†Landfall (N.Z.)
Library
Library Review
Library World
London Magazine

†Meanjin Quarterly (Aus.)
New Statesman
*Saturday Review
Spectator
Times Literary Supple-
   ment
Twentieth Century
Woman Journalist
Writer
*Writer
Writer's Review

MOTORING

Autocar
Automobile Engineer
Car
Car Mechanics
Caravan
Commercial Motor
Commercial Vehicles
Ford Times

Garage
Good Motoring
Modern Caravan
Motor
Motor Cycle
Motor Cycle News
Motor Industry
Motor Racing

Motor Trader
Motor World
Motoring Life
Practical Motorist
Transport History
Vauxhall Motorist
Vehicle Cleaning News
†Wheels (Aus.)

MUSIC

Audio Record
   Review
*Film Quarterly
Hi-Fi News
Hi-Fi Sound
Keyboard
Making Music
Melody Maker

Music
Music and Letters
Music and Musicians
Music Business Weekly
Music in Education
Music Industry
Music Review
Music Teacher

Musical Opinion
Musical Times
New Musical Express
Organ
Records and Recording
Strad
Tape Recording
Tempo

NATURAL HISTORY

Aquarist and Pondkeeper
Birds and Country
  Magazine
Cage and Aviary Birds
Country Life
Countryman
Country-side

Dalesman
Entomologists' Magazine
Essex Countryside
Gamekeeper and
  Countryside
Geological Magazine
Guider

Naturalist
Nature
Scottish Field
Shooting Times
*Sports Afield
*Travel
†Walkabout (Aus.)

NAUTICAL OR MARINE

Ashore and Afloat
*Boating
British Trade Journal
Dock and Harbour
  Authority
Fairplay International
  Shipping Journal
Lloyd's List
Marine Engineer
Motor Boat

Motor Ship
Nautical Magazine
Navy
P.L.A. Monthly
Practical Boat Owner
Safety at Sea
Sea Breezes
Sea Cadet
†Seacraft (Aus.)

Ship & Boat International
Shipbuilding
Shipping World
Small Boat
*Yachting
Yachting Monthly
Yachting World
Yachts and Yachting

PHILATELY

Philatelic Magazine
Philately

Stamp Collecting
Stamp Lover
Stamp Magazine

Stamp Monthly
Stamp Weekly

PHOTOGRAPHY

Amateur Photographer
British Journal of Photo-
  graphy
Creative Camera

Film User
*Modern Photography
Photo Finisher
Photography

*Popular Photography
SLR Camera
*Travel & Camera

POLITICS

*American Scholar
*Atlantic
†Australian Quarterly
British Weekly
Candour
China Quarterly
*Commonweal
Contemporary Review
†Current Events (In.)
East-West Digest
Eastern World
*Foreign Affairs

*Harper's Magazine
International Affairs
International Associa-
  tions
Labour Monthly
Liberal News
New Commonwealth
*New Republic
New Statesman
Political Quarterly
*Political Science Quarterly
Round Table

Socialist Commentary
South Asian Review
†Thought (In.)
Trade Unionist
Tribune
Twentieth Century
Un-Common Sense
Unesco Courier
West Africa
World Survey
World Today

RADIO AND TELEVISION

Electrical and Electronic
  Trader
Electrical and Radio
  Trading
†Electronics (Aus.)
Electronics Weekly
*Electronics World
*Film Quarterly

International Broadcast
  Engineer
Listener
Look and Listen
Practical Television
Practical Wireless
Radio Constructor
Radio Times

Short-Wave Magazine
Stage and Television
  Today
Television Mail
T.V. Times
†T.V. Times (Aus.)
Wireless World

RELIGION AND PHILOSOPHY

†Aryan Path (In.)
Baptist Times
British Weekly
Catholic Fireside
Catholic Gazette
Catholic Herald
Catholic Pictorial
Catholic Standard
†Catholic Weekly (Aus.)
Christian Action
Christian Herald
*Christian Science
  Monitor
Christian Record
Church News
Church of England News-
  paper
Church of Ireland Gazette
Church Teacher
Church Times
Churchman
Clergy Review
Compass Newspapers

Congregational Monthly
Contemporary Review
Cross, The
Crusade
Downside Review
Evangelical Quarterly
Faith and Freedom
Friend
Frontier
Guideposts
Heythrop Journal
Home Words
Humanist
Inquirer
Life and Work
*Living Church
Mankind Quarterly
Methodist Recorder
Modern Churchman
Month
New Blackfriars
New Christian
New Outlook

News Extra
Pax
Reality
Sign
†Southern Cross (S.A.)
Spearhead
Studies in Comparative
  Religion
Sunday
Sunday Companion
*Sunday Digest
Tablet
Theology
Universe
Vanguard
War Cry
Word
World Outlook
Young Soldier

SCIENCE

(*Not included under* AGRICULTURE, AVIATION, CINEMA, ENGINEERING, HEALTH, HISTORY,
MOTORING, NATURAL HISTORY, NAUTICAL, PHOTOGRAPHY, RADIO, SPORTS, TRAVEL,
q.v.)

*American Mercury
*American Scholar
*Analog
*Atlantic
British Chemical
  Engineering
British Food Journal
Chemical Age
Chemical and Process
  Engineering
Chemical Processing
Colliery Guardian
Criminologist

Fire
Fire Protection
Geological Magazine
*Harper's Magazine
Illustrated London News
Impact of Science on
  Society
Industrial Gas
Journal of the British Inter-
  planetary Society
Laboratory Practice
Mankind Quarterly
Manufacturing Chemist

*Mechanix Illustrated
Microscope, The
Mind
Nature
New Scientist
Nuclear Engineering
*Popular Science Monthly
Practical Electronics
Psychologist Magazine
Science Journal
Science Progress
Sound

SERVICES: NAVAL, MILITARY, AIR, AND CIVIL

Air Pictorial
Army Quarterly
British Legion Journal

Journal of the R.U.
  Service Institution
Red Tape
Royal Air Forces
  Quarterly

Sea Cadet
Soldier
TAVR

SPORT, GAMES, HOBBIES AND PASTIMES

(*Not included under* AGRICULTURE, ANIMALS, ART, AVIATION, CINEMA, FEMININE, HOME, MEN, MOTORING, MUSIC, PHILATELY, PHOTOGRAPHY, RADIO, THEATRE, TRAVEL, q.v.)

*American Field
Anglers' Mail
Angling
Angling Times
†Australian Outdoors (Aus.)
†Australian Sportfishing
†Australian Sporting
   Shooter
British Chess Magazine
Climber and Rambler
Coins and Medals
Cycletouring
Cycling
Disc and Music Echo
East Coast Yachtsman
Edinburgh Evening News
Farm and Country
Field, The
*Field and Stream
Fishing
Gamekeeper and
   Countryside

Goal
Golf Illustrated
Golf Monthly
Golf Weekly
Golf World
Guider
Horse and Hound
Lawn Tennis
Leisure
Light Horse
Meccano Magazine
Model Engineer
Model Railway
   Constructor
Model Railway News
†New Zealand Outdoor
Popular Camping
*Popular Electronics
Practical Camper
Rod and Line
Scottish Field
Scouter

†Sea Harvest and Ocean
   Science (Can.)
Shooting Times
Skier
Small Boat
*Sport Magazine
Sport and Recreation
Sporting Life
*Sports Illustrated
Trident
Trout and Salmon
Water Skier
Woodworker
World Bowls
World Fishing
World Sports
*Yachting
Yachting Monthly
Yachting World
Yachts and Yachting

THEATRE, DRAMA AND DANCING
(*Not included under* CINEMA, MUSIC, q.v.)

Amateur Stage
Ballet To-day
Ballroom Dancing Times
Dance and Dancers
Dancing Times

Drama
Gambit
Opera
*Plays
Plays and Players

Radio Times
Stage and Television
   Today
T.V. Times

TOPOGRAPHY

Bedfordshire Magazine
Bucks Life
Cheshire Life
Country Life
Country Quest
Coventry Evening Tele-
   graph
Cumbria
Dalesman
Derbyshire Life and
   Countryside
Eastern Daily Press
England

Essex Countryside
Gloucestershire Life and
   Countryside
Hampshire
Hertfordshire Country-
   side
Inverness Courier
Kent
Kent Life
Lancashire Evening Post
Lancashire Life
London Welshman
Maidstone Gazette

Orbis
Scotland's Magazine
Scottish Field
Selborne Magazine
Sruth
Sussex Life
Thames Valley
   Countryside
This England
Warwickshire and Worce-
   stershire Life
Yorkshire Life
Yorkshire Ridings

TRADE AND COMMERCE

(*Not included under* ARCHITECTURE, ADVERTISING, AGRICULTURE, CINEMA, ECONOMICS, ENGINEERING, MOTORING, q.v.)

Achievement
Ambassador
Baker and Confectioner
Board Practice
Bookseller
Brewing Trade Review
British Plastics
British Printer
Brushes
Business Credit
Business Management
Cabinet Maker and Retail Furnisher
Carpets & Textiles
Caterer and Hotelkeeper
Caterer's Association Bulletin
Catering & Hotel Management
Catering Times
Cement Technology
Cement, Lime and Gravel
Ceramic Digest
Ceramics
Chemist and Druggist
Claycraft
Cleaning and Maintenance
Coaching Journal
Coal Merchant and Shipper
Confectionary and Tobacco News
Converting Industry
Co-Partnership
Cordage, Canvas and Jute World
Corsetry and Underwear
Data Journal
Data Processing
Data Systems
Display
Disposables International
Dock and Harbour Authority
Draper's Record
Drapery & Fashion Weekly
Dyer, Textile Printer
Fabric Forecast
Fairplay Shipping Journal
Fashion Forecast
Food Manufacture

Food Processing
Food Trade Review
Footwear Weekly
Free Trader
Freight Management
Freight News Weekly
Furnishing World
Furniture and Bedding
Games and Toys
Gems
Gifts
Glass
Grocer
Hairdressers' Journal
Hardware Merchandiser
Hardware Trade Journal
Headlight
Hotel and Catering Institute Journal
Hotel & Restaurant Catering
Industria Britanica
Industrial and Scientific Communication
Industrial & Welfare Catering
Industrial Diamond Review
Industrial Safety
Instrument Practice
International Brewers Journal
International Bulletin for the Printing and Allied Trades
*Jeweler's Circular—Keystone
Knitwear and Stockings
Laundry & Cleaning
Laundry & Cleaning International
Leather
Leathergoods
Litho-Printer
Maker-up
Manufacturing Clothier
Marine and Air Catering
Marketing
Materials Handling News
Meat Industry
Men's Wear
Mercantile Guardian
Millinery and Boutique
Muck Shifter

National Newsagent
Off Licence News
Optician
Packaging Review
Paint Manufacture
Paint, Oil and Colour Journal
Paper Maker
Paper Trade Review
Power Laundry
Printing and Bookbinding Trade Review
Printing Trades Journal
Printing World
Product Finishing
*Publishers' Weekly
Quarry Managers' Journal
Refractories Journal
Retail Chemist
Retail Jeweller
Retail Newsagent
Security Gazette
Self-Service and Supermarket
Service Station
Shop Fitting International
Soap, Perfumery and Cosmetics
Soft Drinks
Stone Industries
Style Weekly
Supervisor
Sweets and Tobacco Retailing
Swimming Pool Review
Tableware International
Tailor and Cutter
Textile Manufacturer
Textile Weekly
Timber Trades Journal
Tobacco
Tooling
Travel World
Watchmaker, Jeweller and Silversmith
Wine Magazine
Wire Industry
Wood
Woodworker
Woodworking Industry
Wool Record
World Tobacco
World's Paper Trade Review

TRAVEL AND GEOGRAPHY

Blackwood's Magazine
British Esperantist
British-Soviet Friendship
Bulletin of Hispanic
  Studies
†Canadian Geographical
  Journal (Can.)
Caravan, The
Coming Events in Britain

Eastern World
Geographical Journal
Geographical Magazine
Hibernia
*Holiday
Illustrated London News
Ireland of the Welcomes
†Natal Witness (S.A.)
*National Geographic

†New Zealand Holiday
  (N.Z.)
Queen's Highway
Scotland's Magazine
South Asian Review
*Travel & Camera
†United Asia (In.)
†Walkabout (Aus.)

A TABLE SHOWING JOURNALS UNDER THE SAME PUBLISHERS, ETC.

BENN BROTHERS, LTD.
Bouverie House, 154 Fleet Street, EC4A 2DL *T.* 01–353 3212.

BUILDERS MECHANT REVIEW
CABINET MAKER AND RETAIL FURNISHER
CHEMICAL AGE
COMMERCIAL GROWER
DISPOSABLES INTERNATIONAL
EDUCATION EQUIPMENT
EXPORT MANAGEMENT
FIRE PROTECTION REVIEW
GAS SHOWROOM
GAS WORLD
GIFTS
HARDWARE TRADE JOURNAL
INDUSTRIA BRITANICA

INDUSTRIAL GAS
LEATHER
LEATHERGOODS
MARINE & AIR CATERING
NURSERYMAN & GARDEN CENTRE
PRINTING TRADES JOURNAL
PRINTING WORLD
SHIPPING WORLD AND SHIPBUILDER
SPORTS EQUIPMENT NEWS
SPORTS TRADER
TIMBER TRADES JOURNAL
WOOD
WORLD'S PAPER TRADE REVIEW

BUSINESS PUBLICATIONS LTD.
Mercury House, Waterloo Road, London, S.E.1. *T.* 01–928 3388.

BUSINESS MANAGEMENT
DATA SYSTEMS & DATA WEEK

PERSONNEL MANAGEMENT

EVANS BROTHERS LTD.
Montague House, Russell Square, W.C.1. *T.* 01–636 8521.

ART AND CRAFT IN EDUCATION
CHILD EDUCATION
CHILD EDUCATION QUARTERLY
MUSIC TEACHER

PICTORIAL EDUCATION
PICTORIAL EDUCATION QUARTERLY
TEACHERS WORLD

HANSOM BOOKS
Artillery Mansions, 75 Victoria Street, London S.W.1. *T.* 01–799 4452

ART AND ARTISTS
BOOKS AND BOOKMEN
DANCE AND DANCERS
FILMS AND FILMING
LOOK AND LISTEN

MUSIC AND MUSICIANS
PLAYS AND PLAYERS
RECORDS AND RECORDING

IPC BUSINESS PRESS LTD.
161–166 Fleet Street, London, E.C.4. *T.* 01–353 5011
Mss. should be sent to individual journals

Agricultural Press Ltd.:
AGRICULTURAL MACHINERY JOURNAL
FARMER AND STOCKBREEDER
FARMERS WEEKLY
FARMING NEWS
POULTRY INDUSTRY
POULTRY WORLD
POWER FARMING

Building and Contract Journals Ltd.:
ARCHITECT AND BUILDING NEWS

BUILDING AND CONTRACT JOURNAL
  (IRELAND)
BUILDING EQUIPMENT NEWS
CONTRACT JOURNAL
GROUND ENGINEERING
HIGHWAYS AND TRAFFIC ENGINEERING
INDUSTRIALISED BUILDING SYSTEMS AND
  COMPONENTS
INTERNATIONAL CONSTRUCTION
SURVEYOR—LOCAL GOVERNMENT TECHNO-
  LOGY

Engineering ,Chemical & Marine Press Ltd.:
BRITISH CHEMICAL ENGINEERING
BRITISH PLASTICS
CHEMICAL PROCESSING
DESIGN & COMPONENTS IN ENGINEERING
ENGINEERING
ENGINEERING MATERIALS & DESIGN
ENGINEERING PRODUCTION
EUROPEAN CHEMICAL NEWS
INDUSTRIAL EQUIPMENT NEWS
MACHINERY LLOYD
MAINTENANCE
MATERIALS HANDLING NEWS
MECHANICAL HANDLING
METROLOGY AND INSPECTION
MOTOR SHIP, THE
PACKAGING REVIEW
PETROLEUM TIMES
SHIPBUILDING & SHIPPING RECORD
WELDING AND METAL FABRICATION
WORKS ENGINEERING AND FACTORY
  SERVICES

*Iliffe Science & Technology Publications
  Ltd.:*
APPLIED ERGONOMICS
COMPOSITES
CRYOGENICS
FUEL
FUTURES
GERONTOLOGY
INSTRUCTIONAL TECHNOLOGY
IRON AND STEEL
MANAGEMENT DECISION
NON-DESTRUCTIVE TESTING
OPTICS AND LASER TECHNOLOGY
ORGANISATION AND MANPOWER
POLYMER
SCIENCE JOURNAL
SOVIET SCIENCE REVIEW
TRIBOLOGY
TROPICAL AGRICULTURE
ULTRASONICS
UNDERWATER SCIENCE AND TECHNOLOGY
UNDERWATER SCIENCE AND TECHNOLOGY
  INFORMATION BULLETIN

IPC Consumer Industries Press Ltd.:
CATERER & HOTELKEEPER
CTN incorporating BRITISH STATIONER
DRINKS INTERNATIONAL
FOOD PROCESSING INDUSTRY
FOOTWEAR WEEKLY
FRAMES AND DATA
HAIRDRESSERS JOURNAL
HOTEL & RESTAURANT CATERING
INDUSTRIAL & WELFARE CATERING
LAUNDRY AND CLEANING
LAUNDRY AND CLEANING INTERNATIONAL
MANUFACTURING OPTICS INTERNATIONAL
MEAT INDUSTRY
OFF-LICENCE JOURNAL
OPTICIAN, THE
POWER LAUNDRY & CLEANING NEWS
RETAIL CHEMIST
SCOTTISH LICENSED TRADE NEWS
SELF-SERVICE & SUPERMARKET

SERVICE WORLD INTERNATIONAL
WATCHMAKER, JEWELLER AND SILVER-
  SMITH

IPC Electrical–Electronic Press Ltd.:
COMPUTER AIDED DESIGN
COMPUTER WEEKLY
COMPUTER WEEKLY INTERNATIONAL
DATA PROCESSING
DESIGN ELECTRONICS
ELECTRICAL AND ELECTRONIC TRADER
ELECTRICAL EXPORT REVIEW
ELECTRICAL & RADIO TRADING
ELECTRICAL REVIEW
ELECTRICAL TIMES
ELECTRONICS WEEKLY
INSTRUMENT AND CONTROL ENGINEERING
NUCLEAR ENGINEERING INTERNATIONAL
WATER POWER
WIRELESS WORLD

IPC Specialist & Professional Press Ltd.:
AMATEUR PHOTOGRAPHER
CAGE AND AVIARY BIRDS
CYCLING
DISC AND MUSIC ECHO
FOOTBALL MONTHLY
GOAL
KINE WEEKLY
MELODY MAKER
MOTOR CYCLE
MOTOR CYCLE AND CYCLE TRADER
MUSIC BUSINESS WEEKLY
NURSING MIRROR
RUGBY WORLD
SPORTING RECORD

IPC Transport Press Ltd.:
ABC AIRWAYS MAGAZINE
ABC GOODS TRANSPORT GUIDE
AUTOCAR
AUTOMOBILE ENGINEER
COMMERCIAL MOTOR
COMMERCIAL VEHICLES
FLIGHT INTERNATIONAL
FREIGHT MANAGEMENT
MOTOR
MOTOR BOAT AND YACHTING
MOTOR TRADER
MOTOR TRANSPORT
RAILWAY GAZETTE
RAILWAY MAGAZINE
TRAVEL NEWS
YACHTING WORLD

Textile Business Press Ltd.:
BRITISH FABRICS FOR EUROPE
BRITISH FASHION FOR EUROPE
CARPETS & TEXTILES
DISPOSABLES & NONWOVENS
DRAPERY & FASHION WEEKLY
INTERNATIONAL DYER
INTERSWATCH
STYLE
TEXTILE MONTH
TEXTILE NEWS
WOOL RECORD & TEXTILE WORLD

IPC MAGAZINES LTD.

Tower House, Southampton Street, London, W.C.2. *T.* 01–836 4363

MSS. should be sent to individual journals.

Periodicals and Magazines:
AMATEUR GARDENING
ANGLER'S MAIL
ARGOSY
BOBO BUNNY
BUSTER
CLUB
COR!!
COUNTRY LIFE
FABULOUS 208
FLAIR
GEOGRAPHICAL MAGAZINE
HERS
HOMEMAKER
HOMES AND GARDENS
HONEY
HORSE AND HOUND
IDEAL HOME
JACK & JILL
JUNE & SCHOOL FRIEND
LION AND EAGLE
LOOK & LEARN
LOVING
MIRABELLE
MOTHER
MY HOME & FAMILY
NEW MUSICAL EXPRESS
NEW SCIENTIST
NEW SOCIETY
19
NOVA
PETTICOAT
PLAYHOUR AND ROBIN
POPULAR GARDENING
PRACTICAL BOAT OWNER
PRACTICAL HOME BUILDING
& DECORATING
PRACTICAL ELECTRONICS
PRACTICAL HOUSEHOLDER
PRACTICAL MOTORIST
PRACTICAL TELEVISION
PRACTICAL WIRELESS
PRACTICAL WOODWORKING
PRINCESS TINA
RAVE
RIDING

SALLY
SATURDAY TITBITS
SCORCHER
SMASH
SUNDAY COMPANION
SUNNY STORIES
TEDDY BEAR
TIGER AND JAG
TREASURE
TRIDENT
TRUE MAGAZINE
VALENTINE
VALIANT
WHIZZER AND CHIPS
WOMAN
WOMAN & HOME
WOMAN BRIDE & HOME
WOMAN'S JOURNAL
WOMAN'S OWN
WOMAN'S REALM
WOMAN'S REALM HOME
SEWING & KNITTING
WOMAN'S WEEKLY
WORLD OF WONDER
YACHTING MONTHLY
Libraries:
ACTION PICTURE LIBRARY
AIR ACE PICTURE LIBRARY
BATTLE PICTURE LIBRARY
BLACK TULIP THRILLER
ROMANCES
CAMEO ROMANCES
HOSPITAL ROMANCES
JUNE & SCHOOL FRIEND
PICTURE LIBRARY
LOVE STORY LIBRARY]
LUCKY STAR ROMANCES
MIRACLE LIBRARY
ORACLE LIBRARY
PICTURE ROMANCES
TRUE LIFE LIBRARY
WAR PICTURE LIBRARY
WILD WEST PICTURE
WOMAN'S LIFE ROMANCES
WOMAN'S WEEKLY
WOMAN'S WORLD

IPC NEWSPAPERS LTD.

33 Holborn, London, E.C.1.

ODHAMS NEWSPAPERS LTD.

Long Acre, London, W.C.2. *T.* 01–836 1200

PEOPLE, THE | SPORTING LIFE, THE

THE DAILY MIRROR NEWSPAPERS LTD.

33 Holborn, London, E.C.1. *T.* 01–353 0246

DAILY MIRROR
DAILY RECORD
REVEILLE

SUNDAY MAIL
SUNDAY MIRROR

LINK HOUSE PUBLICATIONS, LTD.

Link House, Dingwall Avenue, Croydon, CR9 2TA.   MSS. are interchangeable.

AUDIO ANNUAL	HI-FI NEWS
CAMPING SITES IN BRITAIN	POPULAR CAMPING
CARAVAN	PREDICTION (also ANNUAL)
CARAVAN YEAR BOOK	SMALL BOAT
COINS (also ANNUAL)	STAMP MAGAZINE
CONTINENTAL CAMPING SITES	STAMP WEEKLY
CUSTOM CAR	STAMP YEAR BOOK
DO IT YOURSELF (also ANNUAL)	STUDIO SOUND
DO IT YOURSELF GARDENING ANNUAL	WATERWAYS SERIES
EXCHANGE AND MART	

MORGAN GRAMPIAN (PUBLISHERS) LTD.

28 Essex Street, Strand, London, W.C.2. *T.* 01–353 6565.

ASSEMBLY & FASTENER ENGINEERING	FOOD MANUFACTURE
BUILDERS' MERCHANTS' JOURNAL	HARDWARE MERCHANDISER
BUILDING DESIGN	INDUSTRIAL PURCHASING NEWS
BUSINESS ADMINISTRATION	MANUFACTURING CHEMIST & AEROSOL
CHEMICAL & PROCESS ENGINEERING	NEWS
CHEMIST & DRUGGIST	METALWORKING PRODUCTION
CONTROL & INSTRUMENTATION	MUCK SHIFTER
CRANES	PAINT MANUFACTURE
DESIGN ENGINEERING	PROCESS BIOCHEMISTRY
ELECTRONIC ENGINEERING	PROCESS ENGINEERING
ENGINEER, THE	WORLD CROPS
ESTATES TIMES	WORLD FISHING
FLUID POWER INTERNATIONAL	

SCRIPTURE UNION

5 Wigmore Street, London, W1H 0AD.   *T.* 01–486 2561.

ADVENTURERS	OUTREACH
BEGINNER ACTIVITY LEAFLETS	PILOT
DAILY BREAD	QUEST
DAILY NOTES	TEACHING BEGINNERS
FAMILY PRAYERS	TEACHING JUNIORS
FRIENDS OF GOD	TEACHING PRIMARIES
KEY NOTES	TEACHING TEENAGERS

WM. STEVENS, PUBLICATIONS

St. John's House, St. John's Square, London E.C.1.   *T.* 01–253 6680.

All MSS. submitted are considered for any of the publications below. There is no need for stories to be submitted to each paper individually.

CHRISTIAN NOVELS	TRUE LOVE SERIES
NEW MOON SERIES	THIS IS LONDON

THOMSON-LENG PUBLICATIONS
Dundee

All MSS. are interchangeable and are placed with the Editor to whose publication they are most suited.

ANNABEL	FAMILY STAR	ROVER
BEANO	HORNET	SCOTS MAGAZINE
BEEZER	HOTSPUR	SECRETS
BIMBO	JACKIE	SECRETS STORY LIBRARY
BUNTY	JUDY	SPARKY
BUNTY LIBRARY	JUDY LIBRARY	STAR LOVE STORIES
COMMANDO LIBRARY	MANDY	SUNDAY POST
DANDY	MY WEEKLY	TOPPER
DIANA	PEOPLE'S FRIEND	TWINKLE
DUNDEE COURIER AND	PEOPLE'S JOURNAL	VICTOR
ADVERTISER	RED LETTER	WEEKLY NEWS
DUNDEE EVENING TELE-	RED STAR WEEKLY	WIZARD
GRAPH & POST	ROMEO